William Shakespeare, Swynfen Jervis

A Dictionary of the Language of Shakespeare

William Shakespeare, Swynfen Jervis

A Dictionary of the Language of Shakespeare

ISBN/EAN: 9783337055530

Printed in Europe, USA, Canada, Australia, Japan

Cover: Foto ©Thomas Meinert / pixelio.de

More available books at **www.hansebooks.com**

A DICTIONARY

OF THE

LANGUAGE OF SHAKSPEARE.

BY

SWYNFEN JERVIS, ESQ.

LONDON:
JOHN RUSSELL SMITH, 36 SOHO SQUARE.

MDCCCLXVIII.

LONDON:
ROBSON AND SON, GREAT NORTHERN PRINTING WORKS,
PANCRAS ROAD, N.W.

PREFACE.

My friend Mr. SWYNFEN JERVIS had revised the proof-sheets of one half of the present volume, when an ailment, from which he had been suffering for a considerable time, at last proved fatal. On his death-bed he expressed an anxious wish that the remainder of the work, which was quite complete in manuscript, should be printed with the same accuracy as the portion he had himself superintended at press; and, in becoming the Editor of the latter half of his Dictionary, I have endeavoured to fulfil that wish. My task has been a comparatively easy one; nothing more having been required of me than to see that the manuscript was faithfully followed, and to correct some trifling errors of quotation. I need hardly add, that I have attempted no alteration in any of the few glosses to which I happen not to subscribe.

Mr. SWNYFEN JERVIS was born in London, May 10th, 1797; and died at his seat, Darlaston Hall, in Staffordshire, January 15th, 1867.

ALEXANDER DYCE.

A DICTIONARY

OF THE

LANGUAGE OF SHAKSPEARE.

'A. *He.*

The which if he can prove, *'a* pops me out
At least from fair five hundred pound a-year.
King John, i. 1.

'*A* made a fine end, and went away, an it had been any christom child; *'a* parted even just between twelve and one, even at the turning o' the tide. *Henry 5,* ii. 3.

A pestilence on him for a mad rogue! *'a* poured a flagon of Rhenish on my head once.
Hamlet, v. 1.

To ABANDON. *To banish; to send away.*

Ay, and the time seems thirty unto me,
Being all this time *abandon'd* from your bed.
Taming of the Shrew, Induction, sc. 2.

To ABATE. *To lessen; to diminish; to deject; to depress; to shorten.*

Abate the edge of traitors, gracious Lord,
That would reduce these bloody days again!
Richard 3, v. 5.

If he have power,
Then vail your ignorance; if none, *abate*
Your dangerous lenity. *Coriolanus,* iii. 1.

Till at length
Your ignorance deliver you, as most
Abated captives, to some nation
That won you without blows. *Ibid.* iii. 3.

O, long and tedious night, *abate* thy hours!
Midsummer-Night's Dream, iii. 2.

ABCEE-BOOK. *A horn-book; a primer; a catechism.*

And then comes answer like an *abcee-book.*
King John, i. 1.

To ABHOR. *To reject; to protest against.*

Therefore I say again,
I utterly *abhor,* yea, from my soul,
Refuse you for my judge. *Henry 8,* ii. 4.

To ABIDE. *To sojourn; to tarry awhile; to pay dearly; to suffer.*

There's no virtue whipped out of the court: they cherish it, to make it stay there; and yet it will no more but *abide.* *Winter's Tale,* iv. 2.

I'll call upon you straight: *abide* within.
Macbeth, iii. 1.

If it be found so, some will dear *abide* it.
Julius Cæsar, iii. 2.

ABILITIES. *Strength; power of resisting attack.*

So may he with more facile question bear it,
For that it stands not in such warlike brace,
But altogether lacks the *abilities*
That Rhodes is dress'd in. *Othello,* i. 3.

ABJECT. *A mean and despicable person; a slave.*

We are the queen's *abjects,* and must obey.
Richard 3, i. 1.

B

ABLE. *Strong; active; competent.*

Be *able* for thine enemy rather in power than use.
All's well that ends well, i. 1.

And such other gambol faculties he has, that
show a weak mind and an *able* body.
Henry 4, P. 2, ii. 4.

If heaven had pleas'd to have given me longer life
And *able* means, we had not parted thus.
Henry 8, iv. 2.

To ABLE. *To uphold; to justify.*

None does offend, none,—I say, none; I'll *able* 'em :
Take that of me, my friend, who have the power
To seal the accuser's lips. *King Lear,* iv. 6.

ABODE. *Delay; tarriance; stay.*

Especially that of Cleopatra's, which wholly de-
pends on your *abode.* *Antony and Cleopatra,* i. 2.

Sweet friends, your patience for my long *abode.*
Merchant of Venice, ii. 5.

To ABODE. *To bode; to portend.*

That this tempest,
Dashing the garment of this peace, *aboded*
The sudden breach on't. *Henry* 8, i. 1.

The night-crow cried, *aboding* luckless time.
Henry 6, P. 3, v. 6.

ABODEMENT. *Omen; prodigy.*

Tush, man; *abodements* must not now affright us.
Henry 6, P. 3, iv. 7.

ABORTIVE. *An abortion; a monstrous birth.*

And call them meteors, prodigies, and signs,
Abortives, presages, and tongues of heaven,
Plainly denouncing vengeance upon John.
King John, iii. 4.

ABORTIVE. *Untimely; born prematurely;
unseasonable.*

Thou elvish-mark'd, *abortive,* rooting hog !
Richard 3, i. 3.

Remember it, and let it make thee crost-fall'n ;
Ay, and allay this thy *abortive* pride.
Henry 6, P. 2, iv. 1.

ABOUT. *To the point; to the purpose; to business.*

About, my brain ! *Hamlet,* ii. 2.

ABRIDGMENT. *A drama; a play; an abstract; a summary.*

Say, what *abridgment* have you for this evening ?
What masque ? what music ?
Midsummer-Night's Dream, v. 1.

Look, where my *abridgment* comes. *Hamlet,* ii. 2.

This fierce *abridgment*
Hath to it circumstantial branches, which
Distinction should be rich in. *Cymbeline,* v. 5.

ABROACH. *A-foot; in action.*

The secret mischiefs that I set *abroach*
I lay unto the grievous charge of others.
Richard 3, i. 3.

Would he abuse the countenance of the king,
Alack, what mischiefs might he set *abroach,*
In shadow of such greatness ! *Henry* 4, P. 2, iv. 2.

ABROAD. *Broadly; wide open.*

His hands *abroad* display'd, as one that grasp'd
And tugg'd for life, and was by strength subdu'd.
Henry 6, P. 2, iii. 2.

To ABROOK. *To brook; to endure.*

Sweet Nell, ill can thy noble mind *abrook*
The abject people gazing on thy face
With envious looks, still laughing at thy shame.
Henry 6, P. 2, ii. 4.

ABRUPTION. *Interruption; pause.*

What should they grant? what makes this pretty
abruption ? *Troilus and Cressida,* iii. 2.

ABSOLUTE. *Complete; perfect; resolved; certain; positive.*

The wicked'st caitiff on the ground
May seem as shy, as grave, as just, as *absolute*
As Angelo. *Measure for Measure,* v. 1.

Therefore, most *absolute* sir, if thou wilt have
The leading of thine own revenges, take
The one half of my commission. *Coriolanus,* iv. 5.

Believe me, an *absolute* gentleman, full of most
excellent differences. *Hamlet,* v. 2.

Be *absolute* for death ; either death or life
Shall thereby be the sweeter.
Measure for Measure, iii. 1.

I am *absolute* 'twas very Cloten. *Cymbeline,* iv. 2.

How *absolute* the knave is ! *Hamlet,* v. 1.

ABSTRACT. *An epitome; an abridgment; a
table; a schedule.*

I have to-night dispatched sixteen businesses a
month's length apiece, by an *abstract* of success.
All's well that ends well, iv. 3.

You shall find there
A man who is the *abstract* of all faults
That all men follow. *Antony and Cleopatra,* i. 4.

Let them be well used; for they are the *abstract*
and brief chronicles of the time. *Hamlet,* ii. 2.

Brief *abstract* and record of tedious days.
Richard 3, iv. 4.
He hath an *abstract* for the remembrance of such places, and goes to them by his note.
Merry Wives of Windsor, iv. 2.

ABUSE. *Deceit; trick; artifice; corrupt practice; offence.*
This is a strange *abuse.* Let's see thy face.
Measure for Measure, v. 1.
Victorious Talbot! pardon my *abuse.*
Henry 6, P. 1, ii. 3.
For the poor *abuses* of the time want countenance.
Henry 4, P. 1, i. 2.
I will be deaf to pleading and excuses ;
Nor tears nor prayers shall purchase out *abuses.*
Romeo and Juliet, iii. 1.

To ABUSE. *To bring shame upon; to disgrace; to impose upon; to deceive.*
Thou never hadst renown, nor canst not lose it.—
Yes, your renownèd name : shall flight *abuse* it ?
Henry 6, P. 1, iv. 5.
The people are *abus'd ;* set on. This paltering
Becomes not Rome. *Coriolanus,* iii. 1.
Fair day-light !—I am mightily *abus'd.*
King Lear, iv. 7.
Old fools are babes again; and must be us'd
With checks as flatteries, — when they are seen *abus'd.* *Ibid.* i. 3.
Is there not charms
By which the property of youth and maidhood
May be *abus'd ?* *Othello,* i. 1.
Yea, and perhaps,
Out of my weakness and my melancholy,
Abuses me to damn me. *Hamlet,* ii. 2.

ABUSED. *Disfigured.*
Poor soul, thy face is much *abus'd* with tears.
Romeo and Juliet, iv. 1.

To ABY. *To buy; to pay for.*
Disparage not the faith thou dost not know,
Lest, to thy peril, thou *aby* it dear.
Midsummer-Night's Dream, iii. 2.

ABYSM. *Abyss.*
What see'st thou else
In the dark backward and *abysm* of time ?
Tempest, i. 2.
When my good stars, that were my former guides,
Have empty left their orbs, and shot their fires
Into the *abysm* of hell.
Antony and Cleopatra, iii. 13.

ACADEME. *Academy.*
They are the books, the arts, the *academes,*
That show, contain, and nourish all the world,
Else none at all in aught proves excellent.
Love's Labour's lost, iv. 3.

ACCEPT. *Acceptance; assent.*
Pleaseth your grace
To appoint some of your council presently
To sit with us once more, with better heed
To re-survey them, we will suddenly
Pass our *accept* and peremptory answer.
Henry 5, v. 2.

To ACCITE. *To induce; to call; to summon.*
And what *accites* your most worshipful thought
to think so ? *Henry* 4, P. 2, ii. 2.
Our coronation done, we will *accite,*
As I before remember'd, all our state.
Ibid. P. 2, v. 2.

To ACCOMMODATE. *To furnish; to supply; to dress up; to deck.*
But who comes here?
The safer sense will ne'er *accommodate*
His master thus. *King Lear,* iv. 6.

ACCOMMODATED. *Advantaged; favoured.*
These three,
Accommodated by the place, more charming
With their own nobleness,—which could have turn'd
A distaff to a lance,—gilded pale looks,
Part shame, part spirit renew'd. *Cymbeline,* v. 3.

ACCOMMODATIONS. *Necessaries; conveniences; food, clothing, &c.*
Thou art not noble ;
For all the *accommodations* that thou bear'st
Are nurs'd by baseness.
Measure for Measure, iii. 1.

ACCOMPLICE. *A friend; a companion; an ally.*
Success unto our valiant general,
And happiness to his *accomplices* !
Henry 6, P. 1, v. 2.

To ACCOMPLISH. *To furnish; to adorn; to deck; to obtain; to gain; to win.*
His face thou hast, for even so look'd he,
Accomplish'd with the number of thy hours.
Richard 2, ii. 1.

The armorers, *accomplishing* tho knights,
With busy hammers closing rivets up,
Give dreadful note of preparation.
Henry 5, iii. Chorus.

O miserable thought I and more unlikely
Than to *accomplish* twenty golden crowns !
Henry 6, P. 3, iii. 2.

ACCOMPT. *Value; weight; importance.*

I talk not of your soul : our compell'd sins
Stand more for number than *accompt*.
Measure for Measure, ii. 4.

ACCORD. *Wish; desire.*

Then let your will attend on their *accords*.
Comedy of Errors, ii. 1.

ACCORDING. *Accordingly.*

Thou art said to have a stubborn soul,
That apprehends no further than this world,
And squar'st thy life *according*.
Measure for Measure, v. 1.

ACCORDINGLY. *Equally; correspondingly.*

I do assure you he is very great in knowledge, and
accordingly valiant. *All's well that ends well*, ii. 5.

To ACCOST. *To approach; to salute; to woo.*

Accost, Sir Andrew, *accost*. *Twelfth-Night*, i. 3.

ACCOSTING. *Solicitation; courtship; wooing.*

O, these encounterers, so glib of tongue,
That give *accosting* welcome ere it comes !
Troilus and Cressida, iv. 5.

ACCOUNTANT. *Responsible; amenable; accountable.*

And his offence is so, as it appears,
Accountant to the law upon that pain.
Measure for Measure, ii. 4.

Though peradventure
I stand *accountant* for as great a sin. *Othello*, ii. 1.

ACCUSE. *Accusation.*

And dogged York, that reaches at the moon,
Whose overweening arm I have pluck'd back,
By false *accuse* doth level at my life.
Henry 6, P. 2, iii. 1.

To ACCUSE. *To blame; to censure; to call to
account; to impeach; to suspect.*

And for thy life let justice be *accus'd*.
Merchant of Venice, iv. 1.
Let not my cold words here *accuse* my zeal.
Richard 2, i. 1.
Who being *accus'd* a crafty murderer.
Henry 6, P. 2, iii. 1.

To ACHIEVE. *To gain; to win; to obtain.*

I got a promise of this fair one here,
To have her love, provided that your fortune
Achiev'd her mistress. *Merchant of Venice*, iii. 2.
If I begin the battery once again,
I will not leave the half-*achieved* Harflour
Till in her ashes she lie buried. *Henry* 5, iii. 2.
I pray thee, bear my former answer back :
Bid them *achieve* me, and then sell my bones.
Ibid. iv. 3.

To ACKNOW. *To confess; to acknowledge.*

Be not *acknown* on't ; I have use for it.
Othello, iii. 3.

ACONITUM. *The aconite, or monk's-hood.*

Though it do work as strong
As *aconitum* or rash gunpowder.
Henry 4, P. 2, iv. 4.

ACQUIT. *Acquitted.*

Courageous Richmond, well hast thou *acquit* thee.
Richard 3, v. 3.

To ACQUIT. *To quit; to be rid of; to release.*

I am glad I am so *acquit* of this tinder-box.
Merry Wives of Windsor, i. 3.
I will *acquit* you. *Twelfth-Night*, iii. 4.

ACQUITTANCE. *Forgiveness; pardon.*

Now must your conscience my *acquittance* seal.
Hamlet, iv. 7.

To ACQUITTANCE. *To release; to discharge;
to acquit.*

But if black scandal or foul-fac'd reproach
Attend the sequel of your imposition,
Your mere enforcement shall *acquittance* me
From all the impure blots and stains thereof.
Richard 3, iii. 7.

ACT. *Action; operation; activity.*

But on us both did haggish age steal on,
And wore us out of *act*. *All's well that ends well*, i. 2.
Dangerous conceits are, in their natures, poisons,
Which at the first are scarce found to distaste,
But, with a little *act* upon the blood,
Burn like the mines of sulphur. *Othello*, iii. 3.
I will try the forces
Of these thy compounds on such creatures as
We count not worth the hanging,—
To try the vigour of them, and apply
Allayments to their *act*. *Cymbeline*, i. 5.
Whilst they, distill'd
Almost to jelly with the *act* of fear,
Stand dumb, and speak not to him. *Hamlet*, i. 2.

To Act. *To enforce; to execute.*
Here is a hand to hold a sceptre up,
And with the same to *act* controlling laws.
Henry 6, P. 2, v. 1.

Action. *Accusation; charge; probation.*
The bloody book of law
You shall yourself read in the bitter letter,
After your own sense; yea, though our proper son
Stood in your *action*. *Othello*, i. 3.
This *action* I now go on is for my better grace.
Winter's Tale, ii. 1.

Adamant. *The magnet.*
As true as steel, as plantage to the moon,
As iron to *adamant*, as earth to the centre.
Troilus and Cressida, iii. 2.

Addiction. *Inclination.*
Some to dance, some to make bonfires, each
man to what sport and revels his *addiction* leads
him. *Othello*, ii. 2.

Addition. *Name; title; distinction; honour; exaggeration.*
Where great *additions* swell us, and virtue none,
It is a dropsied honour. *All's well that ends well*, ii. 3.
He bade me, from him, call thee thane of Cawdor;
In which *addition*, hail, most worthy thane!
Macbeth, i. 3.
This man, lady, hath robbed many beasts of their
particular *additions*. *Troilus and Cressida*, i. 2.
I do attend here on the general,
And think it no *addition*, nor my wish,
To have him see me woman'd. *Othello*, iii. 4.
Truly to speak, and with no *addition*,
We go to gain a little patch of ground,
That hath no profit in it but the name.
Hamlet, iv. 4.

To Address. *To prepare; to get ready.*
I will then *address* me to my appointment.
Merry Wives of Windsor, iii. 5.
Our navy is *address'd*, our power collected.
Henry 4, P. 2, iv. 4.
I do not speak of flight, of fear, of death,
But dare all imminence that gods and men
Address their dangers in.
Troilus and Cressida, v. 10.

To Adhere. *To fit; to be suitable; to belong; to incline to; to esteem.*
Nor time nor place
Did then *adhere*, and yet you would make both.
Macbeth, i. 7.

A shepherd's daughter,
And what to her *adheres*, which follows after,
Is the argument of time.
Winter's Tale, iv. Chorus.
And sure I am two men there are not living
To whom he more *adheres*. *Hamlet*, ii. 2.

To Adjoin. *To join together; to unite.*
It is a massy wheel,
To whose huge spokes ten thousand lesser things
Are mortis'd and *adjoin'd*. *Hamlet*, iii. 3.

Adjunct. *Coupled with; consequent upon.*
So well, that what you bid me undertake,
Though that my death were *adjunct* to my act,
By heaven, I would do it. *King John*, iii. 3.

Admiration. *Wonder; a prodigy.*
Working so grossly in a natural cause,
That *admiration* did not whoop at them.
Henry 5, ii. 2.
Now, good Lafeu, bring in the *admiration*.
All's well that ends well, ii. 1.

To Admire. *To wonder at; to be astonished; to regard with wonder.*
I perceive, these lords
At this encounter do so much *admire*,
That they devour their reason. *Tempest*, v. 1.
You have displac'd the mirth, broke the good meeting
With most *admir'd* disorder. *Macbeth*, iii. 4.

To Admit. *To choose; to elect; to approve.*
The custom of request you have discharg'd:
The people do *admit* you; and are summon'd
To meet anon, upon your approbation.
Coriolanus, ii. 3.

Admittance. *Repute; acceptance; vogue; fashion.*
A gentleman of excellent breeding, admirable
discourse, of great *admittance*.
Merry Wives of Windsor, ii. 2.
The brow that becomes the ship-tire, the tire-valiant, or any tire of Venetian *admittance*.
Ibid. iii. 3.

Admonishment. *Counsel; admonition.*
Thy grave *admonishments* prevail with me.
Henry 6, P. 1, ii. 5.

ADOPTION. *Addition; imposition; possession; inheritance; acquisition.*

I shall not only receive this villanous wrong,
but stand under the *adoption* of abominable terms.
      Merry Wives of Windsor, ii. 2.

Yes, and in time,
When she had fitted you with her craft, to work
Her son into the *adoption* of the crown.
      Cymbeline, v. 5.

ADOPTIOUS. *Adopted.*

With a world
Of pretty, fond, *adoptious* christendoms,
That blinking Cupid gossips.
      All's well that ends well, i. 1.

ADORNINGS. *Decorations; ornaments.*

Her gentlewomen tended her i' the eyes,
And made their bends *adornings.*
      Antony and Cleopatra, ii. 2.

ADULTERATE. *Adulterous.*

And the beholders of this frantic play,
The *adulterate* Hastings, Rivers, Vaughan, Grey,
Untimely smother'd in their dusky graves.
      Richard 3, iv. 4.
Ay, that incestuous, that *adulterate* beast.
      Hamlet, i. 5.

To ADULTERATE. *To be guilty of adultery.*

But Fortune, O!
She is corrupted, chang'd, and won from thee;
She *adulterates* hourly with thine uncle John.
      King John, iii. 1.

To ADVANCE. *To prefer; to dignify; to lift up; to raise.*

Look you, my good lord,
I must entreat you, honour me so much
As to *advance* this jewel.   *Timon of Athens,* i. 2.
Filling the air with swords *advanc'd* and darts.
      Coriolanus, i. 6.
Which being *advanc'd,* declines, and then men die.
      Ibid. ii. 1.
Advanc'd their eyelids, lifted up their noses
As they smelt music.   *Tempest,* iv. 1.

ADVANTAGE. *Amplification; exaggeration; stratagem; policy; occasion; opportunity.*

But he'll remember with *advantages*
What feats he did that day   *Henry 5,* iv. 3.
You go so much backward when you fight.—
That's for *advantage.* *All's well that ends well,* i. 1.

Though we seemed dead, we did but sleep; *advantage* is a better soldier than rashness.
      Henry 5, iii. 5.
Advantage feeds him fat while men delay.
      Henry 4, P. 1, iii. 2.
For where there is *advantage* to be ta'en,
Both more and less have given him the revolt.
      Macbeth, v. 4.
That none so small *advantage* shall step forth
To check his reign, but they will cherish it.
      King John, iii. 4.

To ADVANTAGE. *To benefit; to profit.*

Stand fast, good Fate, to his hanging! make
the rope of his destiny our cable, for our own doth
little *advantage!*   *Tempest,* i. 2.
By this is your brother saved, your honour
untainted, the poor Mariana *advantaged,* and the
corrupt deputy foiled. *Measure for Measure,* iii. 1.
Convey what I will set down to my lady: it
shall *advantage* thee more than ever the bearing of
letter did.   *Twelfth-Night,* iv. 2.

ADVANTAGEABLE. *Convenient; advantageous; suitable.*

And take with you free power to ratify,
Augment, or alter, as your wisdoms best
Shall see *advantageable* for our dignity,
Any thing in or out of our demands. *Henry 5,* v. 2.

ADVANTAGEOUS. *Politic; wise; prudent.*

I do not fly; but *advantageous* care
Withdrew me from the odds of multitude.
      Troilus and Cressida, v. 4.

ADVENTURE. *Chance; hazard; accident.*

Alas, poor shepherd! searching of thy wound,
I have by hard *adventure* found mine own.
      As you like it, ii. 4.

ADVERSITY. *Perversity; contrariety; contradiction.*

Well said, *Adversity!* and what need these tricks?
      Troilus and Cressida, iv. 5.

To ADVERTISE. *To teach; to make known; to inform.*

But I do bend my speech
To one that can my part in him *advertise.*
      Measure for Measure, i. 1.
We are *advertis'd* by our loving friends
That they do hold their course toward Tewksbury.
      Henry 6, P. 3, v. 3.

ADVERTISEMENT. *Precept; admonition; information; notice.*

Therefore give me no counsel:
My griefs cry louder than *advertisement.*
Much Ado about Nothing, v. 1.

That is an *advertisement* to a proper maid in
Florence, one Diana.
All's well that ends well, iv. 3.

For this *advertisement* is five days old.
Henry 4, P. 1, iii. 2.

Yet doth he give us bold *advertisement,*
That with our small conjunction we should on,
To see how fortune is dispos'd to us.
Ibid. P. 1, iv. 1.

ADVERTISING. *Attentive to; active.*

I was then *advertising* and holy to your business.
Measure for Measure, v. 1.

ADVICE. *Information; knowledge; caution; deliberation; consideration; prudence.*

How shall I dote on her with more *advice,*
That thus without *advice* begin to love her!
Two Gentlemen of Verona, ii. 4.

Rinaldo, you did never lack *advice* so much
As letting her pass so.
All's well that ends well, iii. 4.

Thy son is banish'd upon good *advice.*
Richard 2, i. 3.

We consider
It was excess of wine that set him on;
And, on his more *advice,* we pardon him.
Henry 5, ii. 2.

To ADVISE. *To consider; to bethink; to be aware.*

Advise you what you say; the minister is here.
Twelfth-Night, iv. 2.

Have you nothing said
Upon his party 'gainst the Duke of Albany?
Advise yourself. *King Lear,* ii. 1.

Go, bid thy master well *advise* himself.
Henry 5, iii. 5.

You were *advis'd* his flesh was capable
Of wounds and scars. *Henry 4, P. 2, i. 1.*

ADVISED. *Wise; cautious; prudent.*

The silver livery of *advised* age.
Henry 6, P. 2, v. 2.

ADVOCATION. *Advocacy; mediation; intercession.*

Alas, thrice-gentle Cassio!
My *advocation* is not now in tune. *Othello,* iii. 4.

AERY. *A brood of hawks or other birds of prey; a nest.*

Shall that victorious hand be feebled here,
That in your chambers gave you chastisement?
No: know the gallant monarch is in arms;
And like an eagle o'er his *aery* towers,
To souse annoyance that comes near his nest.
King John, v. 2.

Your *aery* buildeth in our *aery's* nest.
Richard 3, i. 3.

But there is, sir, an *aery* of children, little eyases,
that cry out on the top of question, and are most
tyrannically clapped for't. *Hamlet,* ii. 2.

AFAR OFF. *Remotely; indirectly.*

He who shall speak for her's *afar off* guilty
But that he speaks. *Winter's Tale,* ii. 1.

AFFECT. *Affection; passion.*

Necessity will make us all forsworn
Three thousand times within this three years' space:
For every man with his *affects* is born;
Not by might master'd, but by special grace.
Love's Labour's lost, i. 1.

Thou art not certain;
For thy complexion shifts to strange *affects,*
After the moon. *Measure for Measure,* iii. 1.

Wooing poor craftsmen with the craft of smiles,
And patient underbearing of his fortune,
As 'twere to banish their *affects* with him.
Richard 2, i. 4.

To AFFECT. *To be fond of; to adopt; to practise.*

For he does neither *affect* company,
Nor is he fit for't, indeed. *Timon of Athens,* i. 2.

I thought the king had more *affected* the Duke
of Albany than Cornwall. *King Lear,* i. 1.

Though it do well, I do not relish well
Their loud applause and aves vehement:
Nor do I think the man of safe discretion
That does *affect* it. *Measure for Measure,* i. 1.

I will something *affect* the letter, for it argues
facility. *Love's Labour's lost,* iv. 3.

AFFECTING. *Affected.*

I never heard such a drawling, *affecting* rogue.
Merry Wives of Windsor, ii. 1.

The pox of such antic, lisping, *affecting* fantasticoes; these new tuners of accents!
Romeo and Juliet, ii. 4.

AFFECTION. *Disposition; quality; passion; sympathy; affectation.*

With this, there grows
In my most ill-compos'd *affection*, such
A stanchless avarice.   *Macbeth*, iv. 3.
The *affection* of nobleness which nature shows
Above her breeding.   *Winter's Tale*, v. 2.
O, with what wings shall his *affections* fly
Towards fronting peril and oppos'd decay!
    Henry 4, P. 2, iv. 4.
The motions of his spirit are dull as night,
And his *affections* dark as Erebus.
    Merchant of Venice, v. 1.
Affection! thy intention stabs the centre.
    Winter's Tale, i. 2.
For *affection*,
Master of passion, sways it to the mood
Of what it likes or loathes.
    Merchant of Venice, iv. 1.
I remember, one said there were no sallets in the lines to make the matter savoury, nor no matter in the phrase that might indict the author of *affection*.   *Hamlet*, ii. 2.
Pleasant without scurrility, witty without *affection*, audacious without impudency, learned without opinion, and strange without heresy.
    Love's Labour's lost, v. 1.

To AFFECTION. *To love.*

But can you *affection* the oman?
    Merry Wives of Windsor, i. 1.

AFFECTIONED. *Affected; conceited.*

An *affectioned* ass, that cons state without book.
    Twelfth-Night, ii. 3.

AFFEERED. *Confirmed.*

Wear thou thy wrongs, thy title is *affeer'd!*
    Macbeth, iv. 3.

AFFIANCE. *Trust; confidence.*

O, how hast thou with jealousy infected
The sweetness of *affiance!*   *Henry* 5, ii. 2.
Ah, what's more dangerous than this fond *affiance!*
    Henry 6, P. 2, iii. 1.
Give me your pardon.
I have spoke this, to know if your *affiance*
Were deeply rooted.   *Cymbeline*, i. 6.

AFFINED. *Joined by affinity; related; bound; allied.*

For then the bold and coward,
The wise and fool, the artist and unread,
The hard and soft, seem all *affin'd* and kin.
    Troilus and Cressida, i. 3.

Now, sir, be judge yourself,
Whether I in any just term am *affin'd*
To love the Moor.   •   *Othello*, i. 1.
If partially *affin'd*, or leagu'd in office,
Thou dost deliver more or less than truth,
Thou art no soldier.   *Ibid.* ii. 3.

AFFINITY. *Alliance; family; connexion.*

The Moor replies,
That he you hurt is of great fame in Cyprus
And great *affinity*, and that in wholesome wisdom
He might not but refuse you.   *Othello*, iii. 1.

To AFFRAY. *To affright.*

Since arm from arm that voice doth us *affray*,
Hunting thee hence with hunt's up to the day.
    Romeo and Juliet, iii. 5.

AFFRONT. *Attack; assault; charge.*

There was a fourth man in a silly habit,
That gave the *affront* with them.   *Cymbeline*, v. 3.

To AFFRONT. *To meet; to encounter; to confront.*

Unless another,
As like Hermione as is her picture,
Affront his eye.   *Winter's Tale*, v. 1.
For we have closely sent for Hamlet hither,
That he, as 'twere by accident, may here
Affront Ophelia.   *Hamlet*, iii. 1.
That my integrity and truth to you
Might be *affronted* with the match and weight
Of such a winnow'd purity in love.
    Troilus and Cressida, iii. 2.
My liege, your preparation can *affront* no less
Than what you hear of.   *Cymbeline*, iv. 3.

To AFFY. *To betroth.*

Where, then, do you hold best
We be *affied?*   *Taming of the Shrew*, iv. 4.
And wedded be thou to the hags of hell,
For daring to *affy* a mighty lord
Unto the daughter of a worthless king,
Having neither subject, wealth, nor diadem.
    Henry 6, P. 2, iv. 1.

A-FOOT. *In action; in motion.*

I prithee, when thou seest that act *a-foot*,
Even with the very comment of thy soul
Observe mine uncle.   *Hamlet*, iii. 2.
Of Albany's and Cornwall's powers you heard not?—
'Tis said they are *a-foot*.   *King Lear*, iv. 3.
We shall be shorten'd in our aim; which was,
To take in many towns, ere, almost, Rome
Should know we were *a-foot*.   *Coriolanus*, i. 2.

AFTER. *According to.*

Use every man *after* his desert, and who should scape whipping? Use them *after* your own honour and dignity : the less they deserve, the more merit is in your bounty. *Hamlet*, ii. 2.
Be assur'd you shall not find me, daughter,
After the slander of most step-mothers,
Evil-ey'd unto you. *Cymbeline*, i. 1.

To AFTER-EYE. *To keep in view.*

Thou shouldst have made him
As little as a crow, or less, ere left
To *after-eye* him. *Cymbeline*, i. 3.

AGAINST. *Beyond ; in excess of.*

And, for your service done him,
So much *against* the mettle of your sex,
Here is my hand. *Twelfth-Night*, v. 1.

AGATE. *A bauble ; a diminutive figure cut in agate, and set as a ring.*

I was never manned with an *agate* till now.
Henry 4, P. 2, i. 1.
In shape no bigger than an *agate*-stone
On the fore-finger of an alderman.
Romeo and Juliet, i. 4.

AGAZED. *Aghast ; amazed ; terrified.*

All the whole army stood *agaz'd* on him.
Henry 6, P. 1, i. 1.

AGEN. *Again.*

I'll write to my lord she's dead. O Imogen,
Long mayst thou wander, safe return *agen !*
Cymbeline, iii. 5.

To AGGRAVATE. *To augment ; to enlarge.*

Ford's a knave, and I will *aggravate* his style.
Merry Wives of Windsor, ii. 2.

AGLET-BABY. *A figure carved on an aglet or tag.*

Give him gold enough, and marry him to a puppet or an *aglet-baby*. *Taming of the Shrew*, i. 2.

To AGNIZE. *To confess ; to avow ; to acknowledge.*

I do *agnize*
A natural and prompt alacrity
I find in hardness. *Othello*, i. 3.

A-GOOD. *In earnest ; plentifully ; abundantly.*

And at that time I made her weep *a-good*,
For I did play a lamentable part.
Two Gentlemen of Verona, iv. 2.

A-HEIGHT. *On high ; aloft.*

Look up *a-height ;*—the shrill-gorg'd lark so far
Cannot be seen or heard. *King Lear*, iv. 6.

A-HIGH. *On high ; aloft.*

One heav'd *a-high*, to be hurl'd down below.
Richard 3, iv. 4.

AIDANCE. *Help ; assistance ; support.*

Who, in the conflict that it holds with death,
Attracts the same for *aidance* 'gainst the enemy.
Henry 6, P. 2, iii. 2.

AIDANT. *Helpful.*

All you unpublish'd virtues of the earth,
Spring with my tears ! be *aidant* and remediate
In the good man's distress ! *King Lear*, iv. 4.

AIM. *Conjecture ; guess.*

What you would work me to, I have some *aim*.
Julius Cæsar, i. 2.
As in these cases, where the *aim* reports,
'Tis oft with difference. *Othello*, i. 3.
But, fearing lest my jealous *aim* might err,
And so, unworthily, disgrace the man,
I gave him gentle looks.
Two Gentlemen of Verona, iii. 1.

To AIM. *To guess.*

They *aim* at it,
And botch the words up fit to their own thoughts.
Hamlet, v. 5.
That my discovery be not *aimèd* at.
Two Gentlemen of Verona, iii. 1.
I *aim'd* so near, when I suppos'd you lov'd.
Romeo and Juliet, i. 1.

To AIR. *To live ; to breathe ; to enjoy the air ; to give air to.*

It is sixteen years since I saw my country : though I have, for the most part, been *aired* abroad, I desire to lay my bones there.
Winter's Tale, iv. 1.
For her male issue
Or died where they were made, or shortly after
The world had *air'd* them. *Henry 8*, ii. 4.

c

AIRY. *Breathing; vocal; oral.*
> The great Achilles,
> Having his ear full of his *airy* fame,
> Grows dainty of his worth, and in his tent
> Lies mocking our designs.
> *Troilus and Cressida,* i. 3.

To ALARUM. *To alarm; to rouse.*
> And wither'd murder,
> *Alarum'd* by his sentinel, the wolf,
> Towards his design moves like a ghost.
> *Macbeth,* ii. 1.

ALDER-LIEFEST. *Dearest; best-beloved.*
> With you, mine alder-liefest sovereign.
> *Henry 6,* P. 2, i. 1.

ALE. *A religious feast or festival.*
> Because thou hast not so much charity in thee
> as to go to the *ale* with a Christian.
> *Two Gentlemen of Verona,* ii. 5.

ALEVEN. *Eleven.*
> *Aleven* widows and nine maids is a simple com-
> ing-in for one man.   *Merchant of Venice,* ii. 2.

A-LIFE. *Above all things; excessively.*
> I love a ballad in print *a-life;* for then we are
> sure they are true.   *Winter's Tale,* iv. 3.

ALL. *Any; both.*
> Both my revenge and hate
> Loosing upon thee in the name of justice,
> Without *all* terms of pity.
> *All's well that ends well,* ii. 3.
> Why, then, good morrow to you *all,* my lords.
> *Henry 4,* P. 2, iii. 1.
> And him to Pomfret,—where, as *all* you know,
> Harmless Richard was murder'd traitorously.
> *Henry 6,* P. 2, ii. 2.

ALLAY. *Mitigation; alleviation; allayment.*
> Besides, the penitent king, my master, hath
> sent for me; to whose feeling sorrows I might be
> some *allay,* or I o'erween to think so.
> *Winter's Tale,* iv. 1.

To ALLAY. *To abate; to subside.*
> Which at this instant so rageth in him, that
> with the mischief of your person it would scarcely
> *allay.*   *King Lear,* i. 2.

ALLAYMENT. *Alleviation; mitigation.*
> To try the vigour of them, and apply
> *Allayments* to their act.   *Cymbeline,* i. 5.

> If I could temporize with my affection,
> Or brew it to a weak and colder palate,
> The like *allayment* could I give my grief.
> *Troilus and Cressida,* iv. 4.

ALLEGIANT. *Loyal.*
> For your great graces
> Heap'd upon me, poor undeserver, I
> Can nothing render but *allegiant* thanks.
> *Henry 8,* iii. 2.

To ALL-HAIL. *To greet; to salute.*
> While I stood rapt in the wonder of it, came
> missives from the king, who *all-hailed* me, "Thane
> of Cawdor."   *Macbeth,* i. 2.

ALL-HALLOWN SUMMER. *Second, or late summer; l'été de St. Martin.*
> Farewell, thou latter spring! farewell, *all-hallown
> summer!*   *Henry 4,* P. 1, i. 2.

ALL-OBEYING. *All-obeyed; omnipotent.*
> Tell him, from his *all-obeying* breath I hear
> The doom of Egypt.
> *Antony and Cleopatra,* iii. 13.

ALL-THING. *Altogether; quite.*
> If he had been forgotten,
> It had been as a gap in our great feast,
> And *all-thing* unbecoming.   *Macbeth,* iii. 1.

ALLICHOLY. *Melancholy.*
> Now, my young guest,—methinks you're *allicholy.*
> *Two Gentlemen of Verona,* iv. 2.

ALLOTTERY. *Allotment; portion.*
> Give me the poor *allottery* my father left me by
> testament; with that I will go buy my fortunes.
> *As you like it,* i. 1.

To ALLOW. *To approve; to commend; to
show; to prove.*
> She is *allowed* for the day-woman.
> *All's well that ends well,* i. 2.
> Generally *allowed* for your many warlike, court-
> like, and learned preparations.
> *Merry Wives of Windsor,* ii. 2.
> And arms her with the boldness of a wife
> To her *allowing* husband.   *Winter's Tale,* i. 2.
> I like them all, and do *allow* them well.
> *Henry 4,* P. 2, iv. 2.
> O heavens, if you do love old men, if your sweet sway
> *Allow* obedience, if yourselves are old,
> Make it your cause; send down, and take my part!
> *King Lear,* ii. 4.

For I can sing,
And speak to him in many sorts of music,
That will *allow* me very worth his service.
Twelfth-Night, i. 2.

ALLOWANCE. *Approbation ; commendation ; reputation.*

But now grow fearful
That you protect this course, and put it on
By your *allowance.* *King Lear*, i. 4.
A stirring dwarf we do *allowance* give
Before a sleeping giant. *Troilus and Cressida*, ii. 3.
If this be known to you, and your *allowance,*
We then have done you bold and saucy wrongs.
Othello, i. 1.
The censure of which one must, in your *allowance,* outweigh a whole theatre of others.
Hamlet, iii. 2.
His bark is stoutly timber'd, and his pilot
Of very expert and approv'd *allowance.*
Othello, ii. 1.
Among ourselves
Give him *allowance* for the better man ;
For that will physic the great Myrmidon
Who broils in loud applause.
Troilus and Cressida, i. 3.

ALLOWED. *Invested ; armed ; licensed ; privileged ; admitted.*

Therefore, so please thee to return with us,
And of our Athens—thine and ours—to take
The captainship, thou shalt be met with thanks,
Allow'd with absolute power, and thy good name
Live with authority. *Timon of Athens*, v. 1.
There is no slander in an *allowed* fool, though he
do nothing but rail. *Twelfth-Night*, i. 5.
You put our page out : go, you are *allow'd.*
Love's Labour's lost, v. 2.
These are such *allow'd* infirmities that honesty
Is never free of. *Winter's Tale*, i. 2.

ALMAIN. *A German.*

He sweats not to overthrow your *Almain.*
Othello, ii. 3.

ALMS-DRINK. *A double portion of liquor.*

They have made him drink *alms-drink.*
Antony and Cleopatra, ii. 7.

ALREADY. *Previously.*

Falstaff, Bardolph, Peto, and Gadshill shall rob
those men that we have *already* waylaid.
Henry 4, P. 1, i. 2.

AMAIN. *With speed ; hastily.*

Forslow no longer, make we hence *amain.*
Henry 6, P. 3, ii. 3.

To AMAZE. *To perplex ; to alarm ; to startle ; to confound.*

You do *amaze* her : hear the truth of it.
Merry Wives of Windsor, v. 5.
Yet you are *amazed ;* but this shall absolutely
resolve you. *Measure for Measure*, iv. 2.
Now for the counsel of my son and queen !
I am *amaz'd* with matter. , *Cymbeline*, iv. 3.
Amaze the welkin with your broken staves !
Richard 3, v. 3.
Make mad the guilty, and appal the free,
Confound the ignorant ; and *amaze,* indeed,
The very faculties of eyes and ears. *Hamlet*, ii. 2.
Why stand these royal fronts *amazèd* thus ?
King John, ii. 1.
Bear with me, cousin ; for I was *amaz'd*
Under the tidings. *Ibid.* iv. 2.

AMAZEDLY. *Confusedly.*

My lord, I shall reply *amazedly,*
Half sleep, half waking.
Midsummer-Night's Dream, iv. 1.

AMAZEMENT. *Alarm ; terror ; perplexity ; uneasiness.*

Behold, distraction, frenzy, and *amazement,*
Like witless antics, one another meet,
And all cry, Hector ! Hector's dead ! O Hector !
Troilus and Cressida, v. 4.
Then thus she says ; your behaviour hath struck
her into *amazement* and admiration. *Hamlet*, iii. 2.
But, look, *amazement* on thy mother sits :
O, step between her and her fighting soul,—
Conceit in weakest bodies strongest works,—
Speak to her, Hamlet. *Ibid.* iii. 4.
No more *amazement :* tell your piteous heart
There's no harm done. *Tempest*, i. 2.

AMBUSCADO. *Ambuscade ; ambush.*

Sometimes she driveth o'er a soldier's neck,
And then dreams he of cutting foreign throats,
Of breaches, *ambuscadoes,* Spanish blades,
Of healths five-fathom deep.
Romeo and Juliet, i. 4.

AMENDS. *Amendment ; improvement.*

Now, Lord be thankèd for my good *amends !*
Taming of the Shrew, Induction, sc. 2.

To AMERCE. *To punish.*

But I'll *amerce* you with so strong a fine,
. That you shall all repent the loss of mine.
Romeo and Juliet, iii. 1.

AMES-ACE. *Two aces.*

I had rather be in this choice than throw *ames-ace* for my life. *All's well that ends well*, ii. 3.

AMIABLE. *Pretending love ; professing love.*

Give me so much of your time in exchange of it, as to lay an *amiable* siege to the honesty of this Ford's wife. *Merry Wives of Windsor*, ii. 2.

AMISS. *Misfortune.*

To my sick soul, as sin's true nature is,
Each toy seems prologue to some great *amiss*.
Hamlet, iv. 5.

AMORT. *Dejected; cast down; dispirited.*

Now where's the Bastard's braves, and Charles his glecks ?
What, all *amort* ? *Henry* 6, P. 1, iii. 2.
How fares my Kate ? What, sweating, all *amort* ?
Taming of the Shrew, iv. 3.

AN. *If, as if.*

An you use these blows long, I must get a sconce for my head, and ensconce it too.
Comedy of Errors, ii. 2.
An honest mind and plain,—he must speak truth !
An they will take it, so; if not, he's plain.
King Lear, ii. 2.
'A made a fine end, and went away, *an* it had been any christom child. *Henry* 5, ii. 3.

To ANATOMIZE. *To lay bare; to expose.*

If not, the wise man's folly is *anatomiz'd*
Even by the squandering glances of the fool.
As you like it, ii. 7.

ANATOMY. *A skeleton.*

Then with a passion would I shake the world;
And rouse from sleep that fell *anatomy*
Which cannot hear a lady's feeble voice,
Which scorns a modern invocation.
King John, iii. 4.

ANCIENT. *A flag or streamer ; an ensign ; a standard-bearer.*

Ten times more dishonourable ragged than an old faced *ancient*. *Henry* 4, P. 1, iv. 2.
He, in good time, must his lieutenant be,
And I—God bless the mark !—his Moorship's *ancient*. *Othello*, i. 1.

ANCIENTRY. *Antiquity; gentry.*

The wedding, mannerly-modest, as a measure, full of state and *ancientry*.
Much Ado about Nothing, ii. 1.
For there is nothing in the between but getting wenches with child, wronging the *ancientry*, stealing, fighting. *Winter's Tale*, iii. 3.

ANCHOR. *An anchoret ; a hermit.*

An *anchor's* cheer in prison be my hope.
Hamlet, iii. 2.

ANDIRONS. *Machines to burn wood upon.*

Her *andirons*,—
I had forgot them,—were two winking Cupids
Of silver, each on one foot standing.
Cymbeline, ii. 4.

ANGEL. *A gold coin ; a gull ; a simpleton.*

And, ere our coming, see thou shake the bags
Of hoarding abbots ; set at liberty
Imprison'd *angels*. *King John*, iii. 3.
But at last I spied
An ancient *angel* coming down the hill,
Will serve the turn. *Taming of the Shrew*, iv. 3.

ANGERLY. *Angrily.*

Why, how now, Hecate ! you look *angerly*.
Macbeth, iii. 5.
How *angerly* I taught my brow to frown !
Two Gentlemen of Verona, i. 2.
I will not stir, nor wince, nor speak a word,
Nor look upon the iron *angerly*. *King John*, iv. 1.

ANGLE. *Corner ; nook ; a fishing-rod.*

Cooling of the air with sighs
In an odd *angle* of the isle. *Tempest*, i. 2.
But I fear the *angle* that plucks our son thither.
Winter's Tale, iv. 1.
Give me mine *angle*,—we'll to the river.
Antony and Cleopatra, ii. 5.

ANGRY. *Fierce ; gaudy ; showy.*

What, thyself ?—Ay.—Wherefore ?—
That I had no *angry* wit to be a lord.
Timon of Athens, i. 1.

AN IF. *If.*

Noting this penury, to myself I said,
An if a man did need a poison now,
Whose sale is present death in Mantua,
Here lives a caitiff wretch would sell it him.
Romeo and Juliet, v. 1.

A-NIGHT. *In the night; by night.*

I remember, when I was in love I broke my sword upon a stone, and bid him take that for coming *a-night* to Jane Smile. *As you like it,* ii. 4.

ANNEXMENT. *Appendage; adjunct.*

Which, when it falls,
Each small *annexment,* petty consequence,
Attends the boisterous ruin. *Hamlet,* iii. 3.

ANNOY. *Trouble; vexation; injury; mischief.*

Sound, drums and trumpets! farewell sour *annoy!*
Henry 6, P. 3, v. 7.
Good angels guard thee from the boar's *annoy!*
Richard 3, v. 3.

ANON. *Quickly; immediately.*

Do my good morrow to them ; and *anon*
Desire them all to my pavilion. *Henry* 5, iv. 1.
For through this laund *anon* the deer will come.
Henry 6, P. 3, iii. 1.

ANOTHER. *The other.*

I think there is not half a kiss to choose
Who loves *another* best. *Winter's Tale,* iv. 3.

ANSWER. *Retribution; requital; trial; retaliation; vengeance.*

He'll call you to so hot an *answer* of it,
That caves and womby vaultages of France
Shall chide your trespass. *Henry* 5, ii. 4.
For after the stout Earl Northumberland
Arrested him at York, and brought him forward—
As a man sorely tainted—to his *answer,*
He fell sick suddenly, and grew so ill
He could not sit his mule. *Henry* 8, iv. 2.
He'll not feel wrongs,
Which tie him to an *answer.* *King Lear,* iv. 2.
Great the slaughter is
Here made by the Roman ; great the *answer* be
Britons must take. *Cymbeline,* v. 3.

To ANSWER. *To oppose; to pay for; to require.*

Call the creatures, whose bare unhoused trunks,
To the conflicting elements expos'd,
Answer mere nature, bid them flatter thee.
Timon of Athens, iv. 3.
Why, thou wert better in thy grave than to
answer with thy uncovered body this extremity of
the skies. *King Lear,* iii. 4.
If it were so, it was a grievous fault ;
And grievously hath Cæsar *answer'd* it.
Julius Cæsar, iii. 2.

It is a surplus of your grace, which never
My life may last to *answer.* *Winter's Tale,* v. 3.

ANTHROPOPHAGINIAN. *A cannibal; a man-eater.*

Go knock and call ; he'll speak like an *Anthropophaginian* unto thee.
Merry Wives of Windsor, iv. 5.

ANTIC. *A buffoon; a kind of masque.*

And there the *antic* sits,
Scoffing his state, and grinning at his pomp.
Richard 2, iii. 2.
If black, why, Nature, drawing of an *antic,*
Made a foul blot, *Much Ado about Nothing,* iii. 1.
Fear not, my lord : we can contain ourselves,
Were he the veriest *antic* in the world.
Taming of the Shrew, Induction, sc. 1.
We will have, if this fadge not, an *antic.*
Love's Labour's lost, v. 1.

ANTIC. *Grotesque; ridiculous; odd; wild; eccentric.*

What, dares the slave
Come hither, cover'd with an *antic* face,
To fleer and scorn at our solemnity?
Romeo and Juliet, i. 5.
As I, perchance, hereafter shall think meet
To put an *antic* disposition on. *Hamlet,* i. 5.

To ANTICIPATE. *To preclude; to prevent.*

Time, thou *anticipat'st* my dread exploits.
Macbeth, iv. 1.

To ANTIC. *To make antic-like.*

The wild disguise hath almost
Antick'd us all. *Antony and Cleopatra,* ii. 7.

ANTICLY. *Like an antic or buffoon; absurdly; preposterously.*

Go *anticly,* show outward hideousness.
Much Ado about Nothing, v. 1.

ANTIQUARY. *Ancient; antique.*

Here's Nestor,—
Instructed by the *antiquary* times,
He must, he is, he cannot but be wise.
Troilus and Cressida, ii. 3.

ANTRE. *A cavern; a cave.*

Wherein of *antres* vast and deserts idle,
Rough quarries, rocks, and hills whose heads touch heaven,
It was my hint to speak. *Othello,* i. 3.

APE. *A fool.*

The *ape* is dead, and I must conjure him.
Romeo and Juliet, ii. 1.

APOPLEX. *Apoplexy; fit.*

This *apoplex* will certain be his end.
Henry 4, P. 2, iv. 4.

APOPLEXED. *Obscured; weakened; lethargied.*

Sense, sure, you have,
Else could you not have motion : but, sure, that
sense
Is *apoplex'd.*   *Hamlet,* iii. 4.

APOTHECARY. *A druggist; a vender of medicines.*

I do remember an *apothecary,*—
And hereabouts he dwells. *Romeo and Juliet,* v. 1.
Give me an ounce of civet, good *apothecary,* to
sweeten
My imagination.   *King Lear,* iv. 6.

APPARENT. *Heir-apparent.*

Next to thyself and my young rover, he's
Apparent to my heart.   *Winter's Tale,* i. 2.
My gracious father, by your kingly leave,
I'll draw it as *apparent* to the crown.
Henry 6, P. 3, ii. 2.

APPARENT. *Open; evident.*

It may be, these *apparent* prodigies,
And the persuasion of his augurers,
May hold him from the Capitol to-day.
Julius Cæsar, ii. 1.
What starting-hole canst thou now find out to
hide thee from this open and *apparent* shame?
Henry 4, P. 1, ii. 4.

To APPEACH. *To accuse; to impeach.*

Disclose the state of your affection; for your passions
Have to the full *appeach'd.*
All's well that ends well, i. 3.
Now, by mine honour, by my life, my troth,
I will *appeach* the villain.   *Richard 2,* v. 2.

APPEAL. *Accusation.*

Here to make good the boisterous late *appeal*
Against the Duke of Norfolk, Thomas Mowbray.
Richard 2, i. 1.
As I intend to thrive in this new world,
Aumerle is guilty of my true *appeal.*
Richard 2, iv. 1.

The duke's unjust,
Thus to retort your manifest *appeal,*
And put your trial in the villain's mouth
Which here you come to accuse.
Measure for Measure, v. 1.
And not resting here, accuses him of letters he
had formerly wrote to Pompey; upon his own *appeal* seizes him.   *Antony and Cleopatra,* iii. 5.

To APPEAL. *To accuse.*

Tell me, moreover, hast thou sounded him,
If he *appeal* the duke on ancient malice ;
Or worthily, as a good subject should,
On some known ground of treachery in him?
Richard 2, i. 1.

APPERIL. *Peril.*

Let me stay at thine *apperil,* Timon.
Timon of Athens, i. 2.

APPERTAINMENT. *Privilege; prerogative.*

He shent our messengers ; and we lay by
Our *appertainments,* visiting of him.
Troilus and Cressida, ii. 3.

APPERTINENT. *Appurtenance; adjunct; appendage.*

You know how apt our love was to accord,
To furnish him with all *appertinents*
Belonging to his honour.   *Henry 5,* ii. 2.

APPLIANCE. *Application; remedy; means.*

Ask God for temperance ; that's the *appliance* only
Which your disease requires.   *Henry 8,* i. 1.
Thou art too noble to conserve a life
In base *appliances.* *Measure for Measure,* iii. 1.
Diseases desperate grown
By desperate *appliance* are reliev'd. *Hamlet,* iv. 3.
With all *appliances* and means to boot.
Henry 4, P. 2, iii. 1.

To APPOINT. *To equip; to furnish; to involve.*

What well-*appointed* leader fronts us here?
Henry 4, P. 2, iv. 1.
Dost think I am so muddy, so unsettled,
To *appoint* myself in this vexation,
Without ripe moving to't? *Winter's Tale,* i. 2.

APPOINTMENT. *Equipment; preparation; direction; command.*

Let's march without the noise of threatening drum,
That from the castle's tatter'd battlements
Our fair *appointments* may be well perus'd.
Richard 2, iii. 3.

Forward, now,
Where their *appointment* we may best discover.
　　　Antony and Cleopatra, iv. 10.
Therefore your best *appointment* make with speed;
Tomorrow you set on. *Measure for Measure*, iii. 1.
　　That good fellow,
If I command him, follows my *appointment*.
　　　Henry 8, ii. 2.

APPREHENSION. *Surmise; thought; opinion.*

For your partaker Poole, and you yourself,
I'll note you in my book of memory,
To scourge you for this *apprehension*.
　　　Henry 6, P. 1, ii. 4.
　　Who has a breast so pure,
But some uncleanly *apprehensions*
Keep leets and law-days, and in session sit,
With meditations lawful?　　*Othello*, iii. 3.

APPREHENSIVE. *Quick; intelligent.*

　　To be the snuff
Of younger spirits, whose *apprehensive* senses
All but new things disdain.
　　　All's well that ends well, i. 2.
Makes it *apprehensive*, quick, forgetive, full of
nimble, fiery, and delectable shapes.
　　　Henry 4, P. 2, iv. 3.
And men are flesh and blood, and *apprehensive*.
　　　Julius Cæsar, iii. 1.

To APPROACH. *To arrive.*

Don Pedro is *approached*.
　　　Much Ado about Nothing, i. 1.
I will, if that my fading breath permit,
And death *approach* not ere my tale be done.
　　　Henry 6, P. 1, ii. 5.
He was expected then, but not *approach'd*.
　　　Cymbeline, ii. 4.

APPROBATION. *Probation; proof.*

This day my sister should the cloister enter,
And there receive her *approbation*.
　　　Measure for Measure, i. 2.
That lack'd sight only, naught for *approbation*
But only seeing.　　*Winter's Tale*, ii. 1.
　Would I had put my estate and my neighbour's
on the *approbation* of what I have spoke!
　　　Cymbeline, i. 4.

APPROPRIATION. *Peculiarity.*

　And he makes it a great *appropriation* to his
own good parts, that he can shoe him himself.
　　　Merchant of Venice, i. 2.

APPROOF. *Approbation; proof.*

O perilous mouths,
That bear in them one and the self-same tongue,
Either of condemnation or *approof!*
　　　Measure for Measure, ii. 4.
So in *approof* lives not his epitaph
As in your royal speech.
　　　All's well that ends well, i. 2.
　　Sister, prove such a wife
As my thoughts make thee, and as my furthest band
Shall pass on thy *approof*.
　　　Antony and Cleopatra, iii. 2.

To APPROVE. *To prove; to justify; to confirm.*

He is of a noble strain, of *approved* valour, and
confirmed honesty. *Much Ado about Nothing*, ii. 1.
Not to knit my soul to an *approved* wanton.
　　　Ibid. iv. 1.
True swains in love shall, in the world to come,
Approve their truths by Troilus.
　　　Troilus and Cressida, iii. 2.
　　I am full sorry
That he *approves* the common liar, fame.
　　　Antony and Cleopatra, i. 1.
What damnèd error, but some sober brow
Will bless it, and *approve* it with a text?
　　　Merchant of Venice, iii. 2.
But the main article I do *approve*
In fearful sense.　　*Othello*, i. 3.
I shall not fail to *approve* the fair conceit
The king hath of you.　　*Henry* 8, ii. 3.

APPROVER. *One that makes trial; an assailant.*

　　Their discipline
Now mingled with their courage will make known
To their *approvers* they are people such
That mend upon the world.　　*Cymbeline*, ii. 4.

APT. *Unsteady; weak; giddy; volatile.*

I have a heart as little *apt* as yours,
But yet a brain that leads my use of anger
To better vantage.　　*Coriolanus*, iii. 2.
　　She is young and *apt:*
Our own precedent passions do instruct us
What levity's in youth. *Timon of Athens*, i. 1.

AQUILON. *The north wind.*

Blow, villain, till thy spherèd bias cheek
Outswell the colic of puff'd *Aquilon*.
　　　Troilus and Cressida, iv. 5.

To ARAISE. *To raise; to restore to life.*

Whose simple touch
Is powerful to *araise* King Pepin, nay,
To give great Charlemain a pen in's hand,
And write to her a love-line.
All's well that ends well, ii. 1.

To ARBITRATE. *To decide; to determine.*

Thoughts speculative their unsure hopes relate;
But certain issue strokes must *arbitrate.*
Macbeth, v. 4.
Which now the manage of two kingdoms must
With fearful bloody issue *arbitrate.*
King John, i. 1.
And often, at his very loose, decides
That which long process could not *arbitrate.*
Love's Labour's lost, v. 2.

ARBITREMENT. *Decision; determination; investigation; examination.*

I know the knight is incensed against you, even
to a mortal *arbitrement.*   *Twelfth-Night,* iii. 4.
The *arbitrement* is like to be bloody. Fare you
well, sir.   *King Lear,* iv. 7.
And put thy fortune to the *arbitrement*
Of bloody strokes and mortal-staring war.
Richard 3, v. 3.
For well you know we of the offering side
Must keep aloof from strict *arbitrement.*
Henry 4, P. 1, iv. 1.

ARCH. *A chief; a protector.*

The noble duke my master,
My worthy *arch* and patron, comes to-night.
King Lear, ii. 1.

ARCH. *Consummate; thorough-paced; complete.*

The tyrannous and bloody act is done,—
The most *arch* deed of piteous massacre
That ever yet this land was guilty of.
Richard 3, iv. 3.
And indeed this day,—
Sir, I may tell it you, I think,—I have
Incens'd the lords o' the council, that he is
A most *arch* heretic.   *Henry 8,* v. 1.

ARGIER. *Algiers.*

This damn'd witch Sycorax,
For mischiefs manifold, and sorceries terrible
To enter human hearing, from *Argier,*
Thou know'st, was banish'd.   *Tempest,* i. 2.

ARGOSY. *A merchantman; a trading vessel.*

There, where your *argosies* with portly sail
Do overpeer the petty traffickers.
Merchant of Venice, i. 1.
That she shall have; besides an *argosy*
That now is lying in Marseilles' road.
Taming of the Shrew, ii. 1.

ARGUMENT. *Theme; subject; controversy; conversation.*

But were I not the better part made mercy,
I should not seek an absent *argument*
Of my revenge, thou present. *As you like it,* iii. 1.
Content;—and the *argument* shall be thy running away.   *Henry 4,* P. 1, ii. 4.
For all my reign hath been but as a scene
Acting that *argument.*   *Ibid.* P. 2, iv. 4.
Signior Benedick,
For shape, for bearing, *argument,* and valour,
Goes foremost in report through Italy.
Much Ado about Nothing, iii. 1.
Now could thou and I rob the thieves, and go
merrily to London, it would be *argument* for a
week, laughter for a month, and a good jest for
ever.   *Henry 4,* P. 1, ii. 2.

To ARM. *To take up; to carry.*

Let us
Find out the prettiest daisied plot we can,
And make him with our pikes and partisans
A grave: come, *arm* him.   *Cymbeline,* iv. 2.

ARMADO. *A fleet.*

So, by a roaring tempest on the flood,
A whole *armado* of convented sail
Is scatter'd and disjoin'd from fellowship.
King John, iii. 4.

ARM-GAUNT. *Lean.*

So he nodded,
And soberly did mount an *arm-gaunt* steed.
Antony and Cleopatra, i. 5.

AROINT. *Avaunt; be gone.*

Aroint thee, witch! the rump-fed ronyon cries.
Macbeth, i. 3.
Bid her alight,
And her troth-plight,
And, *aroint* thee, witch, *aroint* thee!
King Lear, iii. 4.

A-ROW. *In succession.*

My master and his man are both broke loose,
Beaten the maids *a-row,* and bound the doctor.
Comedy of Errors, v. 1.

ARRAS. *Tapestry.*

Behind the *arras* I'll convey myself,
To hear the process. *Hamlet,* iii. 3.
In cypress chests my *arras* counterpoints.
Taming of the Shrew, ii. 1.
I will ensconce me behind the *arras.*
Merry Wives of Windsor, iii. 3.

ARREARAGES. *Arrears.*

And I think
He'll grant the tribute, send the *arrearages,*
Or look upon our Romans, whose remembrance
Is yet fresh in their grief. *Cymbeline,* ii. 4.

ARRIVANCE. *Company coming; arrivals.*

Come, let's do so:
For every minute is expectancy
Of more *arrivance.* *Othello,* ii. 1.

To ARRIVE. *To reach; to arrive at.*

Those powers that the queen
Hath rais'd in Gallia have *arriv'd* our coast.
Henry 6, P. 3, v. 3.
But ere we could *arrive* the point propos'd,
Cæsar cried, "Help me, Cassius, or I sink!"
Julius Cæsar, i. 2.
And now, *arriving*
A place of potency, and sway o' the state,
Your voices might be curses to yourselves.
Coriolanus, ii. 3.

ART. *Speculation; theory; skill; artfulness; cunning.*

I have as much of this in *art* as you,
But yet my nature could not bear it so.
Julius Cæsar, iv. 3.
The *art* of our necessities is strange,
That can make vile things precious.
King Lear, iii. 2.
More matter with less *art.* *Hamlet,* ii. 2.

ARTERY. *A nerve.*

My fate cries out,
And makes each petty *artery* in this body
As hardy as the Némean lion's nerve.
Hamlet, i. 4.
Why, universal plodding prisons up
The nimble spirits in the *arteries.*
Love's Labour's lost, iv. 3.

ARTICLES. *Terms; conditions; stipulations.*

I embrace these conditions; let us have *articles*
betwixt us. *Cymbeline,* i. 4.
I cannot stay to hear these *articles.*
Henry 6, P. 3, i. 1.

To ARTICULATE. *To set forth in articles; to make conditions; to treat.*

These things, indeed, you have *articulated.*
Henry 4, P. 1, v. 1.
Send us to Rome
The best, with whom we may *articulate.*
Coriolanus, i. 9.

ARTIFICIAL. *Inventive; artful; skilful.*

Artificial strife
Lives in these touches, livelier than life.
Timon of Athens, i. 1.
We, Hermia, like two *artificial* gods,
Have with our neelds created both one flower.
Midsummer-Night's Dream, iii. 2.

ARTLESS. *Simple; foolish.*

So full of *artless* jealousy is guilt,
It spills itself in fearing to be spilt. *Hamlet,* iv. 5.

AS. *As well as; as if; since; inasmuch as.*

As now at last
Given hostile strokes, and that not in the presence
Of dreaded justice, but on the ministers
That do distribute it. *Coriolanus,* iii. 3.
The seasons change their manners, *as* the year
Had found some months asleep, and leap'd them
over. *Henry* 4, P. 2, iv. 4.
One cried, "God bless us!" and "Amen," the other;
As they had seen me, with these hangman's hands,
Listening their fear. *Macbeth,* ii. 1.
Why, look you there! look how it steals away!
My father, in his habit *as* he liv'd!
Hamlet, iii. 4.
Advanc'd their eyelids, lifted up their noses
As they smelt music. *Tempest,* iv. 1.
Justice, and your father's wrath, should he
take me in his dominion, could not be so cruel to
me, *as* you, O the dearest of creatures, would even
renew me with your eyes. *Cymbeline,* iii. 2.

ASPECT. *Regard; look.*

Some other mistress hath thy sweet *aspécts.*
Comedy of Errors, ii. 2.

ASPERSION. *A sprinkling; a shower.*

No sweet *aspersion* shall the heavens let fall
To make this contract grow. *Tempest,* iv. 1.

ASPIC. *An asp.*

This is an *aspic's* trail: and these fig-leaves
Have slime upon them, such as the *aspic* leaves
Upon the caves of Nile.
Antony and Cleopatra, v. 2.

D

To ASPIRE. *To ascend; to rise to; to mount.*

That gallant spirit hath *aspir'd* the clouds,
Which too untimely here did scorn the earth.
Romeo and Juliet, iii. 1.

A-SQUINT. *Awry.*

The eye that told you so look'd but *a-squint.*
King Lear, v. 3.

ASSAULT. *Liability; obnoxiousness.*

A savageness in unreclaimèd blood,
Of general *assault.*   *Hamlet,* ii. 1.

ASSAY. *Attempt; trial; effort; incursion; inroad.*

Let us make the *assay* upon him: if he care not
for't, he will supply us easily.
Timon of Athens, iv. 3.

Their malady convinces
The great *assay* of art; but, at his touch,
They presently amend.   *Macbeth,* iv. 3.

This cannot be,
By no *assay* of reason : 'tis a pageant
To keep us in false gaze.   *Othello,* i. 3.
And thus do we of wisdom and of reach,
With windlaces, and with *assays* of bias,
By indirections find directions out. *Hamlet,* ii. 1.
Galling the gleanèd land with hot *assays.*
Henry 5, i. 2.

To ASSAY. *To attempt; to tempt; to try; to endeavour.*

And passion, having my best judgment collied,
Assays to lead the way.
Did you *assay* him to any pastime ? *Hamlet,* iii. 1.
But that thy face is, visard-like, unchanging,
I would *assay,* proud queen, to make thee blush.
Henry 6, P. 3, i. 4.

ASSEMBLANCE. *Semblance; appearance; outside.*

Care I for the limb, the thews, the stature, bulk,
and big *assemblance* of a man ! Give me the spirit,
Master Shallow.   *Henry 4,* P. 2, iii. 2.

ASSIGNS. *Adjuncts; appendages.*

Against the which he has imponed, as I take
it, six French rapiers and poniards, with their *assigns,* as girdle, hangers, and so. *Hamlet,* v. 2.

ASSINEGO. *An ass.*

An *assinego* may tutor thee.
Troilus and Cressida, ii. 1.

ASSISTANCE. *Associates; partners; colleagues.*

Self-loving, and affecting one sole throne,
Without *assistance.*   *Coriolanus,* iv. 6.

To ASSOCIATE. *To accompany; to unite with; to join with.*

Going to find a bare-foot brother out,
One of our order, to *associate* me.
Romeo and Juliet, v. 2.
A fearful army, led by Caius Marcius
Associated with Aufidius, rages
Upon our territories.   *Coriolanus,* iv. 6.

To ASSUBJUGATE. *To lower; to degrade.*

Nor, by my will, *assubjugate* his merit
By going to Achilles. *Troilus and Cressida,* ii. 3.

To ASSUME. *To attain to; to reach; to put on.*

He it is that hath
Assum'd this age : indeed, a banish'd man ;
I know not how a traitor.   *Cymbeline,* v. 5.

To ASSURE. *To affiance; to betroth.*

And your lips too : for I am well assur'd
That I did so when I was first *assur'd.*
King John, ii. 1.
Called me Dromio ; swore I was *assured* to her.
Comedy of Errors, iii. 2.

AS THAT. *Inasmuch as; because.*

But lest you do repent,
As that the sin hath brought you to this shame.
Measure for Measure, ii. 3.

To ASTONISH. *To stun.*

Enough, captain : you have *astonished* him.
Henry 5, v. 1.

ASTRONOMER. *Astrologer.*

But when he performs, *astronomers* foretell it.
Troilus and Cressida, v. 1.

AT AN INCH. *Closely; to an inch.*

Beldam, I think we watch'd you at *an inch.*
Henry 6, P. 2, i. 4.

AT ANY HAND. *In any hand; at all events; at any rate.*

All books of love, see that *at any hand.*
Taming of the Shrew, i. 2.
Let him fetch off his drum *in any hand.*
All's well that ends well, iii. 6.

AT A POINT. *Collected; brought together; in readiness.*

Whither, indeed, before thy here-approach,

Old Siward, with ten thousand warlike men,
Already *at a point*, was setting forth. *Macbeth*, iv. 3.

AT EACH. *Adjoined; placed end to end.*
Ten masts *at each* make not the altitude
Which thou hast perpendicularly fell.
King Lear, iv. 6.

AT FALL. *Without means ; at a low ebb.*
They answer, in a joint and corporate voice,
That now they are *at fall*, want treasure, cannot
Do what they would. *Timon of Athens*, ii. 2.

AT FOOT. *Closely ; at heels.*
Follow him *at foot;* tempt him with speed aboard.
Hamlet, iv. 3.

AT FRIEND. *At peace with ; on friendly terms.*
By his command
Have I here touch'd Sicilia, and from him
Give you all greetings that a king, *at friend*,
Can send his brother. *Winter's Tale*, v. 1.

AT HELP. *Fair ; favourable.*
The bark is ready, and the wind *at help.*
Hamlet, iv. 3.

AT HOST. *At the lodgings ; at home.*
Dromio, what stuff of mine hast thou embark'd?—
Your goods that lay *at host*, sir, in the Centaur.
Comedy of Errors, v. 1.

AT LARGE. *In full; fully ; entirely.*
I long to know the truth hereof *at large.*
Comedy of Errors, iv. 4.

AT POINT. *Ready ; prepared.*
But even before, I was *at point* to sink for food.
Cymbeline, iii. 6.
A hundred knights !
'Tis politic and safe to let him keep
At point a hundred knights. *King Lear*, i. 4.
Who already,
Wise in our negligence, have secret feet
In some of our best ports, and are *at point*
To show their open banner. *Ibid.* iii. 1.

ATHWART. *Wrongly ; adversely ; vexatiously ; across.*
The baby beats the nurse, and quite *athwart*
Goes all decorum. *Measure for Measure*, i. 3.
When, all *athwart*, there came
A post from Wales loaden with heavy news.
Henry 4, P. 1, i. 1.
Athwart the lane,
He, with two striplings,—lads more like to run
The country base than to commit such slaughter,—
Made good the passage. *Cymbeline*, v. 3.

Athwart men's noses as they lie asleep.
Romeo and Juliet, i. 4.

A-TIME. *For a time ; awhile.*
But there is
No danger in what show of death it makes,
More than the locking-up the spirits *a-time*,
To be more fresh, reviving. *Cymbeline*, i. 5.

ATOMY. *An atom ; a mote.*
It is as easy to count *atomies* as to resolve the
propositions of a lover. *As you like it*, iii. 2.
Drawn with a team of little *atomies*
Athwart men's noses as they lie asleep.
Romeo and Juliet, i. 4.

To ATONE. *To reconcile ; to agree.*
Since we can not *atone* you, we shall see
Justice design the victor's chivalry. *Richard 2*, i. 1.
I would do much
To *atone* them, for the love I bear to Cassio.
Othello, iv. 1.
To forget them quite
Were to remember that the present need
Speaks to *atone* you. *Antony and Cleopatra*, ii. 2.
He and Aufidius can no more *atone*
Than violentest contrariety. *Coriolanus*, iv. 6.

ATONEMENT. *Reconciliation ; agreement.*
If we do now make our *atonement* well,
Our peace will, like a broken limb united,
Grow stronger for the breaking.
Henry 4, P. 2, iv. 1.
Ay, madam : he desires to make *atonement*
Between the Duke of Gloster and your brothers.
Richard 3, i. 3.

To ATTACH. *To arrest; to seize; to be subject to.*
I therefore apprehend and do *attach* thee
For an abuser of the world. *Othello*, i. 2.
Old lord, I cannot blame thee,
Who am myself *attach'd* with weariness.
Tempest, iii. 3.
For France hath flaw'd the league, and hath *attach'd*
Our merchants' goods at Bourdeaux. *Henry 8*, i. 1.
May worthy Troilus be half *attach'd*
With that which here his passion doth express?
Troilus and Cressida, v. 2.

ATTACHMENT. *Arrest; caption ; seizure.*
Sleep kill those pretty eyes,
And give as soft *attachment* to thy senses
As infants' empty of all thought !
Troilus and Cressida, iv. 2.

ATTAINDER. *Taint; stain; sully.*

Either I must, or have mine honour soil'd
With the *attainder* of his slanderous lips.
Richard 2, iv. 1.

So smooth he daub'd his vice with show of virtue,
That, his apparent open guilt omitted,
He liv'd from all *attainder* of suspect.
Richard 3, iii. 5.

ATTAINT. *Taint; stain; vice; defect; weariness.*

What simple thief brags of his own *attaint?*
Comedy of Errors, iii. 2.

There is no man hath a virtue that he hath not
a glimpse of; nor any man an *attaint,* but he carries some stain of it.   *Troilus and Cressida,* i. 2.

But freshly looks, and overbears *attaint.*
Henry 5, iii. Chorus.

ATTAINT. *Affected; touched.*

My tender youth was never yet *attaint*
With any passion of inflaming love.
Henry 6, P. 1, v. 5.

ATTAINTURE. *Disgrace.*

And her *attainture* will be Humphrey's fall.
Henry 6, P. 2, i. 2.

To ATTASK. *To blame; to tax; to condemn.*

You are much more *attask'd* for want of wisdom
Than prais'd for harmful mildness.
King Lear, i. 4.

ATTEMPT. *Pursuit; object; achievement; action.*

Such poor, such base, such lewd, such mean *attempts,*
Such barren pleasures, rude society.
Henry 4, P. 1, iii. 2.

The man was noble,
But with his last *attempt* he wip'd it out.
Coriolanus, v. 3.

To ATTEMPT. *To tempt; to solicit; to induce; to prevail with; to assail.*

Dear sir, of force I must *attempt* you further.
Merchant of Venice, iv. 1.

This man of thine *attempts* her love.
Timon of Athens, i. 1.

Yet since I see you fearful, that neither my coat,
integrity, nor persuasion can with ease *attempt* you,
I will go further than I meant.
Measure for Measure, iv. 2.

Being down, insulted, rail'd,
And put upon him such a deal of man,

That worthied him, got praises of the king
For him *attempting* who was self-subdu'd.
King Lear, ii. 2.

ATTEMPTABLE. *Open to attack; assailable.*

This gentleman at that time vouching his to be
more fair, virtuous, wise, chaste, constant-qualified,
and less *attemptable,* than any the rarest of our
ladies in France.   *Cymbeline,* i. 4.

To ATTEND. *To wait for; to expect; to regard; to listen to.*

He was convoy'd by Richard duke of Gloster,
And the Lord Hastings, who *attended* him
In secret ambush on the forest-side.
Henry 6, P. 3, iv. 6.

Shame serves thy life, and doth thy death *attend.*
Richard 3, iv. 4.

I am *attended* at the cypress grove.
Coriolanus, i. 10.

The crow doth sing as sweetly as the lark,
When neither is *attended. Merchant of Venice,* v. 1.

She will *attend* it better in thy youth
Than in a nuncio of more grave aspéct.
Twelfth-Night, i. 4.

ATTENT. *Attentive.*

Season your admiration for a while
With an *attent* ear.   *Hamlet,* i. 2.

ATTEST. *Testimony; attestation; evidence.*

An esperance so obstinately strong,
That doth invert the *attest* of eyes and ears.
Troilus and Cressida, v. 2.

To ATTEST. *To call to witness; to invoke.*

But I *attest* the gods, your full consent
Gave wings to my propension.
Troilus and Cressida, ii. 2.

ATTORNEY. *Deputy.*

Then, in mine own person, I die.—
No, faith, die by *attorney. As you like it,* iv. 1.

I, by *attorney,* bless thee from thy mother,
Who prays continually for Richmond's good.
Richard 3, v. 3.

Therefore, dear mother,—I must call you so,—
Be the *attorney* of my love to her.   *Ibid.* iv. 4.

To ATTORNEY. *To perform by proxy; to employ as proxy.*

Their encounters, though not personal, have
been royally *attorneyed,* with interchange of gifts,
letters, loving embassies.   *Winter's Tale,* i. 1.

Not changing heart with habit, I am still
Attorney'd at your service.
Measure for Measure, v. 1.

ATTRIBUTE.   *Reputation; credit; honour.*

Much *attribute* he hath; and much the reason
Why we ascribe it to him.
Troilus and Cressida, ii. 3.
And, indeed, it takes
From our achievements, though perform'd at height,
The pith and marrow of our *attribute*. *Hamlet*, i. 4.

ATTRIBUTION.   *Allowance; commendation; approbation.*

If speaking truth
In this fine age were not thought flattery,
Such *attribution* should the Douglas have,
As not a soldier of this season's stamp
Should go so general current through the world.
Henry 4, P. 1, iv. 1.

ATTRIBUTIVE.   *Prompt to ascribe excellence; ready to commend.*

And the will dotes, that is *attributive*
To what infectiously itself affects,
Without some image of the affected merit.
Troilus and Cressida, ii. 2.

A-TWAIN.   *Asunder.*

Such smiling rogues as these,
Like rats, oft bite the holy cords *a-twain*
Which are too intrinse t' unloose. *King Lear*, ii. 2.

AUDACIOUS.   *Bold; daring; uncompromising.*

Audacious without impudency, learned without
opinion, and strange without heresy.
Love's Labour's lost, v. 1.

AUDACIOUSLY.   *Boldly; fearlessly; confidently.*

Yet fear not thou, but speak *audaciously*.
Love's Labour's lost, v. 2.

AUGURER.   *An augur; a soothsayer.*

What say the *augurers?*—They would not have
you to stir forth to-day. *Julius Cæsar*, ii. 2.
The *augurer* tells me we shall have news to-night.
Coriolanus, ii. 1.

AUGURS.   *Auguries; omens; abodements; prodigies.*

Augurs, and understood relations, have
By magot-pies and choughs and rooks brought forth
The secret'st man of blood. *Macbeth*, iii. 4.

AUNT.   *An old woman; a matron.*

The wisest *aunt*, telling the saddest tale,
Sometime for three-foot stool mistaketh me.
Midsummer-Night's Dream, ii. 1.

AVAIL.   *Advantage; benefit.*

When better fall, for your *avails* they fell.
All's well that ends well, iii. 1.
I charge thee,
As heaven shall work in me for thine *avail*,
To tell me truly. *Ibid.* i. 3.

AVAUNT.   *Away; be gone.*

After this process,
To give her the *avaunt!* it is a pity
Would move a monster. *Henry 8*, ii. 3.
Avaunt, thou hateful villain, get thee gone!
King John, iv. 3.

AVE.   *Salutation; shout.*

I do not relish well
Their loud applause and *aves* vehement.
Measure for Measure, i. 1.

To AVER.   *To allege; to bring forward; to produce.*

Averring notes
Of chamber-hanging, pictures, this her bracelet,—
Nay, some marks of secret on her person.
Cymbeline, v. 5.

AVISED.   *Informed; advised.*

Art *avis'd* o' that? more on't.
Measure for Measure, ii. 2.
Are you *avised* o' that?
Merry Wives of Windsor, i. 4.

To AVOID.   *To evade; to parry; to depart; to retire; to leave.*

Yet, as the matter now stands, he will *avoid* your
accusation,—he made trial of you only.
Measure for Measure, iii. 1.
Well done; *avoid;* no more. *Tempest*, iv. 1.
Let us *avoid*. *Winter's Tale*, i. 2.
Avoid, and leave him. *Antony and Cleopatra*, v. 2.
Avoid the gallery. *Henry 8*, v. 1.

AVOUCH.   *Testimony; evidence.*

Before my God, I might not this believe
Without the sensible and true *avouch*
Of mine own eyes. *Hamlet*, i. 1.

To AVOUCH.   *To declare; to affirm; to assert; to maintain.*

Is this well spoken?—I dare *avouch* it, sir.
King Lear, ii. 4.

You will think you have made no offence, if
the duke *avouch* the justice of your dealing?
Measure for Measure, iv. 2.

AWAY WITH.   *Bear; endure.*

She never could *away with* me.
Henry 4, P. 2, iii. 2.

AWFUL.   *Reverent; worshipful.*

Marry, peace it bodes, and love, and quiet life,
An *awful* rule, and right supremacy.
Taming of the Shrew, v. 2.
Know, then, that some of us are gentlemen,
Such as the fury of ungovern'd youth
Thrust from the company of *awful* men.
Two Gentlemen of Verona, iv. 1.

AWKWARD.   *Adverse; untoward.*

Was I for this nigh wreck'd upon the sea,

And twice by *aukward* wind from England's bank
Drove back again unto my native clime?
Henry 6, P. 2, iii. 2.

AWLESS.   *Fearless; unfeared.*

Against whose fury and unmatchèd force
The *awless* lion could not wage the fight,
Nor keep his princely heart from Richard's hand.
King John, i. 1.
Insulting tyranny begins to jet
Upon the innocent and *awless* throne.
Richard 3, ii. 4.

AZURED.   *Azure; blue.*

And 'twixt the green sea and the *azur'd* vault
Set roaring war. *Tempest,* v. 1.
Nor the *azur'd* harebell, like thy veins.
Cymbeline, iv. 2.

B.

BABY.   *A doll; a puppet.*

If trembling I inhibit thee, protest me
The *baby* of a girl. *Macbeth,* iii. 4.
A knack, a toy, a trick, a *baby's* cap.
Taming of the Shrew, iv. 3.

BACCARE.   *Go back; stand back.*

Baccare! you are marvellous forward.
Taming of the Shrew, ii. 1.

To BAFFLE.   *To insult; to mock; to mortify.*

I am disgrac'd, impeach'd, and *baffled* here.
Richard 2, i. 1.
Alas, poor fool, how have they *baffled* thee!
Twelfth-Night, v. 1.

BAIRN.   *An infant; a child.*

Mercy on's, a *bairn;* a very pretty *bairn!*
Winter's Tale, iii. 3.

BALANCE.   *A pair of scales.*

Are there *balance* here to weigh the flesh?
Merchant of Venice, iv. 1.

BALD.   *Bare-headed; uncovered.*

No question asked him by any of the senators, but
they
Stand *bald* before him. *Coriolanus,* iv. 5.

BALDRICK.   *A belt; a girdle.*

Or hang my bugle in an invisible *baldrick,* all
women shall pardon me.
Much Ado about Nothing, i. 1.

BALE.   *Loss; defeat.*

Rome and her rats are at the point of battle;
The one side must have *bale. Coriolanus,* i. 1.

BALEFUL.   *Poisonous; pernicious; deadly.*

I must up-fill this osier cage of ours
With *baleful* weeds and precious-juicèd flowers.
Romeo and Juliet, ii. 3.
Speak, Winchester; for boiling choler chokes
The hollow passage of my prison'd voice,
By sight of these our *baleful* enemies.
Henry 6, P. 1, v. 4.

To BALK.   *To heap up; to enridge; to omit;
to neglect; to leave undone.*

Ten thousand bold Scots, two-and-twenty knights,
Balk'd in their own blood, did Sir Walter see
On Holmedon's plains. *Henry* 4, P. 1, i. 1.
Balk logic with acquaintance that you have.
Taming of the Shrew, i. 1.
This was looked for at your hand, and this was
balked. Twelfth-Night, iii. 2.

To BALLAD.   *To make ballads or songs.*

And scald rhymers
Ballad us out o' tune. *Antony and Cleopatra,* v. 2.

BALLAST.   *Ballasted; supplied with ballast.*

Who sent whole armadoes of caracks to be *ballast*
at her nose. *Comedy of Errors,* iii. 2.

To BALLAST. *To balance; to counterpoise.*

> Then had my prize
> Been less; and so more equal *ballasting*
> To thee, Posthúmus.   *Cymbeline,* iii. 6.

BALLOW. *A cudgel; a staff.*

> Keep out, or ise try whether your costard or
> my *ballow* be the harder.   *King Lear,* iv. 6.

BALM. *Consecrated oil.*

> With mine own tears I wash away my *balm.*
>   *Richard 2,* iv. 1.

BAN. *A curse; a malediction.*

> Sometime with lunatic *bans,* sometime with prayers,
> Enforce their charity.   *King Lear,* ii. 3.
> Take thou that too, with multiplying *bans!*
>   *Timon of Athens,* iv. 1.
> Thou mixture rank, of midnight weeds collected,
> With Hecate's *ban* thrice blasted, thrice infected.
>   *Hamlet,* iii. 2.

To BAN. *To curse.*

> Fell *banning* hag, enchantress, hold thy tongue!
>   *Henry 6,* P. 1, v. 3.
> And, in thy closet pent up, rue my shame,
> And *ban* thine enemies, both mine and thine!
>   *Ibid.* P. 2, ii. 4.

BAND. *Bond.*

> Hast thou, according to thy oath and *band,*
> Brought hither Henry Hereford thy bold son?
>   *Richard 2,* i. 1.
> Tell me, was he arrested on a *band?*
>   *Comedy of Errors,* iv. 2.
> If not, the end of life cancels all *bands.*
>   *Henry 4,* P. 1, iii. 2.

BANDITTO. *An outlaw; a robber.*

> A Roman sworder and *banditto* slave
> Murder'd sweet Tully.   *Henry 6,* P. 2, iv. 1.

BAN-DOG. *A watch-dog; a house-dog.*

> The time when screech-owls cry, and *ban-dogs* howl.
>   *Henry 6,* P. 2, i. 4.

To BANDY. *To beat to and fro; to exchange; to contend.*

> My words would *bandy* her to my sweet love,
> And his to me.   *Romeo and Juliet,* ii. 5.
> Do you *bandy* looks with me, you rascal?
>   *King Lear,* i. 4.
> I will *bandy* with thee in faction; I will o'er-
> run thee with policy; I will kill thee in a hun-
> dred-and-fifty ways.   *As you like it,* v. 1.

BANDYING. *Contention; strife; quarrelling.*

> Tybalt,—Mercutio,—the prince expressly hath
> Forbidden *bandying* in Verona streets.
>   *Romeo and Juliet,* iii. 1.
> But howsoe'er, no simple man that sees
> This factious *bandying* of their favourites,
> But that he doth presage some ill event.
>   *Henry 6,* P. 1, iv. 1.

To BANE. *To poison.*

> What if my house be troubled with a rat,
> And I be pleas'd to give ten thousand ducats
> To have it *ban'd?*   *Merchant of Venice,* iv. 1.

To BANISH. *To carry into banishment.*

> And patient underbearing of his fortune,
> As 'twere to *banish* their affects with him.
>   *Richard 2,* i. 4.

To BANK. *To skirt; to pass; to coast.*

> Have I not heard these islanders shout out,
> Vive le roi! as I have *bank'd* their towns?
>   *King John,* v. 2.

BANNERET. *A small flag, or streamer.*

> Yet the scarfs and *bannerets* about thee did mani-
> foldly dissuade me from believing thee a vessel of too
> great a burden.
>   *All's well that ends well,* ii. 3.

BANQUET. *A slight refection; a dessert.*

> My *banquet* is to close our stomachs up,
> After our great good cheer.
>   *Taming of the Shrew,* v. 2.

To BANQUET. *To feast; to give feasts.*

> Or if you know
> That I profess myself in *banqueting*
> To all the rout, then hold me dangerous.
>   *Julius Cæsar,* i. 2.

BAR. *A place of congress.*

> I have labour'd
> With all my wits, my pains, and strong endeavours,
> To bring your most imperial majesties
> Unto this *bar* and royal interview. *Henry 5,* v. 2.

To BAR. *To except; to exclude.*

> Nay, but I *bar* to-night: you shall not gauge me
> By what we do to-night. *Merchant of Venice,* ii. 2.
> Nor have we herein *barr'd* your better wisdoms.
>   *Hamlet,* i. 2.

BARBARISM. *Ignorance; barbarity; cruelty.*

> I have for *barbarism* spoke more
> Than for that angel knowledge you can say.
>   *Love's Labour's lost,* i. 1.

Lest *barbarism*, making me the precedent,
Should a like language use to all degrees.
Winter's Tale, ii. 1.
That had not God, for some strong purpose, steel'd
The hearts of men, they must perforce have melted,
And *barbarism* itself have pitied him.
Richard 2, v. 2.

BARBED. *Furnished with armour.*

And now,—instead of mounting *barbèd* steeds
To fright the souls of fearful adversaries,—
He capers nimbly in a lady's chamber
To the lascivious pleasing of a lute. *Richard 3*, i. 1.

To BARBER. *To trim the hair or beard.*

Our courteous Antony,
Being *barber'd* ten times o'er, goes to the feast,
And, for his ordinary, pays his heart
For what his eyes eat only.
Antony and Cleopatra, ii. 2.

BARBER-MONGER. *A fop.*

Draw, you whoreson cullionly *barber-monger*, draw.
King Lear, ii. 2.

BARE. *Plain; simple; threadbare.*

She hath more qualities than a water-spaniel,—
which is much in a *bare* Christian.
Two Gentlemen of Verona, iii. 1.
But know, I come not
To hear such flatteries now, and in my presence;
They are too thin and *bare* to hide offences.
Henry 8, v. 2.

BARE. *Bore; carried.*

Who *bare* my letter, then, to Romeo?
Romeo and Juliet, v. 2.

BARFUL. *Clogged with difficulties; full of impediments.*

Yet, a *barful* strife!
Whoe'er I woo, myself would be his wife.
Twelfth-Night, i. 4.

To BARK. *To cover; to incrust.*

And a most instant tetter *bark'd* about
All my smooth body. *Hamlet*, i. 5.

BARKY. *Covered with bark.*

The female ivy so
Enrings the *barky* fingers of the elm.
Midsummer-Night's Dream, iv. 1.

BASE. *A well-known rustic game.*

Lads more like to run
The country *base* than to commit such slaughter.
Cymbeline, v. 3.

BASE. *Low; inferior; mean; humble; lower.*

It is the *base*, though bitter disposition of Beatrice that puts the world into her person, and so gives me out. *Much Ado about Nothing*, ii. 1.
The roof of this court is too high to be yours,
and welcome to the wide fields too *base* to be mine.
Love's Labour's lost, ii. 1.
I cannot think but your age has forgot me;
It could not else be, I should prove so *base*,
To sue, and be denied such common grace.
Timon of Athens, iii. 5.
My lord, in the *base* court he doth attend
To speak with you. *Richard 2*, iii. 3.

BASILISK. *A kind of cannon.*

And thou hast talk'd
Of *basilisks*, of cannon, culverin,
Of prisoners ransom'd, and of soldiers slain.
Henry 4, P. 1, ii. 3.

BASIS. *Pedestal; base.*

How many times shall Cæsar bleed in sport,
That now on Pompey's *basis* lies along,
No worthier than the dust! *Julius Cæsar*, iii. 1.
Troy, yet upon his *basis*, had been down,
And the great Hector's sword had lack'd a master,
But for these instances. *Troilus and Cressida*, i. 3.

BASTA. *Enough.*

Basta; content thee; for I have it full.
Taming of the Shrew, i. 1.

BASTARD. *A sort of sweet wine.*

Why, then, your brown *bastard* is your only drink. *Henry 4*, P. 1, ii. 4.
We shall have all the world drink brown and white *bastard*. *Measure for Measure*, iii. 2.

BATE. *Strife; contention.*

And breeds no *bate* with telling of discreet stories.
Henry 4, P. 2, ii. 4.

To BATE. *To leave out; to except; to fall away; to grow less; to flutter; to blunt.*

Were the world mine, Demetrius being *bated*,
The rest I'll give to be to you translated.
Midsummer-Night's Dream, i. 1.
Do I not *bate?* do I not dwindle?
Henry 4, P. 1, iii. 3.
'Tis a hooded valour; and when it appears, it will *bate*. *Henry 5*, iii. 6.
To watch her, as we watch these kites,
That *bate* and beat, and will not be obedient.
Taming of the Shrew, iv. 3.

When spite of cormorant devouring Time
Th' endeavour of this present breath may buy
That honour which shall *bate* his scythe's keen edge,
And make us heirs of all eternity.
　　　　　　　Love's Labour's lost, i. 1.

BATED.　*Bating; fluttering.*
Bated like eagles having lately bath'd.
　　　　　　　Henry 4, P. 1, iv. 1.

BATLET.　*A small bat; an instrument with which washers beat their coarse linen.*
And I remember the kissing of her *batlet.*
　　　　　　　As you like it, ii. 4.

BATTALIA.　*An entire army.*
Why, our *battalia* trebles that account.
　　　　　　　Richard 3, v. 3.
When sorrows come, they come not single spies,
But in *battalias.*　　*Hamlet,* iv. 5.

To BATTEN.　*To feed; to fatten.*
Follow your function, go,
And *batten* on cold bits.　*Coriolanus,* iv. 5.
Could you on this fair mountain leave to feed,
And *batten* on this moor?　*Hamlet,* iii. 4.

BATTLE.　*An army; the division of an army.*
The colour of the king doth come and go
Between his purpose and his conscience,
Like heralds 'twixt two dreadful *battles* set.
　　　　　　　King John, iv. 2.
Fire answers fire; and through their paly flames
Each *battle* sees the other's umber'd face.
　　　　　　　Henry 5, iii. Chorus.
What may the king's whole *battle* reach unto?
　　　　　　　Henry 4, P. 1, iv. 1.
The French are bravely in their *battles* set,
And will with all expedience charge on us.
　　　　　　　Henry 5, iv. 3.

BATTY.　*Batlike.*
Till o'er their brows death-counterfeiting sleep
With leaden legs and *batty* wings doth creep.
　　　　　　　Midsummer-Night's Dream, iii. 2.

BAVIN.　*Brushwood; a faggot.*
The skipping king, he ambled up and down,
With shallow jesters and rash *bavin* wits,
Soon kindled and soon burn'd.
　　　　　　　Henry 4, P. 1, iii. 2.

BAWBLING.　*Paltry.*
A *bawbling* vessel was he captain of.
　　　　　　　Twelfth-Night, v. 1.

BAWCOCK.　*A burlesque term of endearment.*
The king's a *bawcock,* and a heart of gold.
　　　　　　　Henry 5, iv. 1.
Why, how now, my *bawcock!* how dost thou, chuck?
　　　　　　　Twelfth-Night, iii. 4.

BEADSMAN.　*One employed in praying for another.*
And in thy danger,
If ever danger do environ thee,
Commend thy grievance to my holy prayers,
For I will be thy *beadsman,* Valentine.
　　　　　　　Two Gentlemen of Verona, i. 1.

BEAK.　*The prow.*
I boarded the king's ship; now on the *beak,*
Now in the waist, the deck, in every cabin.
　　　　　　　Tempest, i. 2.

BE-ALL.　*All that is to be done; the sole act.*
That but this blow
Might be the *be-all* and the end-all here,
We'd jump the life to come.　*Macbeth,* i. 7.

BEAM.　*A lance.*
And stands colossus-wise, waving his *beam.*
　　　　　　　Troilus and Cressida, v. 5.

To BEAR.　*To behave; to carry; to take; to subdue.*
Well, *bear* you well in this new spring of time,
Lest you be cropp'd before you come to prime.
　　　　　　　Richard 2, v. 2.
Supply me with the habit, and instruct me
How I may formally in person *bear* me
Like a true friar.　*Measure for Measure,* i. 3.
Hath he *borne* himself penitently in prison?
　　　　　　　Ibid. iv. 2.
So may he with more facile question *bear* it,
For that it stands not in such warlike brace,
But altogether lacks the abilities
That Rhodes is dress'd in.　*Othello,* i. 3.

To BEAR A BRAIN.　*To remember; to recollect.*
My lord and you were then at Mantua:—
Nay, I do *bear a brain.*　*Romeo and Juliet,* i. 3.

To BEAR HARD.　*To have a spite against; to take amiss; to resent.*
Cæsar doth *bear me hard;* but he loves Brutus.
　　　　　　　Julius Cæsar, i. 2.
I do beseech ye, if you *bear me hard,*
Now, whilst your purpled hands do reek and smoke,
Fulfil your pleasure.　*Ibid.* iii. 1.

E

The archbishop of York, is't not?—True; who *bears*
　　hard
His brother's death at Bristol. *Henry* 4, P. 1, i. 3.

TO BEAR IN HAND. *To keep in expectation;
to pretend; to deceive; to delude.*
The duke
Bore many gentlemen, myself being one,
In hand, and hope of action.
　　　　　Measure for Measure, i. 4.
Your daughter, whom she *bore in hand* to love
With such integrity, she did confess
Was as a scorpion to her sight.　*Cymbeline,* v. 5.
　　　　Whereat griev'd,
That so his sickness, age, and impotence,
Was falsely *borne in hand,* sends out arrests
On Fortinbras.　　　　　*Hamlet,* ii. 2.
I made good to you in our last conference
How you were *borne in hand,* how cross'd.
　　　　　Macbeth, iii. 1.

TO BEAR OUT. *To support; to favour; to
countenance.*
　And if I cannot once or twice in a quarter *bear
out* a knave against an honest man, I have but a
very little credit with your worship.
　　　　　Henry 4, P. 2, v. 1.

TO BEAR THE KNAVE. *To brook insulting
language.*
Ay, as an ostler, that for the poorest piece
Will *bear the knave* by the volume.
　　　　　Coriolanus, iii. 3.

TO BEARD. *To oppose; to defy.*
No man so potent breathes upon the ground
But I will *beard* him.　*Henry* 4, P. 1, iv. 1.

BEARING-CLOTH. *A baptismal cloth or mantle.*
Look thee, a *bearing-cloth* for a squire's child!
　　　　　Winter's Tale, iii. 3.
Thy scarlet robes as a child's *bearing-cloth*
I'll use to carry thee out of this place.
　　　　　Henry 6, P. 1, i. 3.

TO BEAT. *To dwell upon without ceasing; to
hammer.*
Do not infest your mind with *beating* on
The strangeness of this business.　*Tempest,* v. 1.
　And now, I pray you, sir,—
For still 'tis *beating* in my mind,—your reason
For raising this sea-storm?　　*Ibid.* i. 2.
　Thine eyes and thoughts
Beat on a crown, the treasure of thy heart.
　　　　　Henry 6, P. 2, ii. 1.

Whereon his brains still *beating* puts him thus
From fashion of himself.　*Hamlet,* iii. 1.

BEAUTIFIED. *Beautiful.*
To the celestial, and my soul's idol, the most
beautified Ophelia.　　*Hamlet,* ii. 2.

TO BEAUTY. *To beautify; to adorn.*
The harlot's cheek, *beautied* with plastering art,
Is not more ugly to the thing that helps it
Than is my deed to my most painted word.
　　　　　Hamlet, iii. 1.

BEAVER. *A helmet; that part of the helmet
which covered the lower part of the face.*
I saw young Harry, with his *beaver* on,
His cuisses on his thighs, gallantly arm'd.
　　　　　Henry 4, P. 1, iv. 1.
What, is my *beaver* easier than it was?
　　　　　Richard 3, v. 3.
Their armèd staves in charge, their *beavers* down.
　　　　　Henry 4, P. 2, iv. 1.

TO BECHANCE. *To happen to; to befall.*
All happiness *bechance* to thee in Milan!
　　　　　Two Gentlemen of Verona, i. 1.
My sons,—God knows what hath *bechancèd* them.
　　　　　Henry 6, P. 3, i. 3.

TO BECK. *To beckon; to make signs.*
Bell, book, and candle shall not drive me back,
When gold and silver *becks* me to come on.
　　　　　King John, iii. 3.
O this false soul of Egypt! this grave charm,
Whose eye *beck'd* forth my wars, and call'd them
　home.　　*Antony and Cleopatra,* iv. 12.

TO BECOME. *To go; to suit; to befit; to
grace; to dignify.*
I cannot joy, until I be resolv'd
Where our right valiant father is *become.*
　　　　　Henry 6, P. 3, ii. 1.
But, madam, where is Warwick, then, *become?*
　　　　　Ibid. P. 3, iv. 6.
　If I *become* not a cart as well as another man, a
plague on my bringing up!　*Henry* 4, P. 1, ii. 4.
But since your falsehood shall *become* you well
To worship shadows and adore false shapes,
Send to me in the morning, and I'll send it.
　　　　　Two Gentlemen of Verona, iv. 2.
Look sweet, speak fair, *become* disloyalty.
　　　　　Comedy of Errors, iii. 1.
Observe how Antony *becomes* his flaw.
　　　　　Antony and Cleopatra, iii. 12.

The vilest things
Become themselves in her.
Antony and Cleopatra, ii. 2.

BECOMED. *Becoming; seemly; become; beseemed; befitted.*

I met the youthful lord at Lawrence' cell;
And gave him what *becomèd* love I might,
Not stepping o'er the bounds of modesty.
Romeo and Juliet, iv. 2.
A good rebuke,
Which might have well *becom'd* the best of men,
To taunt at slackness. *Antony and Cleopatra*, iii. 7.
The forlorn soldier, that so nobly fought,
He would have well *becom'd* this place, and grac'd
The thankings of a king. *Cymbeline*, v. 5.

BECOMINGS. *Perfections; graces.*

But, sir, forgive me;
Since my *becomings* kill me, when they do not
Eye well to you. *Antony and Cleopatra*, i. 3.

To BEDASH. *To besprinkle.*

That all the standers-by had wet their cheeks,
Like trees *bedash'd* with rain. *Richard 3*, i. 2.

BEDLAM. *A madman; a lunatic.*

Let's follow the old earl, and get the *Bedlam*
To lead him where he would: his roguish madness
Allows itself to any thing. *King Lear*, iii. 7.

To BEDRENCH. *To soak; to moisten; to drench.*

Far off from the mind of Bolingbroke
It is, such crimson tempest should *bedrench*
The fresh green lap of fair King Richard's land.
Richard 2, iii. 3.

BED-SWERVER. *An adulteress.*

What she should shame to know herself
But with her most vile principal, that she's
A *bed-swerver*. *Winter's Tale*, ii. 1.

BEDWARD. *Toward bed.*

In heart
As merry as when our nuptial day was done,
And tapers burn'd to *bedward*! *Coriolanus*, i. 6.

BEEF-WITTED. *Ox-witted; dull; stupid.*

The plague of Greece upon thee, thou mongrel
beef-witted lord! *Troilus and Cressida*, ii. 1.

To BEETLE. *To jut out; to project.*

Or to the dreadful summit of the cliff
That *beetles* o'er his base into the sea. *Hamlet*, i. 4.

BEEVES. *Oxen; cattle; beef.*

And now has he land and *beeves*.
Henry 4, P. 2, iii. 2.
They want their porridge and their fat bull-*beeves*.
Henry 6, P. 1, i. 2.

To BEFORTUNE. *To happen to; to befall.*

As much I wish all good *befortune* you.
Two Gentlemen of Verona, iv. 2.

To BEGGAR. *To lessen; to abate; to depreciate.*

And do a deed that fortune never did,—
Beggar the estimation which you priz'd
Richer than sea and land.
Troilus and Cressida, ii. 2.

BE HANGED AN HOUR. *Be hanged awhile; be hanged to you; a petty oath or execration.*

Show your sheep-biting face, and *be hanged an hour!*
Measure for Measure, v. 1.

To BEHAVE. *To govern; to subdue.*

And with such sober and unnoted passion
He did *behave* his anger, ere 'twas spent,
As if he had but prov'd an argument.
Timon of Athens, iii. 5.

BEHAVIOUR. *Presence; person; demeanour; bearing.*

There is a fair *behaviour* in thee, captain;
And I will believe thou hast a mind that suits
With this thy fair and outward character.
Twelfth-Night, i. 2.
Thus, after greeting, speaks the King of France,
In my *behaviour*, to the majesty,
The borrow'd majesty of England here.
King John, i. 1.

BEHEST. *Command.*

Away! and, to be blest,
Let us with care perform his great *behest*.
Cymbeline, v. 4.

BEHOLDING. *Beholden; obliged to.*

She is *beholding* to thee, gentle youth.
Two Gentlemen of Verona, iv. 2.

BEHOVE. *Behoof; advantage; profit.*

To contract, O, the time, for, ah, my *behove*,
O, methought, there was nothing meet.
Hamlet, v. 1.

BEHOVEFUL. *Useful; needful.*
No, madam; we have cull'd such necessaries
As are *behoveful* for our state to-morrow.
Romeo and Juliet, iv. 3.

BEING. *Abode; residence.*
To shift his *being*
Is to exchange one misery with another.
Cymbeline, i. 5.

BELIKE. *Probably; perhaps.*
Belike this is a man of that quirk.
Twelfth-Night, iii. 4.
Belike that now she hath enfranchis'd them.
Two Gentlemen of Verona, ii. 4.

To BELLY. *To swell out; to fill.*
Your breath of full consent *bellied* his sails.
Troilus and Cressida, ii. 2.

BELONGING. *Endowment; gift; qualification; talents.*
Thyself and thy *belongings*
Are not thine own so proper, as to waste
Thyself upon thy virtues, they on thee.
Measure for Measure, i. 1.

To BEMAD. *To make mad; to madden.*
Some that will thank you, making just report
Of how unnatural and *bemadding* sorrow
The king hath cause to plain. *King Lear*, iii. 1.

To BEMETE. *To measure.*
Or I shall so *bemete* thee with thy yard,
As thou shalt think on prating whilst thou liv'st.
Taming of the Shrew, iv. 3.

To BEMOCK. *To taunt; to insult; to laugh at.*
Bemock the modest moon. *Coriolanus*, i. 1.
Or with *bemock'd*-at stabs
Kill the still-closing waters. *Tempest*, iii. 3.

To BEMOIL. *To bemire; to bedraggle.*
Thou shouldst have heard, in how miry a place,
Now she was *bemoiled*. *Taming of the Shrew*, iv. 1.

To BE-MONSTER. *To make monstrous; to deform.*
Thou changèd and self-cover'd thing, for shame,
Be-monster not thy feature. *King Lear*, iv. 2.

BE NAUGHT AWHILE. *Be hanged an hour.*
See *Measure for Measure*, v. 1.
Marry, sir, be better employed, and *be naught awhile*.
As you like it, i. 1.

To BENCH. *To advance; to dignify; to sit.*
His cupbearer, whom I from meaner form
Have *bench'd*, and rear'd to worship.
Winter's Tale, i. 2.
And thou, his yoke-fellow of equity,
Bench by his side. *King Lear*, iii. 6.

BEND. *A glance of the eye; a look.*
And that same eye, whose *bend* doth awe the world,
Did lose his lustre. *Julius Cæsar*, i. 2.
Her gentlewomen, like the Nereides,
So many mermaids, tended her i' the eyes,
And made their *bends* adornings.
Antony and Cleopatra, ii. 2.

To BEND. *To make for; to direct to a certain point.*
My best train
I have from your Sicilian shores dismiss'd;
Who for Bohemia *bend*. *Winter's Tale*, v. 1.
The associates tend, and every thing is *bent*
For England. *Hamlet*, iv. 3.

To BEND UP. *To strain; to stretch.*
Hold hard the breath, and *bend up* every spirit
To his full height! *Henry 5*, iii. 1.
I am settled, and *bend up*
Each corporal agent to this terrible feat.
Macbeth, i. 7.

BENEATH. *Lower; under.*
I have, in this rough work, shap'd out a man,
Whom this *beneath* world doth embrace and hug
With amplest entertainment.
Timon of Athens, i. 1.

BENISON. *Blessing.*
The bounty and the *benison* of heaven
To boot, and boot! *King Lear*, iv. 6.
Therefore be gone
Without our grace, our love, our *benison*.
Ibid. i. 1.

BENT. *Bend, power of bending.*
For I can give his humour the true *bent*,
And I will bring him to the Capitol.
Julius Cæsar, ii. 1.
Eternity was in our lips and eyes,
Bliss in our brows' *bent*.
Antony and Cleopatra, i. 3.
They seem to pity the lady: it seems her affections have their full *bent*.
Much Ado about Nothing, ii. 3.
They fool me to the top of my *bent*. *Hamlet*, iii. 2.

BENUMBED. *Besotted; infatuated.*
If this law
Of nature be corrupted by affection;
And that great minds, of partial indulgence
To their *benumbèd* wills, resist the same;
There is a law in each well-order'd nation,
To curb those raging appetites that are
Most disobedient and refractory.
Troilus and Cressida, ii. 2.

To BE ODD WITH. *To be at odds with; to be at variance; to quarrel.*
The general state, I fear,
Can scarce entreat you to *be odd with* him.
Troilus and Cressida, iv. 5.

To BEQUEATH. *To give; to offer; to tender.*
A sister I *bequeath* you, whom no brother
Did ever love so dearly.
Antony and Cleopatra, ii. 2.
To whom, with all submission, on my knee,
I do *bequeath* my faithful services
And true subjection everlastingly. *King John,* v. 7.

To BERATTLE. *To fill with noise.*
These are now the fashion; and so *berattle* the common stages (so they call them), that many wearing rapiers are afraid of goose-quills, and dare scarce come hither. *Hamlet,* ii. 2.

BERMOOTHES. *Bermudas.*
Thou call'dst me up at midnight to fetch dew
From the still-vex'd *Bermoothes.* *Tempest,* i. 2.

To BESCREEN. *To shelter; to conceal; to screen.*
What man art thou, that, thus *bescreen'd* in night,
So stumblest on my counsel?
Romeo and Juliet, ii. 2.

BESEECH. *Request; entreaty; supplication.*
Therefore this maxim out of love I teach,—
Achievement is command; ungain'd, *beseech.*
Troilus and Cressida, i. 2.

BESEEMING. *Appearance; garb; raiment.*
I am, sir,
The soldier that did company these three
In poor *beseeming.* *Cymbeline,* v. 5.

To BESHREW. *To curse; to wish ill or shame to; to execrate.*
Now much *beshrew* my manners and my pride,
If Hermia meant to say, Lysander lied.
Midsummer-Night's Dream, ii. 2.

BESIDES. *Beside; out of; beyond.*
Quite *besides*
The government of patience! *Cymbeline,* ii. 4.
Alas, sir, how fell you *besides* your five wits?
Twelfth-Night, iv. 2.

To BESLUBBER. *To smear.*
And then to *beslubber* our garments with it, and swear it was the blood of true men.
Henry 4, P. 1, ii. 4.

To BESMIRCH. *To stain; to sully; to tarnish.*
Our gayness and our gilt are all *besmirch'd*
With rainy marching in the painful field.
Henry 5, iv. 3.
And now no soil nor cautel doth *besmirch*
The virtue of his will. *Hamlet,* i. 3.

BESORT. *Attendance; company; society.*
With such accommodation and *besort*
As levels with her breeding. *Othello,* i. 3.

To BESORT. *To become; to befit.*
And the remainder, that shall still depend,
To be such men as may *besort* your age,
Which know themselves and you. *King Lear,* i. 4.

To BESPICE. *To drug; to poison.*
Thou mightst *bespice* a cup,
To give mine enemy a lasting wink;
Which draught to me were cordial.
Winter's Tale, i. 2.

BEST. *Chiefs; leading men.*
Send us to Rome
The *best,* with whom we may articulate
For their own good and ours. *Coriolanus,* i. 9.

BEST. *Bravest.*
For Nym,—he hath heard that men of few words
are the *best* men; and therefore he scorns to say his prayers, lest 'a should be thought a coward.
Henry 5, iii. 1.

BESTED. *Provided; furnished; prepared.*
I never saw a fellow worse *bested,*
Or more afraid to fight, than is the appellant,
The servant of this armorer, my lords.
Henry 6, P. 2, ii. 3.

To BESTOW. *To stow; to conduct; to bear; to exhibit; to show.*
Hence, and *bestow* your luggage where you found it.
Tempest, v. 1.
Good reverend father, make my person yours,
And tell me how you would *bestow* yourself.
King John, iii. 1.

The boy is fair,
Of female favour, and *bestows* himself
Like a ripe sister. *As you like it*, iv. 3.
How might we see Falstaff *bestow* himself to-
night in his true colours, and not ourselves be seen?
Henry 4, P. 2, ii. 2.
My sovereign lord, *bestow* yourself with speed.
Henry 5, iv. 3.

BESTOWING. *Ability; capacity.*

And all my powers do their *bestowing* lose,
Like vassalage at unawares encountering
The eye of majesty. *Troilus and Cressida*, iii. 2.

BESTRAUGHT. *Mad.*

What! I am not *bestraught*.
Taming of the Shrew, Induction, sc. 2.

To BETEEM. *To give; to afford; to yield;
to suffer; to permit.*

Belike for want of rain, which I could well
Beteem them from the tempest of mine eyes.
Midsummer-Night's Dream, i. 1.
So loving to my mother,
That he might not *beteem* the winds of heaven
Visit her face too roughly. *Hamlet*, i. 2.

To BETHINK. *To consider; to call to mind;
to reflect.*

Romeo that spoke him fair, bade him *bethink*.
How nice the quarrel was, and urg'd withal
Your high displeasure. *Romeo and Juliet*, iii. 2.
I have *bethought* me of another fault.
Measure for Measure, v. 1.

To BETIDE. *To happen; to bechance; to befall.*

And let them tell thee tales
Of woeful ages long ago *betid*. *Richard 2*, v. 1.
No, not so much perdition as an hair
Betid to any creature in the vessel
Which thou heard'st cry, which thou saw'st sink.
Tempest, i. 2.
Neither know I
What is *betid* to Cloten; but remain
Perplex'd in all. *Cymbeline*, iv. 3.

BETOSSED. *Disturbed; agitated.*

What said my man, when my *betossèd* soul
Did not attend him as we rode? I think
He told me Paris should have married Juliet.
Romeo and Juliet, v. 3.

To BETRIM. *To adorn; to decorate; to dress
up.*

Thy banks with peonèd and lilied brims,
Which spongy April at thy hest *betrims*.
Tempest, iv. 1.

BETTER. *Best; quickest.*

Go not my horse the *better*,
I must become a borrower of the night
For a dark hour or twain. *Macbeth*, iii. 1.

To BETTER. *To surpass; to excel; to magnify; to exaggerate.*

What you do
Still *betters* what is done. *Winter's Tale*, iv. 3.
Not unlike, each way, to *better* yours.
Coriolanus, iii. 1.
I have seen you both :
But since he is *better'd*, we have therefore odds.
Hamlet, v. 2.
Bettering thy loss, makes the bad-causer worse.
Richard 3, iv. 4.

BETWEEN. *Interval; intermediate time.*

For there is nothing in the *between* but wronging the ancientry, stealing, fighting.
Winter's Tale, iii. 3.

BEVY. *A company; an assembly; kind;
sort; feather.*

None here, he hopes,
In all this noble *bevy* has brought with her
One care abroad. *Henry 8*, i. 4.
And many more of the same *bevy*, that, I know,
the drossy age dotes on. *Hamlet*, v. 2.

BEWITCHMENT. *Fascination; flattery; ca-
jolery.*

That is, sir, I will counterfeit the *bewitchment*
of some popular man, and give it bountiful to the
desirers. *Coriolanus*, ii. 3.

To BEWRAY. *To betray; to show; to discover.*

Here comes the queen, whose looks *bewray* her
anger. *Henry 6*, P. 3, i. 1.
He did *bewray* his practice; and receiv'd
This hurt you see, striving to apprehend him.
King Lear, ii. 1.
Mark the high noises ; and thyself *bewray*,
When false opinion, whose wrong thought defiles
thee,
In thy just proof, repeals and reconciles thee.
Ibid. iii. 6.

Should we be silent and not speak, our raiment
And state of bodies would *betray* what life
We have led since thy exile. *Coriolanus,* v. 3.

BEYOND ALL TALENTS. *Above all riches.*

In himself, 'tis much ;
In you,—which I count his, *beyond all talents,*—
Whilst I am bound to wonder, I am bound
To pity too. *Cymbeline,* i. 6.

BEZONIAN. *A beggar ; a scoundrel.*

Great men oft die by vile *bezonians.*
Henry 6, P. 2, iv. 1.
Under which king, *bezonian ?* speak, or die.
Henry 4, P. 2, v. 3.

BIAS. *Protuberant ; swelling ; puffed out.*

Blow, villain, till thy sphered *bias* cheek
Outswell the colic of puff'd Aquilon.
Troilus and Cressida, iv. 5.

BIAS AND THWART. *Crookedly ; contrarily ; obliquely ; adversely.*

Sith every action that hath gone before,
Whereof we have record, trial did draw
Bias and thwart, not answering the aim.
Troilus and Cressida, iv. 5.

BIAS-DRAWING. *Bias ; partiality.*

But in this extant moment, faith and troth
Strain'd purely from all hollow *bias-drawing,*
Bids thee, great Hector, welcome.
Troilus and Cressida, iv. 5.

BIBBLE-BABBLE. *Idle talk.*

Endeavour thyself to sleep, and leave thy vain
bibble-babble. *Twelfth-Night,* iv. 2.

To BID. *To give ; to offer.*

Stand we in good array; for they no doubt
Will issue out again, and *bid* us battle.
Henry 6, P. 3, v. 1.
Thou and Oxford, with five thousand men,
Shall cross the seas, and *bid* false Edward battle.
Ibid. iii. 3.

To BIDE. *To abide ; to bear ; to endure ; to suffer.*

Of all one pain,—save for a night of groans
Endur'd of her, for whom you *bid* like sorrow.
Richard 3, iv. 4.
Poor naked wretches, wheresoe'er you are,
That *bide* the pelting of this pitiless storm.
King Lear, iv. 6.

BIDING. *Habitation ; residence ; dwelling.*

Give me your hand, I'll lead you to some *biding.*
King Lear, iv. 6.

BIGGIN. *A nightcap.*

Sleep with it now !
Yet not so sound and half so deeply sweet
As he whose brow with homely *biggin* bound
Snores out the watch of night. *Henry* 4, P. 2, iv. 4.

BILBO. *A sword.*

I combat challenge of this latten *bilbo.*
Merry Wives of Windsor, i. 1.

BILBOES. *An instrument formerly in use for the punishment of refractory sailors.*

Methought I lay
Worse than the mutines in the *bilboes.*
Hamlet, v. 2.

BILL. *A petition ; a letter ; a paper ; a pike or halberd ; a halberdier.*

Why, I'll exhibit a *bill* in the parliament for
the putting down of fat men.
Merry Wives of Windsor, ii. 1.
Ride, ride, Messala, ride, and give these *bills*
Unto the legions on the other side.
Julius Cæsar, v. 2.
Whereby he does receive
Particular addition, from the *bill*
That writes them all alike. *Macbeth,* iii. 1.
Only have a care that your *bills* be not stolen.
Much Ado about Nothing, iii. 3.
There's my gauntlet ; I'll prove it on a giant.—
Bring up the brown *bills.* *King Lear,* iv. 6.

BIRTHDOM. *Birthright.*

Let us rather
Hold fast the mortal sword ; and, like good men,
Bestride our down-fall'n *birthdom.* *Macbeth,* iv. 3.

BISSON. *Blind.*

What harm can your *bisson* conspectuities glean
out of this character, if I be known well enough
too ? *Coriolanus,* ii. 1.
How shall this *bisson* multitude digest
The senate's courtesy ? *Ibid.* iii. 1.

To BITE. *To cut ; to pierce.*

Were it a casque compos'd by Vulcan's skill,
My sword should *bite* it. *Troilus and Cressida,* v. 2.
I have seen the day, with my good *biting* falchion
I would have made them skip : I am old now,
And these same crosses spoil me. *King Lear,* v. 3.

BLAME. *Fault; failing; crime.*

'Tis his own *blame;* hath put himself from rest,
And must needs taste his folly. *King Lear,* ii. 4.
    My high-repented *blames,*
Dear sovereign, pardon to me.
    All's well that ends well, v. 3.
    Here abjure
The taints and *blames* I laid upon myself,
For strangers to my nature. *Macbeth,* iv. 3.

BLAME. *Blameworthy; blamable; without excuse.*

In faith, my lord, you are too wilful-*blame.*
    Henry 4, P. 1, iii. 1.

BLANK. *Aim; mark.*

    The harlot king
Is quite beyond mine arm, out of the *blank*
And level of my brain, plot-proof.
    Winter's Tale, ii. 3.
    So, haply slander,—
Whose whisper o'er the world's diameter,
As level as the cannon to his *blank,*
Transports his poison'd shot,—may miss our name,
And hit the woundless air. *Hamlet,* iv. 1.
I have spoken for you all my best,
And stood within the *blank* of his displeasure
For my free speech. *Othello,* iii. 4.

BLANKET. *Curtain.*

That my keen knife see not the wound it makes,
Nor heaven peep through the *blanket* of the dark,
To cry, " Hold, hold !" *Macbeth,* i. 5.

BLAST. *A sudden stroke of disease; an infection.*

    Blasts and fogs upon thee !
Th' untented woundings of a father's curse
Pierce every sense about thee ! *King Lear,* i. 4.
Bring with thee airs from heaven or *blasts* from hell,
Be thy intents wicked or charitable,
Thou com'st in such a questionable shape,
That I will speak to thee. *Hamlet,* i. 4.

To BLAST. *To wither; to perish; to burst; to fail.*

    Blasting in the bud,
Losing his verdure even in the prime,
And all the fair effects of future hopes.
    Two Gentlemen of Verona, i. 1.
    Therefore this project
Should have a back or second, that might hold,
If this should *blast* in proof. *Hamlet,* iv. 7.

BLASTMENT. *A sudden stroke of infection; a blast.*

And in the morn and liquid dew of youth
Contagious *blastments* are most imminent.
    Hamlet, i. 3.

To BLAZE. *To make known; to publish.*

Where thou shalt live, till we can find a time
To *blaze* your marriage, reconcile your friends,
Beg pardon of the prince, and call thee back
With twenty hundred thousand times more joy
Than thou went'st forth in lamentation.
    Romeo and Juliet, iii. 3.

BLAZON. *Disclosure; declaration; proclamation; publication.*

But this eternal *blazon* must not be
To ears of flesh and blood. *Hamlet,* i. 5.
" Above my fortunes, yet my state is well :
I am a gentleman." I'll be sworn thou art ;
Thy tongue, thy face, thy limbs, actions, and spirit,
Do give thee five-fold *blazon.* *Twelfth-Night,* i. 5.

To BLAZON. *To display; to manifest.*

    O thou goddess,
Thou divine Nature, how thyself thou *blazon'st*
In these two princely boys ! *Cymbeline,* iv. 2.

To BLEAR. *To dim; to disfigure with weeping.*

And the *bleared* sights are spectacled to see him.
    Coriolanus, ii. 1.
While counterfeit supposes *blear'd* thine eyne.
    Taming of the Shrew, v. 1.
The rest aloof are the Dardanian wives,
With *bleared* visages, come forth to view
The issue of the exploit. *Merchant of Venice,* iii. 2.

To BLENCH. *To shrink; to start back; to turn aside; to deviate; to err; to mistake.*

Patience herself, what goddess e'er she be,
Doth lesser *blench* at sufferance than I do.
    Troilus and Cressida, i. 1.
I'll tent him to the quick: if he but *blench,*
I know my course. *Hamlet,* ii. 2.
    There can be no evasion
To *blench* from this, and to stand firm by honour.
    Troilus and Cressida, ii. 2.
And hold you ever to our special drift ;
Though sometimes you do *blench* from this to that,
As cause doth minister. *Measure for Measure,* iv. 5.
    Would I do this ?
Could man so *blench ?* *Winter's Tale,* i. 2.

BLIND-WORM. *The slow-worm; a small viper.*
Newts and *blind-worms*, do no wrong.
Midsummer-Night's Dream, ii. 2.

BLOAT. *Bloated; swollen.*
Not this, by no means, that I bid you do :
Let the *bloat* king tempt you again to bed.
Hamlet, iii. 4.

BLOCK. *The wooden mould on which the crown of a hat is formed.*
This' a good *block* :—
It were a delicate stratagem, to shoe
A troop of horse with felt : I'll put 't in proof;
And when I have stol'n upon these sons-in-law,
Then, kill, kill, kill, kill, kill, kill !
King Lear, iv. 6.
He wears his faith but as the fashion of his hat;
it ever changes with the next *block*.
Much Ado about Nothing, i. 1.

BLOCKISH. *Dull; stupid.*
And, by device, let *blockish* Ajax draw
The sort to fight with Hector.
Troilus and Cressida, i. 3.

BLOOD. *Inclination; disposition; race; family.*
Blood, thou still art *blood* :
Let's write good angel on the devil's horn,
'Tis not the devil's crest.
Measure for Measure, ii. 4.
For beauty is a witch,
Against whose charms faith melteth into *blood*.
Much Ado about Nothing, ii. 1.
Know of your youth, examine well your *blood*.
Midsummer-Night's Dream, i. 1.
Now his important *blood* will naught deny
That she'll demand. *All's well that ends well*, iii. 7.
Let thy *blood* be thy direction till thy death !
Troilus and Cressida, ii. 3.
Rome, thou hast lost the breed of noble *bloods* !
Julius Cæsar, i. 2.

BLOOD-BOLTERED. *Smeared with blood.*
Now, I see, 'tis true ;
For the *blood-bolter'd* Banquo smiles upon me,
And points at them for his.
Macbeth, iv. 1.

BLOODY. *Cruel; fierce; savage; relentless.*
And he is bred out of that *bloody* strain
That haunted us in our familiar paths.
Henry 5, ii. 4.
Some *bloody* passion shakes your very frame.
Othello, v. 2.

So is he mine ; and in such *bloody* distance,
That every minute of his being thrusts
Against my near'st of life.
Macbeth, iii. 1.

BLOT. *Stain; spot; fault; blemish.*
I yet beseech your majesty that you make known
It is no vicious *blot*, murder, or foulness,
No unchaste action, or dishonour'd step,
That hath depriv'd me of your grace and favour.
King Lear, i. 1.

To BLOW. *To swell; to inflate.*
Ne'er through an arch so hurried the *blown* tide,
As the recomforted through the gates.
Coriolanus, v. 4.
Exchange me for a goat,
When I shall turn the business of my soul
To such exsufflicate and *blown* surmises.
Othello, iii. 3.
No *blown* ambition doth our arms incite,
But love, dear love, and our ag'd father's right.
King Lear, iv. 4.
Here, on her breast,
There is a vent of blood, and something *blown* :
The like is on her arm. *Antony and Cleopatra*, v. 2.
A plague of sighing and grief ! it *blows* a man
up like a bladder. *Henry 4, P. 1*, ii. 4.

BLUE. *Livid; discoloured.*
A *blue* eye and sunken,—which you have not.
As you like it, iii. 2.

BLUE-CAP. *A Scot.*
Well, he is there too, and one Mordake, and a
thousand *blue-caps* more. *Henry 4, P. 1*, ii. 4.

BLUE-EYED. *Having livid or discoloured eyes.*
This *blue-ey'd* hag was hither brought with child,
And here was left by the sailors. *Tempest*, i. 2.

BLUNT. *Dull; stupid.*
But, Valentine being gone, I'll quickly cross,
By some sly trick, *blunt* Thurio's dull proceeding.
Two Gentlemen of Verona, ii. 6.
With hasty Germans and *blunt* Hollanders.
Henry 6, P. 3, iv. 8.
This third, dull lead, with warning all as *blunt*.
Merchant of Venice, ii. 6.

To BLUR. *To sully; to blot; to impair.*
Such an act
That *blurs* the grace and blush of modesty.
Hamlet, iii. 4.
Long is it since I saw him,
But time hath nothing *blurr'd* those lines of favour
Which then he wore. *Cymbeline*, iv. 2.

To BOARD. *To accost; to attack; to assail.*

For I will *board* her, though she chide as loud
As thunder, when the clouds in autumn'crack.
Taming of the Shrew, i. 2.
You mistake, knight : accost is front her, *board*
her, woo her, assail her. *Twelfth-Night,* i. 3.
Away, I do beseech you, both away :
I'll *board* him presently. *Hamlet,* ii. 2.

BOARISH. *Cruel; ferocious; swinish; brutal.*

Because I would not see thy cruel nails
Pluck out his poor old eyes ; nor thy fierce sister
In his anointed flesh stick *boarish* fangs.
King Lear, iii. 7.

BOB. *A slight blow; a tap; a jibe; a sneering jest.*

The man, sir, that, when gentlemen are tired,
gives them a *bob,* and rests them.
Comedy of Errors, iv. 3.
He that a fool doth very wisely hit,
Doth very foolishly, although he smart,
But to seem senseless of the *bob.*
As you like it, ii. 7.

To BOB. *To cheat; to filch; to beat; to cudgel.*

You shall not *bob* us out of our melody.
Troilus and Cressida, iii. 1.
Live Roderigo,
He calls me to a restitution large
Of gold and jewels that I *bobb'd* from him,
As gifts to Desdemona. *Othello,* v. 1.
And not these bastard Bretagnes; whom our fathers
Have in their own land beaten, *bobb'd,* and thump'd.
Richard 3, v. 3.
I have *bobbed* his brain more than he has beat
my bones. *Troilus and Cressida,* ii. 1.

To BODE. *To forebode; to foretell; to portend.*

Marry, peace it *bodes,* and love, and quiet life,
An awful rule, and right supremacy.
Taming of the Shrew, v. 2.
I would croak like a raven ; I would *bode,* I
would *bode.* *Troilus and Cressida,* v. 2.
If hollowly, invert
What best is *boded* me to mischief. *Tempest,* iii. 1.

BODEMENT. *Prediction ; prognostication.*

This foolish, dreaming, superstitious girl
Makes all these *bodements.*
Troilus and Cressida, v. 3.

Who can impress the forest ; bid the tree
Unfix his earth-bound root? Sweet *bodements!*
good! *Macbeth,* iv. 1.

To BODGE. *To boggle; to fail; to miscarry.*

With this, we charg'd again : but, out, alas !
We *bodg'd* again. *Henry 6,* P. 3, i. 3.

BODKIN. *A dagger.*

Betwixt the firmament and it you cannot thrust
a *bodkin's* point. *Winter's Tale,* iii. 3.
When he himself might his quietus make
With a bare *bodkin.* *Hamlet,* iii. 1.

To BOGGLE. *To blench; to shrink; to startle.*

You *boggle* shrewdly, every feather starts you.
All's well that ends well, v. 3.

BOGGLER. *A deceiver; a dissembler; a jilt.*

You have been a *boggler* ever :
But when we in our viciousness grow hard—
O misery on't !—the wise gods seel our eyes.
Antony and Cleopatra, iii. 13.

BOLD. *Confident ; assured ; audacious.*

Jockey of Norfolk, be not too *bold.*
Richard 3, v. 3.
Therefore my hopes, not surfeited to death,
Stand in *bold* cure. *Othello,* ii. 1.
And in that behalf,
Bold of your worthiness, we single you
As our best-moving fair solicitor.
Love's Labour's lost, ii. 1.
Be *bold* you do so grow in my requital,
As nothing can unroot you.
All's well that ends well, v. 1.
All these *bold* fears
Thou see'st with peril I have answer'd.
Henry 4, P. 2, iv. 4.

To BOLD. *To bolden ; to make bold, to encourage.*

For this business,
It toucheth us, as France invades our land,
Not *bolds* the king, with others, whom, I fear,
Most just and heavy causes make oppose.
King Lear, v. 1.
Indeed, good lady,
The fellow has a deal of that, too much,
Which *bolds* him much to have.
All's well that ends well, iii. 2.

To BOLL. *To swell.*

Why he cannot abide a gaping pig;
Why he, a harmless necessary cat;
Why he, a *bollen* bag-pipe.
    Merchant of Venice, iv. 1.

BOLT. *An arrow; a fetter.*

'Twas but a *bolt* of nothing, shot at nothing,
Which the brain makes of fumes. *Cymbeline*, iv. 2.
Yet mark'd I where the *bolt* of Cupid fell.
    Midsummer-Night's Dream, ii. 1.
Away with him to prison! lay *bolts* enough
upon him.   *Measure for Measure*, v. 1.
   You good gods, give me
The penitent instrument to pick that *bolt*,
Then, free for ever!   *Cymbeline*, v. 4.

To BOLT. *To fan; to winnow; to sift.*

Such and so finely *bolted* didst thou seem.
    Henry 5, ii. 2.
   I take thy hand,—this hand,
As soft as dove's down and as white as it,
Or Ethiop's tooth, or the fann'd snow that's *bolted*
By the northern blasts twice o'er.
    Winter's Tale, iv. 3.

BOLTING-HUTCH. *A meal-tub or bin.*

Why dost thou converse with that trunk of
humours, that *bolting-hutch* of beastliness?
    Henry 4, P. 1, ii. 4.

BOMBARD. *A large drinking-vessel, made of leather.*

That huge *bombard* of sack. *Henry* 4, P. 1, ii. 4.
Yond same black cloud, yond huge one, looks
like a foul *bombard* that would shed his liquor.
    Tempest, ii. 2.
And here ye lie baiting of *bombards*, when
Ye should do service.   *Henry* 8, v. 3.

BOMBAST. *A kind of wadding.*

How now, my sweet creature of *bombast*!
    Henry 4, P. 1, ii. 4.
As *bombast*, and as lining of the time.
    Love's Labour's lost, v. 2.

BOMBAST. *Bombastic; inflated.*

But he, as loving his own pride and purposes,
Evades them, with a *bombast* circumstance,
Horribly stuff'd with epithets of war. *Othello*, i. 1.

BONDAGE. *Obligation; binding power; force; efficacy.*

The vows of women
Of no more *bondage* be, to where they are made,
Than they are to their virtues; which is nothing.
    Cymbeline, ii. 4.

To BONNET. *To show respect by taking off the cap; to stand uncovered.*

And his ascent is not by such easy degrees as
those who, having been supple and courteous to
the people, *bonneted*, without any further deed to
heave them at all into their estimation and report.
    Coriolanus, ii. 2.

BONNY. *Gay; merry.*

And be you blithe and *bonny*.
    Much Ado about Nothing, ii. 3.

BOOK. *A calendar; an indenture; a writing of any kind.*

Then he disdains to shine; for by the *book*
He should have brav'd the east an hour ago.
    Richard 3, v. 3.
By that time will our *book*, I think, be drawn.
    Henry 4, P. 1, iii. 1.
Large gifts have I bestow'd on learnèd clerks,
Because my *book* preferr'd me to the king.
    Henry 6, P. 2, iv. 7.
A beggar's *book* outweighs a noble's blood.
    Henry 8, i. 1.

BOOKISH. *Learned; studious.*

Though I am not *bookish*, yet I can read wait-
ing-gentlewoman in the scape. *Winter's Tale*, iii. 3.
And, force perforce, I'll make him yield the crown,
Whose *bookish* rule hath pull'd fair England down.
    Henry 6, P. 2, i. 1.
   Unless the *bookish* theoric,
Wherein the togèd consuls can propose
As masterly as he.   *Othello*, i. 1.

BOOKMATE. *A fellow student.*

A phantasm, a Monarcho, and one that makes sport
To the prince and his *bookmates*.
    Love's Labour's lost, iv. 1.

BOOK-OATH. *Bible-oath.*

I put thee now to thy *book-oath*: deny it, if
thou canst.   *Henry* 4, P. 2, ii. 1.

BOOT. *Plunder; booty; advantage; profit; addition; surplus; over-measure.*

Others, like soldiers, armèd in their stings,
Make *boot* upon the summer's velvet buds.
    Henry 5, i. 2.

Yea, my gravity,
Wherein—let no man hear me—I take pride,
Could I with *boot* change for an idle plume
Which the air beats for vain.
Measure for Measure, ii. 4.
Give him no breath, but now
Make *boot* of his distraction.
Antony and Cleopatra, iv. 1.
Though the pennyworth on his side be the
worst, yet hold thee, there's some *boot*.
Winter's Tale, iv. 3.
Canst thou, O partial sleep, give thy repose
To the wet sea-boy in an hour so rude;
And in the calmest and most stillest night,
With all appliances and means to *boot*,
Deny it to a king?   *Henry* 4, P. 2, iii. 1.
This, and St. George to *boot!* What think'st thou,
Norfolk?   *Richard* 3, v. 3.

To BOOT.   *To enrich ; to benefit ; to profit.*
And I will *boot* thee with what gift beside
Thy modesty can beg.
Antony and Cleopatra, ii. 5.
For what I have, I need not to repeat;
And what I want, it *boots* not to complain.
Richard 2, iii. 4.

BOOTLESS.   *Vain ; useless ; unprofitable.*
And *bootless* 'tis to tell you we will go.
Henry 4, P. 1, i. 1.
And left me to a *bootless* inquisition. *Tempest*, i. 2.

To BORDER.   *To keep within bounds; to limit;
to restrain.*
That nature, which contemns its origin,
Cannot be *border'd* certain in itself.
King Lear, iv. 2.

To BORE.   *To plague ; to harass ; to under-
mine.*
At this instant
He *bores* me with some trick.   *Henry* 8, i. 1.

BORN.   *Offspring ; issue ; child.*
That is honour's scorn,
Which challenges itself as honour's *born*,
And is not like the sire.
All's well that ends well, ii. 3.

BORROW.   *A loan ; any thing lent ; any thing
borrowed.*
Yet of your royal presence I'll adventure
The *borrow* of a week.   *Winter's Tale*, i. 2.

To BORROW.   *To usurp ; to assume.*
A strange beginning; *borrow'd* majesty!
King John, i. 1.
A *borrow'd* title hast thou bought too dear:
Why didst thou tell me that thou wert a king?
Henry 4, P. 1, v. 3.
This is a slave, whose easy-*borrow'd* pride
Dwells in the fickle grace of her he follows.
King Lear, ii. 4.

BOSOM.   *Desire ; inclination ; wish ; favour.*
I will bestow you where you shall have time
To speak your *bosom* freely.   *Othello*, iii. 1.
And you shall have your *bosom* on this wretch,
Grace of the duke, revenges to your heart,
And general honour.   *Measure for Measure*, iv. 3.
Whose age has charms in it, whose title more,
To pluck the common *bosom* on his side.
King Lear, v. 3.

BOSSED.   *Studded ; embossed.*
Fine linen, Turkey cushions *boss'd* with pearl.
Taming of the Shrew, ii. 1.

BOTCH.   *Patch ; flaw ; imperfection.*
And with him,—
To leave no rubs nor *botches* in the work,—
Fleance his son, that keeps him company.
Macbeth, iii. 1.

BOTCHER.   *A mender of old clothes.*
If he mend, he is no longer dishonest; if he
cannot, let the *botcher* mend him.
Twelfth-Night, i. 5.
I know him: he was a *botcher's* 'prentice in Paris.
All's well that ends well, iv. 3.
And your beards deserve not so honourable a
grave as to stuff a *botcher's* cushion.
Coriolanus, ii. 1.

To BOTCH UP.   *To put together ; to contrive.*
And hear thou there how many fruitless pranks
This ruffian hath *botch'd up*, that thou thereby
Mayst smile at this.   *Twelfth-Night*, iv. 1.

BOTTLE.   *A bundle or truss.*
Methinks I have a great desire to a *bottle* of hay:
good hay, sweet hay, hath no fellow.
Midsummer-Night's Dream, iv. 1.

BOTTLED.   *Bottle-shaped.*
Why strew'st thou sugar on that *bottled* spider?
Richard 3, i. 3.

To **Bottom.** *To probe; to find the bottom of.*

I have heard I am a strumpet; and mine ear,
Therein false struck, can take no greater wound,
Nor tent to *bottom* that.   *Cymbeline,* iii. 4.

Bound. *Ground; land; limit.*

And he hath bought the cottage and the *bounds*
That the old carlot once was master of.
     As you like it, iii. 5.
Besides, his cote, his flocks, and *bounds* of feed,
Are now on sale.   *Ibid.* ii. 4.
     Our gentle flame
Provokes itself, and, like the current, flies
Each *bound* it chafes.   *Timon of Athens,* i. 1.

To **Bound.** *To make leap or curvet; to throb with; to convey.*

Or if I might buffet for my love, or *bound* my
horse for her favours, I could lay on like a butcher,
and sit like a jack-an-apes, never off. *Henry* 5, v. 2.
If love ambitious sought a match of birth,
Whose veins *bound* richer blood than Lady Blanch?
     King John, ii. 1.

Bounden. *Bound; obliged.*

I rest much *bounden* to you: fare you well.
     As you like it, i. 2.

Bourn. *Limit; boundary; confine; a brook.*

The undiscover'd country, from whose *bourn*
No traveller returns.   *Hamlet,* iii. 1.
False as dice are to be wish'd by one that fixes
No *bourn* 'twixt his and mine. *Winter's Tale,* i. 2.
I'll set a *bourn* how far to be belov'd.
     Antony and Cleopatra, i. 1.
Come o'er the *bourn*, Bessy, to me.
     King Lear, iii. 6.

Bow. *A yoke.*

As the ox hath his *bow*, sir, the horse his curb,
and the falcon her bells, so man hath his desires.
     As you like it, iii. 3.

To **Bow.** *To bend.*

Who, sensible, outdares his senseless sword,
And, when it *bows*, stands up. *Coriolanus,* i. 4.

Bowed. *Bent; crooked.*

'Tis strange: a three-pence *bow'd* would hire me,
Old as I am, to queen it.   *Henry* 8, ii. 3.

To **Bower.** *To embower; to lodge; to enclose.*

O nature, what hadst thou to do in hell,

When thou didst *bower* the spirit of a fiend
In mortal paradise of such sweet flesh?
     Romeo and Juliet, iii. 2.

To **Boy.** *To represent; to personate.*

     And I shall see
Some squeaking Cleopatra *boy* my greatness
I' the posture of a whore.
     Antony and Cleopatra, v. 2.

Boy-queller. *Boy-killer.*

Come, come, thou *boy-queller*, show thy face.
     Troilus and Cressida, v. 5.

Brabble. *A brawl; a quarrel.*

     Here in the streets
In private *brabble* did we apprehend him.
     Twelfth-Night, v. 1.

Brabbler. *A wrangler.*

We hold our time too precious to be spent
With such a *brabbler*.   *King John,* v. 2.

Brace. *Preparation; trim; state of defence.*

For that it stands not in such warlike *brace*,
But altogether lacks the abilities
That Rhodes is dress'd in.   *Othello,* i. 3.

Brach. *A hound.*

Truth's a dog must to kennel; he must be
whipped out, when the lady *brach* may stand by
the fire and stink.   *King Lear,* i. 4.
I will hold my peace when Achilles' *brach* bids
me, shall I?   *Troilus and Cressida,* ii. 1.
I had rather hear Lady, my *brach*, howl in
Irish.   *Henry* 4, P. 1, iii. 1.

Braid. *False; deceitful.*

Since Frenchmen are so *braid*,
Marry that will, I live and die a maid.
     All's well that ends well, iv. 2.

To **Brain.** *To frustrate; to defeat; to understand.*

It was the swift celerity of his death,
Which I did think with slower foot came on,
That *brain'd* my purpose.
     Measure for Measure, v. 1.
'Tis still a dream; or else such stuff as madmen
Tongue, and *brain* not.   *Cymbeline,* v. 4.

Brainish. *Furious; hot-headed; insane.*

And, in this *brainish* apprehension, kills
The unseen good old man.   *Hamlet,* iv. 1.

BRAIN-PAN. *The skull.*

For many a time, but for a sallet, my *brain-pan*
had been cleft with a brown bill.
Henry 6, P. 2, iv. 10.

BRAIN-SICK. *Crazy; hot-headed.*

Her *brain-sick* raptures
Cannot distaste the goodness of a quarrel
Which hath our several honours all engag'd
To make it gracious. *Troilus and Cressida, ii. 2.*
Good Lord, what madness rules in *brain-sick* men,
When for so slight and frivolous a cause
Such factious emulations shall arise !
Henry 6, P. 1, iv. 1.

BRAIN-SICKLY. *Weakly; foolishly.*

You do unbend your noble strength, to think
So *brain-sickly* of things. *Macbeth, ii. 1.*

BRAND. *A stigma; a disgrace; a reproach;
a fire-brand.*

The blood he hath lost he dropp'd it for his country;
And what is left, to lose it by his country,
Were to us all, that do't and suffer it,
A *brand* to the end o' the world. *Coriolanus, iii. 1.*
If he were putting to my house the *brand*
That should consume it, I have not the face
To say, " Beseech you, cease." *Ibid. iv. 6.*

BRAVE. *A boast; a taunt; a defiance.*

There end thy *brave*, and turn thy face in peace;
We grant thou canst outscold us. *King John, v. 2.*
Sirrah, I will not bear these *braves* of thine.
Taming of the Shrew, iii. 1.
I'll tell thee, Diomed,
This *brave* shall oft make thee to hide thy head.
Troilus and Cressida, iv. 4.

BRAVE. *Fine; noble; good.*

Believe me, sir,
It carries a *brave* form. *Tempest, i. 2.*
I'll prove the prettier fellow of the two,
And wear my dagger with the *braver* grace.
Merchant of Venice, iii. 4.

To BRAVE. *To make fine; to bedeck; to defy.*

Thou hast *braved* many men ; brave not me.
Taming of the Shrew, iv. 3.
Then he disdains to shine ; for by the book
He should have *brav'd* the east an hour ago.
Richard 3, v. 3.
Hated by one he loves ; *brav'd* by his brother ;
Check'd like a bondman. *Julius Cæsar, iv. 3.*
The Florentines and Senoys are by the ears ;
Have fought with equal fortune, and continue
A *braving* war. *All's well that ends well, i. 2.*

BRAVELY. *Skilfully; splendidly; in good
order.*

Bravely the figure of this harpy hast thou
Perform'd, my Ariel. *Tempest, iii. 3.*
The French are *bravely* in their battles set,
And will with all expedience charge on us.
Henry 5, iv. 3.

BRAVERY. *Finery; splendour; show; ostentation.*

My holy sir, none better knows than you
How I have ever lov'd the life remov'd ;
And held in idle price to haunt assemblies,
Where youth, and cost and witless *bravery* keeps.
Measure for Measure, i. 3.
But, sure, the *bravery* of his grief did put me
Into a towering passion. *Hamlet, v. 2.*
And now, in madness,
Upon malicious *bravery*, dost thou come,
To start my quiet. *Othello, i. 1.*

BRAWL. *A kind of dance.*

Master, will you win your love with a French
brawl ? *Love's Labour's lost, iii. 1.*

To BRAWL. *To report; to proclaim loudly.*

For his divisions, as the times do *brawl*,
Are in three heads. *Henry 4, P. 2, i. 3.*

BRAWN. *The arm.*

And I had purpose
Once more to hew thy target from thy *brawn*.
Coriolanus, iv. 5.
And in my vantbrace put this wither'd *brawn*.
Troilus and Cressida, i. 3.
This is his hand ;
His foot Mercurial; his Martial thigh ;
The *brawns* of Hercules. *Cymbeline, iv. 2.*

To BREAK OUT. *To come off; to hurry away.*

I left him almost speechless ; and *broke out*
To acquaint you with this evil. *King John, v. 6.*

To BREAK UP. *To cut up; to carve; to open.*

Boyet, you can carve ; *break up* this capon.
Love's Labour's lost, iv. 1.

To BREAK WITH. *To communicate secretly;
to come to an explanation.*

And I will *break with* her and with her father,
And thou shalt have her.
Much Ado about Nothing, i. 1.
O, name him not : let us not *break with* him ;

For he will never follow any thing
That other men begin.   *Julius Cæsar*, ii. 1.
Finding thee fit for bloody villany,
I faintly *broke with* thee of Arthur's death.
                              King John, iv. 2.
   With which they mov'd,
Have *broken with* the king.   *Henry* 8, v. 1.

BREAST.   *Voice.*
By my troth, the fool has an excellent *breast*.
                              Twelfth-Night, ii. 3.

BREATH.   *Words; exercise; a breathing.*
If overboldly we have borne ourselves
In the converse of *breath*, your gentleness
Was guilty of it.   *Love's Labour's lost*, v. 2.
   He hopes it is no other
But for your health and your digestion's sake,—
An after-dinner's *breath*. *Troilus and Cressida*, ii. 3.
   As you and lord Æneas
Consent upon the order of the fight,
So be it; either to the uttermost,
Or else a *breath*.   *Ibid.* iv. 5.

To BREATHE.   *To give utterance to; to speak;
to exercise; to keep in breath.*
He's truly valiant that can wisely suffer
The worst that man can *breathe*.
                              Timon of Athens, iii. 5.
You *breathe* in vain.   *Ibid.* iii. 5.
   Thou wast created for men to *breathe* themselves
upon thee.   *All's well that ends well*, ii. 3.

BREATHING.   *Exercise.*
A nursery to our gentry, who are sick
For *breathing* and exploit.   *Ibid.* i. 2.

BREECHED.   *Cased; covered; clad.*
   There, the murderers,
Steep'd in the colours of their trade, their daggers
Unmannerly *breech'd* with gore.   *Macbeth*, ii. 1.

To BREED.   *To educate.*
Which may, if fortune please, both *breed* thee, pretty,
And still rest thine.   *Winter's Tale*, iii. 3.
   And, as thou sayest, charged my brother, on his
blessing, to *breed* me well.   *As you like it*, i. 1.

BREEDBATE.   *A mischief-maker.*
   And, I warrant you, no tell-tale, nor no *breedbate*.   *Merry Wives of Windsor*, i. 4.

BREEDING.   *Education; bringing up.*
   And will you, being a man of your *breeding*, be
married under a bush, like a beggar?
                              As you like it, iii. 3.

His *breeding*, sir, hath been at my charge.
                              King Lear, i. 1.
   And, besides, the king
Hath not deserv'd my service nor your loves;
Who find in my exile the want of *breeding*,
The certainty of this hard life.   *Cymbeline*, iv. 4.

BREESE.   *The gadfly.*
   For in her ray and brightness
The herd hath more annoyance by the *breese*
Than by the tiger.   *Troilus and Cressida*, i. 3.
   Yon ribaudred nag of Egypt,
Whom leprosy o'ertake!—i' the midst o' the fight,
The *breese* upon her, like a cow in June,
Hoists sails and flies.
                              Antony and Cleopatra, iii. 10.

BRIBE.   *Fee; salary; pittance.*
   O, this life
Is nobler than attending for a check,
Richer than doing nothing for a *bribe*.
                              Cymbeline, iii. 3.

To BRIBE.   *To steal.*
Divide me like a *bribed* buck, each a haunch.
                              Merry Wives of Windsor, v. 5.

BRIBER.   *Fee; price; recompense; ransom.*
   In vain! his service done
At Lacedæmon and Byzantium
Were a sufficient *briber* for his life.
                              Timon of Athens, iii. 5.

BRIDGE.   *The upper part of the nose.*
   Take the *bridge* quite away
Of him that, his particular to foresee,
Smells from the general weal. *Timon of Athens*, iv. 3.

BRIEF.   *A short discourse or writing; an in-
ventory; a schedule; a list.*
   And she told me,
In a sweet verbal *brief*, it did concern
Your highness with herself.
                              All's well that ends well, v. 3.
   And the hand of time
Shall draw this *brief* into as huge a volume.
                              King John, ii. 1.
   Whose ceremony
Shall seem expedient on the now-born *brief*,
And be perform'd to-night.
                              All's well that ends well, ii. 3.
Hie, good Sir Michael; bear this sealèd *brief*
With wingèd haste to the lord marshal.
                              Henry 4, P. 1, iv. 4.

There is a *brief* how many sports are ripe.
    Midsummer-Night's Dream, v. 1.
This is a *brief* of money, plate, and jewels,
I am possess'd of: 'tis exactly valu'd.
    Antony and Cleopatra, v. 2.

BRIEF. *Quick; speedy; narrow; contracted.*

Yea, noise?—then I'll be *brief.*—O happy dagger!
    Romeo and Juliet, v. 3.
Ah, women, women!—come; we have no friend
But resolution, and the *briefest* end.
    Antony and Cleopatra, iv. 15.
For feature, laming
The shrine of Venus, or straight-pight Minerva,
Postures beyond *brief* nature.   *Cymbeline*, v. 5.

BRIEF. *Soon; quickly.*

But that a joy past joy calls out on me,
It were a grief, so *brief* to part with thee.
    Romeo and Juliet, iii. 3.

BRIEFLY. *Quickly; just now; not long since.*

Briefly die their joys
That place them on the truth of girls and boys.
    Cymbeline, v. 5.
Go put on thy defences.—*Briefly*, sir.
    Antony and Cleopatra, iv. 4.
'Tis not a mile; *briefly* we heard their drums.
    Coriolanus, i. 6.

BRIEFNESS. *Dispatch; quickness.*

I hope the *briefness* of your answer made
The speediness of your return.   *Cymbeline*, ii. 4.
And I have one thing, of a queasy question,
Which I must act: *briefness* and fortune work!
    King Lear, ii. 1.

BRINDED. *Streaked; variegated.*

Thrice the *brinded* cat hath mew'd. *Macbeth*, iv. 1.

To BRING. *To accompany; to go along with; to attend.*

He would not suffer me to *bring* him to the haven.
    Cymbeline, i. 1.
Yet, give leave, my lord,
That we may *bring* you something on the way.
    Measure for Measure, i. 1.

To BRING OUT. *To bring forth; to produce; to put out; to disconcert.*

Ensear thy fertile and conceptious womb,
Let it no more *bring out* ingrateful man!
    Timon of Athens, iv. 3.

They do not mark me, and that *brings me out.*
    Love's Labour's lost, v. 2.
Thou *bringest me out* of tune. *As you like it*, iii. 2.

To BROACH. *To pierce; to transfix.*

Bringing rebellion *broachèd* on his sword.
    Henry 5, iv. Chorus.

BROCK. *A badger.*

Marry, hang thee, *brock!*   *Twelfth-Night*, ii. 5.

BROGUE. *A kind of shoe.*

I thought he slept; and put
My clouted *brogues* from off my feet, whose rudeness
Answer'd my steps too loud.   *Cymbeline*, iv. 2.

To BROKE. *To employ a pander.*

He does indeed;
And *brokes* with all that can in such a suit
Corrupt the tender honour of a maid.
    All's well that ends well, iii. 5.

BROKER. *A pander; a go-between.*

Now, by my modesty, a goodly *broker!*
    Two Gentlemen of Verona, i. 2.
They say,—a crafty knave does need no *broker.*
    Henry 6, P. 2, i. 2.
That *broker*, that still breaks the pate of faith.
    King John, ii. 1.
Do not believe his vows, for they are *brokers,*
Not of that dye which their investments show.
    Hamlet, i. 3.

BROOCH. *An ornament; a jewel.*

I know him well: he is the *brooch*, indeed,
And gem of all the nation.   *Hamlet*, iv. 7.
And love to Richard
Is a strange *brooch* in this all-hating world.
    Richard 2, v. 5.

To BROOCH. *To ornament; to decorate as with a brooch.*

Not the imperious show
Of the full-fortun'd Cæsar ever shall
Be *brooch'd* with me. *Antony and Cleopatra*, iv. 15.

BROODED. *Brooding.*

Then, in despite of *brooded* watchful day,
I would into thy bosom pour my thoughts.
    King John, iii. 3.

BROTHER. *Brother-in-law.*

Back, Edmund, to my *brother;*
Hasten his musters and conduct his powers.
    King Lear, iv. 2.

Sir, 'tis your *brother* Cassius at the door,
Who doth desire to see you. *Julius Cæsar*, ii. 1.

BRUIT. *Report.*
But yet I love my country ; and am not
One that rejoices in the common wreck,
As common *bruit* doth put it.
Timon of Athens, v. 1.
The *bruit* is, Hector's slain, and by Achilles.
Troilus and Cressida, v. 9.
The *bruit* thereof will bring you many friends.
Henry 6, P. 3, iv. 7.

TO BRUIT. *To report ; to rumour ; to noise.*
In few, his death
Being *bruited* once, took fire and heat away
From the best-temper'd courage in his troops.
Henry 4, P. 2, i. 1.
By this great clatter, one of greatest note
Seems *bruited*. *Macbeth*, v. 7.
And the king's rouse the heavens shall *bruit* again,
Re-speaking earthly thunder. *Hamlet*, i. 2.

BRUSH. *A shock ; a rude assault.*
Old Salisbury, who can report of him,—
That winter lion, who in rage forgets
Aged contusions and all *brush* of time,
And, like a gallant in the brow of youth,
Repairs him with occasion ? *Henry* 6, P. 2, v. 3.
Let grow thy sinews till their knots be strong,
And tempt not yet the *brushes* of the war.
Troilus and Cressida, v. 3.

BUBUCKLE. *A pimple.*
His face is all *bubuckles*, and whelks, and knobs,
and flames o' fire. *Henry* 5, iii. 5.

BUCK. *Any quantity of dirty linen washed at one time.*
But now of late, not able to travel with her furred
pack, she washes *bucks* at home.
Henry 6, P. 2, iv. 2.
Why, what have you to do whither they bear
it ? You were best meddle with *buck*-washing.
Merry Wives of Windsor, iii. 3.

TO BUCKLE. *To bend ; to give way.*
And as the wretch, whose fever-weaken'd joints,
Like strengthless hinges, *buckle* under life,
Impatient of his fit, breaks like a fire
Out of his keeper's arms. *Henry* 4, P. 2, i. 1.

TO BUCKLE WITH. *To contend with ; to bandy ; to assail.*
In single combat thou shalt *buckle with* me.
Henry 6, P. 1, i. 2.

My ancient incantations are too weak,
And hell too strong for me to *buckle with*.
Henry 6, P. 1, v. 3.
I will not bandy with thee word for word,
But *buckle with* thee blows, twice two for one.
Ibid. P. 3, i. 4.
All our general force
Might with a sally of the very town
Be *buckled with*. *Henry* 6, P. 1, iv. 4.

TO BUCKLER. *To defend ; to guard ; to protect.*
Fear not, sweet wench, they shall not touch thee,
Kate :
I'll *buckler* thee against a million.
Taming of the Shrew, iii. 2.
Can Oxford, that did ever fence the right,
Now *buckler* falsehood with a pedigree ?
Henry 6, P. 3, iii. 3.

BUCKRAM. *Strong linen cloth.*
I have cases of *buckram* for the nonce.
Henry 4, P. 1, i. 2.

TO BUDGE. *To stir.*
I will not *budge* for no man's pleasure, I.
Romeo and Juliet, iii. 1.

BUFFET. *A blow.*
O, I could divide myself, and go to *buffets*.
Henry 4, P. 1, ii. 3.
For thou hast been
As one, in suffering all, that suffers nothing,
A man that fortune's *buffets* and rewards
Hast ta'en with equal thanks. *Hamlet*, iii. 2.

BUG. *A bugbear ; a goblin ; a spectre ; a terror.*
Tush, tush ! fear boys with *bugs*.
Taming of the Shrew, i. 2.
The *bug* which you would fright me with, I seek.
Winter's Tale, iii. 2.
With, ho ! such *bugs* and goblins in my life.
Hamlet, v. 2.
For Warwick was a *bug* that fear'd us all.
Henry 6, P. 3, v. 2.
Those that would die or e'er resist are grown
The mortal *bugs* o' the field. *Cymbeline*, v. 3.

BUGBEAR. *A goblin.*
A bugbear take him ! *Troilus and Cressida*, iv. 2.

BULK. *The body ; the projecting part of a building.*
But smother'd it within my panting *bulk*,
Which almost burst to belch it in the sea.
Richard 3, i. 4.

G

He mis'd a sigh so piteous and profound,
That it did seem to shatter all his *bulk*.
Hamlet, ii. 1.
Here, stand behind this *bulk;* straight will he come.
Othello, v. 1.

BUNG. *A cut-purse; a thief.*

Away, you cut-purse rascal! you filthy *bung*, away!
Henry 4, P. 2, ii. 4.

BUNTING. *The wood-lark, a bird like the sky-lark in shape and plumage, but with little or no voice.*

I took this lark for a *bunting*.
All's well that ends well, ii. 5.

To BUOY UP. *To swell up ; to rise.*

The sea, with such a storm as his bare head
In hell-black night endur'd, would have *buoy'd up*,
And quench'd the stellèd fires. *King Lear*, iii. 7.

BURGONET. *A helmet.*

The demi-Atlas of this earth, the arm
And *burgonet* of men. *Antony and Cleopatra*, i. 5.
And that I'll write upon thy *burgonet*,
Might I but know thee by thy household badge.
Henry 6, P. 2, v. 1.

BURST. *Abruptness ; suddenness ; uneven-ness.*

The snatches in his voice,
And *burst* of speaking, were as his.
Cymbeline, iv. 2.

To BURST. *To break.*

Your heart is *burst*, you have lost half your soul.
Othello, i. 1.
How her bridle was *burst*.
Taming of the Shrew, iv. 1.
You will not pay for the glasses you have *burst* ?
Ibid. Induction, sc. 1.
He never saw him but once in the Tilt-yard;
and then he *burst* his head for crowding among
the marshal's men. *Henry* 4, P. 2, iii. 2.

To BURY. *To conceal; to keep secret.*

You shall not only take the sacrament
To *bury* mine intents, but also to effect
Whatever I shall happen to devise.
Richard 2, iv. 1.

BUSILESS. *Unbusied ; at leisure.*

But these sweet thoughts do even refresh my labour;
Most *busiless* when I do it. *Tempest*, iii. 1.

BUT. *Otherwise than; except; unless; than; only.*

I should sin
To think *but* nobly of my grandmother.
Tempest, i. 2.
And *but* he's something stain'd
With grief, that's beauty's canker, thou mightst
call him
A goodly person. *Ibid.* i. 2.
To each of you one fair and virtuous mistress
Fall, when Love please !—marry, to each, *but* one !
All's well that ends well, ii. 3.
But on this day let seamen fear no wreck.
King John, iii. 1.
Well, I must wait,
And watch withal ; for, *but* I be deceiv'd,
Our fine musician groweth amorous.
Taming of the Shrew, iii. 1.
And *but* thou love me, let them find me here.
Romeo and Juliet, ii. 2.
Her head's declin'd, and death will seize her, *but*
Your comfort make the rescue.
Antony and Cleopatra, iii. 11.
But being charg'd, we will be still by land.
Ibid. iv. 11.
Cesario, thou know'st no less *but* all.
Twelfth-Night, i. 4.
But to the girdle do the gods inherit,
Beneath is all the fiends'. *King Lear*, iv. 6.
Could all *but* answer for that peevish brat ?
Richard 3, i. 3.
I am, my lord, *but* as my betters are,
That led me hither. *Henry* 4, P. 2, iv. 3.

BUT EVEN BEFORE. *Just before.*

My dear lord !
Thou art one o' the false ones: now I think on thee,
My hunger's gone ; *but even before*, I was
At point to sink for food. *Cymbeline*, iii. 6.

BUTCHERY. *A slaughter-house.*

This is no place ; this house is but a *butchery :*
Abhor it, fear it, do not enter it.
As you like it, ii. 3.

BUTT. *The point aimed at.*

Here is my journey's end, here is my *butt*,
And very sea-mark of my utmost sail. *Othello*, v. 2.

BUTTON. *A gem ; a jewel ; a bud.*

Happy, in that we are not over-happy ;
On fortune's cap we are not the very *button*.
Hamlet, ii. 2.

The canker galls the infants of the spring,
Too oft before their *buttons* be disclos'd.
Hamlet, i. 3.

BUZZ. *A whisper; a rumour.*

Yes, that, on every dream,
Each *buzz*, each fancy, each complaint, dislike,
He may enguard his dotage with their powers,
And hold our lives in mercy. *King Lear*, i. 4.

To BUZZ. *To whisper; to scatter secretly; to infuse.*

They, knowing dame Eleanor's aspiring humour,
Have hirèd me to undermine the duchess,
And *buzz* these conjurations in her brain.
Henry 6, P. 2, i. 2.

BY. *According to.*

But you well know,
Things of like value, differing in their owners,
Are prizèd *by* their masters. *Timon of Athens*, i. 1.

BY HIM. *By his house.*

Now, good Metellus, go along *by him*.
Julius Cæsar, ii. 1.

BY MEASURE OF. *By means of.*

And know, *by measure*
Of their observant toil, the enemies' weight.
Troilus and Cressida, i. 3.

BY PERSUASION OF. *By reason of; on account of.*

It should not be, *by the persuasion of* his new feasting. *Timon of Athens*, iii. 6.

BY THE VOLUME. *In any quantity; without limitation; indefinitely.*

Ay, as an ostler, that for the poorest piece
Will bear the knave *by the volume. Coriolanus*, iii. 3.

BY-DEPENDENCY. *Casualty; casual circumstance; incident.*

And all the other *by-dependencies*
From chance to chance. *Cymbeline*, v. 5.

To 'BY. *To aby; to pay for; to buy.*

Thou shalt *'by* this dear,
If ever I thy face by daylight see.
Midsummer-Night's Dream, iii. 2.

C.

CACODEMON. *An evil spirit; a demon.*

Hie thee to hell for shame, and leave this world,
Thou *cacodemon!* there thy kingdom is.
Richard 3, i. 3.

CADDIS. *Worsted.*

Inkles, *caddisses*, cambrics, lawns.
Winter's Tale, iv. 3.

CADE. *A barrel.*

Or rather, of stealing a *cade* of herrings.
Henry 6, P. 2, iv. 2.

CADENT. *Falling; trickling.*

Let it stamp wrinkles in her brow of youth;
With *cadent* tears fret channels in her cheeks;
Turn all her mother's pains and benefits
To laughter and contempt! *King Lear*, i. 4.

CAGE. *A basket.*

I must up-fill this osier *cage* of ours
With baleful weeds and precious-juicèd flowers.
Romeo and Juliet, ii. 3.

CAITIFF. *A wretch.*

I flatter not; but say thou art a *caitiff*.
Timon of Athens, iv. 3.
For queen, a very *caitiff* crown'd with care.
Richard 3, iv. 4.
Whoever charges on his forward breast,
I am the *caitiff* that do hold him to't.
All's well that ends well, iii. 2.

CAITIFF. *Base; servile.*

Noting this penury, to myself I said,
An if a man did need a poison now,
Whose sale is present death in Mantua,
Here lives a *caitiff* wretch would sell it him.
Romeo and Juliet, v. 1.

To CALCULATE. *To predict; to foretell events; to cast nativities.*

A cunning man did *calculate* my birth,
And told me that by water I should die.
Henry 6, P. 2, iv. 1.
Why birds and beasts from quality and kind;
Why old men fool, and children *calculate*.
Julius Cæsar, i. 3.

CALIVER. *A musket; a blunderbuss.*

Such as fear the report of a *caliver* worse than
a struck fowl or a hurt wild-duck.
Henry 4, P. 1, iv. 2.
Come, manage me your *caliver*. *Ibid.* P. 2, iii. 2.

To CALL IN QUESTION. *To talk over; to dis-*
cuss.

Now sit we close about this taper here,
And *call in question* our necessities.
Julius Cæsar, iv. 3.

To CALL TO. *To call upon; to visit.*

I'll *call to* you. *Timon of Athens*, i. 2.

CALLET. *A scold; a drab; a trull.*

A *callet*
Of boundless tongue, who late hath beat her husband,
And now baits me! *Winter's Tale*, ii. 3.
Contemptuous base-born *callet* as she is.
Henry 6, P. 2, i. 3.
He call'd her whore : a beggar in his drink
Could not have laid such terms upon his *callet*.
Othello, iv. 2.

CALLING. *Name; appellation.*

I am Sir Roland's son,
His youngest son ; and would not change that
calling,
To be adopted heir to Frederick.
As you like it, i. 2.

To CALM. *To becalm.*

Like to a ship that, having scap'd a tempest,
Is straightway *calm'd*, and boarded with a pirate.
Henry 6, P. 2, iv. 10.
At Rhodes, at Cyprus, must be be-lee'd and *calm'd*
By debitor and creditor, this counter-caster.
Othello, i. 1.

CALVES-GUTS. *Catgut.*

If it do not, it is a vice in her ears, which
horse-hairs and *calves-guts* can never amend
Cymbeline, ii. 3.

CAN. *Gan; began.*

Through the velvet leaves the wind,
All unseen, *can* passage find.
Love's Labour's lost, iv. 3.

To CAN. *To be able to do; to perform.*

I have seen myself, and serv'd against the French,
And they *can* well on horseback. *Hamlet*, iv. 7.

CANAKIN. *A drinking-cup.*

And let me the *canakin* clink, clink ;
And let me the *canakin* clink. *Othello*, ii. 3.

CANARY. *An ancient dance ; a sweet wine.*

Quicken a rock, and make you dance *canary*
With spritely fire and motion.
All's well that ends well, ii. 1.
O knight, thou lackest a cup of *canary*.
Twelfth-Night, i. 3.

CANDLE-MINE. *Candle-stuff; grease; tallow.*

You whoreson *candle-mine*, you, how vilely did
you speak of me even now before this honest, virtuous civil gentlewoman ! *Henry* 4, P. 2, ii. 4.

CANDLE-WASTER. *A reveller ; a wassailer.*

Patch grief with proverbs, make misfortune drunk
With *candle-wasters*.
Much Ado about Nothing, v. 1.

CANKER. *The canker-worm ; the dog-rose.*

The *canker* galls the infants of the spring,
Too oft before their buttons be disclos'd.
Hamlet, i. 3.
The *canker* gnaw thy heart,
For showing me again the eyes of man !
Timon of Athens, iv. 3.
I had rather be a *canker* in a hedge, than a rose
in his grace. *Much Ado about Nothing*, i. 3.
To put down Richard, that sweet lovely rose,
And plant this thorn, this *canker*, Bolingbroke.
Henry 4, P. 1, i. 3.

To CANONIZE. *To consecrate; to sanctify ; to*
hallow ; to glorify.

But tell
Why thy *canóniz'd* bones, hearsèd in death,
Have burst their cerements. *Hamlet*, i. 4.
Whose present courage may beat down our foes,
And fame in time to come *canónize* us.
Troilus and Cressida, ii. 2.

CANOPY. *The sky.*

Where dwellest thou ?—Under the canopy.
Coriolanus, iv. 5.

CANSTICK. *Candlestick.*

I'd rather hear a brazen *canstick* turn'd,
Or a dry wheel grate on the axle-tree.
Henry 4, P. 1, iii. 1.

CANTLE. *A piece ; a portion.*

See how this river comes me cranking in,

And cuts me from the best of all my land
A huge half-moon, a monstrous *cantle* out.
Henry 4, P. 1, iii. 1.
The greater *cantle* of the world is lost
With very ignorance. *Antony and Cleopatra,* iii. 10.

CANTON. *A canto.*

Write loyal *cantons* of contemnèd love,
And sing them loud even in the dead of night.
Twelfth-Night, i. 5.

To CANVASS. *To sift; to examine; to try.*

I'll *canvass* thee in thy broad cardinal's hat,
If thou proceed in this thy insolence.
Henry 6, P. 1, i. 3.

CAP. *The top; the chief; the head.*

Thou art the *cap* of all the fools alive.
Timon of Athens, iv. 3.
Be more expressive to them : for they wear
themselves in the *cap* of the time.
All's well that ends well, ii. 1.

CAPABLE. *Apprehensive; intelligent; susceptible; able to acquire; able to understand; capacious; comprehensive.*

O, 'tis a parlous boy,
Bold, quick, ingenious, forward, *capable.*
Richard 3, iii. 1.
His form and cause conjoin'd, preaching to stones,
Would make them *capable.* *Hamlet,* iii. 4.
For I am sick, and *capable* of fears.
King John, iii. 1.
Heart too *capable*
Of every line and trick of his sweet favour.
All's well that ends well, i. 1.
But we all are men,
In our own natures frail, and *capable*
Of our flesh ; few are angels. *Henry* 8, v. 2.
And of my land,
Loyal and natural boy, I'll work the means
To make thee *capable.* *King Lear,* ii. 1.
To split the ears of the groundlings, who, for
the most part, are *capable* of nothing but inexplicable dumb-shows and noise. *Hamlet,* iii. 2.
So thou wilt be *capable* of a courtier's counsel,
and understand what advice shall thrust upon thee.
All's well that ends well, i. 1.
Even so my bloody thoughts, with violent pace,
Shall ne'er look back, ne'er ebb to humble love,
Till that a *capable* and wide revenge
Swallow them up. *Othello,* iii. 3.

To CAPITULATE. *To confederate; to combine; to treat with; to make conditions.*

Percy, Northumberland,
The Archbishop's grace of York, Douglas, Mortimer,
Capitulate against us, and are up.
Henry 4, P. 1, iii. 2.
Do not bid me
Dismiss my soldiers, or *capitulate*
Again with Rome's mechanics. *Coriolanus,* v. 3.

CAPOCCHIO. *A fool; a simpleton.*

Ah, poor *capocchio !* hast not slept to-night ?
Troilus and Cressida, iv. 2.

CAPON. *A letter.*

Boyet, you can carve ; break up this *capon.*
Love's Labour's lost, iv. 1.

CAPRICCIO. *Caprice; whim; humour.*

Will this *capriccio* hold in thee, art sure ?
All's well that ends well, ii. 3.

CAPTAIN. *Courageous; valiant.*

Why then, women are more valiant
That stay at home, if bearing carry it ;
And the ass more *captain* than the lion.
Timon of Athens, iii. 5.

CAPTAINSHIP. *Government; supreme command; military skill.*

Therefore, so please thee to return with us,
And of our Athens—thine and ours—to take
The *captainship,* thou shalt be met with thanks,
Allow'd with absolute power, and thy good name
Live with authority. *Timon of Athens,* v. 1.
The itch of his affection should not then
Have nick'd his *captainship.*
Antony and Cleopatra, iii. 13.

CAPTIOUS. *Capacious.*

Yet, in this *captious* and intenible sieve
I still pour in the waters of my love,
And lack not to lose still.
All's well that ends well, i. 3.

CAPTIVATE. *Captured; taken prisoner.*

Tush, women have been *captivate* ere now.
Henry 6, P. 1, v. 3.
That hast by tyranny, these many years,
Wasted our country, slain our citizens,
And sent our sons and husbands *captivate.*
Ibid. P. 1, ii. 3.

To CAPTIVATE. *To make prisoner; to reduce to captivity.*

How ill-beseeming is it in thy sex
To triumph, like an Amazonian trull,
Upon their woes whom fortune *captivates!*
Henry 6, P. 3, i. 4.

To CAPTIVE. *To take prisoner; to capture.*

And all our princes *captiv'd* by the hand
Of that black name, Edward, Black Prince of Wales.
Henry 5, ii. 4.

CARACK. *A large ship of burden.*

Faith, he to-night hath boarded a land *carack:*
If it prove lawful prize, he's made for ever.
Othello, i. 2.
Who sent whole armadoes of *caracks* to be ballast at her nose. *Comedy of Errors, iii. 2.*

CARBONADO. *A collop; a slice of meat; a steak.*

If he do not, if I come in his willingly, let him make a *carbonado* of me. *Henry 4, P. 1, v. 3.*

To CARBONADO. *To cut or hack; to scotch.*

Draw, you rogue, or I'll so *carbonado* your shanks.
King Lear, ii. 2.
But it is your *carbonadoed* face.
All's well that ends well, iv. 5.
And how she longed to eat adders' heads and toads *carbonadoed.* *Winter's Tale, iv. 3.*

CARBUNCLED. *Set with carbuncles.*

He has deserv'd it, were it *carbuncled*
Like holy Phœbus' car. *Antony and Cleopatra, iv. 8.*

CARCANET. *A necklace; a chain.*

Say that I linger'd with you at your shop
To see the making of her *carcanet.*
Comedy of Errors, iii. 1.

CARD. *A sea-chart; a map.*

We must speak by the *card*, or equivocation will undo us. *Hamlet, v. 1.*
Indeed, to speak feelingly of him, he is the *card* or calendar of gentry. *Ibid. v. 2.*
I myself have all the other;
And the very ports they blow,
All the quarters that they know
I' the shipman's *card.* *Macbeth, i. 3.*

To CARD. *To debase.*

Carded his state;
Mingled his royalty with carping fools.
Henry 4, P. 1, iii. 2.

CARDECUE. *The fourth part of a French coin.*

For a *cardecue* he will sell the fee-simple of his salvation, the inheritance of it.
All's well that ends well, iv. 3.

CARE. *Wish; inclination.*

I have more *care* to stay than will to go.
Romeo and Juliet, iii. 5.

CAREFUL. *Full of troubles and anxieties; uneasy; restless.*

By Him that rais'd me to this *careful* height
From that contented hap which I enjoy'd.
Richard 3, i. 3.
And *careful* hours with Time's deformèd hand
Have written strange defeatures in my face.
Comedy of Errors, v. 1.

CARL. *A rustic; a peasant.*

I have belied a lady,
The princess of this country, and the air on't
Revengingly enfeebles me; or could this *carl*,
A very drudge of nature's, have subdu'd me
In my profession? *Cymbeline, v. 2.*

CARLOT. *A peasant; a countryman.*

And he hath bought the cottage and the bounds
That the old *carlot* once was master of.
As you like it, iii. 5.

CARNAL. *Licentious; sensual.*

O upright, just, and true-disposing God,
How do I thank thee, that this *carnal* cur
Preys on the issue of his mother's body,
And makes her pew-fellow with others' moan!
Richard 3, iv. 4.
So shall you hear
Of *carnal*, bloody, and unnatural acts.
Hamlet, v. 2.

CAROUSE. *A large draught of wine; a bumper.*

And drink *carouses* to the next day's fate.
Antony and Cleopatra, iv. 8.
And quaff *carouses* to our mistress' health.
Taming of the Shrew, i. 2.

To CAROUSE. *To drink; to quaff.*

The queen *carouses* to thy fortune, Hamlet.
Hamlet, v. 2.
Faith, sir, we were *carousing* till the second cock.
Macbeth, ii. 1.
Now, my sick fool Roderigo,
Whom love hath turn'd almost the wrong side out,

To Desdemona hath to-night *carous'd*
Potations pottle-deep ; and he's to watch.
Othello, ii. 3.

CARPET. *A table-cover.*

Be the jacks fair within, the jills fair without,
the *carpets* laid, and every thing in order ?
Taming of the Shrew, iv. 1.

CARRIAGE. *Behaviour ; conduct ; burden ;
import ; intent ; removal ; flight.*

Consider what you do;
How you may hurt yourself, ay, utterly
Grow from the king's acquaintance, by this *carriage*.
Henry 8, iii. 1.
Teach sin the *carriage* of a holy saint.
Comedy of Errors, iii. 2.
Look, prithee, Charmian,
How this Herculean Roman does become
The *carriage* of his chafe.
Antony and Cleopatra, i. 3.
My spirits obey ; and time
Goes upright with his *carriage*. *Tempest*, v. 1.
As, by the same cov'nant,
And *carriage* of the article design'd,
His fell to Hamlet. *Hamlet*, i. 1.
Well, madam, we must take a short farewell,
Lest, being miss'd, I be suspected of
Your *carriage* from the court. *Cymbeline*, iii. 4.

CARRY-TALE. *A tale-bearer.*

Some *carry-tale*, some please-man, some slight zany.
Love's Labour's lost, v. 2.

To CARRY. *To effect ; to manage ; to take ; to
conquer ; to subdue.*

Why, all this business
Our reverend cardinal *carried*. *Henry 8*, i. 1.
Sir, I beseech you, think you he'll *carry* Rome ?
Coriolanus, iv. 7.
No, by the flame of yonder glorious heaven,
He shall not *carry* him. *Troilus and Cresida*, v. 6.

To CARRY COALS. *To take an affront patiently.*

Gregory, o' my word, we'll not *carry coals*.
Romeo and Juliet, i. 1.
I knew by that piece of service the men would
carry coals. *Henry 5*, iii. 1.

CART. *Car.*

Full thirty times hath Phœbus' *cart* gone round
Neptune's salt wash and Tellus' orbèd ground.
Hamlet, iii. 2.

To CARVE. *To woo ; to give encouragement ;
to court.*

She discourses, she *carves*, she gives the leer of
invitation. *Merry Wives of Windsor*, i. 3.

CASE. *A set ; a pair ; a covering of any
kind ; the skin.*

The knocks are too hot ; and, for mine own
part, I have not a *case* of lives. *Henry 5*, iii. 1.
I have *cases* of buckram for the nonce.
Henry 4, P. 1, i. 2.
They seemed almost, with staring on one an-
other, to tear the *cases* of their eyes.
Winter's Tale, v. 2.
O thou dissembling cub ! what wilt thou be
When time hath sow'd a grizzle on thy *case* ?
Twelfth-Night, v. 1.

To CASE. *To cover ; to enclose : to flay ; to
skin.*

Whole as the marble, founded as the rock ;
As broad and general as the *casing* air.
Macbeth, iii. 4.
If thou wouldst not entomb thyself alive,
And *case* thy reputation in thy tent.
Troilus and Cressida, iii. 3.
You look pale, and gaze,
And put on fear, and *case* yourself in wonder.
Julius Cæsar, i. 3.
We'll make you some sport with the fox, ere
we *case* him. *All's well that ends well*, iii. 6.

CASK. *A casket.*

A jewel, lock'd into the woful'st *cask*
That ever did contain a thing of worth.
Henry 6, P. 2, iii. 2.

CASSOCK. *A loose outward coat.*

Half of the which dare not shake the snow
from off their *cassocks*, lest they shake themselves
to pieces. *All's well that ends well*, iv. 3.

To CAST. *To cast up ; to throw up ; to dismiss ; to reject ; to compute.*

She from whom
We all were sea-swallow'd, though some *cast* again.
Tempest, ii. 1.
His filth within being *cast*, he would appear
A pond as deep as hell.
Measure for Measure, iii. 1.
Our general *cast* us thus early for the love of his
Desdemona. *Othello*, ii. 3.

You are but now *cast* in his mood, a punishment more in policy than in malice. *Othello*, ii. 3.

For, I do know, the state,—
However this may gall him with some check,—
Cannot with safety *cast* him. *Ibid.* i. 1.
Let it be *cast* and paid. *Henry 4, P. 2*, v. 1.

CASTED. *Cast; shed; thrown off.*

The organs, though defunct and dead before,
Break up their drowsy grave, and newly move
With *casted* slough and fresh legerity. *Henry 5*, iv. 1.

CASTLE. *A kind of helmet.*

Farewell, revolted fair! and, Diomed,
Stand fast, and wear a *castle* on thy head.
Troilus and Cressida, v. 2.

CATAIAN. *A sharper; a rogue.*

I will not believe such a *Cataian*.
Merry Wives of Windsor, ii. 1.

CATAPLASM. *A poultice; a salve.*

Where it draws blood no *cataplasm* so rare
Can save the thing from death that is but scratch'd
withal. *Hamlet*, iv. 7.

To CATCH COLD. *To be turned out of doors.*

Nay, an thou canst not smile as the wind sits,
thou'lt *catch cold* shortly. *King Lear*, i. 4.

CATER-COUSINS. *Good friends; upon friendly terms.*

His master and he—saving your worship's reverence—are scarce *cater-cousins*.
Merchant of Venice, ii. 2.

CATES. *Food; victuals; dainties; delicacies.*

But though my *cates* be mean, take them in good part. *Comedy of Errors*, iii. 1.
I had rather live
With cheese and garlic in a windmill, far,
Than feed on *cates* and have him talk to me
In any summer-house in Christendom.
Henry 4, P. 1, iii. 1.
Nor other satisfaction do I crave,
But only, with your patience, that we may
Taste of your wine, and see what *cates* you have.
Henry 6, P. 1, ii. 3.

CATLING. *A fiddle-string.*

What music will be in him when Hector has knocked out his brains, I know not; but, I am sure, none,—unless the fiddler Apollo get his sinews to make *catlings* on. *Troilus and Cressida*, iii. 3.

To CAUDLE. *To refresh; to restore; to revive.*

Will the cold brook,
Candied with ice, *caudle* thy morning taste,
To cure thy o'er-night's surfeit?
Timon of Athens, iv. 3.

'CAUSE. *Because.*

But, peace!—for from broad words, and *'cause* he fail'd
His presence at the tyrant's feast, I hear,
Macduff lives in disgrace. *Macbeth*, iii. 6.

CAUSE. *Reason; motive.*

We thank you both: yet one but flatters us,
As well appeareth by the *cause* you come.
Richard 2, i. 1.

CAUTEL. *Deceit; treachery.*

Perhaps he loves you now;
And now no soil nor *cautel* doth besmirch
The virtue of his will. *Hamlet*, i. 3. ✓

CAUTELOUS. *Insidious; wary; artful; cunning.*

Believe't not lightly, your son
Will or exceed the common, or be caught
With *cautelous* baits and practice. *Coriolanus*, iv. 1.
Swear priests, and cowards, and men *cautelous*.
Julius Cæsar, ii. 1.

CAVALERO. *A gallant; a rake; a libertine.*

I'll drink to Master Bardolph, and to all the *cavaleroes* about London. *Henry 4, P. 2*, v. 3.

To CAVE. *To dwell in a cave.*

It may be heard at court, that such as we
Cave here, hunt here, are outlaws, and in time
May make some stronger head. *Cymbeline*, iv. 2.

CEASE. *Extinction; failure; cessation.*

The *cease* of majesty
Dies not alone; but, like a gulf, doth draw
What's near with it. *Hamlet*, iii. 3. ✓

To CEASE. *To put an end to; to stop; to die.*

Heaven *cease* this idle humour in your honour!
Taming of the Shrew, Induction, sc. 2.
Now let the general trumpet blow his blast,
Particularities and petty sounds to *cease!*
Henry 6, P. 2, v. 2.
Impórtune him for my moneys; be not *ceas'd*
With slight denial. *Timon of Athens*, ii. 1.
And both shall *cease*, without your remedy.
All's well that ends well, v. 3.

CELEBRATION. *Nuptial feast.*

He shall conceal it,
Whiles you are willing it shall come to note,
What time we will our *celebration* keep,
According to my birth.   *Twelfth-Night,* iv. 3.

CENSER. *A fire-pan; a brasier.*

Like to a *censer* in a barber's shop.
        Taming of the Shrew, iv. 3.

CENSURE. *Opinion; judgment.*

How blest am I
In my just *censure,* in my true opinion !
        Winter's Tale, ii. 1.

And betray themselves to every modern *censure*
worse than drunkards.   *As you like it,* iv. 1.
Madam, the king is old enough himself
To give his *censure.*   *Henry 6,* P. 2, i. 3.
Madam,—and you, my mother,—will you go
To give your *censures* in this business? -
        Richard 3, ii. 3.

To CENSURE. *To pass judgment upon; to sentence; to judge; to estimate.*

'Tis a passing shame
That I, unworthy body as I am,
Should *censure* thus on lovely gentlemen.
        Two Gentlemen of Verona, ii. 1.

Doth he so seek his life?—
Has *censur'd* him already.
        Measure for Measure, i. 4.
Do you two know how you are *censured* here in
the city, I mean of us o' the right-hand file?
        Coriolanus, ii. 1.

Whose equality
By our best eyes cannot be *censur'd.*
        King John, ii. 1.

CENTURY. *A hundred; a company of soldiers.*

And when
With wild wood-leaves and weeds I ha' strew'd his
grave,
And on it said a *century* of prayers,
Such as I can, twice o'er, I'll weep and sigh.
        Cymbeline, iv. 2.

If I do send, dispatch
Those *centuries* to our aid.   *Coriolanus,* i. 7.

A *century* send forth;
Search every acre in the high-grown field,
And bring him to our eye.   *King Lear,* iv. 4.

CERECLOTH. *Waxed cloth.*

It were too gross
To rib her *cerecloth* in the obscure grave.
        Merchant of Venice, ii. 6.

CEREMENT. *Cerecloth.*

Let me not burst in ignorance; but tell
Why thy canóniz'd bones, hearsèd in death,
Have burst their *cerements.*   *Hamlet,* i. 4.

CEREMONIES. *Ornaments of state; scarfs; omens; prodigies.*

Disrobe the images,
If you do find them deck'd with *ceremonies.*
        Julius Cæsar, i. 1.

For he is superstitious grown of late;
Quite from the main opinion he held once
Of fantasy, of dreams, and *ceremonies.*   *Ibid.* ii. 1.

Cæsar, I never stood on *ceremonies,*
Yet now they fright me.   *Ibid.* ii. 2.

CEREMONIOUS. *Observant of forms; formal; customary.*

You are too senseless-obstinate, my lord,
Too *ceremonious* and traditional.   *Richard 3,* iii. 1.

Farewell: the leisure and the fearful time
Cuts off the *ceremonious* vows of love.   *Ibid.* v. 3.

CEREMONY. *A memorial; a keepsake.*

What man is there so much unreasonable,
If you had pleas'd to have defended it
With any terms of zeal, wanted the modesty
To urge the thing held as a *ceremony?*
        Merchant of Venice, v. 1.

'CERNS. *Concerns.*

Why, sir, what *'cerns* it you if I wear pearl and
gold?   *Taming of the Shrew,* v. 1.

CERTAIN. *Constant.*

Thou art not *certain;*
For thy complexion shifts to strange affects
After the moon.   *Measure for Measure,* iii. 1.

CERTES. *Assuredly; certainly.*

One, *certes,* that promises no element
In such a business.   *Henry 8,* i. 1.
Certes, she did; the kitchen-vestal scorn'd you.
        Comedy of Errors, iv. 4.

CESS. *Measure.*

The poor jade is wrung in the withers out of all
cess.   *Henry 4,* P. 1, ii. 1.

H

CESSE. *Cease.*

Or, ere they meet, in me, O nature, *cesse!*
　　　　All's well that ends well, v. 3.

CHAFE. *Anger ; rage.*

Look, prithee, Charmian,
How this Herculean Roman does become
The carriage of his *chafe. Antony and Cleop.* i. 3.

CHAIR. *A seat of dignity; a state; a throne.*

A base foul stone, made precious by the foil
Of England's *chair*, where he is falsely set.
　　　　　　　　　　　Richard 3, v. 3.
Is the *chair* empty ? is the sword unsway'd ?
Is the king dead ?　　　　　*Ibid.* iv. 4.
And power, unto itself most commendable,
Hath not a tomb so evident as a *chair*
To extol what it hath done.　*Coriolanus,* iv. 7.

TO CHAIR. *To seat; to fix; to make firm.*

This push
Will *chair* me ever, or disseat me now. *Macb.* v. 3.

CHAIR-DAYS. *Old age ; the latter end of life.*

And, in thy reverence and thy *chair-days*, thus
To die in ruffian battle.　*Henry* 6, P. 2, v. 2.

CHALICED. *Having a calix or cup.*

And Phœbus gins arise,
His steeds to water at those springs
On *chalic'd* flowers that lies. *Cymbeline,* ii. 3.

CHALLENGE. *Claim ; demand.*

Either accept the title thou usurp'st,
Of benefit proceeding from our king,
And not of any *challenge* of desert,
Or we will plague thee with incessant wars.
　　　　　　　　　　　Henry 6, P. 1, v. 4.

TO CHALLENGE. *To claim as due; to call for ; to demand ; to accuse.*

Tell me, my daughters,
Which of you shall we say doth love us most ?
That we our largest bounty may extend
Where nature doth with merit *challenge.*
　　　　　　　　　　　King Lear, i. 1.
Had you not been their father, these white flakes
Had *challeng'd* pity of them.　*Ibid.* iv. 7.
And so much duty as my mother show'd
To you, preferring you before her father,
So much I *challenge* that I may profess
Due to the Moor my lord.　*Othello,* i. 3.
Who may I rather *challenge* for unkindness,
Than pity for mischance.　*Macbeth,* iii. 4.

CHALLENGER. *Claimant.*

He bids you then resign
Your crown and kingdom, indirectly held
From him the native and true *challenger.*
　　　　　　　　　　　Henry 5, ii. 4.
Whose worth, if praises may go back again,
Stood *challenger* on mount of all the age
For her perfections.　　　*Hamlet,* iv. 7.

CHAMBER. *The city of London, which was formerly called the King's Chamber ; a species of cannon.*

Welcome, sweet prince, to London, to your *chamber.*　　　　　　　*Richard* 3, iii. 1.
To venture upon the charged *chambers* bravely.
　　　　　　　　　　　Henry 4, P. 2, ii. 4.

CHAMBERER. *A man of gallantry; an intriguer.*

Haply, for I am black,
And have not those soft parts of conversation
That *chamberers* have.　　*Othello,* iii. 3.

CHAMBER-HANGING. *Tapestry.*

Averring notes
Of *chamber-hanging*, pictures, this her bracelet,—
O cunning, how I got it !—nay, some marks
Of secret on her person.　*Cymbeline,* v. 5.

TO CHAMPION. *To challenge ; to defy.*

Rather than so, come, fate, into the list,
And *champion* me to the utterance. *Macbeth,* iii. 1.

TO CHANCE. *To light upon ; to fall upon by chance ; to happen.*

You shall not know by what strange accident
I *chancèd* on this letter. *Merchant of Venice,* v. 1.
Think what a chance thou *chancest* on.
　　　　　　　　　　　Cymbeline, i. 5.
Ay, Casca ; tell us what hath *chanc'd* to-day,
That Cæsar looks so sad.　*Julius Cæsar,* i. 2.
He that but fears the thing he would not know
Hath by instinct knowledge from others' eyes
That what he fear'd is *chancèd. Henry* 4, P. 2, i. 1.

CHANGE. *Variety.*

From whom I have receiv'd not only greetings,
But with them *change* of honours. *Coriolanus,* ii. 1.

CHANGEFUL. *Precarious ; uncertain.*

And sometimes we are devils to ourselves,
When we will tempt the frailty of our powers,
Presuming on their *changeful* potency.
　　　　　　　　　　　Troilus and Cressida, iv. 4.

CHANGELING. *One who is fond of change.*
Yet his nature
In that's no *changeling;* and I must excuse
What cannot be amended. *Coriolanus,* iv. 7.
To face the garment of rebellion
With some fine colour that may please the eye
Of fickle *changelings* and poor discontents.
Henry 4, P. 1, v. 1.

CHANNEL. *A kennel.*
Cut me off the villain's head; throw the quean
in the *channel. Henry 4,* P. 2, ii. 1.
As if a *channel* should be call'd the sea.
Henry 6, P. 3, ii. 2.

CHANSON. *A song.*
Tho first row of the pious *chanson* will show you
more. *Hamlet,* ii. 2.

CHANTRY. *A small church or chapel.*
If you mean well,
Now go with me and with this holy man
Into the *chantry* by. *Twelfth-Night,* iv. 3.

CHAPE. *The hook of a scabbard or sheath.*
This is Monsieur Parolles, that had the whole
theoric of war in the knot of his scarf, and the
practice in the *chape* of his dagger.
All's well that ends well, iv. 3.

CHAPELESS. *Having no chape.*
An old rusty sword ta'en out of the town ar-
moury, with a broken hilt and *chapeless.*
Taming of the Shrew, iii. 2.

CHAPLESS. *Without lips.*
Or shut me nightly in a charnel-house,
O'er-cover'd quite with dead men's rattling bones,
With reeky shanks, and yellow *chapless* skulls.
Romeo and Juliet, iv. 1.
Why, e'en so: and now my Lady Worm's; *chap-
less,* and knocked about the mazzard with a sexton's
spade. *Hamlet,* v. 1.

CHAPMAN. *A trader; a dealer.*
Fair Diomed, you do as *chapmen* do,
Dispraise the thing that you desire to buy.
Troilus and Cressida, iv. 1.
Beauty is bought by judgment of the eye,
Not utter'd by base sale of *chapmen's* tongues.
Love's Labour's lost, ii. 1.

CHARACT. *Inscription.*
So may Angelo,
In all his dressings, *characts,* titles, forms,
Be an arch-villain. *Measure for Measure,* v. 1.

CHARACTER. *Inscription; register; hand-
writing; a written or printed letter.*
There lie; and there thy *character.*
Winter's Tale, iii. 3.
You know the *character* to be your brother's.
King Lear, i. 2.
The letters of Antigonus, found with it, which
they know to be his *character. Winter's Tale,* v. 2.
I say, without *characters,* fame lives long.
Richard 3, iii. 1.

To CHARACTER. *To engrave; to inscribe.*
Show me one scar *charácter'd* on thy skin.
Henry 6, P. 2, iii. 1.
And these few precepts in thy memory
See thou *charácter. Hamlet,* i. 3.
These trees shall be my books,
And in their barks my thoughts I'll *character.*
As you like it, iii. 2.

CHARACTERLESS. *Without record; unregis-
tered.*
And mighty states *characterless* are grated
To dusty nothing; yet let memory,
From false to false, among false maids in love,
Upbraid my falsehood!
Troilus and Cressida, iii. 2.

CHARACTERY. *Writing; language.*
Fairies use flowers for their *charáctery.*
Merry Wives of Windsor, v. 5.
All my engagements I will construe to thee,
All the *charáctery* of my sad brows.
Julius Cæsar, ii. 1.

CHARE. *Work; business; task; service.*
No more, but e'en a woman, and commanded
By such poor passion as the maid that milks,
And does the meanest *chares.*
Antony and Cleopatra, iv. 15.
And, when thou hast done this *chare,* I'll give thee
leave
To play till doomsday. *Ibid.* v. 2.

CHARGE. *Expense; cost; value; importance;
weight; commission.*
Our abbeys and our priories shall pay
This expedition's *charge. King John,* i. 1.
You embrace you *charge* too willingly.
Much Ado about Nothing, i. 1.

I hope so, sir; for I have about me many parcels
of *charge*.   *Winter's Tale*, iv. 3.
With many suchlike as's of great *charge*.
                                      Hamlet, v. 2.
I have procured thee, Jack, a *charge* of foot.
                                      Henry 4, P. 1, iii. 3.
A good and virtuous nature may recoil
In an imperial *charge*.   *Macbeth*, iv. 3.
I'm weary of this *charge*, the gods can witness.
                                      Timon of Athens, iii. 4.

To CHARGE. *To call upon; to challenge; to
summon; to enjoin.*

Thou canst not, cardinal, devise a name
So slight, unworthy, and ridiculous,
To *charge* me to an answer, as the pope.
                                      King John, iii. 1.
For his best friends, if they
Should say, "Be good to Rome," they *charg'd* him
even
As those should do that had deserv'd his hate,
And therein show'd like enemies. *Coriolanus*, iv. 6.

CHARGEFUL. *Expensive; costly.*

The fineness of the gold, and *chargeful* fashion,
Which doth amount to three odd ducats more.
                                      Comedy of Errors, iv. 1.

CHARGE-HOUSE. *A free-school.*

Do you not educate youth at the *charge-house*
on the top of the mountain?
                                      Love's Labour's lost, v. 1.

CHARINESS. *Delicacy; purity.*

I will consent to act any villany against him,
that may not sully the *chariness* of our honesty.
                                      Merry Wives of Windsor, ii. 1.

CHARITABLE. *Endearing.*

How had you been my friends else? why have
you that *charitable* title from thousands, did not
you chiefly belong to my heart?
                                      Timon of Athens, i. 2.

To CHARM. *To adjure; to control; to silence; to call forth; to enchant; to cause;
to compel.*

I *charm* you, by my once-commended beauty,
That you unfold to me, yourself, your half,
Why you are heavy.   *Julius Cæsar*, ii. 1.
Petrucio is the master,
That teacheth tricks eleven and twenty long,
To tame a shrew, and *charm* her chattering tongue.
                                      Taming of the Shrew, iv. 2.

But I will *charm* him first to keep his tongue.
                                      Taming of the Shrew, i. 1.
But 'tis your grace
That, from my mutest conscience, to my tongue,
Charms this report out.   *Cymbeline*, i. 6.
I bear a *charmèd* life, which must not yield
To one of woman born.   *Macbeth*, v. 8.
And then I will her *charmèd* eye release.
                                      Midsummer-Night's Dream, iii. 2.
I, in mine own woe *charm'd*,
Could not find death where I did hear him groan,
Nor feel him where he struck.   *Cymbeline*, v. 3.
Music, ho! music, such as *charmeth* sleep!
                                      Midsummer-Night's Dream, iv. 1.

CHARMER. *An enchanter; a magician.*

She was a *charmer*, and could almost read
The thoughts of people.   *Othello*, iii. 4.

CHARNECO. *A kind of sweet wine.*

And here, neighbour, here's a cup of *charneco*.
                                      Henry 6, P. 2, ii. 3.

CHARY. *Careful; cautious.*

The *chariest* maid is prodigal enough
If she unmask her beauty to the moon.
                                      Hamlet, i. 3.

CHASE. *The game hunted.*

Nay, Warwick, single out some other *chase*;
For I myself will hunt this wolf to death.
                                      Henry 6, P. 3, ii. 4.
Well may I get aboard!—This is the *chase*:
I am gone for ever.   *Winter's Tale*, iii. 3.

To CHASTISE. *To awe; to intimidate; to rebuke.*

And *chastise* with the valour of my tongue
All that impedes thee from the golden round
Which fate and metaphysical aid doth seem
To have thee crown'd withal.   *Macbeth*, i. 5.
Know, sir, that I
Will not wait pinion'd at your master's court,
Nor once be *chastis'd* with the sober eye
Of dull Octavia.   *Antony and Cleopatra*, v. 2.

CHAUDRON. *The entrails.*

Add thereto a tiger's *chaudron*,
For the ingredients of our caldron. *Macbeth*, iv. 1.

CHEAP. *Little valued; not respected.*

The goodness that is *cheap* in beauty makes
beauty brief in goodness.
                                      Measure for Measure, iii. 1.

CHEATER. *Escheator, an officer of the Exchequer in former days; a cheat; a rogue.*

I will be *cheater* to them both, and they shall be exchequers to me. *Merry Wives of Windsor,* i. 3.

He's no swaggerer, hostess; a tame *cheater,* i' faith.
Henry 4, P. 2, ii. 4.

CHECK. *A rebuke; a rebuff.*

O, this life
Is nobler than attending for a *check,*
Richer than doing nothing for a bribe.
Cymbeline, iii. 3.

Rebukable,
And worthy shameful *check* it were, to stand
On more mechanic compliment.
Antony and Cleopatra, iv. 4.

To CHECK AT. *To stop; to pause; to hesitate.*

What dish o' poison has she dressed him!—
And with what wing the staniel *checks at* it!
Twelfth-Night, ii. 5.

Not, like the haggard, *check at* every feather.
Ibid. iii. 1.

If he be now return'd,—
As *checking at* his voyage, and that he means
No more to undertake it,—I will work him
To an exploit, now ripe in my device,
Under the which he shall not choose but fall.
Hamlet, iv. 7.

CHEER. *Gaiety; jollity; countenance; mien.*

The human mortals want their winter *cheer.*
Midsummer-Night's Dream, ii. 1.

I have not that alacrity of spirit,
Nor *cheer* of mind, that I was wont to have.
Richard 3, v. 3.

All fancy-sick she is, and pale of *cheer.*
Midsummer-Night's Dream, iii. 2.

Methinks your looks are sad, your *cheer* appall'd.
Henry 6, P. 1, i. 1.

To CHEER. *To incite; to prompt.*

And here's the heart that triumphs in their death,
And *cheers* those hands that slew thy sire and brother,
To execute the like upon thyself.
Henry 6, P. 3, ii. 4.

CHEERLY. *Cheerful.*

Prithee, man, look *cheerly.* These old fellows
Have their ingratitude in them hereditary.
Timon of Athens, ii. 2.

CHERRY-PIT. *A well-known game, played by children.*

What, man! 'tis not for gravity to play at *cherry-pit* with Satan. *Twelfth-Night,* iii. 4.

CHERUBIN. *A cherub; an angel.*

Their dwarfish pages were
As *cherubins* all gilt. *Henry 8,* i. 1.

O, a *cherubin*
Thou wast that did preserve me! *Tempest,* i. 2.

CHERUBIN. *Angelical.*

This fell whore of thine
Hath in her more destruction than thy sword
For all her *cherubin* look. *Timon of Athens,* iv. 3.

CHEVERIL. *Kid-leather.*

O, here's a wit of *cheveril,* that stretches from an inch narrow to an ell broad.
Romeo and Juliet, ii. 4.

A sentence is but a *cheveril* glove to a good wit: how quickly the wrong side may be turned outward!
Twelfth-Night, iii. 1.

Which gifts the capacity
Of your soft *cheveril* conscience would receive,
If you might please to stretch it. *Henry 8,* ii. 3.

To CHEW. *To meditate; to ponder; to reflect.*

Till then, my noble friend, *chew* upon this.
Julius Cæsar, i. 2.

CHEWET. *A sort of pie.*

Peace, *chewet,* peace! *Henry 4,* P. 1, v. 1.

To CHIDE. *To make a noise; to resound.*

Yet my duty,
As doth a rock against the *chiding* flood,
Should the approach of this wild river break,
And stand unshaken yours. *Henry 8,* iii. 2.

That caves and womby vaultages of France
Shall *chide* your trespass, and return your mock
In second accent of his ordnance. *Henry 5,* ii. 4.

CHIDING. *Noise; sound; clamour.*

The icy fang
And churlish *chiding* of the winter's wind.
As you like it, ii. 1.

Never did I hear such gallant *chiding.*
Midsummer-Night's Dream, iv. 1.

CHIDING. *Noisy; clamorous.*

And with an accent tun'd in self-same key
Retorts to *chiding* fortune.
Troilus and Cressida, i. 3.

CHIEF. *Chiefly.*

And they in France of the best rank and station
Are most select and generous *chief* in that.
Hamlet, i. 3.
Wherein the honour
Of my dear father's gift stands *chief* in power.
All's well that ends well, ii. 1.

CHILD. *A female infant.*

A boy or a *child,* I wonder? *Winter's Tale,* iii. 3.

CHILDING. *Fruitful; productive; teeming; abundant.*

The *childing* autumn, angry winter, change
Their wonted liveries.
Midsummer-Night's Dream, ii. 1.

CHILDNESS. *Childishness.*

He makes a July's day short as December;
And with his varying *childness* cures in me
Thoughts that would thick my blood.
Winter's Tale, i. 2.

CHINKS. *Money.*

I tell you, he that can lay hold of her
Shall have the *chinks.* *Romeo and Juliet,* i. 5.

CHIRURGEONLY. *Surgically.*

Very well.—And most *chirurgeonly.* *Tempest,* ii. 1.

CHOPINE. *A high shoe or clog.*

Your ladyship is nearer heaven than when I
saw you last, by the altitude of a *chopine.*
Hamlet, ii. 2.

CHOP-LOGIC. *A dealer in words; a logician.*

How now, how now, *chop-logic!* What is this?
Romeo and Juliet, iii. 5.

CHOPPING. *Mincing.*

Speak "pardon" as 'tis current in our land,
The *chopping* French we do not understand.
Richard 2, v. 3.

CHRISTENDOM. *Christianity; baptism; a term of affection or endearment.*

By my *christendom,*
So I were out of prison, and kept sheep,
I should be merry as the day is long.
King John, iv. 1.

With a world
Of pretty, fond-adoptious *christendoms,*
That blinking Cupid gossips.
All's well that ends well, i. 1.

CHRISTOM. *Chrysom, an infant that dies within a month of its birth.*

'A made a fine end, and went away, an it had
been any *christom* child. *Henry* 5, ii. 3.

CHUCK. *A familiar term of endearment.*

Why, how now, my bawcock! how dost thou, *chuck?*
Twelfth-Night, iii. 4.
Be innocent of the knowledge, dearest *chuck,*
Till thou applaud the deed. *Macbeth,* iii. 2.

CHURL. *A selfish or greedy wretch; a niggard; a miser; a peasant.*

Poison, I see, hath been his timeless end:
O *churl!* drink all, and leave no friendly drop
To help me after? *Romeo and Juliet,* v. 3.
Prithee, fair youth,
Think us no *churls,* nor measure our good minds
By this rude place we live in. *Cymbeline,* iii. 6.

CICATRICE. *A mark; an impression.*

Lean but upon a rush,
The *cicatrice* and capable impressure
Thy palm some moment keeps.
As you like it, iii. 5.

CINCTURE. *A garment; a covering for the body; a coat.*

Now happy he whose cloak and *cincture* can
Hold out this tempest. *King John,* iv. 3.

CINDERS OF THE ELEMENT. *The stars.*

And I, in the clear sky of fame, o'ershine you
as much as the full moon doth the *cinders of the element.* *Henry* 4, P. 2, iv. 3.

CIRCLE. *Crown; diadem.*

Next, Cleopatra does confess thy greatness;
Submits her to thy might; and of thee craves
The *circle* of the Ptolemies for her heirs,
Now hazarded to your grace.
Antony and Cleopatra, iii. 12.

CIRCUMMURED. *Walled round.*

He hath a garden *circummur'd* with brick.
Measure for Measure, iv. 1.

CIRCUMSTANCE. *Appendage ; attribute ; discourse ; argument ; circumlocution.*

His approach,
So out of *circumstance* and sudden, tells us
'Tis not a visitation fram'd, but forc'd
By need and accident. *Winter's Tale,* v. 1.
The royal banner, and all quality,
Pride, pomp, and *circumstance* of glorious war !
Othello, iii. 3.
The interruption of their churlish drums
Cuts off more *circumstance.* *King John,* ii. 1.
So by your *circumstance* you call me fool.
Two Gentlemen of Verona, i. 1.
But he, as loving his own pride and purposes,
Evades them, with a bombast *circumstance,*
Horribly stuff'd with epithets of war. *Othello,* i. 1.
And can you, by no drift of *circumstance,*
Get from him why he puts on this confusion?
Hamlet, iii. 1.

CIRCUMSTANCED. *Ruled by circumstances ; governed by events.*

'Tis very good; I must be *circumstanc'd.*
Othello, iii. 4.

CIRCUMVENTION. *Intimation ; notice ; information ; warning.*

What ever have been thought on in this state,
That could be brought to bodily act ere Rome
Had *circumvention?* *Coriolanus,* i. 2.

CITAL. *Impeachment ; blame ; condemnation.*

And, which became him like a prince indeed,
He made a blushing *cital* of himself.
Henry 4, P. 1, v. 2.

To CITE. *To witness ; to testify ; to urge ; to incite.*

Whose agèd honour *cites* a virtuous youth.
All's well that ends well, i. 3.
For Valentine, I need not *cite* him to it.
Two Gentlemen of Verona, ii. 4.

CITIZEN. *Effeminate ; citizen-like.*

I am not well;
But not so *citizen* a wanton as
To seem to die ere sick. *Cymbeline,* iv. 2.

CITTERN. *A musical instrument like a guitar.*

What is this?—A *cittern* head.
Love's Labour's lost, v. 2.

CIVET. *A perfume.*

Give me an ounce of *civet,* good apothecary, to sweeten my imagination. *King Lear,* iv. 6.
Civet is of a baser birth than tar,—the very uncleanly flux of a cat. *As you like it,* iii. 2.

CIVIL. *Grave ; solemn ; serious ; civilised.*

Tongues I'll hang on every tree,
That shall *civil* sayings show. *As you like it,* iii. 2.
Where is Malvolio?—he is sad and *civil,*
And suits well for a servant with my fortunes.
Twelfth-Night, iii. 4.
Come, *civil* night,
Thou sober-suited matron, all in black.
Romeo and Juliet, iii. 2.
Ho ! who's here?
If any thing that's *civil,* speak. *Cymbeline,* iii. 6.
The round world
Should have shook lions into *civil* streets,
And citizens to their dens.
Antony and Cleopatra, v. 1.
Kent, in the Commentaries Cæsar writ,
Is term'd the *civil'st* place of all this isle.
Henry 6, P. 2, iv. 7.

CLACK-DISH. *A wooden box or dish formerly carried by beggars.*

Yes, your beggar of fifty; and his use was to put a ducat in her *clack-dish.*
Measure for Measure, iii. 2.

To CLAMOUR. *To check ; to restrain ; to clam ; to muffle.*

Clamour your tongues, and not a word more.
Winter's Tale, iv. 3.

To CLAP INTO. *To take to ; to enter upon ; to begin at once.*

Truly, sir, I would desire you to *clap into* your prayers. *Measure for Measure,* iv. 3.
Shall we *clap into* it roundly, without hawking, or spitting, or saying we are hoarse?
As you like it, v. 3.

CLAUSE. *Phrase ; sentence ; separate article.*

Do not extort thy reasons from this *clause,*
For that I woo, thou therefore hast no cause ;
But, rather, reason thus with reason fetter,—
Love sought is good, but given unsought is better.
Twelfth-Night, iii. 1.

To CLAW. *To flatter.*

I laugh when I am merry, and *claw* no man in his humour. *Much Ado about Nothing,* i. 3.

CLEAR. *Pure; blameless; serene; cheerful.*

Whose wraths to guard you from,
Is nothing but heart's sorrow,
And a *clear* life ensuing. *Tempest,* iii. 3.
I cannot project mine own cause so well
To make it *clear.* *Antony and Cleopatra,* v. 2.
Go then; and with a countenance as *clear*
As friendship wears at feasts. *Winter's Tale,* i. 2.

CLEARNESS. *Immunity; freedom from imputation.*

For't must be done to-night,
And something from the palace; always thought
That I require a *clearness.* *Macbeth,* iii. 2.

CLEMENT. *Merciful; compassionate.*

I know you are more *clement* than vile men,
Who of their broken debtors take a third,
A sixth, a tenth, letting them thrive again
On their abatement. *Cymbeline,* v. 4.

TO CLEPE. *To call.*

They *clepe* us drunkards, and with swinish phrase
Soil our addition. *Hamlet,* iv. 1.
Shoughs, water-rugs, and demi-wolves, are *clept*
All by the name of dogs. *Macbeth,* iii. 1.
He *clepeth* a calf, cauf; half, hauf.
Love's Labour's lost, v. 1.

CLERK. *A scholar; a learned person.*

Where I have come, great *clerks* have purposèd
To greet me with premeditated welcomes.
Midsummer-Night's Dream, v. 1.

CLERK-LIKE. *Learned; scholarly.*

You are certainly a gentleman; thereto
Clerk-like, experienc'd. *Winter's Tale,* i. 2.

CLERKLY. *Learned; clerk-like.*

Thou art *clerkly,* thou art *clerkly,* Sir John.
Merry Wives of Windsor, iv. 5.

CLERKLY. *Learnedly; cleverly; ingeniously.*

I thank you, gentle servant: 'tis very *clerkly* done.
Two Gentlemen of Verona, ii. 1.
Hath he not twit our sovereign lady here
With ignominious words, though *clerkly* couch'd?
Henry 6, P. 2, iii. 1.

CLIFF. *Key; a musical term.*

And any man may sing her, if he can take her
cliff; she's noted. *Troilus and Cressida,* v. 2.

TO CLIMATE. *To dwell; to inhabit.*

The blessèd gods
Purge all infection from our air whilst you
Do *climate* here! *Winter's Tale,* v. 1.

CLIMATURE. *Climate.*

And even the like precurse of fierce events
Have heaven and earth together demonstrated
Unto our *climature* and countrymen. *Hamlet,* i. 1.

TO CLING. *To shrink up; to consume.*

If thou speak'st false,
Upon the next tree shalt thou hang alive,
Till famine *cling* thee: if thy speech be sooth,
I care not if thou dost for me as much.
Macbeth, v. 5.

CLINQUANT. *Glittering; sparkling.*

To-day, the French,
All *clinquant,* all in gold, like heathen gods,
Shone down the English. *Henry 8,* i. 1.

TO CLIP. *To embrace; to lessen.*

Here I *clip*
The anvil of my sword. *Coriolanus,* iv. 5.
Then again worries he his daughter with *clipping*
her. *Winter's Tale,* v. 2.
That Neptune's arms, who *clippeth* thee about,
Would bear thee from the knowledge of thyself,
And grapple thee unto a pagan shore!
King John, v. 2.
All my reports go with the modest truth;
Nor more nor *clipp'd,* but so. *King Lear,* iv. 7.

CLODPOLE. *A dolt; a blockhead.*

Therefore this letter, being so excellently ignorant, will breed no terror in the youth,—he will find it comes from a *clodpole.* *Twelfth-Night,* iii. 4.

CLOISTERED. *Secluded; solitary; lonely.*

Ere the bat hath flown
His *cloister'd* flight, there shall be done
A deed of dreadful note. *Macbeth,* iii. 2.

CLOSE. *Secret; gloomy; continued.*

Know'st thou not any whom corrupting gold
Would tempt unto a *close* exploit of death?
Richard 3, iv. 2.
But in a man that's just
They're *close* delations, working from the heart.
Othello, iii. 3.
And will continue fast to your affection,
Still *close* as sure. *Cymbeline,* i. 6.

That *close* aspect of his
Doth show the mood of a much-troubled breast.
King John, iv. 2.

Show your wisdom, daughter,
In your *close* patience.
Measure for Measure, iv. 3.

To CLOSE. *To join ; to unite ; to enclose.*

It would become me better than to *close*
In terms of friendship with thine enemies.
Julius Cæsar, iii. 1.

See now, whether pure fear and entire cowardice
doth not make thee wrong this virtuous gentlewoman to *close* with us. *Henry 4*, P. 2, ii. 4.

The housekeeper, the hunter, every one
According to the gift which bounteous nature
Hath in him *clos'd*. *Macbeth*, iii. 1.

CLOSELY. *Privately ; secretly.*

For we have *closely* sent for Hamlet hither,
That he, as 'twere by accident, may here
Affront Ophelia. *Hamlet*, iii. 1.

Silence ; no more : go *closely* in with me :
Much danger do I undergo for thee.
King John, iv. 1.

CLOSENESS. *Retirement ; privacy ; seclusion.*

I, thus neglecting worldly ends, all dedicated
To *closeness*, and the bettering of my mind,
In my false brother awak'd an evil nature.
Tempest, i. 2.

CLOSURE. *Enclosure ; circumference.*

O thou bloody prison,
Fatal and ominous to noble peers !
Within the guilty *closure* of thy walls
Richard the second here was hack'd to death.
Richard 3, iii. 3.

CLOTPOLL. *The head ; a dolt ; a blockhead.*

I have sent Cloten's *clotpoll* down the stream,
In embassy to his mother : his body's hostage
For his return. *Cymbeline*, iv. 2.

What says the fellow there ? Call the *clotpoll*
back. *King Lear*, i. 4.

I will see you hanged, like *clotpolls*, ere I come
any more to your tents. *Troilus and Cressida*, ii. 1.

To CLOUD. *To defame ; to stain ; to sully.*

I would not be a stander-by to hear
My sovereign mistress *clouded* so, without
My present vengeance taken. *Winter's Tale*, i. 2.

CLOUDY. *Gloomy ; displeased ; sullen.*

He did : and with an absolute, " Sir, not I,"
The *cloudy* messenger turns me his back.
Macbeth, iii. 6.

Slept in his face, and render'd such aspéct
As *cloudy* men use to their adversaries.
Henry 4, P. 1, iii. 2.

CLOUT. *A white linen cloth used as a mark
by archers when shooting at long distances.*

Dead !—he would have clapped in the *clout* at
twelve score. *Henry 4*, P. 2, iii. 2.

O, well flown, bird ! i' the *clout*, i' the *clout*.
King Lear, iv. 6.

CLOUTED. *Hobnailed.*

Spare none but such as go in *clouted* shoon.
Henry 6, P. 2, iv. 2.

I thought he slept ; and put
My *clouted* brogues from off my feet, whose rudeness
Answer'd my steps too loud. *Cymbeline*, iv. 2.

To CLOY. *To claw ; to stroke ; to smooth.*

His royal bird
Prunes the immortal wing, and *cloys* his beak,
As when his god is pleas'd. *Cymbeline*, v. 4.

CLOYLESS. *Uncloying.*

Epicúrean cooks
Sharpen with *cloyless* sauce his appetite !
Antony and Cleopatra, ii. 1.

CLOYMENT. *Satiety ; repletion.*

Alas, their love may be call'd appetite,—
No motion of the liver, but the palate,—
That suffers surfeit, *cloyment*, and revolt.
Twelfth-Night, ii. 4.

COACH-FELLOW. *A companion.*

I have grated upon my good friends for three
reprieves for you and your *coach-fellow* Nym.
Merry Wives of Windsor, ii. 2.

To COACT. *To act in concert.*

But if I tell how these two did *coact*,
Shall I not lie in publishing a truth?
Troilus and Cressida, v. 2.

COACTIVE. *Confederate ; allied together ; affined.*

With what's unreal thou *coactive* art,
And follow'st nothing. *Winter's Tale*, i. 2.

I

COAL. *Difference; disagreement; heat.*

For it is you
Have blown this *coal* betwixt my lord and me.
Henry 8, ii. 4.

COBLOAF. *A crusty uneven loaf.*

Thou shouldst strike him.—
Cobloaf!   *Troilus and Cressida,* ii. 1.

COCK. *A small boat; a cockboat; a weather-cock.*

The fishermen, that walk upon the beach,
Appear like mice; and yond tall anchoring bark,
Diminish'd to her *cock;* her *cock,* a buoy
Almost too small for sight.   *King Lear,* iv. 6.
You cataracts and hurricanoes, spout
Till you have drench'd our steeples, drown'd the
cocks.   *Ibid.* iii. 2.

To COCKER. *To fondle; to indulge.*

Shall a beardless boy,
A *cocker'd* silken wanton, brave our fields?
King John, v. 2.

COCKLED. *Shelled.*

Love's feeling is more soft and sensible
Than are the tender horns of *cockled* snails.
Love's Labour's lost, iv. 3.

COCK-SURE. *Quite safe; without risk.*

We steal, as in a castle, *cock-sure.*
Henry 4, P. 1, ii. 1.

COCK-SHUT. *Twilight.*

The Earl of Surrey, and himself,
Much about *cock-shut* time, from troop to troop
Went through the army, cheering up the soldiers.
Richard 3, v. 3.

COD. *A pod; the case in which the seeds of leguminous plants are enclosed.*

From whom I took two *cods,* and, giving her
them again, said with weeping tears, "Wear these
for my sake."   *As you like it,* ii. 4.

To COG. *To cheat; to lie.*

Since you can *cog,* I'll play no more with you.
Love's Labour's lost, v. 2.
Mistress Ford, I cannot *cog,* I cannot prate.
Merry Wives of Windsor, iii. 3.
Come, both you *cogging* Greeks; have at you both!
Troilus and Cressida, v. 6.

COGNITION. *Knowledge; consciousness.*

I will not be myself, nor have *cognition*
Of what I feel: I am all patience.
Troilus and Cressida, v. 2.

COGNIZANCE. *A badge.*

And that great men shall press
For tinctures, stains, relics, and *cognizance.*
Julius Cæsar, ii. 2.
The *cognizance* of her incontinency
Is this.   *Cymbeline,* ii. 4.
As *cognizance* of my blood-drinking hate.
Henry 6, P. 1, ii. 4.

COHERENCE. *Congruity; correspondence.*

It is a wonderful thing to see the semblable
coherence of his men's spirits and his.
Henry 4, P. 2, v. 1.

COHERENT. *Suitable; consistent; agreeing well together.*

Instruct my daughter how she shall persever,
That time and place, with this deceit so lawful,
May prove *coherent. All's well that ends well,* iii. 7.

COIGN. *Corner; angle.*

No jutty, frieze,
Buttress, nor *coign* of vantage, but this bird
Hath made his bed and procreant cradle.
Macbeth, i. 6.
See you yond *coign* o' the Capitol, yond corner-
stone?   *Coriolanus,* v. 4.

COIL. *Tumult; turmoil.*

I am not worth this *coil* that's made for me.
King John, ii. 1.
Who was so firm, so constant, that this *coil*
Would not infect his reason?   *Tempest,* i. 2.
For in that sleep of death what dreams may come,
When we have shuffled off this mortal *coil,*
Must give us pause.   *Hamlet,* iii. 1.

COISTREL. *A mean paltry fellow; a scoundrel.*

He's a coward and a *coistrel* that will not drink
to my niece.   *Twelfth-Night,* i. 3.

COLD. *Shivering; naked; dull.*

Full oft we see
Cold wisdom waiting on superfluous folly.
All's well that ends well, i. 1.
You smell this business with a sense as *cold*
As is a dead man's nose.   *Winter's Tale,* i. 2.

COLIC. *The paunch; the belly.*

Blow, villain, till thy spherèd bias cheek
Outswell the *colic* of puff'd Aquilon.
Troilus and Cressida, iv. 5.

COLLATERAL. *Indirect; clandestine; secret.*

If by direct or by *collateral* hand
They find us touch'd, we will our kingdom give,
Our crown, our life, and all that we call ours,
To you in satisfaction. *Hamlet*, iv. 5.

COLLEAGUED. *Joined with; united to.*

Colleaguèd with the dream of his advantage,
He hath not fail'd to pester us with message,
Importing the surrender of those lands.
Hamlet, i. 2.

To COLLECT. *To observe; to remark.*

The reverent care I bear unto my lord
Made me *collect* these dangers in the duke.
Henry 6, P. 2, iii. 1.

COLLECTION. *Inference; conclusion; deduction; consequence.*

Her speech is nothing,
Yet the unshapèd use of it doth move
The hearers to *collection*. *Hamlet*, iv. 5.
When I wak'd, I found
This label on my bosom; whose containing
Is so from sense in hardness, that I can
Make no *collection* of it. *Cymbeline*, v. 5.

COLLIER. *An obsolete term of reproach.*

Hang him, foul *collier!* *Twelfth-Night*, iii. 4.
Gregory, o' my word, we'll not carry coals.—
No, for then we should be *colliers*.
Romeo and Juliet, i. 1.

To COLLY. *To obscure; to cloud; to darken.*

And passion, having my best judgment *collied*,
Assays to lead the way. *Othello*, ii. 3.
Brief as the lightning in the *collied* night.
Midsummer-Night's Dream, i. 1.

COLOUR. *Pretext; excuse; justification; sort; kind.*

Nay, pray you, seek no *colour* for your going,
But bid farewell, and go.
Antony and Cleopatra, i. 3.
Under the *colour* of commending him,
I have access my own love to prefer.
Two Gentlemen of Verona, iv. 2.
It is no matter if I do halt; I have the wars

for my *colour*, and my pension shall seem the more
reasonable. *Henry 4*, P. 2, i. 2.
If I find not what I seek, show no *colour* for
my extremity, let me for ever be your table-sport.
Merry Wives of Windsor, iv. 2.
As boys and women are for the most part cattle
of this *colour*. *As you like it*, iii. 2.

To COLOUR. *To palliate; to excuse; to hide.*

Read on this book:
That show of such an exercise may *colour*
Your loneliness. *Hamlet*, iii. 1.
You were sent for; and there is a kind of confession in your looks, which your modesties have
not craft enough to *colour*. *Ibid.* ii. 2.

COLOURING. *Exaggeration; heightening.*

Here's such ado to make no stain a stain,
As passes *colouring*. *Winter's Tale*, ii. 2.

To COLT. *To befool; to trick; to cheat; to deceive.*

What a plague mean ye to *colt* me thus?
Henry 4, P. 1, ii. 2.

CO-MATE. *A companion.*

Now, my *co-mates* and brothers in exile.
As you like it, ii. 1.

COMBINATE. *Betrothed; affianced.*

With him, the portion and sinew of her fortune,
her marriage-dowry; with both, her *combinate* husband, this well-seeming Angelo.
Measure for Measure, iii. 1.

COMBINATION. *Alliance; league; union.*

When that is known, and golden time convents,
A solemn *combination* shall be made
Of our dear souls. *Twelfth-Night*, v. 1.
This cunning cardinal
The articles o' the *combination* drew
As himself pleas'd. *Henry 8*, i. 1.

To COMBINE. *To bind; to join; to unite.*

That which *combin'd* us was most great, and let not
A leaner action rend us. *Antony and Cleop.* ii. 2.
Thy faith my fancy to thee doth *combine*.
As you like it, v. 4.
I am *combinèd* by a sacred vow,
And shall be absent. *Measure for Measure*, iv. 3.

To COME OFF. *To pay handsomely.*

They must *come off*; I'll sauce them.
Merry Wives of Windsor, iv. 3.

To COME SHORT. *To fail.*

Hero's a petition from a Florentine,
Who hath, for four or five removes, *come short*
To tender it herself. *All's well that ends well*, v. 3.

COMFORT. *Assistance; help.*

I will piece out the *comfort* with what addition
I can : I will not be long from you.
King Lear, iii. 6.

To COMFORT. *To support; to abet; to help;
to assist.*

Your most obedient counsellor ; yet that dares
Less appear so, in *comforting* your evils,
Than such as most seem yours. *Winter's Tale*, ii. 3.
If I find him *comforting* the king, it will stuff
his suspicion more fully. *King Lear*, iii. 5.

COMFORTABLE. *Cheerful; consolatory; bringing comfort.*

For my sake be *comfortable*.
As you like it, ii. 6.
My lord leans wondrously to discontent: his
comfortable temper has forsook him.
Timon of Athens, iii. 4.
O *comfortable* friar ! where is my lord?
Romeo and Juliet, v. 3.
Had I a steward
So true, so just, and now so *comfortable* ?
Timon of Athens, iv. 3.

COMMANDMENTS. *A cant word. The nails.*

Could I come near your beauty with my nails,
I'd set my ten *commandments* in your face.
Henry 6, P. 2, i. 3.

To COMMENCE. *An academical term. To dignify; to honour ; to sanction.*

And learning, a mere hoard of gold kept by a
devil, till sack *commences* it, and sets it in act and
use. *Henry 4, P. 2, iv. 3.*

To COMMEND. *To commit; to deliver.*

I do in justice charge thee
That thou *commend* it strangely to some place
Where chance may nurse or end it.
Winter's Tale, ii. 3.
And to the hazard
Of all incertainties himself *commended*.
Winter's Tale, iii. 2.
He creates
Lucius pro-consul : and to you the tribunes,

For this immediate levy, he *commends*
His absolute commission. *Cymbeline*, iii. 7.
And to her white hand see thou do *commend*
This seal'd-up counsel. *Love's Labour's lost*, iii. 1.
My lord, when at their home
I did *commend* your highness' letters to them.
King Lear, ii. 4.
Commend the paper to his gracious hand.
All's well that ends well, v. 1.
Sir, I *commend* you to your own content.
Comedy of Errors, i. 2.

COMMENDATION. *Recommendation ; salutation; compliment; message of love.*

If I come off, and leave her in such honour as
you have trust in, she your jewel, this your jewel,
and my gold are yours;—provided I have your com-
mendation for my free entertainment. *Cymbel.* i. 4.
Such *commendations* as become a maid,
A virgin, and his servant, say to him.
Henry 6, P. 1, v. 3.
Mistress Page hath her hearty *commendations*
to you, too. *Merry Wives of Windsor*, ii. 2.

COMMENDS. *Commendations ; compliments ;
salutations; good wishes.*

Tell her I send to her my kind *commends*.
Richard 2, iii. 1.
To wit, besides *commends* and courteous breath,
Gifts of rich value. *Merchant of Venice*, ii. 8.
With all the gracious utterance thou hast
Speak to his gentle hearing kind *commends*.
Richard 2, iii. 3.

COMMISSION. *Warrant; authority.*

Arbitrating that
Which the *commission* of thy years and art
Could to no issue of true honour bring.
Romeo and Juliet, iv. 1.
'Tis very credent
Thou mayst co-join with something; and thou dost,—
And that beyond *commission*. *Winter's Tale*, i. 2.

COMMIXTION. *Composition.*

Were thy *commixtion* Greek and Trojan so,
That thou couldst say, "This hand is Grecian all,
And this is Trojan;" by Jove multipotent,
Thou shouldst not bear from me a Greekish member
Wherein my sword had not impressure made
Of our rank feud. *Troilus and Cressida*, iv. 5.

COMMODITY. *Interest; advantage ; gain ;
profit.*

For the *commodity* that strangers have

With us in Venice, if it be denied,
Will much impeach the justice of the state.
Merchant of Venice, iii. 3.
That smooth-fac'd gentleman, tickling *commodity*.
King John, ii. 1.
I will turn diseases to *commodity*.
Henry 4, P. 2, i. 2.
To me can life be no *commodity*.
Winter's Tale, iii. 2.

COMMON. *The people ; the community.*
Digest things rightly touching the weal o' the
common. *Coriolanus*, i. 1.

COMMONER. *A drab ; a prostitute.*
O thou public *commoner !*
I should make very forges of my cheeks,
That would to cinders burn up modesty,
Did I but speak thy deeds. *Othello*, iv. 2.

COMMONERS. *The people ; the plebeians.*
Doubt not the *commoners* will forget,
With the least cause, these his new honours.
Coriolanus, ii. 1.

COMMUNITY. *Commonness ; participation ;
familiarity.*
Seen, but with such eyes
As, sick and blunted with *community*,
Afford no extraordinary gaze. *Henry 4*, P. 1, iii. 2.

COMPACT. *Composed ; confederate ; leagued.*
The lunatic, the lover, and the poet,
Are of imagination all *compact*.
Midsummer-Night's Dream, v. 1.
If he, *compact* of jars, grow musical,
We shall have shortly discord in the spheres.
As you like it, ii. 7.
And thou pernicious woman,
Compact with her that's gone, think'st thou thy oaths
Were testimonies against his worth and credit,
That's seal'd in approbation ?
Measure for Measure, v. 1.
When he, *compact*, and flattering his displeasure,
Tripp'd me behind. *King Lear*, ii. 2.

TO COMPACT. *To strengthen ; to confirm.*
Inform her full of my particular fear;
And thereto add such reasons of your own
As may *compact* it more. *King Lear*, i. 4.

COMPANION. *A mean fellow ; a rascal.*
Has the porter his eyes in his head, that he gives
entrance to such *companions ?* *Coriolanus*, iv. 5.

It is not fit your lordship should undertake every
companion that you give offence to. *Cymbeline*, ii. 1.
Away with those giglets too, and with the other
confederate *companion !* *Measure for Measure*, v. 1.

TO COMPANION. *To equalise ; to make equal.*
Find me to marry me with Octavius Cæsar, and
companion me with my mistress.
Antony and Cleopatra, i. 2.

COMPANY. *A companion.*
And thence from Athens turn away our eyes,
To seek new friends and stranger *companies*.
Midsummer-Night's Dream, i. 1.
I would gladly have him see his *company* ana-
tomized. *All's well that ends well*, iv. 3.
He is but one : you and my brother search
What *companies* are near. *Cymbeline*, iv. 2.
His *companies* unletter'd, rude, and shallow.
Henry 5, i. 1.

TO COMPANY. *To accompany.*
I am, sir,
The soldier that did *company* these three
In poor beseeming. *Cymbeline*, v. 5.

COMPARATIVE. *Rival.*
And gave his countenance, against his name,
To laugh at gibing boys, and stand the push
Of every beardless vain *comparative*.
Henry 4, P. 1, iii. 2.

COMPARATIVE. *Equivalent ; fond of making
comparisons.*
Thou wert dignified enough,
Even to the point of envy, if 'twere made
Comparative for your virtues, to be styl'd
The under-hangman of his kingdom.
Cymbeline, ii. 3.
Thou hast the most unsavoury similes, and art,
indeed, the most *comparative*, rascallest,—sweet
young prince. *Henry 4*, P. 1, i. 2.

COMPARE. *Comparison.*
Full of protest, of oath, and big *compare*.
Troilus and Cressida, iii. 2.
Our strength as weak, our weakness past *compare*.
Taming of the Shrew, v. 2.
Now I perceive that she hath made *compare*
Between our statures. .
Midsummer-Night's Dream, iii. 2.

To COMPARE BETWEEN. *To make comparisons.*

O Richard! York is too far gone with grief,
Or else he never would *compare* between.
Richard 2, ii. 1.

COMPARISON. *Condition; stipulation.*

Insulting Charles! hast thou by secret means
Us'd intercession to obtain a league,
And, now the matter grows to compromise,
Stand'st thou aloof upon *comparison?*
Henry 6, P. 1, v. 4.

COMPARISONS. *Caparisons; trappings; decorations.*

I dare him therefore
To lay his gay *comparisons* apart,
And answer me declin'd, sword against sword,
Ourselves alone. *Antony and Cleopatra*, iii. 13.

COMPASS. *Extent; reach; moderation; temperance; revolution.*

All those things you have done of late,
By your power legatine, within this kingdom,
Fall into the *compass* of a præmunire.
Henry 8, iii. 2.
Lived well, and in good *compass:* and now I
live out of all order, out of all *compass.*
Henry 4, P. 1, iii. 3.
A sibyl that had number'd in the world
The sun to course two hundred *compasses,*
In her prophetic fury sew'd the work. *Othello*, iii. 4.

To COMPASS. *To contrive; to procure.*

That were hard to *compass;*
Because she will admit no kind of suit,
No, not the duke's. *Twelfth-Night,* i. 2.
Then he *compassed* a motion of the Prodigal
Son. *Winter's Tale,* iv. 3.

COMPASSED. *Rounded; circular.*

With a small *compassed* cape.
Taming of the Shrew, iv. 3.
She came to him th' other day into the *compassed* window. *Troilus and Cressida,* i. 2.

COMPASSIONATE. *Complaining; querulous; repining.*

It boots thee not to be *compassionate:*
After our sentence plaining comes too late.
Richard 2, i. 3.

To COMPEER. *To equal; to be on a par with.*

In my rights,
By me invested, he *compeers* the best.
King Lear, v. 3.

To COMPEL. *To take by force; to exact.*

And we give express charge, that in our marches
through the country, there be nothing *compelled*
from the villages, nothing taken but paid for.
Henry 5, iii. 5.
The subjects' grief
Comes through commissions, which *compel* from
each
The sixth part of his substance, to be levied
Without delay. *Henry* 8, i. 2.

COMPETITOR. *An associate; a confederate; a partner.*

The *competitors* enter. *Twelfth-Night,* iv. 2.
And every hour more *competitors*
Flock to the rebels, and their power grows strong.
Richard 3, iv. 4.
You may see, Lepidus, and henceforth know,
It is not Cæsar's natural vice to hate
Our great *competitor.* *Antony and Cleopatra,* i. 4.

To COMPLAIN. *To lament; to grieve for; to bewail.*

For what I have, I need not to repeat;
And what I want, it boots not to *complain.*
Richard 2, iii. 4.

COMPLEMENT. *Accomplishments; ornamental qualifications.*

O, he is the courageous captain of *complements.*
Romeo and Juliet, ii. 4.
Garnish'd and deck'd in modest *complement.*
Henry 5, ii. 2.
And I profess requital to a hair's breadth; not
only, Mistress Ford, in the simple office of love,
but in all the accoutrement, *complement*, and ceremony of it. *Merry Wives of Windsor,* iv. 2.
A man of *complements*, whom right and wrong
Have chose as umpire of their mutiny.
Love's Labour's lost, i. 1.
These are *complements*, these are humours.
Ibid. iii. 1.

COMPLETE. *Consummate; perfect; without flaw.*

Then marvel not, thou great and *cómplete* man,
That all the Greeks begin to worship Ajax.
Troilus and Cressida, iii. 3.

Believe not that the dribbling dart of love
Can pierce a cómplete bosom.
Measure for Measure, i. 3.

COMPLEXION. *Temperament; disposition.*

Good my *complexion!* dost thou think I have a
doublet and hose in my disposition?
As you like it, iii. 2.

Shylock, for his own part, knew the bird was
fledged; and then it is the *complexion* of them all
to leave the dam. *Merchant of Venice,* iii. 1.

Thou art not certain;
For thy *complexion* shifts to strange affects,
After the moon. *Measure for Measure,* iii. 1.

COMPLICE. *An accomplice; a confederate.*

The lives of all your loving *complices*
Lean on your health. *Henry 4,* P. 2, i. 1.

To Bristol-castle, which they say is held
By Bushy, Bagot, and their *complices.*
Richard 2, ii. 3.

COMPLIMENTAL. *Complimentary.*

I will make a *complimental* assault upon him,
for my business seethes. *Troilus and Cressida,* iii. 1.

COMPLOT. *A plot; a plan; a secret design.*

I know their *complot* is to have my life.
Henry 6, P. 2, iii. 1.

What shall we do, if we perceive
Lord Hastings will not yield to our *complots?*
Richard 3, iii. 1.

To COMPLOT. *To plot; to contrive; to plan.*

Nor never by advisèd purpose meet
To plot, contrive, or *complot* any ill
'Gainst us, our state, our subjects, or our land.
Richard 2, i. 3.

To COMPLY. *To compliment; to treat ceremoniously.*

Let me *comply* with you in this garb; lest my
extent to the players, which, I tell you, must show
fairly outward, should more appear like entertainment than yours. *Hamlet,* ii. 2.

He did *comply* with his dug, before he sucked it.
Ibid. v. 2.

To COMPOSE. *To come to an agreement.*

If we *compose* well here, to Parthia.
Antony and Cleopatra, ii. 2.

COMPOSITION. *Agreement; frame; fabric.*

Mad world! mad kings! mad *composition!*
King John, ii. 1.

He had, my lord; and that it was which caus'd
Our swifter *composition.* *Coriolanus,* iii. 1.

There is no *composition* in these news
That gives them credit. *Othello,* i. 3.

Thus we are agreed:
I crave our *composition* may be written;
And seal'd between us. *Antony and Cleopatra,* ii. 6.

Which was broke off,
Partly for that her promisèd proportions
Came short of *composition.*
Measure for Measure, v. 1.

Do you not read some tokens of my son
In the large *composition* of this man?
King John, i. 1.

COMPOSTURE. *Manure; compost.*

The earth's a thief,
That feeds and breeds by a *composture* stol'n
From general excrement. *Timon of Athens,* iv. 3.

COMPOSURE. *Combination; composition.*

But it was a strong *composure* a fool could disunite. *Troilus and Cressida,* ii. 3.

His *composure* must be rare indeed
Whom these things cannot blemish.
Antony and Cleopatra, i. 4.

Thank the heavens, lord, thou art of sweet *composure.* *Troilus and Cressida,* ii. 3.

To COMPOUND. *To agree; to compose; to adjust.*

Till you *compound* whose right is worthiest,
We for the worthiest hold the right from both.
King John, ii. 1.

We here deliver,
Subscribèd by the consuls and patricians,
Together with the seal o' the senate, what
We have *compounded* on. *Coriolanus,* v. 6.

To have his pomp, and all what state *compounds,*
But only painted, like his varnish'd friends.
Timon of Athens, iv. 2.

Rise, Grumio, rise: we will *compound* this quarrel.
Taming of the Shrew, i. 2.

COMPROMISE. *Agreement; compact; bargain.*

Shall we, upon the footing of our land,
Send fair-play offers, and make *compromise,*
Insinuation, parley, and base truce,
To arms invasive? *King John,* v. 1.

Wars have not wasted it, for warr'd he hath not,

But basely yielded upon *compromise*
That which his ancestors achiev'd with blows.
　　　　　　　　　Richard 2, ii. 1.
Insulting Charles! hast thou by secret means
Us'd intercession to obtain a league,
And, now the matter grows to *compromise*,
Stand'st thou aloof upon comparison?
　　　　　　　　　Henry 6, P. 1, v. 4.

To COMPROMISE. *To agree together; to enter into a compact; to come to an understanding.*

When Laban and himself were *compromis'd*
That all the eanlings which were streak'd and pied
Should fall as Jacob's hire.
　　　　　　　　　Merchant of Venice, i. 3.

COMPT. *Account; audit; reckoning.*

Take the bonds along with you,
And have the dates in *compt*.
　　　　　　　　　Timon of Athens, ii. 1.
That thou didst love her, strikes some scores away
From the great *compt*.
　　　　　　　　　All's well that ends well, v. 3.

COMPTIBLE. *Susceptible; sensible.*

Good beauties, let me sustain no scorn; I am
very *comptible*, even to the least sinister usage.
　　　　　　　　　Twelfth-Night, i. 5.

COMPULSATIVE. *Compulsive; compulsory.*

Which is no other
But to recover of us, by strong hand
And terms *compulsative*, those foresaid lands
So by his father lost.　　　*Hamlet*, i. 1.

COMPULSIVE. *Compulsory.*

Proclaim no shame
When the *compulsive* ardour gives the charge,
Since frost itself as actively doth burn,
And reason panders will.　　*Hamlet*, iii. 4.
Like to the Pontic sea,
Whose icy current and *compulsive* course
Ne'er feels retiring ebb, but keeps due on
To the Propontic and the Hellespont.
　　　　　　　　　Othello, iii. 3.

COMPUNCTIOUS. *Soft; tender; compassionate.*

That no *compunctious* visitings of nature
Shake my fell purpose, nor keep peace between
The effect and it!　　　*Macbeth*, i. 5

To CON. *To study; to learn; to know.*

Their herald is a pretty knavish page,
That well by heart hath *conn'd* his embassage.
　　　　　　　　　Love's Labour's lost, v. 2.
And this they *con* perfectly in the phrase of war.
　　　　　　　　　Henry 5, iii. 5.

To CON THANKS. *To thank; to give thanks.*

Yet *thanks I must you con*,
That you are thieves profess'd.
　　　　　　　　　Timon of Athens, iv. 3.
But I *con* him no *thanks* for't, in the nature he
delivers it.　　*All's well that ends well*, iv. 3.

CONCEALMENT. *Art; mystery.*

Exceedingly well-read, and profited
In strange *concealments*.　　*Henry 4, P.* 1, iii. 1.

CONCEIT. *Thought; understanding; opinion.*

Which his fair tongue,—*conceit's* expositor,—
Delivers in such apt and gracious words
That aged ears play truant at his tales,
And younger hearings are quite ravishèd.
　　　　　　　　　Love's Labour's lost, ii. 1.
I am press'd down with *conceit*,—
Conceit, my comfort and my injury.
　　　　　　　　　Comedy of Errors, iv. 2.
For thy *conceit* is soaking, will draw in
More than the common blocks. *Winter's Tale*, i. 2.
Proteus, the good *conceit* I hold of thee,
Makes me the better to confer with thee.
　　　　　　　　　Two Gentlemen of Verona, iii. 2.

To CONCEIT. *To think; to believe; to imagine; to conceive.*

My credit now stands on such slippery ground,
That one of two bad ways you must *conceit* me,
Either a coward or a flatterer.　*Julius Cæsar*, iii. 1.
I do beseech you, that your wisdom yet,
From one that so imperfectly *conceits*,
Would take no notice.　　　*Othello*, iii. 3.
Him, and his worth, and our great need of him,
You have right well *conceited*. *Julius Cæsar*, i. 3.

CONCEITLESS. *Dull; stupid.*

Think'st thou I am so shallow, so *conceitless*,
To be seduced by thy flattery?
　　　　　　　　　Two Gentlemen of Verona, iv. 2.

CONCEIVING. *Conception; apprehension.*

The younger brother, Cadwal,—
Once Arviragus,—in as like a figure,

Strikes life into my speech, and shows much more
His own *conceiving*.   *Cymbeline*, iii. 3.

CONCENT. *Concord; harmony; agreement.*

For government, though high, and low, and lower,
Put into parts, doth keep in one *concent*.
                                    Henry 5, i. 2.
            I this infer,
That many things, having full reference
To one *concent*, may work contrariously. *Ibid.* i. 2.
I doubt not that; since we are well persuaded
We carry not a heart with us from hence
That grows not in a fair *concent* with ours.
                                    Ibid. ii. 2.

CONCEPTION. *Intent; purpose; design.*

Please your highness, note
This dangerous *conception* in this point.
                                    Henry 8, i. 2.
And in my heart the strong and swelling evil
Of my *conception*.   *Measure for Measure*, ii. 4.

CONCEPTIOUS. *Prolific; fruitful.*

Ensear thy fertile and *conceptious* womb,
Let it no more bring out ingrateful man !
                                    Timon of Athens, iv. 3.

CONCERNANCY. *Business.*

The *concernancy*, sir ? why do we wrap the gentleman in our more rawer breath ?   *Hamlet*, v. 2.

CONCERNING. *Affair; business; concern.*

We shall write to you,
As time and our *concernings* shall importune,
How it goes with us. *Measure for Measure*, i. 1.
        'Twere good you let him know ;
For who, that's but a queen, fair, sober, wise,
Would from a paddock, from a bat, a gib,
Such dear *concernings* hide ?   *Hamlet*, iii. 4.

CONCLUSION. *Experiment; deduction; inference.*

No, in despite of sense and secrecy,
Unpeg the basket on the house's top,
Let the birds fly, and, like the famous ape,
To try *conclusions*, in the basket creep,
And break your own neck down.   *Hamlet*, iii. 4.
        Most probable
That so she died ; for her physician tells me
She hath pursu'd *conclusions* infinite
Of easy ways to die. *Antony and Cleopatra*, v. 2.
        Is't not meet
That I did amplify my judgment in
Other *conclusions* ?   *Cymbeline*, i. 5.

Your wife Octavia, with her modest eyes
And still *conclusion*, shall acquire no honour
Demuring upon me. *Antony and Cleopatra*, iv. 15.

CONCUPISCIBLE. *Eager; ardent.*

He would not, but by gift of my chaste body
To his *concupiscible* intemperate lust,
Release my brother.   *Measure for Measure*, v. 1.

CONCUPY. *Concupiscence.*

He'll tickle it for his *concupy*.
                                    Troilus and Cressida, v. 2.

CONDITION. *Temper; disposition; property;
attribute.*

Our tongue is rough, coz, and my *condition* is
not smooth.   *Henry* 5, v. 2.
Madam, I have a touch of your *condition*,
That cannot brook the accent of reproof.
                                    Richard 3, iv. 4.
I cannot believe that in her ; she's full of most
blessed *condition*.   *Othello*, ii. 1.
All his senses have but human *conditions*.
                                    Henry 5, iv. 1.

To CONDITION. *To bind by stipulation; to
limit; to restrain.*

        Go, live rich and happy;
But thus *condition'd :*—thou shalt build from men ;
Hate all, curse all ; show charity to none ;
But let the famish'd flesh slide from the bone,
Ere thou relieve the beggar.
                                    Timon of Athens, iv. 3.

To CONDOLE. *To grieve; to lament; to mourn.*

        Let us *condole* the knight; for, lambkins, we
will live.   *Henry* 5, ii. 1.
I will move storms, I will *condole* in some
measure.   *Midsummer-Night's Dream*, i. 2.

CONDOLEMENT. *Sorrow; lamentation; mourning.*

        But to persever
In obstinate *condolement*, is a course
Of impious stubbornness ; 'tis unmanly grief.
                                    Hamlet, i. 2.

To CONDUCE. *To ensue.*

Within my soul there doth *conduce* a fight
Of this strange nature, that a thing inseparate
Divides more wider than the sky and earth;
And yet the spacious breadth of this division
Admits no orifex for a point, as subtle

K

As Ariachne's broken woof, to enter.
Troilus and Cressida, v. 2.

CONDUCT. *Conductor; convoy.*

I will be his *conduct.* *Richard 2*, iv. 1.
Come, bitter *conduct*, come, unsavoury guide.
Romeo and Juliet, v. 3.
And there is in this business more than nature
Was ever *conduct* of. *Tempest*, v. 1.
Sheriff, farewell, and better than I fare,—
Although thou hast been *conduct* of my shame.
Henry 6, P. 2, ii. 4.
Away to heaven, respective lenity,
And fire-ey'd fury be my *conduct* now!
Romeo and Juliet, iii. 1.
So, sir, I desire of you
A *conduct* overland to Milford Haven.
Cymbeline, iii. 5.
And in my *conduct* shall your ladies come.
Henry 4, P. 1, iii. 1.

CONDUCTOR. *Commander; general; leader.*

Who is *conductor* of his people?—
As 'tis said, the bastard son of Gloster.
King Lear, iv. 7.

CONFECT. *A dried sweetmeat; a comfit.*

Surely, a princely testimony, a goodly count,
count *confect;* a sweet gallant, surely!
Much Ado about Nothing, iv. 1.

CONFECTION. *A sweetmeat; a drug; a compound.*

Hast thou not learn'd me how
To make perfumes? distil? preserve? yea, so
That our great king himself doth woo me oft
For my *confections?* *Cymbeline*, i. 5.
"If Pisanio
Have," said she, "given his mistress that *confection*,
Which I gave him for cordial, she is serv'd
As I would serve a rat." *Ibid.* v. 5.

CONFECTIONARY. *A maker of sweetmeats.*

But myself,
Who had the world as my *confectionary.*
Timon of Athens, iv. 3.

To CONFER. *To talk; to converse.*

They sit *conferring* by the parlour fire.
Taming of the Shrew, v. 2.

CONFERENCE. *Conversation.*

I do beseech your majesty
To have some *conference* with your grace alone.
Richard 2, v. 3.

CONFESSION. *Profession.*

If there be one among the fair'st of Greece
That loves his mistress more than in *confession*,
And dare avow her beauty and her worth
In other arms than hers,—to him this challenge.
Troilus and Cressida, i. 3.

CONFINE. *Restriction; limitation; restraint.*

But that I love the gentle Desdemona,
I would not my unhousèd free condition
Put into circumscription and *confine*
For the sea's worth. *Othello*, i. 2.

To CONFINE. *To restrain; to withhold.*

So have we thought it good
From our free person she should be *confin'd*,
Lest that the treachery of the two fled hence
Be left her to perform. *Winter's Tale*, ii. 1.

CONFINELESS. *Unbounded; unlimited.*

Esteem him as a lamb, being compar'd
With my *confineless* harms. *Macbeth*, iv. 3.

CONFINER. *A borderer.*

The senate hath stirr'd up the *cónfiners*
And gentlemen of Italy. *Cymbeline*, iv. 2.

To CONFIRM. *To settle; to establish; to certify.*

Confirm the crown to me and to mine heirs,
And thou shalt reign in quiet while thou liv'st.
Henry 6, P. 3, i. 1.
And three corrupted men
Have, for the gilt of France—O guilt indeed!—
Confirm'd conspiracy with fearful France.
Henry 5, i. 2. Chorus.
Yet do they all *confirm*
A Turkish fleet, and bearing up to Cyprus.
Othello, i. 3.

CONFIRMATION. *Declaration; settlement; assurance.*

And let heaven
Witness, how dear I hold this *confirmation.*
Henry 8, v. 2.

CONFISCATE. *Confiscated; forfeited.*

First pay me for the nursing of thy sons;
And let it be *confiscate* all, so soon
As I have receiv'd it. *Cymbeline*, v. 5.
His goods *confiscate* to the duke's dispose.
Comedy of Errors, i. 1.

CONFIXED. *Fixed.*

Or else for ever be *confixèd* here,
A marble monument.   *Measure for Measure*, v. 1.

CONFLUX. *Union; confluence.*

As knots, by the *conflux* of meeting sap,
Infect the sound pine, and divert his grain.
     Troilus and Cressida, i. 3.

To CONFOUND. *To destroy; to ruin; to waste; to confuse; to perplex.*

Let the brow o'erwhelm it
As fearfully as doth a gallèd rock
O'erhang and jutty his *confounded* base.
     Henry 5, iii. 1.
Who, falling there to find his fellow forth,
Unseen, inquisitive, *confounds* himself.
     Comedy of Errors, i. 2.
The attempt, and not the deed, *confounds* us.
     Macbeth, ii. 1.
Now, for the love of Love and her soft hours,
Let's not *confound* the time with conference harsh.
     Antony and Cleopatra, i. 1.
How couldst thou in a mile *confound* an hour?
     Coriolanus, i. 6.
     Where's Publius?—
Here, quite *confounded* with this mutiny.
     Julius Cæsar, iii. 1.

To CONFRONT. *To oppose.*

Blood hath bought blood, and blows have answer'd blows;
Strength match'd with strength, and power *confronted* power.   *King John*, ii. 1.

CONFUSION. *Ruin; destruction; overthrow; distraction; wildness.*

Wouldst thou have thyself fall in the *confusion*
of men, and remain a beast with the beasts?
     Timon of Athens, iv. 3.
As, by the strength of their illusion,
Shall draw him on to his *confusion*. *Macbeth*, iii. 5.
And can you, by no drift of circumstance,
Get from him why he puts on this *confusion*?
     Hamlet, iii. 1.

To CONFUTE. *To overcome; to defeat.*

My sisterly remorse *confutes* mine honour,
And I did yield to him. *Measure for Measure*, v. 1.

To CONGE. *To take leave of.*

I have *conge'd* with the duke, done my adieu
with his nearest.   *All's well that ends well*, iv. 3.

CONGEALMENT. *Clotted blood; gore.*

Whilst they with joyful tears
Wash the *congealment* from your wounds, and kiss
The honour'd gashes whole.
     Antony and Cleopatra, iv. 8.

To CONGREE. *To agree; to join; to unite.*

Congreeing in a full and natural close,
Like harmony.   *Henry 5*, i. 2.

To CONGREET. *To exchange salutations; to greet reciprocally.*

My office hath so far prevail'd,
That, face to face and royal eye to eye,
You have *congreeted*.   *Henry 5*, v. 2.

CONJECTURE. *Suspicion; imagination; thought.*

And on my eyelids shall *conjecture* hang
To turn all beauty into thoughts of harm,
And never shall it more be gracious.
     Much Ado about Nothing, iv. 1.
Now entertain *conjecture* of a time
When creeping murmur and the poring dark
Fills the wide vessel of the universe.
     Henry 5, iv. Chorus.

To CONJOIN. *To unite; to combine.*

This part of his *conjoins* with my disease,
And helps to end me.   *Henry 4, P. 2*, iv. 4.

CONJUNCT. *Conjunctive; familiar.*

I am doubtful that you have been *conjunct*
And bosom'd with her, as far as we call hers.
     King Lear, v. 1.

CONJUNCTION. *Union; alliance; league; force.*

Son, list to this *conjunction*, make this match.
     King John, ii. 1.
Yet doth he give us bold advertisement,
That with our small *conjunction* we should on,
To see how fortune is dispos'd to us.
     Henry 4, P. 1, iv. 1.

CONJUNCTIVE. *Closely united.*

     And for myself,
She's so *conjunctive* to my life and soul,
That, as the star moves not but in his sphere,
I could not but by her.   *Hamlet*, iv. 7.
Let us be *conjunctive* in our revenge against him.
     Othello, i. 3.

CONJURATION. *An adjuration; a charge; an earnest appeal.*

An earnest *conjuration* from the king.
Hamlet, v. 2.

Mock not my senseless *conjuration*, lords.
Richard 2, iii. 2.

Under this *conjuration*, speak, my lord.
Henry 5, i. 2.

I do defy thy *conjurations*,
And apprehend thee for a felon here.
Romeo and Juliet, v. 3.

To CONJURE. *To adjure; to enjoin; to enchant; to exorcise.*

I *cónjure* thee but slowly; run more fast.
King John, iv. 2.

Which imports at full,
By letters *conjuring* to that effect,
The present death of Hamlet. *Hamlet*, iv. 3.

Whose phrase of sorrow
Cónjures the wandering stars, and makes them stand
Like wonder-wounded hearers. *Ibid.* v. 1.

I would to God some scholar would *conjure* her.
Much Ado about Nothing, ii. 1.

CONSANGUINEOUS. *Related by blood; near of kin.*

Am not I *consanguineous?* am I not of her blood?
Twelfth-Night, ii. 3.

CONSCIENCE. *Sense; reason; honour; honesty; justice.*

Why dost thou weep? Canst thou the *conscience* lack,
To think I shall lack friends?
Timon of Athens, ii. 2.

Men must learn now with pity to dispense;
For policy sits above *conscience.* *Ibid.* iii. 2.

Their best *conscience*
Is not to leave undone, but keep unknown.
Othello, iii. 3.

Thrown out his angle for my proper life,
And with such cozenage,—is't not perfect *conscience*,
To quit him with this arm? *Hamlet*, v. 2.

Now must your *conscience* my acquittance seal.
Ibid. iv. 7.

CONSCIONABLE. *Conscientious.*

A knave very voluble; no further *conscionable* than in putting on the mere form of civil and humane seeming, for the better compassing of his salt and most hidden loose affection. *Othello*, ii. 1.

CONSECRATE. *Consecrated; dedicated.*

And that this body, *consecrate* to thee,
By ruffian lust should be contaminate.
Comedy of Errors, ii. 2.

CONSENT. *A plot; a compact; party; faction.*

Here was a *consent*,
Knowing aforehand of our merriment,
To dash it like a Christmas comedy.
Love's Labour's lost, v. 2.

If you shall cleave to my *consent*,—when 'tis,
It shall make honour to you. *Macbeth*, ii. 1.

To CONSENT. *To agree together; to cooperate.*

Did you and he *consent* in Cassio's death? *Othel.* v. 2.

Comets, importing change of time and states,
Brandish your crystal tresses in the sky,
And with them scourge the bad revolting stars
That have *consented* unto Henry's death!
Henry 6, P. 1, i. 1.

CONSEQUENCE. *Upshot; conclusion; event.*

If *consequence* do but approve my dream,
My boat sails freely, both with wind and stream.
Othello, ii. 3.

O bitter *consequence*,
That Edward still should live,—true, noble prince!—
Cousin, thou wast not wont to be so dull.
Richard 3, iv. 2.

The spirits that know
All mortal *consequences* have pronounc'd me thus,
"Fear not, Macbeth; no man that's born of woman
Shall e'er have power upon thee." *Macbeth*, v. 3.

CONSERVE. *A sweetmeat.*

Will't please your honour taste of these *conserves?*
Taming of the Shrew, Induction, sc. 2.

To CONSERVE. *To preserve.*

Thou art too noble to *conserve* a life
In base appliances. *Measure for Measure*, iii. 1.

And it was dy'd in mummy which the skilful
Conserv'd of maidens' hearts. *Othello*, iii. 4.

To CONSIDER. *To reward; to recompense; to requite.*

If this penetrate, I will *consider* your music the better. *Cymbeline*, ii. 3.

Being something gently *considered*, I'll bring you where he is aboard, tender your persons to his presence, whisper him in your behalf, and if it be in man besides the king to effect your suits, here is man shall do it. *Winter's Tale*, iv. 3.

CONSIDERANCE. *Consideration; reflection.*
After this cold *considerance*, sentence me.
Henry 4, P. 2, v. 2.

CONSIDERATE. *Cautious; prudent; circumspect.*
Go to, then; your *considerate* stone.
Antony and Cleopatra, ii. 2.
None are for me
That look into me with *considerate* eyes.
Richard 3, iv. 2.

CONSIDERATION. *Reflection; thought; reason.*
Whereof ingrateful man, with liquorish draughts
And morsels unctuous, greases his pure mind,
That from it all *consideration* slips.
Timon of Athens, iv. 3.

CONSIDERING. *Doubt; consideration; meditation.*
Which forc'd such way,
That many maz'd *considerings* did throng,
And press'd in with this caution. *Henry* 8, ii. 4.
His thinkings are below the moon, not worth
His serious *considering*. *Ibid.* iii. 2.

To CONSIGN. *To consent; to subscribe; to conjoin; to undergo the same conditions.*
And, God *consigning* to my good intents,
No prince nor peer shall have just cause to say,
God shorten Harry's happy life one day!
Henry 4, P. 2, v. 2.
It were, my lord, a hard condition for a maid
to *consign* to. *Henry* 5, v. 2.
As many farewells as be stars in heaven,
With distinct breath and *consign'd* kisses to them,
He fumbles up into a loose adieu;
And scants us with a single famish'd kiss,
Distasted with the salt of broken tears.
Troilus and Cressida, iv. 4.
All lovers young, all lovers must
Consign to thee, and come to dust.
Cymbeline, iv. 2.

To CONSIST UPON. *To insist upon; to demand; to require.*
If we can make our peace
Upon such large terms and so absolute
As our conditions shall *consist upon*,
Our peace shall stand as firm as rocky mountains.
Henry 4, P. 2, iv. 1.

CONSISTORY. *A receptacle; a repository.*
My other self, my counsel's *consistory*,
My oracle, my prophet!—my dear cousin,
I, as a child, will go by thy direction.
Richard 3, ii. 2.

To CONSOLATE. *To soothe; to comfort; to console.*
I will be gone,
That pitiful rumour may report my flight,
And *consolate* thine ear.
All's well that ends well, iii. 2.

CONSORT. *A band; a gang; a company of musicians.*
Was he not companion with the riotous knights
That tend upon my father?—
Yes, madam, he was of that *consort*.
King Lear, ii. 1.
Wilt thou be of our *consort*?
Two Gentlemen of Verona, iv. 1.
Visit by night your lady's chamber-window
With some sweet *consort*. *Ibid.* iii. 2.
And boding screech-owls make the *consort* full.
Henry 6, P. 2, iii. 2.

To CONSORT. *To associate with; to accompany; to confederate; to unite with.*
Please you, I'll meet with you upon the mart,
And afterwards *consort* you till bed-time.
Comedy of Errors, i. 2.
Mercutio, thou *consort'st* with Romeo.
Romeo and Juliet, iii. 1.
Sweet health and fair desires *consort* your grace!
Love's Labour's lost, ii. 1.
Who to Philippi here *consorted* us.
Julius Cæsar, v. 1.
But for our trusty brother-in-law, and the abbot,
With all the rest of that *consorted* crew,
Destruction straight shall dog them at the heels.
Richard 2, v. 3.
Consort with me in loud and dear petition.
Troilus and Cressida, v. 3.

CONSPECTUITY. *Eye-sight.*
What harm can your bisson *conspectuities* glean
out of this character, if I be known well enough
too? *Coriolanus*, ii. 1.

CONSPIRANT. *Engaged in a plot; conspiring.*
Thou art a traitor,
False to thy gods, thy brother, and thy father;
Conspirant 'gainst this high illustrious prince.
King Lear, v. 3.

CONSPIRED. *Conspirant; confederated.*

Thou,
Conspir'd with that irregulous devil, Cloten,
Hast here cut off my lord.   *Cymbeline, iv. 2.*

CONSTANT. *Firm; resolute; grave; consistent; unmixed.*

Some dear friend dead; also nothing in the world
Could turn so much the constitution
Of any *constant* man.   *Merchant of Venice, iii. 2.*
Cassius, be *constant*.   *Julius Cæsar, iii. 1.*
Be you *constant* in the accusation, and my cunning shall not shame me.
    Much Ado about Nothing, ii. 2.
I am no more mad than you are; make the trial of it in any *constant* question.
    Twelfth-Night, iv. 2.
'Twas just the difference
Betwixt the *constant* red, and mingled damask.
    As you like it, iii. 5.

CONSTANCY. *Resolution; firmness.*

Your *constancy*
Hath left you unattended.   *Macbeth, ii. 1.*
One that, in her sex, her years, profession,
Wisdom, and *constancy*, hath amaz'd me more
Than I dare blame my weakness.
    All's well that ends well, ii. 1.

CONSTANTLY. *Certainly; unhesitatingly; firmly.*

I do *constantly* believe you.
    Measure for Measure, iv. 1.
For I am fresh of spirit, and resolv'd
To meet all perils very *constantly*.
    Julius Cæsar, v. 1.
Since patiently and *constantly* thou hast stuck to the bare fortune of that beggar Posthumus, thou canst not, in the course of gratitude, but be a diligent follower of mine.   *Cymbeline, iii. 5.*

CONSTELLATION. *Star; disposition; temperament.*

I know thy *constellation* is right apt
For this affair.   *Twelfth-Night, i. 3.*

CONSTITUTION. *Make; shape.*

I did think, by the excellent *constitution* of thy leg, it was formed under the star of a galliard.
    Twelfth-Night, i. 3.

TO CONSTRINGE. *To bind together; to collect; to gather.*

The dreadful spout,
Constring'd in mass by the almighty sun.
    Troilus and Cressida, v. 2.

CONSTRUCTION. *Opinion; judgment; interpretation; explanation.*

Under your hard *construction* must I sit,
To force that on you, in a shameful cunning,
Which you know none of yours.
    Twelfth-Night, iii. 1.
Good my lord of Rome,
Call forth your soothsayer. Let him show
His skill in the *construction*.   *Cymbeline, v. 5.*

TO CONSTRUE. *To interpret.*

I can *construe* the action of her familiar style.
    Merry Wives of Windsor, i. 3.
But men may *construe* things after their fashion,
Clean from the purpose of the things themselves.
    Julius Cæsar, i. 3.
And his unbookish jealousy must *construe*
Poor Cassio's smiles, gestures, and light behaviour,
Quite in the wrong.   *Othello, iv. 1.*

CONSUL. *A counsellor; a senator.*

And many of the *consuls*, rais'd and met,
Are at the duke's already.   *Othello, i. 2.*
    Unless the bookish theoric,
Wherein the togèd *consuls* can propose
As masterly as he.   *Ibid. i. 1.*

CONSUMMATE. *Done; performed.*

Do you the office, friar; which *consummate*,
Return him here again.   *Measure for Measure, v. 1.*

TO CONTAIN. *To keep; to retain; to restrain; to behave.*

Or your own honour to *contain* the ring.
    Merchant of Venice, v. 1.
Fear not, my lord : we can *contain* ourselves,
Were he the veriest antic in the world.
    Taming of the Shrew, Induction, sc. 1.

CONTAINING. *Inscription; contents.*

When I wak'd, I found
This label on my bosom; whose *containing*
Is so from sense in hardness, that I can
Make no collection of it.   *Cymbeline, v. 5.*

CONTAMINATE. *Contaminated; polluted; sullied.*

And that this body, consecrate to thee,
By ruffian lust should be *contaminate*.
Comedy of Errors, ii. 2.

CONTEMPT. *Vileness; baseness.*

Cowards father cowards, and base things sire base:
Nature hath meal and bran, *contempt* and grace.
Cymbeline, iv. 2.

CONTEMPTIBLE. *Contemptuous; scornful.*

For the man, as you know all, hath a *contemptible* spirit. *Much Ado about Nothing*, ii. 3.

To CONTEND WITH. *To emulate; to vie with; to rival.*

The next time I do fight,
I'll make death love me; for I will *contend*
Even *with* his pestilent scythe.
Antony and Cleopatra, iii. 13.

CONTESTATION. *Quarrel; cause.*

Your wife and brother
Made wars upon me; and their *contestation*
Was theme for you, you were the word of war.
Antony and Cleopatra, ii. 2.

CONTINENT. *Bound; limit; case; covering; schedule; inventory.*

Contagious fogs, which falling in the land
Have every pelting river made so proud,
That they have overborne their *continents*.
Midsummer-Night's Dream, ii. 1.
Fight for a plot
Whereon the numbers cannot try the cause,
Which is not tomb enough and *continent*
To hide the slain. *Hamlet*, iv. 4.
Heart, once be stronger than thy *continent*,
Crack thy frail case! *Antony and Cleopatra*, iv. 14.
Here's the scroll,
The *continent* and summary of my fortune.
Merchant of Venice, iii. 2.

CONTINENT. *Opposing; restraining; confining.*

I pray you have a *continent* forbearance till the
speed of his rage goes slower. *King Lear*, i. 2.
And my desire
All *continent* impediments would o'erbear,
That did oppose my will. *Macbeth*, iv. 3.

CONTINUATE. *Continued; unceasing; free from interruption.*

A most incomparable man; breath'd, as it were,
To an untirable and *continuate* goodness.
Timon of Athens, i. 1.
I have this while with leaden thoughts been press'd;
But I shall, in a more *continuate* time,
Strike off this score of absence. *Othello*, iii. 4.

To CONTINUE. *To keep back; to retain; to reserve.*

And how shall we *continue* Claudio,
To save me from the danger that might come
If he were known alive?
Measure for Measure, iv. 3.

CONTRACT. *Betrothment; affiance.*

Upon a true *contráct*
I got possession of Julietta's bed.
Measure for Measure, i. 2.
I did; with his *contráct* with Lady Lucy,
And his *contráct* by deputy in France.
Richard 3, iii. 7.

CONTRACT. *Contracted; affianced; betrothed.*

For first was he *contráct* to Lady Lucy,
And afterward by substitute betroth'd
To Bona, sister to the King of France.
Richard 3, iii. 7.

To CONTRACT. *To betroth; to affiance.*

The truth is, she and I, long since *contracted*,
Are now so sure that nothing can dissolve us.
Merry Wives of Windsor, v. 5.
I was *contracted* to them both: all three
Now marry in an instant. *King Lear*, v. 3.

CONTRACTION. *A sacred compact; a contract; a bond of fidelity.*

O, such a deed
As from the body of *contraction* plucks
The very soul; and sweet religion makes
A rhapsody of words. *Hamlet*, iii. 4.

To CONTRADICT. *To oppose; to resist; to forbid.*

Lady, come from that nest
Of death, contagion, and unnatural sleep:
A greater power than we can *contradict*
Hath thwarted our intents. *Romeo and Juliet*, v. 3.
'Tis she is sub-contracted to this lord,
And I, her husband, *contradict* your bans.
King Lear, v. 3.

CONTRADICTION. *Opposition.*

He hath been us'd
Ever to conquor, and to have his worth
Of *contradiction.* *Coriolanus*, iii. 3.

CONTRARIETY. *Inconsistency; contradiction.*

He will be here, and yet he is not here :
How can these *contrarieties* agree?
 Henry 6, P. 1, ii. 3.

CONTRARIOUS. *Contrary.*

Volumes of report
Run with these false and most *contrarious* quests
Upon thy doings! *Measure for Measure*, iv. 1.

CONTRARIOUSLY. *In different ways; in various directions.*

I this infer,
That many things, having full reference
To one concent, may work *contrariously.*
 Henry 5, i. 2.

CONTRARY. *Double; false; deceitful; irregular.*

In the divorce his *contrary* proceedings
Are all unfolded. *Henry* 8, iii. 2.

To CONTRARY. *To oppose; to thwart; to contradict.*

You must *contráry* me!—marry, 'tis time.
 Romeo and Juliet, i. 5.

To CONTRIVE. *To plot; to confederate; to combine; to wear away.*

If thou read this, O Cæsar, thou mayst live;
If not, the Fates with traitors do *contrive.*
 Julius Cæsar, ii. 3.
Have you conspir'd, have you with these *contriv'd,*
To bait me with this foul derision?
 Midsummer-Night's Dream, iii. 2.
Please ye we may *contrive* this afternoon,
And quaff carouses to our mistress' health.
 Taming of the Shrew, i. 2.

CONTRIVER. *Intriguer; plotter; schemer; caballer.*

We shall find of him a shrewd *contriver.*
 Julius Cæsar, ii. 1.

CONTROLLER. *A blusterer; a bully.*

He dares not calm his contumelious spirit,
Nor cease to be an arrogant *controller,*
Though Suffolk dare him twenty thousand times.
 Henry 6, P. 2, iii. 2.

CONTROL. *Compulsion; force.*

The proud *control* of fierce and bloody war.
 King John, i. 1.

To CONTROL. *To confute; to contradict.*

The Duke of Milan
And his more braver daughter could *control* thee,
If now 'twere fit to do't. *Tempest*, i. 2.

CONTROLMENT. *Force; compulsion.*

Here have we war for war, and blood for blood,
Controlment for *controlment.* *King John*, i. 1.

CONTROVERSY. *Dispute; opposition; quarrel; contest.*

My liege, here is the strangest *controversy,*
Come from the country to be judg'd by you,
That o'er I heard. *King John*, i. 1.
The torrent roar'd; and we did buffet it
With lusty sinews, throwing it aside,
And stemming it with hearts of *controversy.*
 Julius Cæsar, i. 2.
The dead men's blood, the pining maidens' groans,
For husbands, fathers, and betrothèd lovers,
That shall be swallow'd in this *controversy.*
 Henry 5, ii. 4.

CONVENIENCE, CONVENIENCY. *Advantage; satisfaction.*

Now, for want of these required *conveniences,*
her delicate tenderness will find itself abused, begin
to heave the gorge, disrelish and abhor the Moor.
 Othello, ii. 1.
And rather, as it seems to me now, keepest
from me all *conveniency* than suppliest me with
the least advantage of hope. *Ibid.* iv. 2.

To CONVENT. *To cite; to summon; to suit; to favour; to unite; to assemble.*

What he, with his oath
And all probation, will make up full clear,
Whensoever he's *convented.* *Measure for M.* v. 1.
Who hath commanded
To-morrow morning to the council-board
He be *convented.* *Henry* 8, v. 1.
When golden time *convents,*
A solemn combination shall be made
Of our dear souls. *Twelfth-Night*, v. 1.
So, by a roaring tempest on the flood,
A whole armado of *convented* sail
Is scatter'd and disjoin'd from fellowship.
 King John, iii. 4.

CONVENTICLE. *A meeting; an assembly.*

Ay, all of you have laid your heads together—
Myself had notice of your *conventicles*—
And all to make away my guiltless life.
        Henry 6, P. 2, iii. 1.

CONVERSATION. *Disposition; intercourse.*

Octavia is of a holy, cold, and still *conversation.*
     Antony and Cleopatra, ii. 6.
I mean, his *conversation* with Shore's wife.
        Richard 3, iii. 5.

CONVERSE. *Interchange; conversation.*

If over-boldly we have borne ourselves
In the *convérse* of breath, your gentleness
Was guilty of it. *Love's Labour's lost,* v. 2.
And I'll devise a mean to draw the Moor
Out of the way, that your *convérse* and business
May be more free.   *Othello,* iii. 1.
Your party in *convérse,* him you would sound.
        Hamlet, ii. 1.

To CONVERSE. *To hold intercourse with; to associate with.*

Full often, like a shag-hair'd crafty kern,
Hath he *conversèd* with the enemy. *H.* 6, P. 2, iii. 1.
I will *converse* with iron-witted fools
And unrespective boys: none are for me
That look into me with considerate eyes.
        Richard 3, iv. 2.
 To love him that is honest; to *converse* with
him that is wise, and says little. *King Lear,* i. 4.

CONVERSION. *Transformation; new-born greatness.*

'Tis too respective and too sociable
For your *conversion.*   *King John,* i. 1.

CONVERTITE. *A convert.*

To him will I: out of these *convertites*
There is much matter to be heard and learn'd.
       As you like it, v. 4.
But since you are a gentle *convertite,*
My tongue shall hush again this storm of war.
        King John, v. 1.

To CONVEY. *To fetch; to derive; to manage secretly; to provide; to steal.*

Hugh Capet also, who usurp'd the crown
Of Charles the duke of Lorraine,
To fine his title with some show of truth,
Convey'd himself as heir to the Lady Lingare.
        Henry 5, i. 2.

I will seek him, sir, presently; *convey* the busi-
ness as I shall find means, and acquaint you withal.
        King Lear, i. 2.
 You may
Convey your pleasures in a spacious plenty,
And yet seem cold.   *Macbeth,* iv. 3.
That a king's children should be so *convey'd!*
        Cymbeline, i. 1.

CONVEYANCE. *Dexterity; skill; trickery; ar- tifice; deceit; concession; grant.*

Huddling jest upon jest, with such impossible
conveyance upon me. *Much Ado about Nothing,* ii. 1.
I will not hence, till, with my talk and tears,
Both full of truth, I make King Louis behold
Thy sly *conveyance,* and thy lord's false love.
        Henry 6, P. 3, iii. 3.
Since Henry's death I fear there is *conveyance.*
        Ibid. P. 1, i. 3.
Tell him that, by his license, Fortinbras
Craves the *conveyance* of a promis'd march
Over his kingdom.   *Hamlet,* iv. 4.

CONVEYER. *A juggler; a thief.*

O, good! convey?—*conveyers* are you all,
That rise thus nimbly by a true king's fall.
        Richard 2, iv. 1.

CONVICT. *Convicted; condemned.*

Before I be *convict* by course of law,
To threaten me with death is most unlawful.
        Richard 3, i. 4.

To CONVINCE. *To overpower; to overcome; to triumph over; to obtain; to condemn.*

When Duncan is asleep, his two chamberlains
Will I with wine and wassail so *convince.* *Macb.* i. 7.
    Their malady *convinces*
The great assay of art; but, at his touch,
They presently amend.   *Ibid.* iv. 3.
 Your Italy contains none so accomplished a cour-
tier to *convince* the honour of my mistress.
        Cymbeline, i. 4.
Though the mourning brow of progeny
Forbid the smiling courtesy of love
The holy suit which fain it would *convince.*
      Love's Labour's lost, v. 2.
Else might the world *convince* of levity
As well my undertakings as your counsels.
      Troilus and Cressida, ii. 2.

To CONVIVE. *To feast.*

First, all you peers of Greece, go to my tent;
There in the full *convive* we.
      Troilus and Cressida, iv. 5.

              L

CONVOY. *Conveyance.*

And, sister, as the winds give benefit,
And *convoy* is assistant, do not sleep,
But let me hear from you. *Hamlet*, i. 3.

His grace is at Marseilles; to which place we
have convenient *convoy.*
All's well that ends well, iv. 4.

His passport shall be made,
And crowns for *convoy* put into his purse
Henry 5, iv. 3.

To CONY-CATCH. *To cheat.*

I have matter in my head against you: and
against your *cony-catching* rascals, Bardolph, Nym,
and Pistol. *Merry Wives of Windsor*, i. 1.

I must *cony-catch;* I must shift. *Ibid.* i. 3.

Take heed lest you be *cony-catched* in this business. *Taming of the Shrew*, v. 1.

CONY-CATCHING. *Trickery; jocularity; merriment.*

Come, you are so full of *cony-catching.*
Taming of the Shrew, iv. 1.

COOLING-CARD. *An impediment; an obstruction; an obstacle.*

There all is marr'd; there lies a *cooling-card.*
Henry 6, P. 1, v. 3.

COPATAIN. *High-crowned.*

A silken doublet! a velvet hose! a scarlet cloak!
and a *copatain* hat! O, I am undone!
Taming of the Shrew, v. 1.

To COPE. *To reward; to recompense; to
oppose; to encounter.*

In lieu whereof,
Three thousand ducats, due unto the Jew,
We freely *cope* your courteous pains withal.
Merchant of Venice, iv. 1.

We must not stint
Our necessary actions, in the fear
To *cope* malicious censurers. *Henry 8*, i. 2.

Know, my name is lost;
By treason's tooth bare-gnawn and canker-bit:
Yet am I noble as the adversary
I come to *cope.* *King Lear*, v. 3.

COPULATIVE. *A couple; a pair.*

I press in here, sir, amongst the rest of the
country *copulatives*, to swear and to forswear.
As you like it, v. 4.

COPY. *Lease; tenure; theme; subject; model; pattern.*

But in them nature's *copy's* not eterne.
Macbeth, iii. 2.

It was the *copy* of our conference.
Comedy of Errors, v. 1.

The *copy* of your speed is learn'd by them.
King John, iv. 2.

Such a man might be a *copy* to these younger times.
All's well that ends well, i. 3.

Be *copy* now to men of grosser blood,
And teach them how to war! *Henry 5*, iii. 1.

CORANTO. *A quick lively dance.*

Why dost thou not go to church in a galliard,
and come home in a *coranto?* *Twelfth-Night*, i. 3.

Why, he's able to lead her a *coranto.*
All's well that ends well, ii. 3.

To CO-RIVAL. *To vie with; to emulate.*

Where's then the saucy boat
Whose weak untimber'd sides but even now
Co-rivall'd greatness? *Troilus and Cressida*, i. 3.

CORKY. *Resembling cork; shrivelled; withered.*

Bind fast his *corky* arms. *King Lear*, iii. 7.

CORNER. *Edge; margin; extremity.*

Upon the *corner* of the moon
There hangs a vaporous drop profound.
Macbeth, iii. 5.

CORNER-CAP. *The corner-stone; the head-
stone.*

Thou mak'st the triumviry, the *corner-cap* of society.
Love's Labour's lost, iv. 3.

CORNET. *A troop or company of horse.*

O God, that Somerset,—who in proud heart
Doth stop my *cornets*,—were in Talbot's place !
Henry 6, P. 1, iv. 3.

CORNUTO. *A cuckold.*

The peaking *cornuto* her husband.
Merry Wives of Windsor, iii. 5.

COROLLARY. *A surplus.*

Bring a *corollary*, rather than want a spirit.
Tempest, iv. 1.

CORONET. *A crown.*

Must he be, then, as shadow of himself?
Adorn his temples with a *coronet*,

And yet, in substance and authority,
Retain but privilege of a private man?
Henry 6, P. 1, v. 4.
The sway, revenue, execution of the rest,
Belovèd sons, be yours : which to confirm,
This *coronet* part between you. *King Lear*, i. 1.

CORPSE. *A corse; a ghost.*

My lord your son had only but the *corpse*,
But shadows and the shows of men, to fight.
Henry 4, P. 2, i. 1.

CORRECTION. *Punishment.*

Correction and instruction must both work
Ere this rude beast will profit.
Measure for Measure, iii. 2.

CORRESPONDENT. *Obedient; submissive.*

Pardon, master :
I will be *correspondent* to command,
And do my spriting gently. *Tempest*, i. 2.

CORRESPONSIVE. *Corresponding.*

Dardan, and Tymbria, Helias, Chetas, Troien,
And Antenorides, with massy staples,
And *corresponsive* and fulfilling bolts,
Sperr up the sons of Troy.
Troilus and Cressida, Prologue.

CORRIGIBLE. *Corrective; corrected; punished.*

Why, the power and *corrigible* authority of this
lies in our wills. *Othello*, i. 3.
Wouldst thou be window'd in great Rome, and see
Thy master thus with pleach'd arms, bending down
His *corrigible* neck, his face subdu'd
To penetrative shame?
Antony and Cleopatra, iv. 14.

CORRIVAL. *Rival; competitor.*

And many more *corrivals* and dear men
Of estimation and command in arms.
Henry 4, P. 1, iv. 4.
So he that doth redeem her thence might wear
Without *corrival* all her dignities. *Ibid.* P. 1, i. 3.

CORROSIVE. *Any thing which frets, or gives pain.*

Care is no cure, but rather *córrosive*,
For things that are not to be remedied.
Henry 6, P. 1, iii. 3.
Away! though parting be a fretful *córrosive*,
It is applied to a deathful wound. *Ibid.* P. 2, iii. 2.

To CORRUPT. *To putrefy; to rot; to decay.*

But it is I,
That lying by the violet, in the sun,
Do as the carrion does, not as the flower,
Corrupt with virtuous season.
Measure for Measure, ii. 2.

CORRUPTIBLY. *Corruptedly.*

It is too late : the life of all his blood
Is touch'd *corruptibly*. *King John*, v. 7.

COSIER. *A botcher; a tailor.*

Do ye make an alehouse of my lady's house, that
ye squeak out your *cosiers'* catches without any mitigation or remorse of voice? *Twelfth-Night*, ii. 3.

COSTARD. *The head.*

Take him on the *costard* with the hilts of thy
sword, and then throw him into the malmsey-butt
in the next room. *Richard 3*, i. 4.
Or ise try whether your *costard* or my ballow
be the harder. *King Lear*, iv. 6.

COTE. *A cottage.*

Besides, his *cote*, his flocks, and bounds of feed,
Are now on sale. *As you like it*, ii. 4.

To COTE. *To overtake; to pass.*

We *coted* them on the way; and hither are
they coming, to offer you service. *Hamlet*, ii. 2.

COT-QUEAN. *A man who busies himself un-
duly with domestic arrangements.*

Go, you *cot-quean*, go, get you to bed.
Romeo and Juliet, iv. 4.

COUCHING. *Bending.*

These *couchings* and these lowly courtesies
Might fire the blood of ordinary men.
Julius Cæsar, iii. 1.

COUNSEL. *A secret.*

I will hear you, Master Fenton; and I will at
the least keep your *counsel*.
Merry Wives of Windsor, iv. 6.
Tell me your *counsels*, I will not disclose 'em.
Julius Cæsar, ii. 1.
What man art thou, that, thus bescreen'd in night,
So stumblest on my *counsel*? *Romeo and Jul.* ii. 2.
We shall know by this fellow : the players
cannot keep *counsel*; they'll tell all. *Hamlet*, iii. 2.

COUNT. *Reckoning ; mark ; line ; accusation.*

By my *count*
I was your mother much upon these years
That you are now a maid. *Romeo and Juliet*, i. 3.
Well, I know not
What *counts* harsh fortune casts upon my face ;
But in my bosom shall she never come,
To make my heart her vassal.
Antony and Cleopatra, ii. 6.
The other motive,
Why to a public *count* I might not go,
Is the great love the general gender bear him.
Hamlet, iv. 7.

COUNTENANCE. *Appearance; semblance; seeming.*

Keep me in patience, and with ripen'd time
Unfold the evil which is here wrapt up
In *countenance !* *Measure for Measure*, v. 1.

To COUNTENANCE. *To favour ; to suit ; to correspond with.*

I beseech you, sir, to *countenance* William Visor
of Wincot against Clement Perkes of the hill.
Henry 4, P. 2, v. 1.

The knave is mine honest friend, sir ; therefore, I beseech your worship, let him be *countenanced.* *Ibid. P. 2,* v. 1.
Malcolm ! Banquo !
As from your graves rise up, and walk like sprites,
To *countenance* this horror ! *Macbeth*, ii. 1.

COUNTER. *A round piece of metal, formerly used in calculations.*

I cannot do't without *counters.* *Winter's Tale*, iv. 2.
And I must be be-lee'd and calm'd
By debitor and creditor, this *counter*-caster.
Othello, i. 1.

COUNTER. *The wrong way ; in the wrong direction.*

A hound that runs *counter*, and yet draws dry-foot
well. *Comedy of Errors*, iv. 2.
O, this is *counter*, you false Danish dogs !
Hamlet, iv. 5.
You hunt *counter :* hence ! avaunt !
Henry 4, P. 2, i. 2.

COUNTER-CASTER. *An arithmetician.*

And I must be be-lee'd and calm'd
By debitor and creditor, this *counter-caster.*
Othello, i. 1.

COUNTERCHANGE. *Interchange; reciprocation.*

And she, like harmless lightning, throws her eye
On him, her brothers, me, her master ; hitting
Each object with a joy : the *counterchange*
Is severally in all. *Cymbeline*, v. 5.

COUNTERFEIT. *A portrait ; a likeness.*

Good honest men !—Thou draw'st a *counterfeit*
Best in all Athens. *Timon of Athens*, v. 1.
What find I here ? fair Portia's *counterfeit !*
Merchant of Venice, iii. 2.

To COUNTERFEIT. *To feign ; to dissemble ; to paint a portrait.*

How ill agrees it with your gravity
To *counterfeit* thus grossly with your slave !
Comedy of Errors, ii. 1.
Thou'rt, indeed, the best ;
Thou *counterfeit'st* most lively.—So, so, my lord.
Timon of Athens, v. 1.

To COUNTERMAND. *To stop ; to obstruct.*

A back-friend, a shoulder-clapper, one that *countermands*
The passages of alleys, creeks, and narrow lands.
* *Comedy of Errors*, iv. 2.

COUNTERPOINT. *A counterpane ; a coverlet.*

In cypress chests my arras *counterpoints.*
Taming of the Shrew, ii. 1.

COUNTY. *A count ; a lord.*

The gallant, young, and noble gentleman,
The *County* Paris. *Romeo and Juliet*, iii. 3.

COUPLEMENT. *A pair ; a couple.*

I wish you the peace of mind, most royal *couplement !* *Love's Labour's lost*, v. 2.

COUPLET. *A pair ; a couple.*

Anon, as patient as the female dove,
When that her golden *couplets* are disclos'd,
His silence will sit drooping. *Hamlet*, v. 1.

COURAGE. *Temper; spirit; inclination; will; desire.*

My lord, cheer up your spirits : our foes are nigh,
And this soft *courage* makes your followers faint.
Henry 6, P. 3, ii. 2.
Nor check my *courage* for what they can give,
To have't with saying, Good morrow.
Coriolanus, iii. 3.

I'd rather than the worth of thrice the sum,
Had sent to me first; but for my mind's sake;
I'd such a *courage* to do him good.
Timon of Athens, iii. 3.

COURT-CUPBOARD. *A movable sideboard.*

Away with the joint-stools, remove the *court-cupboard*, look to the plate. *Romeo and Juliet*, i. 5.

COURT HOLY-WATER. *Fair words; flattery; fine phrases.*

O nuncle, *court holy-water* in a dry house is better than this rain-water out o' door.
King Lear, iii. 2.

TO COURTESY. *To salute.*

Toby approaches; *court'sies* there to me.
Twelfth-Night, ii. 5.
There, where your argosies with portly sail
Do overpeer the petty traffickers,
That *court'sy* to them, do them reverence,
As they fly by them with their woven wings.
Merchant of Venice, i. 1.

COUSIN. *A grand-child; a nephew; a kins-man.*

My pretty *cousins*, you mistake me both.
Richard 3, ii. 2.
You'll have your nephews neigh to you; you'll have coursers for *cousins*, and gennets for germans.
Othello, i. 1.
Dream on thy *cousins* smother'd in the Tower.
Richard 3, v. 3.
And we beseech you, bend you to remain
Here, in the cheer and comfort of our eye,
Our chiefest courtier, *cousin*, and our son.
Hamlet, i. 2.

COVENT. *A convent.*

One of our *covent*, and his confessor,
Gives me this instance.
Measure for Measure, iv. 3.
Where the reverend abbot,
With all his *covent*, honourably receiv'd him.
Henry 8, iv. 2.

TO COVER. *To prepare a banquet.*

Sirs, *cover* the while; the duke will drink under this tree. *As you like it*, ii. 5.
Go to thy fellows; bid them *cover* the table, serve in the meat, and we will come in to dinner.
Merchant of Venice, iii. 5.

COVERT. *Secret; concealed.*

How *covert* matters may be best disclos'd,
And open perils surest answer'd.
Julius Cæsar, iv. 1.
Well, well, he was the *covert'st* shelter'd traitor
That ever liv'd. *Richard 3*, iii. 5.
Caitiff, to pieces shake,
That under *covert* and convenient seeming
Hast practis'd on man's life. *King Lear*, iii. 2.

COVERTURE. *An arbour; covering; shelter; defence.*

So angle we for Beatrice; who even now
Is couch'd in the woodbine *coverture*.
Much Ado about Nothing, iii. 1.
And now what rests but, in night's *coverture*,
Thy brother being carelessly encamp'd,
And but attended by a simple guard,
We may surprise and take him at our pleasure?
Henry 6, P. 3, iv. 2.
When steel grows soft as the parasite's silk,
Let him be made a *coverture* for the wars!
Coriolanus, i. 9.

COVETOUSNESS. *Eagerness; intensity of desire.*

When workmen strive to do better than well,
They do confound their skill in *covetousness*.
King John, iv. 2.

COWARD. *Cowardly.*

His *coward* lips did from their colour fly.
Julius Cæsar, i. 2.

TO COWARD. *To fright; to terrify.*

What read you there,
That hath so *cowarded* and chas'd your blood
Out of appearance? *Henry 5*, ii. 2.

COWISH. *Mean; dastardly; pusillanimous.*

It is the *cowish* terror of his spirit,
That dares not undertake. *King Lear*, iv. 2.

COXCOMB. *A fool's cap; the top of the head.*

Sirrah, you were best take my *coxcomb*.
King Lear, i. 4.
Cry to it, nuncle, as the cockney did to the eels when she put 'em i' the paste alive; she knapped 'em o' the *coxcombs* with a stick, and cried, "Down, wantons, down!" *Ibid.* ii. 4.
Has broke my head across, and has given Sir Toby a bloody *coxcomb* too. *Twelfth-Night*, v. 1.

To COY. *To hesitate; to object; to smooth; to fondle; to caress.*

> Nay, if he coy'd
> To hear Cominius speak, I'll keep at home.
> *Coriolanus*, v. 1.
> Come, sit thee down upon this flowery bed,
> While I thy amiable cheeks do coy.
> *Midsummer-Night's Dream*, iv. 1.

To COZEN. *To cheat.*

> He stamp'd and swore,
> As if the vicar meant to cozen him.
> *Taming of the Shrew*, iii. 2.
> Who is thus like to be cozened with the sem-
> blance of a maid. *Much Ado about Nothing*, ii. 2.
> Only, in this disguise, I think 't no sin
> To cozen him that would unjustly win.
> *All's well that ends well*, iv. 2.

COZENAGE. *Fraud; cheating.*

> Out, alas, sir! cozenage, mere cozenage!
> *Merry Wives of Windsor*, iv. 5.

COZENER. *A sharper; a cheat; a swindler; a thief.*

> Run away with by the cozeners.
> *Merry Wives of Windsor*, iv. 5.
> The usurer hangs the cozener. *King Lear*, iv. 6.

CRACK. *A boy; a breach; a flaw.*

> I saw him break Skogan's head at the court-gate,
> when he was a crack not thus high.
> *Henry 4*, P. 2, iii. 2.
> Indeed, la, 'tis a noble child.—
> A crack, madam. *Coriolanus*, i. 3.
> And my fortunes against any lay worth naming,
> this crack of your love shall grow stronger than it
> was before. *Othello*, ii. 3.

To CRACK. *To utter a loud noise; to resound; to boast.*

> For I will board her, though she chide as loud
> As thunder, when the clouds in autumn crack.
> *Taming of the Shrew*, i. 2.
> And Ethiops of their sweet complexion crack.
> *Love's Labour's lost*, iv. 3.

CRACKER. *A boaster; a noisy turbulent fellow.*

> What cracker is this same that deafs our ears
> With this abundance of superfluous breath?
> *King John*, ii. 1.

CRACK-HEMP. *A rascal; a rogue.*

> Come hither, crack-hemp.
> *Taming of the Shrew*, v. 1.

To CRAFT. *To play tricks; to act craftily; to plot; to scheme.*

> You have made fair hands,
> You and your crafts! you have crafted fair!
> *Coriolanus*, iv. 6.

CRANK. *A winding passage.*

> And, through the cranks and offices of man,
> The strongest nerves and small interior veins
> From me receive that natural competency
> Whereby they live. *Coriolanus*, i. 1.

To CRANK. *To wind.*

> See how this river comes me cranking in.
> *Henry 4*, P. 1, iii. 1.

CRANTS. *Garlands.*

> Yet here she is allow'd her virgin crants.
> *Hamlet*, v. 1.

CRARE. *A small sailing-vessel.*

> O melancholy!
> Who ever yet could sound thy bottom? find
> The ooze, to show what coast thy sluggish crare
> Might easiliest harbour in? *Cymbeline*, iv. 2.

CRAVEN. *A coward; a recreant.*

> No cock of mine; you crow too like a craven.
> *Taming of the Shrew*, ii. 1.
> He is a craven and a villain else, in my conscience.
> *Henry 5*, iv. 7.

CRAVEN. *Base; cowardly.*

> Whether it be
> Bestial oblivion, or some craven scruple.
> *Hamlet*, iv. 4.
> He bears him on the place's privilege,
> Or durst not, for his craven heart, say thus.
> *Henry 4*, P. 1, ii. 4.

To CRAVEN. *To terrify; to intimidate.*

> Against self-slaughter
> There is a prohibition so divine
> That cravens my weak hand. *Cymbeline*, iii. 4.

CRAZED. *Weak; feeble; crazy; invalid.*

> Lysander, yield
> Thy crazèd title to my certain right.
> *Midsummer-Night's Dream*, i. 1.

CREATE. *Created ; composed ; compounded.*

And the issue there *create*
Evor shall be fortunate.
                Midsummer-Night's Dream, v. 1.
Tho fire is dead with grief,
Being *create* for comfort, to be us'd
In undoserv'd extremes.   *King John*, iv. 1.
With hearts *create* of duty and of zoal.
                       Henry 5, ii. 2.

CREDENCE. *Trust; confidence.*

And we, groat in our hope, lay our best love and
    credence
Upon thy promising fortuno.
             All's well that ends well, iii. 3.

CREDENT. *Not to be questioned ; weighty ; credible ; credulous.*

For my authority bears so *credent* bulk,
That no particular scandal once can touch
But it confounds the breathor.
           Measure for Measure, iv. 4.
        'Tis very *credent*
Thou mayst co-join with something; and thou dost,
And that beyond commission. *Winter's Tale*, i. 2.
Then weigh what loss your honour may sustain,
If with too *credent* ear you list his songs.
                       Hamlet, i. 3.

CREDIT. *Report; rumour; credibility; credulity.*

      And there I found this *credit*,
That he did rango the town to seek mo out.
                Twelfth-Night, iv. 3.
That she loves him, 'tis apt, and of great *credit*.
                     Othello, ii. 1.
What ! lack I *credit* ?   *Winter's Tale*, ii. 1.
Alas, poor women ! make us but believe
Being compact of *credit*, that you love us.
               Comedy of Errors, iii. 2.

CRESCENT. *Increasing; growing.*

My powers are *crescent*, and my auguring hope
Says it will come to the full.
              Antony and Cleopatra, ii. 1.
   Believe it, sir, I have soon him in Britain : he
was thon of a *crescent* note.,   *Cymbeline*, i. 4.

CRESCIVE. *Increasing; growing.*

      Which, no doubt,
Grew like the summer grass, fastest by night,
Unseen, yet *crescive* in his faculty. *Henry 5*, i. 1.

CRESSET. *A lamp ; a hollow vessel filled with combustibles.*

      At my nativity
Tho front of heaven was full of fiery shapes,
Of burning *cressets*.   *Henry 4*, P. 1, iii. 1.

CREW. *A band ; a company of any kind.*

Oxford, redoubted Pembroko, Sir James Blunt,
And Rice ap Thomas, with a valiant *crew*.
                      Richard 3, iv. 5.

To CRINGE. *To wrinkle; to contract.*

      Whip him, fellows,
Till, like a boy, you see him *cringe* his face,
And whine aloud for mercy.
            Antony and Cleopatra, iii. 13.

CRISP. *Indented ; winding ; curled ; arched.*

Leave your *crisp* channels, and on this green land
Answer this summons.   *Tempest*, iv. 1.
And hid his *crisp* head in the hollow bank.
              Henry 4, P. 1, i. 3.
With all the abhorrèd births below *crisp* heaven,
Whereon Hyperion's quickening fire doth shino.
             Timon of Athens, iv. 3.

To CRISP. *To curl.*

So are those *crispèd* snaky golden locks
Upon supposèd fairness, often known
To be the dowry of a second head.
             Merchant of Venice, iii. 2.

CRITIC. *A cynic ; a censor.*

      Do not give advantago
To stubborn *critics*, to square the general sex
By Cressid's rule : rather think this is not Cressid.
            Troilus and Cressida, v. 2.
And Nestor play at push-pin with the boys,
And *critic* Timon laugh at idle toys !
           Love's Labour's lost, iv. 3.

CRITICAL. *Cynical ; censorious.*

That is some satire, keen and *critical*.
          Midsummer-Night's Dream, v. 1.
For I am nothing, if not *critical*.   *Othello*, ii. 1.

CRONE. *An old woman ; a hag.*

Take't up, I say ; give't to thy *crone*.
              Winter's Tale, ii. 3.

CROSS. *A coin so called.*

He speaks the mere contrary,—*crosses* love not
him.   *Love's Labour's lost*, i. 2.

CROSSLY. *Adversely.*

Thy friends are fled, to wait upon thy foes;
And *crossly* to thy good all fortune goes.
Richard 2, ii. 4.

CROSS-ROW. *The alphabet.*

He hearkens after prophecies and dreams;
And from the *cross-row* plucks the letter G.
Richard 3, i. 1.

To CROW. *To laugh.*

I protest, I take these wise men, that *crow* so at
these set kind of fools, no better than the fools'
zanies. *Twelfth-Night*, i. 5.

CROW-KEEPER. *A scarecrow.*

Scaring the ladies like a *crow-keeper.*
Romeo and Juliet, i. 4.
That fellow handles his bow like a *crow-keeper.*
King Lear, iv. 6.

CROWNER. *A coroner.*

Go thou, and seek the *crowner*, and let him sit
o' my coz; for he's in the third degree of drink,—
he's drowned. *Twelfth-Night*, i. 5.
The *crowner* hath sat on her, and finds it Christian burial. *Hamlet*, v. 1.

CROWNET. *A crown; a coronet.*

Sixty and nine, that wore
Their *crownets* regal, from the Athenian bay
Put forth towards Phrygia.
Troilus and Cressida, Prologue.
Whose bosom was my *crownet*, my chief end.
Antony and Cleopatra, iv. 12.
In his livery
Walk'd crowns and *crownets*; realms and islands
were
As plates dropp'd from his pocket. *Ibid.* v. 2.

CRUDY. *Crude; raw.*

It ascends me into the brain; dries me there all
the foolish and dull and *crudy* vapours which environ it. *Henry 4, P. 2*, iv. 3.

CRUELS. *Cruelty; barbarity; inhumanity.*

If wolves had at thy gate howl'd that stern time,
Thou shouldst have said, "Good porter, turn the
key,"
All *cruels* else subscrib'd. *King Lear*, iii. 7.

CRUSADO. *A Portuguese coin.*

Believe me, I had rather have lost my purse
Full of *crusadoes*. *Othello*, iii. 4.

To CRUSH. *To empty; to finish.*

My master is the great rich Capulet; and if you
be not of the house of Montagues, I pray, come and
crush a cup of wine. *Romeo and Juliet*, i. 2.

CRY. *A pack; a company.*

You have made good work, you and your *cry!*
Coriolanus, iv. 6.
You common *cry* of curs! whose breath I hate
As reek o' the rotten fens. *Ibid.* iii. 3.
Would not this, sir, and a forest of feathers,
with two Provincial roses on my razed shoes, get
me a fellowship in a *cry* of players? *Hamlet*, iii. 2.

To CRY AIM. *To applaud; to encourage.*

Cried I aim? said I well?
Merry Wives of Windsor, ii. 3.
And to these violent proceedings all my neigh-
bours shall *cry aim.* *Ibid.* iii. 2.
It ill beseems this presence to *cry aim*
To these ill-tuned repetitions. *King John*, ii. 1.

To CRY ON. *To call loudly; to vociferate; to
proclaim.*

Who's there? whose noise is this that *cries on*
murder? *Othello*, v. 1.
This quarry *cries on* havoc. *Hamlet*, v. 2.

To CRY OUT. *To give tongue; to yelp.*

Sowter will *cry* upon't, for all this, though it be
as rank as a fox. *Twelfth-Night*, ii. 5.
If I *cry out* thus upon no trail, never trust me
when I open again. *Merry Wives of Windsor*, iv. 2.
He *cried* upon it at the merest loss:
Trust me, I take him for the better dog.
Taming of the Shrew, Induction, sc. 1.

To CRY WOE. *To grieve; to lament; to complain.*

You live that shall *cry woe* for this hereafter.
Richard 3, iii. 3.
The man that makes his toe
What he his heart should make,
Shall of a corn *cry woe*,
And turn his sleep to wake. *King Lear*, iii. 2.

CRYSTALS. *The eyes.*

Go, clear thy *crystals*. *Henry 5*, ii. 3.

CUBICULO. *Lodging; place of residence.*

We'll call thee at thy *cubiculo*: go.
Twelfth-Night, iii. 2.

CUCKOO-BUDS. *Cowslips.*

And *cuckoo-buds,* of yellow hue,
Do paint the meadows with delight.
Love's Labour's lost, v. 2.

CUISSES. *Armour for the thighs.*

I saw young Harry,—with his beaver on,
His *cuisses* on his thighs, gallantly arm'd.
Henry 4, P. 1, iv. 1.

CULLION. *A mean fellow; a scoundrel.*

Away, base *cullions!*—Suffolk, let them go.
Henry 6, P. 2, i. 3.
But one that scorn to live in this disguise,
For such a one as leaves a gentleman,
And makes a god of such a *cullion.*
Taming of the Shrew, iv. 2.

CULLIONLY. *Mean; base.*

Draw, you whoreson *cullionly* barber-monger, draw.
King Lear, ii. 2.

CULVERIN. *A sort of cannon.*

Of basilisks, of cannon, *culverin,*
Of prisoners ransom'd, and of soldiers slain,
And all the 'currents of a heady fight.
Henry 4, P. 1, ii. 3.

TO CUMBER. *To harass; to torment.*

Domestic fury and fierce civil strife
Shall *cumber* all the parts of Italy.
Julius Cæsar, iii. 1.
Let it not *cumber* your better remembrance.
Timon of Athens, iii. 6.

CUNNING. *Skill; knowledge; proficiency.*

But, in the boldness of my *cunning,* I will lay
myself in hazard.   *Measure for Measure,* iv. 2.
Nor I have no *cunning* in protestation.
·*Henry* 5, v. 2.
But trust me, gentlemen, I'll prove more true
Than those that have more *cunning* to be strange.
Romeo and Juliet, ii. 2.
Shame, that they wanted *cunning,* in excess,
Hath broke their hearts.   *Timon of Athens,* v. 4.

CUNNING. *Skilful; well-instructed; learned.*

For to *cunning* men
I will be very kind, and liberal
To mine own children in good bringing up.
Taming of the Shrew, i. 1.
'Tis beauty truly blent, whose red and white
Nature's own sweet and *cunning* hand laid on.
Twelfth-Night, i. 5.

Wherein *cunning,* but in craft? wherein crafty,
but in villany? wherein villanous, but in all things?
wherein worthy, but in nothing?
Henry 4, P. 1, ii. 4.

TO CUP. *To supply with drink.*

Cup us, till the world go round!
Antony and Cleopatra, ii. 7.

TO CUPBOARD. *To hoard; to stow away.*

Still *cupboarding* the viand, never bearing
Like labour with the rest.   *Coriolanus,* i. 1.

TO CURB. *To crouch; to cringe; to bend.*

For in the fatness of these pursy times
Virtue itself of vice must pardon beg,
Yea, *curb* and woo for leave to do him good.
Hamlet, iii. 4.

CURDED. *Congealed.*

The noble sister of Publicola,
The moon of Rome; chaste as the icicle,
That's *curded* by the frost from purest snow,
And hangs on Dian's temple.   *Coriolanus,* v. 3.

CURIOSITY. *Fastidiousness; squeamishness; effeminate softness.*

When thou wast in thy gilt and thy perfume,
they mocked thee for too much *curiosity;* in thy
rags thou' knowest none, but art despised for the
contrary.   *Timon of Athens,* iv. 3.

CURIOUS. *Scrupulous; fastidious; nice; trivial; frivolous.*

For *curious* I cannot be with you,
Signior Baptista, of whom I hear so well.
Taming of the Shrew, iv. 4.
Frank nature, rather *curious* than in haste,
Hath well compos'd thee.
All's well that ends well, i. 2.
What care I
What *curious* eye doth quote deformities?
Romeo and Juliet, i. 4.
I can keep honest counsel, ride, run, mar a *curious* tale in telling it, and deliver a plain message
bluntly.   *King Lear,* i. 4.

CURIOUSLY. *Minutely; nicely; exactly; carefully.*

'Twere to consider too *curiously,* to consider so.
Hamlet, v. 1.
I would gladly have him see his company anatomized, that he might take a measure of his own

M

judgment, wherein so *curiously* he had set this counterfeit. *All's well that ends well*, iv. 3.

'CURRENT. *Occurrent; incident; event.*

Of prisoners ransom'd, and of soldiers slain,
And all the *'currents* of a heady fight.
Henry 4, P. 1, ii. 3.

To CURRY. *To insinuate; to hint; to flatter.*

If to his men, I would *curry* with Master Shallow, that no man could better command his servants.
Henry 4, P. 2, v. 1.

CURSED. *Blasted by a curse; banned; be-
witched.*

And such an ache in my bones, that, unless a
man were *cursed*, I cannot tell what to think on't.
Troilus and Cressida, v. 3.

CURSORARY. *Cursory; hasty.*

I have but with a *cursorary* eye
O'erglanc'd the articles. *Henry 5, v. 2.*

CURST. *Crabbed; froward; shrewish; fierce;
savage.*

Item, she is *curst.*—
Well, the best is, she hath no teeth to bite.
Two Gentlemen of Verona, iii. 1.
If she be *curst*, it is for policy,
For she's not froward, but modest as the dove.
Taming of the Shrew, ii. 1.
They are never *curst*, but when they are hungry.
Winter's Tale, iii. 3.

CURSTNESS. *Ill humour; peevishness.*

Touch you the sourest points with sweetest terms,
Nor *curstness* grow to the matter.
Antony and Cleopatra, ii. 2.

CURTAINS. *Flags; colours.*

Their ragged *curtains* poorly are let loose,
And our air shakes them passing scornfully.
Henry 5, iv. 2.

CURTAL. *A docked horse or dog.*

I'd give bay *curtal* and his furniture,
My mouth no more were broken than these boys'.
All's well that ends well, ii. 3.
Hope is a *curtal* dog in some affairs : Sir John
affects thy wife. *Merry Wives of Windsor, ii. 1.*

CURTLE-AXE. *A cutlass; a broadsword.*

A gallant *curtle-axe* upon my thigh,
A boar-spear in my hand. *As you like it, i. 3.*

CUSTARD-COFFIN. *A custard-case or crust.*

A *custard-coffin*, a bauble, a silken pie.
Taming of the Shrew, iv. 3.

CUSTOMER. *A drab; a courtezan.*

I think thee now some common *customer.*
All's well that ends well, v. 3.
I marry her!—what, a *customer!* Prithee, bear
some charity to my wit; do not think it so unwholesome. *Othello, iv. 1.*

CUT. *A term of reproach, implying a mean
shabby fellow; a lot.*

Send for money, knight : if thou hast her not
i' the end, call me *cut.* *Twelfth-Night, ii. 3.*
We'll draw *cuts* for the senior : till then lead
thou first. *Comedy of Errors, v. 1.*

CUTTER. *A chisel.*

The *cutter*
Was as another nature, dumb; outwent her,
Motion and breath left out. *Cymbeline, ii. 4.*

CUTTLE. *A slanderer; a calumniator; a
liar.*

By this wine, I'll thrust my knife in your mouldy
chaps, an you play the saucy *cuttle* with me.
Henry 4, P. 2, ii. 4.

CYPRUS. · *Crape.*

To one of your receiving
Enough is shown; a *cyprus*, not a bosom,
Hides my heart. *Twelfth-Night, iii. 1.*
Lawn as white as driven snow;
Cyprus black as e'er was crow. *Winter's Tale, iv. 3.*

D.

To DAFF. *To doff; to put off; to lay aside.*
Every day thou *daffest* me with some device,
Iago. *Othello*, iv. 2.
I would have *daffed* all other respects, and made
her half myself. *Much Ado about Nothing*, ii. 3.
Where is his son, the madcap Prince of Wales,
And his comrádes, that *daff* the world aside,
And bid it pass? *Henry* 4, P. 1, iv. 1.
He that unbuckles this, till we do please
To *daff't* for our repose, shall hear a storm.
Antony and Cleopatra, iv. 4.

DAINTY. *Nice; fastidious; ceremonious; scrupulous; elegant.*
The great Achilles,
Having his ear full of his airy fame,
Grows *dainty* of his worth, and in his tent
Lies mocking our designs. *Troilus and Cressida*, i. 3.
And let us not be *dainty* of leave-taking,
But shift away. *Macbeth*, ii. 1.
Forget your laboursome and *dainty* trims,
Wherein you made great Juno angry.
Cymbeline, iii. 4.

DALLIANCE. *Delay; wantonness; endearment.*
My business cannot brook this *dalliance.*
Comedy of Errors, iv. 1.
Then march to Paris, royal Charles of France,
And keep not back your powers in *dalliance.*
Henry 6, P. 1, v. 2.
Whilst, like a puff'd and reckless libertine,
Himself the primrose path of *dalliance* treads,
And recks not his own read. *Hamlet*, i. 3.
Look thou be true; do not give *dalliance*
Too much the rein. *Tempest*, iv. 1.

To DALLY. *To trifle.*
Take heed you *dally* not before your king.
Richard 3, ii. 1.
Tell me, and *dally* not, where is the money?
Comedy of Errors, i. 2.
Dally not with the gods, but get thee gone.
Taming of the Shrew, iv. 4.

DANGER. *Debt; harm; mischief; damage.*
You stand within his *danger*, do you not?
Merchant of Venice, iv. 1.

The letter was not nice, but full of charge
Of dear import; and the neglecting it
May do much *danger*. *Romeo and Juliet*, v. 2.
My lords, when you shall know the great *danger*
Which this man's life did owe you, you'll rejoice
That he is thus cut off. *Coriolanus*, v. 6.

To DANGER. *To endanger.*
Whose quality, going on,
The sides o' the world may *danger*.
Antony and Cleopatra, i. 2.

DANSKER. *A Dane.*
Look you, sir,
Inquire me first what *Danskers* are in Paris.
Hamlet, ii. 1.

DARE. *Boldness; defiance; challenge.*
It lends a lustre and more great opinion,
A larger *dare* to our great enterprise,
Than if the earl were here. *Henry* 4, P. 1, iv. 1.
Sextus Pompeius
Hath given the *dare* to Cæsar, and commands
The empire of the sea. *Antony and Cleopatra*, i. 2.

To DARE. *To scare; to terrify.*
For our approach shall so much *dare* the field,
That England shall couch down in fear, and yield.
Henry 5, iv. 2.
Let his grace go forward,
And *dare* us with his cap like larks. *Henry* 8, iii. 2.

DAREFUL. *Daring; full of defiance.*
We might have met them *dareful*, beard to beard,
And beat them backward home. *Macbeth*, v. 5.

DARK. *Close; secret; impenetrable.*
Meantime we shall express our *darker* purpose.
King Lear, i. 1.
Now, if you could wear a mind
Dark as your fortune is, and but disguise
That which, to appear itself, must not yet be
But by self-danger, you should tread a course
Pretty and full of view. *Cymbeline*, iii. 4.

DARK HOUSE. *A madhouse.*
War is no strife
To the *dark house* and the detested wife.
All's well that ends well, ii. 3.

Love is merely a madness; and, I tell you, deserves as well a *dark house* and a whip as madmen do. *As you like it*, iii. 2.
Kept in a *dark house*, visited by the priest,
And made the most notorious geck and gull
That e'er invention play'd on. *Twelfth-Night*, v. 1.

DARKLING. *In darkness; in the dark.*

So, out went the candle, and we were left *darkling*.
King Lear, i. 4.
O sun, burn the great sphere thou mov'st in!—
darkling stand
The varying shore o' the world.
Antony and Cleopatra, iv. 15.
O, wilt thou *darkling* leave me? do not so.
Midsummer-Night's Dream, ii. 2.

To **DARRAIGN.** *To range troops in the order of battle.*

Darraign your battle, for they are at hand.
Henry 6, P. 3, ii. 2.

DASH. *A smack; a sprinkling.*

Now, had I not the *dash* of my former life in me, would preferment drop on my head.
Winter's Tale, v. 2.

To **DASH.** *To set aside; to abolish; to stain; to sully.*

For by my scouts I was advertised
That she was coming with a full intent
To *dash* our late decree in parliament
Touching King Henry's oath and your succession.
Henry 6, P. 3, ii. 1.
And, not consulting, broke
Into a general prophecy,—That this tempest,
Dashing the garment of this peace, aboded
The sudden breach on't. *Henry 8*, i. 1.

DATE. *Continuance; duration; limitation of time.*

With league whose *date* till death shall never end.
Midsummer-Night's Dream, iii. 2.
His days and times are past,
And my reliance on his fracted *dates*
Have smit my credit. *Timon of Athens*, ii. 1.
Take the bonds along with you,
And have the *dates* in compt. *Ibid.* ii. 1.

To **DAUB.** *To play the hypocrite; to counterfeit; to feign.*

Poor Tom's a-cold.—I cannot *daub* it further.
King Lear, iv. 1.

DAUBERY. *Deceit; trickery; fraud.*

She works by charms, by spells, by the figure,
and such *daubery* as this is.
Merry Wives of Windsor, iv. 2.

DAWNING. *Morning.*

Good *dawning* to thee, friend: art of this house?
King Lear, ii. 2.
Swift, swift, you dragons of the night, that *dawning*
May bare the raven's eye! *Cymbeline*, ii. 2.

DAY-BED. *A couch; a sofa.*

He is not lolling on a lewd *day-bed*,
But on his knees at meditation. *Richard 3*, iii. 7.
Having come from a *day-bed*, where I have
left Olivia sleeping. *Twelfth-Night*, ii. 5.

A **DAY OF SEASON.** *A day without violent or sudden changes of any kind; a seasonable day.*

I am not a *day of season*,
For thou mayst see a sunshine and a hail
In me at once. *All's well that ends well*, v. 3.

DAY-WOMAN. *A dairy-maid.*

She is allowed for the *day-woman*.
Love's Labour's lost, i. 2.

DEAD. *Dull; heavy; sad; spiritless; stupefied; pale; insensible.*

But old folks, many feign as they were *dead*.
Romeo and Juliet, ii. 5.
Thy Juliet is alive,
For whose dear sake thou wast but lately *dead*.
Ibid. iii. 3.
We were *dead* of sleep,
And,—how we know not,—all clapp'd under
hatches. *Tempest*, v. 1.
So should a murderer look,—so *dead*, so grim.
Midsummer-Night's Dream, iii. 2.
Have you ta'en of it?—
Most like I did, for I was *dead*. *Cymbeline*, v. 5.

To **DEAF.** *To deafen.*

What cracker is this same that *deafs* our ears
With this abundance of superfluous breath?
King John, ii. 1.

To **DEAL UPON.** *To deal with; to trust to; to depend upon.*

Two deep enemies,
Foes to my rest, and my sweet sleep's disturbers,

Are they that I would have thee *deal upon* :—
Tyrrel, I mean those bastards in the Tower.
Richard 3, iv. 2.
He alone
Dealt on lieutenantry, and no practice had
In the brave squares of war.
Antony and Cleopatra, iii. 11.

DEAR. *Propitious ; favourable ; good ; noble ;
dire ; grievous.*

By accident most strange, bountiful Fortune—
Now my *dear* lady—hath mine enemies
Brought to this shore.   *Tempest*, i. 2.
Now, madam, summon up your *dearest* spirits.
Love's Labour's lost, ii. 1.
Be now as prodigal of all *dear* grace,
As nature was in making graces *dear*,
When she did starve the general world beside,
And prodigally gave them all to you.   *Ibid.* ii. 1.
Would I had met my *dearest* foe in heaven
Or ever I had seen that day, Horatio ! *Hamlet*, i. 2.
O, pardon me, my liege ! but for my tears
I had forestall'd this *dear* and deep rebuke.
Henry 4, P. 2, iv. 4.
So is the *dear'st* o' the loss.   *Tempest*, ii. 1.

To DEAR. *To endear.*

And the ebb'd man, ne'er lov'd till ne'er worth love,
Comes *dear'd* by being lack'd.
Antony and Cleopatra, i. 4.

DEARLY. *Grievously.*

How *dearly* would it touch thee to the quick,
Shouldst thou but hear I were licentious !
Comedy of Errors, ii. 2.

DEATHSMAN. *An executioner.*

He's dead ; I am only sorry he had no other
deathsman.   *King Lear*, iv. 6.
But if you ever chance to have a child,
Look in his youth to have him so cut off
As, *deathsmen*, you have rid this sweet young prince !
Henry 6, P. 3, v. 5.

DEBATE. *Strife ; contest ; quarrel.*

If you give me directly to understand you have
prevailed, I am no further your enemy ; she is not
worth our *debate*.   *Cymbeline*, i. 4.
Now, lords, if God doth give successful end
To this *debate* that bleedeth at our doors.
Henry 4, P. 2, iv. 4.
And this same progeny of evil comes
From our *debate*, from our dissension.
Midsummer-Night's Dream, ii. 1.

To DEBATE. *To dispose of ; to settle ; to discuss ; to dispute.*

Two thousand souls and twenty thousand ducats
Will not *debate* the question of this straw.
Hamlet, iv. 4.
Nature and sickness
Debate it at their leisure.
All's well that ends well, i. 2.

DEBATEMENT. *Contention ; controversy ; deliberation.*

And, after much *debatement*,
My sisterly remorse confutes mine honour,
And I did yield to him. *Measure for Measure*, v. 1.
That, on the view and knowing of these contents,
Without *debatement* further, more or less,
He should the bearers put to sudden death.
Hamlet, v. 2.

To DEBAUCH. *To degrade by intemperance ;
to debase ; to profane.*

Why, thou *debauched* fish, was there ever a man
a coward that hath drunk so much sack as I to-day?
Tempest, ii. 3.
The mere word's a slave,
Debauch'd on every tomb, on every grave
A lying trophy.   *All's well that ends well*, ii. 3.

DEBILE. *Weak ; impotent.*

For that I have not wash'd
My nose that bled, or foil'd some *debile* wretch,
You shout me forth
In acclamations hyperbolical   *Coriolanus*, i. 9.

DEBITOR. *A debtor.*

And I must be be-lee'd and calm'd
By *debitor* and creditor, this counter-caster.
Othello, i. 1.
O, the charity of a penny cord ! it sums up thou-
sands in a trice : you have no true *debitor* and cre-
ditor but it.   *Cymbeline*, v. 4.

DEBTED. *Indebted.*

Which doth amount to three odd ducats more
Than I stand *debted* to this gentleman.
Comedy of Errors, iv. 1.

DECAY. *Overthrow ; destruction ; ruin.*

Be thou the trumpet of our wrath,
And sullen presage of your own *decay*.
King John, i. 1.
O, with what wings shall his affections fly
Towards fronting peril and oppos'd *decay* !
Henry 4, P. 2, iv. 4.

No, my good lord ; I am the very man,
That, from your first of difference and *decay,*
Have follow'd your sad steps.   *King Lear,* v. 3.

DECEIVABLE.   *Deceitful ; deceptive.*

There's something in't that is *deceivable.*
            Twelfth-Night, iv. 3.
Show me thy humble heart, and not thy knee,
Whose duty is *deceivable* and false.
            Richard 2, ii. 3.

DECEPTIOUS.   *Deceptive ; deceitful.*

As if those organs had *deceptious* functions,
Created only to calumniate.
            Troilus and Cressida, v. 2.

DECIPHERED.   *Marked down ; written.*

Well didst thou, Richard, to suppress thy voice ;
For, had the passions of thy heart burst out,
I fear we should have soon *decipher'd* there
More rancorous spite, more furious raging broils,
Than yet can be imagin'd or suppos'd.
            Henry 6, P. 1, iv. 1.

DECK.   *A pack of cards.*

But, while he thought to steal the single ten,
The king was slily finger'd from the *deck !*
            Henry 6, P. 3, v. 1.

TO DECLINE.   *To fall ; to incline to ; to inflect ; to vary.*

When thou hast hung thy advancèd sword i' the air,
Not letting it *decline* on the *declin'd.*
            Troilus and Cressida, iv. 5.
Not one accompanying his *declining* foot.
            Timon of Athens, i. 1.
Far more, far more to you do I *decline.*
            Comedy of Errors, iii. 2.
Decline all this, and see what now thou art.
            Richard 3, iv. 4.
I'll *decline* the whole question.
            Troilus and Cressida, ii. 3.

DEDICATE.   *Dedicated ; devoted.*

He that is truly *dedicate* to war
Hath no self-love.   *Henry* 6, P. 2, v. 2.
Prayers from preservèd souls,
From fasting maids, whose minds are *dedicate*
To nothing temporal.   *Measure for Measure,* ii. 2.

DEDICATION.   *Devotion ; consecration.*

His life I gave him, and did thereto add
My love, without retention or restraint,
All his in *dedication.*   *Twelfth-Night,* v. 1.

DEED.   *Fulfilment ; execution.*

Performance is ever the duller for his act ; and,
but in the plainer and simpler kind of people, the
deed of saying is quite out of use.
            Timon of Athens, v. 1.

DEEM.   *Surmise ; thought ; opinion.*

I true ! how now ! what wicked *deem* is this!
            Troilus and Cressida, iv. 4.

TO DEEM.   *To judge of ; to estimate.*

In Britain where was he
That could stand up his parallel ;
Or fruitful object be
In eye of Imogen, that best
Could *deem* his dignity?   *Cymbeline,* v. 4.

DEEP.   *Important ; weighty ; skilful ; intense.*

Still, I swear I love you.—
If you but said so, 'twere as *deep* with me.
            Cymbeline, ii. 3.
Tut, I can counterfeit the *deep* tragedian ;
Speak and look back, and pry on every side,
Tremble and start at wagging of a straw,
Intending *deep* suspicion.   *Richard* 3, iii. 5.

DEER.   *Wild animals.*

But mice and rats, and such small *deer,*
Have been Tom's food for seven long year.
            King Lear, iii. 4.

TO DEFACE.   *To destroy ; to cancel.*

Defacing monuments of conquer'd France.
            Henry 6, P. 2, i. 1.
Pay him six thousand, and *deface* the bond.
            Merchant of Venice, iii. 2.

DEFACER.   *A destroyer ; a disturber.*

That foul *defacer* of God's handiwork.
            Richard 3, iv. 4.
            Nor is there living
A man that more detests, more stirs against,
Both in his private conscience and his place,
Defacers of a public peace, than I do. *Henry* 8, v. 2.

DEFEAT.   *Failure ; frustration ; assault ; ruin.*

So may a thousand actions, once afoot,
End in one purpose, and be all well borne
Without *defeat.*   *Henry* 5, i. 2.
            No, not for a king,
Upon whose property and most dear life
A damn'd *defeat* was made.   *Hamlet,* ii. 2.   ✓

Their *defeat*
Does by their own insinuation grow. *Hamlet*, v. 2.

To Defeat. *To disappoint; to foil; to frustrate; to alter; to disguise; to destroy.*

They would have stol'n away; they would, Demetrius,
Thereby to have *defeated* you and me,
You of your wife, and me of my consent.
Midsummer-Night's Dream, iv. 1.

He pleaded still, not guilty, and alleg'd
Many sharp reasons to *defeat* the law.
Henry 8, ii. 1.

Therefore our sometime sister, now our queen,
Have we, as 'twere with a *defeated* joy,—
With one auspicious, and one dropping eye,
The equal scale weighing delight and dole,—
Taken to wife. *Hamlet*, i. 2.

Follow thou the wars; *defeat* thy favour with
a usurped beard. *Othello*, i. 3.

And his unkindness may *defeat* my life,
But never taint my love. *Ibid.* iv. 2.

Defeature. *Change of feature.*

Then is he the ground of my *defeatures.*
Comedy of Errors, ii. 1.

And careful hours with Time's *deformèd* hand
Have written strange *defeatures* in my face.
Ibid. v. 1.

Defect. *Deficiency; default.*

Being unprepar'd,
Our will became the servant to *defect.*
Macbeth, ii. 1.

Defence. *Skill in defence; fencing; policy; resistance.*

And by how much *defence* is better than no
skill, by so much is a horn more precious than to
want. *As you like it*, iii. 3.

And give you such a masterly report,
For art and exercise in your *defence. Hamlet*, iv. 7.

Now·is it manhood, wisdom, and *defence*,
To give the enemy way. *Henry* 6, P. 2, v. 2.

I would not have you, lord, forget yourself,
Nor tempt the danger of my true *defence.*
King John, iv. 3.

To Defend. *To forbid.*

For God *defend* the lute should be like the case!
Much Ado about Nothing, ii. 1.

Hath he soon majesty?—Isis else *defend*,
And serving you so long!
Antony and Cleopatra, iii. 3.

Defendant. *Defensive.*

To line and new repair our towns of war
With men of courage and with means *defendant.*
Henry 5, ii. 4.

Defensible. *Able to defend; defensive.*

Him did you leave, to abide a field
Where nothing but the sound of Hotspur's name
Did seem *defensible. Henry* 4, P. 2, ii. 3.

Defiance. *Refusal; denial.*

Take my *defiance;*
Die, perish! might but my bending down
Reprieve thee from thy fate, it should proceed.
Measure for Measure, iii. 1.

Definitive. *Firm; positive; determined.*

Never crave him; we are *definitive.*
Measure for Measure, v. 1.

Deformed. *Deforming; destructive.*

And careful hours with Time's *deformèd* hand
Have written strange *defeatures* in my face.
Comedy of Errors, v. 1.

Deftly. *Fitly; neatly; quickly; dexterously.*

Come, high or low;
Thyself and office *deftly* show. *Macbeth*, iv. 1.

Defunction. *Death.*

Nor did the French possess the Salique land
Until four hundred one and twenty years
After *defunction* of King Pharamond.
Henry 5, i. 2.

To Defy. *To disdain; to renounce; to reject.*

No, I *defy* all counsel, all redress.
King John, iii. 4.

All studies here I solemnly *defy*,
Save how to gall and pinch this Bolingbroke.
Henry 4, P. 1, i. 3.

Complexions that liked me, and breaths that I
defied not. *As you like it*, v. 4.

Not a whit, we *defy* augury: there's a special
providence in the fall of a sparrow. *Hamlet*, v. 2.

Degree. *Step.*

But when he once attains the upmost round,
He then unto the ladder turns his back,
Looks in the clouds, scorning the base *degrees*
By which he did ascend. *Julius Cæsar*, ii. 1.

DEITY. *Divineness; something more than human; ubiquity.*

Nor can there be that *deity* in my nature,
Of here and every where. *Twelfth-Night,* v. 1.

DEJECT. *Dejected; cast down.*

Reason and respect
Make livers pale, and lustihood *deject.*
Troilus and Cressida, ii. 2.
And I, of ladies most *deject* and wretched.
Hamlet, iii. 1.

To DEJECT. *To lay aside; to abate.*

Nor once *deject* the courage of our minds,
Because Cassandra's mad.
Troilus and Cressida, ii. 2.

DELATION. *Denotement; indication; sign.*

But in a man that's just
They are close *delations;* working from the heart,
That passion cannot rule. *Othello,* iii. 3.

To DELAY. *To lose; to neglect.*

And that you not *delay* the present, but,
Filling the air with swords advanc'd and darts,
We prove this very hour. *Coriolanus,* i. 6.

DELIBERATE. *Advised; wary; discreet; circumspect.*

O, these *deliberate* fools! when they do choose,
They have the wisdom by their wit to lose.
Merchant of Venice, ii. 8.

DELICATES. *Dainties; delicacies.*

All which secure and sweetly he enjoys,
Is far beyond a prince's *delicates. Henry* 6, P. 3, ii. 5.

DELIGHTED. *Delighting; delightful; pleasing; jocund.*

And, noble signior,
If virtue no *delighted* beauty lack,
Your son-in-law is far more fair than black.
Othello, i. 3.
Whom best I love I cross; to make my gift,
The more delay'd, *delighted. Cymbeline,* v. 4.
And the *delighted* spirit
To bathe in fiery floods, or to reside
In thrilling regions of thick-ribbèd ice.
Measure for Measure, iii. 1.

To DELIVER. *To make known; to report; to show; to speak.*

Deliver this with modesty to the queen.
Henry 8, ii. 2.

O that I serv'd that lady,
And might not be *deliver'd* to the world,
Till I had made mine own occasion mellow,
What my estate is! *Twelfth-Night,* i. 2.
All this can I truly *deliver. Hamlet,* v. 2.
The sorrow that *delivers* us thus chang'd
Makes you think so. *Coriolanus,* v. 3.
But, an't please you, *deliver. Ibid.* i. 1.

DELIVERANCE. *Delivery; utterance; report.*

You have it from his own *deliverance.*
All's well that ends well, ii. 4.

To DEMEAN. *To behave.*

But this I know,—they have *demean'd* themselves
Like men born to renown by life or death.
Henry 6, P. 3, i. 3.
Now, out of doubt Antipholus is mad,
Else would he never so *demean* himself.
Comedy of Errors, iv. 3.

DEMERIT. *Desert.*

Besides, if things go well,
Opinion, that so sticks on Marcius, shall
Of his *demerits* rob Cominius. *Coriolanus,* i. 1.
And my *demerits*
May speak, unbonneted, to as proud a fortune
As this that I have reach'd. *Othello,* i. 2.

DEMI-NATURED. *Homogeneous; partaking of the same nature.*

And to such wondrous doing brought his horse,
As he had been incorps'd and *demi-natur'd*
With the brave beast. *Hamlet,* iv. 7.

To DEMISE. *To bring; to grant; to confer upon.*

Tell me what state, what dignity, what honour,
Canst thou *demise* to any child of mine?
Richard 3, iv. 4.

To DEMURE. *To look with affected modesty.*

Your wife Octavia, with her modest eyes
And still conclusion, shall acquire no honour
Demuring upon me.
Antony and Cleopatra, iv. 15.

DEMURELY. *Solemnly; formally.*

Hark! the drums
Demurely wake the sleepers.
Antony and Cleopatra, iv. 9.

DENAY. *Denial.*

To her in haste ; give her this jewel ; say,
My love can give no place, bide no *denay.*
Twelfth-Night, ii. 4.

To DENAY. *To deny.*

If York have ill demean'd himself in France,
Then let him be *denay'd* the regentship.
Henry 6, P. 2, i. 3.

DENIER. *A very small French coin.*

My dukedom to a beggarly *denier,*
I do mistake my person all this while.
Richard 3, i. 2.
You will not pay for the glasses you have burst ?—
No, not a *denier. Taming of the Shrew,* Ind. sc. 1.

DENOTEMENT. *Observation ; notice.*

Our general's wife is now the general ;—I may
say so in this respect, for that he hath devoted and
given up himself to the contemplation, mark, and
denotement of her parts and graces. *Othello,* ii. 3.

To DENOUNCE. *To proclaim ; to declare
openly ; to pronounce.*

If not *denounc'd* against us, why should not we
Be there in person ? *Antony and Cleopatra,* iii. 7.
I will *denounce* a curse upon his head.
King John, iii. 1.

DENUNCIATION. *Declaration ; sanction.*

She is fast my wife,
Save that we do the *denunciation* lack
Of outward order. *Measure for Measure,* i. 2.

DEPART. *Departure ; death.*

At my *depart* I gave this unto Julia.
Two Gentlemen of Verona, v. 4.
I had in charge at my *depart* for France
To marry Princess Margaret for your grace.
Henry 6, P. 2, i. 1.
Tidings, as swiftly as the posts could run,
Were brought me of your loss and his *depart.*
Ibid. P. 3, ii. 1.

To DEPART. *To part ; to separate.*

Ere we *depart,* we'll share a bounteous time
In different pleasures. *Timon of Athens,* i. 1.

To DEPART WITH. *To part with ; to yield ;
to give up.*

Which we much rather had *depart withal,*
And have the money by our father lent,
Than Aquitain so gelded as it is.
Love's Labour's lost, ii. 1.

John, to stop Arthur's title in the whole,
Hath willingly *departed with* a part.
King John, ii. 1.

DEPARTING. *Separation.*

A deadly groan, like life and death's *departing.*
Henry 6, P. 3, ii. 6.

To DEPEND. *To impend; to continue to serve ;
to overhang.*

This day's black fate on more days doth *depend ;*
This but begins the woe others must end.
Romeo and Juliet, iii. 1.
We'll slip you for a season ; but our jealousy
Does yet *depend. Cymbeline,* iv. 3.
And the remainder, that shall still *depend,*
To be such men as may besort your age.
King Lear, i. 4.
Her andirons were two winking Cupids
Of silver, each on one foot standing, nicely
Depending on their brands. *Cymbeline,* ii. 4.

DEPENDENCY. *Reliance ; trust ; confidence.*

Let me report to him
Your sweet *dependency. Antony and Cleopatra,* v. 2.

To DEPOSE. *To examine ; to declare upon
oath.*

And formally, according to our law,
Depose him in the justice of his cause.
Richard 2, i. 3.
Then, seeing 'twas he that made you to *depose,*
Your oath, my lord, is vain and frivolous.
Henry 6, P. 3, i. 2.

DEPRAVATION. *Blame ; censure ; condemnation ; detraction.*

Do not give advantage
To stubborn critics,—apt, without a theme,
For *depravation,*—to square the general sex
By Cressid's rule. *Troilus and Cressida,* v. 2.

To DEPRIVE. *To set aside ; to depose ; to
disinherit.*

What if it tempt you toward the flood, my lord,
Or to the dreadful summit of the cliff
That beetles o'er his base into the sea,
And there assume some other horrible form,
Which might *deprive* your sovereignty of reason,
And draw you into madness ? *Hamlet,* i. 4.
Wherefore should I
Stand in the plague of custom, and permit
The curiosity of nations to *deprive* me,

N

For that I am some twelve or fourteen moonshines
Lag of a brother?   *King Lear*, i. 2.

DEPUTATION. *Authority; commission; delegation; deputy.*

Sometime, great Agamemnon,
Thy topless *deputation* he puts on.
                    Troilus and Cressida, i. 3.
Lent him our terror, drest him with our love;
And given his *deputation* all the organs
Of our own power.   *Measure for Measure*, i. 1.
Proceeded further; cut me off the heads
Of all the favourites, that the absent king
In *deputation* left behind him here
When he was personal in the Irish war.
                    Henry 4, P. 1, iv. 3.
He writes me here, that inward sickness,—
And that his friends by *deputation* could not
So soon be drawn.   *Ibid.* iv. 1.

To DERACINATE. *To eradicate; to extirpate; to uproot.*

While that the coulter rusts,
That should *deracinate* such savagery.
                          Henry 5, v. 2.
          Frights, changes, horrors,
Divert and crack, rend and *deracinate*
The unity and married calm of states
Quite from their fixure! *Troilus and Cressida*, i. 3.

DERIVATIVE. *An inheritance; something transmitted by descent.*

For honour,
'Tis a *derivative* from me to mine;
And only that I stand for.   *Winter's Tale*, iii. 2.

To DERIVE. *To acquire; to bring; to incur; to inherit; to descend from; to deduce.*

O, that estates, degrees, and offices,
Were not *deriv'd* corruptly!
                    Merchant of Venice, ii. 8.
Things which would *derive* me ill will to speak of.
                    All's well that ends well, v. 3.
What friend of mine
That had to him *deriv'd* your anger, did I
Continue in my liking?   *Henry* 8, ii. 4.
She *derives* her honesty, and achieves her goodness.
                    All's well that ends well, i. 1.
I am, my lord, a wretched Florentine,
Deriv'd from the ancient Capulet.   *Ibid.* v. 3.
I am, my lord, as well *deriv'd* as he.
                    Midsummer-Night's Dream, i. 1.
Derive this; come.   *Troilus and Cressida*, ii. 3.

DEROGATE. *Degenerate; degraded.*

Dry up in her the organs of increase;
And from her *derogate* body never spring
A babe to honour her!   *King Lear*, i. 4.

To DEROGATE. *To incur degradation; to degenerate.*

Is there no derogation in't?—
You cannot *derogate*, my lord.   *Cymbeline*, ii. 1.
You are a fool granted; therefore your issues,
being foolish, do not *derogate*.   *Ibid.* ii. 1.

DEROGATELY. *Disparagingly; with disrespect.*

More laugh'd at, that I should
Once name you *derogately*, when to sound your
          name
It not concern'd me. *Antony and Cleopatra*, ii. 2.

DEROGATION. *Degradation.*

Is it fit I went to look upon him? is there no
derogation in't?   *Cymbeline*, ii. 1.

DESCANT. *A discourse; a disquisition.*

And look you get a prayer-book in your hand,
And stand between two churchmen, good my lord;
For on that ground I'll make a holy *descant*.
                          Richard 3, iii. 7.

DESCENSION. *A descent.*

From a god to a bull? a heavy *descension*! it
was Jove's case.   *Henry* 4, P. 2, ii. 2.

DESCRY. *Discovery; view; display.*

How near's the other army?—
Near and on speedy foot; the main *descry*
Stands on the hourly thought.   *King Lear*, iv. 6.

DESERT. *Degree of merit; meritorious act; deserving.*

The base o' the mount
Is rank'd with all *deserts*, all kind of natures,
That labour on the bosom of this sphere
To propagate their states.   *Timon of Athens*, i. 1.
          And then myself, I chiefly,
That set thee on to this *desert*, am bound
To load thy merit richly.   *Cymbeline*, i. 5.

To DESERVE. *To earn.*

On, good Roderigo;—I'll *deserve* your pains.
                          Othello, i. 1.

Say not so, Agrippa :
If Cleopatra heard you, your reproof
Were well *deserv'd* of rashness.
Antony and Cleopatra, ii. 2.

DESERVED. *Deserving; meritorious.*

Now the good gods forbid
That our renownèd Rome, whose gratitude
Towards her *deservèd* children is enroll'd
In Jove's own book, like an unnatural dam
Should now eat up her own. *Coriolanus*, iii. 1.

To DESIGN. *To point out; to designate.*

Since we cannot atone you, we shall see
Justice *design* the victor's chivalry.
Richard 2, i. 1.

DESIGNMENT. *Intent; purpose.*

The desperate tempest hath so bang'd the Turks,
That their *designment* halts. *Othello*, ii. 1.
Serv'd his *designments* in mine own person.
Coriolanus, v. 6.

To DESIRE. *To put off; to defer; to summon.*

It shall be therefore bootless
That longer you *desire* the court. *Henry 8*, ii. 4.
Do my good morrow to them ; and anon
Desire them all to my pavilion. *Henry 5*, iv. 1.

DESPERATE. *Profound; bold; confident.*

This boy is forest-born,
And hath been tutor'd in the rudiments
Of many *desperate* studies by his uncle.
As you like it, v. 4.
Sir Paris, I will make a *desperate* tender
Of my child's love. *Romeo and Juliet*, iii. 4.

DESPISED. *Despicable; contemptible.*

Frighting her pale-fac'd villages with war
And ostentation of *despisèd* arms.
Richard 2, ii. 3.

DESPITE. *Defiance; anger; malignity.*

And, in *despite* of mirth, mean to be merry.
Comedy of Errors, iii. 1.
Thy intercepter, full of *despite*, bloody as the
hunter, attends thee at the orchard end.
Twelfth-Night, iii. 4.

DETECTED. *Suspected; accused.*

I never heard the absent duke much *detected* for
women. *Measure for Measure*, iii. 2.

DETERMINATE. *Intended; effectual; certain.*

My *determinate* voyage is mere extravagancy.
Twelfth-Night, ii. 1.
Wherein none can be so *determinate* as the re-
moving of Cassio. *Othello*, iv. 2.

To DETERMINATE. *To end; to terminate.*

The fly-slow hours shall not *determinate*
The dateless limit of thy dear exile.
Richard 2, i. 3.

DETERMINATION. *Inclining; party.*

Welcome, Sir Walter Blunt ; and would to God
You were of our *determination!*
Henry 4, P. 1, iv. 3.

To DETERMINE. *To destroy; to put an end
to; to come to an end.*

Now, where is he that will not stay so long
Till his friend sickness hath *determin'd* me ?
Henry 4, P. 2, iv. 4.
As it *determines*, so dissolve my life !
Antony and Cleopatra, iii. 13.
For myself, son,
I purpose not to wait on fortune till
These wars *determine*. *Coriolanus*, v. 3.

DEVICE. *Accusation; charge; invention; genius.*

He shows his reason for that ;—to have a dispatch of complaints, and to deliver us from *devices*
hereafter, which shall then have no power to stand
against us. *Measure for Measure*, iv. 4.
Yet he's gentle; never schooled and yet learned;
full of noble *device;* of all sorts enchantingly beloved. *As you like it*, i. 1.

To DEVISE. *To consider; to contrive.*

Devise but how you'll use him when he comes,
And let us two *devise* to bring him thither.
Merry Wives of Windsor, iv. 4.

DEVOTE. *Devoted; dedicated; given up to.*

Or so *devote* to Aristotle's ethics,
As Ovid be an outcast quite abjur'd.
Taming of the Shrew, i. 1.

DEWBERRY. *The dwarf mulberry, a species
of blackberry.*

Feed him with apricocks and *dewberries*.
Midsummer-Night's Dream, iii. 1.

DEXTERIOUSLY. *Dexterously.*
Can you do it?—*Dexteriously*, good madonna.
Twelfth-Night, i. 5.

DIAL. *A watch.*
And then he drew a *dial* from his poke.
As you like it, ii. 7.
Then my *dial* goes not true.
All's well that ends well, ii. 5.

TO DIALOGUE. *To talk; to converse with.*
How dost, fool?—
Dost *dialogue* with thy shadow?
Timon of Athens, ii. 2.

DICH. *Do't; may it do.*
Much good *dich* thy good heart, Apemantus!
Timon of Athens, i. 2.

TO DIE. *To swoon.*
Cleopatra, catching but the least noise of this,
dies instantly; I have seen her *die* twenty times
upon far poorer moment. *Antony and Cleop.* i. 2.

TO DIET. *To feed; to regale; to feed by rule.*
As if I lov'd my little should be *dieted*
In praises sauc'd with lies. *Coriolanus*, i. 9.
They must be *dieted* like mules,
And have their provender tied to their mouths.
Henry 6, P. 1, i. 2.
Thou art all the comfort
The gods will *diet* me with. *Cymbeline*, iii. 4.
Therefore I'll watch him
Till he be *dieted* to my request. *Coriolanus*, v. 1.

DIETER. *One who prescribes rules for diet.*
He cut our roots in characters;
And sauc'd our broths, as Juno had been sick,
And he her *dieter*. *Cymbeline*, iv. 2.

DIFFERENCE. *Dispute; quarrel; controversy.*
And now he feasts, mousing the flesh of men,
In undetermin'd *differences* of kings. *K. John*, ii. 1.
Or to the place of *difference* call the swords
Which must decide it. *Henry* 4, P. 2, iv. 1.
Are you acquainted with the *difference*
That holds this present question in the court?
Merchant of Venice, iv. 1.

DIFFERENT. *Unequal; disproportioned; unsuitable.*
The course of true love never did run smooth;
But either it was *different* in blood.
Midsummer-Night's Dream, i. 1.

DIFFERING. *Inconstant; wavering; fickle.*
Laying by
That nothing gift of *differing* multitudes.
Cymbeline, iii. 6.

DIFFIDENCE. *Suspicion; doubt.*
We have been guided by thee hitherto,
And of thy cunning had no *diffidence*.
Henry 6, P. 1, iii. 3.
Out on thee, rude man! thou dost shame thy mother,
And wound her honour with this *diffidence*.
King John, i. 1.

TO DIFFUSE. *To make uncouth and strange; to deform.*
If but as well I other accents borrow
That can my speech *diffuse*, my good intent
May carry through itself to that full issue
For which I raz'd my likeness. *King Lear*, i. 4.

DIFFUSED. *Wild; irregular; uncouth.*
Let them from forth a sawpit rush at once
With some *diffused* song.
Merry Wives of Windsor, iv. 4.
To swearing, and stern looks, *diffus'd* attire,
And every thing that seems unnatural.
Henry 5, v. 2.
Vouchsafe, *diffus'd* infection of a man.
Richard 3, i. 2.

TO DIGEST. *To brook; to endure.*
For it can never be
They will *digest* this harsh indignity.
Love's Labour's lost, v. 2.
But will the king
Digest this letter of the cardinal's? *Henry* 8, iii. 2.

TO DIGRESS. *To deviate; to swerve; to err; to transgress.*
Thy noble shape is but a form of wax,
Digressing from the valour of a man.
Romeo and Juliet, iii. 3.
Sufficeth, I am come to keep my word,
Though in some part enforced to *digress*.
Taming of the Shrew, iii. 2.
And thy abundant goodness shall excuse
This deadly blot in thy *digressing* son.
Richard 2, v. 3.

DIGRESSION. *Derogation; deviation.*
I will have that subject newly writ o'er, that I
may example my *digression* by some mighty precedent. *Love's Labour's lost*, i. 2.

To Dilate. *To relate.*

Do me the favour to *dilate* at full
What hath befall'n of them and thee till now.
Comedy of Errors, i. 1.
And found good means
To draw from her a prayer of earnest heart
That I would all my pilgrimage *dilate,*
Whereof by parcels she had something heard,
But not intentively. *Othello,* i. 3.

Dimension. *Proportion ; form.*

And in *dimension* and the shape of nature,
A gracious person. *Twelfth-Night,* i. 5.
A spirit I am indeed ;
But am in that *dimension* grossly clad,
Which from the womb I did participate.
Twelfth-Night, v. 1.

Diminutive. *Any thing small, or of little value.*

How the poor world is pestered with such water-
flies,—*diminutives* of nature !
Troilus and Cressida, v. 1.
Most monster-like, be shown
For poor'st *diminutives,* for doits.
Antony and Cleopatra, iv. 12.

Dint. *Influence ; force.*

O, now you weep ; and, I perceive, you feel
The *dint* of pity. *Julius Cæsar,* iii. 2.

Direction. *Judgment ; skill ; propensity ; inclination.*

Call for some men of sound *direction.*
Richard 3, v. 3.
And thus do we of wisdom and of reach,
With windlaces, and with assays of bias,
By indirections find *directions* out. *Hamlet,* ii. 1.

Directive. *Capable of direction ; manageable.*

Which entertain'd, limbs are his instruments,
In no less working than are swords and bows
Directive by the limbs. *Troilus and Cressida,* i. 3.

Disability. *Insufficiency.*

Leave off discourse of *disability.*
Two Gentlemen of Verona, ii. 4.

To Disable. *To impair ; to undervalue ; to disparage.*

'Tis not unknown to you, Antonio,

How much I have *disabled* mine estate.
Merchant of Venice, i. 1.
And yet to be afeard of my deserving
Were but a weak *disabling* of myself. *Ibid.* ii. 6.
If again, it was not well cut, he *disabled* my
judgment : this is called the Reply churlish.
As you like it, v. 4.
Fie, De-la-poole ! *disable* not thyself.
Henry 6, P. 1, v. 3.

To Disallow. *To reject ; to refuse to comply.*

What follows, if we *disallow* of this ?
King John, i. 1.

To Disanimate. *To depress ; to discourage ; to dishearten.*

The presence of a king engenders love
Amongst his subjects and his loyal friends,
As it *disanimates* his enemies. *Henry 6,* P. 1, iii. 1.

To Disannul. *To annul ; to nullify.*

Then Warwick *disannuls* great John of Gaunt,
Which did subdue the greatest part of Spain.
Henry 6, P. 3, iii. 3.
Were it not against our laws,
Against my crown, my oath, my dignity,—
Which prince, would they, may not *disannul,*—
My soul should sue as advocate for thee.
Comedy of Errors, i. 1.

Disappointed. *Unprepared.*

Cut off even in the blossoms of my sin,
Unhousel'd, *disappointed,* unanel'd. *Hamlet,* i. 5.

To Disaster. *To disfigure.*

To be called into a huge sphere, and not to be
seen to move in't, are the holes where eyes should
be, which pitifully *disaster* the cheeks.
Antony and Cleopatra, ii. 7.

To Disbench. *To drive from a seat ; to unseat.*

I hope my words *disbench'd* you not.
Coriolanus, ii. 2.

To Discandy. *To melt ; to dissolve.*

The hearts
That spaniel'd me at heels, to whom I gave
Their wishes, do *discandy,* melt their sweets
On blossoming Cæsar.
Antony and Cleopatra, iv. 12.

The next Cæsarion smite!
Till, by degrees, the memory of my womb,
Together with my brave Egyptians all,
By the *discandying* of this pelleted storm,
Lie graveless.　　*Antony and Cleopatra*, iii. 13.

To DISEASE.　*To strip; to undress.*

Therefore *disease* thee instantly, and change
garments with this gentleman. *Winter's Tale*, iv. 3.
I will *disease* me, and myself present
As I was sometime Milan.　　*Tempest*, v. 1.

DISCERNING.　*Judgment; discrimination; discernment.*

Either his notion weakens, or his *discernings*
Are lethargied—Ha! waking? 'tis not so.
　　King Lear, i. 4.

To DISCHARGE.　*To pay; to reimburse.*

Would we were all *discharg'd!*
　　Timon of Athens, ii. 2.
Besides, it should appear, that if he had
The present money to *discharge* the Jew,
He would not take it. *Merchant of Venice*, iii. 2.

To DISCIPLE.　*To train; to educate.*

He did look far
Into the service of the time, and was
Discipled of the bravest.
　　All's well that ends well, i. 2.

To DISCIPLINE.　*To chastise; to beat; to punish.*

Has he *disciplined* Aufidius soundly?
　　Coriolanus, ii. 1.

To DISCLAIM IN.　*To disclaim; to disown.*

You cowardly rascal, nature *disclaims in* thee.
　　King Lear, ii. 2.

DISCLOSE.　*Disclosure; opening.*

And I do doubt the hatch and the *disclose*
Will be some danger.　　*Hamlet*, iii. 1.

To DISCLOSE.　*To detect; to discern; to open; to hatch.*

How covert matters may be best *disclos'd*,
And open perils surest answered.
　　Julius Cæsar, iv. 1.
The canker galls the infants of the spring,
Too oft before their buttons be *disclos'd*.
　　Hamlet, i. 3.

Anon, as patient as the female dove,
When that her golden couplets are *disclos'd*,
His silence will sit drooping.　　*Hamlet*, v. 1.

DISCOMFIT.　*Defeat; rout; overthrow.*

But fly you must; uncurable *discomfit*
Reigns in the hearts of all our present parts.
　　Henry 6, P. 2, v. 2.

DISCOMFORT.　*Grief; sadness; sorrow.*

Discomfort guides my tongue,
And bids me speak of nothing but despair.
　　Richard 2, iii. 2.
So from that spring, whence comfort seem'd to come,
Discomfort swells.　　*Macbeth*, i. 2.
What mean you, sir, to give them this *discomfort?*
　　Antony and Cleopatra, iv. 2.
I am so much a fool, should I stay longer,
It would be my disgrace and your *discomfort*.
　　Macbeth, iv. 2.

To DISCOMFORT.　*To dishearten; to discourage; to make uneasy.*

His funerals shall not be in our camp,
Lest it *discomfort* us.　　*Julius Cæsar*, v. 3.
My lord, you do *discomfort* all the host.
　　Troilus and Cressida, v. 10.
Yet, though I distrust,
Discomfort you, my lord, it nothing must.
　　Hamlet, iii. 2.

DISCONTENT.　*A malcontent.*

To the ports
The *discontents* repair, and men's reports
Give him much wrong'd.
　　Antony and Cleopatra, i. 4.
To face the garment of rebellion
With some fine colour, that may please the eye
Of fickle changelings and poor *discontents*.
　　Henry 4, P. 1, v. 1.

DISCONTENTING.　*Discontented; displeased.*

Your *discontenting* father strive to qualify,
And bring him up to liking. *Winter's Tale*, iv. 3.

DISCOURSE.　*Understanding; capacity; reason; course.*

Sure, he that made us with such large *discourse*,
Looking before and after, gave us not
That capability and god-like reason
To fust in us unused.　　*Hamlet*, iv. 4.
A beast, that wants *discourse* of reason,
Would have mourn'd longer.　　*Ibid.* i. 2.

Of government the properties to unfold
Would seem in me to affect speech and *discourse*.
                                        Measure for Measure, i. 1.
Yet doth this accident and flood of fortune
So far exceed all instance, all *discourse*,
That I am ready to distrust mine eyes.
                                        Twelfth-Night, iv. 3.
If e'er my will did trespass 'gainst his love,
Either in *discourse* of thought or actual deed,
Comfort forswear me!   *Othello*, iv. 2.

TO DISCOURSE. *To utter; to relate.*

Govern these ventages with your finger and
thumb, give it breath with your mouth, and it will
discourse most eloquent music.   *Hamlet*, iii. 2.
The manner of their taking may appear
At large *discoursèd* in this paper here.
                                        Richard 2, v. 6.
Go with us into the abbey here,
And hear at large *discoursèd* all our fortunes.
                                        Comedy of Errors, v. 1.

DISCOURSIVE. *Suggesting; insinuating.*

But I can tell, that in each grace of these
There lurks a still and dumb-*discoursive* devil
That tempts most cunningly.
                                        Troilus and Cressida, iv. 4.

TO DISCOVER. *To observe; to examine; to
disclose; to make known.*

Thou hast painfully *discover'd :* are his files
As full as thy report?   *Timon of Athens*, v. 2.
    It were good that Benedick knew of it by some
other, if she will not *discover* it.
                                        Much Ado about Nothing, ii. 3.
    If ever he return, and I can speak to him, I will
open my lips in vain, or *discover* his government.
                                        Measure for Measure, iii. 1.

DISCOVERER. *A scout; a spy.*

Here stand, my lords; and send *discoverers* forth
To know the numbers of our enemies.
                                        Henry 4, P. 2, iv. 1.

DISCOVERY. *Disclosure; exposure; observation.*

Why, 'tis an office of *discovery*, love,
And I should be obscur'd. *Merchant of Venice*, ii. 5.
For myself, I'll put my fortunes to your service,
Which are here by this *discovery* lost.
                                        Winter's Tale, i. 2.
    I will tell you why; so shall my anticipation
prevent your *discovery*, and your secrecy to the
king and queen moult no feather.   *Hamlet*, ii. 2.

Here is the guess of their true strength and forces
By diligent *discovery*.   *King Lear*, v. 1.

DISCREDIT. *Offence; misdeed.*

But 'tis all one to me; for had I been the finder-
out of this secret, it would not have relished among
my other *discredits*.   *Winter's Tale*, v. 2.

TO DISCREDIT. *To shame; to bring disgrace
upon.*

You had then left unseen a wonderful piece of
work; which not to have been blessed withal would
have *discredited* your travel.
                                        Antony and Cleopatra, i. 2.

TO DISDAIN. *To be scornful.*

Yet nature might have made me as these are,
Therefore I will not *disdain*. *Winter's Tale*, iv. 3.

DISDAINED. *Disdainful; scornful.*

Revenge the jeering and *disdain'd* contempt
Of this proud king.   *Henry 4*, P. 1, i. 3.

TO DISEASE. *To disturb; to trouble.*

Let her alone, lady : as she is now, she will but
disease our better mirth.   *Coriolanus*, i. 3.

DISEASES. *Wants; necessities.*

Five days we do allot thee, for provision
To shield thee from *diseases* of the world;
And, on the sixth, to turn thy hated back
Upon our kingdom.   *King Lear*, i. 1.

DISEDGED. *Cloyed; satiated.*

                    And I grieve myself
To think, when thou shalt be *disedg'd* by her
That now thou tir'st on, how thy memory
Will be pang'd by me.   *Cymbeline*, iii. 4.

TO DISFURNISH. *To strip; to deprive; to
disqualify.*

My riches are these poor habiliments,
Of which if you should here *disfurnish* me,
You take the sum and substance that I have.
                                        Two Gentlemen of Verona, iv. 1.
    What a wicked beast was I to *disfurnish* myself
against such a good time, when I might ha' shown
myself honourable !   *Timon of Athens*, iii. 2.

DISGRACE. *Offence; complaint; grievance.*

Tell thou thy earl his divination lies,

And I will take it as a sweet *disgrace*,
And make thee rich for doing me such wrong.
Henry 4, P. 2, i. 1.
Well, I'll hear it, sir: yet you must not think
to fob-off our *disgrace* with a tale. *Coriolanus,* i. 1.

DISGRACIOUS. *Unpleasing.*
I do suspect I have done some offence
That seems *disgracious* in the city's eye.
Richard 3, iii. 7.

DISGUISE. *Debauch; revel.*
The wild *disguise* hath almost
Antick'd us all. *Antony and Cleopatra,* ii. 7.

TO DISHABIT. *To displace; to dislodge.*
And, but for our approach, those sleeping stones
By this time from their fixèd beds of lime
Had been *dishabited.* *King John,* ii. 1.

DISHONESTLY. *Dishonourably; reproachfully.*
He said he was gentle, but unfortunate;
Dishonestly afflicted, but yet honest.
Cymbeline, iv. 2.

DISJOINT. *Divided; disjointed.*
Or thinking by our late dear brother's death
Our state to be *disjoint* and out of frame.
Hamlet, i. 2.

TO DISJOINT. *To fall to pieces.*
But let the frame of things *disjoint,*
Ere we will eat our meal in fear, and sleep
In the affliction of these terrible dreams
That shake us nightly. *Macbeth,* iii. 2.

DISJUNCTION. *Separation.*
From the whom, I see,
There's no *disjunction* to be made, but by,
As heavens forfend! your ruin.
Winter's Tale, iv. 3.

TO DISLIKE. *To displease.*
Neither, fair saint, if either thee *dislike.*
Romeo and Juliet, ii. 2.
I pray you, call them in.—
I'll do't; but it *dislikes* me. *Othello,* ii. 3.

TO DISLIKEN. *To disguise; to conceal.*
Dismantle you; and, as you can, *disliken*
The truth of your own seeming.
Winter's Tale, iv. 3.

TO DISLIMN. *To efface; to obliterate.*
That which is now a horse, even with a thought
The rack *dislimns,* and makes it indistinct,
As water is in water. *Antony and Cleopatra,* iv. 14.

TO DISLODGE. *To retire; to depart.*
Good news, good news ;—the ladies have prevail'd,
The Volscians are *dislodg'd,* and Marcius gone.
Coriolanus, v. 4.

DISLOYAL. *Faithless; unchaste; perfidious; treacherous.*
And, circumstances shortened, the lady is *disloyal.*
Much Ado about Nothing, iii. 2.
For such things in a false *disloyal* knave
Are tricks of custom. *Othello,* iii. 3.

DISLOYALTY. *Want of fidelity in love; dishonour.*
Look sweet, speak fair, become *disloyalty.*
Comedy of Errors, iii. 1.
In the mean time I will so fashion the matter
that Hero shall be absent, and there shall appear
such seeming truth of her *disloyalty,* that jealousy
shall be called assurance, and all the preparation
overthrown. *Much Ado about Nothing,* ii. 2.

TO DISMANTLE. *To strip off; to undress; to divest.*
This is most strange,
That she, who even but now was your best object,
Most best, most dearest, should in this trice of time
Commit a thing so monstrous, to *dismantle*
So many folds of favour. *King Lear,* i. 1.
Dismantle you; and, as you can, disliken
The truth of your own seeming.
Winter's Tale, iv. 3.

TO DISMAY. *To be discouraged.*
Dismay not, princes, at this accident,
Nor grieve that Rouen is so recoverèd.
Henry 6, P. 1, iii. 3.

DISME. *Ten.*
Since the first sword was drawn about the question,
Every tithe soul, 'mongst many thousand *dismes,*
Hath been as dear as Helen.
Troilus and Cressida, ii. 2.

TO DISMISS. *To pardon; to remit; to leave unpunished.*
For then I pity those I do not know,
Which a *dismiss'd* offence would after gall.
Measure for Measure, ii. 2.

DISMISSION. *Dismissal.*

You must not stay here longer,—your *dismission*
Is come from Cæsar. *Antony and Cleopatra*, i. 1.

DISNATURED. *Unnatural.*

If she must teem,
Create her child of spleen ; that it may live,
And be a thwart *disnatur'd* torment to her !
King Lear, i. 4.

DISORBED. *Unsphered.*

And fly like chidden Mercury from Jove,
Or like a star *disorb'd*. *Troilus and Cressida*, ii. 2.

DISORDER. *Misconduct; irregularity.*

I set him there, sir : but his own *disorders*
Deserv'd much less advancement. *King Lear*, ii. 4.

My lady bade me tell you, that, though she
harbours you as her kinsman, she's nothing allied
to your *disorders*. *Twelfth-Night*, ii. 3.

DISORDERED. *Disorderly; irregular; discordant.*

Here do you keep a hundred knights and squires ;
Men so *disorder'd*, so debauch'd, and bold,
That this our court, infected by their manners,
Shows like a riotous inn. *King Lear*, i. 4.

He that hath suffer'd this *disorder'd* spring
Hath now himself met with the fall of leaf.
Richard 2, iii. 4.

And here have I the daintiness of ear
To check time broke in a *disorder'd* string.
Ibid. v. 5.

DISPARAGEMENT. *Offence; insult; indignity.*

I would not for the wealth of all the town,
Here in my house, do him *disparagement*.
Romeo and Juliet, i. 5.

To DISPATCH. *To come to an agreement.*

They have *dispatch'd* with Pompey, he is gone ;
The other three are sealing.
Antony and Cleopatra, iii. 2.

To DISPENSE WITH. *To forgive; to excuse; to make use of; to employ; to obtain a dispensation from.*

What sin you do to save a brother's life,
Nature *dispenses with* the deed so far
That it becomes a virtue. .
Measure for Measure, iii. 1.

Unfeeling fools can *with* such wrongs *dispense*.
Comedy of Errors, ii. 1.

Might you *dispense with* your leisure, I would
by and by have some speech with you.
Measure for Measure, iii. 1.

Hast thou not sworn allegiance unto me ?
Canst thou *dispense with* heaven for such an oath ?
Henry 6, P. 2, v. 1.

DISPITEOUS. *Pitiless; cruel; unfeeling.*

How now, foolish rheum !
Turning *dispiteous* torture out of door !
King John, iv. 1.

To DISPLANT. *To unpeople.*

Unless philosophy can make a Juliet,
Displant a town, reverse a prince's doom,
It helps not, it prevails not.
Romeo and Juliet, iii. 3.

To DISPLAY. *To talk without restraint; to rail.*

Being the very fellow which of late
Display'd so saucily against your highness.
King Lear, ii. 4.

DISPLEASURE. *Loss of favour; disgrace.*

Good morrow, good lieutenant : I am sorry
For your *displeasure;* but all will sure be well.
Othello, iii. 1.

To DISPONGE. *To discharge; to pour down.*

O sovereign mistress of true melancholy,
The poisonous damp of night *disponge* upon me,
That life, a very rebel to my will,
May hang no longer on me.
Antony and Cleopatra, iv. 9.

DISPORT. *Amusement; pleasure.*

When my *disports* corrupt and taint my business,
Let housewives make a skillet of my helm.
Othello, i. 3.

To DISPORT. *To divert; to amuse.*

We make ourselves fools, to *disport* ourselves.
Timon of Athens, i. 2.

DISPOSE. *Disposal; disposition; temper.*

All that is mine I leave at thy *dispose*,
My goods, my lands, my reputation.
Two Gentlemen of Verona, ii. 7.

o

And show thee all the treasure we have got,
Which, with ourselves, shall rest at thy *dispose.*
Two Gentlemen of Verona, iv. 1.
Needs must you lay your heart at his *dispose*
Against whose fury and unmatchèd force
The awless lion could not wage the fight.
King John, i. 1.
He hath a person, and a smooth *dispose*
To be suspected ; fram'd to make women false.
Othello, i. 3.

To DISPOSE. *To make terms ; to bargain.*

For when she saw—
Which never shall be found—you did suspect
She had *dispos'd* with Cæsar, and that your rage
Would not be purg'd, she sent you word she was
dead. *Antony and Cleopatra,* iv. 14.

DISPOSED. *Inclined to loose mirth ; bestowed.*

Come to our pavilion : Boyet is *dispos'd.*
Love's Labour's lost, ii. 1.
When these so noble benefits shall prove
Not well *dispos'd,* the mind growing once corrupt,
They turn to vicious forms, ten times more ugly
Than ever they were fair. *Henry* 8, i. 2.

DISPOSITION. *Arrangement ; settlement.*

Most humbly, therefore, bending to your state,
I crave fit *disposition* for my wife. *Othello,* i. 3.

To DISPROPERTY. *To annul ; to abolish ; to deprive of.*

That, to's power, he would
Have made them mules, silenc'd their pleaders, and
Dispropertied their freedoms. *Coriolanus,* ii. 1.

DISPROPORTIONED. *Vague ; uncertain ; inconsistent.*

Indeed, they are *disproportion'd.* *Othello,* i. 3.

To DISPURSE. *To disburse.*

Many a pound of mine own proper store,
Because I would not tax the needy commons,
Have I *dispursèd* to the garrisons,
And never ask'd for restitution.
Henry 6, P. 2, iii. 1.

DISPUTABLE. *Disputatious ; fond of disputation.*

And I have been all this day to avoid him. He
is too *disputable* for my company.
As you like it, ii. 5.

To DISPUTE. *To reason upon ; to debate ; to discuss.*

Can he speak ? hear ?
Know man from man ? *dispute* his own estate ?
Winter's Tale, iv. 3.
Let me *dispute* with thee of thy estate.
Romeo and Juliet, iii. 3.
Thou *disputest* like an infant : go, whip thy gig.
Love's Labour's lost, v. 1.
Dispute it like a man. *Macbeth,* iv. 3.

To DISQUANTITY. *To lessen ; to diminish.*

Be, then, desir'd
By her, that else will take the thing she begs,
A little to *disquantity* your train. *King Lear,* i. 4.

To DISROBE. *To strip ; to deprive ; to lay aside ; to discard.*

O, well did he become that lion's robe
That did *disrobe* the lion of that robe !
King John, ii. 1.
I'll *disrobe* me
Of these Italian weeds, and suit myself
As does a Briton peasant. *Cymbeline,* v. 1.

To DISSEMBLE. *To conceal ; to disguise.*

Dissemble not your hatred, swear your love.
Richard 3, ii. 1.
Well, I'll put it on, and I will *dissemble* myself in't.
Twelfth-Night, iv. 2.

DISSEMBLING. *Irregular ; inconsistent ; partial.*

Cheated of feature by *dissembling* nature.
Richard 3, i. 1.

DISSOLUTION. *Confusion ; ruin.*

Reproach and *dissolution* hangeth over him.
Richard 2, ii. 1.

To DISSOLVE. *To remove ; to put an end to ; to destroy.*

I, after him, do after him wish too,
Since I nor wax nor honey can bring home,
I quickly were *dissolvèd* from my hive,
To give some labourers room.
All's well that ends well, i. 2.
Seek, seek for him ;
Lest his ungovern'd rage *dissolve* the life
That wants the means to lead it. *King Lear,* iv. 4.

To DISTAIN. *To stain; to impair; to lessen.*

You having lands, and bless'd with beauteous wives,
They would distrain the one, *distain* the other.
Richard 3, v. 3.

The worthiness of praise *distains* his worth,
If that the prais'd himself bring the praise forth.
Troilus and Cressida, i. 3.

To DISTASTE. *To taint; to be distasteful; to dislike; to embitter; to disrelish.*

Her brain-sick raptures
Cannot *distaste* the goodness of a quarrel
Which hath our several honours all engag'd
To make it gracious. *Troilus and Cressida*, ii. 2.

Dangerous conceits are, in their nature, poisons,
Which at the first are scarce found to *distaste*.
Othello, iii. 3.

If he *distaste* it, let him to my sister,
Whose mind and mine, I know, in that are one.
King Lear, i. 3.

And scants us with a single famish'd kiss
Distasted with the salt of broken tears.
Troilus and Cressida, iv. 4.

DISTEMPER. *Intemperance; disorder; disquiet; perturbation of mind.*

If little faults, proceeding on *distemper*,
Shall not be wink'd at, how shall we stretch our eye
When capital crimes, chew'd, swallow'd, and digested,
Appear before us? *Henry* 5, ii. 2.

Good my lord, what is your cause of *distemper*?
Hamlet, iii. 2.

To DISTEMPER. *To disturb; to excite; to disorder.*

Once more to-day well met, *distemper'd* lords!
King John, iv. 3.

Young son, it argues a *distemper'd* head
So soon to bid good morrow to thy bed.
Romeo and Juliet, ii. 3.

He cannot buckle his *distemper'd* course
Within the belt of rule. *Macbeth*, v. 2.

Never till this
Saw I him touch'd with anger so *distemper'd*.
Tempest, iv. 1.

DISTEMPERATURE. *Disorder; perturbation of mind; discord; strife.*

And at her heels a huge infectious troop
Of pale *distemperatures* and foes to life.
Comedy of Errors, v. 1.

At your birth,
Our grandam earth, having this *distemperature*,
In passion shook. *Henry* 4, P. 1, iii. 1.

Therefore thy earliness doth me assure
Thou art up-rous'd by some *distemperature*.
Romeo and Juliet, ii. 3.

And thorough this *distemperature* we see
The seasons alter. *Midsummer-Night's Dream*, ii. 1.

DISTILMENT. *Distillation; extract.*

And in the porches of mine ears did pour
The leperous *distilment*. *Hamlet*, i. 5.

DISTINCTION. *Discrimination; difference; variety.*

But, in the wind and tempest of her frown,
Distinction, with a broad and powerful fan,
Puffing at all, winnows the light away.
Troilus and Cressida, i. 3.

And I do fear besides,
That I shall lose *distinction* in my joys. *Ibid.* iii. 2.

Thou hast, Ventidius, that
Without the which a soldier, and his sword,
Grants scarce *distinction*.
Antony and Cleopatra, iii. 1.

This fierce abridgment
Hath to it circumstantial branches, which
Distinction should be rich in. *Cymbeline*, v. 5.

DISTINGUISHMENT. *Distinction; difference.*

And mannerly *distinguishment* leave out
Between the prince and beggar. *Winter's Tale*, ii. 1.

DISTRACT. *Distracted; mad.*

They say, poor gentleman, he's much *distract*.
Twelfth-Night, v. 1.

She is importunate, indeed *distract*.
Hamlet, iv. 5.

With this she fell *distract*,
And, her attendants absent, swallow'd fire.
Julius Cæsar, iv. 3.

To DISTRACT. *To disperse; to divide; to vary; to diversify.*

But to the brightest beams
Distracted clouds give way; so stand thou forth,
The time is fair again.
All's well that ends well, v. 3.

Most worthy sir, you therein throw away
The absolute soldiership you have by land;
Distract your army, which doth most consist
Of war-mark'd footmen.
Antony and Cleopatra, iii. 7.

DISTRACTED. 100 DO A COURTESY.

Supply it with one gender of herbs, or *distract* it with many. *Othello*, i. 3.

DISTRACTED. *Wavering; uncertain; giddy.*
He's lov'd of the *distracted* multitude,
Who like not in their judgment, but their eyes.
Hamlet, iv. 3.

DISTRACTIONS. *Detachments; separate bodies.*
While he was yet in Rome,
His power went out in such *distractions* as
Beguil'd all spies. *Antony and Cleopatra*, iii. 7.

DISTRAUGHT. *Distracted; mad.*
O, if I wake, shall I not be *distraught*,
Environèd with all these hideous fears?
Romeo and Juliet, iv. 3.

To DISTRUST. *To fear for; to be alarmed.*
Yet, though I *distrust*,
Discomfort you, my lord, it nothing must.
Hamlet, iii. 2.

DISVALUED. *Reduced in value; depreciated.*
But in chief
For that her reputation was *disvalu'd*
In levity. *Measure for Measure*, v. 1.

To DISVOUCH. *To contradict; to discredit.*
Every letter he hath writ hath *disvouched* other.
Measure for Measure, iv. 4.

DIVIDABLE. *Divided; remote; distant.*
Peaceful commerce from *dividable* shores.
Troilus and Cressida, i. 3.

DIVIDANT. *Distinct; different; separate.*
Twinn'd brothers of one womb,—
Whose procreation, residence, and birth,
Scarce is *dividant*,—touch them with several fortunes;
The greater scorns the lesser.
Timon of Athens, iv. 3.

To DIVIDE. *To disunite; to quarrel; to break friendship.*
O, I could *divide* myself, and go to buffets.
Henry 4, P. 1, ii. 2.
Love cools, friendship falls off, brothers *divide*.
King Lear, i. 2.

DIVIDED. *Distinct; separate; independent; double.*
For we to-morrow hold *divided* councils,
Wherein thyself shalt highly be employ'd.
Richard 3, iii. 1.

DIVINENESS. *Superlative excellence; perfection.*
Behold *divineness* no elder than a boy.
Cymbeline, iii. 6.

DIVISION. *Variation of melody.*
Thy tongue
Makes Welsh as sweet as ditties highly penn'd,
Sung by a fair queen in a summer's bower,
With ravishing *division*, to her lute.
Henry 4, P. 1, iii. 1.
Some say the lark makes sweet *division*.
Romeo and Juliet, iii. 5.

DIVORCEMENT. *Divorce; separation.*
Or that I do not yet, and ever did,
And ever will,—though he do shake me off
To beggarly *divorcement*,—love him dearly,
Comfort forswear me! *Othello*, iv. 2.

To DIVULGE. *To publish; to proclaim; to report.*
A strumpet's boldness, a *divulgèd* shame.
All's well that ends well, ii. 1.
I will *divulge* Page himself for a secure and wilful Actæon. *Merry Wives of Windsor*, iii. 2.
Ay, Greek; and that shall be *divulgèd* well
In characters as red as Mars his heart
Inflam'd with Venus. *Troilus and Cressida*, v. 2.
In voices well *divulg'd*, free, learn'd, and valiant.
Twelfth-Night, i. 5.

To DIZZY. *To confuse; to perplex; to stun.*
To divide him inventorially would *dizzy* the arithmetic of memory. *Hamlet*, v. 2.
Not the dreadful spout,
Constring'd in mass by the almighty sun,
Shall *dizzy* with more clamour Neptune's ear
In his descent, than shall my prompted sword
Falling on Diomed. *Troilus and Cressida*, v. 2.

To DO A COURTESY. *To bend.*
Though well we may not pass upon his life
Without the form of justice, yet our power
Shall *do a courtesy* to our wrath, which men
May blame, but not control. *King Lear*, iii. 7.

To Do JUSTICE. To Do RIGHT. *To pledge in drinking.*

Do me right,
And dub me knight : Samingo.
Why, now you have *done me right.*
                           Henry 4, P. 2, v. 3.
To the health of our general !—
I am for it, lieutenant; and I'll *do you justice.*
                           Othello, ii. 3.

To Do TO DEATH. *To kill; to put to death.*

Unless false Suffolk straight be *done to death,*
Or banishèd fair England's territories,
They will by violence tear him from your palace,
And torture him with grievous lingering death.
                           Henry 6, P. 2, iii. 2.

To Do WITHAL. *To prevent; to hinder; to help.*

(See Gifford's *Ben Jonson,* vol. iii. p. 470.)
How honourable ladies sought my love,
Which I denying, they fell sick and died.—
I could not *do withal.* *Merchant of Venice,* iii. 4.

DOCTRINE. *Skill; knowledge; learning.*

When the schools,
Embowell'd of their *doctrine,* have left off
The danger to itself. *All's well that ends well,* i. 3.

DOCUMENT. *Precept.*

A *document* in madness;— thoughts and remembrance fitted. *Hamlet,* iv. 5.

To DODGE. *To lurch; to shuffle.*

Now I must
To the young man send humble treaties, *dodge*
And palter in the shifts of lowness.
                           Antony and Cleopatra, iii. 11.

To DOFF. *To put aside; to get rid of; to remove; to take off.*

Thou wear a lion's hide ! *doff* it for shame,
And hang a calf's-skin on those recreant limbs.
                           King John, iii. 1.
Your eye in Scotland
Would create soldiers, make our women fight,
To *doff* their dire distresses. *Macbeth,* iv. 3.

DOIT. *A small coin.*

Most monster-like, be shown
For poor'st diminutives, for *doits.*
                           Antony and Cleopatra, iv. 12.

Supply your present wants, and take no *doit*
Of usance for my moneys; and you'll not hear me.
                           Merchant of Venice, i. 3.
When they will not give a *doit* to relieve a
lame beggar, they will lay out ten to see a dead
Indian. *Tempest,* ii. 2.

DOLE. *Distribution; lamentation; sorrow.*

I consider
What great creation and what *dole* of honour
Flies where you bid it.
                           All's well that ends well, ii. 3.
It was your presurmise,
That, in the *dole* of blows, your son might drop.
                           Henry 4, P. 2, i. 1.
The poor old man, their father, making such
pitiful *dole* over them. *As you like it,* i. 2.
In equal scale weighing delight and *dole.*
                           Hamlet, i. 2.

DOLOUR. *Sorrow; grief.*

As if it felt with Scotland, and yell'd out
Like syllable of *dolour.* *Macbeth,* iv. 3.
How poor Andromache shrills her *dolours* forth !
                           Troilus and Cressida, v. 3.

To DON. *To put on.*

I did not think
This amorous surfeiter would have *donn'd* his helm
For such a petty war.
                           Antony and Cleopatra, ii. 1.

DOOMSDAY. *Day of death; day of execution.*

Doomsday is near; die all, die merrily.
                           Henry 4, P. 1, iv. 1.
I·married them; and their stol'n marriage-day
Was Tybalt's *doomsday.* *Romeo and Juliet,* v. 3.
Why, then, All-Souls' day is my body's *doomsday.*
                           Richard 3, v. 1.

DOTAGE. *Fondness.*

Nay, but this *dotage* of our general's
O'erflows the measure. *Antony and Cleopatra,* i. 1.
I would she had bestowed this *dotage* on me.
                           Much Ado about Nothing, ii. 3.
Her *dotage* now I do begin to pity.
                           Midsummer-Night's Dream, iv. 1.

DOTANT. *A dotard.*

Can you think to front his revenges with the
easy groans of old women, the virginal palms of
your daughters, or with the palsied intercession of
such a decayed *dotant* as you seem to be ?
                           Coriolanus, v. 2.

DOUBLE. *Divided; forked; false; deceitful.*

You spotted snakes with *double* tongue.
Midsummer-Night's Dream, ii. 2.
Swear by your *double* self,
And there's an oath of credit.
Merchant of Venice, v. 1.
An adder did it; for with *doubler* tongue
Than thine, thou serpent, never adder stung.
Midsummer-Night's Dream, iii. 2.

DOVE. *A pigeon.*

I have here a dish of *doves* that I would bestow
upon your worship. *Merchant of Venice*, ii. 2.

DOWLAS. *A coarse kind of linen.*

Dowlas, filthy *dowlas*. *Henry 4*, P. 1, iii. 3.

DOWLE. *A feather.*

As diminish one *dowle* that's in my plume.
Tempest, iii. 3.

DOWN-GYVED. *Hanging down loose, like fetters.*

His stockings foul'd,
Ungarter'd, and *down-gyvèd* to his ancle.
Hamlet, ii. 1.

DRAB. *A slut; a jade; a prostitute.*

Follow the knave; and take this *drab* away.
Henry 6, P. 2, ii. 1.
Finger of birth-strangled babe
Ditch-deliver'd by a *drab*. *Macbeth*, iv. 1.
With die and *drab* I purchased this caparison.
Winter's Tale, iv. 2.

DRACHMA. *An old Greek coin.*

See here these movers that do prize their hours
At a crack'd *drachma!* *Coriolanus*, i. 5.
To every Roman citizen he gives,
To every several man, seventy-five *drachmas*.
Julius Cæsar, iii. 2.

DRAFF. *Dregs; refuse.*

'Tis old, but true,—Still swine eat all the *draff*.
Merry Wives of Windsor, iv. 2.
That you would think that I had a hundred and
fifty tattered prodigals lately come from swine-keep-
ing, from eating *draff* and husks.
Henry 4, P. 1, iv. 2.

DRAGONISH. *Like a dragon.*

Sometimes we see a cloud that's *dragonish*.
Antony and Cleopatra, iv. 14.

DRAM. *Draught; potion.*

And at first meeting lov'd;
Continu'd so, until we thought he died.—
By the queen's *dram* she swallow'd.
Cymbeline, v. 5.
I could do this, and that with no rash potion,
But with a lingering *dram*, that should not work
Maliciously like poison. *Winter's Tale*, i. 2.
I'll send to one in Mantua,
Shall give him such an unaccustom'd *dram*,
That he shall soon keep Tybalt company.
Romeo and Juliet, iii. 5.

DRAVE. *Drove.*

That I *drave* my suitor from his mad humour of
love to a living humour of madness.
As you like it, iii. 2.
Made emulous missions 'mongst the gods themselves,
And *drave* great Mars to faction.
Troilus and Cressida, iii. 3.

To DRAW. *To receive in payment; to collect; to assemble; to suck; to withdraw.*

If every ducat in six thousand ducats
Were in six parts, and every part a ducat,
I would not *draw* them. *Merchant of Venice*, iv. 1.
And that his friends by deputation could not
So soon be *drawn*. *Henry 4*, P. 1, iv. 1.
And presently, when you have *drawn* your number,
Repair to the Capitol. *Coriolanus*, ii. 3.
Well *drawn*, monster, in good sooth.
Tempest, ii. 2.
Go, wash thy face, and *draw* thy action.
Henry 4, P. 2, ii. 1.

DRAWN. *Hunted.*

Nor no more truth in thee than in a *drawn* fox.
Henry 4, P. 1, iii. 3.

To DRESS. *To trim; to cultivate; to address; to prepare.*

Thou old Adam's likeness, set to *dress* this garden,
How dares thy harsh-rude tongue sound these un-
pleasing news? *Richard 2*, iii. 4.
Besides, they are our outward consciences,
And preachers to us all; admonishing
That we should *dress* us fairly for our end.
Henry 5, iv. 1.
Now play me Nestor; hem, and stroke thy beard,
As he being *drest* to some oration.
Troilus and Cressida, i. 3.

DRESSINGS. *Ornaments; insignia; official decorations.*

Even so may Angelo, in all his *dressings*, characts,
titles, forms,
Be an arch-villain. *Measure for Measure,* v. 1.

DRIBBLING. *Weak; unsteady.*

Believe not that the *dribbling* dart of love
Can pierce a cómplete bosom.
Measure for Measure, i. 3.

DRIVEL. *A fool; an idiot; a driveller.*

Like a mad lad, pare thy nails, dad;
Adieu, goodman *drivel.* *Twelfth-Night,* iv. 2.

DROLLERY. *A show.*

A living *drollery.* Now I will believe
That there are unicorns. *Tempest,* iii. 3.

DROOPING. *Declining; sinking.*

I, from the orient to the *drooping* west,
Making the wind my post-horse, still unfold
The acts commencèd on this ball of earth.
Henry 4, P. 2, Induction.

DROPLET. *A tear.*

Though thou abhorr'dst in us our human griefs,
Scorn'dst our brain's flow, and those our *droplets*
which
From niggard nature fall, yet rich conceit
Taught thee to make vast Neptune weep for aye
On thy low grave, on faults forgiven.
Timon of Athens, v. 4.

To DROWSE. *To grow sleepy; to look dull and unconcerned.*

Good things of day begin to droop and *drowse.*
Macbeth, iii. 2.
But rather *drows'd,* and hung their eyelids down,
Slept in his face, and render'd such aspéct
As cloudy men use to their adversaries.
Henry 4, P. 1, iii. 2.

DRUG. *A drudge; an inferior servant.*

To such as may the passive *drugs* of it
Freely command. *Timon of Athens,* iv. 3.

To DRUMBLE. *To be slow or awkward.*

Look, how you *drumble!* carry them to the
laundress in Datchet-mead.
Merry Wives of Windsor, iii. 3.

DUCAT. *A coin.*

How now! a rat? Dead, for a *ducat,* dead!
Hamlet, iii. 4.
I cannot instantly raise up the gross
Of full three thousand *ducats.*
Merchant of Venice, i. 3.

To DUCK. *To bow low; to cringe.*

The learned pate *ducks* to the golden fool.
Timon of Athens, iv. 3.
Smile in men's faces, smooth, deceive, and cog,
Duck with French nods and apish courtesy.
Richard 3, i. 3.
These kind of knaves I know, which in this plain-
ness
Harbour more craft and more corrupter ends
Than twenty silly *ducking* observants
That stretch their duties nicely. *King Lear,* ii. 2.

DUDGEON. *Handle.*

I see thee still;
And on thy blade and *dudgeon* gouts of blood,
Which was not so before. *Macbeth,* ii. 1.

To DUE. *To endue.*

This is the latest glory of thy praise
That I, thy enemy, *due* thee withal.
Henry 6, P. 1, iv. 2.

DUELLO. *The laws of duelling.*

He cannot by the *duello* avoid it.
Twelfth-Night, iii. 5.

DUKE. *A general; a leader.*

Be merciful, great *duke,* to men of mould!
Henry 5, iii. 1.

To DUKE. *To play the duke.*

Lord Angelo *dukes* it well in his absence; he
puts transgression to't. *Measure for Measure,* iii. 2.

DULL. *Drowsy; sad; melancholy.*

O thou *dull* god, why liest thou with the vile
In loathsome beds, and leav'st the kingly couch
A watch-case or a common 'larum-bell?
Henry 4, P. 2, iii. 1.
Unless some *dull* and favourable hand
Will whisper music to my weary spirit.
Ibid. iv. 4.

DULLARD. *A dolt; a blockhead*

And thou must make a *dullard* of the world,
If they not thought the profits of my death

Were very pregnant and potential spurs
To make thee seek it. *King Lear*, ii. 1.
What, mak'st thou me a *dullard* in this act?
Wilt thou not speak to me? *Cymbeline*, v. 5.

TO DUMB. *To silence.*

So he nodded,
And soberly did mount an arm-gaunt steed,
Who neigh'd so high, that what I would have spoke
Was beastly *dumb'd* by him. *Antony and Cleop.* i. 5.

DUMP. *A mournful air.*

Sing no more ditties, sing no mo
Of *dumps* so dull and heavy.
Much Ado about Nothing, ii. 3.

Visit by night your lady's chamber-window
With some sweet consort; to their instruments
Tune a deploring *dump.*
Two Gentlemen of Verona, iii. 2.

DUN'S THE MOUSE. *Still as a mouse.*

Tut, *dun's the mouse*, the constable's own word.
Romeo and Juliet, i. 4.

TO DWELL. *To remain; to continue.*

You shall not seal to such a bond for me:
I'll rather *dwell* in my necessity.
Merchant of Venice, i. 3.

E.

EAGER. *Keen; biting; sharp; sour.*

It is a nipping and an *eager* air. *Hamlet*, i. 4.
'Tis not the trial of a woman's war,
The bitter clamour of two *eager* tongues,
Can arbitrate this cause betwixt us twain.
Richard 2, i. 1.
And, with a sudden vigour, it doth posset
And curd, like *eager* droppings into milk,
The thin and wholesome blood. *Hamlet*, i. 5.

TO EAN. *To bring forth young.*

Who, then conceiving, did in *eaning* time
Fall parti-colour'd lambs, and those were Jacob's.
Merchant of Venice, i. 3.

EANLING. *A new-born lamb.*

That all the *eanlings* which were streak'd and pied
Should fall as Jacob's hire.
Merchant of Venice, i. 3.

TO EAR. *To plough.*

That power I have, discharge; and let them go
To *ear* the land that hath some hope to grow.
Richard 2, iii. 2.
He that *ears* my land spares my team, and
gives me leave to inn the crop.
All's well that ends well, i. 3.
Menecrates and Menas, famous pirates, *
Make the sea serve them, which they *ear* and wound
With keels of every kind.
Antony and Cleopatra, i. 4.

EARING. *Ploughing.*

O, then we bring forth weeds,
When our quick minds lie still; and our ills told us
Is as our *earing*. *Antony and Cleopatra*, i. 2.

EARNEST. *The money given to ratify a bargain.*

Nay, stay thou out for *earnest.*
Timon of Athens, iv. 3.
Indeed, I have had *earnest*; but I cannot with
conscience take it. *Winter's Tale*, iv. 3.
You have conspir'd against our royal person,
Join'd with an enemy proclaim'd, and from his
coffers
Receiv'd the golden *earnest* of our death.
Henry 5, ii. 3.

EARTH. *Land.*

She is the hopeful lady of my *earth.*
Romeo and Juliet, i. 2.

EASY. *Slight; weak; credulous.*

These faults are *easy*, quickly answer'd.
Henry 6, P. 2, iii. 1.
And his ascent is not by such *easy* degrees as
those who, having been supple and courteous to
the people, bonneted, without any further deed to
heave them at all into their estimation and report.
Coriolanus, ii. 2.
Can you think to front his revenges with the
easy groans of old women? *Ibid.* v. 2.
And,—when he thinks, good *easy* man, full surely
His greatness is a-ripening,—nips his root,
And then he falls, as I do. *Henry 8*, iii. 2.

ECSTASY. *Distraction; frenzy; emotion; rapture; transport.*

That unmatch'd form and feature of blown youth
Blasted with *ecstasy*. *Hamlet*, iii. 1.

I do beseech you,
That are of suppler joints, follow them swiftly,
And hinder them from what this *ecstasy*
May now provoke them to.	*Tempest,* iii. 3.
Where violent sorrow seems a modern *ecstasy.*
	Macbeth, iv. 3.
O love, be moderate ; allay thy *ecstasy.*
	Merchant of Venice, iii. 2.

EDGE.	*Malice ; acrimony ; incitement ; impulse.*

Abate the *edge* of traitors, gracious Lord,
That would reduce these bloody days again.
	Richard 3, v. 5.
Good gentlemen, give him a further *edge,*
And drive his purpose on to these delights.
	Hamlet, iii. 1.

EFFECT.	*Deed ; intention ; result ; appendage ; intent ; meaning.*

That no compunctious visitings of nature
Shake my fell purpose, nor keep peace between
The *effect* and it !	*Macbeth,* i. 5.
	Do not look upon me ;
Lest with this piteous action you convert
My stern *effects.*	*Hamlet,* iii. 4.
	To make you understand this in a manifested
effect, I crave but four days' respite.
	Measure for Measure, iv. 2.
I do invest you jointly with my power,
Pre-eminence, and all the large *effects*
That troop with majesty.	*King Lear,* i. 1.
Wilt thou know the *effect* of what I wrote ?
	Hamlet, v. 2.

To EFFECT.	*To realise ; to verify.*

The ancient proverb will be well *effected,*—
A staff is quickly found to beat a dog.
	Henry 6, P. 2, iii. 1.

EFFECTUAL.	*True ; veracious.*

Reprove my allegation, if you can ;
Or else conclude my words *effectual.*
	Henry 6, P. 2, iii. 1.

EFFEMINATE.	*Timid ; cowardly ; womanly ; unmanly.*

Shall we at last conclude *effeminate* peace ?
	Henry 6, P. 1, v. 4.
As well we know your tenderness of heart,
And gentle, kind, *effeminate* remorse.
	Richard 3, iii. 7.
While he, young wanton and *effeminate* boy,

Takes on the point of honour to support
So dissolute a crew.	*Richard* 2, v. 3.

EFFIGIES.	*Resemblance ; image.*

And as mine eye doth his *effigies* witness
Most truly limn'd and living in your face,
Be truly welcome hither.	*As you like it,* ii. 7.

EFFUSE.	*Effusion ; loss.*

The air hath got into my deadly wounds,
And much *effuse* of blood doth make me faint.
	Henry 6, P. 3, ii. 6.

EFFUSED.	*Shed.*

Whose maiden blood, thus rigorously *effus'd,*
Will cry for vengeance at the gates of heaven.
	Henry 6, P. 1, v. 4.

EFTEST.	*Readiest ; quickest.*

Yea, marry, that's the *eftest* way.
	Much Ado about Nothing, iv. 2.

EGAL.	*Equal.*

Whose souls do bear an *egal* yoke of love.
	Merchant of Venice, iii. 4.

EGALLY.	*Equally.*

Which we have noted in you to your kindred,
And *egally* indeed to all estates.	*Richard* 3, iii. 7.

EGGS FOR MONEY.	*A proverbial expression, applied to any one who had been frightened or cajoled into making a bad bargain.*

	Mine honest friend,
Will you take *eggs for money* ?—No, my lord, I'll
	fight.	*Winter's Tale,* i. 2.

EISEL.	*Vinegar.*

Woo't drink up *eisel* ? eat a crocodile ?
	Hamlet, v. 1.

EITHER PART.	*The two parties.*

While we were interchanging thrusts and blows,
Came more and more, and fought on part and part,
Till the prince came, who parted *either part.*
	Romeo and Juliet, i. 1.

To EKE.	*To delay ; to protract ; to increase ; to add to.*

I speak too long ; but 'tis to piece the time,
To *eke* it, and to draw it out in length,
To stay you from election.
	Merchant of Venice, iii. 2.

	P

The little strength that I have, I would it were
with you.—And mine, to *eke* out hers.
　　　As you like it, i. 2.

TO ELBOW. *To repel; to keep at a distance.*
Why, good sir?—A sovereign shame so *elbows* him.
　　　King Lear, iv. 3.

ELD. *Old age.*
Virgins and boys, mid age and wrinkled *eld*,
Soft infancy, that nothing canst but cry,
Add to my clamours! *Troilus and Cressida*, ii. 2.
For all thy blessèd youth
Becomes as agèd, and doth beg the alms
Of palsied *eld*.　　*Measure for Measure*, iii. 1.

ELDER. *Older; later.*
Let still the woman take
An *elder* than herself.　　*Twelfth-Night*, ii. 4.
Behold divineness no *elder* than a boy. *Cymb.* iii. 6.
Yet through both
I see some sparkles of a better hope,
Which *elder* days may happily bring forth.
　　　Richard 2, v. 3.
You some permit
To second ills with ills, each *elder* worse.
　　　Cymbeline, v. 1.

ELDEST. *Oldest; longest.*
Your *eld'st* acquaintance cannot be three hours.
　　　Tempest, v. 1.

ELEMENT. *The sky; share; participation.*
The *element* itself, till seven years hence,
Shall not behold her face at ample view.
　　　Twelfth-Night, i. 1.
The *element* shows to him as it doth to me.
　　　Henry 5, iv. 1.
And I, in the clear sky of fame, o'ershine you
as much as the full moon doth the cinders of the
element.　　*Henry 4*, P. 2, iv. 3.
Who did guide,
I mean, who set the body and the limbs
Of this great sport together, as you guess?—
One, certes, that promises no *element*
In such a business.　　*Henry 8*, i. 1.

TO ELF. *To entangle.*
My face I'll grime with filth;
Blanket my loins; *elf* all my hair in knots.
　　　King Lear, ii. 3.

ELF-LOCKS. *Hair supposed to be entangled
by fairies.*
This is that very Mab
That plats the manes of horses in the night;

And bakes the *elf-locks* in foul sluttish hairs.
　　　Romeo and Juliet, i. 4.

ELSE. *Other; others.*
But is there any *else* longs to see this broken
music in his sides?　　*As you like it*, i. 2.
Bastards and *else*.　　*King John*, ii. 1.

ELVISH-MARKED. *Elf-marked; spiteful; ma-
lignant.*
Thou *elvish-mark'd*, abortive, rooting hog!
　　　Richard 3, i. 3.

EMBARQUEMENT. *Restraint; hindrance; em-
barment.*
Nor fame nor Capitol,
The prayers of priests nor times of sacrifice,
Embarquements all of fury, shall lift up
Their rotten privilege and custom 'gainst
My hate to Marcius.　　*Coriolanus*, i. 10.

EMBASSADE. *Embassy.*
When you disgrac'd me in my *embassade*,
Then I degraded you from being king,
And come now to create you Duke of York.
　　　Henry 6, P. 3, iv. 3.

EMBASSAGE. *An errand; a message.*
I have almost matter enough in me for such an
embassage.　　*Much Ado about Nothing*, i. 1.
Nimble mischance, that art so light of foot,
Doth not thy *embassage* belong to me,
And am I last that knows it?　*Richard 2*, iii. 4.

TO EMBATTLE. *To be ready for battle; to be
under arms.*
The English are *embattled*, you French peers.
　　　Henry 5, iv. 2.
The night
Is shiny; and they say we shall *embattle*
By the second hour i' the morn.
　　　Antony and Cleopatra, iv. 9.

TO EMBLAZE. *To blazon.*
Ne'er shall this blood be wiped from thy point;
But thou shalt wear it as a herald's coat,
To *emblaze* the honour that thy master got.
　　　Henry 6, P. 2, iv. 10.

TO EMBOSS. *To hunt hard; to run down.*
O, he is more mad
Than Telamon for his shield; the boar of Thessaly
Was never so *emboss'd*.
　　　Antony and Cleopatra, iv. 13.

But we have almost *embossed* him,—you shall see his fall to-night. *All's well that ends well*, iii. 6.

EMBOSSED. *Tumid; swelling; foaming at the mouth.*

And all the *embossèd* sores and headed evils,
That thou with license of free foot hast caught,
Wouldst thou disgorge into the general world.
As you like it, ii. 7.

Timon hath made his everlasting mansion
Upon the beachèd verge of the salt flood;
Who once a day with his *embossèd* froth
The turbulent sea shall cover. *Timon of Athens*, v. 1.

Trash Merriman,—the poor cur is *emboss'd*.
Taming of the Shrew, Induction, sc. 1.

To EMBOUND. *To enclose; to confine.*

If I in act, consent, or thought,
Be guilty of the stealing that sweet breath
Which was *embounded* in this beauteous clay,
Let hell want pains enough to torture me!
King John, iv. 3.

To EMBOWEL. *To disbowel; to exhaust; to disburden.*

Embowell'd will I see thee by and by:
Till then, in blood by noble Percy lie.
Henry 4, P. 1, v. 4.

When the schools,
Embowell'd of their doctrine, have left off
The danger to itself. *All's well that ends well*, i. 3.

EMBRACED. *Embracing; enclosing; encompassing.*

Let us go and find him out,
And quicken his *embracèd* heaviness
With some delight or other.
Merchant of Venice, ii. 7.

EMBRACEMENT. *An embrace.*

You gentle gods, give me but this I have,
And sear up my *embracements* from a next
With bonds of death! *Cymbeline*, i. 1.

EMBRASURE. *Embracement; embrace.*

Where injury of chance
Forcibly prevents our lock'd *embrasures*.
Troilus and Cressida, iv. 4.

EMINENCE. *Respect; deference; greatness.*

Let your remembrance apply to Banquo;
Present him *eminence*, both with eye and tongue.
Macbeth, iii. 2.

Whether the tyranny be in his place,
Or in his *eminence* that fills it up,
I stagger in. *Measure for Measure*, i. 2.

To EMMEW. *To shut up; to confine; to restrain.*

Whose settled visage and deliberate word
Nips youth i' the head, and follies doth *emmew*,
As falcon doth the fowl.
Measure for Measure, iii. 1.

To EMPALE. *To enclose; to encompass.*

And when I have the bloody Hector found,
Empale him with your weapons round about.
Troilus and Cressida, v. 7.

EMPERY. *Dominion; sovereignty; empire.*

Ruling in large and ample *empery*
O'er France and all her almost kingly dukedoms.
Henry 5, i. 2.

A lady
So fair, and fasten'd to an *empery*,
Would make the great'st king double.
Cymbeline, i. 6.

Your right of birth, your *empery*, your own.
Richard 3, iii. 7.

EMPIRICUTIC. *Empirical.*

The most sovereign prescription in Galen is but *empiricutic*, and, to this preservative, of no better report than a horse-drench. *Coriolanus*, ii. 1.

EMULATE. *Envious; ambitious.*

Our last king
Was, as you know, by Fortinbras of Norway,
Thereto prick'd on by a most *emulate* pride,
Dar'd to the combat. *Hamlet*, i. 1.

EMULATION. *Envy; jealousy; discord; faction.*

My heart laments that virtue cannot live
Out of the teeth of *emulation*. *Julius Cæsar*, ii. 3.

I was advértis'd their great general slept,
Whilst *emulation* in the army crept.
Troilus and Cressida, ii. 2.

EMULOUS. *Adverse; jealous; envious.*

A good quarrel to draw *emulous* factions and bleed to death upon.
Troilus and Cressida, ii. 3.

Wherefore should you so?
He is not *emulous*, as Achilles is. *Ibid.* ii. 3.

To ENACT. *To perform; to represent; to act.*
And what did you *enact?*—
I did *enact* Julius Cæsar : I was killed i' the Capitol ;
Brutus killed me. *Hamlet,* iii. 2.

ENACTURE. *Action; operation.*
The violence of either grief or joy
Their own *enactures* with themselves destroy.
Hamlet, iii. 2.

To ENCAVE. *To hide; to conceal.*
Do but *encave* yourself,
And mark the fleers, the gibes, and notable scorns
That dwell in every region of his face.
Othello, iv. 1.

ENCHASED. *Studded; fretted; embossed.*
What seest thou there ? King Henry's diadem,
Enchas'd with all the honours of the world ?
Henry 6, P. 2, i. 2.

ENCOMPASSMENT. *Circumvention; artifice.*
And finding,
By this *encompassment* and drift of question,
That they do know my son, come you more nearer
Than your particular demands will touch it.
Hamlet, ii. 1.

ENCOUNTER. *A meeting; a rendezvous; an encounterer; a gallant.*
It is no more, but that your daughter
Appoints him an *encounter.*
All's well that ends well, iii. 7.
But the peaking cornuto her husband, dwelling
in a continual 'larum of jealousy, comes me in the
instant of our *encounter.*
Merry Wives of Windsor, iii. 5.
Arm, wenches, arm ! *encounters* mounted are
Against your peace. *Love's Labour's lost,* v. 2.

ENCOUNTERER. *A forward woman; a coquette; a flirt.*
O, these *encounterers,* so glib of tongue,
That give accosting welcome ere it comes,
And wide unclasp the tables of their thoughts
To every ticklish reader ! *Troilus and Cressida,* iv. 5.

END. *The cause; the instigator; aim; object; purpose.*
Certainly the cardinal is the *end* of this.
Henry 8, ii. 1.
I see your *end,*—'tis my undoing. *Ibid.* v. 2.

END-ALL. *The termination; the conclusion.*
That but this blow
Might be the be-all and the *end-all* here,
We'd jump the life to come. *Macbeth,* i. 7.

To ENDAMAGE. *To harm; to injure.*
Where your good word cannot advantage him,
Your slander never can *endamage* him.
Two Gentlemen of Verona, iii. 2.

ENDAMAGEMENT. *Loss ; damage; injury.*
These flags of France, that are advancèd here,
Have hither march'd to your *endanagement.*
King John, ii. 1.

To ENDART. *To dart.*
But no more deep will I *endart* mine eye
Than your consent gives strength to make it fly.
Romeo and Juliet, i. 3.

ENDEAVOUR. *Preparation; movements.*
Where their appointment we may best discover,
And look on their *endeavour.*
Antony and Cleopatra, iv. 10.

To ENDURE. *To continue; to remain.*
I do beseech you, by the vows
We have made to *endure* friends, that you directly
Set me against Aufidius and his Antiates.
Coriolanus, i. 6.

To ENFEOFF. *To surrender; to give up.*
Grew a companion to the common streets,
Enfeoff'd himself to popularity. *Henry 4,* P. 1, iii. 2.

ENFOLDINGS. *Garments.*
See'st thou not the air of the court in these
enfoldings? *Winter's Tale,* iv. 3.

To ENFORCE. *To bring by force; to charge; to urge; to aggravate.*
Being awake, *enforce* them to this place.
Tempest, v. 1.
If he evade us there,
Enforce him with his envy to the people.
Coriolanus, iii. 3.
Enforce his pride,
And his old hate unto you. *Ibid.* ii. 3.
We will extenuate rather than *enforce.*
Antony and Cleopatra, v. 2.

ENFORCEDLY. *By compulsion ; not sponta-*
neously ; not by choice.
If thou didst put this sour-cold habit on
To castigate thy pride, 'twere well : but thou
Dost it *enforcedly ;* thou'dst courtier be again,
Wert thou not beggar. *Timon of Athens,* iv. 3.

ENFRANCHED. *Enfranchised.*
If he mislike
My speech and what is done, tell him he has
Hipparchus, my *enfranchèd* bondman, whom
He may at pleasure whip, or hang, or torture,
As he shall like, to quit me.
Antony and Cleopatra, iii. 13.

To ENFREE. *To set free; to release; to en-*
franchise.
And there to render him,
For the *enfreed* Antenor, the fair Cressid.
Troilus and Cressida, iv. 1.

To ENGAGE. *To gage; to pledge.*
To make that worse, suffer'd his kinsman March
To be *engag'd* in Wales. *Henry 4,* P. 1, iv. 3.
I have *engag'd* myself to a dear friend,
Engag'd my friend to his mere enemy,
To feed my means. *Merchant of Venice,* iii. 2.

ENGAGED. *Entangled ; bound.*
O limèd soul, that, struggling to be free,
Art more *engag'd !* *Hamlet,* iii. 3.

ENGINE. *An instrument of torture ; a machine*
of any kind.
Which, like an *engine,* wrench'd my frame of nature
From the fix'd place. *King Lear,* i. 4.
Sword, pike, knife, gun, or need of any *engine*
Would I not have. *Tempest,* ii. 1.

To ENGIRT. *To engird ; to surround ; to en-*
circle.
That gold must round *engirt* these brows of mine.
Henry 6, P. 2, v. 1.

ENGRAFFED. *Fixed ; confirmed ; bound ; en-*
gaged.
Then must we look to receive from his age, not
alone the imperfections of long-*engraffed* condition,
but therewithal the unruly waywardness that infirm
and choleric years bring with them.
King Lear, i. 1.
And what accites your most worshipful thought

to think so ?—Why, because you have been so lewd,
and so much *engraffed* to Falstaff.
Henry 4, P. 2, ii. 2.

To ENGROSS. *To collect; to accumulate ; to*
fatten.
For this they have *engrossèd* and pil'd up
The canker'd heaps of strange-achievèd gold.
Henry 4, P. 2, iv. 4.
Not sleeping, to *engross* his idle body,
But praying, to enrich his watchful soul.
Richard 3, iii. 7.

ENGROSSMENTS. *Accumulations ; savings.*
This bitter taste
Yield his *engrossments* to the ending father.
Henry 4, P. 2, iv. 4.

To ENGUARD. *To guard; to defend; to sur-*
round.
Yes, that, on every dream,
Each buzz, each fancy, each complaint, dislike,
He may *enguard* his dotage with their powers,
And hold our lives in mercy. *King Lear,* i. 4.

To ENKINDLE. *To urge; to incite ; to stimu-*
late.
That, trusted home,
Might yet *enkindle* you unto the crown,
Besides the thane of Cawdor. *Macbeth,* i. 3.

To ENLARD. *To fatten ; to increase.*
That were to *enlard* his fat-already pride.
Troilus and Cressida, ii. 3.

To ENLARGE. *To state ; to unfold; to dis-*
close.
Bid them move away ;
Then in my tent, Cassius, *enlarge* your griefs,
And I will give you audience. *Julius Cæsar,* iv. 2.

ENLARGEMENT. *Freedom ; privilege.*
Yet you are curb'd from that *enlargement* by
The consequence of the crown. *Cymbeline,* ii. 3.

To ENMESH. *To enclose ; to ensnare.*
And out of her own goodness make the net
That shall *enmesh* them all. *Othello,* ii. 3.

ENOW. *Enough.*
Then the liars and swearers are fools ; for there
are liars and swearers *enow* to beat the honest men,
and hang up them. *Macbeth,* iv. 2.

Enow to press a royal merchant down.
Merchant of Venice, iv. 1.

To ENPIERCE. *To pierce; to transfix.*
I am too sore *enpiercèd* with his shaft,
To soar with his light feathers.
Romeo and Juliet, i. 4.

To ENRANK. *To prepare for battle; to arrange in order of battle; to darraign.*
No leisure had he to *enrank* his men.
Henry 6, P. 1, i. 1.

To ENROUND. *To surround; to encompass.*
Upon his royal face there is no note
How dread an army hath *enrounded* him.
Henry 5, iii. Chorus.

To ENSCHEDULE. *To inscrol; to state in writing.*
Whose tenours and particular effects
You have, *enscheduľd* briefly, in your hands.
Henry 5, v. 2.

To ENSCONCE. *To hide; to conceal.*
I will *ensconce* me behind the arms.
Merry Wives of Windsor, iii. 3.

ENSEAMED. *Luxurious; sensual.*
Nay, but to live
In the rank sweat of an *enseamèd* bed.
Hamlet, iii. 4.

To ENSEAR. *To sear; to close up.*
Ensear thy fertile and conceptious womb,
Let it no more bring out ingrateful man !
Timon of Athens, iv. 3.

ENSHIELD. *Enshielded; covered; concealed.*
As these black masks
Proclaim an *enshield* beauty ten times louder
Than beauty could, display'd.
Measure for Measure, ii. 4.

ENSKYED. *Celestial; heavenly; sacred.*
I hold you as a thing *ensky'd* and sainted.
Measure for Measure, i. 4.

To ENSUE. *To succeed; to follow.*
Let not to-morrow, then, *ensue* to-day.
Richard 2, ii. 1.
Whilst the wheel'd seat
Of fortunate Cæsar, drawn before him, branded
His baseness that *ensu'd.* *Antony and Cleop.* iv. 14.

To ENTAME. *To subject; to enslave; to subdue.*
'Tis not your inky brows, your black-silk hair,
Your bugle eyeballs, nor your cheek of cream,
That can *entame* my spirits to your worship.
As you like it, iii. 5.

ENTERPRISE. *Achievement; conquest.*
Now, lords, for France ; the *enterprise* whereof
Shall be to you, as us, like glorious. *Henry* 5, ii. 2.

To ENTERTAIN. *To preserve; to accept; to receive; to take into service; to retain.*
And I quake,
Lest thou a feverous life shouldst *entertain,*
And six or seven winters more respect
Than a perpetual honour.
Measure for Measure, iii. 1.
But *entertain* it,
And, though thou think me poor, I am the man
Will give thee all the world.
Antony and Cleopatra, ii. 7.
All that serv'd Brutus, I will *entertain.*
Julius Cæsar, v. 5.
You, sir, I *entertain* for one of my hundred; only
I do not like the fashion of your garments.
King Lear, iii. 6.

ENTERTAINMENT. *Employment; pay; service; conversation; welcome.*
Canidius, and the rest
That fell away, have *entertainment*, but
No honourable trust. *Antony and Cleopatra*, iv. 6.
He must think us some band of strangers i' the
adversary's *entertainment.*
All's well that ends well, iv. 1.
The queen desires you to use some gentle *entertainment* to Laertes before you fall to play.
Hamlet, v. 2.
This *entertainment*
May a free face put on ; derive a liberty
From heartiness, from bounty's fertile bosom,
And well become the agent. *Winter's Tale*, i. 2.
Lest my extent to the players, which, I tell you,
must show fairly outward, should more appear like
entertainment than yours. *Hamlet*, ii. 2.

To ENTREAT. *To persuade; to treat; to entertain.*
Pursue him, and *entreat* him to a peace.
Twelfth-Night, v. 1.

I have a wife, whom, I protest, I love :
I would she were in heaven, so she could
Entreat some power to change this currish Jew.
Merchant of Venice, iv. 1.
For God's sake, fairly let her be *entreated.*
Richard 2, iii. 1.
Entreat her not the worse, in that I pray
You use her well. *Henry 6*, P. 2, ii. 4.
Entreat her fair. *Troilus and Cressida*, iv. 4.
My lord, we must *entreat* the time alone.
Romeo and Juliet, iv. 1.

ENTREATMENT. *Entertainment ; reception ;
company.*
Set your *entreatments* at a higher rate
Than a command to parley. *Hamlet*, i. 3.

To ENVENOM. *To poison ; to infect ; to
taint ; to enrage ; to exasperate.*
The treacherous instrument is in thy hand,
Unbated and *envenom'd.* *Hamlet*, v. 2.
O, what a world is this, when what is comely
Envenoms him that bears it ! *As you like it*, ii. 3.
Envenom him with words. *King John*, iii. 1.

ENVIOUS. *Malicious ; spiteful.*
The abject people, gazing on thy face
With *envious* looks, still laughing at thy shame.
Henry 6, P. 2, ii. 4.
But none can drive him from the *envious* plea
Of forfeiture, of justice, and his bond.
Merchant of Venice, iii. 2.
That trick of state was a deep *envious* one.
Henry 8, ii. 1.
This shall make
Our purpose necessary, and not *envious.*
Julius.Cæsar, ii. 1.

ENVIOUSLY. *Angrily ; peevishly ; petulantly.*
Spurns *enviously* at straws ; speaks things in doubt,
That carry but half sense. *Hamlet*, iv. 5.

ENVY. *Malice ;· hatred.*
Or as a moat defensive to a house,
Against the *envy* of less happier lands.
Richard 2, ii. 1.
Lord Angelo is precise ;
Stands at a guard with *envy.*
Measure for Measure, ii. 1.

To ENVY. *To hate ; to wish ill to.*
Is it for him you do *envy* me so ?
Taming of the Shrew, ii. 1.

Not Afric owns a serpent I abhor
More than thy fame I *envy.* *Coriolanus*, i. 8.
Do not take
His rougher accents for malicious sounds,
But, as I say, such as become a soldier,
Rather than *envy* you. *Ibid.* iii. 2.
For that he has from time to time
Envied against the people, seeking means
To pluck away their power. *Ibid.* iii. 3.

To ENWHEEL. *To encircle ; to encompass ; to
enclose.*
Hail to thee, lady ! and the grace of heaven
Before, behind thee, and on every hand,
Enwheel thee round ! *Othello*, ii. 1.

EPHESIAN. *A jovial fellow ; a boon compa-
nion.*
What company ?
Ephesians, my lord,—of the old church.
Henry 4, P. 2, ii. 2.
It is thine host, thine *Ephesian*, calls.
Merry Wives of Windsor, iv. 5.

EPICURISM. *Luxury ; feasting.*
Epicurism and lust
Make it more like a tavern or a brothel
Than a grac'd palace. *King Lear*, i. 4.

EQUAL. *Exact ; just ; precise.*
Let the forfeit
Be nominated for an *equal* pound
Of your fair flesh. *Merchant of Venice*, i. 3.

EQUALNESS. *Equality.*
But yet let me lament,—that our stars,
Unreconciliable, should divide
Our *equalness* to this. *Antony and Cleopatra*, v. 1.

EQUINOX. *Equality of length ; even measure.*
And do but see his vice ;
'Tis to his virtue a just *equinox*,
The one as long as the other. *Othello*, ii. 3.

EQUIVOCAL. *Equivocating.*
What an *equivocal* companion is this !
All's well that ends well, v. 3.

ERRING. *Wandering ; roving ; erratic.*
If sanctimony and a frail vow betwixt an *erring*
barbarian and a supersubtle Venetian be not too
hard for my wits and all the tribe of hell, thou
shalt enjoy her. *Othello*, i. 3.

Some, how brief tho life of man
Runs his *erring* pilgrimage,
That the stretching of a span
Buckles in his sum of age. *As you like it*, iii. 2.

ERST. *Formerly; before.*

But since that thou canst talk of love so well,
Thy company, which *erst* was irksome to me,
I will endure. *As you like it*, iii. 5.

ESCOTED. *Paid; supported.*

What, aro they children? who maintains 'em?
how aro they *escoted*? *Hamlet*, ii. 2.

ESPERANCE. *Hope.*

An *esperance* so obstinately strong,
That doth invert the attest of eyes and ears.
Troilus and Cressida, v. 2.
The lowest and most dejected thing of fortuno,
Stands still in *esperance*, lives not in fear.
King Lear, iv. 1.

ESPIAL. *A spy.*

Her father and myself,—lawful *espials*,—
Will so bestow ourselves, that, seeing, unscen,
We may of their encounter frankly judge.
Hamlet, iii. 1.

ESSENCE. *Nature; quality.*

But man, proud man, most ignorant of what
He's most assur'd, his glassy *essence*.
Measure for Measure, ii. 2.

To ESTABLISH. *To settle in perpetuity.*

We will *establish* our estate upon
Our eldest, Malcolm; whom we name hereafter
The Prince of Cumberland. *Macbeth*, i. 4.

ESTATE. *State; distinction; condition; sort; rank.*

Our breach of duty this way
Is business of *estate*. *Henry* 8, ii. 2.
The corse they follow did with desperate hand
Fordo its own life; 'twas of some *estate*.
Hamlet, v. 1.
His letter there will show you his *estate*,
Merchant of Venice, iii. 2.
Let me dispute with thee of thy *estate*.
Romeo and Juliet, iii. 3.
Can he speak? hear?
Know man from man? dispute his own *estate*?
Winter's Tale, iv. 3.
Which you on all *estates* will execute
That lie within the mercy of your wit.
Love's Labour's lost, v. 2.

To ESTATE. *To grant; to settle; to confer.*

And some donation freely to *estate*
On the bless'd lovers. *Tempest*, iv. 1.
For my father's house, and all the revenue that
was old Sir Roland's, will I *estate* upon you, and
here live and die a shepherd. *As you like it*, v. 2.

ESTEEM. *Estimation; value; reputation; credit.*

We lost a jewel of her; and our *esteem*
Was made much poorer by it.
All's well that ends well, v. 3.
Twelvo cities, and seven wallèd towns of strength,
Beside five hundred prisoners of *esteem*.
Henry 6, P. 1, iii. 4.
Proceed no straiter 'gainst our uncle Gloster
Than from true evidence, of good *esteem*,
He be approv'd in practice culpable.
Ibid. P. 2, iii. 2.

ESTIMATE. *Estimation; value; reputation; honour.*

For all, that life can rate
Worth name of life, in thee hath *estimate*.
All's well that ends well, ii. 1.
None else of name and noble *estimate*.
Richard 2, ii. 3.
I do love
My country's good with a respect more tender,
More holy, and profound, than mine own life,
My dear wife's *estimate*, her womb's increase,
And treasure of my loins. *Coriolanus*, iii. 3.

ESTIMATION. *Reputation; object of esteem; worth; value; respect; surmise; opinion.*

I know the gentleman
To be of worth, and worthy *estimation*,
And not without desert so well reputed.
Two Gentlemen of Verona, ii. 4.
I am content that he shall take the odds
Of his great name and *estimation*.
Henry 4, P. 1, v. 1.
Your ring may be stolen too: so, your brace of
unprizable *estimations*, the one is but frail, and the
other casual. *Cymbeline*, i. 4.
But your son,
As mad in folly, lack'd the sense to know
Her *estimation* home. *All's well that ends well*, v. 3.
If thy captain knew I were here, he would use
me with *estimation*. *Coriolanus*, v. 2.
I speak not this in *estimation*,
As what I think might be, but what I know
Is ruminated, plotted, and set down.
Henry 4, P. 1, i. 3.

ESTRIDGE. *An ostrich.*

To be furious,
Is to be frighted out of fear; and in that mood
The dove will peck the *estridge.*
Antony and Cleopatra, iii. 13.

All plum'd like *estridges* that wing the wind.
Henry 4, P. 1, iv. 1.

ETERNE. *Eternal.*

But in them nature's copy's not *eterne.*
Macbeth, iii. 2.

And never did the Cyclops' hammers fall
On Mars his armour, forg'd for proof *eterne,*
With less remorse than Pyrrhus' bleeding sword
Now falls on Priam. *Hamlet,* ii. 2.

ETERNITY. *Immortality.*

Who, had he himself *eternity,* and could put
breath into his work, would beguile Nature of her
custom. *Winter's Tale,* v. 2.

EVEN. *Plain ; candid ; equal.*

And by what more dear a better proposer could
charge you withal, be *even* and direct with me,
whether you were sent for, or no. *Hamlet,* ii. 2.

I will be *even* with thee, doubt it not.
Antony and Cleopatra, iii. 7.

EVEN CHRISTIAN. *Fellow-Christian.*

And the more pity that great folk should have
countenance in this world to drown or hang themselves more than their *even Christian. Hamlet,* v. 1.

TO EVEN. *To fill up; to supply; to make
even.*

Be comforted, good madam : the great rage,
You see, is kill'd in him : and yet 'tis danger
To make him *even* o'er the time he has lost.
King Lear, iv. 7.

There's more to be consider'd ; but we'll *even*
All that good time will give us. *Cymbeline,* iii. 4.

The care I have had to *even* your content, I
wish might be found in the calendar of my past
endeavours. *All's well that ends well,* i. 3.

And nothing can or shall content my soul,
Till I am *even'd* with him, wife for wife.
Othello, ii. 1.

EVENT. *Design; purpose; result.*

But leave we him to his *events,* with a prayer
they may prove prosperous.
Measure for Measure, iii. 2.

For this night to bed, and dream on the *event.*
Twelfth-Night, ii. 3.

O heaven, O earth, bear witness to this sound,
And crown what I profess with kind *event,*
If I speak true ! *Tempest,* iii. 1.

EVERY. *Every one; each.*

If *every* of your wishes had a womb,
And fertile every wish, a million.
Antony and Cleopatra, i. 2.

And after, *every* of this happy number
Shall share the good of our returnèd fortune.
As you like it, v. 4.

EVIL. *Fault.*

Your most obedient counsellor ; yet that dares
Less appear so, in comforting your *evils,*
Than such as most seem yours. *Winter's Tale,* ii. 3.

EVIL-EYED. *Malicious ; spiteful.*

No, be assur'd you shall not find me, daughter,
After the slander of most stepmothers,
Evil-ey'd unto you. *Cymbeline,* i. 1.

TO EVITATE. *To avoid.*

Since therein she doth *evitate* and shun
A thousand irreligious cursèd hours.
Merry Wives of Windsor, v. 5.

EXACTLY. *Earnestly; urgently.*

But, ere I last received the sacrament,
I did confess it ; and *exactly* begg'd
Your grace's pardon, and I hope I had it.
Richard 2, i. 1.

TO EXAMINE. *To call in question; to doubt.*

All her deserving
Is a reserved honesty, and that
I have not heard *examin'd.*
All's well that ends well, iii. 5.

TO EXAMPLE. *To exemplify; to justify; to
instance.*

For hear her but *exampled* by herself.
Henry 5, i. 2.

I will have the subject newly writ o'er, that I
may *example* my digression by some mighty precedent. *Love's Labour's lost,* i. 2.

Do villany, do, since you protest to do't,
Like workmen. I'll *example* you with thievery.
Timon of Athens, iv. 3.

Q

EXASPERATE. *Exasperated; angry.*

And this report
Hath so *exasperate* the king, that he
Prepares for some attempt of war. *Macbeth*, iii. 6.

Why art thou, then, *exasperate*, thou idle immaterial skein of sleave-silk?
Troilus and Cressida, v. 1.

EXCELLENT. *Surpassing; exceeding.*

This is the *excellent* foppery of the world.
King Lear, i. 2.

That *excellent* grand tyrant of the earth,
That reigns in gallèd eyes of weeping souls.
Richard 3, iv. 4.

EXCEPT. *Unless.*

Except they meant to bathe in reeking wounds,
Or memorize another Golgotha,
I cannot tell. *Macbeth*, i. 2.

EXCEPTION. *Indignation; displeasure; ob-
jection.*

His honour,
Clock to itself, knew the true minute when
Exception bid him speak.
All's well that ends well, i. 2.

What I have done,
That might your nature, honour, and *exception*,
Roughly awake, I here proclaim was madness.
Hamlet, v. 2.

Your cousin, my lady, takes great *exceptions* to
your ill hours. *Twelfth-Night*, i. 3.

EXCEPTLESS. *Making no exception.*

Forgive my general and *exceptless* rashness,
You perpetual-sober gods! *Timon of Athens*, iv. 3.

EXCLAIM. *Exclamation; clamour.*

Alas, the part I had in Gloster's blood
Doth more solicit me than your *exclaims*,
To stir against the butchers of his life.
Richard 2, i. 2.

I hear his drums:—be copious in *exclaims*.
Richard 3, iv. 4.

EXCOMMUNICATE. *Excommunicated.*

Then, by the lawful power that I have,
Thou shalt stand curs'd and *excommunicate*.
King John, iii. 1.

EXCREMENT. *Whatever grows from the human
body, as hair, nails, &c.*

Your bedded hair, like life in *excrements*,
Starts up, and stands on end. *Hamlet*, iii. 4.

And these assume but valour's *excrement*
To render them redoubted.
Merchant of Venice, iii. 2.

Let me pocket up my pedlor's *excrement*.
Winter's Tale, iv. 3.

TO EXCUSE. *To acquit.*

My lord cardinal,
I do *excuse* you; yea, upon mine honour,
I free you from't. *Henry 8*, ii. 4.

TO EXECUTE. *To practise; to exercise; to
employ; to kill; to do execution.*

Full of comparisons and wounding flouts,
Which you on all estates will *execute*
That lie within the mercy of your wit.
Love's Labour's lost, v. 2.

But, O, the treacherous Fastolfe wounds my heart!
Whom with my bare fists I would *execute*,
If I now had him brought into my power.
Henry 6, P. 1, i. 4.

And Cassio following with determin'd sword
To *execute* upon him. *Othello*, ii. 3.

EXECUTION. *Use; employment; exercise.*

Witness that here Iago doth give up
The *execution* of his wit, hands, heart,
To wrong'd Othello's service! *Othello*, iii. 3.

EXECUTOR. *Executioner.*

The sad-ey'd justice, with his surly hum,
Delivering o'er to *executors* pale
The lazy yawning drone. *Henry 5*, i. 2.

EXEMPT. *Cut off from; removed; excluded.*

Who would not wish to be from wealth *exempt*,
Since riches point to misery and contempt?
Timon of Athens, iv. 2.

And this our life, *exempt* from public haunt,
Finds tongues in trees, books in the running brooks,
Sermons in stones, and good in every thing.
As you like it, ii. 1.

Be it my wrong you are from me *exempt*,
But wrong not that wrong with a more contempt.
Comedy of Errors, ii. 2.

And by his treason, stand'st not thou attainted,
Corrupted, and *exempt* from ancient gentry?
Henry 6, P. 1, ii. 4.

TO EXEMPT. *To cut off; to exclude.*

Things done well, and with a care,
Exempt themselves from fear. *Henry 8*, i. 2.

Exempted be from me the arrogance
To choose from forth the royal blood of France,
My low and humble name to propagate
With any branch or image of thy state.
                    All's well that ends well, ii. 1.

EXEQUIES.   *Funeral rites ; obsequies.*
                    Let's not forget
The noble Duke of Bedford late deceas'd,
But see his *exequies* fulfill'd in Rouen.
                    Henry 6, P. 1, iii. 2.

EXERCISE.   *Religious exhortation.*
I thank thee, good Sir John, with all my heart.
I am in your debt for your last *exercise.*
                    Richard 3, iii. 2.
            This hand of yours requires
A sequester from liberty, fasting and prayer,
Much castigation, *exercise* devout.   *Othello,* iii. 4.

EXHIBITER.   *A petitioner.*
Or, rather, swaying more upon our part
Than cherishing the *exhibiters* against us.
                    Henry 5, i. 1.

EXHIBITION.   *Allowance; pension; payment; recompense.*
I crave fit disposition for my wife ;
Due reference of place and *exhibition;*
With such accommodations and besort
As levels with her breeding.   *Othello,* i. 3.
Kent banish'd thus ! And France in choler parted !
And the king gone to-night ! subscrib'd his power !
Confin'd to *exhibition !*   *King Lear,* i. 2.
What maintenance he from his friends receives,
Like *exhibition* thou shalt have from me.
                    Two Gentlemen of Verona, i. 3.

Marry, I would not do such a thing for a joint-ring, nor for measures of lawn, nor for gowns, petticoats, nor caps, nor any petty *exhibition.*
                    Othello, iv. 3.

EXIGENT.   *End; exigency; extremity.*
These eyes,—like lamps whose wasting oil is spent,—
Wax dim, as drawing to their *exigent.*
                    Henry 6, P. 1, ii. 5.
Why do you cross me in this *exigent ?*
                    Julius Cæsar, v. 1.
            Thou art sworn, Eros,
That when the *exigent* should come,—
That, on my command, thou then wouldst kill me.
                    Antony and Cleopatra, iv. 14.

EXORCISER.   *An enchanter ; a sorcerer ; one who can raise spirits.*
No *exorciser* harm thee !
Nor no witchcraft charm thee !   *Cymbeline,* iv. 2.

EXORCISM.   *Enchantment; incantation.*
Will her ladyship behold and hear our *exorcisms ?*
                    Henry 6, P. 2, i. 3.

EXORCIST.   *An exorciser.*
Thou, like an *exorcist,* hast conjur'd up
My mortified spirit.   *Julius Cæsar,* ii. 1.
            Is there no *exorcist*
Beguiles the truer office of mine eyes ?
                    All's well that ends well, v. 3.

EXPECT.   *Expectation ; likelihood ; probability.*
Speak, Prince of Ithaca ; and be't of less *expect*
That matter needless, of importless burden,
Divide thy lips.   *Troilus and Cressida,* i. 3.

EXPECTANCE.   *Expectation.*
There is *expectance* here from both the sides,
What further you will do.
                    Troilus and Cressida, iv. 5.

EXPECTANCY.   *Hope.*
The *expectancy* and rose of the fair state.
                    Hamlet, iii. 1.

EXPEDIENCE.   *Speed ; expedition; enterprise ; haste ; dispatch.*
All these, well furnish'd by the Duke of Bretagne,
With eight tall ships, three thousand men of war,
Are making hither with all due *expedience.*
                    Richard 2, ii. 1.
Then let me hear of you, my gentle cousin,
What yesternight our council did decree
In forwarding this dear *expedience.*
                    Henry 4, P. 1, i. 1.
            I shall break
The cause of our *expedience* to the queen,
And get her leave to part.
                    Antony and Cleopatra, i. 2.

EXPEDIENT.   *Quick ; hasty ; expeditious.*
His marches are *expedient* to this town.
                    King John, ii. 1.

EXPEDIENTLY.   *Quickly ; immediately.*
Do this *expediently,* and turn him going.
                    As you like it, iii. 1.

EXPENSE. *Disbursement.*

'Tis they have put him on the old man's death,
To have the *expense* and waste of his revenues.
King Lear, ii. 1.

EXPIATE. *Accomplished ; terminated ; expired.*

Make haste ; the hour of death is *expiate*.
Richard 3, iii. 3.

To EXPIRE. *To terminate; to bring to an end.*

And *expire* the term
Of a despisèd life, clos'd in my breast,
By some vile forfeit of untimely death.
Romeo and Juliet, i. 4.

EXPOSITOR. *An interpreter.*

Which his fair tongue, conceit's *expositor*,
Delivers in such apt and gracious words,
That agèd ears play truant at his tales.
Love's Labour's lost, ii. 1.

To EXPOSTULATE. *To discuss; to examine.*

My liege, and madam,—to *expostulate*
What majesty should be, what duty is,
Why day is day, night night, and time is time,
Were nothing but to waste night, day, and time.
Hamlet, ii. 2.

EXPOSURE. *Situation; state; condition.*

And sets Thersites
To weaken and discredit our *exposure*,
How rank soever rounded-in with danger.
Troilus and Cressida, i. 3.

To EXPOUND. *To expose; to lay open; to declare.*

To mart
As in a Romish stew, and to *expound*
His beastly mind to us. *Cymbeline*, i. 6.

To EXPRESS. *To unfold; to make known; to describe.*

Therefore it charges me in manners the rather to
express myself. *Twelfth-Night*, ii. 1.
An old thing 'twas, but it *express'd* her fortune,
And she died singing it. *Othello*, iv. 3.

EXPRESSURE. *Description; expression; utterance; form; impression.*

Wherein by the colour of his beard, the shape
of his leg, the manner of his gait, the *expressure* of

his eye, forehead, and complexion, he shall find
himself most feelingly personated.
Twelfth-Night, ii. 3.
There is a mystery in the soul of state;
Which hath an operation more divine
Than breath or pen can give *expressure* to.
Troilus and Cressida, iii. 3.
Th' *expressure* that it bears, green let it be,
More fertile-fresh than all the field to see.
Merry Wives of Windsor, v. 5.

To EXPULSE. *To expel.*

For ever should they be *expuls'd* from France,
And not have title of an earldom here.
Henry 6, P. 1, iii. 3.

EXSUFFLICATE. *Despicable ; contemptible.*

Exchange me for a goat,
When I shall turn the business of my soul
To such *exsufflicate* and blown surmises,
Matching thy inference. *Othello*, iii. 3.

EXTANT. *Present.*

But in this *extant* moment, faith and troth
Bids thee, with most divine integrity
From heart of very heart, great Hector, welcome.
Troilus and Cressida, iv. 5.

To EXTEND. *To seize.*

Labienus—
This is stiff news—hath, with his Parthian force,
Extended Asia from Euphrätes.
Antony and Cleopatra, i. 2.

EXTENT. *Grasp of the hand ; execution ; seizure ; violence ; outrage.*

Let me comply with you in this garb; lest my
extent to the players, which, I tell you, must show
fairly outward, should more appear like entertainment than yours. *Hamlet*, ii. 2.
And let my officers of such a nature
Make an *extent* upon his house and lands.
As you like it, iii. 1.
Let thy fair wisdom, not thy passion, sway
In this uncivil and unjust *extent*
Against thy peace. *Twelfth-Night*, iv. 1.

To EXTERMINE. *To end; to terminate.*

By giving love, your sorrow and my grief
Were both *extermin'd*. *As you like it*, iii. 5.

EXTERN. *External.*

For when my outward action doth demonstrate
The native act and figure of my heart

In compliment *extern*, 'tis not long after
But I will wear my heart upon my sleeve
For daws to peck at. *Othello*, i. 1.

EXTINCTED. *Extinguished; quenched; exhausted.*

Give renew'd fire to our *extincted* spirits,
And bring all Cyprus comfort ! *Othello*, ii. 1.

To EXTIRP. *To extirpate.*

Nor should that nation boast it so with us,
But be *extirpèd* from our provinces.
Henry 6, P. 1, iii. 3.
But it is impossible to *extirp* it quite, friar, till
eating and drinking be put down.
Measure for Measure, iii. 2.

To EXTORT. *To wring; to wrest; to draw.*

None of noble sort
Would so offend a virgin, and *extort*
A poor soul's patience, all to make you sport.
Midsummer-Night's Dream, iii. 2.
Do not *extort* thy reasons from this clause,
For that I woo thou therefore hast no cause.
Twelfth-Night, iii. 1.

EXTRACTING. *Distracting; perplexing.*

A most *extracting* frenzy of mine own
From my remembrance clearly banish'd his.
Twelfth-Night, v. 1.

EXTRAUGHT. *Derived; descended.*

Sham'st thou not, knowing whence thou art *extraught*,
To let thy tongue detect thy base-born heart ?
Henry 6, P. 3, ii. 2.

EXTRAVAGANT. *Erratic; wandering.*

And at his warning,
Whether in sea or fire, in earth or air,
The *extravagant* and erring spirit hies
To his confine. *Hamlet*, i. 1.

Tying her duty, beauty, wit, and fortunes,
In an *extravagant* and wheeling stranger
Of here and every where. *Othello*, i. 1.

EXTREMES. *Extravagance of conduct; extremity of distress; despair.*

To chide at your *extremes*, it not becomes me,—
O, pardon, that I name them ! *Winter's Tale*, iv. 3.
Therefore, out of thy long-experienc'd time,
Give me some present counsel; or, behold,
'Twixt my *extremes* and me this bloody knife
Shall play the umpire. *Romeo and Juliet*, iv. 1.

EXTREMITY. *Violence; fury.*

Why, thou wert better in thy grave than to answer with thy uncovered body this *extremity* of the skies. *King Lear*, iii. 4.

EYAS. *A young hawk.*

How now, my *eyas*-musket! what news with you?
Merry Wives of Windsor, iii. 3.
But there is, sir, an aery of children, little *eyases*, that cry out on the top of question, and are most tyrannically clapped for it. *Hamlet*, ii. 2.

EYE. *A shade; a tinge.*

The ground, indeed, is tawny,
With an *eye* of green in't. *Tempest*, ii. 1.

To EYE. *To show; to appear; to look.*

But, sir, forgive me ;
Since my becomings kill me, when they do not
Eye well to you. *Antony and Cleopatra*, i. 3.

EYNE. *Eyes.*

Come, thou monarch of the vine,
Plumpy Bacchus with pink *eyne* !
Antony and Cleopatra, ii. 7.
For ere Demetrius look'd on Hermia's *eyne*,
He hail'd down oaths that he was only mine.
Midsummer-Night's Dream, i. 1.

F.

To FACE. *To boast; to trim; to decorate.*
Fair Margaret knows
That Suffolk doth not flatter, *face*, or feign.
Henry 6, P. 1, v. 3.
To *face* the garment of rebellion
With some fine colour that may please the eye
Of fickle changelings and poor discontents.
Henry 4, P. 1, v. 1.

To FACE DOWN. *To put down by sheer effrontery.*
But here's a villain that would *face me down*
He met me on the mart, and that I beat him.
Comedy of Errors, iii. 1.

FACINOROUS. *Bad; wicked.*
And he's of a most *facinorous* spirit, that will not acknowledge it to be the very hand of heaven.
All's well that ends well, ii. 3.

FACT. *Fault; defect; weakness.*
Indeed, his *fact*, till now in the government of Lord Angelo, came not to an undoubtful proof.
Measure for Measure, iv. 2.
As you are past all shame,—
.Those of your *fact* are so,—so past all truth.
Winter's Tale, iii. 2.

FACTION. *Cabal; party; tumult; alliance.*
Let 'em enter. They are the *faction*.
Julius Cæsar, ii. 1.
In that beastly fury
He has been known to commit outrages,
And cherish *factions*. *Timon of Athens*, iii. 5.
All the better; their fraction is more our wish than their *faction:* but it was a strong composure a fool could disunite. *Troilus and Cressida*, ii. 3.

FACTIONARY. *A partisan; an adherent.*
My name is Menenius, always *factionary* on the part of your general. *Coriolanus*, v. 2.

FACTIOUS. *Belonging to a party or faction; united; banded together; associated.*
In all which time you and your husband Grey Were *factious* for the house of Lancaster.
Richard 3, i. 3.
Be *factious* for redress of all these griefs;

And I will set this foot of mine as far
As who goes farthest. *Julius Cæsar*, i. 3.

FACULTY. *Virtue; efficacy; power.*
As notes, whose *faculties* inclusive were,
More than they were in note.
All's well that ends well, i. 3.

To FADE. *To vanish; to disappear.*
It *faded* on the crowing of the cock. *Hamlet*, i. 1.
Yea, all which it inherit shall dissolve,
And, like this insubstantial pageant *faded*,
Leave not a wreck behind. *Tempest*, iv. 1.
One *fading* moment's mirth
With twenty watchful, weary tedious nights.
Two Gentlemen of Verona, i. 1.
Rise, and *fade!* *Cymbeline*, v. 4.

To FADGE. *To suit; to fit.*
We will have, if this *fadge* not, an antic.
Love's Labour's lost, v. 1.
How will this *fadge?* my master loves her dearly;
And I, poor monster, fond as much on him;
And she, mistaken, seems to dote on me.
Twelfth-Night, ii. 2.

FAIL. *Neglect; omission; fault; error; decease; death.*
Mark, and perform it, for the *fail*
Of any point in't shall not only be
Death to thyself, but to thy lewd-tongu'd wife.
Winter's Tale, ii. 3.
Goodly and gallant shall be false and perjur'd
From thy great *fail*. *Cymbeline*, iii. 4.
Which now the public body hath sense withal
Of its own *fail*, restraining aid to Timon.
Timon of Athens, v. 1.
I weigh'd the danger which my realms stood in
By this my issue's *fail;* and that gave me
Many a groaning throe. *Henry 8*, ii. 4.
How grounded he his title to the crown,
Upon our *fail?* *Ibid.* i. 2.

To FAIL. *To die.*
Adding further,
That had the king in his last sickness *fail'd*,
The cardinal's and Sir Thomas Lovell's heads
Should have gone off. *Henry 8*, i. 2.

FAIN. *Fond of; desirous; glad; obliged; forced; compelled.*

Yea, man and birds are *fain* of climbing high.
Henry 6, P. 2, ii. 1.
Ah, York, no man alive so *fain* as I.
Ibid. iii. 1.
Why, horns; which such as you are *fain* to be
beholding to your wives for. *As you like it, iv. 1.*
And wast thou *fain*, poor father,
To hovel thee with swine, and rogues forlorn,
In short and musty straw? *King Lear, iv. 7.*
I am *fain* to dine and sup with water and bran;
I dare not for my head fill my belly.
Measure for Measure, iv. 3.
I perceive, by our general's looks, we shall be
fain to hang you. *All's well that ends well, iv. 3.*

To FAIN. *To be glad; to rejoice.*

The good old man were *fain* that all were well,
So 'twere not long of him. *Henry 6, P. 3, iv. 7.*

To FAINT. *To sadden; to depress; to be dejected.*

It *faints* me, to think what follows. *Henry 8, ii. 3.*
Why *faint* you, lords? *Henry 6, P. 3, i. 1.*

FAIR. *Beauty; fairness.*

O heresy in *fair*, fit for these days!'
Love's Labour's lost, iv. 1.
My decayèd *fair*
A sunny look of his would soon repair.
Comedy of Errors, ii. 1.

FAIR. *Fine; gay; gaudy; showy.*

O then, belike, you fancy riches more :
You will have Gremio to keep you *fair*.
Taming of the Shrew, ii. 1.
Carry him gently to my *fairest* chamber.
Ibid. Induction, sc. 1.

FAIRLY. *Kindly; gently; honourably.*

For God's sake, *fairly* let her be entreated.
Richard 2, iii. 1.

FAIRNESS. *Fulness; full extent.*

I mean to stride your steed; and at all times
To undercrest your good addition
To the *fairness* of my power. *Coriolanus, i. 9.*

FAIRY. *Enchantress.*

To this great *fairy* I'll commend thy acts,
Make her thanks bless thee.
Antony and Cleopatra, iv. 8.

FAITH. *Honour; secrecy; fidelity; truth.*

You do not doubt my *faith*, sir?—
This secret is so weighty, 'twill require
A strong *faith* to conceal it. *Henry 8, ii. 1.*
This day, all things begun come to ill end;
Yea, *faith* itself to hollow falsehood change!
King John, iii. 1.

FAITHED. *Believed; credited.*

Thou unpossessing bastard! dost thou think,
If I would stand against thee, would the reposal
Of any trust, virtue, or worth, in thee
Make thy words *faith'd?* *King Lear, ii. 1.*

FAITHFUL. *Loyal; exact.*

Yet, heaven bear witness,
And if I have a conscience, let it sink me,
Even as the axe falls, if I be not *faithful!*
Henry 8, ii. 1.
Good madam, stay awhile; I will be *faithful*.
Hamlet, ii. 2.

FAITHFULLY. *Earnestly; zealously.*

If his occasion were not virtuous,
I should not urge it half so *faithfully*.
Timon of Athens, iii. 2.

FAITOR. *A vagabond; a rogue; a rascal.*

Down, down, dogs! down, *faitors!* Have we
not Hiren here? *Henry 4, P. 2, ii. 4.*

FALCHION. *A sword.*

I have seen the day, with my good biting *falchion*
I would have made them skip. *King Lear, v. 3.*

To FALL. *To let fall; to strike down; to shrink; to happen; to befall.*

If that the earth could teem with woman's tears,
Each drop she *falls* would prove a crocodile.
Othello, iv. 1.
And, as she fled, her mantle she did *fall*.
Midsummer-Night's Dream, v. 1.
When he, wafting his eyes to the contrary,
And *falling* a lip of much contempt, speeds from me.
Winter's Tale, i. 2.
Infect her beauty, .
You fen-suck'd fogs, drawn by the powerful sun,
To *fall* and blast her pride! *King Lear, ii. 4.*
Let us be keen, and rather cut a little,
Than *fall*, and bruise to death.
Measure for Measure, ii. 1.
A good leg will *fall;* a straight back will stoop.
Henry 5, v. 2.

I know not how,
But I do find it cowardly and vile,
For fear of what might *fall*, so to prevent
The time of life. *Julius Cæsar*, v. 1.

TO FALL FROM. *To leave; to break with; to forsake.*

Thou shalt not need.—England, I will *fall from* thee. *King John*, iii. 1.

TO FALL ON. *To light upon; to meet.*

But, seeing thou *fall'st on* me so luckily,
I will assay thee. *Henry 4*, P. 1, v. 4.

TO FALL OVER. *To revolt; to go over; to desert.*

And dost thou now *fall over* to my foes ?
King John, iii. 1.

FALLACY. *An illusion.*

Until I know this sure uncertainty,
I'll entertain the offer'd *fallacy.*
Comedy of Errors, ii. 2.

FALLING-FROM. *Falling-away; defection.*

The mere want of gold, and the *falling-from* of his friends, drove him into this melancholy.
Timon of Athens, iv. 3.

FALSE. *Insidious; deceitful; treacherous.*

O place and greatness, millions of *false* eyes
Are stuck upon thee ! *Measure for Measure*, iv. 1.

TO FALSE. *To deceive; to forswear.*

Nay, not sure, in a thing *falsing.*
Comedy of Errors, ii. 2.

'Tis gold which makes
Diana's rangers *false* themselves, yield up
Their deer to the stand o' the stealer.
Cymbeline, ii. 3.

FALSEHOOD. *Want of honesty; deceit; perfidy.*

If you suspect my husbandry or *falsehood*,
Call me before the exactest auditors.
Timon of Athens, ii. 2.

O, what a goodly outside *falsehood* hath !
Merchant of Venice, i. 3.

FALSELY. *Artfully; deceitfully; treacherously.*

While truth the while
Doth *falsely* blind the eyesight of his look.
Love's Labour's lost, i. 1.

Nor has Coriolanus
Deserv'd this so dishonour'd rub, laid *falsely*
I' the plain way of his merit. *Coriolanus*, iii. 1.

TO FALSIFY. *To frustrate; to deceive; to disappoint.*

By how much better than my word I am,
By so much shall I *falsify* men's hopes.
Henry 4, P. 1, i. 2.

FAME. *Report; rumour.*

So is the *fame.* Would we had spoke together !
Antony and Cleopatra, ii. 2.

FAMILIAR. *A demon; an intimate friend.*

Away with him ! he has a *familiar* under his tongue; he speaks not o' God's name.
Henry 6, P. 2, iv. 7.

Love is a *familiar*; Love is a devil : there is no evil angel but Love. *Love's Labour's lost*, i. 2.

Sir, the king is a noble gentleman ; and my *familiar*, I do assure ye, my very good friend.
Ibid. v. 1.

FAMILIAR. *Courteous; affable; friendly; attendant; subordinate.*

Be thou *familiar*, but by no means vulgar.
Hamlet, i. 3.

Now, ye *familiar* spirits, that are cull'd
Out of the powerful legions under earth,
Help me this once, that France may get the field.
Henry 6, P. 1, v. 3.

TO FAN. *To winnow; to make trial of; to assay.*

The love I bear him
Made me to *fan* you thus ; but the gods made you,
Unlike all others, chaffless. *Cymbeline*, i. 6.

FANCY. *Love; inclination.*

And the imperial vot'ress passed on,
In virgin meditation, *fancy*-free.
Midsummer-Night's Dream, ii. 2.

Tell me where is *fancy* bred,
Or in the heart, or in the head ?
Merchant of Venice, iii. 2.

All *fancy*-sick she is, and pale of cheer.
Midsummer-Night's Dream, iii. 2.

So full of shapes is *fancy*,
That it alone is high-fantastical.
Twelfth-Night, i. 1.

For you, fair Hermia, look you arm yourself
To fit your *fancies* to your father's will.
Midsummer-Night's Dream, i. 1.

To FANCY. *To love.*

Never did young man *fancy*
With so eternal and so fix'd a soul.
Troilus and Cressida, v. 2.

To FANG. *To seize.*

Destruction *fang* mankind ! *Timon of Athens*, iv. 3.

FANGLED. *Gaudy ; showy ; trifling.*

A book ? O rare one !
Be not, as is our *fangled* world, a garment
Nobler than that it covers. *Cymbeline*, v. 4.

FANTASIED. *Full of wild fancies.*

But as I travell'd hither through the land,
I find the people strangely *fantasied*.
King John, iv. 2.

FANTASTICAL. *Fanciful ; imaginary ; unreal ; ideal.*

So full of shapes is fancy,
That it alone is high-*fantastical*.
Twelfth-Night, i. 1.
Are ye *fantastical*, or that indeed
Which outwardly ye show ? *Macbeth*, i. 3.
My thought, whose murder yet is but *fantastical*,
Shakes so my single state of man, that function
Is smother'd in surmise. *Ibid.* i. 3.

FANTASTICO. *A coxcomb ; a fashion-monger.*

The pox of such antic, lisping, affecting *fantasticoes ;* these new tuners of accents !
Romeo and Juliet, ii. 4.

FANTASY. *Imagination ; fancy.*

Rein up the organs of her *fantasy.*
Merry Wives of Windsor, v. 5.
I know he doth not ; and do arm myself
To welcome the condition of the time ;
Which cannot look more hideously upon me
Than I have drawn it in my *fantasy.*
Henry 4, P. 2, v. 2.
True, I talk of dreams ;
Which are the children of an idle brain,
Begot of nothing but vain *fantasy.*
Romeo and Juliet, i. 4.

FAP. *Drunk.*

And being *fap*, was, as they say, cashiered.
Merry Wives of Windsor, i. 1.

FAR. *Extravagantly ; with exaggeration ; further off.*

You speak him *far.*—
I do extend him, sir, within himself ;

Crush him together, rather than unfold
His measure duly. *Cymbeline*, i. 1.
How of descent
As good as we ?—In that he spake too *far*.
Ibid. v. 5.
Not hold thee of our blood, no, not our kin,
Far' than Deucalion off. *Winter's Tale*, iv. 3.

FARCED. *Swelling ; pompous.*

The intertissu'd robe of gold and pearl,
The *farcèd* title running 'fore the king.
Henry 5, iv. 1.

FARDEL. *A bundle ; a burden.*

Well, let us to the king ; there is that in this *fardel* will make him scratch his beard.
Winter's Tale, iv. 3.
Who would *fardels* bear,
To grunt and sweat under a weary life ?
Hamlet, iii. 1.

To FASHION. *To frame ; to put on ; to assume.*

And it better fits my blood to be disdained of all than to *fashion* a carriage to rob love from any.
Much Ado about Nothing, i. 3.

FAST. *Settled ; firm ; fixed.*

And 'tis our *fast* intent
To shake all cares and business from our age.
King Lear, i. 1.

FASTENED. *Confirmed ; hardened ; determined.*

O strong and *fasten'd* villain !
Would he deny his letter ? *King Lear*, ii. 1.

FAT. *A vat ; wealth.*

In thy *fats* our cares be drown'd,
With thy grapes our hairs be crown'd !
Antony and Cleopatra, ii. 7.
If you do fight against your country's foes,
Your country's *fat* shall pay your pains the hire.
Richard 3, v. 3.

FAT. *Dull.*

Ned, prithee, come out of that *fat* room, and lend me thy hand to laugh a little.
Henry 4, P. 1, ii. 4.
If it be aught to the old tune, my lord,
It is as *fat* and fulsome to mine ear
As howling after music. *Twelfth-Night*, v. 1.

R

FATED. *Preordaining; predestined.*

The *fated* sky
Gives us free scope; only doth backward pull
Our slow designs, when we ourselves are dull.
All's well that ends well, i. 1.
Now all the plagues that in the pendulous air
Hang *fated* o'er men's faults light on thy daughters!
King Lear, iii. 4.
Even then this forkèd plague is *fated* to us
When we do quicken. *Othello,* iii. 3.

FATIGATE. *Fatigued; wearied.*

Then straight his doubled spirit
Requicken'd what in flesh was *fatigate.*
Coriolanus, ii. 2.

FAULTY. *Culpable; guilty.*

Say, if thou dar'st, proud Lord of Warwickshire,
That I am *faulty* in Duke Humphrey's death.
Henry 6, P. 2, ii. 2.

FAVOUR. *Face; countenance; feature; token; mildness; lenity; indulgence; pardon.*

Angelo hath seen them both, and will discover
the *favour.* *Measure for Measure,* iv. 2.
I know that virtue to be in you, Brutus,
As well as I do know your outward *favour.*
Julius Cæsar, i. 2.
When I will wear a garment all of blood,
And stain my *favour* in a bloody mask,
Which, wash'd away, shall scour my shame with it.
Henry 4, P. 1, iii. 2.
With robbers' hands my hospitable *favours*
You should not ruffle thus. *King Lear,* iii. 7.
Here, Fluellen; wear thou this *favour* for me,
and stick it in thy cap. *Henry* 5, iv. 7.
Come on, my son, in whom my house's name
Must be digested, give a *favour* from you.
All's well that ends well, v. 3.
Justice with *favour* have I always done.
Henry 6, P. 2, iv. 7.
Give me your *favour:*—my dull brain was wrought
With things forgotten. *Macbeth,* i. 3.

FAWN. *A cringe; a bow.*

And you will rather show our general louts
How you can frown, than spend a *fawn* upon 'em,
For the inheritance of their loves.
Coriolanus, iii. 2.

FAY. *Faith.*

These fifteen years! by my *fay,* a goodly nap.
Taming of the Shrew, Induction, sc. 2.

Ah, sirrah, by my *fay,* it waxes late :
I'll to my rest. *Romeo and Juliet,* i. 5.
Shall we to the court ? for, by my *fay,*
I cannot reason. *Hamlet,* ii. 2.

FEALTY. *Loyalty; fidelity.*

Our *fealty* and Tenantius' right
With honour to maintain. *Cymbeline,* v. 4.
I am in parliament pledge for his truth
And lasting *fealty* to the new-made king.
Richard 2, v. 2.
And let my sovereign, virtuous Henry,
Command my eldest son, nay, all my sons,
As pledges of my *fealty* and love.
Henry 6, P. 2, v. 1.

FEAR. *An object of fear; any thing which causes alarm; terror; danger.*

Or in the night, imagining some *fear,*
How easy is a bush suppos'd a bear !
Midsummer-Night's Dream, v. 1.
Shall we buy treason ? and indent with *fears,*
When they have lost and forfeited themselves ?
Henry 4, P. 1, i. 3.
All these bold *fears*
Thou see'st with peril I have answerèd.
Ibid. P. 2, iv. 4.
Ensconcing ourselves into seeming knowledge,
when we should submit ourselves to an unknown
fear. *All's well that ends well,* ii. 3.
O, if I wake, shall I not be distraught,
Environèd with all these hideous *fears* ?
Romeo and Juliet, iv. 3.
Present *fears*
Are less than horrible imaginings. *Macbeth,* i. 3.
There is no *fear* in him; let him not die.
Julius Cæsar, ii. 1.

TO FEAR. *To fear for; to care for; to regard; to doubt; to distrust; to frighten.*

The king is sickly, weak, and melancholy,
And his physicians *fear* him mightily.
Richard 3, i. 1.
If any *fear*
Lesser his person than an ill report.
Coriolanus, i. 6.
Well, while I live I'll *fear* no other thing
So sore, as keeping safe Nerissa's ring.
Merchant of Venice, v. 1.
Fear you not her courage. *Henry* 6, P. 2, i. 4.
I speak not " be thou true," as *fearing* thee.
Troilus and Cressida, iv. 4.

We must not make a scarecrow of the law,
Setting it up to *fear* the birds of prey.
                              Measure for Measure, ii. 1.
I tell thee, lady, this aspéct of mine
Hath *fear'd* the valiant.   *Merchant of Venice*, ii. 1.

FEARFUL.   *Formidable ; terrible ; unsafe ; reverential ; impetuous.*

A mighty and a *fearful* head they are.
                              Henry 4, P. 1, iii. 2.
Make not too rash a trial of him, for
He's gentle, and not *fearful*.   *Tempest*, i. 2.
          Nay, when I have a suit
Wherein I mean to touch your love indeed,
It shall be full of poise and difficult weight,
And *fearful* to be granted.   *Othello*, iii. 3.
See to my house, left in the *fearful* guard
Of an unthrifty knave.   *Merchant of Venice*, i. 3.
We are amaz'd ; and thus long have we stood
To watch the *fearful* bending of thy knee,
Because we thought ourself thy lawful king.
                              Richard 2, iii. 3.
          And come down
With *fearful* bravery, thinking by this face
To fasten in our thoughts that they have courage.
                              Julius Cæsar, v. 1.

FEARFULLY.   *Dreadfully ; terribly.*

There is a cliff, whose high and bending head
Looks *fearfully* in the confinèd deep.
                              King Lear, iv. 1.

FEAT.   *Nice ; neat ; clever ; dexterous.*

And look how well my garments sit upon me ;
Much *feater* than before.   *Tempest*, ii. 1.
A page so kind, so duteous, diligent,
So *feat*, so nurse-like.   *Cymbeline*, v. 5.

To FEAT.   *To form ; to fashion.*

To the more mature a glass that *feated* them.
                              Cymbeline, i. 1.

FEATLY.   *Neatly ; nimbly ; dexterously.*

Foot it *featly* here and there.   .   *Tempest*, i. 2.
She dances *featly*.   *Winter's Tale*, iv. 3.

FEATURE.   *Shape ; comeliness ; face ; favour ; countenance.*

Cheated of *feature* by dissembling nature.
                              Richard 3, i. 1.
Thou changèd and self-cover'd thing, for shame,
Be-monster not thy *feature*.   *King Lear*, iv. 3.
Report the *feature* of Octavia, her years,
Her inclination.   *Antony and Cleopatra*, ii. 5.

Am I the man yet ? doth my simple *feature*
content you ?   *As you like it*, iii. 3.
Forgive the comment that my passion made
Upon thy *feature*.   *King John*, iv. 2.

FEDARY.   *Companion ; fellow ; an accomplice ; a confederate.*

          Else let my brother die,
If not a *fedary*, but only he
Owe, and succeed this weakness.
                              Measure for Measure, ii. 4.
Art thou a *fedary* for this act, and look'st
So virgin-like without ?   *Cymbeline*, iii. 2.
More she's a traitor : and Camillo is
A *fedary* with her.   *Winter's Tale*, ii. 1.

FEE.   *Value ; worth.*

I do not set my life at a pin's *fee*.   *Hamlet*, i. 4.

FEE-GRIEF.   *A private grief.*

          What concern they ?
The general cause ? or is it a *fee-grief*
Due to some single breast ?   *Macbeth*, iv. 3.

To FEEBLE.   *To weaken ; to enfeeble.*

Shall that victorious hand be *feebled* here,
That in your chambers gave you chastisement ?
                              King John, v. 2.
          Making parties strong,
And *feebling* such as stand not in their liking
Below their cobbled shoes.   *Coriolanus*, i. 1.

FEED.   *Pasture ; grazing land.*

Besides, his cote, his flocks, and bounds of *feed*,
Are now on sale.   *As you like it*, ii. 4.

FEEDER.   *A servant.*

When all our offices have been oppress'd
With riotous *feeders*.   *Timon of Athens*, ii. 2.
I will your very faithful *feeder* be,
And buy it with your gold right suddenly.
                              As you like it, ii. 4.
          But that the *feeders*
Digest it with a custom, I should blush
To see you so attir'd.   *Winter's Tale*, iv. 3.
Have I my pillow left unpress'd in Rome,
Forborne the getting of a lawful race,
And by a gem of women, to be abus'd
By one who looks on *feeders* ?
                              Antony and Cleopatra, iii. 13.

FEEDING. *Pasture; grazing land.*

They call him Doricles; and boasts himself
To have a worthy *feeding.*   *Winter's Tale,* iv. 3.

FEELING. *Deep-felt; sensible.*

Yet let me weep for such a *feeling* loss.
               Romeo and Juliet, iii. 5.
A most poor man, made tame to fortune's blows;
Who, by the art of known and *feeling* sorrows,
Am pregnant to good pity.   *King Lear,* iv. 6.
I understand thy kisses, and thou mine,
And that's a *feeling* disputation.
               Henry 4, P. 1, iii. 1.

FEET. *Footing.*

Who already,
Wise in our negligence, have secret *feet*
In some of our best ports.   *King Lear,* iii. 1.

FELICITATE. *Made happy.*

And find I am alone *felicitate*
In your dear highness' love.   *King Lear,* i. 1.

FELL. *A hide or skin.*

Why, we are still handling our ewes; and their
fells, you know, are greasy.   *As you like it,* iii. 2.
The goujeers shall devour them, flesh and *fell,*
Ere they shall make us weep. '   *King Lear,* v. 3.
         And my *fell* of hair
Would at a dismal treatise rouse and stir
As life were in't.   *Macbeth,* v. 5.

FELLOW. *A rogue; a rascal; a scoundrel.*

We shall find this friar a notable *fellow.*
               Measure for Measure, v. 1.

To FELLOW. *To pair with; to match; to re-
semble.*

With what's unreal thou coactive art,
And *fellow'st* nothing.   *Winter's Tale,* i. 2.

FELLOWLY. *Sympathetic; brotherly; kindred.*

Mine eyes, even sociable to the show of thine,
Fall *fellowly* drops.   *Tempest,* v. 1.

FELLOWSHIP. *Alliance; coöperation; part-
nership; suretyship.*

This man was riding
From Alcibiades to Timon's cave,

With letters of entreaty, which imported
His *fellowship* i' the cause against your city.
               Timon of Athens, v. 2.
Would not this, sir, and a forest of feathers,
with two Provincial roses on my razed shoes, get
me a *fellowship* in a cry of players? *Hamlet,* iii. 2.
There is scarce truth enough alive to make
societies secure; but security enough to make *fel-
lowships* accursed.   *Measure for Measure,* iii. 2.

FEMALE. *Soft; tender; delicate.*

And boys, with women's voices,
Strive to speak big, and clap their *female* joints
In stiff unwieldy arms against thy crown.
               Richard 2, iii. 2.

FENCE. *Skill in defence; the art of fencing.*

I'll prove it on his body, if he dare,
Despite his nice *fence* and his active practice.
         Much Ado about Nothing, v. 1.
I bruised my shin th' other day with playing at
sword and dagger with a master of *fence.*
         Merry Wives of Windsor, i. 1.

To FENCE. *To guard; to protect; to defend.*

Can Oxford, that did ever *fence* the right,
Now buckler falsehood with a pedigree?
               Henry 6, P. 3, iii. 3.
Where's Captain Margaret, to *fence* you now?
               Ibid. ii. 6.
         O thou wall
That girdlest in those wolves, dive in the earth,
And *fence* not Athens!   *Timon of Athens,* iv. 1.

FESTINATE. *Speedy; hasty.* .

Advise the duke, where you are going, to a
most *festinate* preparation: we are bound to the
like.   *King Lear,* iii. 7.

FESTINATELY. *Quickly; speedily.*

Take this key, give enlargement to the swain,
bring him *festinately* hither.
         Love's Labour's lost, iii. 1.

FESTIVAL. *Holiday; gay; cheerful.*

So that, in this time of lethargy, I picked and
cut most of their *festival* purses. *Winter's Tale,* iv. 3.
I was not born under a rhyming planet, nor I
cannot woo in *festival* terms.
         Much Ado about Nothing, v. 2.
All things that we ordainèd *festival*
Turn from their office to black funeral.
             Romeo and Juliet, iv. 5.

FET. *Fetched; brought; derived.*

And follow'd with a rabble, that rejoice
To see my tears and hear my deep-*fet* groans.
Henry 6, P. 2, ii. 4.

Me seemeth good, that, with some little train,
Forthwith from Ludlow the young prince be *fet*
Hither to London, to be crown'd our king.
Richard 3, ii. 2.

On, on, you noble English,
Whose blood is *fet* from fathers of war-proof!
Henry 5, iii. 1.

FETCH. *A trick; an artifice.*

And, I believe, it is a *fetch* of warrant.
Hamlet, ii. 1.

Deny to speak with me? They are sick? they are
weary?
They have travell'd all the night? Mere *fetches;*
The images of revolt and flying off.
Fetch me a better answer.   *King Lear*, ii. 4.

To FETCH ABOUT. *To veer round; to change.*

And, like a shifted wind unto a sail,
It makes the course of thoughts to *fetch about.*
King John, iv. 2.

To FETCH IN. *To apprehend; to seize; to ensnare; to entangle.*

The which he hearing—
As it is like him—might break out, and swear
He'd *fetch us in.*   *Cymbeline*, iv. 2.

Within our files there are,
Of those that serv'd Mark Antony but late,
Enough to *fetch him in.*
Antony and Cleopatra, iv. 1.

You speak this to *fetch me in*, my lord.
Much Ado about Nothing, i. 1.

To FETTLE. *To prepare; to make ready.*

But *fettle* your fine joints 'gainst Thursday next,
To go with Paris to Saint Peter's church,
Or I will drag thee on a hurdle thither.
Romeo and Juliet, iii. 5.

To FEVER. *To put into a fever.*

Henceforth
The white hand of a lady *fever* thee,
Shake thou to look on't.
Antony and Cleopatra, iii. 13.

FEVEROUS. *Feverish.*

My heart beats thicker than a *feverous* pulse.
Troilus and Cressida, iii. 2.

Some say, the earth was *feverous* and did shake.
Macbeth, ii. 1.

Thou mad'st thine enemies shake, as if the world
Were *feverous* and did tremble.   *Coriolanus*, i. 4.

FEWNESS. *Brevity; conciseness.*

Fewness and truth, 'tis thus.
Measure for Measure, i. 4.

FIELDED. *On the field of battle.*

Now, Mars, I prithee, make us quick in work,
That we with smoking swords may march from
hence,
To help our *fielded* friends!   *Coriolanus*, i. 4.

FIERCE. *Wild; vehement; extravagant; hasty; outrageous; violent.*

Such temperate order in so *fierce* a course
Doth want example.   *King John*, iii. 4.

And your task shall be,
With all the *fierce* endeavour of your wit,
To enforce the painèd impotent to smile.
Love's Labour's lost, v. 2.

And think no more of this night's accidents,
But as the *fierce* vexation of a dream.
Midsummer-Night's Dream, iv. 1.

This *fierce* abridgment
Hath to it circumstantial branches, which
Distinction should be rich in.   *Cymbeline*, v. 5.

What had he to do in these *fierce* vanities?
Henry 8, i. 1.

O, the *fierce* wretchedness that glory brings us!
Timon of Athens, iv. 2.

FIGHTS. *Screens formerly used in sea-fights.*

Pursue, up with your *fights*.
Merry Wives of Windsor, ii. 2.

FIGURE. *Letter; character; semblance; shape.*

Our captain hath in every *figure* skill,
An ag'd interpreter, though young in days.
Timon of Athens, v. 3.

Save me, and hover o'er me with your wings,
You heavenly guards!—What would your gracious
figure?   *Hamlet*, iii. 4.

FILE. *List; roll; register; catalogue.*

The greater *file* of the subject held the duke to
be wise.   *Measure for Measure*, iii. 2.

He makes up the *file* of all the gentry.
Henry 8, i. 1.
This very day,
Great Mars, I put myself into thy *file*.
All's well that ends well, iii. 3.
The valu'd *file*
Distinguishes the swift, the slow, the subtle,
The housekeeper, the hunter. *Macbeth*, iii. 1.

To FILE. *To smooth; to polish; to defile; to sully.*
His discourse peremptory, his tongue *filed*, his eye ambitious. *Love's Labour's lost*, v. 1.
If 't be so,
For Banquo's issue have I *fil'd* my mind.
Macbeth, iii. 1.

To FILE WITH. *To keep rank; to range.*
My endeavours
Have ever come too short of my desires,
Yet *fil'd* with my abilities. *Henry* 8, iii. 2.

FILL. *The shaft of a cart or waggon.*
An you draw backward, we'll put you i' the *fills*.
Troilus and Cressida, iii. 2.
Thou hast got more hair on thy chin than Dobbin my *fill*-horse has on his tail.
Merchant of Venice, ii. 2.

FILTH. *A drab; a prostitute.*
To general *filths*
Convert o' the instant, green virginity!
Timon of Athens, iv. 1.

To FIND. *To find out; to see through; to detect.*
My blood hath been too cold and temperate,
Unapt to stir at these indignities,
And you have *found* me ; for accordingly
You tread upon my patience. *Henry* 4, P. 1, i. 3.
And I'll be plac'd, so please you, in the ear
Of all their conference. If she *find* him not,
To England send him ; or confine him where
Your wisdom best shall think. *Hamlet*, iii. 1.

FIND-FAULT. *A caviller; a censurer; a carper.*
We are the makers of manners, Kate; and the liberty that follows our places stops the mouth of all *find-faults*. *Henry* 5, v. 2.

FINE. *Punishment; penalty; end; conclusion.*
Mine were the very cipher of a function,

To fine the fault, whose *fine* stands in record,
And let go by the actor.
Measure for Measure, ii. 2.
And the *fine* is, I will live a bachelor.
Much Ado about Nothing, i. 1.
Still the *fine's* the crown;
Whate'er the course, the end is the renown.
All's well that ends well, iv. 4.

FINE. *Nice; delicate; subtle; sly.*
Spirits are not finely touch'd
But to *fine* issues. *Measure for Measure*, i. 1.
Nature is *fine* in love ; and, where 'tis *fine*,
It sends some precious instance of itself
After the thing it loves. *Hamlet*, iv. 5.
But thou art too *fine* in thy evidence ; therefore, stand aside. *All's well that ends well*, v. 3.

To FINE. *To punish; to forfeit; to deck; to garnish.*
Mine were the very cipher of a function,
To *fine* the fault, and let go by the actor.
Measure for Measure, ii. 2.
How now! what means this, herald? know'st thou not
That I have *fin'd* these bones of mine for ransom?
Henry 5, iv. 7.
Hugh Capet also
To *fine* his title with some show of truth
Convey'd himself as heir to the Lady Lingare.
Ibid. i. 2.

FINELESS. *Unbounded; infinite.*
Poor and content is rich, and rich enough ;
But riches *fineless* is as poor as winter
To him that ever fears he shall be poor.
Othello, iii. 3.

FINELY. *Nicely; exquisitely.*
Spirits are not *finely* touch'd
But to fine issues. *Measure for Measure*, i. 1.

FIRAGO. *A virago.*
I have not seen such a *firago*. *Twelfth-Night*, iii. 5.

FIRE-DRAKE. *A meteor; an ignis fatuus.*
That *fire-drake* did I hit three times on the head, and three times was his nose discharged against me.
Henry 8, v. 3.

FIRE-NEW. *Bran-new.*
A man of *fire-new* words, fashion's own knight.
Love's Labour's lost, i. 1.

Despite thy victor sword and *fire-new* fortune,
Thy valour and thy heart,—thou art a traitor.
King Lear, v. 3.

FIRST. *Noble; great; excellent.*

My *first* son,
Whither wilt thou go? *Coriolanus*, iv. 1.

FIRSTLING. *First act or thought; the first produce or offspring.*

Our play
Leaps o'er the vaunt and *firstlings* of those broils,
Beginning in the middle.
Troilus and Cressida, Prologue.
The very *firstlings* of my heart shall be
The *firstlings* of my hand. *Macbeth*, iv. 1.

To FIST. *To gripe; to grasp; to lay hold of.*

Unbuckling helms, *fisting* each other's throat.
Coriolanus, iv. 5.
An I but *fist* him once; an he come but within
my vice. *Henry 4*, P. 2, ii. 1.

FIT. *The division of a song or poem.*

Well said, my lord! well, you say so in *fits*.
Troilus and Cressida, iii. 1.

FIT O' THE FACE. *A grimace.*

As far as I see, all the good our English
Have got by the late voyage is but merely
A *fit* or two o' the face. *Henry 8*, i. 3.

To FIT. *To suit; to be fit for.*

Look who comes yonder: she shall be our messenger to this paltry knight.—
Trust me, I thought on her: she'll *fit* it.
Merry Wives of Windsor, ii. 1.

FITCHEW. *A polecat.*

To be a dog, a mule, a cat, a *fitchew*, a toad, a
lizard, an owl, a puttock, or a herring without a roe,
I would not care; but to be Menelaus,—I would
conspire against destiny. *Troilus and Cressida*, v. 1.
'Tis such another *fitchew*! marry, a perfumed one.
Othello, iv. 1.

FITLY. *Exactly; precisely.*

Even so most *fitly*
As you malign our senators for that
They are not such as you. *Coriolanus*, i. 1.

FITMENT. *Equipment; dress; disguise.*

I am, sir,
The soldier that did company these three

In poor beseeming; 'twas a *fitment* for
The purpose I then follow'd. *Cymbeline*, v. 5.

FIXURE. *Position; stability; firmness.*

The *fixure* of her eye has motion in't,
As we are mock'd with art. *Winter's Tale*, v. 3.

Frights, changes, horrors,
Divert and crack, rend and deracinate
The unity and married calm of states
Quite from their *fixure*. *Troilus and Cressida*, i. 3.

FLAKY. *Flakelike; scattering.*

The silent hours steal on,
And *flaky* darkness breaks within the east.
Richard 3, v. 3.

FLAMEN. *A priest.*

Seld-shown *flamens*
Do press among the popular throngs, and puff
To win a vulgar station. *Coriolanus*, ii. 1.

Hear the *flamen*,
That scolds against the quality of the flesh,
And not believes himself. *Timon of Athens*, iv. 3.

FLAP-DRAGON. *A raisin, or other substance, taken into the mouth and eaten while in a state of ignition.*

Thou art easier swallowed than a *flap-dragon*.
Love's Labour's lost, v. 1.

And drinks off candles' ends for *flap-dragons*.
Henry 4, P. 2, ii. 4.

To FLAP-DRAGON. *To swallow up; to devour.*

But to make an end of the ship,—to see how
the sea *flap-dragoned* it. *Winter's Tale*, iii. 3.

FLAT-LONG. *Flat-wise; flat.*

What a blow was there given!
An it had not fallen *flat-long*. *Tempest*, ii. 1.

FLATNESS. *Completeness; fulness; extremity.*

O that he were alive, and here beholding
The *flatness* of my misery, yet with eyes
Of pity, not revenge! *Winter's Tale*, iii. 2.

To FLATTER UP. *To repair.*

If this, or more than this, I would deny,
To *flatter up* these powers of mine with rest,
The sudden hand of death close up mine eye!
Love's Labour's lost, v. 2.

FLAUNTS. *Finery ; showy apparel.*

Or how should I, in these my borrow'd *flaunts*,
Behold the sternness of his presence ?
Winter's Tale, iv. 3.

FLAW. *A piece ; a fragment ; a blast ; disorder ; tumult ; any sudden commotion of mind ; defeat ; overthrow.*

I have full cause of weeping ; but this heart
Shall break into a hundred thousand *flaws*,
Or ere I'll weep.—O fool, I shall go mad !
King Lear, ii. 4.

Like a great sea-mark, standing every *flaw*,
And saving those that eye thee. *Coriolanus*, v. 3.

O, that that earth, which kept the world in awe,
Should patch a wall to expel the winter's *flaw !*
Hamlet, v. 1.

Until the golden circuit on my head,
Like to the glorious sun's transparent beams,
Do calm the fury of this mad-bred *flaw*.
Henry 6, P. 2, iii. 1.

O, these *flaws* and starts,
Impostors to true fear, would well become
A woman's story at a winter's fire. *Macbeth*, iii. 4.

Observe how Antony becomes his *flaw*.
Antony and Cleopatra, iii. 12.

To FLAW. *To break ; to violate ; to crack.*

For France hath *flaw'd* the league, and hath attach'd
Our merchants' goods at Bourdeaux. *Henry* 8, i. 1.

There have been commissions
Sent down among 'em, which hath *flaw'd* the heart
Of all their loyalties. *Ibid.* i. 2.

To FLECK. *To streak ; to variegate.*

And *fleckèd* darkness like a drunkard reels
From forth day's path and Titan's fiery wheels.
Romeo and Juliet, ii. 3.

FLEER. *A sneer ; a look of contempt.*

Do but encave yourself,
And mark the *fleers*, the gibes, and notable scorns,
That dwell in every region of his face.
Othello, iv. 1.

To FLEER. *To mock ; to flout ; to sneer ; to gibe.*

Tush, tush, man ; never *fleer* and jest at me.
Much Ado about Nothing, v. 1.

What, dares the slave
Come hither, cover'd with an antic face,
To *fleer* and scorn at our solemnity ?
Romeo and Juliet, i. 5.

You speak to Casca ; and to such a man
That is no *fleering* tell-tale. *Julius Cæsar*, i. 3.

To FLEET. *To change ; to float.*

So cares and joys abound, as seasons *fleet*.
Henry 6, P. 2, ii. 4.

Clarence is come—false, *fleeting*, perjur'd Clarence—
That stabb'd me in the field by Tewksbury.
Richard 3, i. 4.

Now from head to foot
I am marble-constant ; now the *fleeting* moon
No planet is of mine. *Antony and Cleopatra*, v. 2.

Our sever'd navy too
Have knit again, and *fleet*, threatening most sea-like.
Ibid. iii. 13.

FLESHMENT. *Pride ; insolence ; vainglory.*

And, in the *fleshment* of this dread exploit,
Drew on me here again. *King Lear*, ii. 2.

FLEWED. *Mouthed ; chapped.*

My hounds are bred out of the Spartan kind,
So *flew'd*, so sanded.
Midsummer-Night's Dream, iv. 1.

FLEXURE. *Crouching ; servile bending.*

Think'st thou the fiery fever will go out
With titles blown from adulation ?
Will it give place to *flexure* and low bending ?
Henry 5, iv. 1.

The elephant hath joints, but none for courtesy : his legs are legs for necessity, not for *flexure*.
Troilus and Cressida, ii. 3.

FLIGHTY. *Swift ; speedy ; fleeting.*

The *flighty* purpose never is o'ertook
Unless the deed go with it. *Macbeth*, iv. 1.

To FLINCH. *To err ; to be mistaken ; to fail.*

If I break time, or *flinch* in property
Of what I spoke, unpitied let me die.
All's well that ends well, ii. 1.

To FLING. *To go away.*

He's *flung* in rage from this ingrateful seat
Of monstrous friends. *Timon of Athens*, iv. 2.

FLIRT-GILL. *A jade ; a hussy.*

Scurvy knave ! I am none of his *flirt-gills*.
Romeo and Juliet, ii. 4.

FLOTE. *Wave.*

And for the rest o' the fleet,
Which I dispers'd, they all have met again,
And are upon the Mediterranean *flote*,
Bound sadly home for Naples. *Tempest*, i. 2.

FLOURISH. *Decoration; ornament.*

Poor painted queen, vain *flourish* of my fortune!
Richard 3, i. 3.

TO FLOURISH. *To grace; to deck; to adorn.*

'Tis no sin,
Sith that the justice of your title to him
Doth *flourish* the deceit.
Measure for Measure, iv. 1.

FLOUT. *A mock; a gibe; a sneer.*

O poverty in wit, kingly-poor *flout*!
Will they not, think you, hang themselves to-night?
Love's Labour's lost, v. 2.
Full of comparisons and wounding *flouts*.
Ibid. v. 2.

TO FLOUT. *To mock; to jeer; to gibe; to wrangle.*

By heaven, these scroyles of Angiers *flout* you, kings.
King John, ii. 1.
What, wilt thou *flout* me thus unto my face?
Comedy of Errors, i. 2.
We shall be *flouting*; we cannot hold.
As you like it, v. 1.

FLOWERY. *Soft; effeminate.*

Why give you me this shame?
Think you I can a resolution fetch
From *flowery* tenderness? If I must die,
I will encounter darkness as a bride,
And hug it in mine arms.
Measure for Measure, iii. 1.

FLUSH. *Fresh; vigorous.*

The borders maritime
Lack blood to think on't, and *flush* youth revolt.
Antony and Cleopatra, i. 4.
With all his crimes broad blown, as *flush* as May.
Hamlet, iii. 3.
Now the time is *flush*,
When crouching marrow, in the bearer strong,
Cries, of itself, "No more." *Timon of Athens*, v. 4.

TO FLUSTER. *To make drunk.*

Three lads of Cyprus,—noble swelling spirits,—

Have I to-night *fluster'd* with flowing cups,
And they watch too. *Othello*, ii. 3.

FLUX. *Concourse; confluence.*

'Tis right, quoth he; thus misery doth part
The *flux* of company. *As you like it*, ii. 1.

TO FLY OUT OF. *To forsake; to desert.*

My valour's poison'd
With only suffering stain by him; for him
Shall *fly* out of itself. *Coriolanus*, i. 10.

TO FOB. *To cheat; to defraud; to cozen.*

But, I prithee, sweet wag, shall there be gallows
standing in England when thou art king? and resolution thus *fobbed* as it is with the rusty curb of
old father antic the law? *Henry* 4, P. 1, i. 2.

TO FOB OFF. *To set aside; to put off; to evade.*

Yet you must not think to *fob* off our disgrace
with a tale. *Coriolanus*, i. 1.

FOIL. *Defeat; overthrow.*

One sudden *foil* shall never breed distrust.
Henry 6, P. 1, iii. 3.
Then take my soul, my body, soul, and all,
Before that England give the French the *foil*.
Ibid. v. 3.

TO FOIN. *To thrust; to stab.*

He will *foin* like any devil. *Henry* 4, P. 2, ii. 1.
To see thee fight, to see thee *foin*.
Merry Wives of Windsor, ii. 3.

FOISON. *Abundance; plenty.*

Scotland hath *foisons* to fill up your will,
Of your mere own. *Macbeth*, iv. 3.
But nature should bring forth
Of its own kind, all *foison*, all abundance.
Tempest, ii. 1.

TO FOLD IN. *To infold; to enclose; to en-compass.*

The man is noble, and his fame *folds* in
This orb o' the earth. *Coriolanus*, v. 6.
The fires i' the lowest hell *fold* in the people!
Call me their traitor! *Ibid.* iii. 3.

FOND. *Barren.*

Not with *fond* shekels of the tested gold,
Or stones, whose rates are either rich or poor
As fancy values them; but with true prayers.
Measure for Measure, ii. 2.

To Fond.   *To dote on; to love.*

How will this fadge? my master loves her dearly;
And I, poor monster, *fond* as much on him,
As she, mistaken, seems to dote on me.
Twelfth-Night, ii. 2.

Fool.   *Gooseberry-fool.*

From whence, fragment?—
Why, thou full dish of *fool*, from Troy.
Troilus and Cressida, v. 1.

To Fool.   *To play the fool; to compel to play the fool; to cheat; to deceive.*

Why birds and beasts from quality and kind;
Why old men *fool*, and children calculate.
Julius Cæsar, i. 3.
They *fool* me to the top of my bent.
Hamlet, iii. 2.
I do not now *fool* myself, to let imagination
jade me : for every reason excites to this, that my
lady loves me.   *Twelfth-Night,* ii. 5.

Fool-begged.   *Absurd; foolish; ridiculous.*

But, if thou live to see like right bereft,
This *fool-begg'd* patience of thee will be left.
Comedy of Errors, ii. 1.

Foot.   *A step; a degree.*

A *foot* of honour better than I was;
And many a many foot of land the worse.
King John, i. 1.

To Foot.   *To arrive; to land; to clutch; to grasp.*

Dispatch us with all speed, lest that our king
Come here himself to question our delay;
For he is *footed* in this land already. *Henry 5,* ii. 4.
There is part of a power already *footed.*
King Lear, iii. 3.
And what confederacy have you with the traitors
Late *footed* in the kingdom?   *Ibid.* iii. 7.
The holy eagle stoop'd, as to *foot* us. *Cymbel.* v. 4.

Footing.   *Invasion; landing.*

Shall we, upon the *footing* of our land,
Send fair-play offers, and make compromise
To arms invasive?   *King John,* v. 1.
Whose *footing* here anticipates our thoughts
A se'nnight's speed.   *Othello,* ii. 1.

Footmen.   *Foot-soldiers.*

Distract your army, which doth most consist
Of war-mark'd *footmen.*
Antony and Cleopatra, iii. 7.

Fopped.   *Fooled; cheated; gulled.*

Nay, I think it is scurvy, and begin to find
myself *fopped* in it.   *Othello,* iv. 2.

For.   *Because; from; towards; for the sake of; for want of; favourable to.*

Haply, *for* I am black,
And have not those soft parts of conversation
That chamberers have.   *Othello,* iii. 3.
These cheeks are pale *for* watching for your good.
Henry 6, P. 2, iv. 7.
Be able *for* thine enemy rather in power than
use.   *All's well that ends well,* i. 1.
Let it not be believ'd *for* womanhood!
Troilus and Cressida, v. 2.
And let another half stand laughing by,
All out of work and cold *for* action. *Henry 5,* i. 2.
From whom we thought it meet to hide our love
Till time had made them *for* us.
Measure for Measure, i. 2.

For and.   *And eke; and also.*

A pick-axe and a spade, a spade,
For and a shrouding sheet.   *Hamlet,* v. 1.

For vain.   *In vain; to no purpose.*

Yea, my gravity
Could I with boot change for an idle plume,
Which the air beats *for vain.*
Measure for Measure, ii. 4.

For why.   *Because.*

For why she sweats; a man may go over shoes
in the grime of it.   *Comedy of Errors,* iii. 2.
If she do chide, 'tis not to have you gone;
For why the fools are mad, if left alone.
Two Gentlemen of Verona, iii. 1.
For why the senseless brands will sympathize
The heavy accent of thy moving tongue.
Richard 2, v. 1.

To Forage.   *To wander far; to lay waste; to ravage.*

Forage, and run
To meet displeasure further from the doors,
And grapple with him ere he come so nigh.
King John, v. 1.
While his most mighty father on a hill
Stood smiling to behold his lion's whelp
Forage in blood of French nobility. *Henry 5,* i. 2.

To Forbear.   *To avoid; to spare.*

And at my entreaty *forbear* his presence till

some little time hath qualified the heat of his displeasure. *King Lear,* i. 2.
Ghost unlaid *forbear* thee ! *Cymbeline,* iv. 2.
And spoke such scurvy and provoking terms
Against your honour,
That, with the little godliness I have,
I did full hard *forbear* him. *Othello,* i. 2.

FORBID. *Accurst ; excommunicated.*

He shall live a man *forbid.* *Macbeth,* i. 3.

To FORCE. *To enforce ; to urge ; to farce; to stuff; to hesitate ; to scruple.*

Has he affections in him,
That thus can make him bite the law by the nose,
When he would *force* it ?
Measure for Measure, iii. 1.
If you will now unite in your complaints,
And *force* them with a constancy, the cardinal
Cannot stand under them. *Henry 8,* iii. 2.
And well digest
The abuse of distance, while we *force* a play.
Henry 5, i. Chorus.
Force him with praises : pour in, pour in ; his
ambition is dry. *Troilus and Cressida,* ii. 3.
Peace, peace ! forbear :
Your oath once broke, you *force* not to forswear.
Love's Labour's lost, v. 2.

FORCED. *Farced ; stuffed ; reinforced ; strengthened.*

To what form, but that he is, should wit larded
with malice, and malice *forced* with wit, turn him
to ? *Troilus and Cressida,* v. 1.
Were they not *forc'd* with those that should be ours,
We might have met them dareful, beard to beard,
And beat them backward home. *Macbeth,* v. 5.

To FORDO. *To destroy ; to overcome.*

This is the very ecstasy of love ;
Whose violent property *fordoes* itself.
Hamlet, ii. 1.
Your eldest daughters have *fordone* themselves,
And desperately are dead. *King Lear,* v. 3.
He hath commission from thy wife and me
To hang Cordelia in the prison, and
To lay the blame upon her own despair,
That she *fordid* herself. *Ibid.* v. 3.
Whilst the heavy ploughman snores,
All with weary task *fordone.*
: *Midsummer-Night's Dream,* v. 1.

FORE. *Above ; beyond ; before.*

You must not so far prefer her *fore* ours of Italy.
Cymbeline, i. 4.
Fore noble Lucius
Present yourself, desire his service, tell him
Wherein you are happy. *Ibid.* iii. 4.

FORE END. *The fore part ; the earlier part.*

Where I have liv'd at honest freedom ; paid
More pious debts to heaven than in all
The *fore* end of my time. *Cymbeline,* iii. 3.

FOREGOER. *Ancestor ; progenitor.*

Honours thrive,
When rather from our acts we them derive
Than our *foregoers. All's well that ends well,* ii. 3.

FOREHAND. *The fore part ; the leader.*

The great Achilles, whom opinion crowns
The sinew and the *forehand* of our host.
Troilus and Cressida, i. 3.

'FOREHAND. *Aforehand ; previous ; antecedent.*

And so extenuate the '*forehand* sin.
Much Ado about Nothing, iv. 1.

FOREIGN. *Absent ; living abroad.*

And fearing he would rise, he was so virtuous,
Kept him a *foreign* man still. *Henry 8,* ii. 2.

FOREKNOWING. *Foreknowledge ; foresight.*

If thou art privy to thy country's fate,
Which, happily, *foreknowing* may avoid,
O, speak ! *Hamlet,* i. 1.

FORERUNNER. *Precursor ; predecessor ; messenger.*

Arthur, that great *forerunner* of thy blood,
Richard, that robb'd the lion of his heart,
And fought the holy wars in Palestine,
By this brave duke came early to his grave.
King John, ii. 1.
And there is a *forerunner* come from a fifth.
Merchant of Venice, i. 2.

FORE RANK. *First rank ; the front.*

She is our capital demand, compris'd
Within the *fore rank* of our articles.
Henry 5, v. 2.

To FORESAY. *To appoint; to decree.*
Let ordinance
Come as the gods *foresay* it. *Cymbeline,* iv. 2.

To FORESEE. *To provide for.*
Take the bridge quite away
Of him that, his particular to *foresee,*
Smells from the general weal.
Timon of Athens, iv. 3.

To FORESHOW. *To show beforehand; to fore-token.*
Which *foreshow'd* our princely eagle,
The imperial Cæsar, should again unite
His favour with the radiant Cymbeline,
Which shines here in the west. *Cymbeline,* v. 5.

FORESPENT. *Past; foregone.*
And you shall find his vanities *forespent*
Were but the outside of the Roman Brutus,
Covering discretion with a coat of folly.
Henry 5, ii. 4.

FORE-SPURRER. *A forerunner; a messenger.*
A day in April never came so sweet,
To show how costly summer was at hand,
As this *fore-spurrer* comes before his lord.
Merchant of Venice, ii. 8.

To FORESTALL. *To prevent; to preclude; to anticipate; to hinder; to deprive.*
O, pardon me, my liege! but for my tears,
I had *forestall'd* this dear and deep rebuke.
Henry 4, P. 2, iv. 4.
And never shall you see that I will beg
A rugged and *forestall'd* remission. *Ibid.* v. 2.
And what's in prayer but this twofold force,—
To be *forestalled* ere we come to fall,
Or pardon'd being down? *Hamlet,* iii. 3.
If your mind dislike anything, obey it: I will
forestall their repair hither, and say you are not fit.
Ibid. v. 2.
All the better : may
This night *forestall* him of the coming day !
Cymbeline, iii. 5.

To FORETHINK. *To anticipate; to foresee.*
Forethinking this, I have already fit—
'Tis in my cloak-bag—doublet, hat, hose, all
That answer to them. *Cymbeline,* iii. 4.
And the soul of every man
Prophetically does *forethink* thy fall.
Henry 4, P. 1, iii. 2.

FORETHOUGHT. *Preordained; decreed.*
Thou virtuous Dauphin, alter not the doom
Forethought by heaven ! *King John,* iii. 1.

FOREVOUCHED. *Declared; avowed.*
Sure, her offence
Must be of such unnatural degree,
That monsters it, or your *forevouch'd* affection
Fall into taint. *King Lear,* i. 1.

FOREWARD. *The front; the vanguard.*
My *foreward* shall be drawn out all in length,
Consisting equally of foot and horse.
Richard 3, v. 3.

FORFEIT. *One whose life is forfeited; for-feiture; remission of penalty.*
Your brother is a *forfeit* of the law,
And you but waste your words.
Measure for Measure, iii. 2.
Claudio, whom here you have warrant to execute,
is no greater *forfeit* to the law than Angelo, who
hath sentenced him. *Ibid.* iv. 2.
And I have seen thee spur thy Phrygian steed,
Despising many *forfeits* and subducments.
Troilus and Cressida, iv. 5.
Then say at once what is it thou request'st.—
The *forfeit,* sovereign, of my servant's life ;
Who slew to-day a riotous gentleman,
Lately attendant on the Duke of Norfolk.
Richard 3, ii. 1.

FORFEIT. *Forfeited; fracted; broken; liable to punishment; guilty.*
Why, all the souls that were were *forfeit* once ;
And He that might the vantage best have took
Found out the remedy.
Measure for Measure, ii. 2.
Why, this bond is *forfeit.*
Merchant of Venice, iv. 1.
Double and treble admonition, and still *forfeit*
in the same kind ? *Measure for Measure,* iii. 2.

To FORFEIT. *To sentence; to condemn.*
Shall we buy treason? and indent with fears,
When they have lost and *forfeited* themselves?
Henry 4, P. 1, i. 3.
Undone and *forfeited* to cares for ever !
All's well that ends well, ii. 3.

FORFEITER. *One who forfeits his bond.*
Lovers,
And men in dangerous bonds, pray not alike :

Though *forfeiters* you cast in prison, yet
You clasp young Cupid's tables. *Cymbeline*, iii. 2.

FORFEITURE. *Forfeit; penalty.*
'Tis thought
Thou wilt not only loose the *forfeiture*,
But, touch'd with human gentleness and love,
Forgive a moiety of the principal.
Merchant of Venice, iv. 1.

To FORFEND. *To forbid; to prohibit.*
But have you never found my brother's way
To the *forfended* place? *King Lear*, v. 1.
I would not kill thy unpreparèd spirit;
No,—heaven *forfend!*—I would not kill thy soul.
Othello, v. 2.

FORGERY. *Contrivance; invention; fabrication.*
That I, in *forgery* of shapes and tricks,
Come short of what he did. *Hamlet*, iv. 7.
And there put on him
What *forgeries* you please; marry, none so rank
As may dishonour him; take heed of that. *Ibid.* ii. 1.

To FORGET. *To neglect; to overlook; to efface.*
The latter end of his commonwealth *forgets* the
beginning. *Tempest*, ii. 1.
So the remembrance of my former love
Is by a newer object quite *forgotten*.
Two Gentlemen of Verona, ii. 4.

FORGETIVE. *Inventive; imaginative.*
Makes it apprehensive, quick, *forgetive*, full of
nimble, fiery, and delectable shapes.
Henry 4, P. 2, iv. 3.

FORK. *Tongue; point.*
Thou art by no means valiant;
For thou dost fear the soft and tender *fork*
Of a poor worm. *Measure for Measure*, iii. 1.
Let it fall rather, though the *fork* invade
The region of my heart. *King Lear*, i. 1.

FORKED. *Pointed.*
And yet it irks me, the poor dappled fools
Should, in their own confines, with *forkèd* heads
Have their round haunches gor'd.
As you like it, ii. 1.

FORLORN. *An exile; an outcast.*
Now, therefore, be it known to noble Louis,
That Henry, sole possessor of my love,

Is, of a king, become a banish'd man,
And forc'd to live in Scotland a *forlorn*.
Henry 6, P. 3, iii. 3.

FORLORN. *Small; slight.*
He was so *forlorn*, that his dimensions to any
thick sight were invincible. *Henry 4*, P. 2, iii. 2.

FORMAL. *Sane; reasonable; ordinary; regular.*
I will not let him stir
Till I have us'd the approvèd means I have
To make of him a *formal* man again.
Comedy of Errors, v. 1.
Why, this is evident to any *formal* capacity.
Twelfth-Night, ii. 5.
If not well,
Thou shouldst come like a Fury crown'd with snakes,
Not like a *formal* man.
Antony and Cleopatra, ii. 5.
Thus, like the *formal* vice, Iniquity,
I moralize two meanings in one word.
Richard 3, iii. 1.

FORMER. *Foremost; previous; aforesaid.*
Coming from Sardis on our *former* ensign
Two mighty eagles fell. *Julius Cæsar*, v. 1.
Out of that I'll work myself a *former* fortune.
Coriolanus, v. 3.
You've seen and prov'd a fairer *former* fortune
Than that which is to approach.
Antony and Cleopatra, i. 2.
The *former* agents, if they did complain,
What could the belly answer? *Coriolanus*, i. 1.

To FORSAKE. *To refuse; to reject.*
Thy frank election make;
Thou hast power to choose, and they none to *forsake*.
All's well that ends well, ii. 3.

To FORSLOW. *To delay; to stay; to loiter.*
Forslow no longer, make we hence amain.
Henry 6, P. 3, ii. 3.

To FORSPEAK. *To forbid.*
Thou hast *forspoke* my being in these wars,
And say'st it is not fit. *Antony and Cleopatra*, iii. 7.

FORSPENT. *Spent; exhausted.*
After him came spurring hard
A gentleman, almost *forspent* with speed.
Henry 4, P. 2, i. 1.

FORTED. *Strong; impregnable.*

It deserves, with characters of brass,
A *forted* residence 'gainst the tooth of time
And razure of oblivion. *Measure for Measure*, v. 1.

FORTH-RIGHT. *A straight path.*

Through *forth-rights* and meanders. *Tempest*, iii. 3.
If you give way,
Or hedge aside from the direct *forth-right*,
Like to an enter'd tide, they all rush by,
And leave you hindmost.
Troilus and Cressida, iii. 3.

FORTITUDE. *Power of resistance; strength; vigour.*

Othello, the *fortitude* of the place is best known to
you. *Othello*, i. 3.
Coward of France!—how much he wrongs his fame,
Despairing of his own arm's *fortitude*,
To join with witches and the help of hell!
Henry 6, P. 1, ii. 1.

FORTUNE. *Chance; accident.*

Upon my life, Petrucio means but well,
Whatever *fortune* stays him from his word.
Taming of the Shrew, iii. 2.
The assault that Angelo hath made to you, *fortune* hath conveyed to my understanding.
Measure for Measure, iii. 1.
O thou dull Moor! that handkerchief thou speak'st of
I found by *fortune*, and did give my husband.
Othello, v. 2.

To FORTUNE. *To happen; to fortunize.*

I'll tell you as we pass along,
That you will wonder what hath *fortuned*.
Two Gentlemen of Verona, v. 4.
Therefore, dear Isis, keep decorum, and *fortune*
him accordingly! *Antony and Cleopatra*, i. 2.

FORWARD. *Prompt; ardent; prepared; ready; eager; earnest.*

When a jest is so *forward*, and a-foot too! I
hate it. *Henry* 4, P. 1, ii. 2.
Whoever charges on his *forward* breast,
I am the caitiff that do hold him to't.
All's well that ends well, iii. 2.
Our expectation that it would be thus
Hath made us *forward*. *Cymbeline*, iii. 5.
And mere instinct of love and loyalty
Makes them thus *forward* in his banishment.
Henry 6, P. 2, iii. 2.

FORWEARIED. *Overcome with fatigue.*

Forwearied in this action of swift speed.
King John, ii. 1.

FOUL. *Plain; ugly.*

What miserable praise hast thou for her that's
foul and foolish? *Othello*, ii. 1.
Truly, and to cast away honesty upon a *foul*
slut, were to put good meat into an unclean dish.
As you like it, iii. 3.
Her amber hairs for *foul* have amber quoted.
Love's Labour's lost, iv. 3.
Foul is most *foul*, being *foul*, to be a scoffer.
As you like it, iii. 5.

FOULNESS. *Homeliness; ugliness.*

He's fallen in love with her *foulness*, and she'll
fall in love with my anger. *As you like it*, iii. 5.

To FOUND. *To ground; to demonstrate; to fix; to establish.*

It cannot hold; no reason
Can *found* his state in safety.
Timon of Athens, ii. 1.
Then comes my fit again: I had else been perfect;
Whole as the marble, *founded* as the rock;
As broad and general as the casing air.
Macbeth, iii. 4.

FOUNDATIONS. *Habitations; dwellings.*

O Jove! I think
Foundations fly the wretched; such, I mean,
Where they should be reliev'd. *Cymbeline*, iii. 6.

FOX. *A broadsword.*

O Signieur Dew, thou diest on point of *fox*,
Except, O signieur, thou do give to me
Egregious ransom. *Henry* 5, iv. 4.

FOXSHIP. *Cunning.*

Hadst thou *foxship*
To banish him that struck more blows for Rome
Than thou hast spoken words? *Coriolanus*, iv. 2.

To FRACT. *To break.*

His days and times are past,
And my reliances on his *fracted* dates
Have smit my credit. *Timon of Athens*, ii. 1.
Nym, thou hast spoke the right;
His heart is *fracted* and corroborate. *Henry* 5, ii. 1.

FRACTION. *A broken or imperfect sentence; separation; disunion.*

After distasteful looks, and these hard *fractions*,
With certain half-caps and cold-moving nods
They froze me into silence. *Timon of Athens*, ii. 2.

All the better; their *fraction* is more our wish
than their faction. *Troilus and Cressida*, ii. 3.

FRAME. *Scheme; plan; order; contrivance.*

Chid I for that at frugal nature's *frame* ?
O, one too much by thee !
Much Ado about Nothing, iv. 1.

A woman, that is like a German clock,
Still a-repairing; ever out of *frame*.
Love's Labour's lost, iii. 1.

The practice of it lies in John the bastard,
Whose spirits toil in *frame* of villanies.
Much Ado about Nothing, iv. 1.

To FRAME. *To plan; to prepare; to execute; to apply; to betake.*

His approach,
So out of circumstance and sudden, tells us
'Tis not a visitation *fram'd*, but forc'd
By need and accident. *Winter's Tale*, v. 1.

The silken tackle
Swell with the touches of those flower-soft hands,
That yarely *frame* the office.
Antony and Cleopatra, ii. 2.

Frame yourself
To orderly solicits, and be friended
With aptness of the season. *Cymbeline*, ii. 3.

FRAMPOLD. *Uneasy; vexatious; wearisome.*

She leads a very *frampold* life with him.
Merry Wives of Windsor, ii. 2.

FRANCHISE. *Enfranchisement; freedom.*

Whose repair and *franchise*
Shall, by the power we hold, be our good deed,
Though Rome be therefore angry.
Cymbeline, iii. 1.

FRANK. *A sty.*

Where sups he ? doth the old boar feed in the
old *frank* ? *Henry* 4, P. 2, ii. 2.

To FRANK UP. *To shut up; to confine.*

My son George Stanley is *frank'd up* in hold.
Richard 3, iv. 5.

Marry, as for Clarence, he is well repaid,
He is *frank'd up* to fatting for his pains. *Ibid.* i. 3.

FRANKLIN. *A yeoman; a small landed proprietor; a freeholder.*

Not swear it, now I am a gentleman ? Let boors
and *franklins* say it, I'll swear it.
Winter's Tale, v. 2.

There's a *franklin* in the wild of Kent hath
brought three hundred marks with him in gold.
Henry 4, P. 1, ii. 1.

And provide me presently
A riding-suit, no costlier than would fit
A *franklin's* housewife. *Cymbeline*, iii. 2.

FRAUGHT. *Freight; load.*

Swell, bosom, with thy *fraught*,
For 'tis of aspics' tongues ! *Othello*, iii. 3.

This is that Antonio
That took the Phœnix and her *fraught* from Candy.
Twelfth-Night, v. 1.

To FRAUGHT. *To freight; to load; to burden; to encumber.*

Had I been any god of power, I would
Have sunk the sea within the earth, or e'er
It should the good ship so have swallow'd, and
The *fraughting* souls within her. *Tempest*, i. 2.

Hence, from my sight !
If after this command thou *fraught* the court
With thy unworthiness, thou diest: away !
Cymbeline, i. 1.

FRAUGHTAGE. *Freight; goods; necessaries.*

And the deep-drawing barks do there disgorge
Their warlike *fraughtage*.
Troilus and Cressida, Prologue.

Our *fraughtage*, sir, I have convey'd aboard.
Comedy of Errors, iv. 1.

FRAY. *A duel.*

There is a *fray* to be fought between Sir Hugh
the Welsh priest and Caius the French doctor.
Merry Wives of Windsor, ii. 1.

To FRAY. *To alarm; to terrify.*

She does so blush, and fetches her wind so short,
as if she were *frayed* with a sprite.
Troilus and Cressida, iii. 2.

FREE. *Innocent; guiltless; eager; ready; generous; bountiful.*

But what o' that ? your majesty, and we that
have *free* souls, it touches us not. *Hamlet*, iii. 2.
Make mad the guilty, and appal the *free*,
Confound the ignorant; and amaze, indeed,
The very faculties of eyes and ears. *Ibid.* ii. 2.

Methinks I see
Leontes opening his *free* arms, and weeping
His welcomes forth. *Winter's Tale,* iv. 3.
And now, dear maid, be you as *free* to us.
Measure for Measure, v. 1.
That thought is bounty's foe ;
Being *free* itself, it thinks all others so.
Timon of Athens, ii. 2.

FRET. *The stop of a musical instrument.*
"*Frets* call you these ?" quoth she ; " I'll fume with
them :"
And, with that word, she struck me on the head.
Taming of the Shrew, ii. 1.

To FRET. *To streak; to variegate; to em-
boss; to chase.*
O, pardon, sir, it doth ; and yon gray lines
That *fret* the clouds are messengers of day.
Julius Cæsar, ii. 1.
The roof o' the chamber
With golden cherubins is *fretted. Cymbeline,* ii. 4.

FRIEND. *A lover; a paramour; a sweet-
heart; a mistress.*
Lady, will you walk about with your *friend* ?
Much Ado about Nothing, ii. 1.
Or to be naked with her *friend* in bed,
An hour or more, not meaning any harm.
Othello, iv. 1.
Being so far provoked as I was in France, I
would abate her nothing ; though I profess myself
her adorer, not her *friend. Cymbeline,* i. 4.
The queen
Of audience nor desire shall fail, so she
From Egypt drive her all-disgracèd *friend,*
Or take his life there.
Antony and Cleopatra, iii. 12.
Nor never come in vizard to my *friend.*
Love's Labour's lost, v. 2.

To FRIEND. *To favour; to befriend.*
Well, the gods are above ; time must *friend* or end.
Troilus and Cressida, i. 2.
When vice makes mercy, mercy's so extended,
That for the fault's love is the offender *friended.*
Measure for Measure, iv. 2.
I know that we shall have him well to *friend.*
Julius Cæsar, iii. 1.
What I believe, I'll wail ;
What know, believe ; and what I can redress,
As I shall find the time to *friend,* I will.
Macbeth, iv. 3.

Not *friended* by his wish, to your high person
His will is most malignant. *Henry* 8, i. 2.
Frame yourself
To orderly solicits, and be *friended*
With aptness of the season. *Cymbeline,* ii. 3.

FRIENDING. *Friendship.*
And what so poor a man as Hamlet is
May do, to express his love and *friending* to you,
God willing, shall not lack. *Hamlet,* i. 5.

FRIENDLY. *Like a friend; in a friendly way.*
His name and credit shall you undertake,
And in my house you shall be *friendly* lodg'd.
Taming of the Shrew, iv. 2.

FRIPPERY. *An old-clothes shop.*
O, ho, monster ! we know what belongs to a *frippery.*
Tempest, iv. 1.

FROM. *Out of; beyond; away from; with-
out; free from; contrary to.*
O, my heart bleeds
To think o' the teen that I have turn'd you to,
Which is *from* my remembrance. *Tempest,* i. 2.
For any thing so overdone is *from* the purpose
of playing. *Hamlet,* iii. 2.
But thus condition'd : thou shalt build *from* men ;
Hate all, curse all. *Timon of Athens,* iv. 3.
Whose containing
Is so *from* sense in hardness, that I can
Make no collection of it. *Cymbeline,* v. 5.
That, his apparent open guilt omitted,
He liv'd *from* all attainder of suspect.
Richard 3, iii. 5.
Whereby he does receive
Particular addition, *from* the bill
That writes them all alike : and so of men.
Macbeth, iii. 1.
Take the bridge quite away
Of him that, his particular to foresee,
Smells *from* the general weal.
Timon of Athens, iv. 3.

FROM THE PRESENT. *Not to the purpose; not
now the question.*
Be pleas'd to tell us—
For this is *from the present*—how you take
The offers we have sent you.
Antony and Cleopatra, ii. 6.

FROM THE TEETH. *Unwillingly; grudgingly; reluctantly.*

When the best hint was given him, he not took't,
Or did it *from his teeth*.
         Antony and Cleopatra, iii. 4.

FRONTIER. *The front; a border fortress.*

And majesty might never yet endure
The moody *frontier* of a servant brow.
         Henry 4, P. 1, i. 3.

And thou hast talk'd
Of sallies and retires, of trenches, tents,
Of palisadoes, *frontiers,* parapets.   *Ibid.* ii. 3.

FRONTLET. *A band for the forehead.*

How now, daughter! what makes that *frontlet* on?
Methinks you are too much of late i' the frown.
         King Lear, i. 4.

FRUIT. *Dessert.*

My news shall be the *fruit* to that great feast.
         Hamlet, ii. 2.

FRUITFUL. *Bountiful; generous.*

She's fram'd as *fruitful* as the free elements.
         Othello, ii. 3.

To FRUSH. *To break; to bruise; to crush.*

I like thy armour well;
I'll *frush* it, and unlock the rivets all,
But I'll be master of it. *Troilus and Cressida,* v. 6.

FRUSTRATE. *Frustrated; defeated.*

And the sea mocks our *frustrate* search on land.
         Tempest, iii. 3.

Being so *frustrate,* tell him, he mocks
The pauses that he makes.
         Antony and Cleopatra, v. 1.

To FULFIL. *To fill.*

Priam's six-gated city with massy staples,
And corresponsive and *fulfilling* bolts,
Sperr up the sons of Troy.
         Troilus and Cressida, Prologue.

FULL. *Perfect; complete; strong.*

What a *full* fortune does the thick-lips owe
If he can carry it thus!   *Othello,* i. 1.
Doth not the gentleman
Deserve as *full,* as fortunate a bed
As ever Beatrice shall couch upon?
         Much Ado about Nothing, iii. 1.
For I have serv'd him, and the man commands
Like a *full* soldier.   *Othello,* ii. 1.

What art thou, fellow!—One that but performs
The bidding of the *fullest* man, and worthiest
To have command obey'd.
         Antony and Cleopatra, iii. 13.

FULNESS. *Wealth; plenty; prosperity.*

To lapse in *fulness*
Is sorer than to lie for need; and falsehood
Is worse in kings than beggars.   *Cymbeline,* iii. 6.

FULSOME. *Nauseous; distasteful; superfluous; wanton.*

And stop this gap of breath with *fulsome* dust,
And be a carrion monster like thyself.
         King John, iii. 4.
It is as fat and *fulsome* to mine ear
As howling after music.   *Twelfth-Night,* v. 1.
I, that was wash'd to death with *fulsome* wine,
Poor Clarence, by thy guile betray'd to death!
         Richard 3, v. 3.
He stuck them up before the *fulsome* ewes.
         Merchant of Venice, i. 3.

FUMITER. *Fumitory.*

Crown'd with rank *fumiter* and furrow-weeds.
         King Lear, iv. 4.

FUNCTION. *Power; faculty.*

My thought, whose murder yet is but fantastical,
Shakes so my single state of man, that *function*
Is smother'd in surmise.   *Macbeth,* i. 3.
Tears in his eyes, distraction in's aspéct,
A broken voice, and his whole *function* suiting
With forms to his conceit? and all for nothing!
         Hamlet, ii. 2.
That she may make, unmake, do what she list,
Even as her appetite shall play the god
With his weak *function*.   *Othello,* ii. 3.

To FUR. *To line.*

You are for dreams and slumbers, brother priest;
You *fur* your gloves with reason.
         Troilus and Cressida, ii. 2.

To FURNACE. *To breathe out; to exhale.*

There is a Frenchman his companion, one,
An eminent monsieur, that, it seems, much loves
A Gallian girl at home: he *furnaces*
The thick sighs from him.   *Cymbeline,* i. 4.

To FURNISH. *To equip; to dress; to supply; to enrich.*

All *furnish'd,* all in arms,
All plum'd like estridges that wing the wind.
         Henry 4, P. 1, iv. 1.

I'll show thee some attires; and have thy counsel
Which is the best to *furnish* me to-morrow.
Much Ado about Nothing, iii. 1.

Then, that you have sent innumerable substance
To *furnish* Rome. *Henry 8,* iii. 2.

FURNISHING. *A sample; a foretaste.*

Or something deeper,
Whereof perchance these are but *furnishings,*
King Lear, iii. 1.

FURNITURE. *Equipment; trappings.*

My Lord of Somerset will keep me here,
Without discharge, money, or *furniture,*
Till France be won into the Dauphin's hands.
Henry 6, P. 2, i. 3.

There shalt thou know thy charge; and there receive
Money and order for their *furniture.*
Henry 4, P. 1, iii. 3.

I'd give bay curtal and his *furniture,*
My mouth no more were broken than these boys'.
All's well that ends well, ii. 3.

FURRED. *Soft; furlike.*

Yea, and *furr'd* moss besides, when flowers are none,
To winter-ground thy corse. *Cymbeline,* iv. 2.

FURTHERER. *A promoter; a seconder; an abetter.*

Thy brother was a *furtherer* in the act.
Tempest, v. 1.

TO FUST. *To grow mouldy.*

Sure, he that made us with such large discourse,
Looking before and after, gave us not
That capability and god-like reason
To *fust* in us unus'd. *Hamlet,* iv. 4.

FUSTIAN. *Bombast; high-sounding nonsense.*

Drunk? and speak parrot? and squabble? swagger? swear? and discourse *fustian* with one's own shadow? *Othello,* ii. 3.

FUSTIAN. *Bombastic; high-sounding.*

A *fustian* riddle! *Twelfth-Night,* ii. 5.

FUSTILARIAN. *A term of reproach.*

Away, you scullion! you rampallian! you *fustilarian!* *Henry 4,* P. 2, ii. 1.

FUSTY. *Mouldy; worthless; contemptible.*

'A were as good crack a *fusty* nut with no kernel. *Troilus and Cressida,* ii. 1.

At this *fusty* stuff,
The large Achilles, on his press'd bed lolling,
From his deep chest laughs out a loud applause.
Ibid. i. 3.

G.

GABERDINE. *A cloak; a mantle.*

My best way is to creep under his *gaberdine.*
Tempest, ii. 2.

You call me misbeliever, cut-throat dog,
And spit upon my Jewish *gaberdine.*
Merchant of Venice, i. 3.

GAGE. *A pledge; a pawn.*

Pale trembling coward, there I throw my *gage,*
Disclaiming here the kindred of the king.
Richard 2, i. 1.

TO GAGE. *To pledge; to engage.*

Against the which, a moiety competent
Was *gagèd* by our king. *Hamlet,* i. 1.

But to come fairly off from the great debts,
Wherein my time, something too prodigal,
Hath left me *gag'd.* *Merchant of Venice,* i. 1.

Shall it be spoken in these days,
Or fill up chronicles in time to come,
That men of your nobility and power
Did *gage* them both in an unjust behalf?
Henry 4, P. 1, i. 3.

Both taxing me and *gaging* me to keep
An oath that I have sworn.
Troilus and Cressida, v. 1.

TO GAIN. *To bring back; to restore.*

Poor sick Fidele!
I'll willingly to him; to *gain* his colour
I'd let a parish of such Clotens blood,
And praise myself for charity. *Cymbeline,* iv. 2.

GAIN-GIVING. *'Misgiving.*

It is but foolery; but it is such a kind of *gain-giving* as would perhaps trouble a woman.
Hamlet, v. 2.

To GAINSAY. *To deny.*

The king is present : if it be known to him
That I *gainsay* my deed, how may he wound,
And worthily, my falsehood !   *Henry* 8, ii. 4.

I ne'er heard yet
That any of these bolder vices wanted
Less impudence to *gainsay* what they did
Than to perform it first.   *Winter's Tale*, iii. 2.

GAIT. *Proceeding; way; progress.*

We have here writ to Norway,
To suppress his further *gait* herein.   *Hamlet*, i. 2.

With this field-dew consecrate,
Every fairy take his *gait*.
        Midsummer-Night's Dream, v. 1.

This palpable-gross play hath well beguil'd
The heavy *gait* of night.   *Ibid.* v. 1.

Therefore, good youth, address thy *gait* unto her.
        Twelfth-Night, i. 4.

GALL. *A sarcasm.*

O pestilent *gall* to me !   *King Lear*, i. 4.

To GALL. *To vex; to irritate; to scoff; to sneer.*

All studies here I solemnly defy,
Save how to *gall* and pinch this Bolingbroke.
        Henry 4, P. 1, i. 3.

I have seen you gleeking and *galling* at this
gentleman twice or thrice.   *Henry* 5, v. 1.

GALLANT. *Rare; glorious; noble.*

She is a *gallant* creature, and complete
In mind and feature.   *Henry* 8, iii. 2.

The heir of Alençon, Katharine her name.—
A *gallant* lady. Monsieur, fare you well.
        Love's Labour's lost, ii. 1.

It is a *gallant* child ; one that, indeed, physics
the subject, makes old hearts fresh.
        Winter's Tale, i. 1.

Never did I hear such *gallant* chiding.
        Midsummer-Night's Dream, iv. 1.

When we, in all her trim, freshly beheld
Our royal, good, and *gallant* ship.   *Tempest*, v. 1.

GALLIAN. *Gallic; French.*

'Tis known already that I am possess'd
With more than half the *Gallian* territories. '
        Henry 6, P. 1, v. 4.

There is a Frenchman his companion, one,
An eminent monsieur, that, it seems, much loves
A *Gallian* girl at home.   *Cymbeline*, i. 6.

GALLIARD. *A quick lively dance.*

I did think, by the excellent constitution of thy
leg, it was formed under the star of a *galliard*.
        Twelfth-Night, i. 3.

And bids you be advis'd, there's naught in France
That can be with a nimble *galliard* won.
        Henry 5, i. 2.

GALLIASS. *A large kind of galley.*

Besides two *galliasses* and twelve tight galleys.
        Taming of the Shrew, ii. 1.

GALLIMAUFRY. *A medley; a woman.*

And they have a dance, which the wenches say
is a *gallimaufry* of gambols.   *Winter's Tale*, iv. 3.

He loves the *gallimaufry*: Ford, perpend.
        Merry Wives of Windsor, ii. 1.

To GALLOW. *To frighten.*

The wrathful skies
Gallow the very wanderers of the dark,
And make them keep their caves. *King Lear*, iii. 2.

GALLOWGLASS. *An Irish foot-soldier.*

The merciless Macdonwald from the western isles
Of kerns and *gallowglasses* is supplied.
        Macbeth, i. 2.

GALLOWS. *A rogue; a rascal.*

Ay, and a shrewd unhappy *gallows* too.
        Love's Labour's lost, v. 2.

GAMBOL. *Nimble; active; lively.*

And such other *gambol* faculties he has, that
show a weak mind and an able body.
        Henry 4, P. 2, ii. 4.

GAME. *Play; jest.*

As waggish boys in *game* themselves forswear,
So the boy Love is perjur'd every where.
        Midsummer-Night's Dream, i. 1.

GAMESOME. *Gay; sprightly; lively.*

None a stranger there
So merry and so *gamesome*: he is call'd
The Briton reveller.   *Cymbeline*, i. 6.

I am not *gamesome*: I do lack some part
Of that quick spirit that is in Antony.
        Julius Cæsar, i. 2.

GAMESTER. *A rogue; a reprobate; a prostitute.*

You are a merry *gamester*, my Lord Sands.
        Henry 8, i. 4.

Now will I stir this *gamester:* I hope I shall
see an end of him. *As you like it,* i. 1.
Young *gamester,* your father were a fool
To give thee all. *Taming of the Shrew,* ii. 1.
She's impudent, my lord;
She was a common *gamester* to the camp.
All's well that ends well, v. 3.

To GAPE. *To shout; to bawl; to scream.*

You'll leave your noise anon, ye rascals: do
you take the court for Paris-garden? ye rude slaves,
leave your *gaping.* *Henry 8,* v. 3.
Some men there are love not a *gaping* pig.
Merchant of Venice, iv. 1.

GARBOIL. *Disturbance; tumult; disorder.*

Look here, and, at thy sovereign leisure, read
The *garboils* she awak'd. *Antony and Cleop.* i. 3.
So much uncurable, her *garboils,* Cæsar,
Made out of her impatience, I grieving grant
Did you too much disquiet.
Antony and Cleopatra, ii. 2.

GARISH. *Gaudy; showy.*

That all the world will be in love with night,
And pay no worship to the *garish* sun.
Romeo and Juliet, iii. 2.
A *garish* flag,
To be the aim of every dangerous shot.
Richard 3, iv. 4.

GARLAND. *A crown; a wreath; pride; glory.*

And now my death
Changes the mode; for what in me was purchas'd,
Falls upon thee in a more fairer sort;
So thou the *garland* wear'st successively.
Henry 4, P. 2, iv. 4.
And, in the brunt of seventeen battles since,
He lurch'd all swords of the *garland.*
Coriolanus, ii. 2.
With every minute you do change a mind;
And call him noble that was now your hate,
Him vile that was your *garland.* *Ibid.* i. 1.

To GARNER. *To lay up; to store; to treasure.*

But there, where I have *garner'd* up my heart,
Where either I must live, or bear no life,—
The fountain from the which my current runs,
Or else dries up; to be discarded thence!
Othello, iv. 2.

GARNISH. *Decoration; dress; equipment.*

So are you, sweet,
Even in the lovely *garnish* of a boy.
Merchant of Venice, ii. 5.

GASKINS. *A kind of loose breeches.*

Or, if both break, your *gaskins* fall.
Twelfth-Night, i. 5.

GASTED. *Alarmed.*

Or whether *gasted* by the noise I made,
Full suddenly he fled. *King Lear,* ii. 1.

GASTNESS. *Ghastliness; alarm; terror.*

Do you perceive the *gastness* of her eye?
Othello, v. 1.

To GATHER. *To infer.*

My lord is dead; Edmund and I have talk'd;
And more convenient is he for my hand
Than for your lady's:—you may *gather* more.
King Lear, iv. 5.
The reason that I *gather* he is mad,—
Besides this present instance of his rage,—
Is a mad tale he told to-day at dinner,
Of his own doors being shut against his entrance.
Comedy of Errors, iv. 3.
Thou art my heir; the rest I wish thee *gather.*
Henry 6, P. 1, ii. 5.

GAUD. *A trinket; a bauble; show; splendour.*

And stolen the impression of her fantasy
With bracelets of thy hair, rings, *gauds,* conceits.
Midsummer-Night's Dream, i. 1.
The sun is in the heaven, and the proud day
Is all too wanton and too full of *gauds*
To give me audience. *King John,* iii. 3.
One touch of nature makes the whole world kin,—
That all, with one consent, praise new-born *gauds,*
Though they are made and moulded of things past,
And give to dust, that is a little gilt,
More laud than gilt o'er-dusted.
Troilus and Cressida, iii. 3.

GAUDY. *Festive; merry; jovial.*

Come, let's have one other *gaudy* night.
Antony and Cleopatra, iii. 13.

GAWDED. *Coloured.*

Our veil'd dames
Commit the war of white and damask, in
Their nicely-*gawded* cheeks, to the wanton spoil
Of Phœbus' burning kisses. *Coriolanus,* ii. 1.

GEAR. *Matter; business; stuff; dress; apparel.*

Farewell: I'll grow a talker for this *gear.*
Merchant of Venice, i. 1.

Well, if Fortuno bo a woman, she's a good
wench for this *gear.*　　*Merchant of Venice,* ii. 2.
　　Let mo have
A dram of poison ; such soon-speeding *gear*
As will disperse itself through all the veins,
That the lifo-weary taker may fall dead.
　　　　　　　　　Romeo and Juliet, v. 1.
Let us complain to them what fools were here,
Disguis'd like Muscovites, in shapeless *gear.*
　　　　　　　　Love's Labour's lost, v. 2.
Here's goodly *gear !*　　*Romeo and Juliet,* ii. 4.

GECK.　*A dupe; a fool.*

And to become the *geck* and scorn
O' the other's villany.　　*Cymbeline,* v. 4.
And made the most notorious *geck* and gull
That e'er invention play'd on.　*Twelfth-Night,* ii. 5.

GEMINY.　*A couple; a brace.*

Or else you had looked through the grate, like
a *geminy* of baboons.
　　　　　　　Merry Wives of Windsor, ii. 2.

GENDER.　*Kind; sort.*

　　The other motive,
Why to a public court I might not go,
Is the great love the general *gender* bear him.
　　　　　　　　　　Hamlet, iv. 7.
Supply it with one *gender* of herbs, or distract
it with many.　　　　　*Othello,* i. 3.

To GENDER.　*To breed; to generate; to en-
gender.*

Or keep it as a cistern for foul toads
To knot and *gender* in !　　*Othello,* iv. 1.

GENERAL.　*The multitude; the common people.*

Even so the *general,* subject to a well-wish'd king,
Quit their own part.　*Measure for Measure,* ii. 4.
The play, I remember, pleased not the million ;
'twas caviare to the *general.*　　*Hamlet,* ii. 2.

GENERAL.　*Public; common; compendious;
comprehensive.*

He would drown the stage with tears,
And cleave the *general* ear with horrid speech.
　　　　　　　　　　Hamlet, ii. 2.
　　The other motive,
Why to a public count I might not go,
Is the great love the *general* gender bear him.
　　　　　　　　　　Ibid. iv. 7.

I have been bold—
For that I knew it the most *general* way—
To them to uso your signet and your name.
　　　　　　　　Timon of Athens, ii. 2.

GENERATION.　*Children; offspring.*

　　The barbarous Scythian,
Or he that makes his *generation* messes
To gorge his appetite, shall to my bosom
Be as well neighbour'd, pitied, and reliev'd,
As thou my sometime daughter.　*King Lear,* i. 1.

GENEROSITY.　*Noble birth.*

To break the heart of *generosity,*
And make bold power look pale.　*Coriolanus,* i. 1.

GENEROUS.　*Noble.*

When my dimensions are as well compact,
My mind as *generous,* and my shapo as true,
As honest madam's issue.　　*King Lear,* i. 2.
The *generous* and gravest citizens
Have hent the gates.　*Measure for Measure,* iv. 6.
Your dinner, and the *generous* islanders
By you invited do attend your presence.
　　　　　　　　　　Othello, iii. 3.

GENIUS.　*The presiding spirit of persons or
places.*

One of these men is *Genius* to the other ;
And so of these.　Which is the natural man,
And which the spirit ?　*Comedy of Errors,* v. 1.
　　And under him
My *Genius* is rebuk'd ; as, it is said,
Mark Antony's was by Cæsar.　*Macbeth,* iii. 1.
The *Genius* and the mortal instruments
Are then in council.　　*Julius Cæsar,* ii. 1.

GENNET.　*A Spanish horse.*

You'll have coursers for cousins, and *gennets* for
germans.　　　　　　　*Othello,* i. 1.

GENTILITY.　*Good manners; gentle birth;
gentry.*

To fright them hence with that dread penalty.—
A dangerous law against *gentility.*
　　　　　　　　Love's Labour's lost, i. 1.
　　He lets me feed with his hinds, bars me the
place of a brother, and, as much as in him lies,
mines my *gentility* with my education.
　　　　　　　　　As you like it, i. 1.

GENTLE. 142 GHOST.

GENTLE. *Well born; well descended.*

He said he was *gentle*, but unfortunate.
　　　　　　　　　　　　　Cymbeline, iv. 2.
Whilst by a slave, no *gentler* than my dog,
His fairest daughter is contaminate.
　　　　　　　　　　　　　Henry 5, iv. 5.

To GENTLE. *To raise to the rank of a gentleman.*

Be he ne'er so vile,
This day shall *gentle* his condition. *Henry 5*, iv. 3.

GENTLENESS. *Politeness; courtesy.*

If over boldly we have borne ourselves
In the convérse of breath, your *gentleness*
Was guilty of it. *Love's Labour's lost*, v. 2.
But fare you well: perforce I must confess
I thought you lord of more true *gentleness*.
　　　　　　　　　Midsummer-Night's Dream, ii. 2.

GENTRY. *Gentility; gentle birth; politeness; courtesy.*

Clerk-like, experienc'd, which no less adorns
Our *gentry* than our parents' noble names,
In whose success we are gentle. *Winter's Tale*, i. 2.
Where *gentry*, title, wisdom,
Cannot conclude but by the yea and no
Of general ignorance. *Coriolanus*, iii. 1.
　　　　　　　　　Please you
To show us so much *gentry* and good will
As to expend your time with us awhile.
　　　　　　　　　　　　　Hamlet, ii. 2.

GERMAN. *Brother.*

Wert thou a leopard, thou wert *german* to the
lion, and the spots of thy kindred were jurors on
thy life. *Timon of Athens*, iv. 3.
You'll have coursers for cousins, and gennets for
germans. *Othello*, i. 1.

GERMANE. *Related to; akin; cognate; kindred.*

Those that are *germane* to him, though removed
fifty times, shall all come under the hangman.
　　　　　　　　　　　　　Winter's Tale, iv. 3.
The phrase would be more *germane* to the matter, if we could carry cannon by our sides.
　　　　　　　　　　　　　Hamlet, v. 2.

GERMEN. *Germ; seed.*

Though the treasure
Of nature's *germens* tumble all together,

Even till destruction sicken,—answer me
To what I ask you. *Macbeth*, iv. 1.
Crack nature's moulds, all *germens* spill at once,
That make ingrateful man! *King Lear*, iii. 2.

GEST. *Feat; deed; time; period.*

We have beat him to his camp:—run one before,
And let the queen know of our *gests*.
　　　　　　　　　Antony and Cleopatra, iv. 8.
I'll give you my commission
To let him there a month behind the *gest*
Prefix'd for his parting. *Winter's Tale*, i. 2.

GESTURE. *Mien; look; countenance.*

And their *gesture* sad
Investing lank-lean cheeks and war-worn coats,
Presenteth them unto the gazing moon
So many horrid ghosts. *Henry 5*, iii. Chorus.

To GET. *To make sure of; to secure.*

Well, lords, we have not *got* that which we have.
　　　　　　　　　　　　　Henry 6, P. 2, v. 3.

To GET GOAL FOR GOAL. *To vie with; to emulate.*

What, girl! though grey
Do something mingle with our younger brown, yet
　　　　　　　　　ha' we
A brain that nourishes our nerves, and can
Get goal for goal of youth. *Antony and Cleop.* iv. 8.

To GET WITHIN: *To close with; to grapple; to seize.*

Some *get within* him, take his sword away.
　　　　　　　　　　　　　Comedy of Errors, v. 1.

GHOST. *A dead body; a corpse.*

Some haunted by the *ghosts* they have depos'd.
　　　　　　　　　　　　　Richard 2, iii. 2.
And now will canker-sorrow eat my bud,
And chase the native beauty from his cheek,
And he will look as hollow as a *ghost*.
　　　　　　　　　　　　　King John, iii. 4.
Oft have I seen a timely-parted *ghost*,
Of ashy semblance, meagre, pale, and bloodless,
Being all descended to the labouring heart.
　　　　　　　　　　　　　Henry 6, P. 2, iii. 2.

To GHOST. *To haunt after death.*

Since Julius Cæsar,
Who at Philippi the good Brutus *ghosted*,
There saw you labouring for him.
　　　　　　　　　Antony and Cleopatra, ii. 6.

GIB. *A cat.*

For who, that's but a queen, fair, sober, wise,
Would from a paddock, from a bat, a *gib*,
Such dear concernings hide?   *Hamlet,* iii. 4.

GIB-CAT. *A he-cat.*

'Sblood, I am as melancholy as a *gib-cat* or a
lugged bear.   *Henry 4,* P. 1, i. 2.

To GIBBER. *To chatter.*

The graves stood tenantless, and the sheeted dead
Did squeak and *gibber* in the Roman streets.
Hamlet, i. 1.

To GIBBET-ON. *To hook or hang on.*

He shall come off, and on, swifter than he that
gibbets-on the brewer's bucket.
Henry 4, P. 2, iii. 2.

GIBE. *A sneer; a taunt.*

Where be your *gibes* now? your gambols? your
songs? your flashes of merriment that were wont to
set the table on a roar?   *Hamlet,* v. 1.

Ready in *gibes,* quick-answer'd, saucy, and
As quarrelous as the weasel.   *Cymbeline,* iii. 5.

To GIBE. *To sneer; to scoff; to taunt; to jest.*

You did pocket up my letters, and with taunts
Did *gibe* my missive out of audience.
Antony and Cleopatra, ii. 2.

GIBER. *A joker; a jester; a scoffer; a mocker.*

Come, come, you are well understood to be a
perfecter *giber* for the table than a necessary bencher
in the Capitol.   *Coriolanus,* ii. 1.

GIBINGLY. *Scornfully; tauntingly.*

Which most *gibingly,* ungravely, he did fashion
After the inveterate hate he bears you.
Coriolanus, ii. 3.

GIG. *A top.*

To see great Hercules whipping a *gig.*
Love's Labour's lost, iv. 3.

GIGLET. *A wanton; a jade; a light wench.*

Away with those *giglets* too!
Measure for Measure, v. 1.

GIGLET. *False; inconstant; wanton.*

The fam'd Cassibelan, who was once at point,—
O *giglet* fortune!—to master Cæsar's sword.
Cymbeline, iii. 1.

Young Talbot was not born
To be the pillage of a *giglet* wench.
Henry 6, P. 1, iv. 7.

GILDED. *Yellow.*

Thou didst drink
The stale of horses, and the *gilded* puddle
Which beasts would cough at.
Antony and Cleopatra, i. 4.

GILLYVOR. *The gillyflower.*

The fairest flowers o' the season
Are our carnations and streak'd *gillyvors.*
Winter's Tale, iv. 3.

GILT. *Gold; gilding.*

And give to dust, that is a little gilt,
More laud than *gilt* o'er-dusted.
Troilus and Cressida, iii. 3.

And three corrupted men
Have, for the *gilt* of France—O guilt indeed!—
Confirm'd conspiracy with fearful France.
Henry 5, i. Chorus.

Wipe off the dust that hides our sceptre's *gilt,*
And make high majesty look like itself.
Richard 2, ii. 1.

The double *gilt* of this opportunity you let time
wash off, and you are now sailed into the north of
my lady's opinion.   *Twelfth-Night,* iii. 2.

GIMMAL-BIT. *A bit made of links or rings.*

And in their pale dull mouths the *gimmal-bit*
Lies foul with chew'd grass, still and motionless.
Henry 5, iv. 2.

GIMMERS. *A gimcrack; a mechanical contrivance.*

I think, by some odd *gimmers* or device,
Their arms are set, like clocks, still to strike on.
Henry 6, P. 1, i. 2.

GIN. *A snare; a springe.*

So strives the woodcock with the *gin.*
Henry 6, P. 3, i. 4.

To GIN. *To begin.*

As whence the sun *gins* his reflection
Shipwrecking storms and direful thunders break.
Macbeth, i. 2.

Their great guilt,
Like poison given to work a great time after,
Now *gins* to bite the spirits. *Tempest*, iii. 3.

GING. *A gang.*

There's a knot, a *ging*, a pack, a conspiracy
against me. *Merry Wives of Windsor*, iv. 2.

GIRD. *A gibe; a taunt; a sarcasm.*

Sweet king!—the bishop hath a kindly *gird.*
Henry 6, P. 1, iii. 1.
I thank thee for that *gird*, good Tranio.
Taming of the Shrew, v. 2.

To GIRD. *To taunt; to gibe; to sneer at.*

Men of all sorts take a pride to *gird* at me.
Henry 4, P. 2, i. 2.
Being mov'd, he will not spare to *gird* the gods.
Coriolanus, i. 1.

To GIRT. *To gird; to invest.*

We here create thee the first Duke of Suffolk,
And *girt* thee with the sword. *Henry 6, P. 2*, i. 1.
And, in reguerdon of that duty done,
I *girt* thee with the valiant sword of York.
Ibid. P. 1, iii. 1.

To GIVE. *To tell; to inform; to lay upon;
to impute; to grant; to permit; to grow
moist.*

My mind *gave* me,
In seeking tales and informations
Against this man, whose honesty the devil
And his disciples only envy at,
Ye blow the fire that burns ye. *Henry 8*, v. 2.
And yet my mind *gave* me his clothes made a
false report of him. *Coriolanus*, iv. 5.
Far from his succour, from the king, from all
That might have mercy on the fault thou *gav'st* him.
Henry 8, iii. 2.
Yes, he would *give't* thee, from this rank offence,
So to offend him still. *Measure for Measure*, iii. 1.
What, dost thou weep?—come nearer;—then I love
thee
Because thou art a woman, and disclaim'st
Flinty mankind; whose eyes do never *give*
But thorough lust and laughter.
Timon of Athens, iv. 3.

To GIVE OFF. *To give up; to resign; to give
over.*

Did not the prophet
Say, that before Ascension-day at noon
My crown I should *give off*? *King John*, v. 1.

Follow the noise so far as we have quarter;
Let's see how it will *give off.*
Antony and Cleopatra, iv. 3.

To GIVE OUT. *To lay aside; to give up; to
resign.*

I thought ye would never have *given out* these
arms till you had recovered your ancient freedom.
Henry 6, P. 2, iv. 7.

To GIVE THE BUCKLERS. *To yield; to submit; to surrender.*

And so, I pray thee, call Beatrice: I *give* thee
the bucklers. *Much Ado about Nothing*, v. 2.

GIVEN. *Inclined; disposed.*

Fear him not, Cæsar; he's not dangerous;
He is a noble Roman, and well *given.*
Julius Cæsar, i. 2.
And now I remember me, his name is Falstaff:
if that man should be lewdly *given*, he deceiveth
me; for, Harry, I see virtue in his looks.
Henry 4, P. 1, ii. 4.

GIVING-OUT. *Declaration of intention; expression.*

But we do learn
His *givings-out* were of an infinite distance
From his true-meant design.
Measure for Measure, i. 4.
Or such ambiguous *giving-out*, to note
That you know aught of me:—this not to do,
So grace and mercy at your most need help you,
Swear. *Hamlet*, i. 5.

To GLARE. *To stare.*

Against the Capitol I met a lion,
Who *glar'd* upon me, and went surly by,
Without annoying me. *Julius Cæsar*, i. 3.
Thou hast no speculation in those eyes
Which thou dost *glare* with! *Macbeth*, iii. 4.
On him, on him! Look you, how pale he *glares!*
Hamlet, iii. 4.

GLASS. *Hour-glass.*

Were my wife's liver
Infected as her life, she would not live
The running of one *glass*. *Winter's Tale*, i. 2.

GLASSED. *Enclosed in glass; cased in glass.*

Who, tendering their own worth from where they
were *glass'd*,
Did point you to buy them, along as you pass'd.
Love's Labour's lost, ii. 1.

To GLEAN. *To ravage; to lay waste; to gather; to collect.*

Galling the *gleanèd* land with hot assays.
Henry 5, i. 2.

Yes, that goodness
Of *gleaning* all the land's wealth into one.
Henry 8, iii. 2.

GLEEK. *Music; a gibe; a scoff.*

No money, on my faith ; but the *gleek,*—I will give you the minstrel. *Romeo and Juliet, iv. 5.*
Now where's the Bastard's braves, and Charles his *gleeks ?* *Henry 6, P. 1, iii. 2.*

To GLEEK. *To scoff; to jeer; to jest.*

I have seen you *gleeking* and galling at this gentleman twice or thrice. *Henry 5, v. 1.*
Nay, I can *gleek* upon occasion.
Midsummer-Night's Dream, iii. 1.

To GLISTER. *To glitter; to shine.*

Than to be perk'd up in a *glistering* grief,
And wear a golden sorrow. *Henry 8, ii. 3.*
All that *glisters* is not gold.
Merchant of Venice, ii. 6.
Down, down I come ; like *glistering* Phaëthon,
Wanting the manage of unruly jades.
Richard 2, iii. 3.

GLOSE. *Flattery; compliment.*

Now to plain-dealing ; lay these *gloses* by.
Love's Labour's lost, iv. 3.

To GLOW. *To make hot; to flush.*

On each side her
Stood pretty dimpled boys, like smiling Cupids,
With divers-colour'd fans, whose wind did seem
To *glow* the delicate cheeks which they did cool,
And what they undid did.
Antony and Cleopatra, ii. 2.

To GLOZE. *To interpret; to comment; to flatter.*

Which Salique land the French unjustly *gloze*
To be the realm of France, and Pharamond
The founder of this law and female bar.
Henry 5, i. 2.
Paris and Troilus, you have both said well ;
And on the cause and question now in hand '
Have *gloz'd,*—but superficially.
Troilus and Cressida, ii. 2.
Hark, how the villain would *gloze* now, after his treasonable abuses. *Measure for Measure, v. 1.*

He that no more must say is listen'd more
Than they whom youth and ease have taught to *gloze.* *Richard 2, ii. 1.*

To GLUT. *To englut; to swallow up.*

He'll be hang'd yet,
Though every drop of water swear against it,
And gape at wid'st to *glut* him. *Tempest, i. 2.*

To GNARL. *To snarl; to growl.*

For *gnarling* sorrow hath less power to bite
The man that mocks at it and sets it light.
Richard 2, i. 3.
Thus is the shepherd beaten from thy side,
And wolves are *gnarling* who shall gnaw thee first.
Henry 6, P. 2, iii. 1.

To GO. *To walk.*

Thou must run to him, for thou hast stayed so
long, that *going* will scarce serve the turn.
Two Gentlemen of Verona, iii. 1.
For you know that love
Will creep in service where it cannot *go.*
Ibid. iv. 2.
Ride more than thou *goest.* *King Lear, i. 4.*

To GO BEFORE. *To excel.*

If that thy gentry, Britain, *go before*
This lout as he exceeds our lords, the odds
Is, that we scarce are men, or you are gods.
Cymbeline, v. 2.

To GO BEYOND. *To leave behind; to distance.*

O Cromwell,
The king has *gone beyond* me : all my glories
In that one woman I have lost for ever.
Henry 8, iii. 2.

To GO EVEN WITH. *To comply with; to follow.*

I was then a young traveller; rather shunned
to *go even with* what I heard than in my every
action to be guided by others' experiences.
Cymbeline, i. 4.

GO TO. (An expression indicating impatience or irritation.) *Come, come.*

Go to, go to, thou art a foolish fellow.
Twelfth-Night, iv. 1.
Go to, go to ! How she holds up the neb, the
bill to him ! *Winter's Tale, i. 2.*
Go to, we pardon thee : therefore, in brief,
Tell me their words as near as thou canst guess them.
Henry 6, P. 3, iv. 1.

U

To Go to the world. *To be a woman of the world ; to be married.*

Thus *goes* every one *to the world* but I.
Much Ado about Nothing, ii. 1.

If I may have your ladyship's good will *to go to the world*, Isbel your woman and I will do as we may.   *All's well that ends well*, i. 3.

I do desire it with all my heart; and I hope it is no dishonest desire, to desire *to be a woman of the world.*   *As you like it*, v. 3.

To Go under. *To pass for ; to represent.*

Their promises, enticements, oaths, tokens, and all these engines of lust, are not the things they *go under :* many a maid hath been seduced by them.
All's well that ends well, iii. 5.

Gobbet. *A piece ; a morsel.*

By devilish policy art thou grown great,
And, like ambitious Sylla, overgorg'd
With *gobbets* of thy mother's bleeding heart.
Henry 6, P. 2, iv. 1.

Meet I an infant of the house of York,
Into as many *gobbets* will I cut it,
As wild Medea young Absyrtus did.   *Ibid.* v. 2.

To God. *To deify ; to make a god of.*

This last old man,
Whom with a crack'd heart I have sent to Rome,
Lov'd me above the measure of a father ;
Nay, *godded* me, indeed.   *Coriolanus*, v. 3.

God ild. *God reward ; God recompense.*

God ild you for your last company.
As you like it, iii. 3.
Herein I teach you
How you shall bid *God ild* us for your pains.
Macbeth, i. 6.

Gold. *Money ; pomp ; splendour.*

Thou that didst bear the key of all my counsels,
That almost mightst have coin'd me into *gold.*
Henry 5, ii. 2.
For me,—the *gold* of France did not seduce.
Ibid. ii. 2.
I tell you he does sit in *gold*, his eye
Red as 'twould burn Rome.   *Coriolanus*, v. 1.

Goliasses. *Goliaths.*

For none but Samsons and *Goliasses*
It sendeth forth to skirmish.   *Henry 6, P.* 1, i. 2.

Good. *Goodness ; merit ; advantage ; benefit.*

May it please your highness
To hear me speak his *good* now ?   *Henry 8*, iv. 2.
Ever witness for him
Those twins of learning that he mis'd in you,
Ipswich and Oxford ! one of which fell with him,
Unwilling to outlive the *good* that did it.
Henry 8, iv. 2.
Alas the day ! what *good* could they pretend ?
Macbeth, ii. 2.

Good. *Rich ; wealthy ; comely.*

Antonio is a *good* man.   *Merchant of Venice*, i. 3.
We are accounted poor citizens, the patricians, *good.*
Coriolanus, i. 1.
Thou art a traitor and a miscreant,
Too *good* to be so, and too bad to live.
Richard 2, i. 1.
She's a *good* sign, but I have seen small reflection of her wit.   *Cymbeline*, i. 2.

Good cheap. *Cheap.*

But the sack that thou hast drunk me would have bought me lights as *good cheap* at the dearest chandler's in Europe.   *Henry 4, P.* 1, iii. 3.

Good deed. *Verily ; indeed.*

Yet, *good deed*, I love thee not a jar o' the clock behind
What lady should her lord.   *Winter's Tale*, i. 2.

Good lady. *Good friend ; protectress ; patroness.*

I will inform your father.—
Your mother too :
She's my *good lady ;* and will conceive, I hope,
But the worst of me.   *Cymbeline*, ii. 3.

Good life. *Activity ; diligence ; alacrity.*

So, with *good life*,
And observation strange, my meaner ministers
Their several kinds have done.   *Tempest*, iii. 3.

Good lord. *Good friend ; protector ; patron.*

My lord, beseech you, give me leave to go
Through Glostershire : and, when you come to court,
Stand my *good lord*, pray, in your good report.
Henry 4, P. 2, iv. 3.

Good master. *A patron ; a protector ; a good lord.*

Come, follow us : we'll be thy *good masters*.
Winter's Tale, v. 2.

GOOD DEN. *Good day.*

" *Good den,* Sir Richard :"—God-a-mercy, fellow.
King John, i. 1.

God ye *good den,* fair gentlewoman.
Romeo and Juliet, ii. 4.

Good den, brother. *Much Ado about Nothing,* iii. 2.

GOODNESS. *Good ; commendation ; favourable mention.*

We have made inquiry of you ; and we hear
Such *goodness* of your justice, that our soul
Cannot but yield you forth to public thanks,
Forerunning more requital.
Measure for Measure, v. 1.

GORBELLIED. *Fat ; big-bellied.*

Hang ye, *gorbellied* knaves, are ye undone ?
Henry 4, P. 1, ii. 2.

GORGE. *The throat.*

He hath borne me on his back a thousand times;
and now, how abhorred in my imagination it is ! my
gorge rises at it. *Hamlet,* v. 1.
She whom the spital-house and ulcerous sores
Would cast the *gorge* at, this embalms and spices
To the April day again. *Timon of Athens,* iv. 3.

GOSPELLED. *Religious ; pious.*

Are you so *gospell'd,*
To pray for this good man and for his issue,
Whose heavy hand hath bow'd you to the grave,
And beggar'd yours for ever ? *Macbeth,* iii. 1.

GOURD AND FULLAM. *False dice.*

For *gourd and fullam* holds.
Merry Wives of Windsor, i. 3.

GOUT. *A drop.*

I see thee still ;
And on thy blade and dudgeon *gouts* of blood,
Which was not so before. *Macbeth,* ii. 1.

GOVERNANCE. *Rule ; government.*

What, shall King Henry be a pupil still,
Under the surly Gloster's *governance* ?
Henry 6, P. 2, i. 3.

GOVERNMENT. *Complaisance ; moderation ; regularity of behaviour ; modesty.* ＼

Yet oftentimes it doth present harsh rage,
Defect of manners, want of *government,*
Pride, haughtiness, opinion, and disdain.
Henry 4, P. 1, iii. 1.

Fear not my *government.*   *Othello,* iii. 3.
'Tis *government* that makes them seem divine,
The want thereof makes thee abominable.
Henry 6, P. 3, i. 4.

Thy meekness saint-like, wife-like *government.*
Henry 8, ii. 4.

GRACE. *Excellence; desert; merit; ornament.*

In his own *grace* he doth exalt himself,
More than in your addition. *King Lear,* v. 3.

Know you not, master, to some kind of men
Their *graces* serve them but as enemies ?
As you like it, ii. 3.

Who, dipping all his faults in their affection,
Would, like the spring that turneth wood to stone,
Convert his gyves to *graces.* *Hamlet,* iv. 7.

TO GRACE. *To please ; to gratify.*

What comfortable hour canst thou name,
That ever *grac'd* me in thy company ?
Richard 3, iv. 4.

GRACED. *Chaste ; virtuous ; orderly.*

Epicurism and lust
Make it more like a tavern or a brothel
Than a *grac'd* palace. *King Lear,* i. 4.

GRACEFUL. *Virtuous ; pleased ; favourable.*

You have a holy father,
A *graceful* gentleman ; against whose person,
So sacred as it is, I have done sin.
Winter's Tale, v. 1.

I know you could not lack, I am certain on't,
Very necessity of this thought, that I,
Your partner in the cause 'gainst which he fought,
Could not with *graceful* eyes attend those wars
Which fronted mine own peace.
Antony and Cleopatra, ii. 2.

GRACIOUS. *Graceful ; pleasing ; virtuous ; favoured ; prosperous.*

In law, what plea so tainted and corrupt
But, being season'd with a *gracious* voice,
Obscures the show of evil ?
Merchant of Venice, iii. 2.

For since the birth of Cain the first male child
To him that did but yesterday suspire,
There was not such a *gracious* creature born.
King John, iii. 4.

O, now you weep ; and, I perceive you feel
The dint of pity : these are *gracious* drops.
Julius Cæsar, iii. 2.

Kings are no less unhappy, their issue not being *gracious*, than they are in losing them when they have approved their virtues. *Winter's Tale*, iv. 1.
Thy state is the more *gracious*; for 'tis a vice to know him. *Hamlet*, v. 2.
Wherein if I be foiled, there is but one shamed that was never *gracious*; if killed, but one dead that is willing to be so. *As you like it*, i. 2.
Go,—fresh horses;—and *gracious* be the issue !
Winter's Tale, iii. 1.

To GRAFF. *To graft.*

I'll *graff* it with you, and then I shall *graff* it with a medlar. *As you like it*, iii. 2.

GRAFT. *Grafted.*

Her royal stock *graft* with ignoble plants.
Richard 3, iii. 7.
And noble stock was *graft* with crab-tree slip.
Henry 6, P. 2, iii. 2.

GRAINED. *Rough; furrowed; ingrained; dyed in grain.*

Though now this *grainèd* face of mine be hid
In sap-consuming winter's drizzled snow,
And all the conduits of my blood froze up.
Comedy of Errors, v. 1.
Let me twine
Mine arms about that body, where against
My *grainèd* ash a hundred times hath broke,
And scar'd the moon with splinters.
Coriolanus, iv. 5.
Thou turn'st mine eyes into my very soul ;
And there I see such black and *grainèd* spots
As will not leave their tinct. *Hamlet*, iii. 4.

GRAMERCY, GRAMERCIES. *Thanks; many thanks.*

Gramercies, Tranio, well dost thou advise.
Taming of the Shrew, i. 1.
Gramercy: wouldst thou aught with me ?
Merchant of Venice, ii. 2.

GRANT. *Concession; admission.*

The fairest *grant* is the necessity.
Much Ado about Nothing, i. 1.

To GRANT. *To consent; to yield; to afford.*

The soldiers should have toss'd me on their pikes
Before I would have *granted* to that act.
Henry 6, P. 3, i. 1.
Thou hast, Ventidius, that
Without the which a soldier, and his sword,
Grants scarce distinction.
Antony and Cleopatra, iii. 1.

To GRATE. *To annoy; to tease; to harass; to disturb; to vex.*

What peer hath been suborn'd to *grate* on you ?
Henry 4, P. 2, iv. 1.
I have *grated* upon my good friends for three reprieves for you and your coach-fellow Nym.
Merry Wives of Windsor, ii. 2.
Grating so harshly all his days of quiet
With turbulent and dangerous lunacy.
Hamlet, iii. 1.
News, my good lord, from Rome.—*Grates* me :—
the sum. *Antony and Cleopatra*, i. 1.

To GRATIFY. *To requite; to recompense.*

And she did *gratify* his amorous works
With that recognizance and pledge of love
Which I first gave her. *Othello*, v. 2.
To *gratify* his noble service that
Hath thus stood for his country. *Coriolanus*, ii. 2.
In these sear'd hopes
I barely *gratify* your love. *Cymbeline*, ii. 4.

GRATULATE. *Pleasing; worthy of gratulation.*

There's more behind that is more *gratulate*.
Measure for Measure, v. 1.

To GRATULATE. *To greet; to compliment; to salute.*

Upon the like devotion as yourselves,
To *gratulate* the gentle princes there.
Richard 3, iv. 1.
The five best senses
Acknowledge thee their patron ; and come freely
To *gratulate* thy plenteous bosom.
Timon of Athens, i. 2.

GRAVE. *Destructive; deadly; fatal.*

O this false soul of Egypt ! this *grave* charm,—
Whose eye beck'd forth my wars, and call'd them home. *Antony and Cleopatra*, iv. 12.

To GRAVE. *To bury; to entomb.*

Those whom you curse
Have felt the worst of death's destroying wound,
And lie full low, *grav'd* in the hollow ground.
Richard 2, iii. 2.
Do you damn others, and let this damn you,
And ditches *grave* you all ! *Timon of Athens*, iv. 3.

To GRAVEL. *To pose; to embarrass; to puzzle.*

Nay, you were better speak first; and when you

were *gravelled* for lack of matter, you might take occasion to kiss.   *As you like it*, iv. 1.

GREAT MORNING.   *Broad day.*

It is *great morning;* and the hour prefix'd
Of her delivery to this valiant Greek
Comes fast upon.   *Troilus and Cressida*, iv. 3.

GREAT ONEYERS.   *Great ones; persons of distinction.*

But with nobility and tranquillity, burgomasters and *great oneyers.*   *Henry 4*, P. 1, ii. 1.

GREAVES.   *Armour for the legs.*

Turning your books to *greaves*, your ink to blood,
Your pens to lances, and your tongue divine
To a loud trumpet and a point of war.   .
    Henry 4, P. 2, iv. 1.

To GREE.   *To agree.*

And all the means
Plotted and *greed* on for my happiness.
    Two Gentlemen of Verona, ii. 4.
And to conclude, we have *greed* so well together,
That upon Sunday is the wedding-day.
    Taming of the Shrew, ii. 1.

GREEK.   *A jester; a buffoon.*

I prithee, foolish *Greek*, depart from me.
    Twelfth-Night, iv. 1.

GREEKISH.   *Grecian.*

I'll heat his blood with *Greekish* wine to-night.
    Troilus and Cressida, i. 3.
And all the *Greekish* girls shall tripping sing,
"Great Hector's sister did Achilles win;
But our great Ajax bravely beat down him."
    Ibid. iii. 3.

GREEN.   *Young; inexperienced; new; fresh.*

How *green* you are, and fresh in this old world!
    King John, iii. 4.
You may be jogging whiles your boots are *green*.
    Taming of the Shrew, iii. 2.
Where bloody Tybalt, yet but *green* in earth,
Lies festering in his shroud.
    Romeo and Juliet, iv. 3.

GREENLY.   *Timidly; foolishly; unwisely.*

But, before God, Kate, I cannot look *greenly*,
nor gasp out my eloquence, nor have I no cunning
in protestation.   *Henry 5*, v. 2.
And we have done but *greenly*,
In hugger-mugger to inter him.   *Hamlet*, iv. 5.

GREY.   *Of a blue colour.*

Item, two *grey* eyes, with lids to them.
    Twelfth-Night, i. 5.
Her eyes are *grey* as glass; and so are mine.
    Two Gentlemen of Verona, iv. 2.
Thisbe, a *grey* eye or so, but not to the purpose.
    Romeo and Juliet, ii. 4.

GRIEF.   *Offence; complaint; grievance; pain; harm; mischief.*

Know, then, I here forget all former *griefs*,
Cancel all grudge, repeal thee home again.
    Two Gentlemen of Verona, v. 4.
The king hath sent to know
The nature of your *griefs*.   *Henry 4*, P. 1, iv. 3.
I, then all smarting with my wounds being cold,
Out of my *grief* and my impatience
To be so pester'd with a popinjay,
Answer'd neglectingly, I know not what.
    Ibid. iv. 3.
Can honour set to a leg? no: or an arm? no:
or take away the *grief* of a wound?   *Ibid.* v. 2.
This must be known; which, being kept close,
might move
More *grief* to hide than hate to utter love.
    Hamlet, ii. 1.

GRIEF-SHOT.   *Pierced with grief; sorrow-stricken.*

But as a discontented friend, *grief-shot*
With his unkindness? say't be so?
    Coriolanus, v. 1.

GRIFFIN.   *The gripe or vulture.*

The dove pursues the *griffin*.
    Midsummer-Night's Dream, ii. 1.

GRISE.   *A step; a degree.*

Let me speak like yourself; and lay a sentence,
Which, as a *grise* or step, may help these lovers
Into your favour.   *Othello*, i. 3.
No, not a *grise*; for 'tis a vulgar proof,
That very oft we pity enemies.
    Twelfth-Night, iii. 1.
If one be,
So are they all; for every *grise* of fortune
Is smooth'd by that below.   *Timon of Athens*, iv. 3.

GROOM.   *A servant; a fellow, in contempt; a bridegroom.*

The honourable blood of Lancaster
Must not be shed by such a jaded *groom*.
    Henry 6, P. 2, iv. 1.

Home to your cottages, forsake this *groom.*
Henry 6, P. 2, iv. 2.
An ordinary *groom* is for such payment.
Henry 8, v. 1.
'Tis like you'll prove a jolly surly *groom*
That take it on you at the first so roundly.
Taming of the Shrew, iii. 2.
Were you a woman, youth,
I should woo hard but be your *groom.*
Cymbeline, iii. 6.

GROSS. *Wholesale.*

And we that sell by *gross,* the Lord doth know,
Have not the grace to grace it with such show.
Love's Labour's lost, v. 2.

GROSSNESS. *Extravagance; dulness; ignorance.*

And yet the guiltiness of my mind, the sudden
surprise of my powers, drove the *grossness* of the
foppery into a received belief that they were fairies.
Merry Wives of Windsor, v. 5.
Weigh it but with the *grossness* of this age,
You break not sanctuary in seizing him.
Richard 3, iii. 1.

GROUNDLINGS. *Those spectators who, in our ancient theatres, occupied the ground, or, as we should now say, the pit.*

O, it offends me to the soul to hear a robustious
periwig-pated fellow tear a passion to tatters, to
very rags, to split the ears of the *groundlings.*
Hamlet, iii. 2.

TO GROW. *To cause to grow; to accrue; to become due.*

Touch thou the sourest points with sweetest terms,
Nor curstness *grow* to the matter.
Antony and Cleopatra, ii. 2.
Even just the sum that I do owe to you
Is *growing* to me by Antipholus.
Comedy of Errors, iv. 1.

GROWING. *Growth; progress; advancement.*

I have begun to plant thee, and will labour
To make thee full of *growing.* *Macbeth,* i. 4.
I turn my glass, and give my scene such *growing*
As you had slept between.
Winter's Tale, iv. Chorus.

GRUDGE. *Dissension; quarrel; reluctance; anger; resentment.*

My noble queen, let former *grudges* pass.
Henry 6, P. 3, iii. 3.

Told thee no lies, made no mistakings, serv'd
Without *grudge* or grumblings. *Tempest,* i. 2.
Know then, I here forget all former griefs,
Cancel all *grudge,* repeal thee home again.
Two Gentlemen of Verona, v. 4.

TO GRUDGE. *To cherish secretly; to harbour.*

And as my duty springs, so perish they
That *grudge* one thought against your majesty !
Henry 6, P. 1, iii. 1.

GRUDGING. *Reluctance; unwillingness.*

And yet now, in despite of his heart, he eats his
meat without *grudging.*
Much Ado about Nothing, iii. 4.

TO GUARD. *To face; to trim; to garnish.*

The body of your discourse is sometime *guarded*
with fragments, and the guards are but slightly
basted on neither. *Much Ado about Nothing,* i. 1.
Give him a livery more *guarded* than his fellows.
Merchant of Venice, ii. 2.
To *guard* a title that was rich before,
To gild refinèd gold, to paint the lily,
To throw a perfume on the violet,
To smooth the ice, or add another hue
Unto the rainbow, or with taper-light
To seek the beauteous eye of heaven to garnish,
Is wasteful and ridiculous excess. *King John,* iv. 2.

GUARDAGE. *Wardship.*

Whether a maid so tender, fair, and happy,
Would ever have, to incur a general mock,
Run from her *guardage* to the sooty bosom
Of such a thing as thou,—to fear, not to delight.
Othello, i. 2.

GUARDANT. *A protector; a guardian.*

But when my angry *guardant* stood alone,
Tendering my ruin, and assail'd of none,
Dizzy-ey'd fury and great rage of heart
Suddenly made him from my side to start
Into the clustering battle of the French.
Henry 6, P. 1, iv. 7.

GUARDS. *Facing; trimming.*

O, 'tis the cunning livery of hell,
The damned'st body to invest and cover
In priestly *guards.* *Measure for Measure,* iii. 1.
And the *guards* are but slightly basted on neither. *Much Ado about Nothing,* i. 1.

GUERDON. *Requital; recompense.*

Death, in *guerdon* of her wrongs,
Gives her fame which never dies.
Much Ado about Nothing, v. 3.

To GUERDON. *To reward; to recompense.*

And am I *guerdon'd* at the last with shame?
     Henry 6, P. 3, iii. 3.
My lord protector will, I doubt it not,
See you well *guerdon'd* for these good deserts.
     Ibid. P. 2, i. 4.

GUIDON. *A kind of standard; a banner; a standard-bearer.*

I stay but for my *guidon:*—to the field!
     Henry 5, iv. 2.

GUILDER. *A coin.*

Who, wanting *guilders* to redeem their lives,
Have scal'd his rigorous statutes with their bloods.
     Comedy of Errors, i. 1.
Nor now I had not, but that I am bound
To Persia, and want *guilders* for my voyage.
     Ibid. iv. 1.

GUILED. *Beguiling; deceitful; treacherous.*

Thus ornament is but the *guilèd* shore
To a most dangerous sea. *Merchant of Venice, iii. 2.*

GUINEA-HEN. *A cant term for a courtezan.*

Ere I would say, I would drown myself for the
love of a *guinea-hen,* I would change my humanity
with a baboon.   *Othello, i. 3.*

GUISE. *Custom; practice.*

To shame the *guise* o' the world, I will begin
The fashion,—less without and more within.
     Cymbeline, v. 1.
My Lord of Suffolk, say, is this the *guise,*
Is this the fashion in the court of England?
     Henry 6, P. 2, i. 3.
How rarely does it meet with this time's *guise,*
When man was wish'd to love his enemies!
     Timon of Athens, iv. 3.

GULES. *Red.*

Follow thy drum;
With man's blood paint the ground, *gules, gules.*
     Timon of Athens, iv. 3.
Head to foot now is he total *gules.* *Hamlet, ii. 2.*

GULF. *The stomach.*

Witches' mummy, maw and *gulf*
Of the ravin'd salt-sea shark.   *Macbeth, iv. 1.*

GULL. *An unfledged bird; a nestling; a cheat; a trick; a dupe; a fool.*

And, being fed by us, you us'd us so
As that ungentle *gull,* the cuckoo's bird,
Useth the sparrow,—did oppress our nest.
     Henry 4, P. 1, v. 1.
For, I do fear,
When every feather sticks in his own wing,
Lord Timon will be left a naked *gull,*
Which flashes now a phœnix.
     Timon of Athens, ii. 1.
I should think this a *gull,* but that the white-
bearded fellow speaks it.
     Much Ado about Nothing, ii. 3.
And made the most notorious geck and *gull*
That e'er invention play'd on. *Twelfth-Night, v. 1.*
O *gull!* O dolt! as ignorant as dirt! *Othello, v. 2.*

To GULL. *To trick; to deceive.*

If I do not *gull* him into a nayword, do not
think I have wit enough to lie straight in my bed.
     Twelfth-Night, ii. 3.

GULL-CATCHER. *A trickster; a cheat.*

Here comes my noble *gull-catcher.*
     Twelfth-Night, ii. 5.

GUN-STONE. *A cannon-ball.*

And tell the pleasant prince, this mock of his
Hath turn'd his balls to *gun-stones. Henry 5, i. 2.*

GUST. *Taste; relish; enjoyment.*

But that he hath the gift of a coward to allay
the *gust* he hath in quarrelling, 'tis thought among
the prudent he would quickly have the gift of a
grave.   *Twelfth-Night, i. 3.*
To kill, I grant, is sin's extremest *gust.*
     Timon of Athens, iii. 5.

To GUST. *To taste.*

'Tis far gone, when I shall *gust* it last.
     Winter's Tale, i. 2.

GYVES. *Fetters.*

Who, dipping all his faults in their affection,
Would, like the spring that turneth wood to stone,
Convert his *gyves* to graces. *Hamlet, iv. 7.*

To GYVE. *To fetter; to enchain.*

Ay, smile upon her, do; I will *gyve* thee in thine
own courtship.   *Othello, ii. 1.*

H.

HAGGARD. *A wild hawk.*

Not, like the *haggard*, check at every feather.
Twelfth-Night, iii. 1.
I know her spirits are as coy and wild
As *haggards* of the rock.
Much Ado about Nothing, iii. 1.

HAGGISH. *Haglike; ugly.*

But on us both did *haggish* age steal on,
And wore us out of act.
All's well that ends well, i. 2.

HAGGLED. *Maimed; mangled.*

And York, all *haggled* over,
Comes to him, where in gore he lay insteep'd,
And takes him by the beard.   *Henry 5*, iv. 6.

HAIR. *Nature; grain.*

If you should fight, you go against the *hair* of
your professions. *Merry Wives of Windsor*, ii. 3.
The quality and *hair* of our attempt
Brooks no division.   *Henry 4*, P. 1, iv. 1.
He is melancholy without cause, and merry
against the *hair*.   *Troilus and Cressida*, i. 2.

HALBERD. *A battle-axe fixed to a long pole.*

Advance thy *halberd* higher than my breast,
Or, by Saint Paul, I'll strike thee to my foot,
And spurn upon thee, beggar, for thy boldness.
Richard 3, i. 2.

To HALE. *To haul; to pull; to drag.*

That the appallèd air
May pierce the head of the great combatant,
And *hale* him hither. *Troilus and Cressida*, iv. 5.
The plebeians have got your fellow-tribune,
And *hale* him up and down.   *Coriolanus*, v. 4.

HALF-BLOODED. *Base-born; mean; degenerate.*

The let-alone lies not in your good will.—
Nor in thine, lord.—*Half-blooded* fellow, yes.
King Lear, v. 3.

HALF-CAP. *A slight salutation.*

After distasteful looks, and these hard fractions,
With certain *half-caps* and cold-moving nods
They froze me into silence. *Timon of Athens*, ii. 2.

HALFPENCE. *Pieces; bits.*

O, she tore the letter into a thousand *halfpence*.
Much Ado about Nothing, ii. 3.

HALIDOM. *Holiness; sanctity.*

By my *halidom*, I was fast asleep.
Two Gentlemen of Verona, iv. 2.
Now, by my *halidom*, here comes Katharina!
Taming of the Shrew, v. 2.

HALTING. *Hesitation; prevarication; shuffling.*

No further *halting*: satisfy me home
What is become of her.   *Cymbeline*, iii. 5.

To HAMMER. *To make mention; to dwell upon.*

I'll presently,
Acquaint the queen of your most noble offer;
Who but to-day *hammer'd* of this design.
Winter's Tale, ii. 2.

To HAND. *To handle; to lay hands on.*

Sooth, when I was young,
And *handed* love as you do, I was wont
To load my she with knacks. *Winter's Tale*, iv. 3.
Let him that makes but trifles of his eyes
First *hand* me.   *Ibid.* ii. 3.

HAND-FAST. *Custody; contract; obligation.*

If that shepherd be not in *hand-fast*, let him fly.
Winter's Tale, iv. 3.
The agent for his master;
And the remembrancer of her to hold
The *hand-fast* to her lord.   *Cymbeline*, i. 5.

HANDKERCHER. *A handkerchief; a napkin.*

Some of my shame; if you will know of me
What man I am, and how, and why, and where
This *handkercher* was stain'd. *As you like it*, iv. 3.

HANDS. *Height; inches.*

The worst that they can say of me is, that I am
a second brother, and that I am a proper fellow of
my *hands*.   *Henry 4*, P. 2, ii. 2.

HANDSAW. *A hernshaw; a heron.*

When the wind is southerly I know a hawk
from a *handsaw.* *Hamlet,* ii. 2.

HANDY-DANDY. *A game still played by children.*

Change places; and, *handy-dandy,* which is the
justice, which is the thief? *King Lear,* iv. 6.

HAP. *Fortune; chance; accident.*

Wish me partaker in thy happiness
When thou dost meet good *hap.*
Two Gentlemen of Verona, i. 1.

By Him that rais'd me to this careful height
From that contented *hap* which I enjoy'd.
Richard 3, i. 3.

And by me too, had not our *hap* been bad.
Comedy of Errors, i. 1.

Till I know 'tis done,
Howe'er my *haps,* my joys were ne'er begun.
Hamlet, iv. 3.

Be it art or *hap,* he hath spoken true.
Antony and Cleopatra, ii. 3.

To HAP. *To happen.*

And whatsoever else shall *hap* to-night,
Give it an understanding, but no tongue.
Hamlet, i. 2.

What else may *hap,* to time I will commit.
Twelfth-Night, i. 2.

HAPPILY. *Haply; perchance.*

Besides old Gremio is hearkening still;
And *happily* we might be interrupted.
Taming of the Shrew, iv. 4.

If thou art privy to thy country's fate,
Which, *happily,* foreknowing may avoid,
O, speak! *Hamlet,* i. 1.

Happily he's the second time come to them;
for they say an old man is twice a child. *Ibid.* ii. 2.

HAPPY. *Successful; fortunate; well skilled; accomplished.*

Whether 'twas pride,
Which out of daily fortune ever taints
The *happy* man. *Coriolanus,* iv. 7.

Not so *happy,* yet much happier. *Macbeth,* i. 3.

For if she be not honest, chaste, and true,
There's no man *happy.* *Othello,* iv. 2.

Fore noble Lucius
Present yourself, desire his service, tell him
Wherein you are *happy.* *Cymbeline,* iii. 4.

HARBOURAGE. *Entertainment; shelter.*

Whose labour'd spirits
Crave *harbourage* within your city-walls.
King John, ii. 1.

HARDIMENT. *Deeds of valour; boldness; audacity.*

He did confound the best part of an hour
In changing *hardiment* with great Glendower.
Henry 4, P. 1, i. 3.

For thus popp'd Paris in his *hardiment,*
And parted thus you and your argument.
Troilus and Cressida, iv. 5.

HARDINESS. *Courage; stoutness; valour.*

Hardiness ever
Of *hardiness* is mother. *Cymbeline,* iii. 6.

If we, with thrice such powers left at home,
Cannot defend our own doors from the dog,
Let us be worried, and our nation lose
The name of *hardiness* and policy. *Henry 5,* i. 2.

HARDNESS. *Want; hardship; penury.*

Plenty and peace breeds cowards; *hardness* ever
Of hardiness is mother. *Cymbeline,* iii. 6.

HARLOT. *A rogue; a cheat; a base person.*

While she with *harlots* feasted in my house.
Comedy of Errors, v. 1.

HARLOT. *Depraved; dissolute; debased.*

For the *harlot* king
Is quite beyond mine arm. *Winter's Tale,* ii. 3.

HARM. *Calamity; mishap.*

A league from Epidamnum had we sail'd,
Before the always-wind-obeying deep
Gave any tragic instance of our *harm.*
Comedy of Errors, i. 1.

HARMFUL. *Mischievous; hurtful.*

Yet, under pardon,
You are much more attask'd for want of wisdom
Than prais'd for *harmful* mildness. *King Lear,* i. 4.

HARNESS. *Armour.*

Great men should drink with *harness* on their throats.
Timon of Athens, i. 2.

For, of no right, nor colour like to right,
He doth fill fields with *harness* in the realm.
Henry 4, P. 1, iii. 2.

At least we'll die with *harness* on our back.
Macbeth, v. 5.

x

Leap thou, attire and all,
Through proof of *harness*, to my heart.
Antony and Cleopatra, iv. 8.

To HARNESS. *To put on armour; to arm.*
Before the sun rose, he was *harness'd* light,
And to the field goes he. *Troilus and Cressida*, i. 2.
This *harness'd* masque and unadvisèd revel
The king doth smile at. *King John*, v. 2.

To HARRY. *To use with violence; to maltreat.*
A proper man.—
Indeed, he is so : I repent me much
That so I *harried* him.
Antony and Cleopatra, iii. 3.

HASTE. *Rashness.*
And modest wisdom plucks me
From over-credulous *haste*. *Macbeth*, iv. 3.

HATCH. *A half-door.*
Either get thee from the door, or sit down at
the *hatch*. *Comedy of Errors*, iii. 1.
Something about, a little from the right,
In at the window, or else o'er the *hatch*.
King John, i. 1.
For, with throwing thus my head,
Dogs leap the *hatch*, and all are fled.
King Lear, iii. 6.

HATCHED. *Decked; garnished; adorned.*
And such again
As venerable Nestor, *hatch'd* in silver,
Should with a bond of air knit all the Greekish ears
To his experienc'd tongue.
Troilus and Cressida, i. 3.
Folly, in wisdom *hatch'd*,
Hath wisdom's warrant and the help of school,
And wit's own grace to grace a learnèd fool.
Love's Labour's lost, v. 2.

HATEFUL. *Full of hatred; malignant.*
For little office
The *hateful* commons will perform for us,
Except like curs to tear us all to pieces.
Richard 2, ii. 2.

HAUGHT. *Haughty; proud; disdainful.*
No lord of thine, thou *haught* insulting man,
Nor no man's lord. *Richard 2*, iv. 1.

HAUGHTY. *Lofty; high-minded.*
When first this order was ordain'd, my lords,
Knights of the garter were of noble birth,

Valiant and virtuous, full of *haughty* courage,
Such as were grown to credit by the wars.
Henry 6, P. 1, iv. 1.

To HAVE. *To help; to know; to understand;
to find.*
And light them at the fiery glow-worm's eyes,
To *have* my love to bed and to arise.
Midsummer-Night's Dream, iii. 1.
Or wilt thou sleep? we'll *have* thee to a couch
Softer and sweeter than the lustful bed
On purpose trimm'd up for Semiramis.
Taming of the Shrew, Induction, sc. 2.
He will steal himself into a man's favour, and
for a week escape a great deal of discoveries; but
when you find him out, you *have* him ever after.
All's well that ends well, iii. 6.
You *have* me, have you not?—My lord, I *have*.
Hamlet, ii. 1.
At the Elephant is best to lodge : there shall you
have me. *Twelfth-Night*, iii. 3.

To HAVE AFTER. *To follow.*
Let's follow; 'tis not fit thus to obey him.—
Have after. *Hamlet*, i. 4.

To HAVE IN THE WIND. *To know; to under-
stand.*
I sent to her,
By this same coxcomb that we *have i' the wind*,
Tokens and letters which she did re-send.
All's well that ends well, iii. 6.

HAVING. *Wealth; fortune.*
For simply your *having* in beard is a younger
brother's revenue. *As you like it*, iii. 2.
Our content is our best *having*. *Henry 8*, ii. 3.
My *having* is not much ;
I'll make division of my present with you :
Hold, there's half my coffer. *Twelfth-Night*, iii. 5.

HAVIOUR. *Behaviour; conduct; appearance.*
And furbish new the name of John o' Gaunt,
Even in the lusty *haviour* of his son.
Richard 2, i. 3.
With the same *haviour* that your passion bears,
Goes on my master's grief. *Twelfth-Night*, iii. 4.
Put thyself
Into a *haviour* of less fear, ere wildness
Vanquish my staider senses. *Cymbeline*, iii. 4.
I will keep the *haviour* of reputation.
Merry Wives of Windsor, i. 3.

HAWKING. *Keen; penetrating; hawk-like.*

> To sit and draw
> His archèd brows, his *hawking* eye, his curls,
> In our heart's table. *All's well that ends well,* i. 1.

THE HAY. *A rustic dance.*

> Or I will play
> On the tabor to the Worthies, and let them dance
>   the hay. *Love's Labour's lost,* v. 1.

HEAD. *An armed force; a power.*

> And 'tis no little reason bids us speed,
> To save our heads by raising of a *head*.
>   *Henry* 4, P. 1, i. 3.

> If we, without his help, can make a *head*
> To push against the kingdom, with his help
> We shall o'erturn it topsy-turvy down. *Ibid.* iv. 1.

> When Tarquin made a *head* for Rome, he fought
> Beyond the mark of others. *Coriolanus,* ii. 2.

HEADY. *Impetuous; violent.*

> Of prisoners ransom'd, and of soldiers slain,
> And all the 'currents of a *heady* fight.
>   *Henry* 4, P. 1, ii. 3.

> Never came reformation in a flood,
> With such a *heady* current scouring faults.
>   *Henry* 5, i. 1.

HEALTH. *Welfare; happiness; prosperity; goodness; salvation.*

> For on his choice depends
> The safety and the *health* of the whole state.
>   *Hamlet,* i. 3.

> For youth no less becomes
> The light and careless livery that it wears
> Than settled age his sables and his weeds,
> Importing *health* and graveness. *Ibid.* iv. 7.

> Be thou a spirit of *health* or goblin damn'd,
> Thou com'st in such a questionable shape
> That I will speak to thee. *Ibid.* i. 4.

HEALTHSOME. *Wholesome; healthful.*

> Shall I not, then, be stifled in the vault,
> To whose foul mouth no *healthsome* air breathes in,
> And there die strangled ere my Romeo comes?
>   *Romeo and Juliet,* iv. 3.

HEAP. *Throng; company.*

> Among this princely *heap*, if any here,
> By false intelligence, or wrong surmise,

> Hold me a foe; I desire
> To reconcile me to his friendly peace.
>   *Richard* 3, ii. 1.

HEART. *Courage; power.*

> Good sirs, take *heart*.
>   *Antony and Cleopatra,* iv. 15.

> I see still,
> A diminution in our captain's brain
> Restores his *heart*. *Antony and Cleopatra,* iii. 13.

> Why,
> You grave, but reckless senators, have you thus
> Given Hydra *heart* to choose an officer?
>   *Coriolanus,* iii. 1.

HEARTED. *Laid up in the heart; fixed in the heart.*

> My cause is *hearted;* thine hath no less reason.
>   *Othello,* i. 3.

> Yield up, O love, thy crown and *hearted* throne
> To tyrannous hate! Swell, bosom, with thy fraught,
> For 'tis of aspics' tongues! *Ibid.* iii. 3.

To HEARTEN. *To animate; to encourage.*

> My royal father, cheer these noble lords,
> And *hearten* those that fight in your defence!
>   *Henry* 6, P. 3, ii. 2.

HEARSE. *A coffin; a bier.*

> Stand from the *hearse*, stand from the body.
>   *Julius Cæsar,* iii. 2.

> To add to your laments,
> Wherewith you now bedew King Henry's *hearse*,
> I must inform you of a dismal fight
> Betwixt the stout Lord Talbot and the French.
>   *Henry* 6, P. 1, i. 1.

To HEARSE. *To enclose in a hearse or coffin.*

> Would she were *hearsed* at my foot, and the
> ducats in her coffin! *Merchant of Venice,* iii. 1.

> But tell
> Why thy canónized bones, *hearsèd* in death,
> Have burst their cerements. *Hamlet,* i. 4.

HEAT. *Anger; rage; resentment.*

> The *heat* is past; follow no further now.
>   *Henry* 4, P. 2, iv. 3.

HEAT. *Heated.*

> The iron of itself, though *heat* red hot,
> Approaching near these eyes, would drink my tears,
> And quench his fiery indignation
> Even in the water of mine innocence.
>   *King John,* iv. 1.

To HEAT. *To run over; to traverse.*

You may ride us
With one soft kiss a thousand furlongs, ere
With spur we *heat* an acre. *Winter's Tale*, i. 2.

HEAVILY. *Sorrowfully; mournfully.*

You cannot reason almost with a man
That looks not *heavily* and full of dread.
Richard 3, ii. 3.
Midnight, assist our moan;
Help us to sigh and groan,
Heavily, heavily. *Much Ado about Nothing*, v. 3.

HEAVINESS. *Dejection; sorrow.*

I will, and know her mind early to-morrow;
To-night she is mew'd up to her *heaviness*.
Romeo and Juliet, iii. 4.
Our strength is all gone into *heaviness*,
That makes the weight.
Antony and Cleopatra, iv. 15.

HEAVY. *Sorrowful; mournful; grievous; dark; gloomy.*

Here come the *heavy* issue of dead Harry.
Henry 4, P. 2, v. 2.
She ceas'd, in *heavy* satisfaction, and would never
Receive the ring again.
All's well that ends well, v. 3.
Our treasure seiz'd, our soldiers put to flight,
And, as thou seest, ourselves in *heavy* plight.
Henry 6, P. 3, iii. 3.
There have I made my promise
Upon the *heavy* middle of the night
To call upon him. *Measure for Measure*, iv. 1.
Two or three groan: it is a *heavy* night.
Othello, v. 1.

HEBENON. *Ebony.*

Upon my secure hour thy uncle stole,
With juice of cursèd *hebenon* in a vial.
Hamlet, i. 5.

HECTIC. *A hectic fever.*

For like the *hectic* in my blood he rages,
And thou must cure me. *Hamlet*, iv. 3.

To HEDGE. *To shift; to hide; to skulk; to shut out; to exclude.*

The king in this perceives him, how he coasts
And *hedges* his own way. *Henry* 8, iii. 2.
I myself sometimes, leaving the fear of heaven
on the left hand, and hiding mine honour in my
necessity, am fain to shuffle, to *hedge*, and to lurch.
Merry Wives of Windsor, ii. 2.

Nay, this shall not *hedge* us out: we'll hear
you sing, certainly. *Troilus and Cressida*, iii. 1.

HEED. *Lode-star; heedfulness; eager attention.*

Who dazzling so, that eye shall be his *heed*,
And give him light that it was blinded by.
Love's Labour's lost, i. 1.
He did unseal them: and tho first he view'd,
He did it with a serious mind; a *heed*
Was in his countenance. *Henry* 8, iii. 2.

HEFT. *Heaving; reaching; inclination to vomit.*

But if one make known how he hath drunk,
He cracks his gorge, his sides, with violent *hefts*.
Winter's Tale, ii. 1.

HEIGHT. *Utmost degree; full extent; rank; dignity.*

By day and night, he's traitor to the *height*.
Henry 8, i. 2.
Come on, sir; I shall now put you to the
height of your breeding.
All's well that ends well, ii. 2.
Or with pale beggar-fear impeach my *height*
Before this outdar'd dastard. *Richard* 2, i. 1.

To HELM. *To guide; to conduct; to manage.*

The business he hath *helmed* must, upon a warranted need, give him a better proclamation.
Measure for Measure, iii. 2.

HELP. *Cure; remedy.*

You have brought
A trembling upon Rome, such as was never
So incapable of *help*. *Coriolanus*, iv. 6.
But I am faint, my gashes cry for *help*.
Macbeth, i. 2.

To HELP. *To cure.*

What can man's wisdom
In the restoring his bereavèd sense?
He that *helps* him take all my outward worth.
King Lear, iv. 4.
Love doth to her eyes repair,
To *help* him of his blindness.
Two Gentlemen of Verona, iv. 2.

To HEM. *To sigh.*

She speaks much of her father; says she hears
There's tricks i' the world; and *hems*, and beats
her heart. *Hamlet*, iv. 5.

HEN. *A coward; a dastard.*

Lord have mercy on thee for a *hen!*
All's well that ends well, ii. 3.

HENCE. *Elsewhere; henceforth.*

All members of our cause, both here and *hence,*
That are insinew'd to this action.
Henry 4, P. 2, iv. 1.
Make less thy body *hence,* and more thy grace.
Ibid. v. 5.

HENCHMAN. *A page.*

I do but beg a little changeling boy
To be my *henchman.*
Midsummer-Night's Dream, ii. 1.

To HEND. *To seize; to take possession of.*

The generous and gravest citizens
Have *hent* the gates. *Measure for Measure,* iv. 6.

HENT. *Occasion; opportunity.*

Up, sword; and know thou a more horrid *hent.*
Hamlet, iii. 3.

To HENT. *To seize; to take; to hold.*

Jog on, jog on, the footpath way,
And merrily *hent* the stile-a. *Winter's Tale,* iv. 2.

HERBELET. *A small herb.*

You were as flowers, now wither'd: even so
These *herb'lets* shall, which we upon you strow.
Cymbeline, iv. 2.

HEREAFTER. *Future.*

For I myself have many tears to wash
Hereafter time, for time past wrong'd by thee.
Richard 3, iv. 4.

HEREBY. *As it may happen; as it may be.*

I will visit thee at the lodge.—
That's *hereby.* *Love's Labour's lost,* i. 2.

HERMIT. *A beadsman; one who prays for another.*

For those of old,
And the late dignities heap'd up to them,
We rest your *hermits.* *Macbeth,* i. 6.

HEST. *Behest; command; order.*

Such as we see when men restrain their breath
On some great sudden *hest.* *Henry 4, P. 1, ii. 3.*
Refusing her grand *hests,* she did confine thee,
By help of her more potent ministers,

And in her most unmitigable rage,
Into a cloven pine. *Tempest,* i. 2.
And shape his service wholly to my *hests.*
Love's Labour's lost, v. 2.

HEY-DAY. *Wildness; impetuosity; tumult.*

You cannot call it love; for at your age
The *hey-day* in the blood is tame, it's humble,
And waits upon the judgment. *Hamlet,* iii. 4.

To HIDE. *To strip off the skin; to lay bare; to expose.*

But let your reason serve
To make the truth appear where it seems hid,
And *hide* the false seems true.
Measure for Measure, v. 1.

To HIE. *To hasten; to approach rapidly.*

Minion, your dear lies dead,
And your unblest fate *hies.* *Othello,* v. 1.

HIGH. *Exact; precise.*

And the *high* east
Stands, as the Capitol, directly here.
Julius Cæsar, ii. 1.

HIGH-DAY. *Holiday; special.*

I am half afeard,
Thou wilt say anon he is some kin to thee,
Thou spend'st such *high-day* wit in praising him.
Merchant of Venice, ii. 8.

HIGH-VICED. *Enormously wicked.*

Be as a planetary plague, when Jove
Will o'er some *high-vic'd* city hang his poison
In the sick air. *Timon of Athens,* iv. 3.

HIGHT. *Is called; is named.*

This child of fancy, that Armado *hight.*
Love's Labour's lost, i. 1.

HILDING. *A mean paltry fellow; a jade; a hussy; a slut.*

If your lordship find him not a *hilding,* hold
me no more in your respect.
All's well that ends well, iii. 6.
For shame, thou *hilding* of a devilish spirit.
Taming of the Shrew, ii. 1.
Laura, to his lady, was but a kitchen-wench;
Dido, a dowdy; Helen and Hero, *hildings* and
harlots. *Romeo and Juliet,* ii. 4.

HILTS. *The hilt; the handle.*

And hides a sword from *hilts* unto the point
With crowns imperial, crowns, and coronets.
         Henry 5, ii. Chorus.
Stand not to answer : here, take thou the *hilts,*
         Julius Cæsar, v. 3.
Hold thou my sword-*hilts,* whilst I run on it.
         Ibid. v. 5.

HIM. *Himself.*

But I do bend my speech
To one that can my part in *him* advértise.
         Measure for Measure, i. 1.

HINDERING. *Stunting.*

You minimus, of *hindering* knot-grass made.
         Midsummer-Night's Dream, iii. 2.

HINT. *Theme; subject.*

Our *hint* of woe
Is common ; every day some sailor's wife,
The master of some merchant, and the merchant,
Have just our theme of woe.   *Tempest,* ii. 1.
Wherein of antres vast and deserts idle,
Rough quarries, rocks, and hills whose heads touch
     heaven,
It was my *hint* to speak.   *Othello,* i. 3.

HIS. *Its.*

And at this time his tongue obey'd *his* hand.
         All's well that ends well, i. 2.

To HISTORY. *To record; to chronicle; to register.*

And therefore will he wipe his tables clean,
And keep no tell-tale to his memory,
That may repeat and *history* his loss
To new remembrance.   *Henry* 4, P. 2, iv. 1.

To HIT. *To agree; to concur; to cooperate.*

Pray you, let us *hit* together.   *King Lear,* i. 1.

HITHERTO. *Hither; to this place.*

England, from Trent and Severn *hitherto,*
By south and east is to my part assign'd.
         Henry 4, P. 1, iii. 1.

HITHERWARD. *This way.*

News, madam ;
The British powers are marching *hitherward.*
         King Lear, iv. 4.
Some parcels of their power are forth already,
And only *hitherward.*   *Coriolanus,* i. 2.

To HOAR. *To make hoar.*

Hoar the flamen,
That scolds against the quality of flesh,
And not believes himself.   *Timon of Athens,* iv. 3.

HOB-NOB. *At random; hit or miss.*

Hob, nob, is his word; give't or take't.
         Twelfth-Night, iii. 4.

HOBBY-HORSE. *A simpleton; a trifler; a foolish fellow.*

I have studied eight or nine wise words to speak
to you, which these *hobby-horses* must not hear.
         Much Ado about Nothing, iii. 2.

To HOISE. *To hoist; to set; to heave ; to lift.*

He, mistrusting them,
Hois'd sail, and made again for Bretagne.
         Richard 3, iv. 4.
And all together, with the Duke of Suffolk,
We'll quickly *hoise* Duke Humphrey from his seat.
         Henry 6, P. 2, i. 1.

HOIST. *Hoisted.*

For 'tis the sport to have the enginer
Hoist with his own petar.   *Hamlet,* iii. 4.

HOLD. *Prison; grasp; custody; a den; a lurking-place.*

My son George Stanley is frank'd up in *hold.*
         Richard 3, iv. 5.
King Richard he is in the mighty *hold*
Of Bolingbroke.   *Richard* 2, iii. 4.
But what is this ?
Here is a path to 't : 'tis some savage *hold :*
I were best not call.   *Cymbeline,* iii. 6.

To HOLD. *To refrain; to regard ; to esteem; to wager ; to uphold ; to continue ; to last.*

We shall be flouting ; we cannot *hold.*
         As you like it, v. 1.
He *holds* me well ;
The better shall my purpose work on him.
         Othello, i. 3.
I *hold* you a penny,
A horse and a man is more than one,
And yet not many.   *Taming of the Shrew,* iii. 2.
You must *hold* the credit of your father.
         All's well that ends well, i. 1.
God *hold* it, to your honour's good content !
         Richard 3, iii. 2.

Did you not of late days hear
A buzzing of a separation
Between the king and Katharine ?—
Yes, but it *held* not. *Henry 8,* ii. 1.

TO HOLD HANDS. *To equal; to rank with; to be equal to.*
And make her rich
In titles, honours, and promotions,
As she in beauty, education, blood,
Holds hand with any princess of the world.
King John, ii. 1.

TO HOLD IN. *To be secret ; to tell no tales.*
Nobility and tranquillity, burgomasters and great oneyers, such as can *hold in.* *Henry 4,* P. 1, ii. 1.

TO HOLD UP. *To keep up ; to continue.*
He hath ta'en the infection : *hold it up.*
Much Ado about Nothing, ii. 3.

HOLDING. *Fitness ; congruity ; the burden of a song.*
This has no *holding,*
To swear by him whom I protest to love,
That I will work against him.
All's well that ends well, iv. 2.
The *holding* every man shall bear as loud
As his strong sides can volley.
Antony and Cleopatra, ii. 7.

HOLDING UP. *Assistance; support ; cooperation.*
It lies much in your *holding up.*
Measure for Measure, iii. 1.

HOLIDAY. *Gay; sprightly ; airy.*
With many *holiday* and lady terms
He question'd me. *Henry 4,* P. 1, i. 3.

HOLP. *Helped.*
For though it have *holp* madmen to their wits,
In me it seems it will make wise men mad.
Richard 2, v. 5.
By foul play, as thou say'st, were we heav'd thence;
But blessedly *holp* hither. *Tempest,* i. 2.

HOLY. *Devoted ; faithful; excellent ; worthy.*
I was then advertising and *holy* to your business.
Measure for Measure, v. 1.
Holy Gonzalo, honourable man ! *Tempest,* v. 1.

HOMAGER. *A vassal.*
Thou blushest, Antony ; and that blood of thine
Is Cæsar's *homager.* *Antony and Cleopatra,* i. 1.

HOME. *Fully ; thoroughly.*
For this last,
Before and in Corioli, I cannot speak him *home.*
Coriolanus, ii. 2.
But your son,
As mad in folly, lack'd the sense to know
Her estimation *home.* *All's well that ends well,* v. 3.

HONEST. *Innocent; chaste; virtuous; faithful.*
And, truly, I'll devise some *honest* slanders
To stain my cousin with.
Much Ado about Nothing, iii. 1.
Wives may be merry, and yet *honest* too.
Merry Wives of Windsor, iv. 2.
But called it an *honest* method, as wholesome as
sweet, and by very much more handsome than fine.
Hamlet, ii. 2.
By the world,
I think my wife be *honest,* and think she is not.
Othello, iii. 3.

HONESTY. *Virtue; chastity; good manners; generosity.*
If it be so,
We need no grave to bury *honesty.*
Winter's Tale, ii. 1.
That if you be honest and fair, your *honesty*
should admit no discourse to your beauty.
Hamlet, iii. 1.
If I lov'd many words, lord, I should tell you,
You have as little *honesty* as honour. *Henry 8,* iii. 2.
Every man has his fault, and *honesty* is his.
Timon of Athens, iii. 1.

TO HONEY. *To fondle ; to caress.*
Stew'd in corruption, *honeying* and making love
Over the nasty sty. *Hamlet,* iii. 4.

HONOUR. *Lordship.*
His *honour* and myself are at the one,
And at the other is my good friend Catesby.
Richard 3, iii. 2.
God hold it, to your *honour's* good content !
Ibid. iii. 2.

HONOURED. *Honourable ; illustrious.*
And as oft is dumb
Where dust and damn'd oblivion is the tomb
Of *honour'd* bones indeed.
All's well that ends well, ii. 3.

HOODMAN-BLIND. *Blindman's buff.*

' What devil was't
That thus hath cozen'd you at *hoodman-blind ?*
Hamlet, iii. 4.

To HOODWINK. *To hide; to cover.*

Bo patient, for the prize I'll bring thee to
Shall *hoodwink* this mischance.   *Tempest,* iv. 1.

To HOOP. *To clasp; to encircle.*

Or *hoop* his body more with thy embraces,
I will devise a death as cruel for thee
As thou art tender to't.   *Winter's Tale,* iv. 3.

HOPE. *Expectation; anticipation.*

By how much better than my word I am,
By so much shall I falsify men's *hopes.*
Henry 4, P. 1, i. 2.

To HOPE. *To expect.*

I cannot *hope*
Cæsar and Antony shall well greet together.
Antony and Cleopatra, ii. 1.

HOROLOGE. *A clock.*

He'll watch the *horologe* a double set,
If drink rock not his cradle.   *Othello,* ii. 3.

HOSE. *Breeches.*

O, rhymes are guards on wanton Cupid's *hose.*
Love's Labour's lost, iv. 3.

To HOST. *To lodge.*

Go bear it to the Centaur, where we *host.*
Comedy of Errors, i. 2.

Come, pilgrim, I will bring you
Where you shall *host.*
All's well that ends well, iii. 5.

HOUSEKEEPER. *A housedog.*

The *housekeeper,* the hunter.   *Macbeth,* iii. 1.

HOUSEKEEPING. *Hospitality.*

Thy deeds, thy plainness, and thy *housekeeping,*
Hath won the greatest favour of the commons.
Henry 6, P. 2, i. 1.

To HOVEL. *To take shelter in a hovel.*

And wast thou fain, poor father,
To *hovel* thee with swine, and rogues forlorn,
In short and musty straw ?   *King Lear,* iv. 7.

HOWLET. *The owl.*

Adder's fork and blind-worm's sting,
Lizard's leg and *howlet's* wing.   *Macbeth,* iv. 1.

To HOX. *To hough; to hamstring.*

Or, if thou inclin'st that way, thou art a coward,
Which *hoxes* honesty behind.   *Winter's Tale,* i. 2.

HOY-DAY. *Hey-day.*

Hoy-day, what a sweep of vanity comes this way !
They dance ! they are mad women.
Timon of Athens, i. 2.
Hoy-day, a riddle ! neither good nor bad !
Richard 3, iv. 4.

To HUDDLE. *To crowd; to accumulate.*

Glancing an eye of pity on his losses,
That have of late so *huddled* on his back,
Enow to press a royal merchant down.
Merchant of Venice, iv. 1.

To HUG. *To couch; to lie close.*

To lie, like pawns, lock'd up in chests and trunks;
To *hug* with swine; to seek sweet safety out
In vaults and prisons.   *King John,* v. 2.

HUGGER-MUGGER. *Secrecy.*

And we have done but greenly,
In *hugger-mugger* to inter him.   *Hamlet,* iv. 5.

To HULL. *To float.*

No, good swabber; I am to *hull* here a little
longer.   *Twelfth-Night,* i. 5.
And there they *hull,* expecting but the aid
Of Buckingham to welcome them ashore.
Richard 3, iv. 4.

HUMOROUS. *Capricious; changeable; moist; humid.*

The duke is *humorous:* what he is, indeed,
More suits you to conceive than I to speak of.
As you like it, i. 2.
As *humorous* as winter, and as sudden
As flaws congealèd in the spring of day.
Henry 4, P. 2, iv. 4.
Come, he hath hid himself among these trees,
To be consorted with the *humorous* night.
Romeo and Juliet, ii. 1.

HUNGRY. *Barren.*

By heaven, I will tear thee joint by joint,
And strew this *hungry* churchyard with thy limbs.
Romeo and Juliet, v. 3.

Then let the pebbles on the *hungry* beach
Fillip the stars. *Coriolanus*, v. 3.

HUNGERLY. *Hungry.*

Having no other reason
But that his beard grew thin and *hungerly*,
And seem'd to ask him sops as he was drinking.
Taming of the Shrew, iii. 2.

HUNGERLY. *Greedily; with keen appetite.*

Sir, you have sav'd my longing, and I feed
Most *hungerly* on your sight. *Timon of Athens*, i. 1.

HUNT. *The produce of the chase.*

It shall be so.
Boys, we'll go dress our *hunt*. *Cymbeline*, iii. 6.

HUNTER. *A hound.*

The housekeeper, the *hunter*. *Macbeth*, iii. 1.

HUNT'S UP. *A tune played early in the morning to call the sportsmen from their beds; a morning song.*

Since arm from arm that voice doth us affray,
Hunting thee hence with *hunt's* up to the day.
Romeo and Juliet, iii. 5.

HURLY. *Noise; confusion; commotion; tumult.*

Ay, and amid this *hurly*, I intend
That all is done in reverend care of her.
Taming of the Shrew, iv. 1.
That, with the *hurly*, death itself awakes.
Henry 4, P. 2, iii. 1.
Methinks I see this *hurly* all on foot.
King John, iii. 4.

HURLYBURLY. *Noise; tumult; uproar.*

When the *hurlyburly's* done,
When the battle's lost and won. *Macbeth*, i. 1.

HURLYBURLY. *Tumultuous.*

Which gape and rub the elbow at the news
Of *hurlyburly* innovation. *Henry 4*, P. 1, v. 1.

HURRICANO. *A water-spout.*

The dreadful spout,
Which shipmen do the *hurricano* call.
Troilus and Cressida, v. 2.
You cataracts and *hurricanoes*, spout
Till you have drench'd our steeples, drown'd the
cocks! *King Lear*, iii. 2.

HURTLING. *Confusion; noise; tumult.*

But kindness, nobler ever than revenge,
And nature, stronger than his just occasion,
Made him give battle to the lioness,
Who quickly fell before him: in which *hurtling*
From miserable slumber I awak'd.
As you like it, iv. 3.

HUSBAND. *An economist; a husbandman.*

I am undone! while I play the good *husband*
at home, my son and my servant spend all at the
university. *Taming of the Shrew*, v. 1.
In that I deem you an ill *husband*, and am glad
To have you therein my companion. *Henry* 8, iii. 2.
This Davy serves you for good uses; he is your
serving-man and your *husband*. *Henry 4*, P. 2, v. 3.

HUSBANDRY. *Economy; thrift; frugality.*

If you suspect my *husbandry* or falsehood,
Call me before the exactest auditors,
And set me on the proof. *Timon of Athens*, ii. 2.
Lorenzo, I commit into thy hands
The *husbandry* and manage of my house.
Merchant of Venice, iii. 4.
There's *husbandry* in heaven,
Their candles are all out. *Macbeth*, ii. 1.

HUSWIFE. *A drab; a jade.*

He came ever in the rearward of the fashion;
and sung those tunes to the overscutched *huswives*
that he heard the carmen whistle, and sware they
were his fancies or his good-nights.
Henry 4, P. 2, iii. 2.
Doth Fortune play the *huswife* with me now?
Henry 5, v. 1.

HYEN. *A hyena.*

I will laugh like a *hyen*, and that when thou
art inclined to sleep. *As you like it*, iv. 1.

I.

I COULD NOT WITHAL. *I could not help it.*
And tell quaint lies,
How honourable ladies sought my love,
Which I denying, they fell sick and died,—
I could not do withal. *Merchant of Venice,* iii. 4.

IDEA. *Image; copy; likeness.*
Withal I did infer your lineaments,—
Being the right *idea* of your father,
Both in your form and nobleness of mind.
Richard 3, iii. 7.

IDLE. *Unprofitable; barren.*
I begin to find an *idle* and fond bondage in the oppression of aged tyranny. *King Lear,* i. 2.
Usurping ivy, brier, or *idle* moss.
Comedy of Errors, ii. 2.
Wherein of antres vast and deserts *idle*
It was my hint to speak. *Othello,* i. 3.
The murmuring surge,
That on the unnumber'd *idle* pebbles chafes,
Cannot be heard so high. *King Lear,* iv. 6.

IGNOMY. *Ignominy.*
Ignomy and shame pursue thy life,
And live aye with thy name!
Troilus and Cressida, v. 10.
Ignomy in ransom, and free pardon,
Are of two houses: lawful mercy is
Nothing akin to foul redemption.
Measure for Measure, ii. 4.
Thy *ignomy* sleep with thee in the grave,
But not remember'd in thy epitaph!
Henry 4, P. 1, v. 4.

IGNORANT. *Dull; stupid; wanting discernment.*
Why, either were you *ignorant* to see't?
Or, seeing it, of such childish friendliness
To yield your voices? *Coriolanus,* ii. 3.
Either thou art most *ignorant* by age,
Or thou wert born a fool. *Winter's Tale,* ii. 1.

ILL. *Wrong; harm; injury.*
And therefore haste I to the parliament,
Either to be restored to my blood,
Or make my *ill* the advantage of my good.
Henry 6, P. 1, ii. 5.

ILL. *Vicious; bad; unlucky.*
Of his own body he was *ill*, and gave
The clergy *ill* example. *Henry 8,* iv. 2.
This *ill* day
A most outrageous fit of madness took him.
Comedy of Errors, v. 1.

ILL-ERECTED. *Built for a bad purpose.*
This is the way
To Julius Cæsar's *ill-erected* tower. *Richard 2,* v. 1.

ILL-INHABITED. *Ill-lodged.*
O knowledge *ill-inhabited*,—worse than Jove in a thatched house! *As you like it,* iii. 3.

ILL-NURTURED. *Ill-educated.*
Presumptuous dame, *ill-nurtur'd* Eleanor!
Henry 6, P. 2, i. 2.

ILL-TAKEN. *Unjust; groundless; unfounded.*
Good expedition be my friend, and comfort
The gracious queen, part of his theme, but nothing
Of his *ill-ta'en* suspicion! *Winter's Tale,* i. 2.

ILLNESS. *Evil disposition; iniquity.*
Thou wouldst be great;
Art not without ambition; but without
The *illness* should attend it. *Macbeth,* i. 5.

To ILLUME. *To illuminate; to light.*
When yond same star that's westward from the pole
Had made his course to *illume* that part of heaven
Where now it burns. *Hamlet,* i. 1.

ILLUSTRATE. *Illustrious.*
The magnanimous and most *illustrate* king Cophetua set eye upon the pernicious and indubitate beggar Penelophon. *Love's Labour's lost,* iv. 1.

IMAGE. *Scheme; plan; representation.*
The *image* of the jest
I'll show you here at large.
Merry Wives of Windsor, iv. 6.
This play is the *image* of a murder done in Vienna.
Hamlet, iii. 2.
Is this the promis'd end?—Or *image* of that horror?
King Lear, v. 3.

IMAGERY. *Pictures ; statues.*

And that all the walls
With painted *imagery* had said at once,
" Jesu preserve thee ! welcome, Bolingbroke !"
Richard 2, v. 2.

IMAGINARY. *Imaginative ; fanciful.*

And let us, ciphers to this great accompt,
On your *imaginary* forces work. *Henry 5*, Chorus.

To IMBARE. *To lay bare ; to expose.*

And rather choose to hide them in a net
Than amply to *imbare* their crookèd titles,
Usurp'd from you and your progenitors.
Henry 5, i. 2.

IMMANITY. *Ferocity ; savageness.*

Ay, marry, uncle ; for I always thought
It was both impious and unnatural
That such *immanity* and bloody strife
Should reign among professors of one faith.
Henry 6, P. 1, v. 1.

To IMMASK. *To conceal ; to disguise.*

I have cases of buckram for the nonce, to *immask* our noted outward garments.
Henry 4, P. 1, i. 2.

IMMEDIACY. *Distinction ; personal greatness.*

He led our powers ;
Bore the commission of my place and person ;
The which *immediacy* may well stand up,
And call itself your brother. *King Lear*, v. 3.

IMMINENCE. *Impending evil of any kind.*

I do not speak of flight, of fear, of death ;
But dare all *imminence* that gods and men
Address their dangers in.
Troilus and Cressida, v. 10.

IMMOMENT. *Trifling ; unimportant ; of little
value.*

Immoment toys, things of such dignity
As we greet modern friends withal.
Antony and Cleopatra, v. 2.

IMMURE. *A wall ; an enclosure.*

Within whose strong *immures*
The ravish'd Helen, Menelaus' queen,
With wanton Paris sleeps.
Troilus and Cressida, Prologue.

IMP. *A boy ; a youth ; a child.*

Why, sadness is one and the self-same thing,
dear *imp*. *Love's Labour's lost*, i. 2.
The king's a bawcock, and a heart of gold,
A lad of life, an *imp* of fame. *Henry 5*, iv. 1.
The heavens thee guard and keep, most royal
imp of fame ! *Henry 4*, P. 2, v. 5.

To IMP. *To repair ; to renovate ; to restore.*

If, then, we shall shake off our slavish yoke,
Imp out our drooping country's wing,
And make high majesty look like itself,
Away with me in post to Ravenspurg.
Richard 2, ii. 1.
You that prefer
A noble life before a long, and wish
To *imp* a body with a dangerous physic
That's sure of death without it,—at once pluck out
The multitudinous tongue. *Coriolanus*, iii. 1.

To IMPAINT. *To paint ; to decorate ; to adorn.*

And never yet did insurrection want
Such water-colours to *impaint* his cause.
Henry 4, P. 1, v. 1.

To IMPALE. *To enclose ; to encompass ; to
invest.*

And, whiles I live, to account this world but hell,
Until my head, that this misshap'd trunk bears,
Be round *impalèd* with a glorious crown.
Henry 6, P. 3, iii. 2.
Did I *impale* him with the regal crown ?
Ibid. iii. 3.

To IMPART. *To give ; to bestow.*

And with no less nobility of love
Than that which dearest father bears his son
Do I *impart* toward you. *Hamlet*, i. 2.

IMPARTIAL. *Partial.*

Come, cousin Angelo ;
In this I'll be *impartial ;* be you judge
Of your own cause. *Measure for Measure*, v. 1.

IMPARTMENT. *Disclosure ; communication.*

It beckons you to go away with it,
As if it some *impartment* did desire
To you alone. *Hamlet*, i. 4.

IMPASTED. *Kneaded ; made into a paste.*

Bak'd and *impasted* with the parching streets.
Hamlet, ii. 2.

To IMPAWN. *To pledge; to gage.*

Therefore take heed how you *impawn* our person.
Henry 5, i. 2.
Go to the king; and let there be *impawn'd*
Some surety for a safe return again.
Henry 4, P. 1, iv. 3.
If therefore you do trust my honesty,
That lies enclosèd in this trunk, which you
Shall bear away *impawn'd*,—away to-night!
Winter's Tale, i. 2.

IMPEACH. *Accusation; charge; impeachment.*

Why, what an intricate *impeach* is this!
I think you all have drunk of Circe's cup.
Comedy of Errors, v. 1.
It is war's prize to take all vantages;
And ten to one is no *impeach* of valour.
Henry 6, P. 3, i. 4.

To IMPEACH. *To accuse; to bring into question.*

Thou art a villain to *impeach* me thus.
Comedy of Errors, v. 1.
He plies the duke at morning and at night;
And doth *impeach* the freedom of the state,
If they deny him justice. *Merchant of Venice*, iii. 2.
You do *impeach* your modesty too much
To leave the city, and commit yourself
Into the hands of one that loves you not.
Midsummer-Night's Dream, ii. 1.
Whate'er Lord Harry Percy then had said
May reasonably die, and never rise
To do him wrong, or any way *impeach*
What then he said, so he unsay it now.
Henry 4, P. 1, i. 3.

IMPEACHMENT. *Reproach; imputation; impediment.*

Which would be great *impeachment* to his age,
In having known no travel in his youth.
Two Gentlemen of Verona, i. 3.
Tell thy king,—I do not seek him now;
But would be willing to march on to Calais,
Without *impeachment*. *Henry* 5, iii. 5.

IMPERCEIVERANT. *Undiscerning.*

Yet this *imperceiverant* thing loves him in my
despite. *Cymbeline*, iv. 1.

IMPERIOUS. *Imperial.*

Those high-*imperious* thoughts have punish'd me
With bitter fasts, with penitential groans.
Two Gentlemen of Verona, ii. 4.

Not the *imperious* show
Of the full-fortun'd Cæsar ever shall
Be brooch'd with me. *Antony and Cleopatra*, iv. 15.
The *imperious* seas breed monsters; for the dish
Poor tributary rivers as sweet fish. *Cymbeline*, iv. 2.
Imperious Cæsar, dead and turn'd to clay,
Might stop a hole to keep the wind away.
Hamlet, v. 1.

IMPLORATOR. *An implorer; a solicitor.*

Do not believe his vows; for they are brokers,
Not of that dye which their investments show,
But mere *implorators* of unholy suits. *Hamlet*, i. 3.

IMPONED. *Impawned; staked; wagered.*

Against the which he has *imponed*, as I take
it, six French rapiers and poniards with their assigns, as girdle, hangers, and so. *Hamlet*, v. 2.

IMPORT. *Importance; consequence.*

The letter was not nice, but full of charge
Of dear *import*. *Romeo and Juliet*, v. 2.
And tell us, what occasion of *import*
Hath all so long detain'd you from your wife,
And sent you hither so unlike yourself?
Taming of the Shrew, iii. 2.
If't be not for some purpose of *import*,
Give't me again. *Othello*, iii. 3.

To IMPORT. *To imply; to indicate; to concern.*

To be your prisoner should *import* offending.
Winter's Tale, i. 2.
The fit and apt construction of thy name,
Being Leo-natus, doth *import* so much.
Cymbeline, v. 5.
Belike this show *imports* the argument of the play.
Hamlet, iii. 2.
Next, it *imports* no reason,
That with such vehemency he should pursue
Faults proper to himself.
Measure for Measure, v. 1.
Larded with many several sorts of reasons,
Importing Denmark's health, and England's too.
Hamlet, v. 2.
It doth *import* him much to speak with me.
Troilus and Cressida, iv. 2.

IMPORTANCE. *Importunity; subject; matter.*

Maria writ
The letter at Sir Toby's great *importance*.
Twelfth-Night, v. 1.

At our *importance* hither is he come.
King John, ii. 1.

But the wisest beholder, that knew no more but seeing, could not say if the *importance* were joy or sorrow. *Winter's Tale*, v. 2.

It had been pity you should have been put together with so mortal a purpose as then each bore, upon *importance* of so slight and trivial a nature.
Cymbeline, i. 4.

IMPORTANT. *Urgent; importunate.*

Who I made lord of me and all I had, At your *important* letters. *Comedy of Errors*, v. 1.

Therefore great France My mourning and *important* tears hath pitied.
King Lear, iv. 4.

Now his *important* blood will naught deny That she'll demand. *All's well that ends well*, iii. 7.

IMPORTING. *Important; weighty; serious.*

Her business looks in her with an *importing* visage. *All's well that ends well*, v. 3.

IMPORTLESS. *Trifling; unimportant.*

Speak, Prince of Ithaca; and be't of less expect That matter needless, of *importless* burden, Divide thy lips. *Troilus and Cressida*, i. 3.

IMPORTUNACY. *Importunity.*

Your *importunacy* cease till after dinner.
Timon of Athens, ii. 2.

And art thou not asham'd To wrong him with thy *importunacy* ?
Two Gentlemen of Verona, iv. 2.

To **IMPORTUNE.** *To entreat; to beseech; to render necessary; to require.*

I am dying, Egypt, dying; only I here *impórtune* death awhile, until Of many thousand kisses the poor last I lay upon thy lips. *Antony and Cleopatra*, iv. 15.

We shall write to you, As time and our concernings shall *impórtune*.
Measure for Measure, i. 1.

IMPOSE. *Command; injunction.*

According to your ladyship's *impose*, I am thus early come to know what service It is your pleasure to command me in.
Two Gentlemen of Verona, iv. 2.

To **IMPOSE.** *To condemn; to sentence.*

Impose me to what penance your invention Can lay upon my sin. *Much Ado about Nothing*, v. 1.

IMPOSITION. *Injunction; condition; restraint; penalty.*

They have acquainted me with their determinations; which is, indeed, to trouble you with no more suit, unless you may be won by some other sort than your father's *imposition*, depending on the caskets. *Merchant of Venice*, i. 2.

Let death and honesty Go with your *impositions*, I am yours Upon your will to suffer.
All's well that ends well, iv. 4.

For the encouragement of the like, which else would stand under grievous *imposition*.
Measure for Measure, i. 2.

Had we pursu'd that life, And our weak spirits ne'er been higher rear'd With stronger blood, we should have answer'd heaven Boldly, " Not guilty;" the *imposition* clear'd Hereditary ours. *Winter's Tale*, i. 2.

IMPOSSIBLE. *Incredible; inconceivable.*

Huddling jest upon jest, with such *impossible* conveyance, upon me, that I stood like a man at a mark, with a whole army shooting at me.
Much Ado about Nothing, ii. 1.

IMPOTENT. *One who is afflicted with disease.*

And your task shall be, With all the fierce endeavour of your wit To enforce the painèd *impotent* to smile.
Love's Labour's lost, v. 2.

IMPRESE. *Device; motto.*

Raz'd out my *imprese*, leaving me no sign, Save men's opinions and my living blood, To show the world I am a gentleman.
Richard 2, iii. 1.

IMPRESS. *Power of the state to compel service; impression.*

Ajax was here the voluntary, and you as under an *impress*. *Troilus and Cressida*, ii. 1.

Why such *impress* of shipwrights, whose sore task Does not divide the Sunday from the week.
Hamlet, i. 1.

Your mariners are muleters, reapers, people Ingross'd by swift *impress*.
Antony and Cleopatra, iii. 7.

This weak *impress* of love is as a figure Trenchèd in ice. *Two Gentlemen of Verona*, iii. 2.

To IMPRESS. *To press; to force into service; to mark; to wound.*

That will never be :
Who can *impress* the forest; bid the tree
Unfix his earth-bound root ?   *Macbeth,* iv. 1.
Whose age has charms in it, whose title more,
To pluck the common bosom on his side,
And turn our *impress'd* lances in our eyes
Which do command them.   *King Lear,* v. 3.
As easy mayst thou the intrenchant air
With thy keen blade *impress,* as make me bleed.
Macbeth, v. 8.

IMPRESSURE. *Impression.*

Lean but upon a rush,
The cicatrice and capable *impressure*
Thy palm some moment keeps.
As you like it, iii. 5.
And the *impressure* her Lucrece, with which
she uses to seal.   *Twelfth-Night,* ii. 5.
By Jove multipotent,
Thou shouldst not bear from me a Greekish member
Wherein my sword had not *impressure* made
Of our rank feud.   *Troilus and Cressida,* iv. 5.

IMPUDENCY. *Indecency; coarseness.*

Pleasant without scurrility, witty without affection, audacious without *impudency.*
Love's Labour's lost, v. 1.

To IMPUGN. *To resist.*

Of a strange nature is the suit you follow:
Yet in such rule, that the Venetian law
Cannot *impugn* you, as you do proceed.
Merchant of Venice, iv. 1.

IMPUTATION. *Reputation; credit.*

I mean, sir, for his weapon; but in the *imputation* laid on him by them, in his meed he's unfellowed.   *Hamlet,* v. 2.
And trust to me, Ulysses,
Our *imputation* shall be oddly pois'd
In this wild action.   *Troilus and Cressida,* i. 3.

IN A FEW, IN FEW. *In short.*

But, *in a few,*
Signior Hortensio, thus it stands with me.
Taming of the Shrew, i. 2.
In few, his death
Being bruited once, took fire and heat away
From the best-temper'd courage in his troops.
Henry 4, P. 2, i. 1.

IN BLOOD. *In strength; in vigour.*

Thou rascal, that art worst *in blood* to run,
Lead'st first to win some vantage. *Coriolanus,* i. 1.
If we be English deer, be, then, *in blood ;*
Not rascal-like, to fall down with a pinch.
Henry 6, P. 1, iv. 2.

IN BOOKS. *In favour.*

I see, lady, the gentleman is not *in your books.*
Much Ado about Nothing, i. 1.
A herald, Kate? O, put me *in thy books.*
Taming of the Shrew, ii. 1.

IN BY THE WEEK. *Hired; bound to serve.*

O that I knew he were but *in by the week !*
Love's Labour's lost, v. 2.

IN CHARGE. *In rest; fixed.*

Their armèd staves *in charge,* their beavers down.
Henry 4, P. 2, iv. 1.

IN COMPT. *Subject to account; prepared; ready.*

Take the bonds along with you,
And have the dates *in compt.*
Timon of Athens, ii. 1.
Your servants ever
Have theirs, themselves, and what is theirs, *in compt,*
To make their audit at your highness' pleasure,
Still to return your own.   *Macbeth,* i. 6.

IN CUNNING. *Wilfully; intentionally.*

For if he be not one that truly loves you,
That errs in ignorance, and not *in cunning,*
I have no judgment in an honest face.
Othello, iii. 3.

IN DEPUTATION. *By deputy; by proxy.*

Say to great Cæsar this :—*in deputation*
I kiss his conquering hand : tell him, I am prompt
To lay my crown at's foot, and there to kneel.
Antony and Cleopatra, iii. 13.

IN FEE-FARM. *In perpetuity.*

How now ! a kiss in *fee-farm !*
Troilus and Cressida, iii. 2.

IN GRAIN. *In the grain; not superficial.*

'Tis *in grain,* sir ; 'twill endure wind and weather.
Twelfth-Night, i. 5.

IN HEART. *Heartily; fervently.*

In *heart* desiring still
You may behold confusion of your foes.
Henry 6, P. 1, iv. 1.

Dost thou not wish *in heart*
The chain were longer, and the letter short?
Love's Labour's lost, v. 2.

My lord, *in heart;* and let the health go round.
Timon of Athens, i. 2.

IN OPEN. *Openly; publicly.*

Last, that the Lady Anne,
Whom the king hath in secrecy long married,
This day was view'd *in open* as his queen,
Going to chapel. *Henry 8, iii. 2.*

IN PLACE. *Present.*

But what said Henry's queen?
For I have heard that she was there *in place.*
Henry 6, P. 3, iv. 1.

And yet here's one *in place* I cannot pardon.
Measure for Measure, v. 1.

IN POST. *In great haste.*

I from my mistress come to you *in post.*
Comedy of Errors, i. 2.

IN PRESENCE. *Present.*

'Tis very true :· you were *in presence* then ;
And you can witness with me this is true.
Richard 2, iv. 1.

Is not his brother, Thomas of Clarence, with him?—
No, my good lord ; he is *in presence* here.
Henry 4, P. 2, iv. 4.

IN PRINT. *With the utmost exactness.*

I will do it, sir, *in print.*
Love's Labour's lost, iii. 1.

All this I speak *in print.*
Two Gentlemen of Verona, ii. 1.

O sir, we quarrel *in print,* by the book ; as you
have books for good manners. *As you like it, v. 4.*

IN RESPECT. *In comparison; comparatively.*

He was a man ; this, *in respect,* a child,—
And men ne'er spend their fury on a child.
Henry 6, P. 3, v. 5.

IN THAT. *Inasmuch as; since.*

But *in that* thou art like to be my kinsman,
live unbruised, and love my cousin.
Much Ado about Nothing, v. 2.

IN THE DEFAULT. *At a need ; if necessary.*

That I may say, *in the default,* he is a man I know.
All's well that ends well, ii. 3.

IN THE DUMPS. *Out of spirits; dull; melancholy.*

Why, how now, daughter Katharine! *in your
dumps?* *Taming of the Shrew, ii. 1.*

IN THE EFFECT OF. *In accordance with ; according to.*

But answer *in the effect of* your reputation, and
satisfy the poor woman. *Henry 4, P. 2, ii. 1.*

IN THE HEAT. *Quickly ; immediately.*

We must do something, and *i' the heat.*
King Lear, i. 1.

IN THE SMALLEST. *In the least; in the smallest
degree.*

I may make my case as Claudio's, to cross this
in the smallest. *Measure for Measure, iv. 2.*

IN THE TOP OF. *Above.*

But it was—as I received it, and others, whose
judgments in such matters cried *in the top of* mine
—an excellent play. *Hamlet, ii. 2.*

IN THE TRIM. *Sound ; in good order.*

But, by the mass, our hearts are *in the trim.*
Henry 5, iv. 3.

IN USE. *At interest.*

I am content, so he will let me have
The other half *in use.* *Merchant of Venice, iv. 1.*

INCAPABLE. *Ignorant ; unconscious of ; unfit
for.*

Incapable and shallow innocents,
You cannot guess who caus'd your father's death.
Richard 3, ii. 2.

Which time she chanted snatches of old tunes ;
As one *incapable* of her own distress.
Hamlet, iv. 7.

Is not your father grown *incapable*
Of reasonable affairs? *Winter's Tale, iv. 3.*

TO INCARNADINE. *To redden ; to make red.*

No ; this my hand will rather
The multitudinous seas *incarnadine,*
Making the green one red. *Macbeth, ii. 1.*

To INCENSE. *To instigate ; to inform ; to apprise.*

Think you, my lord, this little prating York
Was not *incensèd* by his subtle mother
To taunt and scorn you thus opprobriously?
Richard 3, iii. 1.
And indeed this day,—
Sir, I may tell it you, I think,—I have
Incens'd the lords o' the council, that he is
A most arch heretic. *Henry* 8, v. 1.

INCH. *Island.*

Nor would we deign him burial of his men,
Till he disbursèd, at Saint Colme's *inch*,
Ten thousand dollars to our general use.
Macbeth, i. 2.

INCH-MEAL. *Inch by inch ; by inches.*

All the infections that the sun sucks up
From bogs, fens, flats, on Prosper fall, and make him
By *inch-meal* a disease! *Tempest*, ii. 2.

INCIDENCY. *Accident ; casualty.*

I cónjure thee, that thou declare
What *incidency* thou dost guess of harm
Is creeping toward me. *Winter's Tale*, i. 2.

INCLINATION. *Disposition of mind ; humour.*

Report the feature of Octavia, her years,
Her *inclination*. *Antony and Cleopatra*, ii. 5.
But, mighty lord, this merry *inclination*
Accords not with the sadness of my suit.
Henry 6, P. 3, iii. 2.

INCLINING. *Inclination ; leaning; wish; side; party.*

If you give him not John Drum's entertainment, your *inclining* cannot be removed.
All's well that ends well, iii. 6.
Were you not sent for? Is it your own *inclining*? Is it a free visitation? *Hamlet*, ii. 2.
Hold your hands,
Both you of my *inclining*, and the rest.
Othello, i. 2.

To INCLIP. *To enclose ; to surround.*

Whate'er the ocean pales, or sky *inclips*,
Is thine, if thou wilt ha't.
Antony and Cleopatra, ii. 7.

To INCLUDE. *To conclude ; to close ; to end.*

Come, let us go : we will *include* all jars
With triumphs, mirth, and rare solemnity.
Two Gentlemen of Verona, v. 4.

INCONTINENT. *Immediately ; without delay.*

He says he will return *incontinent*. *Othello*, iv. 3.
Come, mourn with me for that I do lament,
And put on sullen black *incontinent*. *Rich.* 2, v. 6.

INCONY. *Sweet ; pretty; delicate.*

My sweet ounce of man's flesh! my *incony* Jew!
Love's Labour's lost, iii. 1.

INCORPORAL. *Immaterial ; unsubstantial.*

Alas, how is't with you,
That you do bend your eye on vacancy,
And with the *incorporal* air do hold discourse?
Hamlet, iii. 4.

INCORPORATE. *Incorporated ; associated ; conjunctive.*

No, it is Casca ; one *incorporate*
To our attempt. *Julius Cæsar*, i. 3.
" True is it, my *incorporate* friends," quoth he,
" That I receive the general food at first,
Which you do live upon." *Coriolanus*, i. 1.
When these mutualities so marshal the way,
hard at hand comes the master and main exercise,
the *incorporate* conclusion. *Othello*, ii. 1.

INCORPSED. *Incorporate ; embodied.*

And to such wondrous doing brought his horse,
As he had been *incorps'd* and demi-natur'd
With the brave beast. *Hamlet*, iv. 7.

INCORRECT. *Perverse ; opposed to.*

'Tis unmanly grief :
It shows a will most *incorrect* to heaven.
Hamlet, i. 2.

INCREASE. *Productions ; produce.*

And the mazèd world,
By their *increase*, now knows not which is which.
Midsummer-Night's Dream, ii. 1.

INCREDULOUS. *Incredible.*

No obstacle, no *incredulous* or unsafe circumstance,—What can be said? *Twelfth-Night*, iii. 4.

INDENT. *Indentation.*

It shall not wind with such a deep *indent*,
To rob me of so rich a bottom here.
Henry 4, P. 1, iii. 1.

To INDENT. *To covenant ; to bargain ; to make a compact.*

Shall we buy treason? and *indent* with fears?
Henry 4, P. 1, i. 3.

INDEX. *A list of chapters prefixed to a book for the convenience of the reader ; a table of contents.*

Ay mo, what act,
That roars so loud, and thunders in the *index?*
Hamlet, iii. 4.

By tho way, I'll sort occasion,
As *index* to tho story wo late talk'd of,
To part the queen's proud kindred from tho prince.
Richard 3, ii. 2.

An *index* and obscure prologue to tho history of lust and foul thoughts. *Othello,* ii. 1.

To INDICT. *To convict ; to prove guilty.*

Nor no matter in the phrase that might *indict* tho author of affection. *Hamlet,* ii. 2.

INDIFFERENCY. *Impartiality ; honesty ; moderate dimensions.*

Till this advantage, this vile-drawing bias,
This sway of motion, this commodity
Makes it take head from all *indifferency.*
King John, ii. 1.

An I had but a belly of any *indifferency,* I were simply tho most active follow in Europe : my womb, my womb, my womb, undoes me.
Henry 4, P. 2, iv. 3.

INDIFFERENT. *Impartial ; corresponding ; ordinary ; common.*

Having here no judge *indifferent,* nor no more assurance
Of equal friendship and proceeding. *Henry* 8, ii. 4.

And, noble uncle, I beseech your grace
Look at my wrongs with an *indifferent* eye.
Richard 2, ii. 3.

Let their heads bo sleekly combed, their blue coats brushed, and their garters of an *indifferent* knit. *Taming of the Shrew,* iv. 1.

Good lads, how do ye both?—
As the *indifferent* children of tho earth.
Hamlet, ii. 2.

INDIFFERENTLY. *With equal favour.*

If it bo aught toward the general good,
Set honour in one eye, and death i' tho other,
And I will look on both *indifferently.*
Julius Cæsar, i. 2.

INDIGEST. *A confused mass ; a heap.*

Be of good, comfort, prince ; for you are born

To set a form upon that *indigest*
Which ho hath left so shapeless and so rude.
King John, v. 7.

INDIGN. *Unworthy ; ignominious.*

And all *indign* and base adversities
Make head against my estimation ! *Othello,* i. 3.

INDIRECT. *Crooked ; weak ; defective.*

Fie, what an *indirect* and peevish course
Is this of hers !   •   *Richard* 3, iii. 1.

And, in conclusion, drove us to seek out
This head of safety ; and withal to pry
Into his title, the which now wo find
Too *indirect* for long continuance.
Henry 4, P. 1, iv. 3.

INDIRECTION. *Indirectness ; dishonesty ; artifice ; trick.*

By heaven, I had rather coin my heart,
And drop my blood for drachmas, than to wring
From the hard hands of peasants their vile trash
By any *indirection.* *Julius Cæsar,* iv. 3.

Though indirect,
Yet *indirection* thereby grows direct.
King John, iii. 1.

And thus do we of wisdom and of reach,
By *indirections* find directions out. *Hamlet,* ii. 1.

INDIRECTLY. *Improperly ; wrongly ; dishonestly ; fraudulently.*

And then we shall repent each drop of blood,
That hot rash haste so *indirectly* shed.
King John, ii. 1.

He bids you then resign
Your crown and kingdom, *indirectly* held
From him the native and true challenger.
Henry 5, ii. 4.

INDISTINGUISHABLE. *Deformed ; shapeless.*

Why, no, you ruinous butt; you whoreson *indistinguishable* cur, no.
Troilus and Cressida, v. 1.

To INDRENCH. *To sink ; to immerse ; to insteep.*

When I do tell thee, there my hopes lie drown'd,
Reply not in how many fathoms deep
They lie *indrench'd.* *Troilus and Cressida,* i. 1.

z

INDUBITATE. *Undoubted; unquestionable.*

The magnanimous and most illustrate King Cophetua set eye upon the pernicious and *indubitate* beggar Penelophon. *Love's Labour's lost,* iv. 1.

INDUCEMENT. *Instigation; persuasion; influence.*

My son corrupts a well-derivèd nature
With his *inducement.*
All's well that ends well, iii. 2.

INDUCTION. *Introduction; opening scene; beginning.*

Plots have I laid, *inductions* dangerous.
Richard 3, i. 1.
A dire *induction* am I witness to,
And will to France. *Ibid.* iv. 4.
These promises are fair, the parties sure,
And our *induction* full of prosperous hope.
Henry 4, P. 1, iii. 1.

To INDUE. *To subdue.*

'Tis even so;
For let our finger ache, and it *indues*
Our other healthful members even to that sense
Of pain. *Othello,* iii. 4.

INDUED. *Invested; clothed.*

Or like a creature native and *indu'd*
Unto that element. *Hamlet,* iv. 7.

INDURANCE. *Delay; loss of time.*

I should have ta'en some pains to bring together
Yourself and your accusers; and to have heard you,
Without *indurance,* further. *Henry 8,* v. 1.

INEQUALITY. *Incongruity; inconsistency.*

Harp not on that; nor do not banish reason
For *inequality.* *Measure for Measure,* v. 1.

To INFAMONIZE. *To shame; to disgrace.*

Dost thou *infamonize* me among potentates?
Thou shalt die. *Love's Labour's lost,* v. 2.

INFECT. *Infected; tainted.*

And in the imitation of these twain
Many are *infect.* *Troïlus and Cressida,* i. 3.

To INFECT. *To disease; to taint.*

This is in thee a nature but *infected.*
Timon of Athens, iv. 3.

Infected minds
To their deaf pillows will discharge their secrets.
Macbeth, v. 1.
This sickness doth *infect*
The very life-blood of our enterprise.
Henry 4, P. 1, iv. 1.

INFECTED. *Affected; softened; subdued.*

The incense of a vow, a holy vow,
Never to be *infected* with delight,
Nor conversant with ease and idleness,
Till I have set a glory to this head,
By giving it the worship of revenge.
King John, iv. 3.

INFECTION. *Taint; disease.*

Dar'st thou support a publish'd traitor? Hence;
Lest that the *infection* of his fortune take
Like hold on thee. *King Lear,* iv. 6.
O master! what a strange *infection*
Is fall'n into thy ear! *Cymbeline,* iii. 2.

To INFER. *To offer; to bring forward; to state; to allege.*

Full well hath Clifford play'd the orator,
Inferring arguments of mighty force.
Henry 6, P. 3, ii. 2.
There, at your meetest vantage of the time,
Infer the bastardy of Edward's children.
Richard 3, iii. 5.
Withal I did *infer* your lineaments,—
Being the right idea of your father. *Ibid.* iii. 7.
'Tis *inferr'd* to us,
His days are foul, and his drink dangerous.
Timon of Athens, iii. 5.

INFINITE. *Infinity.*

And instances of *infinite* of love.
Two Gentlemen of Verona, ii. 7.
It is past the *infinite* of thought.
Much Ado about Nothing, ii. 3.
Will you with counters sum
The past-proportion of his *infinite?*
Troïlus and Cressida, ii. 2.

To INFORM. *To animate; to inspire; to give intelligence; to play the spy.*

The god of soldiers,
With the consent of supreme Jove, *inform*
Thy thoughts with nobleness! *Coriolanus,* v. 3.
It is the bloody business which *informs*
Thus to mine eyes. *Macbeth,* ii. 1.

INFORMAL. *Insane; frantic.*

These poor *informal* women are no more
But instruments of some more mightier member
That sets them on.   *Measure for Measure*, v. 1.

To INFUSE. *To endow; to inspire.*

Methinks a woman of this valiant spirit
Should, if a coward heard her speak those words,
Infuse his breast with magnanimity.
                         Henry 6, P. 3, v. 4.
        Thou didst smile,
Infused with a fortitude from heaven,
When I have deck'd the sea with drops full salt.
                         Tempest, i. 2.

INGENER. *Inventor; poet; man of genius.*

One that excels the quirks of blazoning pens,
And in the essential vesture of creation
Does tire the *ingener*.   *Othello*, ii. 1.

INGENIOUS. *Intellectual; mental.*

Here let us breathe, and haply institute
A course of learning and *ingenious* studies.
                         Taming of the Shrew, i. 1.
The king is mad: how stiff is my vile sense,
That I stand up, and have *ingenious* feeling
Of my huge sorrows!   *King Lear*, iv. 6.
        O, treble woe
Fall ten times treble on that cursèd head,
Whose wicked deed thy most *ingenious* sense
Depriv'd thee of!   *Hamlet*, v. 1.

INGENIOUSLY. *Ingenuously; candidly.*

Thou art true and honest; *ingeniously* I speak,
No blame belongs to thee.   *Timon of Athens*, ii. 2.

INGRAFT. *Ingrafted; inveterate.*

And 'tis great pity that the noble Moor
Should hazard such a place as his own second
With one of an *ingraft* infirmity.   *Othello*, ii. 3.

INGRAFTED. *Settled; fixed; rooted.*

        Yet I fear him;
For in the *ingrafted* love he bears to Cæsar,—
Alas, good Cassius, do not think of him.
                         Julius Cæsar, ii. 1.

INGRATE. *Ungrateful.*

Whose hap shall be to have her
Will not so graceless be to be *ingrate*.
                         Taming of the Shrew, i. 2.

INGROSSED. *Collected; brought together.*

Your mariners are muleters, reapers, people
Ingross'd by swift impress.
                         Antony and Cleopatra, iii. 7.

INHABITABLE. *Not habitable; uninhabited.*

And meet him, were I tied to run a-foot
Even to the frozen ridges of the Alps,
Or any other ground *inhabitable*.   *Richard 2*, i. 1.

INHEARSED. *Enclosed; clasped.*

See, where he lies *inhearsèd* in the arms
Of the most bloody nurser of his harms.
                         Henry 6, P. 1, iv. 7.

To INHERIT. *To possess; to win.*

The solemn temples, the great globe itself,
Yea, all which it *inherit*, shall dissolve.
                         Tempest, iv. 1.
Nothing but fair is that which you *inherit*.
                         Love's Labour's lost, iv. 1.
It must be great that can *inherit* us
So much as of a thought of ill in him.
                         Richard 2, i. 1.
This, or else nothing, will *inherit* her.
                         Two Gentlemen of Verona, iii. 2.

INHERITANCE. *Possession.*

And you will rather show our general louts
How you can frown, than spend a fawn upon 'em,
For the *inheritance* of their loves. *Coriolanus*, iii. 2.

To INHIBIT. *To prohibit; to forbid.*

Virginity is peevish, proud, idle, made of self-
love, which is the most *inhibited* sin in the canon.
                         All's well that ends well, i. 1.
I therefore apprehend and do attach thee
For an abuser of the world, a practiser
Of arts *inhibited* and out of warrant.   *Othello*, i. 2.
If trembling I *inhibit* thee, protest me
The baby of a girl.   *Macbeth*, iii. 4.

INHIBITION. *Prohibition.*

I think their *inhibition* comes by the means of
the late innovation.   *Hamlet*, ii. 2.

INHOOPED. *Enclosed for the purpose of fighting.*

        And his quails ever .
Beat mine, *inhoop'd*, at odds.
                         Antony and Cleopatra, ii. 3.

INITIATE. *New; unaccustomed.*

My strange and self-abuse
Is the *initiate* fear, that wants hard use.
Macbeth, iii. 4.

To INJOINT. *To unite; to join.*

The Ottomites, reverend and gracious,
Steering with due course toward the isle of Rhodes,
Have there *injointed* them with an after fleet.
Othello, i. 3.

INJUNCTION. *Inducement; motive; consideration.*

Whose contents
Shall witness to him I am near at home,
And that, by great *injunctions*, I am bound
To enter publicly. *Measure for Measure*, iv. 3.

INJURIOUS. *Pernicious; unjust.*

Till the *injurious* Romans did extort
This tribute from us, we were free.
Cymbeline, iii. 1.
Injurious duke, that threatest where's no cause.
Henry 6, P. 2, i. 4.
O *injurious* law,
That respites me a life, whose very comfort
Is still a dying horror! *Measure for Measure*, ii. 3.

INJURY. *Wrong; outrage.*

Conceit, my comfort and my *injury*.
Comedy of Errors, iv. 2.
Gentlemen all, I do suspect this trash
To be a party in this *injury*. *Othello*, v. 1.

INKHORN. *Pedantic.*

And, ere that we will suffer such a prince
To be disgraced by an *inkhorn* mate,
We, and our wives, and children, all will fight.
Henry 6, P. 1, iii. 1.

INLAND. *Civilised; not rustic.*

But indeed an old religious uncle of mine taught
me to speak, who was in his youth an *inland* man.
As you like it, iii. 2.
Yet am I *inland* bred,
And know some nurture. *Ibid.* ii. 7.

To INN. *To house; to garner.*

He that ears my land spares my team, and gives
me leave to *inn* the crop.
All's well that ends well, i. 3.

INNOCENT. *An idiot; a fool; a natural.*

A dumb *innocent*, that could not say him nay.
All's well that ends well, iv. 3.
Pray, *innocent*, and beware the foul fiend.
King Lear, iii. 6.

INSANE. *Causing madness.*

Or have we eaten on the *insane* root
That takes the reason prisoner? *Macbeth*, i. 3.

INSCULPED. *Carved; engraved.*

A coin that bears the figure of an angel
Stampèd in gold,—but that's *insculp'd* upon.
Merchant of Venice, ii. 7.

INSCULPTURE. *Inscription.*

My noble general, Timon is dead;
Entomb'd upon the very hem of the sea;
And on his grave-stone this *insculpture*.
Timon of Athens, v. 4.

INSEPARATE. *Inseparable; incapable of division.*

Within my soul there doth ensue a fight
Of this strange nature, that a thing *inseparate*
Divides more wider than the sky and earth.
Troilus and Cressida, v. 2.

INSHELLED. *Concealed.*

Which were *inshell'd* when Marcius stood for Rome,
And durst not once peep out. *Coriolanus*, iv. 6.

To INSHIP. *To embark.*

And so, my lord protector, see them guarded,
And safely brought to Dover; where, *inshipp'd*,
Commit them to the fortune of the sea.
Henry 6, P. 1, v. 1.

INSINEWED. *Associated; knit; united.*

All members of our cause, both here and hence,
That are *insinew'd* to this action.
Henry 4, P. 2, iv. 1.

To INSINUATE. *To wheedle; to entice by soft words.*

Thinkest thou, for that I *insinuate*, or touse from
thee thy business, I am therefore no courtier?
Winter's Tale, iv. 3.

INSINUATION. *Fine speeches; flattery; servility; obsequiousness.*

Shall we, upon the footing of our land,
Send fair-play offers, and make compromise,

Insinuation, parley, and base truce,
To arms invasive ?   *King John*, v. 1.
They are not near my conscience; their defeat
Does by their own *insinuation* grow. *Hamlet*, v. 2.

INSISTURE.   *Persistency; regularity; method.*
The heavens themselves, the planets, and this centre,
Observe degree, priority, and place,
Insisture, course, proportion, season, form,
Office, and custom, in all line of order.
                                  Troilus and Cressida, i. 3.

INSTALMENT.   *Stall; installation.*
Each fair *instalment*, coat, and several crest,
With loyal blazon evermore be blest !
                                  Merry Wives of Windsor, v. 5.
What think'st thou ? is it not an easy matter
To make William Lord Hastings of our mind,
For the *instalment* of this noble duke
In the seat royal of this famous isle ?
                                  Richard 3, iii. 1.

INSTANCE.   *Proof; example; motive; cause;*
indication; warning; information; notice.
And *instances* of infinite of love
Warrant me welcome to my Proteus.
                                  Two Gentlemen of Verona, ii. 7.
Instance, O *instance* ! strong as Pluto's gates ;
Cressid is mine, tied with the bonds of heaven ;
Instance, O *instance* ! strong as heaven itself ;
The bonds of heaven are slipp'd, dissolv'd, and loos'd.
                                  Troilus and Cressida, v. 2.
Yet doth this accident and flood of fortune
So far exceed all *instance*, all discourse,
That I am ready to distrust mine eyes.
                                  Twelfth-Night, iv. 3.
The *instances* that second marriage move
Are base respects of thrift, but none of love.
                                  Hamlet, iii. 2.
Tell him his fears are shallow, wanting *instance*.
                                  Richard 3, iii. 2.
Troy, yet upon his basis, had been down,
And the great Hector's sword had lack'd a master,
But for these *instances*. *Troilus and Cressida*, i. 3.
A league from Epidamnum had we sail'd,
Before the always-wind-obeying deep
Gave any tragic *instance* of our harm.
                                  Comedy of Errors, i. 1.
One of our covent, and his confessor,
Gives me this *instance*. *Measure for Measure*, iv. 3.
To comfort you the more, I have receiv'd
A certain *instance* that Glendower is dead.
                                  Henry 4, P. 2, iii. 1.

INSTANT.   *Immediate; present; sudden.*
Take the *instant* way;
For honour travels in a strait so narrow,
Where one but goes abreast.
                                  Troilus and Cressida, iii. 3.
The *instant* burst of clamour that she made—
Unless things mortal move them not at all—
Would have made milch the burning eyes of heaven,
And passion in the gods.   *Hamlet*, ii. 2.

TO INSTATE.   *To invest; to endow.*
For his possessions,
We do *instate* and widow you withal,
To buy you a better husband.
                                  Measure for Measure, v. 1.

TO INSTEEP.   *To soak; to steep; to indrench.*
And York, all haggled over,
Comes to him, where in gore he lay *insteep'd*.
                                  Henry 5, iv. 6.
The gutter'd rocks, and congregated sands,
Traitors *insteep'd* to clog the guiltless keel.
                                  Othello, ii. 1.

INSULTMENT.   *Insult; exultation; triumph.*
He on the ground, my speech of *insultment*
ended on his dead body, to the court I'll knock
her back, foot her home again. *Cymbeline*, iii. 5.

INSUPPRESSIVE.   *Not to be suppressed; irre-*
pressible.
But do not stain
The *insuppressive* mettle of our spirits,
To think that or our cause or our performance
Did need an oath.   *Julius Cæsar*, ii. 1.

INTELLIGENCER.   *Messenger.*
Richard yet lives, hell's black *intelligencer*.
                                  Richard 3, iv. 4.
To us, the imagin'd voice of God himself,
The very opener and *intelligencer*
Between the grace, the sanctities of heaven,
And our dull workings.   *Henry 4*, P. 2, iv. 2.

INTELLIGENCING.   *Giving information.*
A mankind witch ! Hence with her, out o' door :
A most *intelligencing* bawd ! *Winter's Tale*, ii. 3.

INTELLIGENT.   *Ingenuous; conveying infor-*
mation; intelligencing.
Do you know, and dare not be *intelligent* to
me ?   *Winter's Tale*, i. 2.

Who have servants, who seem no less,
Which are to France tho spies and speculations
Intelligent of our state. *King Lear*, iii. 1.
Our posts shall be swift and *intelligent* betwixt
us. *Ibid.* iii. 7.
This is the letter he spoke of, which approves
him an *intelligent* party to the advantages of France.
Ibid. iii. 5.

INTEMPERANCE. *Wildness; irregularity; imprudence.*

The which if he be pleas'd I shall perform,
I do beseech your majesty, may salve
The long-grown wounds of my *intemperance.*
Henry 4, P. 1, iii. 2.

TO INTEND. *To pretend.*

Ay, and amid this hurly, I *intend*
That all is done in reverend care of her.
Taming of the Shrew, iv. 1.
Intend a kind of zeal both to the prince and Claudio.
Much Ado about Nothing, ii. 2.
The mayor is here at hand. *Intend* some fear.
Richard 3, iii. 7.
Tut, I can counterfeit the deep tragedian ;
Speak and look back, and pry on every side,
Tremble and start at wagging of a straw,
Intending deep suspicion. *Ibid.* iii. 5.

INTENDED. *Included; comprised.*

That is *intended* in the general's name ;
I muse you make so slight a question.
Henry 4, P. 2, iv. 1.

INTENDMENT. *Intention; purpose.*

Ay, and said nothing but what I protest *intendment* of doing. *Othello*, iv. 2.
That either you might stay him from his *intendment*, or brook such disgrace well as he shall
run into. *As you like it*, i. 1.
We do not mean the coursing snatchers only,
But fear the main *intendment* of the Scot.
Henry 5, i. 2.

INTENIBLE. *Unretentive.*

Yet, in this captious and *intenible* sieve,
I still pour in the waters of my love,
And lack not to lose still.
All's well that ends well, i. 3.

INTENT. *Meaning.*

You may be pleas'd to catch at mine *intent,*
By what did here befall me.
Antony and Cleopatra, ii. 2.

INTENTION. *Intenseness; earnestness.*

Affection I thy *intention* stabs the centre.
Winter's Tale, i. 2.
She did course o'er my exteriors with such a
greedy *intention*, that the appetite of her eye did
seem to scorch me up like a burning-glass.
Merry Wives of Windsor, i. 3.
Whilst my *intention*, hearing not my tongue,
Anchors on Isabel. *Measure for Measure*, ii. 4.

INTENTIVELY. *Attentively; with close attention.*

Whereof by parcels she had something heard,
But not *intentively.* *Othello*, i. 3.

INTERDICTION. *Interdict; sentence.*

O nation miserable,
When shalt thou see thy wholesome days again,
Since that the truest issue of thy throne
By his own *interdiction* stands accurs'd,
And does blaspheme his breed ! *Macbeth*, iv. 3.

TO INTERESS. *To have an interest in; to affect.*

Now, our joy,
Although the last, not least ; to whose young love
The vines of France and milk of Burgundy
Strive to be *interess'd* ; what can you say to draw
A third more opulent than your sisters ?
King Lear, i. 1.

INTEREST. *Right ; title; claim.*

You taught me how to know the face of right,
Acquainted me with *interest* to this land,
Yea, thrust this enterprise into my heart.
King John, v. 2.
Now, by my sceptre, and my soul to boot,
He hath more worthy *interest* to the state
Than thou, the shadow of succession.
Henry 4, P. 1, iii. 2.
And let the tongue of war
Plead for our *interest* and our being here.
King John, v. 2.

INTER'GATORY. *An interrogatory.*

But nor the time nor place
Will serve our long *inter'gatories.* *Cymbeline*, v. 5.
And charge us there upon *inter'gatories*,
And we will answer all things faithfully.
Merchant of Venice, v. 1.

INTERMISSION. *Procrastination ; delay.*

You lov'd, I lov'd ; for *intermission*
No more pertains to me, my lord, than you.
Merchant of Venice, iii. 2.

Deliver'd letters, spite of *intermission,*
Which presently they read. *King Lear,* ii. 4.

But, gentle heavens, cut short all *intermission !*
Macbeth, iv. 3.

INTERMISSIVE. *Intermitted ; suspended.*

Wounds will I lend the French, instead of eyes,
To weep their *intermissive* miseries.
Henry 6, P. 1, i. 1.

To INTERMIT. *To turn aside ; to avert.*

Run to your houses, fall upon your knees,
Pray to the gods to *intermit* the plague
That needs must light on this ingratitude.
Julius Cæsar, i. 1.

INTERPRETER. *An elucidator ; an unfolder.*

And these thy offices,
So rarely kind, are as *interpreters*
Of my behind-hand slackness. *Winter's Tale,* v. 1.

INTERTISSUED. *Interwoven ; variegated.*

The *intertissu'd* robe of gold and pearl.
Henry 5, iv. 1.

INTESTATE. *Vain ; empty ; unsubstantial.*

Why should calamity be full of words ?—
Windy attorneys to their client woes,
Airy succeeders of *intestate* joys,
Poor breathing orators of miseries !
Let them have scope : though what they do impart
Help nothing else, yet do they ease the heart.
Richard 3, iv. 4.

INTIL. *Into.*

And hath shipped me *intil* the land,
As if I had never been such. *Hamlet,* v. 1.

INTO. *In.*

Ensconcing ourselves *into* seeming knowledge,
when we should submit ourselves to an unknown
fear. *All's well that ends well,* ii. 3.

INTRENCHANT. *Invulnerable.*

As easy mayst thou the *intrenchant* air
With thy keen sword impress, as make me bleed.
Macbeth, v. 8.

INTRINSE. *Intricate ; entangled.*

Such smiling rogues as these,
Like rats, oft bite the holy cords a-twain
Which are too *intrinse* t'unloose. *King Lear,* ii. 2.

INTRINSECATE. *Entangled ; intricate.*

Come, thou mortal wretch,
With thy sharp teeth this knot *intrinsecate*
Of life at once untie. *Antony and Cleopatra,* v. 2.

To INURN. *To bury ; to entomb.*

Why the sepulchre,
Wherein we saw thee quietly *inurn'd,*
Hath op'd his ponderous and marble jaws,
To cast thee up again. *Hamlet,* i. 4.

INVECTIVELY. *Satirically ; censoriously.*

Thus most *invectively* he pierceth through
The body of the country, city, court.
As you like it, ii. 1.

INVENTION. *Imagination ; fabrication ; falsehood.*

O for a Muse of fire, that would ascend
The brightest heaven of *invention !*
Henry 5, i. Chorus.

I am about it ; but indeed my *invention*
Comes from my pate as birdlime does from frize,—
It plucks out brains and all. *Othello,* ii. 1.

Let them accuse me by *invention,* I
Will answer in mine honour. *Coriolanus,* iii. 2.

You love my son : *invention* is asham'd,
Against the proclamation of thy passion,
To say thou dost not. *All's well that ends well,* i. 3.

To INVERT. *To convert ; to subvert ; to overturn.*

O heaven, O earth, bear witness to this sound,
And crown what I profess with kind event,
If I speak true ! if hollowly, *invert*
What best is boded me to mischief ! *Tempest,* iii. 1.

An esperance so obstinately strong,
That doth *invert* the attest of eyes and ears.
Troilus and Cressida, v. 2.

To INVEST. *To clothe ; to adorn ; to install.*

If you but knew how you the purpose cherish
Whiles thus you mock it ! how, in stripping it,
You more *invest* it ! *Tempest,* ii. 1.

He is already nam'd ; and gone to Scone
To be *invested.* *Macbeth,* ii. 2.

Our substitutes in absence well *invested*,
And every thing lies level to our wish.
Henry 4, P. 2, iv. 4.

INVESTMENTS. *Garments.*

Whose white *iuvestments* figure innocence,
The dove and very blessèd spirit of peace.
Henry 4, P. 2, iv. 1.
Do not believe his vows; for they are brokers,—
Not of that dye which their *investments* show.
Hamlet, i. 3.

INVINCIBLE. *Undistinguishable; imperceptible.*

He was so forlorn, that his dimensions to any
thick sight were *invincible*. *Henry* 4, P. 2, iii. 2.

INVITING. *Invitation.*

He hath sent me an earnest *inviting*, which
many my near occasions did urge me to put off.
Timon of Athens, iii. 6.

To INVOCATE. *To invoke; to call upon.*

Be it lawful that I *invocate* thy ghost,
To hear the lamentations of poor Anne!
Richard 3, i. 2.

INWARD. *An intimate friend; the bosom.*

Sir, I was an *inward* of his. A sly fellow was
the duke, and I believe I know the cause of his
withdrawing. *Measure for Measure*, iii. 2.
Wherefore breaks that sigh from the *inward* of
thee? *Cymbeline*, iii. 4.

INWARD. *Confidential; intimate; familiar.*

For what is *inward* between us, let it pass.
Love's Labour's lost, v. 1.
Who is most *inward* with the noble duke?
Richard 3, iii. 4.

INWARDNESS. *Intimacy.*

You know my *inwardness* and love
Is very much unto the prince and Claudio.
Much Ado about Nothing, iv. 1.

To IRK. *To grieve; to give pain.*

And yet it *irks* me, the poor dappled fools
Should, in their own confines, with forkèd heads
Have their round haunches gor'd.
As you like it, ii. 1.
To see this sight, it *irks* my very soul.
Henry 8, P. 3, ii. 2.

IRON-WITTED. *Dull; impenetrable.*

I will converse with *iron-witted* fools
And unrespective boys. *Richard* 3, iv. 2.

IRRECONCILED. *Unrepented; unatoned for.*

Or if a servant, under his master's command
transporting a sum of money, be assailed by robbers,
and die in many *irreconciled* iniquities, you may
call the business of the master the author of the
servant's damnation. *Henry* 5, iv. 1.

IRREGULOUS. *Irregular; lawless.*

Thou,
Conspir'd with that *irregulous* devil, Cloten,
Hast here cut off my lord. *Cymbeline*, iv. 2.

IRREMOVABLE. *Firm; determined; obstinate;
inflexible.*

He's *irremovable*, resolv'd for flight.
Winter's Tale, iv. 3.

ISSUE. *Proceeding; course pursued; result;
consequence.*

There shall I try,
In my oration, how the people take
The cruel *issue* of these bloody men.
Julius Cæsar, iii. 1.
Spirits are not finely touch'd but to fine *issues*.
Measure for Measure, i. 1.
I am to pray you not to strain my speech
To grosser *issues* nor to larger reach
Than to suspicion. *Othello*, iii. 3.

ISSUED. *Descended; derived.*

Thou his only heir,
A princess,—no worse *issu'd*. *Tempest*, i. 2.

ITERANCE. *Reiteration; repetition.*

What needs this *iterance*, woman? I say thy
husband. *Othello*, v. 2.

ITERATION. *Reiteration; repetition.*

Truth tir'd with *iteration*.
Troilus and Cressida, iii. 2.
O, thou hast damnable *iteration*, and art, indeed,
able to corrupt a saint. *Henry* 4, P. 1, i. 2.

J.

JACK. *A Jack-a-lantern; an ignis fatuus; a fellow, in contempt.*

Your fairy, which you say is a harmless fairy, has done little better than played the *Jack* with us. *Tempest*, iv. 1.

I've within my mind
A thousand raw tricks of these bragging *Jacks*,
Which I will practise. *Merchant of Venice*, iii. 4.

Take hence this *Jack*, and whip him.
Antony and Cleopatra, iii. 8.

JACK-A-LENT. *A stuffed figure; a puppet; a term of contempt or familiarity.*

You little *Jack-a-Lent*, have you been true to us? *Merry Wives of Windsor*, iii. 3.

See now how wit may be made a *Jack-a-Lent*, when 'tis upon ill employment. *Ibid.* v. 5.

JACK-AN-APES. *An ape.*

I could lay on like a butcher, and sit like a *jack-an-apes*, never off. *Henry 5*, v. 2.

JACK GUARDANT. *A Jack in office.*

You shall perceive that a *Jack guardant* cannot office me from my son Coriolanus. *Coriolanus*, v. 2.

JACK O' THE CLOCK. *A figure placed outside a clock to strike the hours.*

While I stand fooling here, his *Jack o' the clock*. *Richard 2*, v. 5.

Because that, like a *Jack*, thou keep'st the stroke
Betwixt thy begging and my meditation.
Richard 3, iv. 2.

JADE. *A steed; a nag.*

Down, down I come; like glistering Phaëthon,
Wanting the manage of unruly *jades*.
Richard 2, iii. 3.

The poor *jade* is wrung in the withers out of all cess. *Henry 4*, P. 1, ii. 1.

TO JADE. *To rule; to get the better of; to harass; to drive out.*

I do not now fool myself, to let imagination *jade* me; for every reason excites to this, that my lady loves me. *Twelfth-Night*, ii. 5.

If we live thus tamely,
To be thus *jaded* by a piece of scarlet,
Farewell nobility. *Henry 8*, iii. 2.

How, with his banners and his well-paid ranks,
The ne'er-yet-beaten horse of Parthia ·
We have *jaded* out o' the field.
Antony and Cleopatra, iii. 1.

JADED. *Mean; paltry.*

The honourable blood of Lancaster
Must not be shed by such a *jaded* groom.
Henry 6, P. 2, iv. 1.

TO JANGLE. *To quarrel; to sound discordantly.*

Good wits will be *jangling;* but, gentles, agree.
Love's Labour's lost, ii. 1.

Now see that noble and most sovereign reason,
Like sweet bells *jangled*, out of tune and harsh.
Hamlet, iii. 1.

JANGLING. *Altercation; bickering.*

And so far am I glad it so did sort,
As this their *jangling* I esteem a sport.
Midsummer-Night's Dream, iii. 2.

JAPE. *A jest.*

And where some stretch-mouthed rascal would, as it were, mean mischief, and break a foul *jape* into the matter, he makes the maid to answer, "Whoop, do me no harm, good man." *Winter's Tale*, iv. 3.

JAR. *A tick; a vibration.*

Yet, good deed, Leontes,
I love thee not a *jar* o' the clock behind
What lady should her lord. *Winter's Tale*, i. 2.

TO JAR. *To strike; to tick; to vibrate regularly.*

My thoughts are minutes; and, with sighs, they *jar*
Their watches are unto mine eyes. *Richard 2*, v. 5.

TO JAUNCE. *To ride hard; to jade.*

And yet I bear a burden like an ass,
Spur-gall'd and tir'd by *jauncing* Bolingbroke.
Richard 2, v. 5.

JAY. *A jade; a courtezan.*

Some *jay* of Italy,
Whose mother was her painting, hath betray'd him.
Cymbeline, iii. 4.

AA

We'll teach him to know turtles from *jays.*
        Merry Wives of Windsor, iii. **3.**

JEALOUS. *Suspicious; doubtful; alarmed at.*

Come, go along, and see the truth hereof;
For our first merriment hath made thee *jealous.*
'   *Taming of the Shrew,* iv. **5.**
Jealous in honour, sudden and quick in quarrel,
Seeking the bubble reputation
Even in the cannon's mouth. *As you like it,* ii. **7.**
That you do love me, I am nothing *jealous.*
                Julius Cæsar, i. **2.**
And be not *jealous* on me, gentle Brutus. *Ibid.* i. **2.**
My lord, your nobles, *jealous* of your absence,
Seek through your camp to find you. *Hen.* 5, iv. **1.**

JEALOUS-HOOD. *Jealousy.*

But I will watch you from such watching now.—
A *jealous-hood,* a *jealous-hood* !
                Romeo and Juliet, iv. **4.**

JEALOUSY. *Doubt; suspicion; apprehension.*

And not all love to see you,
But *jealousy* what might befall your travel,
Being skilless in these parts. *Twelfth-Night,* iii. **3.**
We'll slip you for a season ; but our *jealousy*
Does yet depend.   *Cymbeline,* iv. **3.**
.So full of artless *jealousy* is guilt,
It spills itself in fearing to be spilt. *Hamlet,* iv. **5.**

JERK. *A flight; a sally.*

And why, indeed, Naso, but for smelling out
the odoriferous flowers of fancy, the *jerks* of invention ?   *Love's Labour's lost,* iv. **2.**

JEST. *A masque; a pageant; an interlude.*

As gentle and as jocund as to *jest,*
Go I to fight : truth hath a quiet breast.
                Richard 2, i. **3.**

To JET. *To encroach upon ; to strut.*

Insulting tyranny begins to *jet*
Upon the innocent and awless throne.
                Richard 3, ii. **4.**
How he *jets* under his advancèd plumes !
                Twelfth-Night, ii. **5.**
The gates of monarchs
Are arch'd so high, that giants may *jet* through,
And keep their impious turbans on, without
Good morrow to the sun.   *Cymbeline,* iii. **3.**

JEWEL. *A trinket ; a personal ornament of
        any kind.*

Here, wear this *jewel* for me,—'tis my picture.'
                Twelfth-Night, iii. **4.**

JIG. *A song ; a ballad.*

He's for a *jig* or a tale of bawdry, or he sleeps:
say on: come to Hecuba.   *Hamlet,* ii. **2.**

JIGGING. *Rhyming ; ballad-making.*

What should the wars do with these *jigging* fools ?
                Julius Cæsar, iv. **3.**

JOINDER. *Conjunction ; joining.*

A contract and eternal bond of love,
Confirm'd by mutual *joinder* of your hands.
                Twelfth-Night, v. **1.**

To JOINT. *To join ; to unite.*

Which, being dead many years, shall after re-
vive, be *jointed* to the old stock, and freshly grow.
                Cymbeline, v. **4.**
But soon that war had end, and the time's state
Made friends of them, *jointing* their force 'gainst
Cæsar.   *Antony and Cleopatra,* i. **2.**

JOINTRESS. *The holder of a jointure.*

Therefore our sometime sister, now our queen,
The imperial *jointress* of this warlike state,
Have we, as 'twere with a defeated joy,
Taken to wife.   *Hamlet,* i. **2.**

JOINT-RING. *A love-token formerly very com-
        mon ; a double ring.*

Marry, I would not do such a thing for a *joint-
ring.*   *Othello,* iv. **3.**

JOINT-STOOL. *A stool made with joints.*

I knew you at the first,
You were a movable.—Why, what's a movable ?—
A *joint-stool.*   *Taming of the Shrew,* ii. **1.**
Come hither, mistress ; is your name Goneril ?—
She cannot deny it.—Cry you mercy ; I took you
for a *joint-stool.*   *King Lear,* iii. **6.**

To JOLE. *To dash ; to clash.*

How the knave *joles* it to the ground, as if it
were Cain's jaw-bone, that did the first murder !
                Hamlet, v. **1.**
Their heads are both one,—they may *jole* horns
together, like any deer i' the herd.
                All's well that ends well, i. **3.**

JOLLITY. *Mirth ; merriment ; festivity.*

Apprehend nothing but *jollity*. *Winter's Tale*, iv. 3.

A fortnight hold we this solemnity,
In nightly revels and new *jollity*.
Midsummer-Night's Dream, v. 1.

JOURNAL. *Daily ; diurnal.*

Stick to your *journal* course : the breach of custom
Is breach of all. *Cymbeline*, iv. 2.

Ere twice the sun hath made his *journal* greeting
To th' under generation, you shall find
Your safety manifested. *Measure for Measure*, iv. 3.

JOVIAL. *Jove-like.*

The brawns of Hercules : but his *Jovial* face—
Murder in heaven ?—How !—'Tis gone.
Cymbeline, iv. 2.

TO JOY. *To rejoice ; to enjoy.*

Go to a gossips' feast, and *joy* with me ;
After so long grief, such felicity !
Comedy of Errors, v. 1.

My heart doth *joy*, that yet, in all my life
I found no man but he was true to me.
Julius Cæsar, v. 5.

There's nothing in the world can make me *joy*.
King John, iii. 4.

Poor fellow ! never *joyed* since the price of oats
rose. *Henry 4*, P. 1, ii. 1.

Choose out some secret place, some reverend room,
More than thou hast, and with it *joy* thy life.
Richard 2, v. 6.

I can no more :—live thou to *joy* thy life ;
Myself to *joy* in naught but that thou liv'st.
Henry 6, P. 2, iii. 2.

JUDICIOUS. *Judicial.*

His last offences to us
Shall have *judicious* hearing. *Coriolanus*, v. 6.

JUMP. *Chance ; hazard.*

Do not exceed
The prescript of this scroll : our fortune lies
Upon this *jump*. *Antony and Cleopatra*, iii. 8.

JUMP. *Exactly ; precisely.*

Myself the while to draw the Moor apart,
And bring him *jump* when he may Cassio find
Soliciting his wife :—ay, that's the way.
Othello, ii. 3.

But since, so *jump* upon this bloody question,
You from the Polack wars, and you from England,

Are here arriv'd, give order that these bodies
High on a stage be plac'd to the view.
Hamlet, v. 2.

TO JUMP. *To risk ; to hazard ; to agree ; to join ; to tally.*

That but this blow
Might be the be-all and the end-all here,
But here, upon this bank and shoal of time,
We'd *jump* the life to come. *Macbeth*, i. 7.

Or *jump* the after-inquiry on your own peril.
Cymbeline, v. 4.

I will not choose what many men desire,
Because I will not *jump* with common spirits.
Merchant of Venice, ii. 8.

Do not embrace me till each circumstance
Of place, time, fortune, do cohere and *jump*,
That I am Viola. *Twelfth-Night*, v. 1.

But though they *jump* not on a just account,
Yet do they all confirm
A Turkish fleet, and bearing up to Cyprus.
Othello, i. 3.

JUNKET. *A sweetmeat ; a dainty.*

You know there wants no *junkets* at the feast.
Taming of the Shrew, iii. 2.

JUST. *A tournament.*

What news from Oxford ? hold those *justs* and triumphs ? *Richard 2*, v. 2.

JUSTICE. *Punishment ; judgment.*

In God's name,
Turn me away ; and let the foul'st contempt
Shut door upon me, and so give me up
To the sharpest kind of *justice*. *Henry 8*, ii. 4.

Sharp enough, lord, for thy *justice* ! *Ibid*. iii. 2.

JUSTICER. *A judge.*

It shall be done ; I will arraign them straight.—
Come, sit thou there, most learnèd *justicer*.
King Lear, iii. 6.

False *justicer*, why hast thou let her scape ?
Ibid. iii. 6.

O, give me cord, or knife, or poison,
Some upright *justicer* ! *Cymbeline*, v. 5.

TO JUSTIFY. *To declare ; to affirm ; to certify ; to confirm.*

But you, my brace of lords, were I so minded,
I here could pluck his highness' frown upon you,
And *justify* you traitors. *Tempest*, v. 1.

Come, Camillo,
And take her by the hand, whose worth and honesty
Is richly noted, and here *justified*
By us, a pair of kings.   *Winter's Tale*, v. 3.

Let be call'd before us
That gentleman of Buckingham's : in person
I'll hear him his confessions *justify*.   *Henry* 8, i. 1.

More particulars
Must *justify* my knowledge.   *Cymbeline*, ii. 4.

How is this *justified ?*—
The stranger part of it by her own letters.
          All's well that ends well, iv. 3.

JUTTY.   *The projecting part of a building.*

No *jutty*, frieze,

Buttress, nor coign of vantage, but this bird
Hath made his bed and procreant cradle.
          Macbeth, i. 6.

TO JUTTY.   *To jut out; to beetle; to hang over.*

Let the brow o'erwhelm it
As fearfully as doth a gallèd rock
O'erhang and *jutty* his confounded base,
Swill'd with the wild and wasteful ocean.
          Henry 5, iii. 1.

JUVENAL.   *A youth.*

How canst thou part sadness and melancholy,
my tender *juvenal?*   *Love's Labour's lost*, i. 2.

K.

KAM.   *Crooked.*

This is clean *kam*.   *Coriolanus*, iii. 1.

KEECH.   *A roll or lump of fat.*

I wonder
That such a *keech* can with his very bulk
Take up the rays o' the beneficial sun,
And keep it from the earth.   *Henry* 8, i. 1.

Why, thou clay-brained guts, thou nott-pated
fool, thou whoreson, obscene, greasy tallow-*keech*.
          Henry 4, P. 1, ii. 4.

TO KEEL.   *To cool.*

While greasy Joan doth *keel* the pot.
          Love's Labour's lost, v. 2.

KEEP.   *Care ; custody.*

For in Baptista's *keep* my treasure is.
          Taming of the Shrew, i. 2.

TO KEEP.   *To dwell; to care for; to guard; to watch; to observe; to remain with; to resist; to feed; to entertain; to behave.*

A breath thou art
Servile to all the skyey influences
That do this habitation, where thou *keep'st*,
Hourly afflict.   *Measure for Measure*, iii. 1.

Where youth, and cost, and witless bravery *keeps*.
          Ibid. i. 3.

If I do lose thee, I do lose a thing
That none but fools would *keep*.   *Ibid.* iii. 1.

Thy demon, that's thy spirit which *keeps* thee, is

Noble, courageous, high, unmatchable,
Where Cæsar's is not. *Antony and Cleopatra*, ii. 3.

If it prove
She's otherwise, I'll *keep* my stables where
I lodge my wife ; I'll go in couples with her.
          Winter's Tale, ii. 1.

Now, peace be here,
Poor house, that *keep'st* thyself ! *Cymbeline*, iii. 6.

What time we will our celebration *keep*,
According to my birth.   *Twelfth-Night*, iv. 3.

The Earl of Pembroke *keeps* his regiment.
          Richard 3, v. 3.

The seven-fold shield of Ajax cannot *keep*
The battery from my heart.
          Antony and Cleopatra, iv. 14.

Was this face the face
That every day under his household roof
Did *keep* ten thousand men ?   *Richard* 2, iv. 1.

O, 'tis a foul thing when a cur cannot *keep* himself in all companies !
          Two Gentlemen of Verona, iv. 2.

KEEPER.   *A gaoler.*

So I leave you
To the protection of the prosperous gods,
As thieves to *keepers*.   *Timon of Athens*, v. 1.

KEN.   *View ; sight ; eyeshot.*

Milford,
When from the mountain-top Pisanio show'd thee,
Thou wast within a *ken*.   *Cymbeline*, iii. 6.

For, lo ! within a *ken* our army lies.
          Henry 4, P. 2, iv. 1.

To KEN. *To see; to descry; to know.*

As far as I could *ken* thy chalky cliffs,
When from thy shore the tempest beat us back,
I stood upon the hatches in the storm.
Henry 6, P. 2, iii. 2.
'Tis he, I *ken* the manner of his gait.
Troilus and Cressida, iv. 5.
I *ken* the wight : he is of substance good.
Merry Wives of Windsor, i. 3.

KERN. *An Irish boor ; an Irish foot-soldier of the lowest kind.*

We must supplant those rough rug-headed *kerns*,
Which live like venom where no venom else,
But only they, hath privilege to live.
Richard 2, ii. 1.
And with a puissant and a mighty power
Of gallowglasses and stout *kerns*
Is marching hitherward in proud array.
Henry 6, P. 2, iv. 9.

KERSEY. *Coarse woollen cloth.*

With a linen stock on one leg, and a *kersey*
boot-hose on the other. *Taming of the Shrew*, iii. 2.
Henceforth my wooing mind shall be express'd
In russet yeas and honest *kersey* noes.
Love's Labour's lost, v. 2.

KETTLE. *A kettle-drum.*

Give me the cups ;
And let the *kettle* to the trumpet speak.
Hamlet, v. 2.

KEY-COLD. *Lifeless.*

Poor *key-cold* figure of a holy king !
Richard 3, i. 2.

KIBE. *A sore heel.*

The age is grown so picked, that the toe of the
peasant comes so near the heel of the courtier, he
galls his *kibe*. *Hamlet*, v. 1.
If it were a *kibe*, 'twould put me to my slipper.
Tempest, ii. 1.

KICKY-WICKY. *A wife.*

He wears his honour in a box unseen,
That hugs his *kicky-wicky* here at home.
All's well that ends well, ii. 3.

KIDNEY. *Constitution ; temperament.*

A man of my *kidney*,—think of that,—that am
as subject to heat as butter.
Merry Wives of Windsor, iii. 5.

KILN. *A stove.*

Creep into the *kiln*-hole.
Merry Wives of Windsor, iv. 2.
Is there not milking-time, when you are going
to bed, or *kiln*-hole, to whistle off these secrets ?
Winter's Tale, iv. 3.

KIN. *Kindred.*

One touch of nature makes the whole world *kin*.
Troilus and Cressida, iii. 3.
A little more than *kin*, and less than kind.
Hamlet, i. 2.

KIND. *Nature; way; respect; rank; class.*

So with good life,
And observation strange, my meaner ministers
Their several *kinds* have done. *Tempest*, iii. 3.
You must think this, look you, that the worm
will do his *kind*. *Antony and Cleopatra*, v. 2.
Your cuckoo sings by *kind*.
All's well that ends well, i. 3.
Send me your prisoners with the speediest means,
Or you shall hear in such a *kind* from me
As will displease you. *Henry* 4, P. 1, i. 3.
But in this *kind*, wanting your father's voice,
The other must be held the worthier.
Midsummer-Night's Dream, i. 1.
I know not if't be true ;
But I, for mere suspicion in that *kind*,
Will do as if for surety. *Othello*, i. 3.
And in this seat of peace tumultuous wars
Shall kin with kin and *kind* with *kind* confound.
Richard 2, iv. 1.

To KINDLE. *To instigate; to incite.*

This wrestler shall clear all: nothing remains
but that I *kindle* the boy thither ; which now I'll
go about. *As you like it*, i. 1.

KINDLESS. *Unnatural.*

Remorseless, treacherous, lecherous, *kindless* villain !
Hamlet, ii. 2.

KINDLY. *Natural; harmless; gentle.*

And by that fatherly and *kindly* power
That you have in her, bid her answer truly.
Much Ado about Nothing, iv. 1.
Melt Egypt into Nile ! and *kindly* creatures
Turn all to serpents ! *Antony and Cleopatra*, ii. 5.

KINDLY. *Naturally.*

This do, and do it *kindly*, gentle sirs.
Taming of the Shrew, Induction, sc. 1.

Shalt see thy other daughter use thee *kindly* ;
for though she's as like this as a crab's like an apple,
yet I can tell what I can tell. *King Lear*, i. 5.

TO KING. *To supply with a king ; to make a king of.*

King'd of our fear, until our fears, resolv'd,
Be by some certain king purg'd and depos'd.
King John, ii. 1.
For, my good liege, she is so idly *king'd*,
Her sceptre so fantastically borne,
That fear attends her not. *Henry* 5, ii. 4.
Then crushing penury
Persuades me I was better when a king ;
Then am I *king'd* again. *Richard* 2, v. 5.

KINGDOM. *Region ; expanse ; tract.*

The watery *kingdom*, whose ambitious head
Spits in the face of heaven, is no bar
To stop the foreign spirits ; but they come,
As o'er a brook, to see fair Portia.
Merchant of Venice, ii. 6.

KINGDOMED. *Possessing kingly power.*

Kingdom'd Achilles in commotion rages,
And batters down himself.
Troilus and Cressida, ii. 3.

KIRTLE. *A gown.*

What stuff wilt thou have a *kirtle* of ?
Henry 4, P. 2, ii. 4.

TO KITCHEN. *To treat ; to entertain.*

There is a fat friend at your master's house,
That *kitchen'd* me for you to-day at dinner.
Comedy of Errors, v. 1.

KITCHEN-TRULL. *A scullion ; a kitchen-maid.*

Which by his tongue being made,
And then a mind put in't, either our brags
Were crack'd of *kitchen-trulls*, or his description
Prov'd us unspeaking sots. *Cymbeline*, v. 5.

KNACK. *A trifle ; a knick-knack.*

Why 'tis a cockle or a walnut-shell,
A *knack*, a toy, a trick, a baby's cap.
Taming of the Shrew, iv. 3.

TO KNAP. *To break ; to rap.*

I would she were as lying a gossip in that as
ever *knapped* ginger, or made her neighbours believe she wept for the death of a third husband.
Merchant of Venice, iii. 1.

She *knapped* 'em o' the coxcombs with a stick,
and cried, " Down, wantons, down !"
King Lear, ii. 4.

KNAVE. *A servant.*

Whip me such honest *knaves*. *Othello*, i. 1.
See to my house, left in the fearful guard
Of an unthrifty *knave*. *Merchant of Venice*, i. 3.

TO KNEE. *To supplicate by kneeling ; to kneel to.*

A mile before his tent fall down, and *knee*
The way into his mercy. *Coriolanus*, v. 1.
I could as well be brought
To *knee* his throne, and, squire-like, pension beg
To keep base life afoot. *King Lear*, ii. 4.

KNIFE. *A sword ; a dagger.*

I wear no *knife* to slaughter sleeping men.
Henry 6, P. 2, iii. 2.
Come, thick night,
And pall thee in the dunnest smoke of hell,
That my keen *knife* see not the wound it makes.
Macbeth, i. 5.

KNIGHT. *Votary ; servant ; worshipper.*

Pardon, goddess of the night,
Those that slew thy virgin *knight* ;
For the which, with songs of woe,
Round about her tomb they go.
Much Ado about Nothing, v. 3.

KNIT. *Texture.*

Their blue coats brushed, and their garters of
an indifferent *knit*. *Taming of the Shrew*, iv. 1.

TO KNIT. *To tie ; to join together ; to unite.*

When your head did but ache,
I *knit* my handkercher about your brows.
King John, iv. 1.
I'll have this knot *knit* up to-morrow morning.
Romeo and Juliet, iv. 2.
Our sever'd navy too
Have *knit* again, and fleet, threatening most sea-like.
Antony and Cleopatra, iii. 13.
And these, mine enemies, are all *knit* up
In their distractions. *Tempest*, iii. 3.

TO KNOLL. *To toll.*

Had I as many sons as I have hairs,
I would not wish them to a fairer death :
And so, his knell is *knoll'd*. *Macbeth*, v. 8.

If ever you have look'd on better days,
If ever been where bells have knoll'd to church,—
Let gentleness my strong enforcement be :
In the which hope I blush, and hide my sword.
As you like it, ii. 7.

KNOT. *Association; band; confederacy; a flower-bed.*
So oft as that shall be,
So often shall the knot of us be call'd
The men that gave their country liberty.
Julius Cæsar, iii. 1.
Trust me, a good knot. *Merry Wives of Win.* iii. 2.
O you panderly rascals ! there's a knot, a ging,
a pack, a conspiracy against me. *Ibid.* iv. 2.
Her knots disorder'd, and her wholesome herbs
Swarming with caterpillars. *Richard 2*, iii. 4.

To KNOW. *To consider; to acknowledge; to learn; to inquire; to denote; to be acquainted.*
Let but your honour know,
Had time coher'd with place, or place with wishing,
Whether you had not sometime in your life
Err'd in this point which now you censure him.
Measure for Measure, ii. 1.
We know him for no less, though we are but
strangers to him. *Timon of Athens*, iii. 2.
Therefore, fair Hermia, question your desires,
Know of your youth, examine well your blood.
Midsummer-Night's Dream, i. 1.

And, see, a book of prayer in his hand,—
True ornament to know a holy man.
Richard 3, iii. 7.
You and I have known, sir.
Antony and Cleopatra, ii. 6.
Sir, we have known together in Orleans.
Cymbeline, i. 4.

KNOWING. *Knowledge; experience.*
One of your great knowing
Should learn, being taught, forbearance.
Cymbeline, ii. 3.
That, on the view and knowing of these contents,
Without debatement further, more or less,
He should the bearers put to sudden death,
Not shriving-time allow'd. *Hamlet*, v. 2.
Here comes the Briton : let him be so entertained amongst you as suits, with gentlemen of
your knowing, to a stranger of his quality.
Cymbeline, i. 4.
Within the volume of which time I've seen
Hours dreadful and things strange ; but this sore night
Hath trifled former knowings. *Macbeth*, ii. 2.

KNOWLEDGE. *Honour.*
Had I not brought
The knowledge of your mistress home, I grant
We were to question further. *Cymbeline*, ii. 4.

L.

LA. *See; look; behold; lo.*
La you, an you speak ill of the devil, how he
takes it at heart ! *Twelfth-Night*, iii. 4.

LABEL. *A tablet; the appendage of an indenture or deed to which the seal was attached.*
When I wak'd, I found
This label on my bosom. *Cymbeline*, v. 5.
And ere this hand, by thee to Romeo seal'd,
Shall be the label to another deed,
Or my true heart with treacherous revolt
Turn to another, this shall slay them both.
Romeo and Juliet, iv. 1.

To LABOUR. *To move slowly or with difficulty.*
What do you think the hour ?—Labouring for nine.
Timon of Athens, iii. 4.

When shall I come to the top of that same hill ?—
You do climb up it now : look, how we labour.
King Lear, iv. 6.

LABOURSOME. *Assiduous; unremitting; elaborate.*
He hath, my lord, wrung from me my slow leave
By laboursome petition. *Hamlet*, i. 2.
Forget
Your laboursome and dainty trims, wherein
You made great Juno angry. *Cymbeline*, iii. 4.

To LACE. *To streak; to variegate.*
To see th' enclosèd lights, now canopied
Under these windows, white and azure, lac'd
With blue of heaven's own tinct. *Cymbeline*, ii. 2.
Look, love, what envious streaks
Do lace the severing clouds in yonder east.
Romeo and Juliet, iii. 5.

To LACKEY.   *To wait upon; to serve.*

This common body,
Like to a vagabond flag upon the stream,
Goes to and back, *lackeying* the varying tide,
To rot itself with motion.
Antony and Cleopatra, i. 4.

LADY.   *Effeminate.*

With many holiday and *lady* terms
He question'd me.   *Henry* 4, P. 1, i. 3.

LAG.   *The fag end; the lowest class.*

The rest of your foes, O gods,—the senators of
Athens, together with the common *lag* of people,—
what is amiss in them, you gods, make suitable for
destruction.   *Timon of Athens*, iii. 6.

LAG.   *Latter; late.*

For mine own part, I could be well content
To entertain the *lag* end of my life
With quiet hours.   *Henry* 4, P. 1, v. 1.
Some tardy cripple bore the countermand,
That came too *lag* to see him buried.
Richard 3, ii. 1.

To LAME.   *To outgo; to surpass.*

For feature, *laming*
The shrine of Venus, or straight-pight Minerva,
Postures beyond brief nature.   *Cymbeline*, v. 5.

LANGUISH.   *Pain; suffering; anguish.*

One desperate grief cures with another's *languish*.
Romeo and Juliet, i. 2.
What, of death too,
That rids our dogs of *languish*? ·
Antony and Cleopatra, v. 2.

To LANK.   *To shrink; to fall away.*

And all this
Was borne so like a soldier, that thy cheek
So much as *lank'd* not. *Antony and Cleopatra*, i. 4.

LANTERN.   *A turret full of windows.*

A grave? O, no, a *lantern*, slaughter'd youth,
For here lies Juliet, and her beauty makes
This vault a feasting presence full of light.
Romeo and Juliet, v. 3.

To LAP.   *To wrap up; to cover; to envelope.*

Who told me, when we both lay in the field
Frozen almost to death, how he did *lap* me

Even in his garments, and did give himself,
All thin and naked, to the numb cold night.
Richard 3, ii. 1.
Till that Bellona's bridegroom, *lapp'd* in proof,
Confronted him with self comparisons.
Macbeth, i. 2.
He, sir, was *lapp'd*
In a most curious mantle, wrought by the hand
Of his queen mother.   *Cymbeline*, v. 5.

LAPSED.   *Condemned; convicted; lost; immersed.*

Only myself stood out;
For which, if I be *lapsèd* in this place,
I shall pay dear.   *Twelfth-Night*, iii. 3.
Do you not come your tardy son to chide,
That, *laps'd* in time and passion, lets go by
The important acting of your dread command?
Hamlet, iii. 4.

To LARD.   *To fatten.*

It is the pasture *lards* the rother's sides,
The want that makes him lean.
Timon of Athens, iv. 3.
In which array, brave soldier, doth he lie,
Larding the plain.   *Henry* 5, iv. 6.
Falstaff sweats to death,
And *lards* the lean earth as he walks along.
Henry 4, P. 1, ii. 2.

LARDED.   *Mingled; interspersed.*

Larded with sweet flowers.   *Hamlet*, iv. 5.
An exact command
Larded with many several sorts of reasons,
Importing Denmark's health, and England's too.
Ibid. v. 2.

LARGE.   *Free; unrestrained; licentious.*

The man doth fear God, howsoever it seems
not in him by some *large* jests he will make.
Much Ado about Nothing, ii. 3.
I never tempted her with word too *large*.
Ibid. iv. 1.

To LATCH.   *To catch; to anoint.*

But I have words
That would be howl'd out in the desert air,
Where hearing should not *latch* them.
Macbeth, iv. 3.
But hast thou yet *latch'd* the Athenian's eyes
With the love-juice, as I did bid thee do?
Midsummer-Night's Dream, iii. 2.

LATE. *Lately appointed; recent.*

And now to our French causes :
Who are the *late* commissioners?   *Henry* 5, ii. 2.
You the like loss?—As great to me as *late*.
Tempest, v. 1.

LATE. *Lately; recently.*

It pleas'd the king his master very *late*
To strike at me, upon his misconstruction.
King Lear, ii. 2.
Ay, brother,—to our grief, as it is yours :
Too *late* he died that might have kept that title.
Richard 3, iii. 1.
O boy, thy father gave thee life too soon,
And hath bereft thee of thy life too *late!*
Henry 6, P. 3, ii. 5.
The mercy that was quick in us but *late*,
By your own counsel is suppress'd and kill'd.
Henry 5, ii. 2.

LATED. *Belated; benighted.*

Now spurs the *lated* traveller apace
To gain the timely inn.   *Macbeth*, iii. 3.
I am so *lated* in the world, that I
Have lost my way for ever.
Antony and Cleopatra, iii. 11.

LATTEN. *A compound of copper and cala-mine.*

I combat challenge of this *latten* bilbo.
Merry Wives of Windsor, i. 1.

LATTER. *Last.*

The king himself hath a heavy reckoning to make, when all those legs and arms and heads, chopped off in a battle, shall join together at the *latter* day.   *Henry* 5, iv. 1.

LAUD. *Praise; commendation; reverence.*

One touch of nature makes the whole world kin,—
That all, with one consent, praise new-born gauds,
Though they are made and moulded of things past,
And give to dust, that is a little gilt,
More *laud* than gilt o'er-dusted.
Troilus and Cressida, iii. 3.

LAUND. *A lawn; a glade.*

Under this thick-grown brake we'll shroud our-selves ;
For through this *laund* anon the deer will come.
Henry 6, P. 3, iii. 1.

LAVOLT. *A dance.*

I cannot sing,
Nor heel the high *lavolt*, nor sweeten talk,
Nor play at subtle games.
Troilus and Cressida, iv. 4.

LAVOLTA. *The lavolt; a dance.*

They bid us to the English dancing-schools,
And teach *lavoltas* high and swift corantos.
Henry 5, iii. 4.

LAY. *A wager.*

A dreadful *lay!*—address thee instantly.
Henry 6, P. 2, v. 2.
And, my fortunes against any *lay* worth nam-ing, this crack of your love shall grow stronger than it was before.   *Othello*, ii. 3.
I will have it no *lay*.—By the gods, it is one.
Cymbeline, i. 4.

To LAY. *To waylay; to beset; to stake; to play for.*

These five days have I hid me in these woods ;
and durst not peep out, for all the country is *laid* for me.   *Henry* 6, P. 2, iv. 10.
I'll cheer up
My discontented troops, and *lay* for hearts.
Timon of Athens, iii. 5.

To LAY BY. *To stand; to stop.*

Got with swearing "*lay by*," and spent with crying " bring in."   *Henry* 4, P. 1, i. 2.

To LAY DOWN. *To plan; to study; to pro-vide.*

We must not only arm to invade the French,
But *lay down* our proportions to defend
Against the Scot.   *Henry* 5, i. 2.

LAZAR. *A leper; a beggar.*

And, to relief of *lazars* and weak age,
Of indigent faint souls past corporal toil,
A hundred almshouses right well supplied.
Henry 5, i. 1.
Then if she that *lays* thee out says thou art a fair corse, I'll be sworn and sworn upon't she never shrouded any but *lazars*. *Troilus and Cressida*, ii. 3.
For I care not to be the louse of a *lazar*, so I were not Menelaus.   *Ibid*. v. 1.

LEADING. *Generalship; military experience.*

I wonder much,
Being men of such great *leading* as you are,

DD

That you foresee not what impediments
Drag back our expedition.   *Henry 4, P. 1, iv. 3.*

LEAGUER.   *A camp.*

He shall suppose no other but that he is carried
into the *leaguer* of the adversaries.
All's well that ends well, iii. 6.

LEAKED.   *Leaky.*

Leak'd is our bark ;
And we, poor mates, stand on the dying deck,
Hearing the surges threat.   *Timon of Athens, iv. 2.*

LEAN.   *Mean ; unworthy.*

That which combin'd us was most great, and let not
A *leaner* action rend us.
Antony and Cleopatra, ii. 2.

To LEARN.   *To teach.*

Have I not been
Thy pupil long ? Hast thou not *learn'd* me how
To make perfumes ?   *Cymbeline, i. 5.*
Then true nobless would
Learn him forbearance from so foul a wrong.
Richard 2, iv. 1.
The red plague rid you
For *learning* me your language !   *Tempest, i. 2.*

LEARNING.   *Intelligence ; information.*

I did inquire it ;
And have my *learning* from some true reports,
That drew their swords with you.
Antony and Cleopatra, ii. 2.

LEARNED.   *Wise ; skilful ; intelligent.*

This fellow's of exceeding honesty,
And knows all qualities, with a *learned* spirit,
Of human dealings.   *Othello, iii. 3.*

LEASH.   *A leather thong or strap used to couple hounds together.*

Even like a fawning greyhound in the *leash.*
Coriolanus, i. 6.
More straining on for plucking back ; not following
My *leash* unwillingly.   *Winter's Tale, iv. 3.*

To LEASH.   *To fasten together ; to couple.*

And at his heels,
Leash'd in like hounds, should famine, sword, and
fire,
Crouch for employment.   *Henry 5, i. Chorus.*

LEASING.   *Lying ; falsehood.*

Now Mercury endue thee with *leasing,* for thou
speakest well of fools !   *Twelfth-Night, i. 5.*
And in his praise
Have almost stamp'd the *leasing.*   *Coriolanus, v. 2.*

LEATHER-COAT.   *A kind of apple.*

There is a dish of *leather-coats* for you.
Henry 4, P. 2, v. 3.

To LEAVE.   *To cease ; to part with ; to relinquish ; to neglect.*

I cannot *leave* to love, and yet I do ;
But there I *leave* to love where I should love.
Two Gentlemen of Verona, ii. 6.
Endeavour thyself to sleep, and *leave* thy vain
bibble-babble.   *Twelfth-Night, iv. 2.*
It seems you lov'd not her, to *leave* her token.
She is dead, belike ?
Two Gentlemen of Verona, iv. 2.
The more degenerate and base art thou,
To make such means for her as thou hast done,
And *leave* her on such slight conditions. *Ibid. v. 4.*
And there I see such black and grained spots
As will not *leave* their tinct.   *Hamlet, iii. 4.*
O heavens, what some men do,
While some men *leave* to do !
Troilus and Cressida, iii. 3.

LEECH.   *A doctor.*

Make war breed peace ; make peace stint war ; make
each
Prescribe to other, as each other's *leech.*
Timon of Athens, v. 4.

LEER.   *Complexion ; colour ; countenance.*

It pleases him to call you so ; but he hath a
Rosalind of a better *leer* than you.
As you like it, iv. 1.

LEET.   *An ancient court for the trial of petty causes.*

And say, you would present her at the *leet,*
Because she brought stone jugs and no seal'd quarts.
Taming of the Shrew, Induction, sc. 2.
Who has a breast so pure,
But some uncleanly apprehensions
Keep *leets* and law-days, and in session sit
With meditations lawful ?   *Othello, iii. 3.*

LEFT.   *Dowered ; estated ; portioned.*

In Belmont is a lady richly *left.*
Merchant of Venice, i. 1.

LEG. *A bow; an obeisance.*

You make a *leg*, and Bolingbroke says ay.
Richard 2, iii. 3.
He that cannot make a *leg*, put off's cap, kiss
his hand, and say nothing, has neither leg, hands,
lip, nor cap. *All's well that ends well*, ii. 2.
You are ambitious for poor knaves' caps and *legs*.
Coriolanus, ii. 1.

LEGERITY. *Activity; lightness.*

The organs, though defunct and dead before,
Break up their drowsy grave, and newly move
With casted slough and fresh *legerity*.
Henry 5, iv. 1.

LEGITIMATION. *Legitimacy.*

Legitimation, name, and all is gone.
King John, i. 1.

LEISURE. *Occasion; exigency; convenience; want of leisure.*

Farewell : the *leisure* and the fearful time
Cuts off the ceremonious vows of love.
Richard 3, v. 3.
More than I have said
The *leisure* and enforcement of the time
Forbids to dwell upon. *Ibid.* v. 3.
You have scarce time
To steal from spiritual *leisure* a brief span
To keep your earthly audit. *Henry 8*, iii. 2.
Here to make good the boisterous appeal,
Which then our *leisure* would not let us hear,
Against the Duke of Norfolk, Thomas Mowbray.
Richard 2, i. 1.

LEMAN. *A gallant; a paramour; a sweetheart; a mistress.*

As jealous as Ford, that searched a hollow walnut
for his wife's *leman. Merry Wives of Windsor*, iv. 2.
I sent thee sixpence for thy *leman :* had'st it?
Twelfth-Night, ii. 2.

To LEND. *To give; to afford; to bestow.*

Most narrow measure *lent* me.
Antony and Cleopatra, iii. 4.

LENDINGS. *Artificial supplies; clothing, &c.*

Off, off, you *lendings !*—come, unbutton here.
King Lear, iii. 4.

LENGTH. *Continuance; duration.*

I will o'ertake thee, Cleopatra, and
Weep for my pardon. So it must be, for now
All *length* is torture. *Antony and Cleopatra*, iv. 14.

To LENGTHEN. *To delay; to retard.*

Yes, I beseech ; or I shall short my word
By *lengthening* my return. *Cymbeline*, i. 6.

LENTEN. *Brief; laconic; sparing; meagre.*

He shall see none to fear.—
A good *lenten* answer. *Twelfth-Night*, i. 5.
To think, my lord, if you delight not in man,
what *lenten* entertainment the players shall receive
from you. *Hamlet*, ii. 2.

L'ENVOY. *A kind of postscript or conclusion.*

Is not *l'envoy* a salve?
No, page : it is an epilogue or discourse, to make
plain
Some obscure precedence that hath tofore been said.
Love's Labour's lost, iii. 1.

LEPEROUS. *Leprous; causing leprosy.*

And in the porches of mine ears did pour
The *leperous* distilment. *Hamlet*, i. 5.

LESSER. *Less; in a smaller degree; less easily.*

Patience herself, what goddess e'er she be,
Doth *lesser* blench at sufferance than I do.
Troilus and Cressida, i. 1.
Others, that *lesser* hate him,
Do call it valiant fury. *Macbeth*, v. 2.
There's never a man in Christendom
Can *lesser* hide his love or hate than he.
Richard 3, iii. 4.

To LESSON. *To teach; to instruct.*

And, even in kind love, I do conjure thee,
Who art the table wherein all my thoughts
Are visibly charácter'd and engrav'd,
To *lesson* me. *Two Gentlemen of Verona*, ii. 7.
Bid Gloster think on this, and he will weep.—
Ay, millstones ; as he *lesson'd* us to weep.
Richard 3, i. 4.

LET. *Impediment; hindrance.*

And what love can do, that dares love attempt ;
Therefore thy kinsmen are no *let* to me.
Romeo and Juliet, ii. 2.
And my speech entreats
That I may know the *let*, why gentle Peace
Should not expel these inconveniences,
And bless us with her former qualities.
Henry 5, v. 2.

To **Let.** *To hinder; to prevent; to stay; to keep.*

What *lets* but one may enter at her window?
Two Gentlemen of Verona, iii. 1.
By heaven, I'll make a ghost of him that *lets* me.
Hamlet, i. 4.
I'll give you my commission
To *let* him there a month behind the gest
Prefix'd for's parting. *Winter's Tale,* i. 2.

Let-alone. *Prevention; hindrance.*

The *let-alone* lies not in your good will.
King Lear, v. 3.

Lethargied. *Obscured; paralysed.*

Either his notion weakens, or his discernings
Are *lethargied.* *King Lear,* i. 4.

Lethe. *Death.*

Here didst thou fall; and here thy hunters stand,
Sign'd in thy spoil, and crimson'd in thy *lethe.*
Julius Cæsar, iii. 1.

Letheed. *Oblivious; lethean.*

That sleep and feeding may prorogue his honour
Even till a *lethe'd* dulness!
Antony and Cleopatra, ii. 1.

Letter. *Favour; recommendation; alliteration.*

Preferment goes by *letter* and affection,
And not by old gradation, where each second
Stood heir to the first. *Othello,* i. 1.
I will something affect the *letter,* for it argues
facility. *Love's Labour's lost,* iv. 2.

To **Level.** *To square with; to befit; to accord with.*

I crave fit disposition for my wife;
Due reference of place and exhibition;
With such accommodation and besort
As *levels* with her breeding. *Othello,* i. 3.

To **Levy.** *To raise; to lead.*

Brutus and Cassius
Are *levying* powers: we must straight make head.
Julius Cæsar, iv. 1.
Therefore, friends,
As far as to the sepulchre of Christ
Forthwith a power of English shall we *levy.*
Henry 4, P. 1, i. 1.

Lewd. *Vile; bad; wicked.*

Such poor, such base, such *lewd,* such mean attempts. *Henry 4,* P. 1, iii. 2.
We'll talk with Margaret,
How her acquaintance grew with this *lewd* fellow.
Much Ado about Nothing, v. 1.
The which he hath detain'd for *lewd* employments.
Richard 2, i. 1.
Why, because you have been so *lewd,* and so
much engraffed to Falstaff. *Henry 4,* P. 2, ii. 2.

Lewdly. *Wickedly.*

A sort of naughty persons, *lewdly* bent.
Henry. 6, P. 2, ii. 1.

Lewdster. *A libertine; a profligate.*

Against such *lewdsters* and their lechery
Those that betray them do no treachery.
Merry Wives of Windsor, v. 3.

Liable. *Subordinate; subject; fit; qualified.*

Pardon me, Cæsar: for my dear dear love
To your proceeding bids me tell you this;
And reason to my love is *liable. Julius Cæsar,* ii. 2.
Finding thee fit for bloody villany,
Apt, *liable* to be employ'd in danger,
I faintly broke with thee of Arthur's death.
King John, iv. 2.

Libbard. *A leopard.*

I Pompey am.—
With *libbard's* head on knee.
Love's Labour's lost, v. 2.

Liberal. *Licentious; free to excess; gross; wanton.*

Who hath indeed, most like a *liberal* villain,
Confess'd the vile encounters they have had
A thousand times in secret.
Much Ado about Nothing, iv. 1.
Is he not a most profane and *liberal* counsellor?
Othello, ii. 1.
There with fantastic garlands did she come
Of crow-flowers, nettles, daisies, and long purples
That *liberal* shepherds give a grosser name,
But our cold maids do dead men's fingers call them.
Hamlet, iv. 7.

Liberty. *License; libertinage; debauchery.*

Disguised cheaters, prating mountebanks,—
And many such-like *liberties* of sin.
Comedy of Errors, i. 2.

Lust and *liberty*
Creep in the minds and marrows of our youth,
That 'gainst the stream of virtue they may strive,
And drown themselves in riot!
Timon of Athens, iv. 1.

LICENSE. *Licentiousness.*

That fellow is a fellow of much *license*: let him
be called before us. *Measure for Measure*, iii. 2.

To LIE. *To live; to reside; to be in prison.*

The virtuous lady, Countess of Auvergne,
By me entreats, great lord, thou wouldst vouchsafe
To visit her poor castle where she *lies*.
Henry 6, P. 1, ii. 2.
So thou mayst say, the king *lies* by a beggar, if
a beggar dwell near him. *Twelfth-Night*, iii. 1.
When the court *lay* at Windsor.
Merry Wives of Windsor, ii. 2.
I will deliver you, or else *lie* for you.
Richard 3, i. 1.

LIEF. *Willingly.*

I hope not; I had as *lief* bear as much lead.
Merry Wives of Windsor, iv. 2.
Come no more in my sight: I had as *lief* be
wooed by a snail. *As you like it*, iv. 1.

LIEF. *Beloved; dear.*

And with your best endeavour have stirr'd up
My *liefest* liege to be mine enemy.
Henry 6, P. 2, iii. 1.

LIEGEMAN. *Subject.*

Friends to this ground.—And *liegemen* to the Dane.
Hamlet, i. 1.

LIEGER. *A resident ambassador.*

Lord Angelo, having affairs to heaven,
Intends you for his swift ambassador,
Where you shall be an everlasting *lieger*.
Measure for Measure, iii. 1.
I have given him that, which, if he take,
Shall quite unpeople her of *liegers* for her sweet.
Cymbeline, i. 5.

LIEN. *Lain.*

Many a poor man's son would have *lien* still,
And ne'er have spoke a loving word to you.
King John, iv. 1.

LIEU. *Return for; requital.*

Which was, that he, in *lieu* of the premises,
Of homage, and I know not how much tribute,

Should presently extirpate me and mine
Out of the dukedom. *Tempest*, i. 2.

LIEUTENANTRY. *Lieutenancy; lieutenants; subordinates; deputies.*

If such tricks as these strip you out of your *lieutenantry*, it had been better you had not kissed your
three fingers so oft. *Othello*, ii. 1.
'Twas I
That the mad Brutus ended: he alone
Dealt on *lieutenantry*, and no practice had
In the brave squares of war.
Antony and Cleopatra, iii. 11.

LIFTER. *A thief; a robber.*

Is he so young a man, and so old a *lifter*?
Troilus and Cressida, i. 2.

LIGHT. *Unchaste; inconstant.*

Let me give light, but let me not be *light*;
For a *light* wife doth make a heavy husband.
Merchant of Venice, v. 1.

To LIGHT. *To happen; to come to pass.*

And that shall be the day, whene'er it *lights*,
That this same child of honour and renown
And your unthought-of Harry chance to meet.
Henry 4, P. 1, iii. 2.

To LIGHTEN. *To enlighten; to make wise.*

Now, the Lord *lighten* thee! thou art a great fool.
Henry 4, P. 2, ii. 1.

LIGHTER. *Lesser; inferior; meaner.*

To put on yellow stockings, and to frown
Upon Sir Toby and the *lighter* people.
Twelfth-Night, v. 1.

LIGHTLY. *Easily; readily; usually; commonly.*

My wife is in a wayward mood to-day,
And will not *lightly* trust the messenger.
Comedy of Errors, iv. 4.
Short summers *lightly* have a forward spring.
Richard 3, iii. 1.

LIKE. *Any similar thing or person.*

That every *like* is not the same, O Cæsar,
The heart of Brutus yearns to think upon!
Julius Cæsar, ii. 2.
He was a man, take him for all in all,
I shall not look upon his *like* again. *Hamlet*, i. 2.
The mightiest space in fortune nature brings
To join like *likes*, and kiss like native things.
All's well that ends well, i. 1.

LIKE. *Alike; equally; probably; as.*

My fellow-ministers
Are *like* invulnerable. *Tempest*, iii. 3.
Now, lords, for France; the enterprise whereof
Shall be to you, as us, *like* glorious. *Henry 5*, ii. 2.
Will money buy 'em? Very *like*; one of them
Is a plain fish, and, no doubt, marketable.
Tempest, v. 1.
But, *like* in sickness, did I loathe this food.
Midsummer-Night's Dream, iv. 1.

LIKE. *Likely; apt; fit.*

O, that it were as *like* as it is true!
Measure for Measure, v. 1.
If the duke continue these favours towards you,
you are *like* to be much advanced.
Twelfth-Night, ii. 4.
Lads more *like* to run
The country base than to commit such slaughter.
Cymbeline, v. 3.

To LIKE. *To please; to liken; to compare; to thrive; to grow fat.*

Not so, my liege: this lodging *likes* me better,
Since I may say, Now lie I like a king.
Henry 5, iv. 1.
What manner of man, an it *like* your majesty?
Henry 4, P. 1, ii. 4.
How do you, man? the music likes you not.
Two Gentlemen of Verona, iv. 2.
When the prince broke thy head for *liking* his
father to a singing-man of Windsor.
Henry 4, P. 2, ii. 1.
And *like* me to the peasant boys of France.
Henry 6, P. 1, iv. 6.
By my troth, you *like* well, and bear your years
very well. *Henry 4, P. 2*, iii. 2.
Well-*liking* wits they have; gross, gross; fat, fat.
Love's Labour's lost, v. 2.

LIKING. *Appearance; condition.*

I shall think the worse of fat men, as long as I
have an eye to make difference of men's *liking*.
Merry Wives of Windsor, ii. 1.
Well, I'll repent, and that suddenly, while I am
in some *liking*. *Henry 4, P. 1*, iii. 3.

LIKELIHOOD. *Parallel; comparison.*

As, by a lower but by loving *likelihood*,
Were now the general of our gracious empress—
As in good time he may—from Ireland coming,
Bringing rebellion broachèd on his sword.
Henry 5, iv. Chorus.

LIKENESS. *Semblance; seeming; appearance.*

How may *likeness* wade in crimes,
Making practice on the times!
Measure for Measure, iii. 2.
If but as well I other accents borrow
That can my speech diffuse, my good intent
May carry through itself to that full issue
For which I raz'd my *likeness*. *King Lear*, i. 4.

LIMBEC. *An alembic; a still.*

That memory, the warder of the brain,
Shall be a fume, and the receipt of reason
A *limbec* only. *Macbeth*, i. 7.

LIMBER. *Weak; pliant; flexible.*

Verily! You put me off with *limber* vows.
Winter's Tale, i. 2.

LIMB-MEAL. *In pieces; piecemeal.*

O, that I had her here, to tear her *limb-meal*!
Cymbeline, ii. 4.

LIME. *Birdlime.*

Poor bird! thou'dst never fear the net nor *lime*,
The pitfall nor the gin. *Macbeth*, iv. 2.
Come, put some *lime* on your fingers, and away
with the rest. *Tempest*, iv. 1.

To LIME. *To smear with birdlime; to entangle; to ensnare; to cement.*

Madam, myself have *lim'd* a bush for her.
Henry 6, P. 2, i. 3.
She's *limed*, I warrant you: we have caught
her, madam. *Much Ado about Nothing*, iii. 1.
O *limèd* soul, that, struggling to be free,
Art more engag'd! *Hamlet*, iii. 3.
I will not ruinate my father's house,
Who gave his blood to *lime* the stones together.
Henry 6, P. 3, v. 1.

LIMIT. *Limb; limitation; restriction.*

Hurried here to this place, i' the open air,
Before I have got strength of *limit*.
Winter's Tale, iii. 2.
And many *limits* of the charge set down
But yesternight. *Henry 4, P. 1*, i. 1.

To LIMIT. *To appoint; to nominate.*

I'll draw the form and model of our battle,
Limit each leader to his several charge,
And part in just proportion our small power.
Richard 3, v. 3.

LIMITED. *Appointed; narrow; circumscribed.*

I'll make so bold to call,
For 'tis my *limited* service. *Macbeth,* ii. 1.

Yet thanks I must you con
That you are thieves profess'd; that you work not
In holier shapes: for there is boundless theft
In *limited* professions. *Timon of Athens,* iv. 3.

LIMITATION. *Probation; trial; restriction; reservation.*

You have stood your *limitation;* and the tribunes
Endue you with the people's voice.
Coriolanus, ii. 3.
Am I yourself
But, as it were, in sort or *limitation?*
Julius Cæsar, ii. 1.

LINE. *Lineament; feature; lineage; genealogy; pedigree.*

Looking on the *lines* of my boy's face,
Methought I did recoil twenty-three years.
Winter's Tale, i. 2.
He sends you this most memorable *line,*
In every branch truly demonstrative. *Henry 5,* ii. 4.

To LINE. *To strengthen; to support.*

I fear my brother Mortimer doth stir
About his title, and hath sent for you
To *line* his enterprise. *Henry 4,* P. 1, ii. 3.
We will not *line* his thin bestainèd cloak
With our pure honours. *King John,* iv. 3.
Whether he did *line* the rebel
With hidden help and vantage, I know not.
Macbeth, i. 3.

LINEAL. *Lineally descended.*

Till satisfied
That fair Queen Isabel, his grandmother,
Was *lineal* of the Lady Ermengare. *Henry 5,* i. 2.

LINED. *Limned; painted; stuffed; padded.*

All the pictures fairest *lin'd*
Are but black to Rosalind. *As you like it,* iii. 2.
Son of sixteen,
Pluck the *lin'd* crutch from thy old limping sire,
With it beat out his brains! *Timon of Athens,* iv. 1.

To LINGER. *To extend; to lengthen; to protract.*

Who gently would dissolve the bands of life,
Which false hope *lingers* in extremity.
Richard 2, ii. 2.

I say, at once let your brief plagues be mercy,
And *linger* not our sure destructions on!
Troilus and Cressida, v. 10.
O, no; he goes into Mauritania, and takes away
with him the fair Desdemona, unless his abode be
lingered here by some accident. *Othello,* iv. 2.

LINSTOCK. *The match used by gunners.*

And the nimble gunner
With *linstock* now the devilish cannon touches,
And down goes all before them.
Henry 5, ii. Chorus.

To LIQUOR. *To drench; to moisten.*

She will, she will; justice hath *liquored* her.
Henry 4, P. 1, ii. 1.

LIQUORISH. *Lickerish; well-flavoured; palatable.*

Dry up thy marrows, vines, and plough-torn leas;
Whereof ingrateful man, with *liquorish* draughts
And morsels unctuous, greases his pure mind,
That from it all consideration slips!
Timon of Athens, iv. 3.

LIST. *Bound; limit; boundary; inclination; wish.*

I am bound to your niece; I mean she is the
list of my voyage. *Twelfth-Night,* iii. 1.
You and I cannot be confined within the weak
list of a country's fashion. *Henry 5,* v. 2.
The ocean, overpeering of his *list,*
Eats not the flats with more impetuous haste.
Hamlet, iv. 5.
In faith, too much;
I find it still when I have *list* to sleep.
Othello, ii. 1.

To LISTEN. *To attend to.*

He that no more must say is *listen'd* more
Than they whom youth and ease have taught to gloze.
Richard 2, ii. 1.
As they had seen me, with these hangman's hands,
Listening their fear: I could not say "Amen!"
When they did say "God bless us!" *Macbeth,* ii. 1.
Lady, vouchsafe to *listen* what I say.
Henry 6, P. 1, v. 3.

LITHER. *Soft; yielding.*

Two Talbots, wingèd through the *lither* sky,
In thy despite, shall scape mortality.
Henry 6, P. 1, iv. 7.

LITTLE. *Short; inadequate.*

And much too *little* of that good I saw
Is my report of his great worthiness.
Love's Labour's lost, ii. 1.

IN LITTLE. *In miniature.*

Teaching all that road to know
The quintessence of every sprite
Heaven would *in little* show. *As you like it,* iii. 2.

And those that would make mows at him while
my father lived, give twenty, forty, fifty, a hundred
ducats a-piece for his picture *in little. Hamlet,* ii. 2.

LIVELIHOOD. *Freshness; animation; liveliness.*

The tyranny of her sorrows takes all *livelihood*
from her cheek. *All's well that ends well,* i. 1.
What of his heart perceive you in his face
By any *livelihood* he show'd to-day?
Richard 3, iii. 4.

LIVELY. *Naturally; like life.*

Thou'rt, indeed, the best;
Thou counterfeit'st most *lively.*—So, so, my lord.
Timon of Athens, v. 1.

LIVER-VEIN. *The love-vein.*

This is the *liver-vein,* which makes flesh a deity,
A green goose a goddess. *Love's Labour's lost,* iv. 3.

LIVERY. *Recovery of a lapsed inheritance by legal process; delivery.*

I am denied to sue my *livery* here,
And yet my letters-patents give me leave.
Richard 2, ii. 3.

LIVING. *Wealth; fortune; possessions.*

If I gave them all my *living,* I'd keep my coxcombs myself. *King Lear,* i. 4.
That only to stand high in your account,
I might in virtues, beauties, *livings,* friends,
Exceed account. *Merchant of Venice,* iii. 2.

LIVING. *Positive; certain; convincing.*

Give me a *living* reason she's disloyal.
Othello, iii. 3.

LOACH. *A small fish, like an eel, noted for being very prolific.*

Your chamber-lie breeds fleas like a *loach.*
Henry 4, P. 1, ii. 1.

LOATHLY. *Hateful; loathsome.*

Sour-ey'd disdain, and discord, shall bestrew
The union of your bed with weeds so *loathly,*
That you shall hate it both. *Tempest,* iv. 1.
Seeing how *loathly* opposite I stood
To his unnatural purpose. *King Lear,* ii. 1.

LOATHNESS. *Unwillingness.*

Pray you, look not sad,
Nor make replies of *loathness.*
Antony and Cleopatra, iii. 11.
And the fair soul herself
Weigh'd between *loathness* and obedience.
Tempest, ii. 1.

LOB. *A lubber; a lout.*

Farewell, thou *lob* of spirits; I'll begone.
Midsummer-Night's Dream, ii. 1.

TO LOB. *To hang down; to droop.*

And their poor jades
Lob down their heads, dropping the hides and hips.
Henry 5, iv. 2.

LOCK. *A lock of hair.*

I know him; 'a wears a *lock.*
Much Ado about Nothing, iii. 3.

LOCKRAM. *A coarse kind of linen.*

The kitchen malkin pins
Her richest *lockram* 'bout her reechy neck,
Clambering the walls to eye him. *Coriolanus,* ii. 1.

TO LODGE. *To lay; to beat down.*

Though bladed corn be *lodg'd,* and trees blown
down. *Macbeth,* iv. 1.
His well-proportion'd beard made rough and rugged,
Like to the summer's corn by tempest *lodg'd.*
Henry 6, P. 2, iii. 2.

TO LOFFE. *To laugh.*

And then the whole quire hold their hips and *loffe.*
Midsummer-Night's Dream, ii. 1.

LOGGATS. *An ancient game.*

Did these bones cost no more the breeding, but
to play at *loggats* with 'em? mine ache to think
on't. *Hamlet,* v. 1.

TO LONG. *To belong.*

And hold your own, in any case,
With such austerity as *longeth* to a father.
Taming of the Shrew, iv. 5.

He wills you lay apart
The borrow'd glories, that, by gift of heaven,
By law of nature and of nations, *long*
To him and to his heirs.   *Henry 5, ii. 4.*

It is an honour *longing* to our house,
Bequeathèd down from many ancestors.
                All's well that ends well, iv. 2.

To his surname Coriolanus *longs* more pride
Than pity to our prayers.   *Coriolanus, v. 3.*

LONGING.   *Longed for; desired.*

To furnish me upon my *longing* journey.
                Two Gentlemen of Verona, ii. 7.

LONGLY.   *Longingly; lovingly.*

Master, you look'd so *longly* on the maid,
Perhaps you mark'd not what's the pith of all.
                Taming of the Shrew, i. 1.

LONG OF.   *Owing to; through; by means of.*

You, mistress, all this coil is *long of* you.
                Midsummer-Night's Dream, iii. 2.

O, she was naught ; and *long of* her it was
That we meet here so strangely.   *Cymbeline, v. 5.*

The good old man would fain that all were well,
So 'twere not *long of* him.   *Henry 6, P. 3, iv. 7.*

To LOOF.   *To luff; to bring a ship close to
the wind.*

She once being *loof'd*,
The noble ruin of her magic, Antony,
Claps on his sea-wing, and flies after her.
                Antony and Cleopatra, iii. 10.

To LOOK.   *To look for; to seek; to wait; to
be on the watch.*

I will *look* him, and privily relieve him.
                King Lear, iii. 3.

Then he speaks
What's in his heart ; and that is there which *looks*
With us to break his neck.   *Coriolanus, iii. 3.*

To LOOK UPON.   *To look on, as a spectator
only.*

He is my prize ; I will not *look upon.*
                Troilus and Cressida, v. 6.

Why stand we like soft-hearted women here,
Wailing our losses, while the foe doth rage ;
And *look upon,* as if the tragedy
Were play'd in jest by counterfeiting actors ?
                Henry 6, P. 3, ii. 3.

LOON.   *Rascal; villain.*

The devil damn thee black, thou cream-fac'd *loon !*
Where gott'st thou that goose-look ?   *Macbeth, v. 3.*

LOOPED.   *Full of apertures.*

How shall your houseless heads and unfed sides,
Your *loop'd* and window'd raggedness, defend you
From seasons such as these ?   *King Lear, iii. 4.*

LOOSE.   *Release; dismissal; the moment when
an arrow leaves the bow.*

And often, at his very *loose,* decides
That which long process could not arbitrate.
                Love's Labour's lost, v. 2.

LOOSE.   *Incautious; unreticent.*

Where you are liberal of your loves and counsels,
Be sure you be not *loose.*   *Henry 8, ii. 1.*

There are a kind of men so *loose* of soul,
That in their sleeps will mutter their affairs :
One of this kind is Cassio.   *Othello, iii. 3.*

LOP.   *Boughs; branches.*

Why, we take
From every tree *lop,* bark, and part o' the timber.
                Henry 8, i. 2.

LORDING.   *A lordling; a lord.*

You were pretty *lordings* then.   *Winter's Tale, i. 2.*

Lordings, farewell ; and say, when I am gone,
I prophesied—France will be lost ere long.
                Henry 6, P. 2, i. 1.

LORDLY.   *Haughty; overbearing; insolent.*

Who join'st thou with, but with a *lordly* nation,
That will not trust thee but for profit's sake ?
                Henry 6, P. 1, iii. 3.

LORDSHIP.   *Sway; rule; supremacy.*

I wonder, sir, sith wives are monsters to you,
And that you fly them as you swear them *lordship,*
Yet you desire to marry.
                All's well that ends well, v. 3.

To LOSE.   *To bewilder; to deprive of; to
waste; to lavish.*

Indeed so much,
That, as methought, her eyes had *lost* her tongue,
For she did speak in starts distractedly.
                Twelfth-Night, ii. 2.

CC

A still-soliciting eye, and such a tongue
That I am glad I have not, though not to have it
Hath *lost* me in your liking. *King Lear*, i. 1.

You cannot speak of reason to the Dane,
And *lose* your voice. *Hamlet*, i. 2.

I would they would forget me, like the virtues
Which our divines *lose* by 'em. *Coriolanus*, ii. 3.

LOSEL. *A scoundrel; a villain.*

And, *losel*, thou art worthy to be hang'd,
That wilt not stay her tongue. *Winter's Tale*, ii. 3.

LOSS. *License; freedom; desertion; exposure.*

As I subscribe not that, nor any other,
But in the *loss* of question.
Measure for Measure, ii. 4.

Poor wretch, that, for thy mother's fault, art thus
expos'd
To *loss* and what may follow! *Winter's Tale*, iii. 3.

And blessing, against this cruelty, fight on thy side,
Poor thing, condemn'd to *loss*! *Ibid.* ii. 3.

LOST. *Dead.*

And there my mate, that's never to be found
Again, lament till I am *lost*. *Winter's Tale*, v. 3.

LOTTERY. *Lot; allotment; portion.*

So let high-sighted tyranny range on,
Till each man drop by *lottery*. *Julius Cæsar*, ii. 1.

Therefore, the *lottery*, that he hath devised in
these three chests of gold, silver, and lead, will, no
doubt, never be chosen by any rightly, but one who
shall rightly love. *Merchant of Venice*, i. 2.

If beauty, wisdom, modesty, can settle
The heart of Antony, Octavia is
A blessèd *lottery* to him.
Antony and Cleopatra, ii. 2.

LOTS TO BLANKS. *Unquestionable; not to be doubted; all the world to nothing.*

If you have heard your general talk of Rome,
And of his friends there, it is *lots to blanks*,
My name hath touch'd your ears: it is Menenius.
Coriolanus, v. 2.

LOUD. *Rough; turbulent.*

So that my arrows,
Too slightly timber'd for so *loud* a wind,
Would have reverted to my bow again,
And not where I had aim'd them. *Hamlet*, iv. 7.

To LOUT. *To desert; to leave in the lurch.*

Renownèd Talbot doth expect my aid ;
And I am *louted* by a traitor villain,
And cannot help the noble chevalier.
Henry 6, P. 1, iv. 3.

LOVE. *Lover; paramour.*

And, forsooth, to search his house for his wife's *love*.
Merry Wives of Windsor, iii. 5.

To LOVE. *To please; to be pleasing to.*

For wisdom's sake, a word that all men love ;
Or for love's sake, a word that *loves* all men.
Love's Labour's lost, iv. 3.

LOVE-IN-IDLENESS. *The pansy or hearts-ease.*

And maidens call it *love-in-idleness*.
Midsummer-Night's Dream, ii. 1.

LOVE-SPRING. *Love-shoot; affection; tenderness.*

Shall, Antipholus,
Even in the spring of love, thy *love-springs* rot !
Comedy of Errors, iii. 2.

LOVELY. *Loving.*

Two *lovely* berries moulded on one stem.
Midsummer-Night's Dream, iii. 2.

When I should bid good morrow to my bride,
And seal the title with a *lovely* kiss.
Taming of the Shrew, iii. 2.

That I, unworthy body as I am,
Should censure thus on *lovely* gentlemen.
Two Gentlemen of Verona, i. 2.

LOVER. *A friend.*

Farewell, my lord : I as your *lover* speak ;
The fool slides o'er the ice that you should break.
Troilus and Cressida, iii. 3.

I tell thee, fellow,
Thy general is my *lover*. *Coriolanus*, v. 2.

LOWN. *A lout; a rascal.*

He held them sixpence all too dear,
With that he call'd the tailor *lown*. *Othello*, ii. 3.

LOYALTY. *Fidelity in love; constancy.*

And then end life when I end *loyalty*!
Midsummer-Night's Dream, ii. 2.

LUMPISH. *Dull; spiritless.*

For she is *lumpish*, heavy, melancholy.
Two Gentlemen of Verona, iii. 2.

LUNE. *A mad freak; wildness; caprice; humour.*

Why, woman, your husband is in his old *lunes* again.   *Merry Wives of Windsor,* iv. 2.
These dangerous unsafe *lunes* i' the king, beshrew them !
He must be told on't, and he shall.
          Winter's Tale, ii. 2.
Yea, watch his pettish *lunes,* his ebbs, his flows, as if
The passage and whole carriage of this action
Rode on his tide.   *Troilus and Cressida,* ii. 3.

To LURCH. *To lurk; to shift; to disappoint; to balk.*

I myself sometimes, hiding mine honour in my necessity, am fain to shuffle, to hedge, and to *lurch.*
          Merry Wives of Windsor, ii. 2.
And in the brunt of seventeen battles since,
He *lurch'd* all swords of the garland.   *Coriol.* ii. 2.

LUSH. *Rank; luxuriant.*

How *lush* and lusty the grass looks ! *Tempest,* ii. 1.
Quite over-canopied with *lush* woodbine,
With sweet musk-roses, and with eglantine.
          Midsummer-Night's Dream, ii. 1.

LUST. *Will; liking; inclination; pleasure.*

Let me be privileg'd by my place and message,
To be a speaker free ; when I am hence,
I'll answer to my *lust. Troilus and Cressida,* iv. 4.
Our unbitted *lusts;* whereof I take this, that
you call love, to be a sect or scion.   *Othello,* i. 3.
Let the superfluous and *lust*-dieted man,
That slaves your ordinance, that will not see
Because he doth not feel, feel your power quickly.
          King Lear, iv. 1.

LUSTIC. *Strong; healthy.*

Lustic, as the Dutchman says.
          All's well that ends well, ii. 3.

LUSTIHOOD. *Strength; vigour; energy.*

Reason and respect
Make livers pale, and *lustihood* deject.
          Troilus and Cressida, ii. 2.

LUSTY. *Bold; audacious; pert; saucy.*

Proud of their numbers, and secure in soul,
The confident and over *lusty* French
Do the low-rated English play at dice.
          Henry 5, iii. Chorus.
Now, by the world, it is a *lusty* wench.
          Taming of the Shrew, ii. 1.

LUXURIOUS. *Unchaste; licentious.*

She knows the heat of a *luxurious* bed.
          Much Ado about Nothing, iv. 1.

LUXURIOUSLY. *Licentiously; wantonly.*

Besides what hotter hours,
Unregister'd in vulgar fame, you have
Luxuriously pick'd out. *Antony and Cleop.* iii. 13.

LUXURY. *Licentiousness.*

Let not the royal bed of Denmark be
A couch for *luxury* and damnèd incest.
          Hamlet, i. 5.
Fie on lust and *luxury !*
          Merry Wives of Windsor, v. 5.
To't, *luxury,* pell-mell ! for I lack soldiers.
          King Lear, iv. 6.

LYM. *A bloodhound.*

Mastiff, greyhound, mongrel grim,
Hound or spaniel, brach or *lym. King Lear,* iii. 6.

M.

MACHINE. *Frame; body.*

Thine evermore, most dear lady, whilst this *machine* is to him.   *Hamlet,* ii. 2.

MACULATION. *Spot; taint; blemish.*

For I will throw my glove to Death himself,
That there's no *maculation* in thy heart.
          Troilus and Cressida, iv. 4.

MAD. *Wild; inconstant.*

How now, how now, *mad* wag !
          Henry 4, P. 1, i. 2.
She was in love ; and he she lov'd prov'd *mad,*
And did forsake her.   *Othello,* iv. 3.

To MAD. *To make mad.*

A father, and a gracious agèd man,

Whose reverence the head-lugg'd bear would lick,
Most barbarous, most degenerate! have you *madded*.
King Lear, iv. 2.
'Tis mine ; and this will witness outwardly,
As strongly as the conscience does within,
To the *madding* of her lord. *Cymbeline*, ii. 2.

MADE FOR. *Meant for ; intended to represent ; representing.*

He sits in his state, as a thing *made for* Alexander. *Coriolanus*, v. 4.

MADE-UP. *Accomplished ; thoroughpaced ;
consummate.*

Ay, and you hear him cog, see him dissemble,
Know his gross patchery, love him, feed him,
Keep in your bosom : yet remain assur'd
That he's a *made-up* villain. *Timon of Athens*, v. 1.

MAGNIFICENT. *Imperious ; haughty ; arrogant.*

A domineering pedant o'er the boy,
Than whom no mortal so *magnificent*.
Love's Labour's lost, iii. 1.

MAGNIFICO. *A grandee of Venice.*

Be assur'd of this,
That the *magnifico* is much belov'd. *Othello*, i. 2.

MAGOT-PIE. *A magpie.*

Augurs, and understood relations, have
By *magot-pies*, and choughs, and rooks, brought
forth
The secret'st man of blood. *Macbeth*, iii. 4.

MAIDHOOD. *Virginity.*

By *maidhood*, honour, truth, and every thing,
I love thee so, that, maugre all thy pride,
Nor wit nor reason can my passion hide.
Twelfth-Night, iii. 1.

MAIL. *Defensive armour.*

To have done, is to hang
Quite out of fashion, like a rusty *mail*
In monumental mockery.
Troilus and Cressida, iii. 3.

MAILED. *Clad in armour ; clothed ; covered ;
gauntleted.*

The *mailèd* Mars shall on his altar sit
Up to the ears in blood. *Henry* 4, P. 1, iv. 1.

Mail'd up in shame, with papers on my back.
Henry 6, P. 2, ii. 4.
His bloody brow
With his *mail'd* hand then wiping, forth he goes.
Coriolanus, i. 3.

MAIM. *Wrong ; injury ; loss ; detriment.*

A dearer merit, not so deep a *maim*
As to be cast forth in the common air,
Have I deservèd at your highness' hands.
Richard 2, i. 3.
Your father's sickness is a *maim* to us.—
A perilous gash, a very limb lopp'd off :
And yet, in faith, it's not. *Henry* 4, P. 1, iv. 1.

MAIMED. *Imperfect ; defective ; incomplete.*

The queen, the courtiers : who is that they follow?
And with such *maimèd* rites? *Hamlet*, v. 1.

MAIN. *The main point or question ; the main-
land ; the continent.*

I doubt it is no other but the *main*,—
His father's death, and our o'erhasty marriage.
Hamlet, ii. 2.
Goes it against the *main* of Poland, sir,
Or for some frontier? *Ibid.* iv. 4.
I know you. Where's the king ?—
Contending with the fretful elements ;
Bids the wind blow the earth into the sea,
Or swell the curlèd waters 'bove the *main*,
That things might change or cease.
King Lear, iii. 1.

TO MAIN. *To lame.*

And good reason ; for thereby is England *mained*,
and fain to go with a staff, but that my puissance
holds it up. *Henry* 6, P. 2, iv. 2.

MAJOR. *Greater.*

Fall Greeks ; fail fame ; honour or go or stay ;
My *major* vow lies here, this I'll obey.
Troilus and Cressida, v. 1.

MAJORITY. *Preeminence ; supremacy.*

Douglas, whose high deeds,
Whose hot incursions, and great name in arms,
Holds from all soldiers chief *majority*
And military title capital,
Through all the kingdoms that acknowledge Christ.
Henry 4, P. 1, iii. 2.

To MAKE. *To do; to enrich; to fasten; to bar; to earn; to get.*

But, in the beaten way of friendship, what make you at Elsinore? *Hamlet,* ii. 2.

She was in his company at Page's house, and what they *made* there, I know not.
Merry Wives of Windsor, ii. 1.

There would this monster *make* a man.
Tempest, ii. 2.

You're a *made* old man: if the sins of your youth are forgiven you, you're well to live.
Winter's Tale, iii. 3.

If our sport had gone forward, we had all been *made* men. *Midsummer-Night's Dream,* iv. 2.

And doubt not, sir, but she will well excuse Why at this time the doors are *made* against you. *Comedy of Errors,* iii. 1.

Make the doors upon a woman's wit, and it will out at the casement. *As you like it,* iv. 1.

Whether that thy youth and kind
Will the faithful offer take
Of me, and all that I can *make*. *Ibid.* iv. 3.

He's in for a commodity of brown paper and old ginger, nine-score and seventeen pounds; of which he *made* five marks, ready money.
Measure for Measure, iv. 3.

To MAKE DAINTY. *To object; to refuse.*

Which of you all
Will now deny to dance? she that *makes dainty,*
She, I'll swear, hath corns. *Romeo and Juliet,* i. 5.

To MAKE FAIR WEATHER. *To dissemble; to cajole; to flatter.*

But I must *make fair weather* yet awhile,
Till Henry be more weak, and I more strong.
Henry 6, P. 2, v. 1.

To MAKE MEANS. *To take measures; to contrive; to scheme.*

If without peril it be possible,
Sweet Blunt, *make* some good *means* to speak with him,
And give him from me this most needful note.
Richard 3, v. 3.

What *means* do you *make* to him?—
Not any; but abide the change of time.
Cymbeline, ii. 4.

The more degenerate and base art thou,
To *make* such *means* for her as thou hast done,
And leave her on such slight conditions.
Two Gentlemen of Verona, v. 4.

One that *made means* to come by what he hath,
And slaughter'd those that were the means to help him. *Richard 3,* v. 3.

To MAKE NICE. *To object; to scruple; to hesitate.*

And he that stands upon a slippery place
Makes nice of no vile hold to stay him up.
King John, iii. 4.

To MAKE REMAIN. *To stay behind; to remain; to stop.*

Let's fetch him off, or *make remain* alike.
Coriolanus, i. 4.

To MAKE UP. *To advance; to come forward.*

I beseech your majesty, *make up,*
Lest your retirement do amaze your friends.
Henry 4, P. 1, v. 4.

Pardon me, royal sir,
Election *makes* not *up* on such conditions.
King Lear, i. 1.

To MAKE WORTHY. *To extol; to praise; to magnify.*

Your virtue is,
To *make* him *worthy* whose offence subdues him,
And curse that justice did it. *Coriolanus,* i. 1.

MAKE-PEACE. *A peace-maker; a reconciler of differences.*

To be a *make-peace* shall become my age.
Richard 2, i. 1.

MAKING. *Form; ceremony; rite.*

She had all the royal *makings* of a queen,
As holy oil, Edward Confessor's crown,
The rod, and bird of peace, and all such emblems,
Laid nobly on her. *Henry 8,* iv. 1.

MALAPERT. *Pert; saucy.*

Nay, then I must have an ounce or two of this *malapert* blood from you. *Twelfth-Night,* iv. 1.

MALCONTENT. *Discontented; displeased.*

Now, brother of Clarence, how like you our choice,
That you stand pensive, as half *malcontent?*
Henry 6, P. 3, iv. 1.

MALE. *Parent; father.*

And I, the hapless *male* to one sweet bird,
Have now the fatal object in my eye,

Where my poor young was lim'd, was caught, and
kill'd.   *Henry 6*, P. 3, v. 6.

MALICE. *Destruction; mischief; violence.*

Do like the mutines of Jerusalem,
Be friends awhile, and both conjointly bend
Your sharpést deeds of *malice* on this town.
                                        King John, ii. 1.

MALICIOUS. *Destructive.*

King John, your king and England's, doth approach,
Commander of this hot *malicious* day.
                                        King John, ii. 1.

MALICIOUSLY. *Violently; hastily.*

I could do this, and that with no rash potion,
But with a lingering dram, that should not work
Maliciously like poison.   *Winter's Tale*, i. 2.

MALKIN. *A trollop; a slattern.*

The kitchen *malkin* pins
Her richest lockram 'bout her reechy neck,
Clambering the walls to eye him. *Coriolanus*, ii. 1.

TO MAMMER. *To hesitate; to doubt.*

I wonder in my soul,
What you would ask me, that I should deny,
Or stand so *mammering* on.   *Othello*, iii. 3.

TO MAMMOCK. *To tear in pieces.*

O, I warrant, how he *mammocked* it !
                                        Coriolanus, i. 3.

MAMMET. *A doll; a puppet.*

This is no world
To play with *mammets*, and to tilt with lips.
                                        Henry 4, P. 1, ii. 3.
And then to have a wretched puling fool,
A whining *mammet*, in her fortune's tender,
To answer " I'll not wed,—I cannot love,
I am too young,—I pray you, pardon me."
                                        Romeo and Juliet, iii. 5.

MAN. *A servant; a dependant.*

My brother's servants
Were then my fellows ; now they are my *men*.
                                        Tempest, ii. 1.

TO MAN. *To wait upon; to serve; to tame.*

I was never *manned* with an agate till now.
                                        Henry 4, P. 2, i. 1.
Another way I have to *man* my haggard.
                                        Taming of the Shrew, ii. 1.

MAN OF WAR. *A warrior; a soldier.*

All these well furnish'd by the Duke of Bretagne,
With eight tall ships, three thousand *men of war*,
Are making hither with all due expedience.
                                        Richard 2, ii. 1.
And what stir
Keeps good old York there with his *men of war* ?
                                        Ibid. ii. 3.

MANAGE. *Control; government; career; progress; preparation.*

Down, down I come; like glistering Phaëthon,
Wanting the *manage* of unruly jades.
                                        Richard 2, iii. 3.
Which now the *manage* of two kingdoms must
With fearful bloody issue arbitrate.
                                        King John, i. 1.
Full merrily
Hath this brave *manage*, this career, been run.
                                        Love's Labour's lost, v. 2.
O noble prince, I can discover all
The unlucky *manage* of this fatal brawl.
                                        Romeo and Juliet, iii. 1.
Expedient *manage* must be made, my liege,
Ere further leisure yield them further means
For their advantage, and your highness' loss.
                                        Richard 2, i. 4.

TO MANAGE. *To wield.*

Yea, distaff-women *manage* rusty bills
Against thy seat.   *Richard 2*, iii. 2.

MANHOOD. *Resolution; courage.*

With slight and *manhood* stole to Rhesus' tents,
And brought from thence the Thracian fatal steeds.
                                        Henry 6, P. 3, iv. 2.

MANKIND. *Masculine; immodest; shameless.*

A *mankind* witch ! Hence with her, out o' door !
                                        Winter's Tale, ii. 3.
You shall stay too : I would I had the power
To say so to my husband.—
                Are you *mankind* ?   *Coriolanus*, iv. 2.

MANNER. *Custom; habit; fashion; kind; sort.*

My lady,—to the *manner* of the days,—
In courtesy, gives undeserving praise.
                                        Love's Labour's lost, v. 2.
But to my mind,—though I am native here,
And to the *manner* born,—it is a custom
More honour'd in the breach than the observance.
                                        Hamlet, i. 4.

And to give notice, that no *manner* person
Have any time recourse unto the princes.
      Richard 3, iii. 5.
What *manner* of man, an it like your majesty?
      Henry 4, P. 1, ii. 4.

MANNISH. *Manly; masculine.*

And let us, Polydore, though now our voices
Have got the *mannish* crack, sing him to the ground,
As once our mother.   *Cymbeline,* iv. 2.

MANSIONRY. *Abode; residence.*

The temple-haunting martlet does approve,
By his lov'd *mansionry,* that the heaven's breath
Smells wooingly here.   *Macbeth,* i. 6.

MANY. *The multitude.*

O thou fond *many!* with what loud applause
Didst thou beat heaven with blessing Bolingbroke,
Before he was what thou wouldst have him be !
      Henry 4, P. 2, i. 3.

TO MAP. *To set down as on a map; to describe.*

I am near to the place where they should meet,
if Pisanio have *mapped* it truly. *Cymbeline,* iv. 1.

MAPPERY. *Map-making.*

They call this bed-work, *mappery,* closet-war.
     Troilus and Cressida, i. 3.

MARCHES. *Borders; confines.*

They of those *marches,* gracious sovereign,
Shall be a wall sufficient to defend
Our inland from the pilfering borderers.
      Henry 5, i. 2.

MARCHPANE. *A sort of cake.*

Good thou, save me a piece of *marchpane.*
     Romeo and Juliet, i. 5.

MARGENT. *Margin; edge; border.*

Writ on both sides the leaf, *margent* and all.
     Love's Labour's lost, v. 1.
Or in the beachèd *margent* of the sea.
    Midsummer-Night's Dream, ii. 1.
And what obscur'd in this fair volume lies
Find written in the *margent* of his eyes.
     Romeo and Juliet, i. 3.
I knew you must be edified by the *margent* ere
you had done.   *Hamlet,* v. 2.

MARISH. *A marsh; a swamp.*

Our isle be made a *marish* of salt tears,
And none but women left to wail the dead.
      Henry 6, P. 1, i. 1.

MARK. *Image; a coin so called; reputation; note.*

He was the *mark* and glass, copy and book,
That fashion'd others. *Henry* 4, P. 2, ii. 3.
 I have lost a seal-ring of my grandfather's worth
forty *mark.*   *Ibid.* P. 1, iii. 3.
Opinion, that did help me to the crown,
Had still kept loyal to possession ;
And left me in reputeless banishment,
A fellow of no *mark,* nor likelihood.
     Ibid. P. 1, iii. 2.

MARROW. *Pith; energy; vigour.*

Now the time is flush,
When crouching *marrow,* in the bearer strong,
Cries, of itself, "No more." *Timon of Athens,* v. 4.

MARSHAL. *A harbinger; a forerunner.*

Reason becomes the *marshal* to my will.
    Midsummer-Night's Dream, ii. 2.

MART. *Trade; traffic; market.*

And why such daily cost of brazen cannon,
And foreign *mart* for implements of war. *Haml.* i. 1.
 Soon at five o'clock,
Please you, I'll meet with you upon the *mart.*
     Comedy of Errors, i. 2.

TO MART. *To buy or sell; to traffic; to trade dishonourably.*

You have let him go, and nothing *marted* with him.
      Winter's Tale, iv. 3.
To sell and *mart* your offices for gold.
     Julius Cæsar, iv. 3.

MARY-BUD. *The marigold.*

And winking *Mary-buds* begin
To ope their golden eyes. *Cymbeline,* ii. 3.

TO MASK. *To masquerade; to go about in disguise.*

The king hath many *masking* in his coats.
     Henry 4, P. 1, v. 3.

MASTERDOM. *Dominion; rule; supremacy.*

    And you shall put
This night's great business into my dispatch ;

Which shall to all our nights and days to come
Give solely sovereign sway and *masterdom.*
    Macbeth, i. 5.

MASTERSHIP. *Ability; skill; mastery.*

You were us'd to say,
That, when the sea was calm, all boats alike
Show'd *mastership* in floating. *Coriolanus,* iv. 1.

MATCH. *Scheme; device; agreement; bargain; compact.*

What cunning *match* have you made with this
jest of the drawer?   *Henry* 4, P. 1, ii. 4.
Now shall we know, if Gadshill have set a
match.   *Ibid.* i. 2.
There I have another bad *match :* a bankrupt, a
prodigal, who dare scarce show his head on the
Rialto.   *Merchant of Venice,* iii. 1.
You, Polydore, have prov'd best woodman, and
Are master of the feast : Cadwal and I
Will play the cook and servant ; 'tis our *match.*
    Cymbeline, iii. 6.

MATCHED. *Joined; combined.*

The only soil of his fair virtue's gloss
Is a sharp wit *match'd* with too blunt a will.
    Love's Labour's lost, ii. 1.

TO MATE. *To confound; to bewilder; to crush; to compete with; to oppose.*

So, good night :
My mind she has *mated,* and amaz'd my sight.
    Macbeth, v. 1.
Not mad, but *mated ;* how, I do not know.
    Comedy of Errors, iii. 2.
For that is good deceit
Which *mates* him first that first intends deceit.
    Henry 6, P. 2, iii. 1.
That in the way of loyalty and truth
Toward the king, my ever-royal master,
Dare *mate* a sounder man than Surrey can be,
And all that love his follies. *Henry* 8, iii. 2.

MATERIAL. *Sensible; full of matter; original; parental.*

A *material* fool.   *As you like it,* iii. 3.
She that herself will sliver and disbranch
From her *material* sap, perforce must wither,
And come to deadly use. *King Lear,* iv. 2.

MATIN. *Morning.*

The glow-worm shows the *matin* to be near,
And gins to pale his uneffectual fire. *Hamlet,* i. 5.

MAW. *The stomach.*

And none of you will bid the winter come,
To thrust his icy fingers in my *maw.*
    King John, v. 7.

MAZARD. *The head.*

Why, e'en so : and now my Lady Worm's ;
chapless, and knocked about the *mazard* with a
sexton's spade.   *Hamlet,* v. 1.
Let me go, sir,
Or I'll knock you o'er the *mazard.* *Othello,* ii. 3.

MAZE. *A labyrinth.*

And the quaint *mazes* in the wanton green,
For lack of tread, are undistinguishable.
    Midsummer-Night's Dream, ii. 2.

TO MAZE. *To perplex; to bewilder; to alarm.*

And the *mazèd* world,
By their increase, now knows not which is which.
    Midsummer-Night's Dream, ii. 1.
A little herd of England's timorous deer,
Maz'd with a yelping kennel of French curs.
    Henry 6, P. 1, iv. 2.

MEACOCK. *Tame; timorous; effeminate.*

How tame, when men and women are alone,
A *meacock* wretch can make the curstest shrew !
    Taming of the Shrew, ii. 1.

MEAGRE. *Poor; hungry; barren.*

But thou, thou *meagre* lead,
Which rather threatenest than dost promise aught,
Thy plainness moves me more than eloquence.
    Merchant of Venice, iii. 2.

MEALED. *Mixed; carded; compounded.*

Were he *meal'd* with that
Which he corrects, then were he tyrannous.
    Measure for Measure, iv. 2.

MEAN. *A tenor in music; moan; sorrow.*

Nay, he can sing a *mean* most meanly.
    Love's Labour's lost, v. 2.
Three-man songmen all, and very good ones ;
but they are most of them *means* and bases.
    Winter's Tale, iv. 2.
Our *means* secure us, and our mere defects
Prove our commodities. *King Lear,* iv. 1.

MEAN. *Moderate; not great.*

Good Lord Boyet, my beauty, though but *mean,*
Needs not the painted flourish of your praise.
    Love's Labour's lost, ii. 1.

MEASLE. *A leper.*

> So shall my lungs
> Coin words till their decay against those *measles.*
> > *Coriolanus,* iii. 1.

MEASURE. *Music; a kind of dance; moderation; extent; limit.*

> Shall braying trumpets and loud churlish drums,—
> Clamours of hell,—be *measures* to our pomp?
> > *King John,* iii. 1.

> Our stern alarums chang'd to merry meetings,
> Our dreadful marches to delightful *measures.*
> > *Richard 3,* i. 1.

> And twenty glow-worms shall our lanterns be
> To guide our *measure* round about the tree.
> > *Merry Wives of Windsor,* v. 5.

> O love, be moderate; allay thy ecstasy;
> In *measure* rain thy joy; scant this excess!
> > *Merchant of Venice,* iii. 2.

> Thurio, give back, or else embrace thy death;
> Come not within the *measure* of my wrath.
> > *Two Gentlemen of Verona,* v. 4.

MEASURELESS. *Boundless.*

> *Measureless* liar, thou hast made my heart
> Too great for what contains it. *Coriolanus,* v. 6.

> This diamond he greets your wife withal,
> By the name of most kind hostess; and shut up
> In *measureless* content. *Macbeth,* ii. 1.

MECHANIC. *Mean; servile.*

> Rebukable,
> And worthy shameful check it were, to stand
> On more *mechanic* compliment.
> > *Antony and Cleopatra,* iv. 4.

MECHANICAL. *A mechanic; a workman.*

> A crew of patches, rude *mechanicals,*
> That work for bread upon Athenian stalls,
> Were met together to rehearse a play,
> Intended for great Theseus' nuptial-day.
> > *Midsummer-Night's Dream,* iii. 2.

MECHANICAL. *Of the working class.*

> What! know you not,
> Being *mechanical,* you ought not walk
> Upon a labouring day without the sign
> Of your profession? *Julius Cæsar,* i. 1.

> Hang him, *mechanical* salt-butter rogue!
> > *Merry Wives of Windsor,* ii. 2.

TO MEDDLE. *To mix; to mingle with; to enter into.*

> More to know
> Did never *meddle* with my thoughts. *Tempest,* i. 2.

TO MEDDLE OR MAKE. *To interfere.*

> For my part, I'll *meddle* nor make no more i'
> the matter. *Troilus and Cressida,* i. 2.

> I will cut his troat in de park; and I will teach
> a scurvy jack-a-nape priest to *meddle or make.*
> > *Merry Wives of Windsor,* i. 4.

MEDICINABLE. *Medicinal; salutary.*

> Some griefs are *med'cinable.* *Cymbeline,* iii. 2.

> Any cross, any impediment will be *medicinable*
> to me. *Much Ado about Nothing,* ii. 2.

> Of one, whose subdu'd eyes,
> Albeit unus'd to the melting mood,
> Drop tears as fast as the Arabian trees
> Their *med'cinable* gum. *Othello,* v. 2.

MEDICINE. *A physician; the elixir employed by the alchemists in the transmutation of metals.*

> I have seen a *medicine*
> That's able to breathe life into a stone.
> > *All's well that ends well,* ii. 1.

> Meet we the *medicine* of the sickly weal.
> > *Macbeth,* v. 2.

> How much unlike art thou Mark Antony!
> Yet, coming from him, that great *medicine* hath
> With his tinct gilded thee.
> > *Antony and Cleopatra,* i. 5.

TO MEDICINE. *To cure; to restore.*

> Great griefs, I see, *medicine* the less, for Cloten
> Is quite forgot. *Cymbeline,* iv. 2.

> Not poppy, nor mandragora,
> Nor all the drowsy syrups of the world,
> Shall ever *medicine* thee to that sweet sleep
> Which thou ow'dst yesterday. *Othello,* iii. 3.

MEDITERRANEUM. *The Mediterranean Sea.*

> Now, by the salt wave of the *Mediterraneum,* a
> sweet touch, a quick venue of wit.
> > *Love's Labour's lost,* v. 1.

MEED. *Desert; merit; excellence; gift; present.*

> That's not my fear; my *meed* hath got me fame.
> > *Henry 6, P. 3,* iv. 7.

But in the imputation laid on him by them, in
his *need* he's unfellowed. *Hamlet,* v. 2.
Plutus, the god of gold,
Is but his steward : no *meed,* but he repays
Sevenfold above itself. *Timon of Athens,* i. 1.

MEEK. *Tame; humbled.*
Doing the honour of thy lordliness
To one so *meek.* *Antony and Cleopatra,* v. 2.

MEET WITH. *Even with.*
Faith, niece, you tax Signior Benedick too much ;
but he'll be *meet with* you, I doubt it not.
Much Ado about Nothing, i. 1.

TO MEET WITH. *To counteract; to frustrate ;
to clash with ; to be opposed to.*
Spirit,
We must prepare to *meet with* Caliban.
Tempest, iv. 1.
How rarely does it *meet with* this time's guise,
When man was wish'd to love his enemies !
Timon of Athens, iv. 3.

MEINY. *Retainers ; followers ; dependants.*
On whose contents,
They summon'd up their *meiny ;* straight took horse.
King Lear, ii. 4.

MEMORIAL. *A monument.*
I pray you, let us satisfy our eyes
With the *memorials* and the things of fame
That do renown this city. *Twelfth-Night,* iii. 3.

MEMORIAL. *Preservative of memory.*
And sighs, and takes my glove,
And gives *memorial* dainty kisses to it,
As I kiss thee. *Troilus and Cressida,* v. 2.

TO MEMORIZE. *To make memorable.*
I persuade me, from her
Will fall some blessing to this land, which shall
In it be *memoriz'd.* *Henry 8,* iii. 2.
Except they meant to bathe in reeking wounds,
Or *memorize* another Golgotha,
I cannot tell. *Macbeth,* i. 2.

MEMORY. *Memorial ; monument.*
O my sweet master ! O you *memory*
Of old Sir Roland ! *As you like it,* ii. 3.
These weeds are *memories* of those worser hours :
I prithee, put them off. *King Lear,* iv. 7.

A good *memory,*
And witness of the malice and displeasure
Which thou shouldst bear me. *Coriolanus,* iv. 5.
Though in this city he
Hath widow'd and unchilded many a one,
Which to this hour bewail the injury,
Yet he shall have a noble *memory.* *Ibid.* v. 6.

TO MEND. *To grace; to enrich.*
Believe't, dear lord,
You *mend* the jewel by the wearing it.
Timon of Athens, i. 1.

MENDS. *Amends ; remedy.*
If she be fair, 'tis the better for her ; an she be
not, she has the *mends* in her own hands.
Troilus and Cressida, i. 1.

MERCATANTE. *A merchant ; a trader.*
A *mercatantè,* or a pedant,
I know not what ; but formal in apparel,
In gait and countenance surely like a father.
Taming of the Shrew, iv. 2.

MERCENARY. *A hired soldier.*
So that, in these ten thousand they have lost,
There are but sixteen hundred *mercenaries.*
Henry 5, iv. 8.

MERCHANT. *A merchant-man ; a trading-
vessel ; a chap ; a fellow.*
Every day, some sailor's wife,
The master of some *merchant,* and the merchant,
Have just our theme of woe. *Tempest,* ii. 1.
This is a riddling *merchant* for the nonce.
Henry 6, P. 1, ii. 3.
What saucy *merchant* was this, that was so full
of his ropery ? *Romeo and Juliet,* ii. 4.

MERE. *Absolute ; entire ; only.*
Take but degree away, untune that string,
And, hark, what discord follows ! each thing meets
In *mere* oppugnancy. *Troilus and Cressida,* i. 3.
Our means secure us, and our *mere* defects
Prove our commodities. *King Lear,* iv. 1.
He cried upon it at the *merest* loss,
And twice to-day pick'd out the dullest scent :
Trust me, I take him for the better dog.
Taming of the Shrew, Induction, sc. 1.
Your pleasure was my *mere* offence, my punishment
Itself, and all my treason ; that I suffer'd
Was all the harm I did. *Cymbeline,* v. 5.

To MERE.   *To bound; to limit; to divide.*

The itch of his affection should not then
Have nick'd his captainship; at such a point,
When half to half the world oppos'd, he being
The *meràd* question.   *Antony and Cleopatra*, iii. 13.

MERELY.   *Absolutely; entirely.*

We are *merely* cheated of our lives by drunkards.
           Tempest, i. 2.
      'Tis an unweeded garden,
That grows to seed; things rank and gross in nature
Possess it *merely.*   *Hamlet*, i. 2.
     That I drave my suitor from his mad humour
of love to a living humour of madness; which was,
to forswear the full stream of the world, and to
live in a nook *merely* monastic.
           As you like it, iii. 2.

MERIT.   *Meed; recompense; reward.*

A dearer *merit*, not so deep a maim
As to be cast forth in the common air,
Have I deservèd at your highness' hands.
           Richard 2, i. 3.

MERITS.   *Deserts.*

Be't known that we, the greatest, are misthought
For things that others do; and, when we fall,
We answer others' *merits* in our name,
Are therefore to be pitied.
           Antony and Cleopatra, v. 2.

MERMAID.   *A syren.*

     Thou remember'st
Since once I sat upon a promontory,
And heard a *mermaid*, on a dolphin's back,
Uttering such dulcet and harmonious breath,
That the rude sea grew civil at her song.
           Midsummer-Night's Dream, ii. 2.

O, train me not, sweet *mermaid*, with thy note!
           Comedy of Errors, iii. 2.
     At the helm
A seeming *mermaid* steers.
           Antony and Cleopatra, ii. 2.

MESS.   *A party or set of four dining together; a company; a gang.*

     But that our feasts
In every *mess* have folly, I should blush
To see you so attir'd.   *Winter's Tale*, iv. 3.
     Now your traveller,—
He and his toothpick at my worship's *mess.*
           King John, i. 1.

Lower *messes*
Perchance are to this business purblind? say.
           Winter's Tale, i. 2.
You three fools lack'd me fool to make up the *mess.*
           Love's Labour's lost, iv. 3.
We have had pastimes here and pleasant game:
A *mess* of Russians left us but of late.   *Ibid.* v. 2.
Where are your *mess* of sons to back you now?
           Henry 6, P. 3, i. 4.

METAPHYSICAL.   *Supernatural.*

And chastise with the valour of my tongue
All that impedes thee from the golden round, ·
Which fate and *metaphysical* aid doth seem
To have thee crown'd withal.   *Macbeth*, i. 5.

To METE.   *To measure; to judge of; to estimate.*

     And their memory
Shall as a pattern or a measure live,
By which his grace must *mete* the lives of others,
Turning past evils to advantages.
           Henry 4, P. 2, iv. 4.

METE-YARD.   *A yard-measure.*

Give me thy *mete-yard*, and spare not me.
           Taming of the Shrew, iv. 3.

METTLE.   *Courage; spirit; substance.*

     Though care killed a cat, thou hast *mettle* enough
in thee to kill care.   *Much Ado about Nothing*, v. 1.
What a blunt fellow is this grown to be!
He was quick *mettle* when he went to school.
           Julius Cæsar, i. 2.
     Whose self-same *mettle*,
Whereof thy proud child, arrogant man, is puff'd,
Engenders the black toad and adder blue.
           Timon of Athens, iv. 3.

To MEW.   *To shut up; to imprison.*

Why should your fears, then, move you to *mew* up
Your tender kinsman?   *King John*, iv. 2.
For aye to be in shady cloister *mew'd.*
           Midsummer-Night's Dream, i. 1.
And therefore has he closely *mew'd* her up,
Because he will not be annoy'd with suitors.
           Taming of the Shrew, i. 1.

MICHER.   *A truant; an idler; a loiterer.*

     Shall the blessed sun of heaven prove a *micher*,
and eat blackberries? a question not to be asked.
           Henry 4, P. 1, ii. 4.

MICKLE. *Much; great.*

The one ne'er got me credit, the other *mickle* blame.
Comedy of Errors, iii. 1.

O, *mickle* is the powerful grace that lies
In herbs, plants, stones, and their true qualities.
Romeo and Juliet, ii. 3.

MIDDEST. *Midst.*

Have through the very *middest* of you.
Henry 6, P. 2, iv. 7.

MILCH. *Pale.*

The instant burst of clamour that she made—
Unless things mortal move them not at all—
Would have made *milch* the burning eyes of heaven,
And passion in the gods.   *Hamlet,* ii. 2.

MILITARIST. *A soldier.*

This is Monsieur Parolles, the gallant *militarist.*
All's well that ends well, iv. 3.

MIMIC. *An actor; a player.*

Anon his Thisbe must be answerèd,
And forth my *mimic* comes.
Midsummer-Night's Dream, iii. 2.

To MINCE. *To walk or talk affectedly; to extenuate; to soften; to abate.*

And turn two *mincing* steps into a manly stride.
Merchant of Venice, iii. 4.

Hold up your head, and *mince.*
Merry Wives of Windsor, v. 1.

I know no ways to *mince* it in love, but directly
to say, I love you.   *Henry* 5, v. 2.

Thy honesty and love doth *mince* this matter,
Making it light to Cassio.   *Othello,* ii. 3.

Speak to me home, *mince* not the general tongue.
Antony and Cleopatra, i. 2.

MINCING. *Affectation; scrupulousness.*

Which gifts,—
Saving your *mincing,*—the capacity
Of your soft cheveril conscience would receive,
If you might please to stretch it.   *Henry* 8, ii. 3.

MIND. *Disposition; temper; love; imagination; command; wish.*

'Tis pity bounty had not eyes behind,
That man might ne'er be wretched for his *mind.*
Timon of Athens, i. 2.

O my master!
Your *mind* to her is now as low as were
Thy fortunes.   *Cymbeline,* iii. 2.

Still be kind,
And eke out our performance with your *mind.*
Henry 5, ii. Chorus.

For servants must their masters' *minds* fulfil.
Comedy of Errors, iv. 1.

To MIND. *To remind; to call to mind; to mean; to heed; to take notice of.*

I *minded* him how royal 'twas to pardon
When it was least expected.   *Coriolanus,* v. 1.

I beseech you, rather
Let me be punish'd, that have *minded* you
Of what you should forget.   *Winter's Tale,* iii. 2.

Minding true things by what their mockeries be.
Henry 5, iii. Chorus.

Belike she *minds* to play the Amazon.
Henry 6, P. 3, iv. 1.

I'll fall flat; perchance he will not *mind* me.
Tempest, ii. 2.

MINDED. *Inclined to; disposed.*

Which, too much *minded* by herself alone,
May be put from her by society.
Romeo and Juliet, iv. 1.

Who's there, besides foul weather?—
One *minded* like the weather, most unquietly.
King Lear, iii. 1.

We come but to know
How you stand *minded* in the weighty difference
Between the king and you.   *Henry* 8, iii. 1.

MINDLESS. *Unmindful; regardless.*

I have heard, and griev'd,
How cursèd Athens, *mindless* of thy worth,
Forgetting thy great deeds, when neighbour states,
But for thy sword and fortune, trod upon them.
Timon of Athens, iv. 3.

To MINE. *To undermine; to mar; to taint; to corrupt.*

He lets me feed with his hinds, bars me the
place of a brother, and, as much as lies in his power,
mines my gentility with my education.
As you like it, i. 1.

MINGLE. *Compound; conjunction; union.*

He was not sad,—for he would shine on those
That make their looks by his; he was not merry,—
Which seem'd to tell them his remembrance lay
In Egypt with his joy; but between both:
O heavenly *mingle!*   *Antony and Cleopatra,* i. 5.

Trumpeters,
With brazen din blast you the city's ear,
Make *mingle* with our rattling tabourines.
　　　　　Antony and Cleopatra, iv. 8.

MINIKIN. *Small; diminutive.*

And for one blast of thy *minikin* mouth
Thy sheep shall take no harm. *King Lear*, iii. 6.

MINIMUS. *A pigmy.*

You *minimus*, of hindering knot-grass made.
　　　　　Midsummer-Night's Dream, iii. 2.

To MINISTER. *To administer medicine; to prescribe.*

Canst thou not *minister* to a mind diseas'd?
　　　　　Macbeth, v. 3.

MINSTRELSY. *A minstrel.*

But, I protest, I love to hear him lie;
And I will use him for my *minstrelsy.*
　　　　　Love's Labour's lost, i. 1.

MINUTE-JACK. *A jack o' the clock.* (Which see.)

Cap and knee slaves, vapours, and *minute-jacks!*
　　　　　Timon of Athens, iii. 6.

MIRABLE. *Admirable; wonderful.*

Not Neoptolemus so *mirable*
Could promise to himself
A thought of added honour torn from Hector.
　　　　　Troilus and Cressida, iv. 5.

To MIRACLE. *To beget wonder.*

I'm not their father; yet who this should be,
Doth *miracle* itself, lov'd before me.
　　　　　Cymbeline, iv. 2.

To MIRE. *To stick in the mud; to be bogged.*

Paint till a horse may *mire* upon your face.
　　　　　Timon of Athens, iv. 3.

To MISBECOME. *To dishonour; to sully; to bring shame upon.*

Which parti-coated presence of loose love
Put on by us, if, in your heavenly eyes,
Have *misbecom'd* our oaths and gravities,
Those heavenly eyes, that look into these faults,
Suggested us to make them.
　　　　　Love's Labour's lost, v. 2.

To MISCARRY. *To die; to perish.*

But so it must be, if the king *miscarry.*
　　　　　Richard 3, i. 3.
Have you not heard speak of Mariana, the sister
of Frederick the great soldier who *miscarried* at
sea?　　　　　*Measure for Measure*, iii. 1.
I would not have him *miscarry* for the half of
my dowry.　　　　　*Twelfth-Night*, iii. 4.
Then threw he down himself, and all their lives
That by indictment and by dint of sword
Have since *miscarried* under Bolingbroke.
　　　　　Henry 4, P. 2, iv. 1.

To MISCHIEF. *To hurt; to injure.*

Grant I may ever love, and rather woo
Those that would *mischief* me than those that do!
　　　　　Timon of Athens, iv. 3.

MISCONCEIVED. *Mistaken; ignorant.*

No, *misconceived!* Joan of Arc hath been
A virgin from her tender infancy,
Chaste and immaculate in very thought.
　　　　　Henry 6, P. 1, v. 4.

MISCONSTRUCTION. *Misrepresentation.*

It pleas'd the king his master very late
To strike at me, upon his *misconstruction.*
　　　　　King Lear, ii. 2.

To MISCONSTRUE. *To misjudge.*

Lest, through thy wild behaviour,
I be *misconstru'd* in the place I go to,
And lose my hopes.　　*Merchant of Venice*, ii. 2.
If he outlive the envy of this day,
England did never owe so sweet a hope,
So much *misconstru'd* in his wantonness.
　　　　　Henry 4, P. 1, v. 2.

MISCREATE. *False; invalid.*

Or nicely charge your understanding soul
With opening titles *miscreate*, whose right
Suits not in native colours with the truth.
　　　　　Henry 5, i. 2.

MISDOUBT. *Hesitation; want of confidence.*

Now, York, or never, steel thy fearful thoughts,
And change *misdoubt* to resolution.
　　　　　Henry 6, P. 2, iii. 1.

To MISDOUBT. *To suspect; to doubt.*

The bird that hath been limèd in a bush,
With trembling wings *misdoubteth* every bush.
　　　　　Henry 6, P. 3, v. 6.
I do not *misdoubt* my wife; but I would be
loth to turn them together.
　　　　　Merry Wives of Windsor, ii. 1.

Do you *misdoubt* this sword and these my wounds?
　　　Antony and Cleopatra, iii. 7.
If you *misdoubt* me that I am not she,
I know not how I shall assure you further.
　　　All's well that ends well, iii. 7.

MISERY. *Avarice.*

He covets less
Than *misery* itself would give.　*Coriolanus*, ii. 2.

MISER. *A wretch; a mean fellow.*

Decrepit *miser!* base ignoble wretch!
　　　Henry 6, P. 1, v. 4.

MISGOVERNED. *Unruly; barbarous.*

At that sad stop, my lord,
Where rude *misgovern'd* hands from windows' tops
Threw dust and rubbish on King Richard's head.
　　　Richard 2, v. 2.

MISGOVERNMENT. *Misconduct; frailty.*

Thus, pretty lady,
I am sorry for thy much *misgovernment.*
　　　Much Ado about Nothing, iv. 1.

MISLIKE. *Disapprobation; dislike.*

Setting your scorns, and your *mislike* aside,
Tell me some reason why the Lady Grey
Should not become my wife and England's queen.
　　　Henry 6, P. 3, iv. 1.

TO MISLIKE. *To dislike.*

Mislike me not for my complexion.
　　　Merchant of Venice, ii. 1.

TO MISPRISE. *To mistake; to despise.*

You spend your passion on a *mispris'd* mood.
　　　Midsummer-Night's Dream, iii. 2.
Disdain and scorn ride sparkling in her eyes,
Misprising what they look on.
　　　Much Ado about Nothing, iii. 1.

MISPRISION. *Mistake; misconception.*

There is some strange *misprision* in the princes.
　　　Much Ado about Nothing, iv. 1.
Of thy *misprision* must perforce ensue
Some true-love turn'd, and not a false turn'd true.
　　　Midsummer-Night's Dream, iii. 2.
Misprision in the highest degree!
　　　Twelfth-Night, i. 5.

MISPROUD. *Overweening; arrogant.*

Impairing Henry, strengthening *misproud* York,
The common people swarm like summer flies.
　　　Henry 6, P. 3, ii. 6.

MISS. *Loss; want.*

O, I should have a heavy *miss* of thee,
If I were much in love with vanity!
　　　Henry 4, P. 1, v. 4.

TO MISS. *To spare; to do without; to lack; to want.*

But, as 'tis, we cannot *miss* him.　*Tempest*, i. 2.
What I can help thee to, thou shalt not *miss*.
　　　All's well that ends well, i. 3.

MIS-SHAPEN. *Ill directed.*

Thy wit, that ornament to shape and love,
Mis-shapen in the conduct of them both,
Like powder in a skilless soldier's flask,
Is set a-fire by thine own ignorance,
And thou dismember'd with thine own defence.
　　　Romeo and Juliet, iii. 3.

MISSING. *Flight; absence.*

Lord Cloten,
Upon my lady's *missing*, came to me
With his sword drawn; foam'd at the mouth, and swore,
If I discover'd not which way she was gone,
It was my instant death.　*Cymbeline*, v. 5.

MISSINGLY. *From time to time; occasionally.*

But I have *missingly* noted, he is of late much
retired from court.　*Winter's Tale*, iv. 1.

MISSION. *Cabal; party; faction.*

Whose glorious deeds, but in these fields of late,
Made emulous *missions* 'mongst the gods themselves,
And drave great Mars to faction.
　　　Troilus and Cressida, iii. 3.

MISSIVE. *Messenger.*

While I stood rapt in the wonder of it, came
missives from the king, who all-hailed me, "Thane
of Cawdor."　*Macbeth*, i. 5.
You did pocket up my letters, and with taunts
Did gibe my *missive* out of audience.
　　　Antony and Cleopatra, ii. 2.

TO MISTAKE. *To be deceived in; to misjudge; to misunderstand.*

O peace, Prince Dauphin!
You are too much *mistaken* in this king.
　　　Henry 5, ii. 4.
Yet, had he *mistook* him, and sent to me, I

should ne'er have denied his occasion so many talents. *Timon of Athens*, iii. 2.
Your rage *mistakes* us. *Henry 8*, iii. 1.
    I am sorry
To hear this of him; and could wish he were
Something *mistaken* in't. *Ibid.* i. 1.

MISTEMPERED. *Disorderly; fierce; angry.*
Throw your *mistemper'd* weapons to the ground.
Romeo and Juliet, i. 1.
This inundation of *mistemper'd* humour
Rests by you only to be qualified. *King John*, v. 1.

TO MISTHINK. *To think ill of; to blame.*
Be it known, that we, the greatest, are *misthought*
For things that others do.
Antony and Cleopatra, v. 2.
How will the country for these woful chances
Misthink the king, and not be satisfied!
Henry 6, P. 3, ii. 5.

MISTREADING. *Misdeed.*
    Mark'd
For the hot vengeance and the rod of heaven
To punish my *mistreadings*. *Henry 4*, P. 1, iii. 2.

MISTRUST. *Doubt; suspicion.*
None but that ugly treason of *mistrust*,
Which makes me fear the enjoying of my love.
Merchant of Venice, iii. 2.

TO MISTRUST. *To suspect; to doubt.*
All's true that is *mistrusted*. *Winter's Tale*, ii. 1.

MISUSE. *Ill usage; outrage; villany.*
Upon whose dead corpse' there was such *misuse*
By those Welshwomen done, as may not be
Without much shame retold or spoken of.
Henry 4, P. 1, i. 1.

TO MISUSE. *To abuse; to deceive.*
Proof enough to *misuse* the prince, to vex Claudio, to undo Hero, and kill Leonato.
Much Ado about Nothing, ii. 2.

MO. *More.*
Sing no more ditties, sing no *mo*
Of dumps so dull and heavy.
Much Ado about Nothing, ii. 3.

TO MOBLE. *To wrap up ; to muffle.*
But who, O, who had seen the *mobled* queen
Run barefoot up and down, threatening the flames
With bisson rheum. *Hamlet*, ii. 2.

TO MOCK. *To pretend; to simulate; to feign.*
I long till Edward fall by war's mischance,
For *mocking* marriage with a dame of France.
Henry 6, P. 3, iii. 3.
Being so frustrate, tell him, he *mocks*
The pauses that he makes.
Antony and Cleopatra, v. 1.

MODE. *Form; method.*
And now my death changes the *mode*.
Henry 4, P. 2, iv. 4.

MODEL. *Mould; image; representative.*
And nothing can we call our own but death,
And that small *model* of the barren earth
Which serves as paste and cover to our bones.
Richard 2, iii. 2.
O England!—*model* to thy inward greatness,
Like little body with a mighty heart!
Henry 5, i. Chorus.
And then all this thou see'st is but a clod
And *model* of confounded royalty. *King John*, v. 7.
    Thou dost consent
In some large measure to thy father's death,
In that thou seest thy wretched brother die,
Who was the *model* of thy father's life.
Richard 2, i. 2.
Come, bring forth this counterfeit *model*.
All's well that ends well, iv. 3.
In which I have commended to his goodness
The *model* of our chaste loves, his young daughter.
Henry 8, iv. 2.

MODERN. *Trite; common; ordinary.*
    And then the justice,
With eyes severe and beard of formal cut,
Full of wise saws and *modern* instances.
As you like it, ii. 7.
Those that are in extremity of either are abominable fellows, and betray themselves to every *modern* censure worse than drunkards. *Ibid.* iv. 1.
Which cannot hear a lady's feeble voice,
Which scorns a *modern* invocation.
King John, iii. 4.
Her infinite cunning, with her *modern* grace,
Subdu'd me to her rate.
All's well that ends well, v. 3.
Immoment toys, things of such dignity
As we greet *modern* friends withal.
Antony and Cleopatra, v. 2.
They say miracles are past; and we have our philosophical persons, to make *modern* and familiar, things supernatural and causeless.
All's well that ends well, ii. 3.

Where violent sorrow seems a *modern* ecstasy.
Macbeth, iv. 3.

Why follow'd not, when she said "Tybalt's dead,"
Thy father, or thy mother, nay, or both,
Which *modern* lamentation might have mov'd?
Romeo and Juliet, iii. 2.

MODEST. *Unostentatious; unassuming; diffident; becoming.*

Garnish'd and deck'd in *modest* complement.
Henry 5, ii. 2.

How *modest* in exception, and withal
How terrible in constant resolution! *Ibid.* ii. 4.

Resolve me, with all *modest* haste, which way
Thou might'st deserve, or they impose, this usage.
King Lear, ii. 4.

MODESTLY. *Simply; plainly; without exaggeration.*

And, since you know you cannot see yourself
So well as by reflection, I, your glass,
Will *modestly* discover to yourself
That of yourself which you yet know not of.
Julius Cæsar, i. 2.

MODESTY. *Gentleness; moderation; forbearance; simplicity.*

Deliver this with *modesty* to the queen.
Henry 8, ii. 2.

The enemies of Cæsar shall say this;
Then, in a friend, it is cold *modesty.*
Julius Cæsar, iii. 1.

It will be pastime passing excellent,
If it be husbanded with *modesty.*
Taming of the Shrew, Induction, sc. 1.

Win straying souls with *modesty* again,
Cast none away. *Henry 8,* v. 2.

Suit the action to the word, the word to the action; with this special observance, that you o'erstep not the *modesty* of nature. *Hamlet,* iii. 2.

MOIETY. *Share; proportion.*

Against the which, a *moiety* competent
Was gag'd by our king. *Hamlet,* i. 1.

Methinks my *moiety,* north from Burton here,
In quantity equals not one of yours.
Henry 4, P. 1, iii. 1.

For equalities are so weighed, that curiosity in neither can make choice of either's *moiety.*
King Lear, i. 1.

TO MOIST. *To moisten.*

I have
Immortal longings in me : now no more
The juice of Egypt's grape shall *moist* this lip.
Antony and Cleopatra, v. 2.

Write till your ink be dry, and with your tears
Moist it again. *Two Gentlemen of Verona,* iii. 2.

MOLDWARP. *The mole.*

Sometimes he angers me
With telling me of the *moldwarp* and the ant.
Henry 4, P. 1, iii. 1.

MOLESTATION. *Tumult; uproar; disturbance.*

I never did like *molestation* view
On the enchafèd flood. . *Othello,* ii. 1.

MOME. *A dolt; a blockhead.*

Mome, malt-horse, capon, coxcomb, idiot, patch !
Comedy of Errors, iii. 1.

MOMENTANY. *Brief; momentary.*

Making it *momentany* as a sound,
Swift as a shadow, short as any dream.
Midsummer-Night's Dream, i. 1.

TO MONARCHIZE. *To play the king.*

Allowing him a breath, a little scene,
To *monarchize,* be fear'd, and kill with looks.
Richard 2, iii. 2.

TO MONSTER. *To exaggerate; to make monstrous.*

I had rather have one scratch my head i' the sun,
When the alarum were struck, than idly sit
To hear my nothings *monster'd.* *Coriolanus,* ii. 2.

Sure, her offence
Must be of such unnatural degree,
That *monsters* it, or your fore-vouch'd affection
Fall'n into taint.— — -- *King Lear,* i. 1.

MONSTRUOSITY. *Extravagance; wildness; irregularity.*

This is the *monstruosity* in love, lady.
Troilus and Cressida, iii. 2.

MONUMENT. *A memorial; a remembrance; a keepsake.*

Defacing *monuments* of conquer'd France ;
Undoing all, as all had never been.
Henry 6, P. 2, i. 1.

Nor let the rain of heaven wet this place,
To wash away my woful *monuments*.
Henry 6, P. 2, iii. 2.

MONUMENTAL.　*Ancestral; memorial.*

He hath given her his *monumental* ring, and
thinks himself made in the unchaste composition.
All's well that ends well, iv. 3.

MOOD.　*Rage; anger; fit; humour.*

Come, come, thou art as hot a Jack in thy *mood*
as any in Italy.　　　　*Romeo and Juliet*, iii. 1.

And I from Mantua, for a gentleman,
Who, in my *mood*, I stabb'd unto the heart.
Two Gentlemen of Verona, iv. 1.

You are but now cast in his *mood*, a punishment
more in policy than in malice.　　　*Othello*, ii. 3.

O the blest gods! so will you wish on me,
When the rash *mood* is on.　　　*King Lear*, ii. 4.

MOODY.　*Sad; pensive; melancholy.*

Sweet recreation barr'd, what doth ensue
But *moody*, moping, and dull melancholy,
Kinsman to grim and comfortless despair?
Comedy of Errors, v. 1.

Give me some music,—music, *moody* food
For us that trade in love.　　*Ant. and Cleop.* ii. 5.

MOON-CALF.　*A monster.*

I hid me under the dead *moon-calf's* gaberdine
for fear of the storm.　　　*Tempest*, ii. 2.

MOONISH.　*Like the moon; inconstant; fickle.*

At which time would I, being but a *moonish*
youth, grieve, be effeminate, changeable, longing,
and liking.　　　*As you like it*, iii. 2.

To MOP.　*To make wry faces; to grin.*

Flibbertigibbet, of *mopping* and mowing.
King Lear, iv. 1.

MORAL.　*The meaning.*

The *moral* of my wit is—plain and true.
Troilus and Cressida, iv. 4.

Why Benedictus? you have some *moral* in Benedictus.　　　*Much Ado about Nothing*, iii. 4.

MORAL.　*Wise; reasonable.*

But no man's virtue nor sufficiency
To be so *moral* when he shall endure
The like himself.　*Much Ado about Nothing*, v. 1.

France spreads his banners in our noiseless land;
While thou, a *moral* fool, sitt'st still, and criest,
" Alack, why does he so?"　　*King Lear*, iv. 2.

To MORAL.　*To moralize; to reason.*

When I did hear
The motley fool thus *moral* on the time,
My lungs began to crow like chanticleer,
That fools should be so deep contemplative.
As you like it, ii. 7.

MORALER.　*A moralist.*

Come, you are too severe a *moraler*.　*Othello*, ii. 3.

To MORALIZE.　*To furnish morals or meanings.*

Thus, like the formal vice, Iniquity,
I *moralize* two meanings in one word.
Richard 3, iii. 1.

MORE.　*Greater.*

But wrong not that wrong with a *more* contempt.
Comedy of Errors, ii. 2.

More reasons for this action
At our *more* leisure shall I render you.
Measure for Measure, i. 3.

To make a *more* requital to your love. *K. John*, ii. 1.

For where there is advantage to be ta'en,
Both *more* and less have given him the revolt.
Macbeth, v. 4.

The *more* and less came in with cap and knee.
Henry 4, P. 1, iv. 3.

And my *more*-having would be as a sauce
To make me hunger more.　　　*Macbeth*, iv. 3.

MORE ABOVE.　*Moreover.*

And *more above*, hath his solicitings,
As they fell out by time, by means, and place,
All given to mine ear.　　　*Hamlet*, ii. 2.

MORISCO.　*A morris-dancer.*

And, in the end being rescu'd, I have seen
Him caper upright like a wild *Morisco*.
Henry 6, P. 2, iii. 1.

MORT.　*A tune or flourish formerly played at
the death or mort of the deer.*

And then to sigh, as 'twere the *mort* o' the deer.
Winter's Tale, i. 2.

MORTAL.　*Deadly; fatal; heinous.*

Come, you spirits
That tend on *mortal* thoughts, unsex me here.
Macbeth, i. 5.

EE

This news is *mortal* to the queen.
Winter's Tale, iii. 2.

If my offence be of such *mortal* kind,
That nor my service past, nor present sorrows,
Can ransom me into his love again,
But to know so must be my benefit. *Othello*, iii. 4.

MORTALITY. *Death.*

Mortality and mercy in Vienna
Live in thy tongue and heart. *Measure for M.* i. 1.
We cannot hold *mortality's* strong hand.
King John, iv. 2.
Here, on my knee, I beg *mortality*,
Rather than life preserv'd with infamy.
Henry 6, P. 1, iv. 5.

TO MORTIFY. *To macerate; to humble; to subdue; to tame.*

For their dear causes
Would to the bleeding and the grim alarm
Excite the *mortified* man. *Macbeth*, v. 2.
My loving lord, Dumain is *mortified*.
Love's Labour's lost, i. 1.
And let my liver rather heat with wine
Than my heart cool with *mortifying* groans.
Merchant of Venice, i. 1.
The breath no sooner left his father's body,
But that his wildness, *mortified* in him,
Seem'd to die too. *Henry* 5, i. 1.

MOST. *Greatest; longest.*

This not to do,
So grace and mercy at your *most* need help you,
Swear. *Hamlet*, i. 5.
'Tis honour with *most* lands to be at odds.
Timon of Athens, iii. 5.
Not fearing death, nor shrinking for distress,
But always resolute in *most* extremes.
Henry 6, P. 1, iv. 1.
Yet, ere we put ourselves in arms, dispatch we
The business we have talk'd of.—With *most* gladness. *Antony and Cleopatra*, ii. 2.
And that I have possess'd him my *most* stay
Can be but brief. *Measure for Measure*, iv. 1.

MOTE. *An atom.*

O heaven!—that there were but a *mote* in yours,
A grain, a dust, a gnat, a wandering hair!
King John, iv. 1.
A *mote* will turn the balance, which Pyramus,
which Thisbe, is the better.
Midsummer-Night's Dream, v. 1.
A *mote* it is to trouble the mind's eye. *Hamlet*, i. 1.

MOTHER. *The superior of a nunnery.*

No longer staying but to give the *mother*
Notice of my affair. *Measure for Measure*, i. 4.

MOTION. *Frame; body; puppet-show; puppet; proposal; impulse; notion; help; service; cogitation; mind.*

This sensible warm *motion* to become
A kneaded clod; and the delighted spirit
To bathe in fiery floods, or to reside
In thrilling regions of thick-ribbèd ice.
Measure for Measure, iii. 1.
Then he compassed a *motion* of the Prodigal Son.
Winter's Tale, iv. 2.
O excellent *motion!* O exceeding puppet!
Two Gentlemen of Verona, ii. 1.
I have a *motion* much imports your good.
Measure for Measure, v. 1.
Yes, I agree, and thank you for your *motion.*
Henry 6, P. 3, iii. 3.
And of other *motions*, as promising her marriage,
and things which would derive me ill-will to speak
of. *All's well that ends well*, v. 3.
Within this bosom never enter'd yet
The dreadful *motion* of a murderous thought.
King John, iv. 2.
Like a common and an outward man,
That the great figure of a council frames
By self-unable *motion*.
All's well that ends well, iii. 1.
Masters o' the people,
We do request your kindest ears; and, after,
Your loving *motion* toward the common body,
To yield what passes here. *Coriolanus*, ii. 2.
But from the inward *motion* to deliver
Sweet, sweet, sweet poison for the age's tooth.
King John, i. 1.
I see it in
My *motion*, have it not in my tongue.
Antony and Cleopatra, ii. 3.

TO MOTION. *To propose; to counsel.*

One that still *motions* war, and never peace,
O'ercharging your free purses with large fines.
Henry 6, P. 1, i. 3.

MOTIVE. *Mover; causer; agent; instrument.*

Her wanton spirits look out
At every joint and *motive* of her body.
Troilus and Cressida, iv. 5.
Nor are they living
Who were the *motives* that you first went out.
Timon of Athens, iv. 5.

Doubt not but heaven
Hath brought me up to be your daughter's dower,
As it hath fated her to be my *motive*
And helper to a husband.
All's well that ends well, iv. 4.
Ere my tongue
Shall wound my honour with such feeble wrong,
Or sound so base a parle, my teeth shall tear
The slavish *motive* of recanting fear,
And spit it bleeding in his high disgrace,
Where shame doth harbour, even in Mowbray's face.
Richard 2, i. 1.

MOULD. *Model.*
New honours come upon him,
Like our strange garments, cleave not to their *mould*
But with the aid of use. *Macbeth*, i. 3.
The expectancy and rose of the fair state,
The glass of fashion and the *mould* of form.
Hamlet, iii. 1.

MOUNTAINEER. *An outlaw; a robber.*
What are you
That fly me thus? some villain *mountaineers*?
Cymbeline, iv. 2.
What hast thou done?—
I am perfect what: cut off one Cloten's head,
Son to the queen, after his own report;
Who call'd me traitor, *mountaineer*. *Ibid.* iv. 2.
This was my master,
A very valiant Briton and a good,
That here by *mountaineers* lies slain. *Ibid.* iv. 2.

MOUNTANT. *Raised; spread out.*
Hold up, you sluts, your aprons *mountant*.
Timon of Athens, iv. 3.

TO MOUNTEBANK. *To play the mountebank; to cheat; to impose upon.*
I'll *mountebank* their loves,
Cog their hearts from them, and come home belov'd
Of all the trades in Rome. *Coriolanus*, iii. 2.

MOUSE. *A term of endearment.*
What's your dark meaning, *mouse*, of this light word? *Love's Labour's lost*, v. 2.

TO MOUSE. *To tear.*
And now he feasts, *mousing* the flesh of men,
In undetermin'd differences of kings.
King John, ii. 1.
Well *moused*, lion.
Midsummer-Night's Dream, v. 1.

MOUSE-HUNT. *A libertine; an intriguer.*
Ay, you have been a *mouse-hunt* in your time.
Romeo and Juliet, iv. 4.

MOVABLES. *Household goods; furniture.*
Towards our assistance we do seize to us
The plate, coin, revenues, and *movables*,
Whereof our uncle Gaunt did stand possess'd.
Richard 2, ii. 1.
My lord, I claim the gift, my due by promise,
For which your honour and your faith is pawn'd;
The earldom of Hereford, and the *movables*,
Which you have promisèd I shall possess.
Richard 3, iv. 2.

TO MOVE. *To anger; to irritate; to prevail on;. to persuade.*
A woman *mov'd* is like a fountain troubled,
Muddy, ill-seeming, thick, bereft of beauty.
Taming of the Shrew, v. 2.
Throw your mistemper'd weapons to the ground,
And hear the sentence of your *movèd* prince.
Romeo and Juliet, i. 1.
Things have fall'n out, sir, so unluckily
That we have had no time to *move* our daughter.
Ibid. iii. 4.

MOW. *A wry face; a grimace.*
And those that would make *mows* at him while
my father lived, give twenty, forty, fifty, a hundred ducats apiece for his picture in little.
Hamlet, ii. 2.
For apes and monkeys,
'Twixt two such shes, would chatter this way, and
Condemn with *mows* the other. *Cymbeline*, i. 6.

TO MOW. *To make mouths.*
Flibbertigibbet, of mopping and *mowing*.
King Lear, iv. 1.
Sometimes like apes that *mow* and chatter at me.
Tempest, ii. 2.

MUCH. *Great; exceeding.*
Thanks, good friend Escalus, for thy *much* goodness.
Measure for Measure, v. 1.

MUCH. *Not at all; pshaw. (A term expressing indignation or contempt.)*
How say you now? Is it not past two o'clock?
And here *much* Orlando! *As you like it*, iv. 3.
I promise you, my lord, you mov'd me much.—
Much! *Timon of Athens*, i. 2.

Since when, I pray you, sir?—God's light, with two points on your shoulder? *Much !*
Henry 4, P. 2, ii. 4.

MUCH. *Very.*

I am *much* sorry, sir,
You put me to forget a lady's manners,
By being so verbal. *Cymbeline,* ii. 3.
Achilles bids me say, he is *much* sorry.
Troilus and Cressida, ii. 3.

MUDDY. *Dull; stupid; besotted.*

Dost think I am so *muddy,* so unsettled,
To appoint myself in this vexation,
Without ripe moving to't? *Winter's Tale,* i. 2.
Farewell, ye *muddy* knave. *Henry 4, P. 1, ii. 1.*

TO MUFFLE. *To blindfold; to hoodwink; to conceal.*

We have caught the woodcock, and will keep him
muffled
Till we do hear from them.
All's well that ends well, iv. 1.

MUFFLER. *A covering for the face; a kind of hood.*

Muffle me, night, a while. *Romeo and Juliet,* v. 3.
Fortune is painted blind, with a *muffler* afore
her eyes, to signify to you that Fortune is blind.
Henry 5, iii. 5.
There is no woman's gown big enough for him;
otherwise he might put on a hat, a *muffler,* and a
kerchief, and so escape.
Merry Wives of Windsor, iv. 2.
I spy a great pearl under her *muffler. Ibid.* iv. 2.

MULLED. *Dull; spiritless.*

Peace is a very apoplexy, lethargy; *mulled,* deaf,
sleepy, insensible. *Coriolanus,* iv. 5.

MULETEER. *A muleteer.*

Your mariners are *muleters,* reapers, people
Ingross'd by swift impress.
Antony and Cleopatra, iii. 7.

MULTIPOTENT. *All-powerful.*

By Jove *multipotent,*
Thou shouldst not bear from me a Greekish member
Wherein my sword had not impressure made
Of our rank feud. *Troilus and Cressida,* iv. 5.

MULTITUDINOUS. *Manifold; belonging to the multitude.*

No; this my hand will rather
The *multitudinous* seas incarnadine,
Making the green one red. *Macbeth,* ii. 1.
Therefore at once pluck out
The *multitudinous* tongue; let them not lick
The sweet which is their poison. *Coriolanus,* iii. 1.

MUM. *Silent.*

The citizens are *mum,* say not a word.
Richard 3, iii. 7.

MUMBLE-NEWS. *A tale-bearer; a busybody.*

Some *mumble-news,* some trencher-knight, some
Dick. *Love's Labour's lost,* v. 2.

MUMMY. *A medical preparation of two kinds, brought from the East, and formerly in good repute.*

Scale of dragon, tooth of wolf,
Witches' *mummy,* maw and gulf
Of the ravin'd salt-sea shark. *Macbeth,* iv. 1.
The worms were hallow'd that did breed the silk;
And it was dy'd in *mummy,* which the skilful
Conserv'd of maidens' hearts. *Othello,* iii. 4.

MUNIMENT. *Support; stay; defence.*

Our steed the leg, the tongue our trumpeter,
With other *muniments* and petty helps
In this our fabric. *Coriolanus,* i. 1.

MURAL. *A wall.*

Now is the *mural* down between the two neighbours.
Midsummer-Night's Dream, v. 1.

MURDERING-PIECE. *A species of cannon used in ships of war.*

O, my dear Gertrude, this,
Like to a *murdering-piece,* in many places
Gives me superfluous death. *Hamlet,* iv. 5.

MURE. *A wall.*

The incessant care and labour of his mind
Hath wrought the *mure,* that should confine it in,
So thin, that life peeps through, and will break out.
Henry 4, P. 2, iv. 4.

MURK. *Darkness; gloom.*

Ere twice in *murk* and occidental damp
Moist Hesperus hath quench'd his sleepy lamp.
All's well that ends well, ii. 1.

MURMUR. *Report; rumour.*

And then 'twas fresh in *murmur*—as, you know,
What great ones do, the less will prattle of—
That he did seek the love of fair Olivia.
Twelfth-Night, i. 2.

MURRAIN. *Infected with the murrain.*

And crows are fatted with the *murrain* flock.
Midsummer-Night's Dream, ii. 1.

TO MUSE. *To wonder.*

Do not *muse* at me, my most worthy friends;
I have a strange infirmity, which is nothing
To those that know me. *Macbeth*, iii. 4.
I *muse* my lord of Gloster is not come.
Henry 6, P. 2, iii. 1.
I cannot too much *muse*
Such shapes, such gesture, and such sound, ex-
pressing—
Although they want the use of tongue—a kind
Of excellent dumb discourse. *Tempest*, iii. 3.

MUSIC. *Delight; happiness.*

Very nobly
Have you deserv'd : it is my father's *music*
To speak your deeds; not little of his care
To have them recompens'd as thought on.
Winter's Tale, iv. 3.

MUSS. *A scramble.*

Of late, when I cried, "Ho!"
Like boys unto a *muss*, kings would start forth,
And cry, "Your will?"
Antony and Cleopatra, iii. 13.

MUTINE. *A mutineer.*

Do like the *mutines* of Jerusalem,

He friends awhile, and both conjointly bend
Your sharpest deeds of malice on this town.
King John, ii. 1.
Methought I lay,
Worse than the *mutines* in the bilboes.
Hamlet, v. 2.

TO MUTINE. *To rebel.*

Rebellious hell,
If thou canst *mutine* in a matron's bones,
To flaming youth let virtue be as wax,
And melt in her own fire. *Hamlet*, iii. 4.

MUTINER. *Mutineer.*

Worshipful *mutiners*,
Your valour puts well forth. *Coriolanus*, i. 1.

MUTINY. *A quarrel; dissension; strife.*

You'll make a *mutiny* among my guests.
Romeo and Juliet, i. 5.
A man of compliments, whom right and wrong
Have chose as umpire of their *mutiny*.
Love's Labour's lost, i. 1.

MUTUALITY. *Reciprocation; interchange.*

When these *mutualities* so marshal the way,
hard at hand comes the master and main exercise,
the incorporate conclusion. *Othello*, ii. 1.

MYRMIDONS. *The officers of justice.*

My lady has a white hand, and the *Myrmidons'*
are no bottle-ale houses. *Twelfth-Night*, ii. 3.

MYSTERY. *Mode; fashion; custom; practice.*

Is't possible the spells of France should juggle
Men into such strange *mysteries?* *Henry* 8, i. 3.

N.

NAPKIN. *A handkerchief.*

And to that youth he calls his Rosalind
He sends this bloody *napkin*.
As you like it, iv. 3.
Keep thou the *napkin*, and go boast of this.
Henry 6, P. 3, i. 4.
I am glad I have found this *napkin;*
It was her first remembrance from the Moor.
Othello, iii. 3.

NATIVE. *Natural; kindred; cognate.*

Seek none, conspiracy ;
Hide it in smiles and affability :
For if thou put thy *native* semblance on,
Not Erebus itself were dim enough
To hide thee from prevention. *Julius Cæsar*, ii. 1.
For no pulse
Shall keep his *native* progress, but surcease.
Romeo and Juliet, iv. 1.

The head is not more *native* to the heart,
The hand more instrumental to the mouth,
Than is the throne of Denmark to thy father.
Hamlet, i. 2.

The mightiest space in fortune nature brings
To join like likes, and kiss like *native* things.
All's well that ends well, i. 1.

NATURAL. *A fool; an idiot.*

That a monster should be such a *natural!*
Tempest, iii. 2.

NATURE. *Natural affection; disposition of mind; mode; manner; way.*

Yet that the world may witness that my end
Was wrought by *nature*, not by vile offence,
I'll utter what my sorrow gives me leave.
Comedy of Errors, i. 1.

Not nature,
To whom all sores lay siege, can bear great fortune,
But by contempt of *nature*. *Timon of Athens*, iv. 3.

Who may, in the ambush of my name, strike home,
And yet my *nature* never in the sight,
To do it slander. *Measure for Measure*, i. 3.

But I con him no thanks for't, in the *nature* he
delivers it. *All's well that ends well*, iv. 3.

NAUGHT. *Bad; wicked; depraved.*

O, she was *naught;* and long of her it was
That we meet here so strangely. *Cymbeline*, v. 5.

Beloved Regan,
Thy sister's *naught:* O Regan, she hath tied
Sharp-tooth'd unkindness, like a vulture, here.
King Lear, ii. 4.

NAVE. *The navel; the centre.*

And ne'er shook hands, nor bade farewell to him,
Till he unseam'd him from the *nave* to the chaps,
And fix'd his head upon our battlements.
Macbeth, i. 2.

NAVIGATION. *Ships; fleets.*

Though the yesty waves
Confound and swallow *navigation* up.
Macbeth, iv. 1.

NAYWARD. *The contrary; the opposite side.*

But I'd say he had not,
And I'll be sworn you would believe my saying,
Howe'er you lean to the *nayward.*
Winter's Tale, ii. 1.

NAY-WORD. *A watch-word; a proverb; a by-word.*

And, in any case, have a *nay-word*, that you
may know one another's mind.
Merry Wives of Windsor, ii. 2.

If I do not gull'him into a *nay-word*, and make
him a common recreation, do not think I have wit
enough to lie straight in my bed.
Twelfth-Night, ii. 3.

NEAR. *In favour with; nearer.*

If I had a suit to Master Shallow, I would humour his men with the imputation of being *near*
their master. *Henry 4*, P. 2, v. 1.

Better far off than near, be ne'er the *near.*
Richard 2, v. 1.

NEAT. *A cow or an ox; oxen.*

What say you to a *neat's* foot?—
'Tis passing good : I prithee let me have it.
Taming of the Shrew, iv. 3.

Methought he bore him in the thickest troop
As doth a lion in a herd of *neat.*
Henry 6, P. 3, ii. 1.

NEAT. *Spruce; finical; foppish.*

You *neat* slave, strike. *King Lear*, ii. 2.

NEB. *The mouth.*

How she holds up the *neb*, the bill to him!
Winter's Tale, i. 2.

NECESSITIED. *In want of.*

This ring was mine ; and, when I gave it Helen,
I told her, if her fortune ever stood
Necessitied to help, that by this token
I would relieve her. *All's well that ends well*, v. 3.

NEEDLESS. *Unneeding; not wanting.*

O, yes, into a thousand similes.
First, for his weeping in the *needless* stream.
As you like it, ii. 1.

NEEDLY. *Perforce; necessarily; of necessity.*

Or,—if sour woe delights in fellowship,
And *needly* will be rank'd with other griefs,—
Why follow'd not, when she said—Tybalt's dead,
Thy father, or thy mother, nay, or both,
Which modern lamentation might have mov'd?
Romeo and Juliet, iii. 2.

NEELD. *A needle.*

We, Hermia, like two artificial gods,
Have with our *neelds* created both one flower.
Midsummer-Night's Dream, iii. 2.
Their thimbles into arm'd gauntlets chang'd,
Their *neelds* to lances, and their gentle hearts
To fierce and bloody inclination. *King John,* v. 2.

To **NEEZE.** *To sneeze.*

And waxen in their mirth, and *neeze,* and swear
A merrier hour was never wasted there.
Midsummer-Night's Dream, ii. 1.

To **NEGLECT.** *To lose; to forego; to hinder; to prevent.*

What infinite heart's-ease must kings *neglect,*
That private men enjoy ! *Henry 5,* iv. 1.
I have been long a sleeper; but, I trust,
My absence doth *neglect* no great design
Which by my presence might have been concluded.
Richard 3, iii. 4.

NEGLECTION. *Non-observance; disregard; negligence.*

And this *neglection* of degree it is,
That by a pace goes backward, with a purpose
It hath to climb. *Troilus and Cressida,* i. 3.
Sleeping *neglection* doth betray to loss
The conquest of our scarce-cold conqueror.
Henry 6, P. 1, iv. 3.

NEIF. *The fist; the hand.*

Sweet knight, I kiss thy *neif. Henry 4,* P. 2, ii. 4.
Give me your *neif,* Monsieur Mustard-seed.
Midsummer-Night's Dream, iv. 1.

NEIGHBOURED. *Regarded; loved; cherished.*

The barbarous Scythian,
Or he that makes his generation messes
To gorge his appetite, shall to my bosom
Be as well *neighbour'd,* pitied, and reliev'd,
As thou my sometime daughter. *King Lear,* i. 1.

NEPHEW. *Grandson; cousin.*

You'll have your *nephews* neigh to you.
Othello, i. 1.
There is among the Greeks
A lord of Trojan blood, *nephew* to Hector.
Troilus and Cressida, i. 2.

NERVE. *Sinew; tendon.*

The strongest *nerves* and small inferior veins
From me receive that natural competency
Whereby they live. *Coriolanus,* i. 1.

NERVY. *Strong; vigorous; powerful.*

Death, that dark spirit, in's *nervy* arm doth lie.
Coriolanus, ii. 1.

NETHER-STOCKS. *Stockings.*

Ere I lead this life long, I'll sew *nether-stocks,*
and mend them and foot them too.
Henry 4, P. 1, ii. 4.
When a man's over-lusty at legs, then he wears
wooden *nether-stocks. King Lear,* ii. 4.

NEW. *Just; just now; lately.*

And even before this truce, but *new* before,
No longer than we well could wash our hands,
Heaven knows, they were besmear'd and overstain'd
With slaughter's pencil. *King John,* iii. 1.
Is the day so young?—But *new* struck nine.
Romeo and Juliet, i. 1.

NEW-TROTHED. *Newly plighted.*

So says the prince, and my *new-trothed* lord.
Much Ado about Nothing, iii. 1.

NEXT. *Nearest; shortest; readiest.*

A prophet I, madam; and I speak the truth
the *next* way. *All's well that ends well,* i. 3.
'Tis the *next* way to turn tailor, or be redbreast
teacher. *Henry 4,* P. 1, iii. 1.
To mourn a mischief that is past and gone,
Is the *next* way to draw new mischief on.
Othello, i. 3.

NICE. *Slight; trivial; fastidious; squeamish; soft; effeminate; exact; minute.*

The letter was not *nice,* but full of charge
Of dear import. *Romeo and Juliet,* v. 2.
Romeo, that spoke him fair, bade him bethink
How *nice* the quarrel was, and urg'd withal
Your high displeasure. *Ibid.* iii. 1.
O Kate, *nice* customs court'sy to great kings.
Henry 5, v. 2.
And therefore, goaded with most sharp occasions,
Which lay *nice* manners by, I put you to
The use of your own virtues, for the which
I shall continue thankful.
All's well that ends well, v. 1.
Since you are strangers, and come here by chance,
We'll not be *nice. Love's Labour's lost,* v. 2.
For when mine hours
Were *nice* and lucky, men did ransom lives
Of me for jests. *Antony and Cleopatra,* iii. 13.

Hence, therefore, thou *nice* crutch !
Henry 4, P. 2, i. 1.
O, relation too *nice*, and yet too true !
Macbeth, iv. 3.

NICELY. *Idly ; foolishly ; exactly ; scrupulously.*

Can sick men play so *nicely* with their names ?
Richard 2, ii. 1.
What safe and *nicely* I might well delay
By rule of knighthood, I disdain and scorn.
King Lear, v. 3.
These kind of knaves I know, which in this plainness
Harbour more craft and more corrupter ends
Than twenty silly ducking observants
That stretch their duties *nicely*. *Ibid.* v. 3.

NICENESS. *Fastidiousness ; scrupulousness.*

You must forget to be a woman, change
Command into obedience ; fear and *niceness*,—
The handmaids of all women, or, more truly,
Woman its pretty self,—into a waggish courage.
Cymbeline, iii. 4.

NICETY. *Niceness ; coyness ; fastidiousness.*

Lay by all *nicety* and prolixious blushes.
Measure for Measure, ii. 4.

To NICK. *To beguile ; to defeat ; to frustrate.*

The itch of his affection should not then
Have *nick'd* his captainship.
Antony and Cleopatra, iii. 13.

NIECE. *Granddaughter.*

Who meets us here ?—my *niece* Plantagenet,
Led in the hand of her kind aunt of Gloster ?
Richard 3, iv. 1.

NIGGARD. *Sparing ; niggardly.*

Niggard of question ; but, of our demands,
Most free in his reply. *Hamlet*, iii. 1.
Scorn'dst our brain's flow, and those our droplets
which
From *niggard* nature fall. *Timon of Athens*, v. 4.

To NIGGARD. *To stint ; to supply sparingly.*

The deep of night is crept upon our talk,
And nature must obey necessity ;
Which we will *niggard* with a little rest.
Julius Cæsar, iv. 3.

NIGHTED. *Dark ; gloomy ; benighted.*

Good Hamlet, cast thy *nighted* colour off,
And let thine eye look like a friend on Denmark.
Hamlet, i. 2.

Edmund, I think, is gone,
In pity of his misery, to dispatch
His *nighted* life. *King Lear*, iv. 5.

NIGHT-RAVEN. *The night-jar.*

I had as lief have heard the *night-raven*, come
what plague could have come after it.
Much Ado about Nothing, ii. 3.

To NILL. *To be unwilling.*

Your dowry greed on ;
And, will you, *nill* you, I will marry you.
Taming of the Shrew, ii. 1.
If the man go to this water, and drown himself,
it is, will he, *nill* he, he goes,—mark you that.
Hamlet, v. 1.

No. *Denial ; negative.*

But that her tender shame
Will not proclaim against her maiden loss,
How might she tongue me ! Yet reason dares her no.
Measure for Measure, iv. 4.
Henceforth my wooing mind shall be express'd
In russet yeas and honest kersey noes.
Love's Labour's Lost, v. 2.

No LESS. *As many as.*

Good my liege,
Your preparation can affront no less
Than what you hear of. *Cymbeline*, iv. 3.

No MORE THAN. *As much as.*

Or were you both our mothers,
I care *no more* for *than* I do for heaven,
So I were not his sister.
All's well that ends well, i. 3.

NOBILITY. *Greatness ; nobleness ; generosity ; dignity.*

I sin in envying his *nobility*. *Coriolanus*, i. 1.
And with no less *nobility* of love
Than that which dearest father bears his son,
Do I impart toward thee. *Hamlet*, i. 2.
O, that your young *nobility* could judge
What 'twere to lose it, and be miserable !
Richard 3, i. 3.

NOBLE. *A gold coin of the value of 6s. 8d.*

While great promotions
Are daily given to ennoble those
That scarce, some two days since, were worth a *noble*.
Richard 3, i. 3.

NOBLENESS. *Distinction; honour; dignity.*

Which honour must
Not unaccompanied invest him only,
But signs of *nobleness*, like stars, shall shine
On all deservers. *Macbeth,* i. 4.

NOBLESS. *Nobility; magnanimity.*

Then true *nobless* would
Learn him forbearance from so foul a wrong.
Richard 2, iv. 1.

NOISE. *Tumult; disorder; report; rumour; music; a company of musicians.*

Tom, away!
Mark the high *noises;* and thyself bewray,
When false opinion, whose wrong thought defiles thee,
In thy just proof, repeals and reconciles thee.
King Lear, iii. 6.

What was his cause of anger?—
The *noise* goes, this. *Troilus and Cressida,* i. 2.
'Tis like she comes to speak of Cassio's death ;
The *noise* was high. *Othello,* v. 2.

Cleopatra, catching but the least *noise* of this,
dies instantly. *Antony and Cleopatra,* i. 2.
Why sinks that caldron? and what *noise* is this?
Macbeth, iv. 1.
And see if thou canst find out Sneak's *noise.*
Henry 4, P. 2, ii. 4.

To NOISE. *To thunder; to threaten; to denounce.*

And gives his potent regiment to a trull,
That *noises* it against us.
Antony and Cleopatra, iii. 6.

NONCE. *Purpose.*

I have cases of buckram for the *nonce,* to immask
our noted outer garments. *Henry 4, P. 1,* i. 2.
When in your motion you are hot and dry,
And that he calls for drink, I'll have prepar'd him
A chalice for the *nonce.* *Hamlet,* iv. 7.

NONPAREIL. *A paragon; one who has no fellow.*

If thou didst it, thou art the *nonpareil.*
Macbeth, iii. 4.

NON-REGARDANCE. *Disregard; slight; contempt.*

Since you to *non-regardance* cast my faith,
Live you, the marble-breasted tyrant, still.
Twelfth-Night, v. 1.

NOOK-SHOTTEN. *Abounding in nooks; many-cornered.*

To buy a slobbery and a dirty farm
In that *nook-shotten* isle of Albion. *Henry 5,* iii. 4.

To NOSE. *To scent; to smell.*

He said 'twas folly,
For one poor grain or two, to leave unburnt,
And still to *nose* the offence. *Coriolanus,* v. 1.
But, indeed, if you find him not within this
month, you shall *nose* him as you go up the stairs
into the lobby. *Hamlet,* iv. 3.

NOT. *Not only.*

Come, go with us ; speak fair : you may salve so,
Not what is dangerous present, but the loss
Of what is past. *Coriolanus,* iii. 2.

And that *not* in the presence
Of dreaded justice, but on the ministers
That do distribute it. *Ibid.* iii. 3.

NOT ALMOST. *Scarcely; hardly.*

And yet his trespass, in our common reason,—
Save that, they say, the wars must make examples
Out of their best,—is *not almost* a fault
To incur a private check. *Othello,* iii. 3.

NOT EVER. *Not always.*

And *not ever*
The justice and truth o' the question carries
The due o' the verdict with it. *Henry 8,* v. 1.

NOTE. *Information; notice; observation; indication; mark; stain; stigma.*

She that from Naples
Can have no *note,* unless the sun were post,
Till new-born chins be rough and razorable.
Tempest, ii. 1.

He shall conceal it
Whiles you are willing it shall come to *note.*
Twelfth-Night, iv. 3.

These present wars shall find I love my country,
Even to the *note* o' the king, or I'll fall in them.
Cymbeline, iv. 3.

Sir, I do know you ;
And dare, upon the warrant of my *note,*
Commend a dear thing to you. *King Lear,* iii. 1.
Upon his royal face there is no *note*
How dread an army hath enrounded him.
Henry 5, iii. Chorus.
No *note* upon my parents, his all noble.
All's well that ends well, i. 3.

FF

Ill, to example ill,
Would from my forehead wipe a perjur'd *note;*
For none offend where all alike do dote.
             Love's Labour's lost, iv. 3.
Once more, the more to aggravate the *note,*
With a foul traitor's name stuff I thy throat.
             Richard 2, i. 1.

To NOTE. *To mark; to brand; to stigmatize.*
You have condemn'd and *noted* Lucius Pella
For taking bribes here of the Sardians.
             Julius Cæsar, iv. 3.

NOTHING. *Barren; empty; worthless.*
    Laying by
That *nothing* gift of differing multitudes.
             Cymbeline, iii. 6.

NOTHING. *Nowise; not at all; no longer.*
My father Capulet will have it so,
And I am *nothing* slow, to slack his haste.
             Romeo and Juliet, iv. 1.
That you do love me, I am *nothing* jealous.
             Julius Cæsar, i. 2.
    The vows of women
Of no more bondage be, to where they are made,
Than they are to their virtues, which is *nothing.*
             Cymbeline, ii. 4.
    Poor Turlygood! poor Tom!
That's something yet :—Edgar I *nothing* am.
             King Lear, ii. 3.

NOTICE. *Information; account.*
Bring me just *notice* of the numbers dead
On both our parts.   *Henry* 5, iv. 7.

NOTION. *Sense; knowledge; understanding.*
Your judgments, my grave lords,
Must give this cur the lie : and his own *notion*
Shall join to thrust the lie unto him.
             Coriolanus, v. 6.
Either his *notion* weakens, or his discernings
Are lethargied.   *King Lear,* i. 4.
How you were borne in hand, how cross'd, the
    instruments,
Who wrought with them, and all things else that
    might
To half a soul and to a *notion* craz'd
Say "Thus did Banquo."   *Macbeth,* iii. 1.

NOTORIOUSLY. *Notably.*
Fool, there was never man so *notoriously* abused.
             Twelfth-Night, iv. 2.

NOTT-PATED. *Smooth-headed.*
Why, thou clay-brained guts, thou *nott-pated* fool.
             Henry 4, P. 1, ii. 4.

To NOURISH. *To maintain; to support.*
Whiles I in Ireland *nourish* a mighty band,
I will stir up in England some black storm
Shall blow ten thousand souls to heaven or hell.
             Henry 6, P. 2, iii. 1.

NOWL. *The head.*
An ass's *nowl* I fixèd on his head.
             Midsummer-Night's Dream, iii. 2.

NOYANCE. *Injury; mischief.*
The single and peculiar life is bound,
With all the strength and armour of the mind,
To keep itself from *noyance.*   *Hamlet,* iii. 3.

NUMB. *Benumbing; benumbed; torpid.*
    And did give himself,
All thin and naked, to the *numb* cold night.
             Richard 3, ii. 1.
Yet are these feet,—whose strengthless stay is
    numb,—
Swift-wingèd with desire to get a grave.
             Henry 6, P. 1, ii. 5.

NUMBERED. *Numerous; abounding; redundant.*
    Which can distinguish 'twixt
The fiery orbs above, and the twinn'd stones
Upon the *number'd* beach.   *Cymbeline,* i. 6.

NUMBNESS. *Torpidity.*
Bequeath to death your *numbness,* for from him
Dear life redeems you.   *Winter's Tale,* v. 3.

NUNCIO. *A messenger.*
She will attend it better in thy youth
Than in a *nuncio* of more grave aspect.
             Twelfth-Night, i. 4.

NUNCLE. *Uncle.*
Can you make no use of nothing, *nuncle?*
             King Lear, i. 4.

NURSERY. *Care; solicitude.*
I lov'd her most, and thought to set my rest
On her kind *nursery.*   *King Lear,* i. 1.

NURTURE. *Instruction; education; culture.*
A devil, a born devil, on whose nature
Nurture can never stick.   *Tempest,* iv. 1.
    Yet am I inland bred,
And know some *nurture.* *As you like it,* ii. 7.

O.

O. *A circle; a naught; a cipher.*

Who more engilds the night
Than all yon fiery *oes* and eyes of light.
Midsummer-Night's Dream, iii. 2.
Or may we cram
Within this wooden *O* the very casques
That did affright the air at Agincourt?
Prologue to Henry 5.
O, that your face were not so full of *O's!*
Love's Labour's lost, v. 2.
His face was as the heavens; and therein stuck
A sun and moon, which kept their course, and
lighted
The little *O*, the earth. *Antony and Cleopatra,* v. 2.
Now thou art an *O* without a figure.
King Lear, i. 4.

OATHABLE. *Qualified to give evidence upon oath.*

You are not *oathable,*—spare your oaths,
I'll trust to your conditions. *Timon of Athens,* iv. 3.

OBJECT. *Sight; evidence; whatever inspires pity or contempt.*

The leanness that afflicts us, the *object* of our
misery, is as an inventory to particularize their
abundance. *Coriolanus,* i. 1.
Swear against *objects.* *Timon of Athens,* iv. 3.
Manly as Hector, but more dangerous;
For Hector, in his blaze of wrath, subscribes
To tender *objects.* *Troilus and Cressida,* iv. 5.
And his eye revil'd
Me, as his abject *object.* *Henry* 8, i. 1.

OBLIGATION. *A contract; a bond.*

Nay, he can make *obligations,* and write court-hand.
Henry 6, P. 2, iv. 2.

OBLIGED. *Bonded; obligatory.*

O, ten times faster Venus' pigeons fly
To seal love's bonds new-made, than they are wont
To keep *obligèd* faith unforfeited.
Merchant of Venice, ii. 5.

OBSCENE. *Atrocious; foul; flagitious.*

O, forfend it, God,
That, in a Christian climate, souls refin'd
Should show so heinous, black, *obscene* a deed!
Richard 2, iv. 1.

OBSCURE. *Dwelling in the dark.*

The *obscure* bird clamour'd the livelong night.
Macbeth, ii. 1.

To OBSCURE. *To conceal; to disguise.*

Why, 'tis an office of discovery, love,
And I should be *obscur'd. Merchant of Venice,* ii. 5.

OBSEQUIOUS. *Full of observance; ceremonious; zealous.*

And so *obsequious* will thy father be
E'en for the loss of thee, having no more,
As Priam was for all his valiant sons.
Henry 6, P. 3, ii. 5.
And the survivor bound,
In filial obligation, for some term
To do *obsequious* sorrow. *Hamlet,* i. 2.
I see you are *obsequious* in your love, and I profess requital to a hair's breadth.
Merry Wives of Windsor, iv. 2.

OBSEQUIOUSLY. *Reverentially; piously.*

Whilst I awhile *obsequiously* lament
The untimely fall of virtuous Lancaster.
Richard 3, i. 2.

OBSERVANCE. *Respect; reverence; observation; practice; care.*

Where I did meet thee once with Helena,
To do *observance* to a morn of May.
Midsummer-Night's Dream, i. 1.
All purity, all trial, all *observance.*
As you like it, v. 2.
Is this certain?—
Or I have no *observance.*
Antony and Cleopatra, iii. 3.
By my troth, I take my young lord to be a very
melancholy man.—By what *observance,* I pray you?
All's well that ends well, iii. 2.

It is a custom
More honour'd in the breach than the *observance*.
Hamlet, i. 4.
With this special *observance*, that you o'erstep
not the modesty of nature. *Ibid.* iii. 2.

OBSERVANT. *A slavish attendant.*
These kind of knaves I know, which in this plainness
Harbour more craft and more corrupter ends
Than twenty silly ducking *observants*
That stretch their duties nicely. *King Lear*, ii. 2.

OBSERVATION. *Observance; ceremony; attention; diligence; worldly knowledge.*
Go, one of you, find out the forester;
For now our *observation* is perform'd.
Midsummer-Night's Dream, iv. 1.
So, with good life,
And *observation* strange, my meaner ministers
Their several kinds have done. *Tempest*, iii. 3.
For he is but a bastard to the time,
That doth not smack of *observation*. *K. John*, i. 1.

TO OBSERVE. *To celebrate; to honour; to respect.*
No doubt they rose up early to *observe*
The rite of May. *Midsummer-Night's Dream*, iv. 1.
Hinge thy knee,
And let his very breath, whom thou'lt *observe*,
Blow off thy cap. *Timon of Athens*, iv. 3.
For he is gracious, if he be *observ'd*;
He hath a tear for pity, and a hand
Open as day for melting charity.
Henry 4, P. 2, iv. 4.

OBSERVINGLY. *Attentively; carefully.*
There is some soul of goodness in things evil,
Would men *observingly* distil it out. *Henry 5*, iv. 1.

OBSTACLE. *Perverse; obstinate.*
Fie, Joan, that thou wilt be so *obstacle!*
Henry 6, P. 1, v. 4.

OBSTRUCT. *An obstacle; an impediment.*
Which soon he granted,
Being an *obstruct* 'tween his lust and him.
Antony and Cleopatra, iii. 6.

OCCASION. *Exigency; need; necessity; provocation; incitement.*
My purse, my person, my extremest means
Lie all unlock'd to your *occasions*.
Merchant of Venice, i. 1.

Withhold thy speed, dreadful *occasion!*
O, make a league with me, till I have pleas'd
My discontented peers! *King John*, iv. 2.
O, that woman that cannot make her fault her
husband's *occasion*, let her never nurse her child
herself, for she will breed it like a fool!
As you like it, iv. 1.

OCCIDENT. *The west.*
I may wander from east to *occident*, never
Find such another master. *Cymbeline*, iv. 2.
See, see, king Richard doth himself appear,
As doth the blushing discontented sun,
From out the fiery portal of the east;
When he perceives the envious clouds are bent
To dim his glory, and to stain the track
Of his bright passage to the *occident*.
Richard 2, iii. 3.

OCCULTED. *Secret; hidden.*
If his *occulted* guilt
Do not itself unkennel in one speech,
It is a damnèd ghost that we have seen.
Hamlet, iii. 2.

OCCUPATION. *Trade; calling; vocation.*
You that stood so much
Upon the voice of *occupation* and
The breath of garlic-eaters! *Coriolanus*, iv. 6.

OCCURRENCE. *Course; passage; tenour.*
All the *occurrence* of my fortune since
Hath been between this lady and this lord.
Twelfth-Night, v. 1.

OCCURRENT. *Occurrence; event; incident.*
He has my dying voice;
So tell him, with the *occurrents*, more and less,
Which have solicited.—The rest is silence.
Hamlet, v. 2.

ODD. *Unobserved; unheeded; unlucky.*
The king's son have I landed by himself;
Whom I left cooling of the air with sighs
In an *odd* angle of the isle. *Tempest*, i. 2.
There are yet missing of your company
Some few *odd* lads that you remember not.
Ibid. v. 1.
I fear the trust Othello puts him in,
On some *odd* time of his infirmity,
Will shake this island. *Othello*, ii. 3.

ODD-EVEN. *Midnight.*
At this *odd-even* and dull watch o' the night.
Othello, i. 1.

ODDLY. *Unequally; not evenly.*

And trust to me, Ulysses,
Our imputation shall be *oddly* pois'd
In this wild action. *Troilus and Cressida*, i. 3.

ODDS. *Quarrel; variance; strife.*

I cannot speak
Any beginning to this peevish *odds*. *Othello*, ii. 3.
Of honourable reckoning are you both;
And pity 'tis you liv'd at *odds* so long.
Romeo and Juliet, i. 2.
Come, damnèd earth,
Thou common whore of mankind, that putt'st *odds*
Among the rout of nations, I will make thee
Do thy right nature. *Timon of Athens*, iv. 3.

ŒILLIAD. *A side-glance; an ogle.*

And here another to Page's wife, who even
now gave me good eyes too, examined my parts
with most judicious *œilliads*.
Merry Wives of Windsor, i. 3.
She gave strange *œilliads* and most speaking looks
To noble Edmund. *King Lear*, iv. 5.

OF ALL HANDS. *In any case; on all sides.*

We cannot cross the cause why we were born;
Therefore *of all hands* must we be forsworn.
Love's Labour's lost, iv. 3.

OF ALL LOVES. *By all means.*

Mistress Page would desire you to send her
your little page, *of all loves:* her husband has a
marvellous infection to the little page.
Merry Wives of Windsor, ii. 2.
Speak, *of all loves!* I swoon almost with fear.
Midsummer-Night's Dream, ii. 2.

OF VANTAGE. *With advantage; without being
seen; secretly.*

'Tis meet that some more audience than a mother,
Since nature makes them partial, should o'erhear
The speech, *of vantage.* *Hamlet*, iii. 3.

OFF. *Not to the purpose.*

That's *off*, that's *off*;
I would you rather had been silent.
Coriolanus, ii. 2.

OFFENCE. *The fruits of guilt; the spoil.*

May one be pardon'd, and retain the *offence?*
Hamlet, iii. 3.

TO OFFER. *To commence; to attack; to assail.*

For well you know we of the *offering* side
Must keep aloof from strict arbitrement.
Henry 4, P. 1, iv. 1.
So that his power, like to a fangless lion,
May *offer*, but not hold. *Ibid.* P. 2, iv. 1.

OFFICE. *Devotion; service; business; a commission appointed for some special service.*

Whom I with all the *office* of my heart
Entirely honour. *Othello*, iii. 4.
Those his goodly eyes, now bend, now turn,
The *office* and devotion of their view
Upon a tawny front. *Antony and Cleopatra*, i. 1.
For little *office*
The hateful commons will perform for us,
Except like curs to tear us all to pieces.
Richard 2, ii. 2.
Hast thou or word, or wit, or impudence,
That yet can do thee *office?*
Measure for Measure, v. 1.
This gate
Instructs you how to adore the heavens, and bows
you
To morning's holy *office.* *Cymbeline*, iii. 3.
I was of late as petty to his ends
As is the morn-dew on the myrtle-leaf
To his grand sea.—Be't so: declare thine *office.*
Antony and Cleopatra, iii. 12.
All was royal;
To the disposing of it nought rebell'd,
Order gave each thing view; the *office* did
Distinctly his full function. *Henry 8*, i. 1.

TO OFFICE. *To do; to perform.*

No, no, although
The air of paradise did fan the house,
And angels *offic'd* all.
All's well that ends well, iii. 2.

OFFICER. *A retainer; a dependant.*

The serving-men in their new fustian, their
white stockings, and every *officer* his wedding-gar-
ment on. *Taming of the Shrew*, iv. 1.
Having been three months married to her, sitting in my state, calling my *officers* about me, in
my branched velvet gown. *Twelfth-Night*, ii. 5.
He hath been in unusual pleasure, and
Sent forth great largess to your *officers.*
Macbeth, ii. 1.

OFFICED. *Active; operative; operant.*
My speculative and *offic'd* instruments. *Othello*, i. 3.

OFFICES. *Rooms in large mansions where the provisions were kept.*
All *offices* are open ; and there is full liberty of feasting from this present hour of five till the bell have told eleven. *Othello*, ii. 2.
When all our *offices* have been oppress'd
With riotous feeders. *Timon of Athens*, ii. 2.

OFTEN. *Frequent.*
And, indeed, the sundry contemplation of my travels, on which my *often* rumination wraps me in a most humorous sadness. *As you like it*, iv. 1.

OLD. *Wold.*
Swithold footed thrice the *old*. *King Lear*, iii. 4.

OLD. *Great; abundant; practised.*
If thou neglect'st, or dost unwillingly .
What I command, I'll rack thee with *old* cramps. *Tempest*, i. 2.
Here will be an *old* abusing of God's patience and the king's English.
Merry Wives of Windsor, i. 4.
Yonder's *old* coil at home.
Much Ado about Nothing, v. 2.
By the mass, here will be *old* utis.
Henry 4, P. 2, ii. 4.
Master, master! *old* news, and such news as you never heard of! *Taming of the Shrew*, iii. 2.
If a man were porter of hell-gate, he should have *old* turning the key. *Macbeth*, ii. 1.
Doth she not think me an *old* murderer,
Now I have stain'd the childhood of our joy
With blood remov'd but little from her own?
Romeo and Juliet, iii. 3.

To OMIT. *To spare; to pass over; to lay aside; to neglect.*
What if we do *omit*
This reprobate till he were well inclin'd?
Measure for Measure, iv. 3.
Tempests themselves, high seas, and howling winds,
As having sense of beauty, do *omit*
Their mortal natures, letting go safely by
The divine Desdemona. *Othello*, ii. 1.
Whose influence
If now I court not, but *omit*, my fortunes
Will over after droop. *Tempest*, i. 2.
There is a tide in the affairs of men,
Which, taken at the flood, leads on to fortune;

Omitted, all the voyage of their life
Is bound in shallows and in miseries.
Julius Cæsar, iv. 3.
Therefore *omit* him not ; blunt not his love,
Nor lose the good advantage of his grace,
By seeming cold, or careless of his will.
Henry 4, P. 2, iv. 4.

OMITTANCE. *Forbearance.*
But that's all one ; *omittance* is no quittance.
As you like it, iii. 5.

ON. *Over; against.*
For they that were your enemies are his,
And have prevail'd as much *on* him as you.
Richard 3, i. 1.

ON FOOT. *In action; in motion.*
In which disguise,
While other jests are something rank *on foot*,
Her father hath commanded her to slip
Away with Slender, and with him at Eton
Immediately to marry.
Merry Wives of Windsor, iv. 6.
How near's the other army?
Near and *on* speedy *foot*; the main descry
Stands on the hourly thought. *King Lear*, iv. 6.

ONCE. *Once for all; some time; at any time; for once.*
Look, what will serve is fit : 'tis *once*, thou lovest.
Much Ado about Nothing, i. 1.
Once this,—your long experience of her wisdom,
Her sober virtue, years, and modesty,
Plead on her part some cause to you unknown,
Why at this time the doors are made against you.
Comedy of Errors, iii. 1.
Once, if he do require our voices, we ought not to deny him. *Coriolanus*, ii. 3.
I pray thee, *once* to-night give my sweet Nan this ring. *Merry Wives of Windsor*, iii. 4.
I hope to see London *once* ere I die.
Henry 4, P. 2, v. 3.
What we oft do best,
By sick interpreters, *once* weak ones, is
Not ours, or not allow'd. *Henry* 8, i. 2.
Where nothing,
But who knows nothing, is *once* seen to smile.
Macbeth, iv. 3.
Can it be
That so degenerate a strain as this
Should *once* set footing in your generous bosoms?
Troilus and Cressida, ii. 2.

If idle talk will *once* be necessary,
I'll not sleep neither : this mortal house I'll ruin,
Do Cæsar what he can. *Antony and Cleopatra*, v. 2.
Have I *once* liv'd to see two honest men ?
Timon of Athens, v. 1.

ONCE A DAY. *Some time in the day; daily.*

Who *once a day* with his embossèd froth
The turbulent surge shall cover.
Timon of Athens, v. 1.

ONION-EYED. *Ready to cry.*

Look, they weep ;
And I, an ass, am *onion-ey'd :* for shame,
Transform us not to women.
Antony and Cleopatra, iv. 2.

ONLY. *But ; except.*

Love, no god, that would not extend his might,
only where qualities were level.
All's well that ends well, i. 3.

OOZE. *Soft mud.*

And think'st it much to tread the *ooze*
Of the salt deep.   *Tempest*, i. 2.

OPE. *Open.*

So, now the gates are *ope :* now prove good seconds.
Coriolanus, i. 4.

With swifter spleen than powder can enforce,
The mouth of passage shall we fling wide *ope*,
And give you entrance.   *King John*, ii. 1.

OPERANT. *Active.*

My *operant* powers their functions leave to do ;
And thou shalt live in this fair world behind,
Honour'd, belov'd.   *Hamlet*, iii. 2.

Earth, yield me roots !
Who seeks for better of thee, sauce his palate
With thy most *operant* poison !
Timon of Athens, iv. 3.

OPINION. *Reputation ; credit ; suspicion ; self-conceit.*

And do a wilful stillness entertain,
With purpose to be dress'd in an *opinion*
Of wisdom, gravity, profound conceit.
Merchant of Venice, i. 1.
Thou hast redeem'd thy lost *opinion*.
Henry 4, P. 1, v. 4.
And spend your rich *opinion* for the name
Of a night-brawler.   *Othello*, ii. 3.

O, let us have him ; for his silver hairs
Will purchase us a good *opinion*.
Julius Cæsar, ii. 1.
How have I been behav'd, that he might stick
The small'st *opinion* of my great'st abuse ?
Othello, iv. 2.
Pride, haughtiness, *opinion*, and disdain.
Henry 4, P. 1, iii. 1.
Learned without *opinion*, and strange without
heresy.   *Love's Labour's lost*, v. 1.

TO OPPOSE. *To expose ; to offer ; to present.*

Her grace sat down to rest awhile
In a rich chair of state, *opposing* freely
The beauty of her person to the people.
Henry 8, iv. 1.

TO OPPOSE AGAINST. *To resist ; to contend with ; to confront ; to be exposed to.*

'Tis your counsel
My lord should to the heavens be contrary,
Oppose against their wills.   *Winter's Tale*, v. 1.
A servant that he bred, thrill'd with remorse,
Oppos'd against the act, bending his sword
To his great master.   *King Lear*, iv. 3.
Was this a face
To be *oppos'd against* the warring winds ?
Ibid. iv. 7.

OPPOSED. *Opposite ; contrary.*

And embraced, as it were, from the ends of *opposed* winds.   *Winter's Tale*, i. 1.
To offend, and judge, are distinct offices,
And of *opposèd* natures. *Merchant of Venice*, ii. 8.

OPPOSELESS. *Irresistible.*

O you mighty gods !
If I could bear it longer, and not fall
To quarrel with your great *opposeless* wills,
My snuff and loathèd part of nature should
Burn itself out.   *King Lear*, iv. 6.

OPPOSER. *Antagonist ; opponent ; rival.*

Your noble Tullus Aufidius will appear well in
these wars, his great *opposer*, Coriolanus, being now
in no request of his country.   *Coriolanus*, iv. 3.

OPPOSITE. *An opponent ; an adversary.*

You hope the duke will return no more ; or you
imagine me too unhurtful an *opposite*.
Measure for Measure, iii. 2.

Tho king enacts more wonders than a man,
Daring an *opposite* to every danger.
Richard 3, v. 4.

OPPOSITE. *Reserved; distant; adverse; contrary; opposed to.*

Bo *opposite* with a kinsman, surly with servants.
Twelfth-Night, ii. 5.
Seeing how loathly *opposite* I stood
To his unnatural purpose, in fell motion,
With his preparèd sword, ho charges home
My unprovided body, lanc'd mine arm.
King Lear, ii. 1.
All form is formless, order orderless,
Savo what is *opposite* to England's love.
King John, iii. 1.
A maid so tender, fair, and happy,
So *opposite* to marriage, that she shunn'd
Tho wealthy curlèd darlings of our nation.
Othello, i. 2.

OPPOSITION. *Combat.*

When on the gentle Severn's sedgy bank,
In single *opposition,* hand to hand,
Ho did confound tho best part of an hour
In changing hardiment with great Glendower.
Henry 4, P. 1, i. 3.
Above him in birth, alike conversant in general
services, and more remarkable in single *oppositions.*
Cymbeline, iv. 1.

OPPRESSION. *Misery; embarrassment; distress; difficulty.*

Good heart, at what?—At thy good heart's *oppression.* *Romeo and Juliet,* i. 1.
Famine is in thy cheeks,
Need and *oppression* starveth in thine eyes.
Ibid. v. 1.
Retire, wo have engag'd ourselves too far :
Cæsar himself has work, and our *oppression*
Exceeds what wo expected.
Antony and Cleopatra, iv. 7.

OPPUGNANCY. *Opposition; contrariety.*

Take but degree away, untune that string,
And, hark, what discord follows! each thing meets
In mere *oppugnancy.* *Troilus and Cressida,* i. 3.

OR. *Ere; sooner than.*

And I think
He'll grant the tribute, send tho arrearages,
Or look upon our Romans, whose remembrance
Is yet fresh in their grief. *Cymbeline,* ii. 4.

OR EVER. *Before; before ever; sooner than.*

I would
Have sunk tho sea within the earth, *or e'er*
It should tho good ship so have swallow'd, and
The fraughting souls within her. *Tempest,* i. 2.
And good men's lives
Expire before tho flowers in their caps,
Dying *or e'er* they sicken. *Macbeth,* iv. 3.
Would I had met my dearest foe in heaven
Or ever I had seen that day, Horatio! *Hamlet,* i. 2.
Those that would die *or e'er* resist aro grown
The mortal bugs o' tho field. *Cymbeline,* v. 3.

ORB. *Ring; circle.*

And I servo tho fairy queen,
To dew her *orbs* upon tho green.
Midsummer-Night's Dream, ii. 1.

ORBED. *Round; circular.*

And all those sayings will I over-swear ;
And all those swearings keep as true in soul
As doth that *orbèd* continent the fire
That severs day from night. *Twelfth-Night,* v. 1.
Full thirty times hath Phœbus' cart gone round
Neptune's salt wash and Tellus' *orbèd* ground.
Hamlet, iii. 2.

ORCHARD. *A garden.*

In my chamber-window lies a book ; bring it
hither to me in tho *orchard.*
Much Ado about Nothing, ii. 3.
Ho ran this way, and leap'd this *orchard* wall.
Romeo and Juliet, ii. 1.

ORDERED. *Orderly; instructed; disciplined.*

Our countrymen
Aro men more *order'd* than when Julius Cæsar
Smil'd at their lack of skill, but found their courage
Worthy his frowning at. *Cymbeline,* ii. 4.

ORDERLY. *Unfailing; regular.*

Frame yourself
To *orderly* solicits, and bo friended
With aptness of tho season. *Cymbeline,* ii. 3.

ORDINANCE. *Fate; appointment; rank; quality.*

Let *ordinance*
Come as the gods foresay it : howsoe'er,
My brother hath done well. *Cymbeline,* iv. 2.
Why all these things change, from their *ordinance,*
Their natures, and preformèd faculties,
To monstrous quality. *Julius Cæsar,* i. 3.

To show bare heads
In congregations, to yawn, be still, and wonder,
When one but of my *ordinance* stood up
To speak of peace or war.   *Coriolanus*, iii. 2.

ORDINANT. *Instrumental; helpful; operant.*
Why, even in that was heaven *ordinant*.
    Hamlet, v. 2.

ORGULOUS. *Proud; haughty.*
From isles of Greece
The princes *orgulous*, their high blood chaf'd,
Have to the port of Athens sent their ships.
    Troilus and Cressida, Prologue.

ORIFEX. *Orifice.*
And yet the spacious breadth of this division
Admits no *orifex* for a point, as subtle
As Ariachne's broken woof, to enter.
    Troilus and Cressida, v. 2.

ORT. *A fragment; a scrap; a relic.*
One that feeds
On abject *orts* and imitations. *Julius Cæsar*, iv. 1.
    It is some poor fragment, some slender *ort* of
his remainder.   *Timon of Athens*, iv. 3.
And with another knot, five-finger-tied,
The fractions of her faith, *orts* of her love,
The fragments, scraps, are bound to Diomed.
    Troilus and Cressida, v. 2.

OSPREY. *The sea-eagle.*
I think he'll be to Rome
As is the *osprey* to the fish, who takes it
By sovereignty of nature.   *Coriolanus*, iv. 7.

OSTENT. *Look; demeanour.*
Like one well studied in a sad *ostent*
To please his grandam. *Merchant of Venice*, ii. 2.

OSTENTATION. *Show; spectacle; display.*
Make good this *ostentation*, and you shall
Divide in all with us.   *Coriolanus*, i. 6.
    The king would have me present the princess
with some delightful *ostentation*, or show, or page-
ant, or antic, or fire-work. *Love's Labour's lost*, v. 1.
    But you are come
A market-maid to Rome; and have prevented
The *ostentation* of our love, which, left unshown,
Is often left unlov'd. *Antony and Cleopatra*, iii. 6.
No trophy, sword, nor hatchment o'er his bones,
No noble rite nor formal *ostentation*. *Hamlet*, iv. 5.

OTHER. *Others.*
Some *other* give me thanks for kindnesses.
    Comedy of Errors, iv. 3.
Every letter he hath writ hath disvouched *other*.
    Measure for Measure, iv. 4.
And therefore is the glorious planet Sol
In noble eminence enthron'd and spher'd
Amidst the *other*.   *Troilus and Cressida*, i. 3.
This, match'd with *other*, did, my gracious lord:
For more uneven and unwelcome news
Came from the north, and thus it did import.
    Henry 4, P. 1, i. 1.

OTHER. *Otherwise.*
If you think *other*,
Remove your thought,—it doth abuse your bosom.
    Othello, iv. 2.
Ay; and you'll look pale
Before you find it *other*.   *Coriolanus*, iv. 6.

OTHER MORE. *Many others.*
And her withholds from me, and *other more*,
Suitors to her, and rivals in my love.
    Taming of the Shrew, i. 2.
And *others more*, going to seek the grave
Of Arthur, who they say is kill'd to-night
On your suggestion.   *King John*, iv. 2.

OTHERGATES. *Otherwise; in another manner.*
But if he had not been in drink, he would have
tickled you *othergates* than he did.
    Twelfth-Night, v. 1.

OTHERWHERE. *Elsewhere.*
Excuse me; the king has sent me *otherwhere*.
    Henry 8, ii. 2.
I know his eye doth homage *otherwhere*.
    Comedy of Errors, ii. 1.

OTHERWHILES. *At other times; sometimes.*
Otherwhiles the famish'd English, like pale ghosts,
Faintly besiege us one hour in a month.
    Henry 6, P. 1, i. 2.

OTTOMITES. *The Ottomans.*
I do agnize
A natural and prompt alacrity
I find in hardness; and do undertake
These present wars against the *Ottomites*.
    Othello, i. 3.

OUCH. *An ornament of gold or jewelry.*
Your brooches, pearls, and *ouches*.
    Henry 4, P. 2, ii. 4.

GG

OUGHT. *Owed.*

And said this other day you *ought* him a thousand pound. *Henry* 4, P. 1, iii. 3.

OUNCE. *The lynx.*

Be it *ounce*, or cat, or boar.
Midsummer-Night's Dream, ii. 2.

OUPH. *An elf; a fairy.*

Like urchins, *ouphs*, and fairies, green and white.
Merry Wives of Windsor, iv. 4.

OUSEL. *The blackbird.*

The *ousel*-cock so black of hue,
With orange-tawny bill.
Midsummer-Night's Dream, iii. 1.

OUT. *Quite; completely; thoroughly; over; at odds; out of temper; out at heels; away; absent.*

I do not think thou canst, for then thou wast not
Out three years old. *Tempest*, i. 2.
Her waspish-headed son has broke his arrows,
Swears he will shoot no more, but play with sparrows,
And be a boy right *out*. *Ibid.* iv. 1.
Thou hast beat me *out* twelve several times.
Coriolanus, iv. 5.
On the catastrophe and heel of pastime,
When it was *out*. *All's well that ends well*, i. 2.
Nay, you need not fear us, Lorenzo : Launcelot
and I are *out*. *Merchant of Venice*, iii. 5.
Nay, I beseech you, sir, be not *out* with me :
yet, if you be *out*, sir, I can mend you.
Julius Cæsar, i. 1.
And his own letter,
The honourable board of council *out*,
Must fetch him in the papers. *Henry* 8, i. 1.
He hath been *out* nine years, and away he shall
again. *King Lear*, i. 1.

OUT OF. *Away from; beyond; without.*

My heart laments that virtue cannot live
Out of the teeth of emulation. *Julius Cæsar*, ii. 3.
His training such,
That he may furnish and instruct great teachers,
And never seek for aid *out of* himself.
Henry 8, i. 2.
When did he regard
The stamp of nobleness in any person
Out of himself? *Ibid.* iii. 2.

I therefore apprehend and do attach thee
For an abuser of the world, a practiser
Of arts inhibited and *out of* warrant. *Othello*, i. 2.
His approach,
So *out of* circumstance and sudden, tells us
'Tis not a visitation fram'd, but forc'd
By need and accident. *Winter's Tale*, v. 1.

OUT OF ALL NICK. *Without measure; immoderately.*

Launce, his man, told me, he loved her *out of all nick*. *Two Gentlemen of Verona*, iv. 2.

OUT OF DOOR. *External; visible.*

All of her that is *out of door* most rich !
Cymbeline, i. 6.

OUT OF FASHION. *Wildly; extravagantly.*

O my sweet,
I prattle *out of fashion*, and I dote
In mine own comforts. *Othello*, ii. 1.

OUT OF SUITS. *Out of favour.*

Wear this for me, one *out of suits* with fortune,
That could give more, but that her hand lacks means.
As you like it, i. 2.

To OUTCRAFT. *To overreach; to deceive; to beguile.*

My husband's hand !
That drug-damn'd Italy hath *outcrafted* him,
And he's at some hard point. *Cymbeline*, iii. 4.

To OUTDARE. *To brave; to defy.*

Or with pale beggar-fear impeach my height
Before this *outdar'd* dastard. *Richard* 2, i. 1.
It was myself, my brother, and his son,
That brought you home, and boldly did *outdare*
The dangers of the time. *Henry* 4, P. 1, v. 1.

To OUTDWELL. *To stay beyond.*

And it is marvel he *outdwells* his hour.
Merchant of Venice, ii. 5.

To OUTFACE. *To outstare; to browbeat; to outbrave.*

Outfacèd infant state, and done a rape
Upon the maiden virtue of the crown.
King John, ii. 1.
Be stirring as the time ; be fire with fire ;
Threaten the threatener, and *outface* the brow
Of bragging horror. *Ibid.* v. 1.

And, with a word, *outfaced* you from your prize.
           Henry 4, P. 1, ii. 4.
Dost thou come here to whine?
To *outface* me with leaping in her grave?
           Hamlet, v. 1.

To OUTGO.   *To outrun; to leave behind; to distance.*
     The time shall not
Outgo my thinking on you.
         Antony and Cleopatra, iii. 2.

To OUTJEST.   *To overcome by jesting.*
     But who is with him?—
None but the fool; who labours to *outjest*
His heart-struck injuries.   *King Lear*, iii. 1.

To OUTLOOK.   *To outstare; to outface; to browbeat.*
     Before I drew this gallant head of war,
And cull'd these fiery spirits from the world,
To *outlook* conquest, and to win renown
Even in the jaws of danger and of death.
         King John, v. 2.

To OUTLUSTRE.   *To exceed in brightness; to outshine.*
     If she went before others I have seen, as that
diamond of yours *outlustres* many I have beheld, I
could not but believe she excelled many.
         Cymbeline, i. 4.

To OUTPEER.   *To surpass; to excel.*
     Great men,
That had a court no bigger than this cave,
That did attend themselves, and had the virtue
Which their own conscience seal'd them,
Could not *outpeer* these twain.   *Cymbeline*, iii. 6.

To OUTPRIZE.   *To exceed in value; to outworth.*
     Either your unparagoned mistress is dead, or
she's *outprized* by a trifle.   *Cymbeline*, i. 4.

OUTRAGE.   *Tumult; disorder; open violence.*
     Seal up the mouth of *outrage* for a while,
Till we can clear these ambiguities,
And know their spring, their head, their true
     descent.   *Romeo and Juliet*, v. 3.
     Are you not asham'd
With this immodest clamorous *outrage*
To trouble and disturb the king and us?
         Henry 6, P. 1, iv. 1.

To OUTSCORN.   *To disregard; to despise.*
     Strives in his little world of man to *outscorn*
The to-and-fro-conflicting wind and rain.
         King Lear, iii. 1.

To OUTSELL.   *To exceed in value; to outprize.*
     Her pretty action did *outsell* her gift,
And yet enrich'd it too : she gave it me, and said
She priz'd it once.   *Cymbeline*, ii. 4.
         From every one
The best she hath, and she, of all compounded,
Outsells them all.   *Ibid.* iii. 5.

To OUTSPEAK.   *To surpass; to go beyond.*
     Which
I find at such proud rate, that it *outspeaks*
Possession of a subject.   *Henry* 8, iii. 2.

To OUTSTAND.   *To outstay; to stay beyond.*
     I have *outstood* my time; which is material
To the tender of our present.   *Cymbeline*, i. 6.

To OUTSTARE.   *To outface; to browbeat.*
     He's gone to the king;
I'll follow and *outstare* him.   *Henry* 8, i. 1.
     I would *outstare* the sternest eyes that look,
To win thee, lady.   *Merchant of Venice*, ii. 1.
     Now he'll *outstare* the lightning.
         Antony and Cleopatra, iii. 13.

To OUTSWEETEN.   *To excel in sweetness.*
     No, nor the leaf of eglantine, whom not to slander,
Outsweeten'd not thy breath.   *Cymbeline*, iv. 2.

To OUT-TONGUE.   *To overpower; to silence.*
     My services, which I have done the signiory,
Shall *out-tongue* his complaints.   *Othello*, i. 2.

To OUTVENOM.   *To exceed in malignity.*
     No, 'tis slander;
Whose edge is sharper than the sword; whose
     tongue
Outvenoms all the worms of Nile.   *Cymbeline*, iii. 4.

To OUTVIE.   *To outbid.*
     Why, then the maid is mine from all the world,
By your firm promise : Gremio is *outvied*.
         Taming of the Shrew, ii. 1.

To OUTVILLAIN. *To exceed in villany.*
He hath *outvillained* villany so far, that the
rarity redeems him. *All's well that ends well,* iv. 3.

OUTWARD. *Outside; exterior; external form.*
I do not think
So fair an *outward,* and such stuff within,
Endows a man but he. *Cymbeline,* i. 1.

OUTWARD. *Excluded; not admitted.*
The reasons of our state I cannot yield,
But like a common and an *outward* man,
That the great figure of a council frames
By self-unable motion.
All's well that ends well, iii. 1.

To OUTWEAR. *To wear out; to waste.*
The sun is high, and we *outwear* the day.
Henry 5, iv. 2.

To OUTWORK. *To surpass; to go beyond; to excel.*
She did lie in her pavilion
O'er-picturing that Venus where we see.
The fancy *outwork* nature.
Antony and Cleopatra, ii. 2.

To OUTWORTH. *To exceed in value.*
A beggar's book *outworths* a noble's blood.
Henry 8, i. 1.

To OVERBEAR. *To bear down; to reject; to overrule; to crush; to subdue.*
We breath'd our counsel; but it pleas'd your highness
To *overbear* it. *King John,* iv. 2.
Egeus, I will *overbear* your will.
Midsummer-Night's Dream, iv. 1.
And pouring war
Into the bowels of ungrateful Rome,
Like a bold flood *o'erbear.* *Coriolanus,* iv. 5.

To OVERBLOW. *To drive away; to keep off.*
While yet the cool and temperate wind of grace
O'erblows the filthy and contagious clouds
Of heady murder, spoil, and villany.
Henry 5, iii. 2.

To OVERBULK. *To crush; to overwhelm.*
The seeded pride
In rank Achilles must or now be cropp'd,
Or, shedding, breed a nursery of like evil,
To *overbulk* us all. *Troilus and Cressida,* i. 3.

To OVERBUY. *To pay too much for a thing.*
You bred him as my playfellow; and he is
A man worth any woman; *overbuys* me
Almost the sum he pays. *Cymbeline,* i. 1.

To OVERCOME. *To pass over.*
Can such things be,
And *overcome* us like a summer's cloud,
Without our special wonder? *Macbeth,* iii. 4.

To OVERCOUNT. *To outnumber.*
We'll speak with thee at sea: at land, thou know'st
How much we do *o'ercount* thee.
Antony and Cleopatra, ii. 6.

To OVERCROW. *To triumph over; to subdue.*
The potent poison quite *o'ercrows* my spirit.
Hamlet, v. 2.

OVEREARNEST. *Hasty; impetuous; vehement.*
Yes, Cassius; and from henceforth,
When you are *overearnest* with your Brutus,
He'll think your mother chides, and leave you so.
Julius Cæsar, iv. 3.

To OVEREYE. *To witness; to observe.*
But I am doubtful of your modesties;
Lest *overeying* of his odd behaviour,—
For yet his honour never heard a play,—
You break into some merry passion,
And so offend him.
Taming of the Shrew, Induction, sc. 1.

OVERFLOURISHED. *Adorned; ornamented.*
But the beauteous-evil
Are empty trunks, *o'erflourish'd* by the devil.
Twelfth-Night, iii. 5.

To OVERGO. *To go beyond; to surpass; to exceed.*
O, what cause have I
To *overgo* thy woes and drown thy cries!
Richard 3, ii. 2.

OVERGROWN. *Overgrown with hair.*
Pray, sir, to the army:
I and my brother are not known; yourself
So out of thought, and thereto so *o'ergrown,*
Cannot be question'd. *Cymbeline,* iv. 4.

OVERGROWTH. *Exuberance; predominance.*
By the *o'ergrowth* of some complexion,
Oft breaking down the pales and forts of reason.
Hamlet, i. 4.

To OVERHOLD. *To keep up; to maintain.*

Go tell him this; and add,
That if he *overhold* his price so much,
We'll none of him. *Troilus and Cressida,* ii. 3.

To OVERLIVE. *To outlive; to survive.*

And concludes in hearty prayers
That your attempts may *overlive* the hazard
And fearful meeting of their opposite.
Henry 4, P. 2, iv. 1.

To OVERLOOK. *To peruse; to charm; to fascinate; to bewitch; to look down upon.*

It is a letter from my brother, that I have not all *o'er-read*; and for so much as I have perused, I find it not fit for your *o'erlooking. King Lear,* i. 2.

When thou shalt have *overlooked* this, give these fellows some means to the king.
Hamlet, iv. 6.

Beshrew your eyes,
They have *o'erlook'd* me, and divided me!
Merchant of Venice, iii. 2.

Vile worm, thou wast *o'erlook'd* even in thy birth.
Merry Wives of Windsor, v. 5.

Shall a few sprays of us,
The emptying of our fathers' luxury,
Our scions, put in wild and savage stock,
Spirt up suddenly into the clouds,
And *overlook* their grafters? *Henry 5,* iii. 4.

And by this hand I swear,
That sways the earth this climate *overlooks,*
Before we will lay down our just-borne arms,
We'll put thee down, 'gainst whom these arms we bear,
Or add a royal number to the dead.
King John, ii. 1.

OVERPARTED. *Overtasked.*

But, for Alisander,—alas, you see how 'tis,—a little *o'erparted.* *Love's Labour's lost,* v. 2.

To OVERPASS. *To pass; to spend.*

In prison hast thou spent a pilgrimage,
And like a hermit *overpass'd* thy days.
Henry 6, P. 1, ii. 5.

To OVERPEER. *To look over; to look down upon.*

There, where your argosies with portly sail
Do *overpeer* the petty traffickers,
That curt'sy to them, do them reverence,

As they fly by them with their woven wings.
Merchant of Venice, i. 1.

What custom wills, in all things should we do't,
The dust on antique time would lie unswept,
And mountainous error be too highly heapt
For truth to *overpeer.* *Coriolanus,* ii. 3.

To OVERPERCH. *To fly over.*

With love's light wings did I *o'erperch* these walls;
For stony limits cannot hold love out.
Romeo and Juliet, ii. 2.

To OVERPOST. *To get quickly over.*

You may thank the unquiet time for your quiet *o'erposting* that action. *Henry 4,* P. 2, i. 2.

To OVERPRIZE. *To outworth; to exceed in value.*

With that which, but by being so retir'd,
O'erpriz'd all popular rate, in my false brother
Awak'd an evil nature. *Tempest,* i. 2.

To OVER-REACH. *To overtake; to cote; to cheat; to cozen.*

Madam, it so fell out, that certain players
We *o'er-raught* on the way: of these we told him.
Hamlet, iii. 1.

Upon my life, by some device or other
The villain is *o'er-raught* of all my money.
Comedy of Errors, i. 2.

We'll *over-reach* the greybeard, Gremio,
The narrow-prying father, Minola,
The quaint musician, amorous Licio;
All for my master's sake, Lucentio.
Taming of the Shrew, iii. 2.

To OVER-RED. *To redden; to smear with red.*

Go prick thy face, and *over-red* thy fear,
Thou lily-liver'd boy. *Macbeth,* v. 3.

To OVER-RIDE. *To overtake.*

My lord, I *over-rode* him on the way.
Henry 4, P. 2, i. 1.

OVERSCUTCHED. *Overwhipt.*

'A came ever in the rearward of the fashion;
and sung those tunes to the *overscutched* huswives
that he heard the carmen whistle, and sware they
were his Fancies or his Good-nights.
Henry 4, P. 2, iii. 2.

HH

To OVERSHOOT. *To go too far; to say too much.*

I have o'ershot myself to tell you of it.
Julius Cæsar, iii. 2.
But are you not ashamed? nay, are you not,
All three of you, to be thus much o'ershot?
Love's Labour's lost, iv. 3.

OVERSIZED. *Plastered over; bespread.*

And thus o'ersizèd with coagulate gore,
With eyes like carbuncles, the hellish Pyrrhus
Old grandsire Priam seeks. *Hamlet*, ii. 2.

To OVERSWEAR. *To swear over again.*

And all those sayings will I oversweår.
Twelfth-Night, v. 1.

OVERTURE. *Promulgation; disclosure.*

And I wish, my liege,
You had only in your silent judgment tried it,
Without more overture. *Winter's Tale*, ii. 1.

Out, treacherous villain!
Thou call'st on him that hates thee : it was he
That made the overture of thy treasons to us.
King Lear, iii. 7.

To OVERVEIL. *To cover; to conceal.*

The day begins to break, and night is fled,
Whose pitchy mantle overveil'd the earth.
Henry 6, P. 1, ii. 2.

To OVERWATCH. *To tire with want of sleep.*

I fear we shall out-sleep the coming morn,
As much as we this night have overwatch'd.
Midsummer-Night's Dream, v. 1.
All weary and o'erwatch'd,   .
Take vantage, heavy eyes, not to behold
This shameful lodging. *King Lear*, ii. 2.
Poor knave, I blame thee not; thou art o'erwatch'd.
Julius Cæsar, iv. 3.

To OVERWEEN. *To think with arrogance; to presume.*

Mowbray, you overween to take it so ;
This offer comes from mercy, not from fear.
Henry 4, P. 2, iv. 1.
My eye's too quick, my heart o'erweens too much,
Unless my hand and strength could equal them.
Henry 6, P. 3, iii. 2.

OVERWEENING. *Insolent; presuming; eager; impetuous.*

Here's an overweening rogue! *Twelfth-Night*, ii. 5.
Oft have I seen a hot o'erweening cur
Run back and bite, because he was withheld ;
Who, being suffer'd with the bear's fell paw,
Hath clapp'd his tail between his legs and cried.
Henry 6, P. 2, v. 1.

OVERWORN. *Worn out; stale.*

I might say element, but the word is overworn.
Twelfth-Night, iii. 1.
The jealous o'erworn widow and herself
Are mighty gossips in this monarchy.
Richard 3, i. 1.

OVERWRESTED. *Overstrained; extravagant.*

And, like a strutting player, whose conceit
Lies in his hamstring,
Such to-be-pitied and o'erwrested seeming
He acts thy greatness in. *Troilus and Cressida*, i. 3.

To OWE. *To own; to possess.*

This is no mortal business, nor no sound
That the earth owes. *Tempest*, i. 2.
Else let my brother die,
If not a fedary, but only he,
Owe and succeed this weakness.
Measure for Measure, ii. 4.
Other of them may have crooked noses; but to
owe such straight arms, none. *Cymbeline*, iii. 1.
What a full fortune does the thick-lips owe,
If he can carry it thus! *Othello*, i. 1.
Not poppy nor mandragora,
Nor all the drowsy syrups of the world,
Shall ever medicine thee to that sweet sleep
Which thou ow'dst yesterday. *Ibid.* iii. 3.

OWED. *Due; dedicated; devoted.*

Never may
That state or fortune fall into my keeping,
That is not ow'd to you! *Timon of Athens*, i. 1

OYES. *Oyez; attend; give attention.*

On whose bright crest Fame with her loud'st Oyes
Cries, "This is he." *Troilus and Cressida*, iv. 5.
Crier Hobgoblin, make the fairy Oyes.
Merry Wives of Windsor, v. 5.

P.

To PACE. *To guide ; to direct.*

If you can, *pace* your wisdom
In that good path that I would wish it go ;
And you shall have your bosom on this wretch,
Grace of the duke, revenges to your heart,
And general honour.   *Measure for Measure,* iv. 3.

PACK. *A confederacy for some bad purpose.*

O you panderly rascals ! there's a knot, a ging,
a *pack,* a conspiracy against me.
                 Merry Wives of Windsor, iv. 2.

To PACK. *To confederate for some bad purpose ; to act in concert.*

That goldsmith there, were he not *pack'd* with her,
Could witness it, for he was with me then.
                       Comedy of Errors, v. 1.
              This naughty man
Shall face to face be brought to Margaret,
Who I believe was *pack'd* in all this wrong,
Hir'd to it by your brother.
            Much Ado about Nothing, v. 1.

To PACK CARDS. *To act in concert ; to combine for a bad purpose.*

She, Eros, has
Pack'd cards with Cæsar, and false-play'd my glory
Unto an enemy's triumph.
             Antony and Cleopatra, iv. 14.

PACKING. *Plotting ; secret combination.*

Here's *packing,* with a witness, to deceive us all.
                    Taming of the Shrew, v. 1.
        What hath been seen,
Either in snuffs and *packings* of the dukes ;
Or the hard rein which both of them have borne
Against the old kind king.   *King Lear,* iii. 1.

PACTION. *Agreement ; compact.*

That never may ill office, or fell jealousy,
Thrust in between the *paction* of these kingdoms,
To make divorce of their incorporate league.
                       Henry 5, v. 2.

To PADDLE. *To play with ; to feel ; to finger.*

Didst thou not see her *paddle* with the palm
of his hand ? didst not mark that ?   *Othello,* ii. 1.

But to be *paddling* palms and pinching fingers,
As now they are, O, that is entertainment
My bosom likes not, nor my brows !
                       Winter's Tale, i. 2.
And let him, for a pair of reechy kisses,
Or *paddling* in your neck with his damn'd fingers,
Make you to ravel all this matter out,
That I essentially am not in madness,
But mad in craft.   *Hamlet,* iii. 4.

PADDOCK. *A toad.*

For who, that's but a queen, fair, sober, wise,
Would from a *paddock,* from a bat, a gib,
Such dear concernings hide ?   *Hamlet,* iii. 4.

To PAGE. *To follow as a page.*

Will these moss'd trees,
That have outliv'd the eagle, *page* thy heels,
And skip where thou point'st out ?
                    Timon of Athens, iv. 3.

To PAGEANT. *To represent ; to exhibit ; to
mimic.*

And with ridiculous and awkward action—
Which, slanderer, he imitation calls—
He *pageants* us.   *Troilus and Cressida,* i. 3.

PAIN. *Penalty ; punishment.*

And his offence is so, as it appears,
Accountant to the law upon that *pain.*
                  Measure for Measure, ii. 4.

PAINFULLY. *Laboriously ; diligently ; carefully.*

Thou hast *painfully* discover'd : are his files
As full as thy report ?   *Timon of Athens,* v. 2.

PALATE. *Flavour ; relish.*

If I could temporize with my affection,
Or brew it to a weak and colder *palate,*
The like allayment could I give my grief.
                   Troilus and Cressida, iv. 4.

To PALATE. *To taste ; to relish.*

And it is great
To do that thing that ends all other deeds ;
Which shackles accidents, and bolts up change ;

PALE. 232 PARAGON.

Which sleeps, and never *palates* more the dug,
The beggar's nurse and Cæsar's.
Antony and Cleopatra, v. 2.
You are plebeians,
If they be senators: and they are no less,
When, both your voices blended, the great'st taste
Most *palates* theirs. *Coriolanus*, iii. 1.

PALE. *An enclosure.*

Why should we, in the compass of a *pale*,
Keep law and form and due proportion,
Showing, as in a model, a firm state,
When our sea-wallèd garden, the whole land,
Is full of weeds? *Richard 2*, iii. 4.

To PALE. *To enclose; to make pale; to dim.*

Whate'er the ocean *pales*, or sky inclips,
Is thine, if thou wilt ha't.
Antony and Cleopatra, ii. 7.
Behold the English beach
Pales in the flood with men, with wives, and boys.
Henry 5, iv. Chorus.
The glow-worm shows the matin to be near,
And gins to *pale* his ineffectual fire.
Hamlet, i. 5.

PALLED. *Impaired; weakened.*

For this,
I'll never follow thy *pall'd* fortunes more.
Antony and Cleopatra, ii. 7.

PALLET. *An inferior kind of bed.*

Why rather, sleep, liest thou in smoky cribs,
Upon uneasy *pallets* stretching thee,
And hush'd with buzzing night-flies to thy slumber,
Than in the pérfum'd chambers of the great,
Under the canopies of costly state,
And lull'd with sounds of sweetest melody?
Henry 4, P. 2, iii. 1.

To PALTER. *To shift; to shuffle; to waver; to hesitate; to equivocate.*

The people are abus'd; set on. This *paltering*
Becomes not Rome. *Coriolanus*, iii. 1.
Now I must
To the young man send humble treaties, dodge
And *palter* in the shifts of lowness.
Antony and Cleopatra, iii. 11.
What need we any spur, but our own cause,
To prick us to redress? what other bond
Than secret Romans, that have spoke the word,
And will not *palter*? *Julius Cæsar*, ii. 1.

And be these juggling fiends no more believ'd,
That *palter* with us in a double sense!
Macbeth, v. 8.

To PANG. *To torment; to give pain; to afflict.*

Yet, if that fortune's quarrel do divorce
It from the bearer, 'tis a sufferance *panging*
As soul and body's severing. *Henry 8*, ii. 3.
And I grieve myself
To think, when thou shalt be dislodg'd by her
That now thou tir'st on, how thy memory
Will then be *pang'd* by me. *Cymbeline*, iii. 4.

PANTLER. *The officer in great families who had charge of the bread.*

A good shallow young fellow: he would have
made a good *pantler*, he would have chipped bread
well. *Henry 4*, P. 2, ii. 4.
Yet you are curb'd from that enlargement by
The consequence o' the crown; and must not soil
The precious note of it with a base slave,
A hilding for a livery, a squire's cloth,
A *pantler*, not so eminent. *Cymbeline*, ii. 3.
When my old wife liv'd, upon
This day she was both *pantler*, butler, cook;
Both dame and servant. *Winter's Tale*, iv. 3.

PAP. *The nipple.*

Thou hast thumped him with thy bird-bolt
under the left *pap*. *Love's Labour's lost*, iv. 3.

To PAPER. *To register; to set down in writing.*

And his own letter,
The honourable board of council out,
Must fetch him in he *papers*. *Henry 8*, i. 1.

PARADOX. *Something inherently false and ridiculous; a ludicrous imitation; a parody.*

You undergo too strict a *paradox*,
Striving to make an ugly deed look fair.
Timon of Athens, iii. 5.
Success or loss, what is or is not, serves
As stuff for these two to make *paradoxes*.
Troilus and Cressida, i. 3.

PARAGON. *A model; a pattern; something supremely excellent.*

By Jupiter, an angel! or, if not,
An earthly *paragon*! *Cymbeline*, iii. 6.

Tunis was never graced before with such a *paragon* to their queen.   *Tempest,* ii. 1.

To PARAGON.   *To parallel; to compare; to equal.*

Prove but our marriage lawful, we are contented
To wear our mortal state to come with her,
Katharine our queen, before the primest creature
That's *paragon'd* o' the world.   *Henry* 8, ii. 4.

By Isis, I will give thee bloody teeth,
If thou with Cæsar *paragon* again
My man of men.   *Antony and Cleopatra,* i. 5.

He hath achiev'd a maid
That *paragons* description and wild fame.
    Othello, ii. 1.

PARALLEL.   *Plain; equal; direct.*

How am I, then, a villain
To counsel Cassio to this *parallel* course,
Directly to his good?   *Othello,* ii. 3.

PARAQUITO.   *A little parrot.*

Come, come, you *paraquito,* answer me
Directly unto this question that I ask.
    Henry 4, P. 1, ii. 3.

To PARCEL.   *To divide; to separate; to compute; to reckon; to cast up.*

Their woes are *parcell'd,* mine are general.
    Richard 3, ii. 2.

O Cæsar, what a wounding shame is this,—
. . . . . that mine own servant should
Parcel the sum of my disgraces by
Addition of his envy!   *Antony and Cleopatra,* v. 2.

PARD.   *A leopard.*

Full of strange oaths, and bearded like the *pard.*
    As you like it, ii. 7.

As false
As air, as water, wind, or sandy earth,
As fox to lamb, as wolf to heifer's calf,
Pard to the hind, or stepdame to her son.
    Troilus and Cressida, iii. 2.

'PAREL.   *Apparel.*

I'll bring him the best *'parel* that I have,
Come on't what will.   *King Lear,* iv. 1.

PARITOR.   *An apparitor; a summoner.*

Sole imperator and great general
Of trotting *paritors!*   *Love's Labour's lost,* iii. 1.

PARLE.   *Parley; conversation.*

Our trumpet call'd you to this gentle *parle.*
    King John, ii. 1.

Of all the fair resort of gentlemen
That every day with *parle* encounter me,
In thy opinion which is worthiest love?
    Two Gentlemen of Verona, i. 2.

To PARLE.   *To converse; to talk.*

Their purpose is, to *parle,* to court, and dance.
    Love's Labour's lost, v. 2.

PARLOUS.   *Perilous;   dangerous;   keen; shrewd.*

Thou art in a *parlous* state, shepherd.
    As you like it, iii. 2.

No doubt, no doubt: O, 'tis a *parlous* boy;
Bold, quick, ingenious, forward, capable.
    Richard 3, iii. 1.

PARMACETI.   *Spermaceti.*

And telling me the sovereign'st thing on earth
Was *parmaceti* for an inward bruise.
    Henry 4, P. 1, i. 3.

PART.   *Relationship; side; party; action; conduct.*

Alas, the *part* I had in Woodstock's blood
Doth more solicit me than your exclaims,
To stir against the butchers of his life!
    Richard 2, i. 2.

Throw in the frozen bosoms of our *part*
Hot coals of vengeance!   *Henry* 6, P. 2, v. 2.

A more unhappy lady
If this division chance, ne'er stood between,
Praying for both *parts.*
    Antony and Cleopatra, iii. 4.

This *part* of his conjoins with my disease,
And helps to end me.   *Henry* 4, P. 2, iv. 4.

PART.   *Partly; in part.*

And, *part,* being prompted by your present trouble,
Out of my lean and low ability
I'll lend you something.   *Twelfth-Night,* iii. 5.

To PART.   *To share; to divide; to possess in common; to go away; to depart.*

So, call the field to rest: and let's away,
To *part* the glories of this happy day.
    Julius Cæsar, v. 5.

I had thought
They had *parted* so much honesty among 'em.
    Henry 8, v. 2.

Peace ! stand aside : the company *parts*.
          Two Gentlemen of Verona, iv. 2.
In debating which was best, wo shall *part* with
neither.   *Comedy of Errors*, iii. 1.
          Wo must all *part*
Into this sea of air.   *Timon of Athens*, iv. 2.
Kent banish'd thus ! and Franco in cholcr *parted !*
And the king gone to-night ! subscrib'd his power !
Confin'd to exhibition !   *King Lear*, i. 2.

To PARTAKE. *To share ; to extend participation to.*
          Go together,
You precious winners all ; your exultation
Partake to every one.   *Winter's Tale*, v. 3.

PARTAKER. *An accomplice.*
For your *partaker* Pole, and you yourself,
I'll note you in my book of memory,
To scourge you for this apprehension.
          Henry 6, P. 1, ii. 4.

PARTED. *Endowed ; gifted ; accomplished.*
          A strange fellow here
Writes me, That man, how dearly ever *parted*,
How much in having, or without or in,
Cannot make boast to have that which he hath,
Nor feels not what he owes, but by reflection.
          Troilus and Cressida, iii. 3.

To PARTIALIZE. *To make partial ; to warp ; to bias.*
Such neighbour-nearness to our sacred blood
Shall nothing privilege him, nor *partialize*
The unstooping firmness of my upright soul.
          Richard 2, i. 1.

PARTICIPATE. *Participant ; participating ; sharing.*
And, mutually *participate*, did minister
Unto the appetite and affection common
Of the whole body.   *Coriolanus*, i. 1.

PARTICIPATION. *Familiarity ; community.*
For thou hast lost thy princely privilege
With vile *participation*.   *Henry* 4, P. 1, iii. 2.

PARTICULAR. *Individual person ; single self.*
For his *particular*, I'll receive him gladly,
But not one follower.   *King Lear*, ii. 4.
You must not marvel, Helen, at my course,
Which holds not colour with the time, nor does

The ministration and required office
On my *particular*.   *All's well that ends well*, ii. 5.

PARTICULAR. *Individual ; single.*
Combine together 'gainst the enemy ;
For these domestic and *particular* broils
Are not the question here.   *King Lear*, v. 1.
          For the success,
Although *particular*, shall give a scantling
Of good or bad unto the general.
          Troilus and Cressida, i. 3.

PARTICULARITY. *Individuality ; separate existence ; respect ; matter.*
Now let the general trumpet blow his blast,
Particularities and petty sounds
To cease !   *Henry* 6, P. 2, v. 2.
          Being as goot a man as yourself in the derivation of my birth, and in other *particularities*.
          Henry 5, iii. 1.

PARTICULARLY. *Within narrow limits ; restrictedly.*
          My free drift
Halts not *particularly*, but moves itself
In a wide sea of wax.   *Timon of Athens*, i. 1.

PARTISAN. *A pike ; a javelin.*
I had as lief have a reed that will do me no service as a *partisan* I could not heave.
          Antony and Cleopatra, ii. 7.
Shall I strike at it with my *partisan* ? *Hamlet*, i. 1.

PARTITION. *Separation ; distinction.*
That were our royal faiths martyrs in love,
We shall be winnow'd with so rough a wind,
That e'en our corn shall seem as light as chaff,
And good from bad find no *partition*.
          Henry 4, P. 2, iv. 1.
          And can we not
Partition make with spectacles so precious
'Twixt fair and foul ?   *Cymbeline*, i. 6.

To PARTNER. *To associate with ; to consort.*
          To be *partner'd*
With tomboys, hir'd with that self-exhibition
Which your own coffers yield !   *Cymbeline*, i. 6.

PARTS. *Powers ; qualities ; arts ; endowments ; gifts ; possessions ; wealth.*
I cónjure thee, by all the *parts* of man
Which honour does acknowledge.
          Winter's Tale, i. 2.

Haply, for I am black,
And have not those soft *parts* of conversation
That chamberers have. *Othello*, iii. 3.

Affliction is enamour'd of thy *parts*,
And thou art wedded to calamity.
Romeo and Juliet, iii. 3.

Who, in his circumstance, expressly proves
That no man is the lord of any thing
Till he communicate his *parts* to others.
Troilus and Cressida, iii. 3.

The *parts* that fortune hath bestow'd upon her,
Tell her, I hold as giddily as fortune.
Twelfth-Night, ii. 4.

PARTY. *Side; part; faction; disorder; tumult.*

Your uncle York is join'd with Bolingbroke ;
And all your northern castles yielded up,
And all your southern gentlemen in arms
Upon his *party*. *Richard 2*, iii. 2.

Which on thy royal *party* granted once,
His glittering arms he will commend to rust,
His barbèd steeds to stables, and his heart
To faithful service of your majesty. *Ibid.* iii. 3.

Proceed by process ;
Lest *parties*—as he is belov'd—break out,
And sack great Rome with Romans.
Coriolanus, iii. 1.

PASH. *This means, to all appearance, the patch or thicket of hair that is more or less conspicuous on the front or forehead of a full-grown bull. Possibly it is but a misprint for* patch.

Thou want'st a rough *pash*, and the shoots that I have,
To be full like me. *Winter's Tale*, i. 2.

To PASH. *To strike ; to smite ; to crush.*

If I go to him, with my armèd fist
I'll *pash* him o'er the face.
Troilus and Cressida, ii. 3.

And stands colossus-wise, waving his beam,
Upon the *pashèd* corses of the kings
Epistrophus and Cedius. *Ibid.* v. 5.

PASS. *A push or thrust in fencing ; offence ; practice.*

'Tis dangerous when the baser nature comes
Between the *pass* and fell incensèd points
Of mighty opposites. *Hamlet*, v. 2.

Or, with a little shuffling, you may choose
A sword unbated, and, in a *pass* of practice,
Requite him for your father. *Hamlet*, iv. 7.

"Steal by line and level" is an excellent *pass* of pate. *Tempest*, iv. 1.

I should be guiltier than my guiltiness,
To think I can be undiscernible,
When I perceive your grace, like power divine,
Hath look'd upon my *passes*.
Measure for Measure, v. 1.

Yond's that same knave
That leads him to these *passes*.
All's well that ends well, iii. 5.

To PASS. *To pass judgment ; to reject ; to care for ; to assure ; to die ; to succeed ; to surpass ; to exceed bounds ; to omit.*

What know the laws that thieves do *pass* on thieves?
Measure for Measure, ii. 1.

Though well we may not *pass* upon his life
Without the form of justice, yet our power
Shall do a courtesy to our wrath. *King Lear*, iii. 7.

But if you fondly *pass* our proffer'd offer,
'Tis not the rondure of your old-fac'd walls
Can hide you from our messengers of war.
King John, ii. 1.

As for these silken-coated slaves, I *pass* not.
Henry 6, P. 2, iv. 2.

If you say no more than this,
That like a father you will deal with him,
And *pass* my daughter a sufficient dower,
The match is made, and all is done.
Taming of the Shrew, iv. 4.

Vex not his ghost : O, let him *pass*!
King Lear, v. 3.

Disturb him not, let him *pass* peaceably.
Henry 6, P. 2, iii. 3.

This practice hath most shrewdly *pass'd* upon thee.
Twelfth-Night, v. 1.

But I have that within which *passeth* show ;
Those but the trappings and the suits of woe.
Hamlet, i. 2.

The women have so cried and shrieked at it,
that it *passed*. *Merry Wives of Windsor*, i. 2.

I do beseech you,
Let me o'erleap that custom ; for I cannot
Put on the gown, stand naked, and entreat them,
For my wounds' sake, to give their suffrage : please you
That I may *pass* this doing. *Coriolanus*, ii. 2.

PASSABLE. *Current; easily passed through.*
Bo it so; go back : tho virtue of your name
Is not hero *passable.*   *Coriolanus*, v. 2.
Hurt him! his body's a *passable* carcass, if ho
bo not hurt.   *Cymbeline*, i. 2.

PASSADO. *A push or thrust in fencing.*
Ah, tho immortal *passado! Romeo and Juliet*, ii. 4.

PASSAGE. *Occurrence; hap; incident; right
of way; traffic; decay.*
And thou, Posthúmus, thou that didst set up
My disobedience 'gainst tho king my father,
And make mo put into contempt tho suits
Of princely fellows, shalt hereafter find
It is no act of common *passage*, but
A strain of rareness.   *Cymbeline*, iii. 4.
O, that " had I" how sad a *passage* 'tis!
          All's well that ends well, i. 1.
But thou dost, in thy *passages* of life,
Make mo believe that thou art only mark'd
For the hot vengeance and tho rod of heaven
To punish my mistreadings.   *Henry* 4, P. 1, iii. 2.
What, are my doors oppos'd against my *passage?*
          Timon of Athens, iii. 4.
What, ho! no watch! no *passage?* murder! murder!
          Othello, v. 1.
Now in tho stirring *passage* of tho day.
          Comedy of Errors, iii. 1.
O, uncle, would some part of my young years
Might but redeem tho *passage* of your age!
          Henry 6, P. 1, ii. 5.

PASSING. *Surpassing; egregious.*
O *passing* traitor, perjur'd and unjust!
          Henry 6, P. 3, v. 1.

PASSION. *Suffering; agony.*
          O you gods,
I feel my master's *passion! Timon of Athens*, iii. 1.
          At your birth,
Our grandam earth, having this distemperature,
In *passion* shook.   *Henry* 4, P. 1, iii. 1.
          Upon a thought
He will again bo well : if much you note him,
You shall offend him, and extend his *passion.*
          Macbeth, iii. 4.

TO PASSION. *To grieve; to lament.*
          'Twas Ariadne, *passioning*
For Theseus' perjury and unjust flight.
          Two Gentlemen of Verona, iv. 2.

PASSIONATE. *Overwhelmed with grief; mourn-
ful; lamentable.*
Sho is sad and *passionate* at your highness' tent.
          King John, ii. 1.
Nephew, what means this *passionate* discourse,
This peroration with such circumstance?
          Henry 6, P. 2, i. 1.

PAST-PROPORTION. *Immensity; boundless extent.*
          Will you with counters sum
Tho *past-proportion* of his infinite?
          Troilus and Cressida, ii. 2.

PASTRY. *A room where pastry is made.*
They call for dates and quinces in tho *pastry.*
          Romeo and Juliet, iv. 4.

PATCH. *A fool.*
Momo, malt-horse, capon, coxcomb, idiot, *patch!*
Either got thee from tho door, or sit down at tho
hatch.   *Comedy of Errors*, iii. 1.
Go prick thy face, and over-red thy fear,
Thou lily-liver'd boy. What soldiers, *patch?*
          Macbeth, v. 3.
What a pied ninny's this!—Thou scurvy *patch!*
          Tempest, iii. 2.

PATCHED. *Parti-coated; motley.*
But man is but a *patched* fool, if ho will offer
to say what methought I had.
          Midsummer-Night's Dream, iv. 1.

PATCHERY. *Roguery; baseness; villany.*
Here is such *patchery*, such juggling, and such
knavery!   *Troilus and Cressida*, ii. 3.
Ay, and you hear him cog, see him dissemble,
Know his gross *patchery*, love him, feed him,
Keep in your bosom : yet remain assur'd
That ho's a made-up villain. *Timon of Athens*, v. 1.

PATHETICAL. *False; hypocritical; affected.*
If you break one jot of your promise, or come
ono minute behind your hour, I will think you tho
most *pathetical* break-promise, and tho most hollow
lover.   *As you like it*, iv. 1.
Sweet invocation of a child; most pretty and *pathetical!*   *Love's Labour's lost*, i. 2.
And his page o' t'other side, that handful of wit!
Ah, heavens, it is a most *pathetical* nit!
          Ibid. iv. 1.

PATIENCE.	*Endurance; suffering.*

Gentlemen both, we will not wake your *patience*.
Much Ado about Nothing, v. 1.

PATINE.	*A plate of metal.*

Look, how the floor of heaven
Is thick inlaid with *patines* of bright gold.
Merchant of Venice, v. 1.

To PATRONAGE.	*To defend.*

Yes, as an outlaw in a castle keeps,
And uses it to *patronage* his theft.
Henry 6, P. 1, iii. 1.

Yes, sir; as well as you dare *patronage*
The envious barking of your saucy tongue
Against my lord the Duke of Somerset. *Ibid.* iii. 4.

PATTERN.	*Sample; instance; masterpiece.*

If thou delight to view thy heinous deeds,
Behold this *pattern* of thy butcheries.
Richard 3, i. 2.

But once put out thy light,
Thou cunning'st *pattern* of excelling nature,
I know not where is that Promethean heat
That can thy light relume.	*Othello*, v. 2.

PAVED.	*Stony; pebbly.*

Her brother's ghost his *pavèd* bed would break,
And take her hence in horror.
Measure for Measure, v. 1.

By *pavèd* fountain, or by rushy brook.
Midsummer-Night's Dream, ii. 1.

PAVILIONED.	*Tented; encamped.*

Never king of England
Had nobles richer and more loyal subjects,
Whose hearts have left their bodies here in England,
And lie *pavilion'd* in the fields of France.
Henry 5, i. 2.

To PAY.	*To beat; to punish; to requite.*

And I paid nothing for it neither, but was *paid*
for my learning.	*Merry Wives of Windsor*, v. 5.

I have *paid* Percy, I have made him sure.
Henry 4, P. 1, v. 3.

And though he came our enemy, remember
He was *paid* for that.	*Cymbeline*, iv. 2.

And on the answer, he *pays* you as surely as
your feet hit the ground they step on.	.
Twelfth-Night, iii. 5.

PAYMENT.	*Punishment.*

If he come to-morrow, I'll give him his *pay-
ment*.	*As you like it*, i. 1.

To PEACH.	*To impeach; to accuse.*

If I be ta'en, I'll *peach* for this.
Henry 4, P. 1, ii. 2.

Then is there here one Master Caper, at the suit
of Master Three-pile the mercer, for some four suits
of peach-coloured satin, which now *peaches* him a
beggar.	*Measure for Measure*, iv. 3.

To PEAK.	*To waste away; to grow lean; to
mope; to drowse.*

Weary seven-nights nine times nine
Shall he dwindle, *peak*, and pine.	*Macbeth*, i. 3.

Yet I,
A dull and muddy-mettled rascal, *peak*,
Like John-a-dreams, unpregnant of my cause.
Hamlet, ii. 2.

PEAKING.	*Mean; sneaking; contemptible.*

No, Master Brook; but the *peaking* cornuto her
husband, Master Brook, dwelling in a continual
'larum of jealousy, comes me in the instant of our
encounter, after we had embraced, kissed, protested,
and, as it were, spoke the prologue of our comedy.
Merry Wives of Windsor, iii. 5.

PEARL.	*Anything which is highly valued or
admired; pride; flower; ornament.*

Black men are *pearls* in beauteous ladies' eyes.
Two Gentlemen of Verona, v. 2.

I see thee compass'd with thy kingdom's *pearl*,
That speak my salutation in their minds.
Macbeth, v. 8.

PEAT.	*A pet; a darling.*

A pretty *peat*! it is best
Put finger in the eye,
An she knew why.	*Taming of the Shrew*, i. 1.

PEDANT.	*A schoolmaster.*

A domineering *pedant* o'er the boy.
Love's Labour's lost, iii. 1.

PEELED.	*Bald-headed; shaven.*

Peel'd priest, dost thou command me be shut out?
Henry 6, P. 1, i. 3.

PEEVISH.	*Silly; foolish.*

Why, this it is to be a *peevish* girl,
That flies her fortune when it follows her.
Two Gentlemen of Verona, v. 2.

What a wretched and *peevish* fellow is this
King of England!	*Henry* 5, iii. 6.

II

A *peevish* schoolboy, worthless of such honour,
Join'd with a masker and a reveller!
Julius Cæsar, v. 1.

To PEISE. *To poise; to balance; to weigh down.*

The world, who of itself is *peised* well,
Made to run even upon even ground.
King John, ii. 1.

I'll strive, with troubled thoughts, to take a nap,
Lest leaden slumber *peise* me down to-morrow,
When I should mount with wings of victory.
Richard 3, v. 3.

PELLETED. *Consisting of little balls or pellets.*

By the discandying of this *pelleted* storm.
Antony and Cleopatra, iii. 13.

PELTING. *Mean; paltry; pitiful; insignificant.*

This land of such dear souls is now leas'd out,
Like to a tenement or *pelting* farm.
Richard 2, ii. 1.

And from low farms, poor *pelting* villages,
Enforce their charity.　*King Lear*, ii. 3.

Contagious fogs; which, falling in the land,
Have every *pelting* river made so proud,
That they have overborne their continents.
Midsummer-Night's Dream, ii. 1.

We have had *pelting* wars, since you refus'd
The Grecians' cause.　*Troilus and Cressida*, iv. 5.

PENETRATIVE. *Penetrating; piercing.*

Wouldst thou be window'd in great Rome, and see
Thy master thus with pleach'd arms, bending down
His corrigible neck, his face subdu'd
To *penetrative* shame!
Antony and Cleopatra, iv. 14.

PENITENT. *Doing penance.*

But we that know what 'tis to fast and pray,
Are *penitent* for your default to-day.
Comedy of Errors, i. 2.

PENNON. *A small flag.*

Bar Harry England, that sweeps through our land
With *pennons* painted in the blood of Harfleur.
Henry 5, iii. 4.

To PEPPER. *To wound; to mangle; to beat.*

Pray God you have not murdered some of them.
—Nay, that's past praying for: I have *peppered*

two of them; two I am sure I have paid,—two
rogues in buckram suits.　*Henry 4*, P. 1, ii. 4.

I am *peppered*, I warrant, for this world:—a
plague o' both your houses!
Romeo and Juliet, iii. 1.

PEPPER-GINGERBREAD. *Spice gingerbread.*

Swear me, Kate, like a lady as thou art,
A good mouth-filling oath; and leave "in sooth,"
And such protest of *pepper-gingerbread*,
To velvet-guards and Sunday-citizens.
Henry 4, P. 1, iii. 1.

PERDITION. *Loss.*

Sir, his definement suffers no *perdition* in you;
though, I know, to divide him inventorially would
dizzy the arithmetic of memory, and it but yaw
neither, in respect of his quick sail.　*Hamlet*, v. 2.

PERDU. *One who is in a position of difficulty or danger.*

Was this a face
To be oppos'd against the warring winds?
To stand against the deep dread-bolted thunder?
In the most terrible and nimble stroke
Of quick, cross lightning? to watch—poor *perdu*!—
With this thin helm?　*King Lear*, iv. 7.

PERDURABLE. *Lasting.*

And I confess me knit to thy deserving with
cables of *perdurable* toughness.　*Othello*, i. 3.

O *perdurable* shame!—let's stab ourselves.
Henry 5, iv. 5.

PERDURABLY. *Everlastingly.*

If it were damnable, he, being so wise,
Why would he for the momentary trick
Be *perdurably* fin'd?　*Measure for Measure*, iii. 1.

PERDY. *Truly; in sooth.*

For if the king like not the comedy,
Why then, belike,—he likes it not, *perdy*.
Hamlet, iii. 2.

The knave turns fool that runs away;
The fool no knave, *perdy*.　*King Lear*, ii. 4.

PEREGRINATE. *Outlandish; foreign.*

Too odd, as it were, too *peregrinate*, as I may call it.
Love's Labour's lost, v. 1.

PERFECT. *Sure; certain; pure; blameless; upright.*

Thou art *perfect*, then, our ship hath touch'd upon
The deserts of Bohemia?　*Winter's Tale*, iii. 3.

What hast thou done?—
I am *perfect* what : cut off one Cloten's head.
Cymbeline, iv. 2.

I am *perfect*
That the Pannonians and Dalmatians, for
Their liberties, are now in arms ;—a precedent
Which not to read would show the Britons cold.
Ibid. iii. 1.

And I have learned by the *perfectest* report,
they have more in them than mortal knowledge.
Macbeth, i. 5.

Then comes my fit again : I had else been *perfect ;*
Whole as the marble, founded as the rock.
Ibid. iii. 4.

Not I ; I must be found :
My parts, my title, and my *perfect* soul
Shall manifest me rightly. *Othello*, i. 2.

My fault being nothing,
But that two villains, whose false oaths prevail'd
Before my *perfect* honour, swore to Cymbeline
I was confederate with the Romans.
Cymbeline, iii. 3.

To PERFECT. *To instruct fully.*

Her cause and yours
I'll *perfect* him withal ; and he shall bring you
Before the duke. *Measure for Measure*, iv. 3.

Being once *perfected* how to grant suits,
How to deny them, who t' advance, and who
To trash for over-topping. *Tempest*, i. 2.

PERFECTION. *Consummation ; performance ;
supreme excellence ; attractions ; graces.*

The image of it gives me content already, and I
trust it will grow to a most prosperous *perfection.*
Measure for Measure, iii. 1.

Vowing more than the *perfection* of ten, and
discharging less than the tenth part of one.
Troilus and Cressida, iii. 2.

You knot of mouth-friends ! smoke and luke-warm
water
Is your *perfection.* *Timon of Athens*, iii. 6.

All her *perfections* challenge sovereignty.
Henry 6, P. 3, iii. 2.

Methinks I feel this youth's *perfections*
With an invisible and subtle stealth
To creep in at mine eyes. *Twelfth-Night*, i. 5.

PERFORCE. *Of necessity ; by force ; forcibly.*

Nature does require
Her times of preservation, which *perforce*
I, her frail son, amongst my brethren mortal,
Must give my tendance to. *Henry* 8, iii. 2.

But she *perforce* withholds the lovèd boy,
Crowns him with flowers, and makes him all her
joy. *Midsummer-Night's Dream*, ii. 1.

PERFUME. *A mistress ; a concubine.*

Thy flatterers yet wear silk, drink wine, lie soft,
Hug their diseas'd *perfumes*, and have forgot
That ever Timon was. *Timon of Athens*, iv. 3.

PERIAPT. *A magical fillet or bandage ; an
amulet.*

Now help, ye charming spells and *periapts !*
Henry 6, P. 1, v. 3.

To PERIOD. *To put an end to ; to terminate.*

Your honourable letter he desires
To those have shut him up ; which failing,
Periods his comfort. *Timon of Athens*, i. 1.

To PERISH. *To destroy.*

Because thy flinty heart, more hard than they,
Might in thy palace *perish* Margaret.
Henry 6, P. 2, iii. 2.

PERJURE. *A perjurer.*

Why, he comes in like a *perjure*, wearing papers.
Love's Labour's lost, iv. 3.

To PERJURE. *To corrupt ; to taint with perjury.*

Women are not
In their best fortunes strong ; but want will *perjure*
The ne'er-touch'd vestal.
Antony and Cleopatra, iii. 12.

To PERK. *To dress up ; to decorate ; to
adorn.*

I swear, 'tis better to be lowly born,
And range with humble livers in content,
Than to be *perk'd up* in a glistering grief,
And wear a golden sorrow. *Henry* 8, ii. 3.

PERMISSIVE. *Permitted ; not prevented.*

For we bid this be done,
When evil deeds have their *permissive* pass,
And not their punishment.
Measure for Measure, i. 3.

To PERPEND. *To reflect ; to consider attentively.*

Therefore *perpend*, my princess, and give ear.
Twelfth-Night, v. 1.

He loves the gallimaufry : Ford, *perpend.*
Merry Wives of Windsor, ii. 1.

To PERSEVER. *To persevere; to persist.*

But to *persèver*
In obstinate condolement, is a course
Of impious stubbornness ; 'tis unmanly grief.
Hamlet, i. 2.

Sho did, my lord, when Valentine was here.—
Ay, and perversely she *persèvers* so.
Two Gentlemen of Verona, iii. 2.

PERSISTED. *Persevered in; long continued.*

And strange it is,
That nature must compel us to lament
Our most *persisted* deeds.
Antony and Cleopatra, v. 1.

PERSISTENCY. *Obstinacy; contumacy.*

Thou thinkest me as far in the devil's book as
thou and Falstaff for obduracy and *persistency;* let
the end try the man. *Henry 4,* P. 2, ii. 2.

PERSISTIVE. *Persevering; steady; persistent.*

And call them shames, which are, indeed, naught
else
But the protractive trials of great Jove
To find *persistive* constancy in men.
Troilus and Cressida, i. 3.

PERSONAL. *Present; engaged in person.*

When he was *personal* in the Irish war.
Henry 4, P. 1, iv. 3.

To PERSONATE. *To represent; to describe.*

The lofty cedar, royal Cymbeline,
Personates thee : and thy lopp'd branches point
Thy two sons forth. *Cymbeline,* v. 5.

Amongst them all
Whose eyes are on this sovereign lady fix'd,
One do I *personate* of Lord Timon's frame,
Whom Fortune with her ivory hand wafts to her.
Timon of Athens, i. 1.

Wherein, by the colour of his beard, the shape
of his leg, the manner of his gait, the expressure of
his eye, forehead, and complexion, he shall find
himself most feelingly *personated.*
Twelfth-Night, ii. 3.

PERSONATING. *A representation; a likeness; a picture.*

It must be a *personating* of himself.
Timon of Athens, v. 1.

PERSPECTIVE. *A reflecting glass.*

One face, one voice, one habit, and two persons,—
A natural *pérspective,* that is and is not !
Twelfth-Night, v. 1.

Where the impression of mine eye infixing,
Contempt his scornful *pérspective* did lend me,
Which warp'd the line of every other favour.
All's well that ends well, iv. 3.

PERSPECTIVELY. *As in a perspective or reflecting glass.*

Yes, my lord, you see them *perspectively,* the
cities turned into a maid ; for they are all girdled
with maiden walls that war hath never entered.
Henry 5, v. 2.

To PERSUADE. *To reason; to expostulate; to intercede.*

The duke himself, and the magnificoes
Of greatest port, have all *persuaded* with him.
Merchant of Venice, iii. 2.

To PERTAIN. *To appertain; to belong.*

And little of this great world can I speak,
More than *pertains* to feats of broil and battle.
Othello, i. 3.

He wills you, in the name of God Almighty,
That you divest yourself, and lay apart
The borrow'd glories, that, by gift of heaven,
By law of nature and of nations, 'long
To him and to his heirs ; namely, the crown,
And all wide-stretchèd honours that *pertain,*
By custom and the ordinance of times,
Unto the crown of France. *Henry 5,* ii. 4.

PERTLY. *Actively; briskly; nimbly; busily.*

Appear, and *pertly!* *Tempest,* iv. 1.

To PERVERT. *To turn aside; to divert.*

Let's follow him, and *pervert* the present wrath
He hath against himself. *Cymbeline,* ii. 4.

To PESTER. *To crowd; to throng; to encumber.*

Who rather had,
Though they themselves did suffer by't, behold
Dissentious numbers *pestering* streets, than see
Our tradesmen singing in their shops, and going
About their functions friendly. *Coriolanus,* iv. 6.

PESTILENCE. *Infection; poison.*

I'll pour this *pestilence* into his ear,
That she repeals him for her body's lust.
Othello, ii. 3.

PETAR. *A case filled with explosive materials.*

Let it work;
For 'tis the sport to have the enginer
Hoist with his own *petar.* *Hamlet,* iii. 4.

PETITIONARY. *Supplicatory.*

Nay, I prithee now with most *petitionary* vehemence, tell me who it is. *As you like it,* iii. 2.

I was hardly moved to come to thee; but being assured none but myself could move thee, I have been blown out of our gates with sighs; and conjure thee to pardon Rome, and thy *petitionary* countrymen. *Coriolanus,* v. 2.

PEWFELLOW. *Companion.*

How do I thank thee, that this carnal cur
Preys on the issue of his mother's body,
And makes her *pewfellow* with others' moan!
Richard 3, iv. 4.

PHANTASMA. PHANTASM. *A vision; an apparition; anything vain and fantastical.*

Between the acting of a dreadful thing
And the first motion, all the interim is
Like a *phantasma,* or a hideous dream.
Julius Cæsar, ii. 1.

I abhor such fanatical *phantasms.*
Love's Labour's lost, v. 1.

A *phantasm,* a Monarcho, and one that makes sport
To the prince and his bookmates. *Ibid.* iv. 1.

To PHEEZE. *To beat; to chastise; to humble.*

I'll *pheeze* you, in faith.
Taming of the Shrew, Induction, scene 1.

An 'a be proud with me, I'll *pheeze* his pride.
Troilus and Cressida, ii. 3.

To PHYSIC. *To cure.*

The labour we delight in *physics* pain.
Macbeth, ii. 1.

Some griefs are med'cinable; that is one of them,
For it doth *physic* love. *Cymbeline,* iii. 2.

PHYSICAL. *Medicinal; salutary; wholesome.*

Is Brutus sick,—and is it *physical*
To walk unbraced? *Julius Cæsar,* ii. 1.

The blood I drop is rather *physical*
Than dangerous to me. *Coriolanus,* i. 5.

To PICK. *To pitch; to throw; to cast.*

You i' the camlet, get up o' the rail;
I'll *pick* you o'er the pales else. *Henry 8,* v. 3.

And let me use my sword, I'd make a quarry
With thousands of these quarter'd slaves, as high
As I could *pick* my lance. *Coriolanus,* i. 1.

PICKED. *Trim; smart; foppish; convenient; chosen.*

And when my knightly stomach is suffic'd,
Why then I suck my teeth, and catechize
My *picked* man of countries. *King John,* i. 1.

He is too *picked,* too spruce, too affected, too odd, as it were, too peregrinate, as I may call it.
Love's Labour's lost, v. 1.

The age is grown so *picked,* that the toe of the peasant comes so near the heel of the courtier, he galls his kibe. *Hamlet,* v. 1.

At *pick'd* leisure,
Which shall be shortly, single I'll resolve you.
Tempest, v. 1.

PICKING. *Trifling; insignificant.*

Note this,—the king is weary
Of dainty and such *picking* grievances.
Henry 4, P. 2, iv. 1.

PICK-THANK. *A tale-bearer; a parasite.*

Yet such extenuation let me beg,
As in reproof of many tales devis'd,—
Which oft the ear of greatness needs must hear,—
By smiling *pick-thanks* and base news-mongers.
Henry 4, P. 1, iii. 2.

PICTURE. *Show; seeming; appearance.*

By which means I saw whose purse was best in *picture.* *Winter's Tale,* iv. 3.

To PIECE. *To augment; to extend; to join; to unite.*

Shall we thither, and with our company *piece* the rejoicing? *Winter's Tale,* v. 2.

I speak too long; but 'tis to *piece* the time,
To eke it, and to draw it out in length.
Merchant of Venice, iii. 2.

Fly with false aim; move the still-*piecing* air,
That sings with piercing; do not touch my lord!
All's well that ends well, iii. 2.

To PIERCE. *To relieve; to give ease to.*

But words are words; I never yet did hear
That the bruis'd heart was *piercèd* through the ear.
Othello, i. 3.

PIGHT. *Placed; pitched; fixed; resolved.*

For feature, laming
The shrine of Venus, or straight-*pight* Minerva.
Cymbeline, v. 5.

You vile abominable tents,
Thus proudly *pight* upon our Phrygian plains,
Let Titan rise as early as he dare,
I'll through and through you!
Troilus and Cressida, v. 10.

When I dissuaded him from his intent,
And found him *pight* to do it, with curst speech
I threaten'd to discover him. *King Lear*, ii. 1.

PILCHER. *A sheath; a scabbard; a pilchard.*

Will you pluck your sword out of his *pilcher*
by the ears? make haste, lest mine be about your
ears ere it be out. *Romeo and Juliet*, iii. 1.

And fools are as like husbands as *pilchers* are
to herring,—the husband's the bigger.
Twelfth-Night, iii. 1.

TO PILL. *To rob; to steal; to spoil; to plunder.*

Large-handed robbers your grave masters are,
And *pill* by law. *Timon of Athens*, iv. 1.

Hear me, you wrangling pirates, that fall out
In sharing that which you have *pill'd* from me!
Richard 3, i. 3.

The commons hath he *pill'd* with grievous taxes,
And lost their hearts. *Richard 2*, ii. 1.

PIN. *The centre.*

The very *pin* of his heart cleft with the blind
bow-boy's butt-shaft. *Romeo and Juliet*, ii. 4.

PIN-AND-WEB. *A disease of the eye.*

And all eyes
Blind with the *pin-and-web*, but theirs, theirs only,
That would unseen be wicked. *Winter's Tale*, i. 2.

This is the foul fiend Flibbertigibbet: he gives
the *web and the pin*, squints the eye, and makes
the hare-lip. *King Lear*, iii. 4.

TO PINE. *To starve; to afflict.*

Part us, Northumberland; I towards the north,
Where shivering cold and sickness *pine* the clime;
My wife to France,—from whence, set forth in pomp,
She came adornèd hither like sweet May,
Sent back like Hallowmas or short'st of day.
Richard 2, v. 1.

PINK. *Small.*

Come, thou monarch of the vine,
Plumpy Bacchus with *pink* eyne!
Antony and Cleopatra, ii. 7.

TO PINK. *To pierce; to perforate.*

That railed upon me till her *pinked* porringer
fell off her head. *Henry 8*, v. 3.

PIONER. *Pioneer.*

A worthy *pioner!*—Once more remove, good friends.
Hamlet, i. 5.

Have you quit the mines? have the *pioners*
given o'er? *Henry 5*, iii. 1.

PITCH. *Size; extent; height.*

Naught enters there,
Of what validity and *pitch* soe'er,
But falls into abatement and low price,
Even in a minute! *Twelfth-Night*, i. 1.

I tell you, madam, were the whole frame here,
It is of such a spacious lofty *pitch*,
Your roof were not sufficient to contain't.
Henry 6, P. 1, ii. 3.

They know their master loves to be aloft,
And bears his thoughts above his falcon's *pitch*.
Henry 6, P. 2, ii. 1.

These growing feathers pluck'd from Cæsar's wing
Will make him fly an ordinary *pitch*.
Julius Cæsar, i. 1.

PITCH AND PAY. *Ready money.*

Let senses rule; the word is *Pitch and pay*;
Trust none. *Henry 5*, ii. 3.

PITH. *The chief part; the quintessence; weight; importance; strength; force.*

And, indeed, it takes
From our achievements, though perform'd at height,
The *pith* and marrow of our attribute. *Hamlet*, i. 4.

And enterprises of great *pith* and moment,
With this regard, their currents turn awry,
And lose the name of action. *Ibid.* iii. 1.

For since these arms of mine had seven years' *pith*,
Till now some nine moons wasted, they have us'd
Their dearest action in the tented field.
Othello, i. 3.

PITY. *Calamity; misfortune; shame; scandal.*

After this process,
To give her the avaunt! it is a *pity*
Would move a monster. *Henry 8*, ii. 3.

That he is old,—the more the *pity*,—his white hairs do witness it.   *Henry 4, P. 1, ii. 4.*

Why, there thou sayst: and the more *pity* that great folk should have countenance in this world to drown or hang themselves, more than their even Christian.   *Hamlet, v. 1.*

PLACE.   *Precedence ; rank ; height ; a mansion.*

Yet these fix'd evils sit so fit in him,
That they take *place*, when virtue's steely bones
Look bleak i' the cold wind.
　　　　　　　All's well that ends well, i. 1.
Most humbly, therefore, bending to your state,
I crave fit disposition for my wife ;
Due reference of *place* and exhibition. *Othello, i. 3.*
A falcon, towering in her pride of *place*,
Was by a mousing owl hawk'd at and kill'd.
　　　　　　　　　Macbeth, ii. 2.
This is no *place;* this house is but a butchery.
　　　　　　　　As you like it, ii. 3.
Colevile shall be still your name, a traitor your degree, and the dungeon your *place.*
　　　　　　　　Henry 4, P. 2, iv. 3.
I do not like the Tower of any *place.*—
Did Julius Cæsar build that *place,* my lord ?
　　　　　　　　　Richard 3, iii. 1.

PLACKET.   *A woman's pocket.*

Will they wear their *plackets* where they should bear their faces ?   *Winter's Tale, iv. 3.*

You might have pinched a *placket*, it was senseless.   *Ibid. iv. 3.*

Liege of all loiterers and malcontents, Dread prince of *plackets*, king of codpieces !
　　　　　　　Love's Labour's lost, iii. 1.

Keep thy foot out of brothels, thy hand out of *plackets*, thy pen from lenders' books, and defy the foul fiend.   *King Lear, iii. 4.*

PLAGUE.   *Vexation ; torment.*

I am not mad ; too well, too well I feel The different *plague* of each calamity.
　　　　　　　　　King John, iii. 4.

To PLAGUE.   *To punish ; to avenge.*

And God, not we, hath *plagu'd* thy bloody deed.
　　　　　　　　　Richard 3, i. 3.

PLAIN.   *Smooth ; level.*
　　　　　　　Nor has Coriolanus
Deserv'd this so dishonour'd rub, laid falsely
In the *plain* way of his merit.   *Coriolanus, iii. 1.*

To PLAIN.   *To complain.*
　　　　　　　Making just report
Of how unnatural and bemadding sorrow
The king hath cause to *plain*.   *King Lear, iii. 1.*

PLAINING.   *Complaint ; remonstrance.*

It boots thee not to be compassionate :
After our sentence *plaining* comes too late.
　　　　　　　　　Richard 2, i. 3.

PLAINLY.   *Openly ; publicly.*
　　　　　　　My partner in this action,
You must report to the Volscian lords, how *plainly*
I have borne this business.   *Coriolanus, v. 3.*

PLAIN-SONG.   *Simple melody.*

An honest country lord . . . .
. . . . may bring his *plain-song*,
And have an hour of hearing.   *Henry 8, i. 3.*

The finch, the sparrow, and the lark,
The *plain-song* cuckoo gray.
　　　　　　　Midsummer-Night's Dream, iii. 1.

PLANCHED.   *Made of planks.*

He hath a garden circummur'd with brick,
Whose western side is with a vineyard back'd ;
And to that vineyard is a *planchèd* gate,
That makes his opening with this bigger key.
　　　　　　　Measure for Measure, iv. 1.

PLANT.   *The foot.*

Some o' their *plants* are ill-rooted already ; the least wind i' the world will blow them down.
　　　　　　　Antony and Cleopatra, ii. 7.

PLANTAGE.   *Herbs ; plants.*

As true as steel, as *plantage* to the moon,
As sun to day, as turtle to her mate.
　　　　　　　Troilus and Cressida, iii. 2.

PLANTATION.   *Colony ; settlement.*

Had I *plantation* of this isle, my lord,
And were the king on't, what would I do ?
I' the commonwealth I would by contraries
Execute all things.   *Tempest, ii. 1.*

PLANTED.   *Skilled ; knowing.*

A man in all the world's new fashion *planted*,
That hath a mint of phrases in his brain.
　　　　　　　Love's Labour's lost, i. 1.

LASH. 244 PLOT.

PLASH. *A small lake; a pool; a pond.*

As he that leaves
A shallow *plash*, to plunge him in the deep.
Taming of the Shrew, i. 1.

To PLATE. *To arm; to clothe in armour.*

Marshal, ask yonder knight in arms,
Both who he is, and why he cometh hither
Thus *plated* in habiliments of war. *Richard 2*, i. 3.

Those his eyes
That o'er the files and musters of the war
Have glow'd like *plated* Mars, now bend, now turn,
The office and devotion of their view
Upon a tawny front. *Antony and Cleopatra*, i. 1.

Plate sin with gold,
And the strong lance of justice hurtless breaks;
Arm it in rags, a pigmy's sword does pierce it.
King Lear, iv. 6.

PLATES. *Coins; money.*

In his livery
Walk'd crowns and crownets; realms and islands were
As *plates* dropp'd from his pocket.
Antony and Cleopatra, v. 2.

PLATFORM. *A rampart; plan; device; stratagem.*

But where was this?—
My lord, upon the *platform* where we watch'd.
Hamlet, i. 2.

Upon the *platform*, twixt eleven and twelve,
I'll visit you. *Ibid.* i. 2.

To the *platform*, masters; come, let's set the watch.
Othello, ii. 3.

And now there rests no other shift but this,—
To gather our soldiers, scatter'd and dispers'd,
And lay new *platforms* to endamage them.
Henry 6, P. 1, ii. 1.

PLAUSIVE. *Plausible; specious.*

Or by some habit, that too much o'erleavens
The form of *plausive* manners. *Hamlet*, i. 4.

His *plausive* words
He scatter'd not in ears, but grafted them,
To grow there, and to bear.
All's well that ends well, i. 2.

It must be a very *plausive* invention that carries it.
Ibid. iv. 1.

To PLAY. *To throw for; to gamble.*

Proud of their numbers, and secure in soul,

The confident and over-lusty French
Do the low-rated English *play* at dice.
Henry 5, iv. Chorus.

PLEACHED. *Interwoven; folded.*

And bid her steal into the *pleachèd* bower.
Much Ado about Nothing, iii. 1.

Wouldst thou be window'd in great Rome, and see
Thy master thus with *pleach'd* arms, bending down
His corrigible neck? *Antony and Cleopatra*, iv. 14.

PLEASANCE. *Gaiety; merriment.*

O God, that men should put an enemy in their
mouths to steal away their brains! that we should,
with joy, *pleasance*, revel, and applause, transform
ourselves into beasts! *Othello*, ii. 3.

PLEASE-MAN. *A pick-thank; a flatterer; a parasite.*

Some carry-tale, some *please-man*, some slight zany,
Some mumble-news, some trencher-knight, some
Dick,
Told our intents before. *Love's Labour's lost*, v. 2.

PLENTY. *Plentiful.*

If reasons were as *plenty* as blackberries, I would
give no man a reason upon compulsion, I.
Henry 4, P. 1, ii. 4.

PLIGHT. *Pledge.*

Haply, when I shall wed,
That lord whose hand must take my *plight* shall
carry
Half my love with him, half my care and duty.
King Lear, i. 1.

To PLIGHT. *To plait; to entangle; to involve; to pledge.*

Time shall unfold what *plighted* cunning hides:
Who cover faults, at last shame them derides.
King Lear, i. 1.

I will remain
The loyal'st husband that did e'er *plight* troth:
My residence in Rome at one Philario's.
Cymbeline, i. 1.

PLOT. *Spot; space; a small extent of land.*

This blessèd *plot*, this earth, this realm, this England.
Richard 2, ii. 1.

Call for our chiefest men of discipline
To cull the *plots* of best advantages.
King John, ii. 1.

And, in this private *plot*, be we the first
That shall salute our rightful sovereign
With honour of his birthright to the crown.
                              Henry 6, P. 2, ii. 2.
      While, to my shame, I see
The imminent death of twenty thousand men,
That for a fantasy and trick of fame
Go to their graves like beds; fight for a *plot*
Whereon the numbers cannot try the cause,
Which is not tomb enough and continent
To hide the slain.   *Hamlet*, iv. 4.

TO PLUME UP. *To make proud; to please; to gratify.*
      Let me see now;
To get his place, and to *plume up* my will
In double knavery.   *Othello*, i. 3.

PLUMPY. *Fat; plump.*
Come, thou monarch of the vine,
Plumpy Bacchus with pink eyne!
            Antony and Cleopatra, ii. 7.

PLURISY. *Superabundance; redundance; excess.*
For goodness, growing to *plurisy*,
Dies in his own too-much.   *Hamlet*, iv. 7.

TO PLY. *To solicit earnestly; to entreat.*
Ply Desdemona well, and you are sure on't.
                              Othello, iv. 1.
He *plies* her hard; and much rain wears the marble.
                              Henry 6, P. 3, iii. 2.

TO POACH. *To thrust; to push; to stab.*
      For where
I thought to crush him in an equal force
True sword to sword, I'll *poach* at him some way,
Or wrath or craft may get him. *Coriolanus*, i. 10.

TO POCKET UP. *To submit to; to brook; to endure.*
Well, ruffian, I must *pocket up* these wrongs.
                              King John, iii. 1.
      And yet you will stand to it; you will not
pocket up wrong : art thou not ashamed?
                              Henry 4, P. 1, iii. 3.

POINT. *A string with a tag; a sound; a note; direction; order.*
To flatter Cæsar, would you mingle eyes
With one that ties his *points*?
            Antony and Cleopatra, iii. 13.

Upon mine honour, for a silken *point*
I'll give my barony.   *Henry* 4, P. 2, i. 1.
Turning your books to greaves, your ink to blood,
Your pens to lances, and your tongue divine
To a loud trumpet and a *point* of war.
                              Ibid. iv. 1.
      Tullus Aufidius,
The second name of men, obeys his *points*
As if he were his officer.   *Coriolanus*, iv. 6.

TO 'POINT. *To appoint.*
And, to be noted for a merry man,
He'll woo a thousand, *'point* the day of marriage,
Yet never means to wed where he hath woo'd.
            Taming of the Shrew, iii. 2.

POINT-DEVISE. *Exact; precise; exactly.*
Then your hose should be ungartered, your
bonnet unbanded, your sleeve unbuttoned, your
shoe untied, and every thing about you demon-
strating a careless desolation;—but you are no
such man,—you are rather *point-devise* in your ac-
coutrements, as loving yourself than seeming the
lover of any other.   *As you like it*, iii. 2.
      I will be proud, I will read politic authors, I
will baffle Sir Toby, I will wash off gross acquaintance, I will be *point-devise* the very man.
                              Twelfth-Night, ii. 5.
      I abhor such fanatical phantasms, such inso-
ciable and *point-devise* companions.
                              Love's Labour's lost, v. 1.

POINTING-STOCK. *An object of ridicule; a butt; a laughing-stock.*
      Whilst I, his forlorn duchess,
Was made a wonder and a *pointing-stock*
To every idle rascal follower. *Henry* 6, P. 2, ii. 4.

POISE. *Moment; weight.*
Occasions, noble Gloster, of some *poise*,
Wherein we must have use of your advice.
                              King Lear, ii. 1.
      Nay, when I have a suit
Wherein I mean to touch your love indeed,
It shall be full of *poise* and difficulty,
And fearful to be granted.   *Othello*, iii. 3.
Pleas'd you to do't at peril of your soul,
Were equal *poise* of sin and charity.
                              Measure for Measure, ii. 4.

TO POISE. *To balance; to weigh.*
      Here, take her hand,
Proud scornful boy, unworthy this good gift;

KK

That dost in vile misprision shackle up
My love and her desert; that canst not dream,
We, *poising* us in her defective scale,
Shall weigh thee to the beam.
                    All's well that ends well, ii. 3.

POKE. *A bag; a pouch; a pocket.*

And then he drew a dial from his *poke*,
And, looking on it with lack-lustre eye,
Says very wisely, " It is ten o'clock."
                    As you like it, ii. 7.

POLICY. *Cunning; stratagem; caution; prudence.*

Unless you do redeem it by some laudable at-
tempt either of valour or *policy.*
                    Twelfth-Night, iii. 2.
    I have heard you say,
Honour and *policy*, like unsever'd friends,
I' the war do grow together. *Coriolanus*, iii. 2.
Men must learn now with pity to dispense;
For *policy* sits above conscience.
                    Timon of Athens, iii. 2.
Ay, but that *policy* may last so long,
That, I being absent, and my place supplied,
My general will forget my love and service.
                    Othello, iii. 3.

POLITIC. *Artful; cunning; prudent; cautious.*

The devil knew not what he did when he made
man *politic.*   *Timon of Athens*, iii. 3.
    As for you, interpreter, you must seem very
politic.   *All's well that ends well*, iv. 1.
    I have been *politic* with my friend, smooth
with mine enemy.   *As you like it*, v. 4.
    And be you well assur'd
He shall in strangeness stand no farther off
Than in a *politic* distance.   *Othello*, iii. 3.

POLLED. *Clear; unincumbered.*

He will mow all down before him, and leave his
passage *polled.*   *Coriolanus*, iv. 5.

POMANDER. *A kind of perfume.*

I have sold all my trumpery; not a counterfeit
stone, not a riband, glass, *pomander*, brooch, table-
book, ballad, knife, tape, glove, shoe-tie, bracelet,
horn-ring, to keep my pack from fasting.
                    Winter's Tale, iv. 3.

POMEWATER. *A species of apple.*

Ripe as a *pomewater.*   *Love's Labour's lost*, iv. 2.

POORLY. *Meanly; irresolutely.*

Get on your nightgown, lest occasion call us,
And show us to be watchers :—be not lost
So *poorly* in your thoughts.   *Macbeth*, ii. 1.

POPINJAY. *A parrot.*

I then, all smarting with my wounds being cold,
Out of my grief and my impatience
To be so pester'd with a *popinjay*,
Answer'd neglectingly, I know not what.
                    Henry 4, P. 1, i. 3.

POPULARITY. *Publicity; public observation.*

Grew a companion to the common streets,
Enfeoff'd himself to *popularity.*
                    Henry 4, P. 1, iii. 2.
His hours fill'd up with riots, banquets, sports;
And never noted in him any study,
Any retirement, any sequestration,
From open haunts and *popularity.*   *Henry 5*, i. 1.

PORING. *Purblind; dim-sighted.*

When creeping murmur and the *poring* dark
Fills the wide vessel of the universe.
                    Henry 5, iv. Chorus.

PORPENTINE. *A porcupine.*

Do not, *porpentine*, do not; my fingers itch.
                    Troilus and Cressida, ii. 1.
Thy knotted and combined locks to part,
And each particular hair to stand on end,
Like quills upon the fretful *porpentine.*
                    Hamlet, i. 5.
And fought so long, till that his thighs with darts
Were almost like a sharp-quill'd *porpentine.*
                    Henry 6, P. 2, iii. 1.

PORRINGER. *A head-dress; a cap.*

There was a haberdasher's wife of small wit,
near him, that railed upon me till her pinked *porringer* fell off her head, for kindling such a com-
bustion in the state.   *Henry 8*, v. 3.

PORT. *Pomp; state; demeanour; carriage;
bearing; a gate.*

'Tis not unknown to you, Antonio,
How much I have disabled mine estate,
By something showing a more swelling *port*
Than my faint means would grant continuance.
                    Merchant of Venice, i. 1.
Thou shalt be master, Tranio, in my stead,
Keep house, and *port*, and servants, as I should.
                    Taming of the Shrew, i. 1.

What, think you much to pay two thousand crowns,
And bear the name and *port* of gentlemen ?
Henry 6, P. 2, iv. 1.
Where souls do couch on flowers, we'll hand in
hand,
And with our sprightly *port* make the ghosts gaze.
Antony and Cleopatra, iv. 14.
Him I accuse
The city *ports* by this hath enter'd, and
Intends t' appear before the people, hoping
To purge himself with words : dispatch.
Coriolanus, v. 5.

PORTABLE. *Endurable ; tolerable ; support-*
able.
How light and *portable* my pain seems now,
When that which makes me bend makes the king
bow ! . *King Lear*, iii. 6.
All these are *portable*,
With other graces weigh'd. *Macbeth*, iv. 3.

PORTAGE. *A port-hole.*
Stiffen the sinews, summon up the blood,
Disguise fair nature with hard-favour'd rage :
Then lend the eye a terrible aspèct,
Let it pry through the *portage* of the head
Like the brass cannon. *Henry 5*, iii. 1.

PORTANCE. *Demeanour ; behaviour ; bearing.*
But your loves,
Thinking upon his services, took from you
The apprehension of his present *portance*.
Coriolanus, ii. 3.
Of being taken by the insolent foe,
And sold to slavery ; of my redemption thence,
And *portance* in my travels' history. *Othello*, i. 3.

PORTRAITURE. *Picture ; portrait ; resem-*
blance.
But I am very sorry, good Horatio,
That to Laertes I forgot myself ;
For, by the image of my cause, I see
The *portraiture* of his. *Hamlet*, v. 2.

To POSSESS. *To inform ; to inspire ; to im-*
bue ; to keep from ; to withhold.
I have *possess'd* him my most stay
Can be but brief. *Measure for Measure*, iv. 1.
Is he yet *possess'd*
How much we would ? *Merchant of Venice*, i. 3.
Possess us, *possess* us ; tell us something of him.
Twelfth-Night, ii. 3.
Yet, in reason, no man should *possess* him with

any appearance of fear, lest he, by showing it, should
dishearten his army. *Henry 5*, iv. 1.
But dar'st not strike ; thy conscience
Is so *possess'd* with guilt. *Tempest*, i. 2.
I will *possess* him with yellowness.
Merry Wives of Windsor, i. 3.
If aught *possess* thee from me, it is dross,
Usurping ivy, brier, or idle moss.
Comedy of Errors, ii. 2.

POSSESSED. *Frantic ; mad.*
Mistress, both man and master is *possess'd*.
Comedy of Errors, iv. 4.
He is coming, madam, but in very strange man-
ner. He is, sure, *possessed*, madam.
Twelfth-Night, iii. 4.

POSSESSION. *Frenzy ; madness.*
How long hath this *possession* held the man ?
Comedy of Errors, v. 1.

To POSSET. *To turn ; to curdle.*
And, with a sudden vigour, it doth *posset*
And curd the thin and wholesome blood.
Hamlet, i. 5.

POSSIBILITIES. *Possessions.*
I know the young gentlewoman ; she has good
gifts.—
Seven hundred pounds and *possibilities* is goot
gifts. *Merry Wives of Windsor*, i. 1.

POST. *A messenger ; haste ; speed.*
I am no fee'd *post*, lady ; keep your purse.
Twelfth-Night, i. 5.
Get *posts* and letters, and make friends with
speed,—
Never so few, and never yet more need.
Henry 4, P. 2, i. 1.
And there are twenty weak and wearied *posts*
Come from the north. *Ibid.* ii. 4.
The mayor towards Guildhall hies him in all *post*.
Richard 3, iii. 5.
But, stay : what news ?—Why com'st thou in such
post ? *Henry 6*, P. 3, i. 2.

To POST. *To travel with speed ; to pass over ;*
to put off ; to linger.
For you my staff of office did I break,
In Richard's time ; and *posted* day and night
To meet you on the way, and kiss your hand.
Henry 4, P. 1, v. 1.
Were't not madness, then,
To make the fox surveyor of the fold ?

Who being accus'd a crafty murderer,
His guilt should be but idly *posted* over,
Because his purpose is not executed.
Henry 6, P. 2, iii. 1.

I have not stopp'd mine ears to their demands,
Nor *posted* off their suits with long delays.
Henry 6, P. 3, iv. 8.

POSTER. *A courier ; a messenger.*

The weird sisters, hand in hand,
Posters of the sea and land,
Thus do go about, about.   *Macbeth*, i. 3.

POSTHORSE. *Post-haste ; speed.*

He cannot live, I hope ; and must not die
Till George be pack'd with *posthorse* up to heaven.
Richard 3, i. 1.

POSTURE. *Direction ; aim ; shape ; form.*

Antony,
The *posture* of your blows are yet unknown ;
But for your words, they rob the Hybla bees,
And leave them honeyless.   *Julius Cæsar*, v. 1.

For feature, laming
The shrine of Venus, or straight-pight Minerva,
Postures beyond brief nature.   *Cymbeline*, v. 5.

And I shall see
Some squeaking Cleopatra boy my greatness
I' the *posture* of a whore.
Antony and Cleopatra, v. 2.

POSY. *A motto.*

Is this a prologue, or the *posy* of a ring?—
'Tis brief, my lord.—As woman's love.
Hamlet, iii. 2.

A quarrel, ho, already ! what's the matter?—
About a hoop of gold, a paltry ring
That she did give to me ; whose *posy* was
For all the world like cutler's poetry
Upon a knife, " Love me, and leave me not."
Merchant of Venice, v. 1.

POTENCY. *Power ; authority ; strength ; force.*

Our *potency* made good, take thy reward.
King Lear, i. 1.

And sometimes we are devils to ourselves,
When we will tempt the frailty of our powers,
Presuming on their changeful *potency*.
Troilus and Cressida, iv. 4.

For use almost can change the stamp of nature,
And either master the devil, or throw him out
With wondrous *potency*.   *Hamlet*, iii. 4.

POTENT. *A prince ; a potentate.*

So *potent*-like would I o'ersway his state,
That he should be my fool, and I his fate.
Love's Labour's lost, v. 2.

POTHECARY. *An apothecary ; a compounder and vender of medicines ; a druggist.*

And here he writes that he did buy a poison
Of a poor *pothecary*.   *Romeo and Juliet*, v. 3.

POTHER. *Uproar ; bustle ; tumult.*

Let the great gods,
That keep this dreadful *pother* o'er our heads,
Find out their enemies now.   *King Lear*, iii. 2.

Such a *pother*,
As if that whatsoever god who leads him
Were slily crept into his human powers,
And gave him graceful posture.   *Coriolanus*, ii. 1.

POTTING. *Drinking.*

'Fore God, an excellent song.—
I learned it in England, where, indeed, they are
most potent in *potting*.   *Othello*, ii. 3.

POTTLE. *A measure containing two quarts.*

Now, my sick fool Roderigo,
Whom love hath turn'd almost the wrong side out,
To Desdemona hath to-night carous'd
Potations *pottle*-deep ; and he's to watch.
Othello, ii. 3.

He gives your Hollander a vomit, ere the next
pottle can be filled.   *Ibid.* ii. 3.

POULTER. *A poulterer.*

If thou dost it half so gravely, so majestically,
both in word and matter, hang me up by the heels
for a rabbit-sucker or a *poulter's* hare.
Henry 4, P. 1, ii. 4.

To POWDER. *To salt.*

If thou embowel me to-day, I'll give you leave
to *powder* me and eat me too to-morrow.
Henry 4, P. 1, v. 4.

POWER. *Authority ; warrant ; a military force ; an army.*

His mother was a witch ; and one so strong
That could control the moon, make flows and ebbs,
And deal in her command, without her *power*.
Tempest, v. 1.

'Tis time to look about ; the *powers* of the kingdom approach apace.   *King Lear*, iv. 7.

Most wisely hath Ulysses here discover'd
The fever whereof all our *power* is sick.
Troilus and Cressida, i. 3.

POW, WOW. *An expression of contempt.*

The gods grant them true!—
True! pow, wow.   *Coriolanus*, ii. 1.

PRACTIC. *Practical.*

So that the art and *practic* part of life
Must be the mistress to this theoric.
Henry 5, i. 1.

PRACTICE. *Treachery ; a criminal device ; a fetch; an artifice.*

It is the shameful work of Hubert's hand ;
The *practice* and the purpose of the king.
King John, iv. 3.
Shall we thus permit
A blasting and a scandalous breath to fall
On him so near us ? This needs must be *practice*.
Measure for Measure, v. 1.
This act persuades me
That this remotion of the duke and her
Is *practice* only.   *King Lear*, ii. 4.

TO PRACTISE. *To conspire against; to plot; to plan ; to meditate ; to impose upon.*

Wouldst thou have *practis'd* on me for thy use?
Henry 5, ii. 2.
Yet if you there
Did *practise* on my state, your being in Egypt
Might be my question. *Antony and Cleopatra*, ii. 2.
And in the mean time,
With this ungracious paper strike the sight
Of the death-*practis'd* duke.   *King Lear*, iv. 6.
And so I would be here, but that I doubt
My uncle *practises* more harm to me.
King John, iv. 1.
And I, with your two helps, will so *practise* on
Benedick.   *Much Ado about Nothing*, ii. 1.

PRACTISANT. *A confederate ; an associate.*

Here enter'd Pucelle and her *practisants*.
Henry 6, P. 1, iii. 2.

TO PRANK. *To deck ; to decorate ; to dress up.*

But 'tis that miracle and queen of gems,
That nature *pranks* her in, attracts my soul.
Twelfth-Night, ii. 4.
And me, poor lowly maid,
Most goddess-like *prank'd* up. *Winter's Tale*, iv. 3.

For they do *prank* them in authority,
Against all noble sufferance.   *Coriolanus*, iii. 1.

TO PRAY IN AID. *To petition ; to solicit ; to sue.*

Let me report to him
Your sweet dependency ; and you shall find
A conqueror that will *pray in aid* for kindness,
Where he for grace is kneel'd to.
Antony and Cleopatra, v. 2.

PREACHMENT. *A solemn discourse.*

Was't you that revell'd in our parliament,
And made a *preachment* of your high descent?
Henry 6, P. 3, i. 4.

PRECEDENCE. *What has been previously said.*

I do not like "But yet," it does allay
The good *precedence ;* fie upon "But yet!"
Antony and Cleopatra, ii. 5.
It is an epilogue or discourse, to make plain
Some obscure *precedence* that hath tofore been sain.
Love's Labour's lost, iii. 1.

PRECEDENT. *The original copy of any writing ; a rough draught.*

My lord Melun, let this be copied out,
And keep it safe for our remembrance :
Return the *precedent* to these lords again.
King John, v. 2.
And mark how well the sequel holds together :—
Eleven hours I have spent to write it over,
For yesternight by Catesby was it sent me ;
The *precedent* was full as long a-doing :
And yet within these five hours Hastings liv'd,
Untainted, unexamin'd, free, at liberty.
Richard 3, iii. 6.

PRECEPT. *A magistrate's warrant ; a summons ; a mandate.*

Marry, sir, thus ; those *precepts* cannot be served.
Henry 4, P. 2, v. 1.
We may as bootless spend our vain command
Upon the enragèd soldiers in their spoil,
As send *precepts* to the Leviathan
To come ashore.   *Henry* 5, iii. 2.

PRECEPTIAL. *Consisting of precepts.*

But, tasting it,
Their counsel turns to passion, which before
Would give *preceptial* medicine to rage,
Fetter strong madness in a silken thread,
Charm ache with air, and agony with words.
Much Ado about Nothing, v. 1.

PRECISE. *Austere ; rigid.*

Lord Angelo is *precise ;*
Stands at a guard with envy ; scarce confesses
That his blood flows, or that his appetite
Is more to bread than stone.
Measure for Measure, i. 3.

PRECISENESS. *Austerity ; purity.*

Is all your strict *preciseness* come to this ?
Henry 6, P. 1, v. 4.

PRECONTRACT. *A previous act of betrothment.*

He is your husband on a *pre-contract.*
Measure for Measure, iv. 1.

PRECURSE. *A preceding course ; a forerunning.*

And even the like *precurse* of fierce events
Have heaven and earth together demonstrated
Unto our climature and countrymen. *Hamlet,* i. 1.

PREDESTINATE. *Predestined.*

So some gentleman or other shall scape a *predestinate* scratched face.
Much Ado about Nothing, i. 1.

TO PREDOMINATE. *To overpower ; to subdue.*

Let your close fire *predominate* his smoke,
And be no turncoats. *Timon of Athens,* iv. 3.

TO PREFER. *To recommend ; to present ; to offer.*

Shylock thy master spoke with me this day,
And hath *preferr'd* thee. *Merchant of Venice,* ii. 2.
    If you, Hortensio,—
Or Signor Gremio, you,—know any such,
Prefer them hither, for to cunning men
I will be very kind, and liberal
To mine own children in good bringing up.
Taming of the Shrew, i. 1.
Where is Metellus Cimber ? let him go,
And presently *prefer* his suit to Cæsar.
Julius Cæsar, iii. 1.
Fellow, wilt thou bestow thy time with me ?—
Ay, if Messala will *prefer* me to you. *Ibid.* v. 5.
Why then *preferr'd* you not your sums and bills
When your false masters eat of my lord's meat ?
Timon of Athens, iii. 4.
    Meet presently at the palace ; every man look
o'er his part ; for the short and the long is, our
play is *preferred. Midsummer-Night's Dream,* iv. 2.

PREFORMED. *Original ; ancient ; prescribed.*

Why all these things change, from their ordinance,
Their nature, and *preformèd* faculties,
To monstrous quality. *Julius Cæsar,* i. 3.

PREGNANCY. *Readiness ; acuteness.*

Pregnancy is made a tapster, and hath his quick
wit wasted in giving reckonings.
Henry 4, P. 2, i. 2.

PREGNANT. *Evident ; obvious ; open to ; susceptible of ; shrewd ; well instructed ; artful.*

'Tis very *pregnant,*
The jewel that we find, we stoop and take't,
Because we see't ; but what we do not see
We tread upon, and never think of it.
Measure for Measure, ii. 1.
Were't not that we stand up against them all,
'Twere *pregnant* they should square between themselves. *Antony and Cleopatra,* ii. 1.
A most poor man, made tame to fortune's blows ;
Who, by the art of known and feeling sorrows,
Am *pregnant* to good pity. *King Lear,* iv. 6.
How *pregnant* sometimes his replies are !
Hamlet, ii. 2.
    The terms
For common justice, you're as *pregnant* in
As art and practice hath enrichèd any
That we remember. *Measure for Measure,* i. 1.
Disguise, I see, thou art a wickedness,
Wherein the *pregnant* enemy does much.
Twelfth-Night, ii. 2.

TO PREJUDICE. *To damage ; to destroy.*

Now let us on, my lords, and join our powers ;
And seek how we may *prejudice* the foe.
Henry 6, P. 1, iii. 3.

PREMISED. *Preordained.*

O, let the vile world end,
And the *premisèd* flames of the last day
Knit earth and heaven together !
Henry 6, P. 2, v. 2.

PRENOMINATE. *Forementioned ; aforesaid.*

Your party in converse, him you would sound,
Having ever seen in the *prenominate* crimes
The youth you breathe of guilty, be assur'd
He closes with you in this consequence.
Hamlet, ii. 1.

TO PRENOMINATE. *To declare beforehand.*

Think'st thou to catch my life so pleasantly,

As to *prenominate* in nice conjecture
Where thou wilt hit me dead ?
    Troilus and Cressida, iv. 5.

PRE-ORDINANCE. *A foregone judgment ; a recorded sentence.*

These couchings and these lowly courtesies
Might fire the blood of ordinary men,
And turn *pre-ordinance* and first decree
Into the law of children.   *Julius Cæsar*, iii. 1.

PREPARATION. *Accomplishment ; qualification ; armada ; armament.*

  You are a gentleman of excellent breeding, admirable discourse, of great admittance, authentic in your place and person, generally allowed for your many war-like, court-like, and learned *preparations.*
    Merry Wives of Windsor, ii. 2.
The Turk with a most mighty *preparation* makes for Cyprus.   *Othello*, i. 3.
    Hear'st thou of them ?—
Ay, my good lord ; your royal *preparation*
Makes us hear something.   *Macbeth*, v. 3.
    Good my liege,
Your *preparation* can affront no less
Than what you hear of.   *Cymbeline*, iv. 3.
'Tis known before ; our *preparation* stands
In expectation of them.   *King Lear*, iv. 4.

PREPARE. *Preparation.*
Pembroke and Stafford, you in our behalf
Go levy men, and make *prepare* for war.
    Henry 6, P. 3, iv. 1.

PRESCRIPT. *A written order ; direction ; precept.*
    Do not exceed
The *prescript* of this scroll : our fortune lies
Upon this jump.   *Antony and Cleopatra*, iii. 8.

PRESCRIPT. *Prescriptive.*
Your mistress bears well.—
Me well ; which is the *prescript* praise and perfection of a good and particular mistress.
    Henry 5, iii. 6.

PRESCRIPTION. *Appointment ; direction; recommendation.*
I'm thankful to you ; and I'll go along
By your *prescription*.   *Henry 8*, i. 1.

PRESENCE. *A room of state; dignity; demeanour ; bearing.*
Suppose the singing-birds musicians,
The grass whereon thou tread'st the *presence* strew'd.
    Richard 2, i. 3.
For here lies Juliet, and her beauty makes
This vault a feasting *presence* full of light.
    Romeo and Juliet, v. 3.
An't please your grace, the two great cardinals
Wait in the *presence*.   *Henry 8*, iii. 1.
    Now he goes
With no less *presence*, but with much more love,
Than young Alcides.   *Merchant of Venice*, iii. 2.
O, sir, your *presence* is too bold and peremptory.
    Henry 4, P. 1, i. 3.

PRESENT. *Instant; immediate.*
Go pronounce his *present* death,
And with his former title greet Macbeth.
    Macbeth, i. 2.
Besides, his expedition promises
Present approach.   *Timon of Athens*, v. 2.
    Which imports at full,
By letters cónjuring to that effect,
The *present* death of Hamlet.   *Hamlet*, iv. 3.

TO PRESENT. *To represent ; to perform.*
The majesty and power of law and justice,
The image of the king whom I *presented*.
    Henry 4, P. 2, v. 2.
    When I *presented* Ceres,
I thought to have told thee of it ; but I fear'd
Lest I might anger thee.   *Tempest*, iv. 1.
    The quick comedians
Extemporally will stage us, and *present*
Our Alexandrian revels.
    Antony and Cleopatra, v. 2.

PRESENTATION. *Representation; image; show.*
I call'd thee then, poor shadow, painted queen,
The *presentation* of but what I was.
    Richard 3, iv. 4.
He uses his folly like a stalking-horse, and under the *presentation* of that he shoots his wit.
    As you like it, v. 4.

PRESENTLY. *Instantly ; immediately.*
Such sanctity hath heaven given his hand,
They *presently* amend.   *Macbeth*, iv. 3.
Therefore, I pray you, stand not to discourse,
But mount you *presently*.
    Two Gentlemen of Verona, v. 1.

PRESENTMENT. *The act of presenting; representation; likeness.*

When comes your book forth?—
Upon the heels of my *presentment*, sir.
Timon of Athens, i. 1.

Look here, upon this picture, and on this,
The counterfeit *presentment* of two brothers.
Hamlet, iii. 4.

PRESIDENT. *Head; sovereign.*

A charge we bear i' the war,
And, as the *president* of my kingdom, will
Appear there for a man.
Antony and Cleopatra, iii. 7.

PRESS. *Crowd; throng; rush.*

Who is it in the *press* that calls on me?
Julius Cæsar, i. 2.

Go, break among the *press*, and find a way out
To let the troop pass fairly. *Henry* 8, v. 3.

And his siege is now
Against the mind, the which he pricks and wounds
With many legions of strange fantasies,
Which, in their throng and *press* to that last hold,
Confound themselves. *King John,* v. 7.

PRESS-MONEY. *Money given to a soldier when he was taken or forced into the service.*

Nature's above art in that respect.—
There's your *press-money.* *King Lear,* iv. 6.

PRESSURE. *Impression; idea; notion.*

To show virtue her own feature, scorn her own
image, and the very age and body of the time his
form and *pressure.* *Hamlet,* iii. 2.

Yea, from the table of my memory
I'll wipe away all trivial fond records,
All saws of books, all forms, all *pressures* past,
That youth and observation copied there.
Ibid. i. 5.

PREST. *Prompt; ready; prepared.*

Then do but say to me what I should do,
That in your knowledge may by me be done,
And I am *prest* unto it. *Merchant of Venice,* i. 1.

PRESUPPOSED. *Prescribed; presuggested.*

And now I do bethink me, it was she
First told me thou wast mad: thou cam'st in smiling,
And in such forms which here were *presuppos'd*
Upon thee in the letter. *Twelfth-Night,* v. 1.

PRESURMISE. *Surmise; belief; opinion.*

It was your *presurmise*,
That, in the dole of blows, your son might drop.
Henry 4, P. 2, i. 1.

PRETENCE. *Intention; design; purpose.*

For love of you, not hate unto my friend,
Hath made me publisher of this *pretence.*
Two Gentlemen of Verona, iii. 1.

Which I have rather blamed as mine own jealous curiosity than as a very *pretence* and purpose
of unkindness. *King Lear,* i. 4.

And thence
Against the undivulg'd *pretence* I fight
Of treasonous malice. *Macbeth,* ii. 1.

I dare pawn down my life for him, that he hath
writ this to feel my affection to your honour, and
to no other *pretence* of danger. *King Lear,* i. 2.

To PRETEND. *To intend; to purpose; to propose; to foreshow; to indicate.*

Now presently I'll give her father notice
Of their disguising and *pretended* flight.
Two Gentlemen of Verona, ii. 6.

Esteem none friends but such as are his friends,
And none your foes but such as shall *pretend*
Malicious practices against his state.
Henry 6, P. 1, iv. 1.

Alas, the day! what good could they *pretend?*
Macbeth, ii. 2.

Or doth this churlish superscription
Pretend some alteration in good will?
Henry 6, P. 1, i. 5.

PRETTY. *Little; crafty; wise; pleasing.*

How mean you, sir? I pretty, and my saying
apt? or I apt, and my saying pretty?—
Thou *pretty*, because little.
Love's Labour's lost, i. 2.

Hast thou the *pretty* worm of Nilus there
That kills, but pains not?—
Truly I have him: but I would not be the party
that should desire you to touch him, for his biting
is immortal; those that do die of it do seldom or
never recover. *Antony and Cleopatra,* v. 2.

Yet that is but a curst necessity,
Since we have locks to safeguard necessaries,
And *pretty* traps to catch the petty thieves.
Henry 5, i. 2.

Now, if you could wear a mind
Dark as your fortune is, and but disguise
That which, to appear itself, must not yet be

But by self-danger, you should tread a course
Pretty and full of view.   *Cymbeline*, iii. 4.

'Twas *pretty*, though a plague,
To see him every hour; to sit and draw
His archèd brows, his hawking eye, his curls,
In our heart's table. *All's well that ends well*, i. 1.

To PREVAIL. *To avail.*

Unless philosophy can make a Juliet,
Displant a town, reverse a prince's doom,
It helps not, it *prevails* not.
     Romeo and Juliet, iii. 3.
If wishes would *prevail* with me,
My purpose should not fail with me,
But thither would I hie.   *Henry 5*, iii. 1.

PREVAILMENT. *Allurement; influence.*

Knacks, trifles, nosegays, sweetmeats,—messengers
Of strong *prevailment* in unharden'd youth.
     Midsummer-Night's Dream, i. 1.

To PREVENT. *To anticipate.*

Besides, he brings his destiny with him.—
What's that?—
Why, horns; which such as you are fain to be
beholding to your wives for: but he comes armed
in his fortune, and *prevents* the slander of his wife.
     As you like it, iv. 1.
But I do find it cowardly and vile,
For fear of what might fall, so to *prevent*
The time of life.   *Julius Cæsar*, v. 1.

PREVENTION. *Precaution.*

Achievements, plots, orders, *preventions*,
Excitements to the field, or speech for truce,
Success or loss, what is or is not, serves
As stuff for these two to make paradoxes.
     Troilus and Cressida, i. 3.

PREVISION. *Foresight.*

I have with such *prevision* in mine art
So safely order'd, that there is no soul—
No, not so much perdition as a hair
Betid to any creature in the vessel. *Tempest*, i. 2.

PRICK. *A quill; a prickle; a point; a skewer.*

     Then like hedgehogs, which
Lie tumbling in my barefoot way, and mount
Their *pricks* at my footfall.   *Tempest*, ii. 2.
Now Phaëthon hath tumbled from his car,
And made an evening at the noontide *prick*.
     Henry 6, P. 3, i. 4.

The country gives me proof and precedent
Of Bedlam beggars, who, with roaring voices,
Stick in their numb'd and mortified bare arms
Pins, wooden *pricks*, nails, sprigs of rosemary.
     King Lear, ii. 3.

To PRICK. *To mark; to nominate; to appoint.*

Will you be *prick'd* in number of our friends;
Or shall we on, and not depend on you?
     Julius Cæsar, iii. 1.
These many, then, shall die; their names are *prick'd*.
     Ibid. iv. 1.
     So you thought him;
And took his voice who should be *prick'd* to die,
In our black sentence and proscription. *Ibid.* iv. 1.

PRICK-SONG. *Music noted down, and sung in parts.*

He fights as you sing *prick-song*, keeps time,
distance, and proportion; rests me his minim rest,
one, two, and the third in your bosom.
     Romeo and Juliet, ii. 4.

PRIG. *A thief.*

Out upon him! *prig*, for my life, *prig:* he
haunts wakes, fairs, and bear-baitings.
     Winter's Tale, iv. 2.

PRIMAL. *Original; earliest.*

O, my offence is rank, it smells to heaven;
It hath the *primal* eldest curse upon't.
     Hamlet, iii. 3.
It hath been taught us from the *primal* state,
That he which is was wish'd until he were.
     Antony and Cleopatra, i. 4.

PRIME. *The spring or morning of life.*

How well resembles it the *prime* of youth!
     Henry 6, P. 3, ii. 1.
Youth, beauty, wisdom, courage, virtue, all
That happiness and *prime* can happy call.
     All's well that ends well, ii. 1.

PRIME. *Important; urgent; first; wanton.*

     I would your highness
Would give it quick consideration, for
There is no *primer* business.   *Henry 8*, i. 2.
     My prime request,
Which I do last pronounce, is,—O you wonder!—
If you be maid or no.   *Tempest*, i. 2.

LL

It is impossible you should see this,
Were they as *prime* as goats, as hot as monkeys.
Othello, iii. 3.

PRIMERO. *A game at cards.*

I never prospered since I forswore myself at *primero*. *Merry Wives of Windsor*, iv. 5.

I did, Sir Thomas; and left him at *primero*
With the Duke of Suffolk. *Henry 8*, v. 1.

PRIMOGENITY. *Primogeniture.*

The *primogenity* and due of birth.
Troilus and Cressida, i. 3.

PRIMROSE. *Flowery; gay; pleasant.*

I had thought to have let in some of all professions, that go the *primrose* way to the everlasting bonfire. *Macbeth*, ii. 1.

Whilst, like a puff'd and reckless libertine,
Himself the *primrose* path of dalliance treads,
And recks not his own read. *Hamlet*, i. 3.

PRIMY. *Early; budding.*

A violet in the youth of *primy* nature,
Forward, not permanent, sweet, not lasting,
The perfume and suppliance of a minute.
Hamlet, i. 3.

To PRINCE. *To play the prince.*

And nature prompts them,
In simple and low things, to *prince* it much
Beyond the trick of others. *Cymbeline*, iii. 3.

PRINCIPALITY. *A prince; a monarch.*

If not divine,
Yet let her be a *principality*,
Sovereign to all the creatures on the earth.
Two Gentlemen of Verona, ii. 4.

PRINCOX. *A coxcomb; a saucy youth.*

You are a *princox*; go. *Romeo and Juliet*, i. 5.

To PRISON. *To emprison; to confine; to restrain.*

Why, universal plodding *prisons* up
The nimble spirits in the arteries.
Love's Labour's lost, iv. 3.

Speak, Winchester; for boiling choler chokes
The hollow passage of my *prison'd* voice.
Henry 6, P. 1, v. 4.

PRIVATE. *Privacy; a private message.*

Go off; I discard you: let me enjoy my *private*:
go off. *Twelfth-Night*, iii. 4.

Whose *private* with me of the Dauphin's love
Is much more general than these lines import.
King John, iv. 3.

PRIZE. *Price; worth; value; spoil; booty; privilege.*

Would it had been so, that they
Had been my father's sons! then had my *prize*
Been less; and so more equal ballasting
To thee, Posthúmus. *Cymbeline*, iii. 6.

And oft 'tis seen the wicked *prize* itself
Buys out the law. *Hamlet*, iii. 3.

It is war's *prize* to take all vantages.
Henry 6, P. 3, i. 4.

Methinks, 'tis *prize* enough to be his son.
Ibid. ii. 1.

PROBAL. *Probable.*

And what's he, then, that says I play the villain?
When this advice is free I give and honest,
Probal to thinking, and, indeed, the course
To win the Moor again? *Othello*, ii. 3.

PROBATION. *Proof; verification.*

And of the truth herein
This present object made *probation*. *Hamlet*, i. 1.

This I made good to you
In our last conference, pass'd in *probation* with you.
Macbeth, iii. 1.

He, sir, was lapp'd
In a most curious mantle, wrought by the hand
Of his queen mother, which, for more *probation*,
I can with ease produce. *Cymbeline*, v. 5.

To PROCEED. *To pass through; to take; to happen.*

Hadst thou, like us from our first swath, *proceeded*
The sweet degrees that this brief world affords,
Thou wouldst have plung'd thyself in general riot.
Timon of Athens, iv. 3.

As they pass by, pluck Casca by the sleeve;
And he will, after his sour fashion, tell you
What hath *proceeded* worthy note to-day.
Julius Cæsar, i. 2.

PROCEEDING. *Justice.*

I am a most poor woman, and a stranger,
Born out of your dominions; having here
No judge indifferent, nor no more assurance
Of equal friendship and *proceeding*. *Henry 8*, ii. 4.

PROCESS. *Relation ; narrative ; proceeding ; course of law ; citation ; summons.*

So the whole ear of Denmark
Is by a forgèd *process* of my death
Rankly abus'd. *Hamlet*, i. 5.
Behind the arms I'll convey myself
To hear the *process*. *Ibid.* iii. 3.
And, England, if my love thou hold'st at aught,
Thou mayst not coldly set our sovereign *process*.
Ibid. iv. 3.
Perchance ! nay, and most like :—
You must not stay here longer,—your dismission
Is come from Cæsar ; therefore hear it, Antony.—
Where's Fulvia's *process*? Cæsar's I would say ?—
both ?—
Call in the messengers. *Antony and Cleopatra*, i. 1.
Proceed by *process*;
Lest parties—as he is belov'd—break out,
And sack great Rome with Romans.
Coriolanus, iii. 1.

PROCLAMATION. *Report; character ; reputation.*

The very stream of his life and the business he
hath helmed must, upon a warranted need, give
him a better *proclamation*.
Measure for Measure, iii. 2.

PROCURATOR. *Substitute; deputy.*

As *procurator* to your excellence.
Henry 6, P. 2, i. 1.

TO PROCURE. *To complete; to consummate ; to bring about; to bring.*

Proceed, Solinus, to *procure* my fall,
And by the doom of death end woes and all.
Comedy of Errors, i. 1.
Is she not down so late, or up so early?
What unaccustom'd cause *procures* her hither?
Romeo and Juliet, iii. 5.

PRODIGIOUS. *Monstrous ; portentous ; ominous.*

Lame, foolish, crookèd, swart, *prodigious*,
Patch'd with foul moles and eye-offending marks.
King John, iii. 1.
If ever he have child, abortive be it,
Prodigious, and untimely brought to light.
Richard 3, i. 2.
A man no mightier than thyself or me
In personal action ; yet *prodigious* grown,'
And fearful, as these strange eruptions are.
Julius Cæsar, i. 3.

He will spend his mouth, and promise, like
Brabbler the hound ; but when he performs, astronomers foretell it ; it is *prodigious*, there will come
some change. *Troilus and Cressida*, v. 1.

PRODIGIOUSLY. *Abortively ; monstrously.*

Let wives with child
Pray that their burdens may not fall this day,
Lest that their hopes *prodigiously* be cross'd.
King John, iii. 1.

PRODITOR. *A betrayer ; a traitor.*

I do, thou most usurping *proditor*,
And not protector, of the king and realm.
Henry 6, P. 1, i. 3.

PROFACE. *Much good may it do you.*

Master page, good master page, sit.—*Proface !*
What you want in meat, we'll have in drink.
Henry 4, P. 2, v. 3.

PROFANE. *Coarse-tongued ; gross in language ; unrestrained.*

I have long dream'd of such a kind of man,
So surfeit-swell'd, so old, and so *profane ;*
But, being awake, I do despise my dream.
Henry 4, P. 2, v. 5.
What *profane* wretch art thou ? *Othello*, i. 1.
How say you, Cassio ; is he not a most *profane*
and liberal counsellor ?—
He speaks home, madam : you may relish him
more in the soldier than in the scholar. *Ibid.* ii. 1.

TO PROFANE. *To misspend; to waste; to insult; to contemn.*

O, let no noble eye *profane* a tear
For me, if I be gor'd with Mowbray's spear.
Richard 2, i. 3.
By heaven, Pointz, I feel me much to blame
So idly to *profane* the precious time.
Henry 4, P. 2, ii. 4.
For I mine own gain'd knowledge should *profane*,
If I would time expend with such a snipe,
But for my sport and profit. *Othello*, i. 3.
Hear your own dignity so much *profan'd*.
Henry 4, P. 2, v. 2.

PROFANELY. *Uncharitably.*

O, there be players that I have seen play, and
heard others praise, and that highly,—not to speak
it *profanely*,—that, neither having the accent of
Christians, nor the gait of Christian, pagan, nor

man, have so strutted and bellowed, that I have
thought some of nature's journeymen had made
men, and not made them well, they imitated humanity so abominably. *Hamlet,* iii. 2.

To PROFESS. *To make declarations of friend-
ship.*
And as he does conceive
He is dishonour'd by a man which ever
Profess'd to him, why, his revenges must
In that be made more bitter. *Winter's Tale,* i. 2.

PROFESSED. *Professing.*
To your *professèd* bosoms I commit him.
King Lear, i. 1.

PROFESSION. *Object; intention; purpose.*
I have spoke
With one that in her sex, her years, *profession,*
Wisdom, and constancy, hath amaz'd me more
Than I dare blame my weakness.
All's well that ends well, ii. 1.

PROFITED. *Proficient; skilful.*
Exceedingly well-read, and *profited*
In strange concealments. *Henry 4,* P. 1, iii. 1.

PROFOUND. *Enchanted; magical.*
Upon the corner of the moon
There hangs a vaporous drop *profound;*
I'll catch it ere it come to ground. *Macbeth,* iii. 5.

PROGENY. *Race; descent; offspring; child-
ren.*
Wert thou the Hector,
That was the whip of your bragg'd *progeny,*
Thou shouldst not scape me here. *Coriolanus,* i. 8.
Besides, all French and France exclaims on thee,
Doubting thy birth and lawful *progeny.*
Henry 6, P. 1, iii. 3.
Not me begotten of a shepherd swain,
But issu'd from the *progeny* of kings. *Ibid.* v. 4.
And though the mourning brow of *progeny*
Forbid the smiling courtesy of love
The holy suit which fain it would convince,
Yet, since love's argument was first on foot,
Let not the cloud of sorrow justle it
From what it purpos'd. *Love's Labour's lost,* v. 2.

PROGRESS. *A royal journey.*
Nothing but to show you how a king may go a
progress through the guts of a beggar.
Hamlet, iv. 3.

PROJECT. *Supposition; hope; expectation.*
Who lin'd himself with hope,
Eating the air on promise of supply,
Flattering himself with *project* of a power
Much smaller than the smallest of his thoughts.
Henry 4, P. 2, i. 3.

To PROJECT. *To put forward; to represent;
to exhibit.*
I cannot *project* mine own cause so well
To make it clear. *Antony and Cleopatra,* v. 2.

PROJECTION. *Plan; outline; delineation.*
Which, of a weak and niggardly *projection,*
Doth, like a miser, spoil his coat with scanting
A little cloth. *Henry 5,* ii. 4.

PROLIXIOUS. *Hesitating; dilatory.*
Lay by all nicety and *prolixious* blushes.
Measure for Measure, ii. 4.

To PROLOGUE. *To introduce; to preface.*
Thus he his special nothing ever *prologues.*
All's well that ends well, ii. 1.

To PROLONG. *To defer; to put off; to post-
pone.*
To-morrow, in my judgment, is too sudden;
For I myself am not so well provided
As else I would be, were the day *prolong'd.*
Richard 3, iii. 4.

PROMPTURE. *Instigation; prompting.*
Though he hath fall'n by *prompture* of the blood,
Yet hath he in him such a mind of honour,
That, had he twenty heads to tender down,
On twenty bloody blocks, he'd yield them up,
Before his sister should her body stoop
To such abhorr'd pollution.
Measure for Measure, ii. 4.

PRONE. *Prompt; ready; eager; ardent.*
For in her youth
There is a *prone* and speechless dialect
Such as moves men. *Measure for Measure,* i. 2.
Unless a man would marry a gallows, and beget
young gibbets, I never saw one so *prone.*
Cymbeline, v. 4.

PROOF. *Temper; hardness; armour duly
proved; experience; knowledge; test; trial.*
Add *proof* unto mine armour with thy prayers;

And with thy blessings steel my lance's point.
Richard 2, i. 3.

Till that Bellona's bridegroom, lapp'd in *proof*,
Confronted him with self-comparisons. *Macbeth*, i. 2.

And in strong *proof* of chastity well arm'd,
From love's weak childish bow she lives unharm'd.
Romeo and Juliet, i. 1.

But 'tis a common *proof*
That lowliness is young ambition's ladder.
Julius Cæsar, ii. 1.

And that I see, in passages of *proof*,
Time qualifies the spark and fire of it. *Hamlet*, iv. 7.

Out of your *proof* you speak; we, poor unfledg'd,
Have never wing'd from view o' the nest, nor know
 not
What air's from home. *Cymbeline*, iii. 3.

Nay, then thou lov'st it not;
And all my pains is sorted to no *proof*.
Taming of the Shrew, iv. 3.

PROOF. *Impenetrable.*

Now put your shields before your hearts, and fight
With hearts more *proof* than shields.
Coriolanus, i. 4.

PROPAGATION. *Improvement; augmentation.*

This we came not to,
Only for *propagation* of a dower
Remaining in the coffer of her friends.
Measure for Measure, i. 2.

TO PROPAGATE. *To improve; to advance; to better.*

The base o' the mount
Is rank'd with all deserts, all kind of natures,
That labour on the bosom of this sphere
To *propagate* their states. *Timon of Athens*, i. 1.

TO PROPEND. *To lean; to incline; to side with.*

Yet, ne'ertheless,
My spritely brethren, I *propend* to you
In resolution to keep Helen still.
Troilus and Cressida, ii. 2.

PROPENSION. *Propensity; inclination.*

But I attest the gods, your full consent
Gave wings to my *propension*.
Troilus and Cressida, ii. 2.

PROPER. *Handsome; personable; good-looking; pure; unmixed.*

Ay, by my beard, will we;
For he's a *proper* man.
Two Gentlemen of Verona, iv. 1

Upon my life, she finds, although I cannot,
Myself to be a marvellous *proper* man.
Richard 3, i. 2.

Proper deformity seems not in the fiend
So horrid as in woman. *King Lear*, iv. 2.

PROPERLY. *Singly; alone; without participation.*

Though I owe
My revenge *properly*, my remission lies
In Volscian breasts. *Coriolanus*, v. 2.

PROPERTIES. *Stage requisites.*

In the mean time I will draw a bill of *properties*,
such as our play wants.
Midsummer-Night's Dream, i. 2.

PROPERTY. *Peculiar quality; nature; faculty; virtue.*

Sweet love, I see, changing his *property*,
Turns to the sourest and most deadly hate.
Richard 2, iii. 2.

Here I disclaim all my paternal care,
Propinquity, and *property* of blood,
And as a stranger to my heart and me
Hold thee, from this, for ever. *King Lear*, i. 1.

If I break time, or flinch in *property*
Of what I spoke, unpitied let me die.
All's well that ends well, ii. 1.

The *property* by what it is should go,
Not by the title. *Ibid.* ii. 3.

TO PROPERTY. *To make a property of; to draw; to attract; to endow with qualities.*

They have here *propertied* me; keep me in
darkness, and do all they can to face me out of my
wits. *Twelfth-Night*, iv. 2.

I am too high-born to be *propertied*.
King John, v. 2.

His large fortune
Subdues and *properties* to his love and tendance
All sorts of hearts. *Timon of Athens*, i. 1.

His voice was *propertied*
As all the tunèd spheres, and that to friends;
But when he meant to quail and shake the orb,
He was as rattling thunder.
Antony and Cleopatra, v. 2.

PROPHESYING. *Prophetic; prescient.*

She had a *prophesying* fear
Of what hath come to pass.
Antony and Cleopatra, iv. 14.

PROPORTION. *Fortune; dowry; harmony; measure; metre.*

Partly for that her promis'd *proportions*
Came short of composition.
Measure for Measure, v. 1.

How sour sweet music is,
When time is broke and no *proportion* kept!
Richard 2, v. 5.

What, in metre?—
In any *proportion* or in any language.
Measure for Measure, i. 2.

PROPOSE. *Conversation.*

And bid her steal into the pleachèd bower,
Where honeysuckles, ripen'd by the sun,
Forbid the sun to enter: there will she hide her,
To listen our *propose*.
Much Ado about Nothing, iii. 1.

To PROPOSE. *To suppose; to imagine; to converse; to talk.*

Be now the father, and *propose* a son;
Hear your own dignity so much profan'd,
See your most dreadful laws so loosely slighted,
Behold yourself so by a son disdain'd;
And then imagine me taking your part,
And, in your power, so silencing your son:
After this cold considerance, sentence me.
Henry 4, P. 2, v. 2.

There shalt thou find my cousin Beatrice
Proposing with the prince and Claudio.
Much Ado about Nothing, iii. 1.

Unless the bookish theoric,
Wherein the togèd consuls can *propose*
As masterly as he. *Othello*, i. 1.

PROPRIETY. *Property; exclusive right; tranquillity; proper state.*

Alas, it is the baseness of thy fear
That makes thee strangle thy *propriety*.
Twelfth-Night, v. 1.

Silence that dreadful bell! it frights the isle
From her *propriety*. *Othello*, ii. 3.

PROPUGNATION. *Defence; power; strength.*

What *propugnation* is in one man's valour,
To stand the push and enmity of those
This quarrel would excite?
Troilus and Cressida, ii. 2.

To PROROGUE. *To defer; to delay; to protract.*

My life were better ended by their hate,
Than death *prorogued*, wanting of thy love.
Romeo and Juliet, ii. 2.

I hear thou must, and nothing may *prorogue* it,
On Thursday next be married to this county.
Romeo and Juliet, iv. 1.

Tie up the libertine in a field of feasts,
Keep his brain fuming; Epicurean cooks
Sharpen with cloyless sauce his appetite;
That sleep and feeding may *prorogue* his honour
Even till a lethe'd dulness.
Antony and Cleopatra, ii. 1.

PROSECUTION. *Pursuit.*

Thou art sworn, Eros,
That, when the exigent should come,—which now
Is come indeed,—when I should see behind me
The inevitable *prosecution* of
Disgrace and horror, that, on my command,
Thou then wouldst kill me: do't; the time is come.
Antony and Cleopatra, iv. 14.

PROSPEROUS. *Propitious; favourable.*

Most gracious duke,
To my unfolding lend a *prosperous* ear.
Othello, i. 3.

To PROSTITUTE. *To give up; to yield; to surrender.*

I say we must not
So stain our judgment, or corrupt our hope,
To *prostitute* our past-cure malady
To empirics. *All's well that ends well*, ii. 1.

PROTEST. *Protestation.*

Swear me, Kate, like a lady as thou art,
A good mouth-filling oath, and leave "in sooth,"
And such *protest* of pepper-gingerbread,
To velvet-guards and Sunday-citizens.
Henry 4, P. 1, iii. 1.

Full of *protest*, of oath, and big compare.
Troilus and Cressida, iii. 2.

To PROTEST. *To prove; to show; to give evidence of.*

And many unrough youths, that even now
Protest their first of manhood. *Macbeth*, v. 2.

To PROTRACT. *To delay; to put off; to postpone.*

Let us bury him,
And not *protract* with admiration what
Is now due debt. *Cymbeline*, iv. 2.

PROTRACTIVE. *Continued; protracted; lengthened.*

And call them shames, which are, indeed, naught else
But the *protractive* trials of great Jove.
Troilus and Cressida, i. 3.

PROVAND. *Food; provender.*

Who have their *provand*
Only for bearing burdens, and sore blows
For sinking under them. *Coriolanus,* ii. 1.

To PROVIDE. *To prepare beforehand; to be ready.*

Lest it should ravel and be good to none,
You must *provide* to bottom it on me.
Two Gentlemen of Verona, iii. 2.

PROVINCIAL. *Accountable.*

His subject am I not, nor here *provincial.*
Measure for Measure, v. 1.

PROVOST. *A gaoler.*

Where is the *provost?*—Here, if it like your
honour. *Measure for Measure,* ii. 1.

To PRUNE. *To dress; to trim; to sleek; to smooth.*

When shall you see me write a thing in rhyme?
Or groan for love? or spend a minute's time
In *pruning* me? *Love's Labour's lost,* iv. 3.
Which makes him *prune* himself, and bristle up
The crest of youth against your dignity.
Henry 4, P. 1, i. 1.
His royal bird
Prunes the immortal wing, and cloys his beak
As when his god is pleas'd. *Cymbeline,* v. 4.

To PUDDLE. *To disturb; to trouble; to defile; to muddy.*

Something, sure, of state
Hath *puddled* his clear spirit. *Othello,* iii. 4.

PUDENCY. *Modesty.*

A *pudency* so rosy, the sweet view on't
Might well have warm'd old Saturn.
Cymbeline, ii. 4.

PUGGING. *Thieving.*

The white sheet bleaching on the hedge
Doth set my *pugging* tooth on edge.
Winter's Tale, iv. 2.

To PULL IN RESOLUTION. *To waver; to lose confidence; to be dismayed.*

I *pull in resolution;* and begin
To doubt the equivocation of the fiend
That lies like truth. *Macbeth,* v. 5.

PULPITER. *Preacher.*

O most gentle *pulpiter!*—what tedious homily
of love have you wearied your parishioners withal,
and never cried, " Have patience, good people!"
As you like it, iii. 2.

PULSIDGE. *The pulse.*

Your *pulsidge* beats as extraordinarily as heart
would desire. *Henry 4,* P. 2, ii. 4.

To PUN. *To pound; to beat.*

He would *pun* thee into shivers with his fist, as
a sailor breaks a biscuit. *Troilus and Cressida,* ii. 1.

PURCHASE. *Booty; plunder.*

They will steal any thing, and call it *purchase.*
Henry 5, iii. 1.
Thou shalt have a share in our *purchase,* as I
am a true man. *Henry 4,* P. 1, ii. 1.

To PURCHASE. *To acquire by other means than inheritance; to obtain; to come by.*

For what in me was *purchas'd,*
Falls upon thee in a more fairer sort.
Henry 4, P. 2, iv. 4.
His faults, in him, seem as the spots of heaven
More fiery by night's blackness; hereditary
Rather than *purchas'd.*
Antony and Cleopatra, i. 4.
Your accent is something finer than you could
purchase in so removed a dwelling.
As you like it, iii. 2.
With die and drab I *purchased* this caparison.
Winter's Tale, iv. 2.

PURGATION. *Exculpation; proof; trial.*

Proceed in justice; which shall have due course,
Even to the guilt or the *purgation.*
Winter's Tale, iii. 2.
If any man doubt that, let him put me to my
purgation. *As you like it,* v. 4.
For, for me to put him to his *purgation* would
perhaps plunge him into far more choler.
Hamlet, iii. 2.

PURPOSE. *Effect; consequence; end proposed.*

Now, sir,
What have you dream'd of late of this war's purpose?   *Cymbeline*, iv. 2.

To PURSE UP. *To ensnare; to entangle.*

When she first met Mark Antony, she *pursed* up his heart, upon the river of Cydnus.
Antony and Cleopatra, ii. 2.

To PURSUE. *To punish; to proscribe.*

It imports no reason
That with such vehemency he should *pursue* Faults proper to himself. *Measure for Measure*, v. 1.

PURSUIVANT. *A state messenger.*

Take this fellow in, and send for his master with a *pursuivant* presently. *Henry 6, P. 2*, i. 3.

PUSH. *Proof; trial; emergency.*

We'll put the matter to the present *push*.
Hamlet, v. 1.
There's time enough for that;
Lest they desire upon this *push* to trouble Your joys with like relation. *Winter's Tale*, v. 3.

PUSH. *Pshaw; pish.*

Push! did you see my cap?
Timon of Athens, iii. 6.

To PUT A GIRDLE ROUND. *To go round; to circle.*

I'll *put a girdle round* about the earth In forty minutes. *Midsummer-Night's Dream*, ii. 1.

To PUT ON. *To show; to indicate; to incite; to encourage; to instigate.*

Let not our looks *put on* our purposes.
Julius Cæsar, ii. 1.
Macbeth
Is ripe for shaking, and the powers above
Put on their instruments.   *Macbeth*, iv. 3.
But now grow fearful
That you protect this course, and *put it on* By your allowance.   *King Lear*, i. 4.
Gods! if you
Should have ta'en vengeance on my faults, I never Had liv'd to *put on* this.   *Cymbeline*, v. 1.
We'll *put on* those shall praise your excellence.
Hamlet, iv. 7.

PUTTER-ON. *An instigator; an inciter.*

You are abus'd, and by some *putter-on*,
That will be damn'd for't.   *Winter's Tale*, ii. 1.
Wherein,
My good lord cardinal, they vent reproaches Most bitterly on you, as *putter-on*
Of these exactions.   *Henry 8*, i. 2.

PUTTING-ON. *Suggestion; intimation; notice.*

Say you ne'er had done't
. . . . but by our *putting-on*.
Coriolanus, ii. 3.
Lord Angelo, belike thinking me remiss in mine office, awakens me with this unwonted *putting-on*.
Measure for Measure, iv. 2.

PUTTOCK. *A kite.*

Who finds the partridge in the *puttock's* nest, But may imagine how the bird was dead, Although the kite soar with unbloodied beak?
Henry 6, P. 2, iii. 2.
O bless'd, that I might not! I chose an eagle, And did avoid a *puttock*.   *Cymbeline*, i. 1.

PUZZEL. *A drab; a jade; a hussy.*

Pucelle or *puzzel*, dolphin or dogfish, Your hearts I'll stamp out with my horse's heels.
Henry 6, P. 1, i. 4.

PYRAMIDES. *Pyramids.*

Rather make
My country's high *pyramides* my gibbet, And hang me up in chains.
Antony and Cleopatra, v. 2.

PYRAMIS. *A pyramid.*

A statelier *pyramis* to her I'll rear Than Rhodope's of Memphis ever was.
Henry 6, P. 1, i. 5.

PYRENEAN. *The Pyrenees.*

And so, ere answer knows what question would,— Saving in dialogue of compliment, And talking of the Alps and Apennines, The *Pyrenean* and the river Po,— It draws toward supper in conclusion so. But this is worshipful society, And fits the mounting spirit like myself.
King John, i. 1.

Q.

QUAIL. *A courtezan ; a drab.*

Here's Agamemnon,—an honest fellow enough,
and one that loves *quails;* but he has not so much
brain as ear-wax.　　　*Troilus and Cressida,* v. 1.

To QUAIL. *To shrink ; to faint ; to quell; to overpower ; to subdue.*

And let not search and inquisition *quail,*
To bring again these foolish runaways.
　　　　　　　　　　As you like it, ii. 2.

This may plant courage in their *quailing* breasts.
　　　　　　　　　　Henry 6, P. 3, ii. 3.

But when he meant to *quail* and shake the orb,
He was as rattling thunder.
　　　　　　　　　　Antony and Cleopatra, v. 2.

O Fates, come, come,
Cut thread and thrum,
Quail, crush, conclude, and quell!
　　　　　　　　Midsummer-Night's Dream, v. 1.

QUAILING. *Shrinking ; holding back ; retreating.*

For, as he writes, there is no *quailing* now,
Because the king is certainly possess'd
Of all our purposes.　　　*Henry* 4, P. 1, iv. 1.

QUAINT. *Pretty ; elegant ; subtle ; ingenious ; strange ; unusual.*

I never saw a better-fashion'd gown,
More *quaint,* more pleasing, nor more commendable.
　　　　　　　　Taming of the Shrew, iv. 3.

My *quaint* Ariel, hark in thine ear.
　　　　　　　　　　Tempest, i. 2.

But you, my lord, were glad to be employ'd,
To show how *quaint* an orator you are.
　　　　　　　　　　Henry 6, P. 2, iii. 2.

And the *quaint* mazes in the wanton green,
For lack of tread, are undistinguishable.
　　　　　　　　Midsummer-Night's Dream, ii. 1.

And some, keep back
The clamorous owl, that nightly hoots and wonders
At our *quaint* spirits.　　　*Ibid.* ii. 2.

QUAINTLY. *Artfully ; ingeniously ; elegantly ; skilfully.*

But breathe his faults so *quaintly,*
That they may seem the taints of liberty ;
The flash and outbreak of a fiery mind.
　　　　　　　　　　Hamlet, ii. 1.

Why, then, a ladder, *quaintly* made of cords,
To cast up, with a pair of anchoring hooks,
Would serve to scale another Hero's tower,
So bold Leander would adventure it.
　　　　　　　Two Gentlemen of Verona, iii. 1.

Yes, yes ; the lines are very *quaintly* writ.
　　　　　　　　　　　Ibid. ii. 1.

'Tis vile, unless it may be *quaintly* order'd,
And better in my mind not undertook.
　　　　　　　　Merchant of Venice, ii. 4.

To QUAKE. *To frighten ; to alarm.*

Where ladies shall be frighted,
And, gladly *quak'd,* hear more.　　*Coriolanus,* i. 9.

QUALIFICATION. *Disposition ; temper.*

For out of that will I cause these of Cyprus to
mutiny ; whose *qualification* shall come into no
true taste again but by the displanting of Cassio.
　　　　　　　　　　Othello, ii. 1.

QUALITY. *Associates ; fellows ; vocation ; nature ; qualification ; property ; disposition ; temper.*

All hail, great master! grave sir, hail! I come
To answer thy best pleasure ; be't to fly,
To swim, to dive into the fire, to ride
On the curl'd clouds,—to thy strong bidding task
Ariel and all his *quality.*　　　*Tempest,* i. 2.

Will they pursue the *quality* no longer than
they can sing?　　　　*Hamlet,* ii. 2.

Come, give us a taste of your *quality;* come, a
passionate speech.　　　　*Ibid.* ii. 2.

But, fair soul,
In your fine frame hath love no *quality?*
　　　　　　　All's well that ends well, iv. 2.

MM

The *quality* of mercy is not strain'd,—
It droppeth as the gentle rain from heaven.
                              Merchant of Venice, iv. 1.

She hath more *qualities* than a water-spaniel,—
which is much in a bare Christian.
                    Two Gentlemen of Verona, iii. 1.

And then I lov'd thee,
And show'd thee all the *qualities* o' the isle.
                                          Tempest, i. 2.

To-night we'll wander through the streets, and note
The *qualities* of people. *Antony and Cleopatra*, i. 1.

There's something tells me—but it is not love—
I would not lose you; and you know yourself,
Hate counsels not in such a *quality*.
                            Merchant of Venice, iii. 2.

QUANTITY.   *Degree; quality; parts; portion.*

Things base and vile, holding no *quantity*,
Love can transpose to form and dignity.
                  Midsummer-Night's Dream, i. 1.

For women's fear and love holds *quantity*,
In neither aught, or in extremity. *Hamlet*, iii. 2.

If I were sawed into *quantities*, I should make
four dozen of such bearded hermits'-staves as Master
Shallow.   *Henry 4*, P. 2, v. 1.

QUARREL.   *A square-headed arrow.*

Yet, if that fortune's *quarrel* do divorce
It from the bearer, 'tis a sufferance panging
As soul and body's severing.   *Henry 8*, ii. 3.

QUARRELOUS.   *Quarrelsome; petulant.*

Ready in gibes, quick-answer'd, saucy, and
As *quarrelous* as the weasel. *Cymbeline*, iii. 4.

QUARRY.   *A heap of slaughtered game.*

And let me use my sword, I'd make a *quarry*
With thousands of these quarter'd slaves, as high
As I could pick my lance.   *Coriolanus*, i. 1.

This *quarry* cries on havoc.   *Hamlet*, v. 2.

To relate the manner,
Were, on the *quarry* of these murder'd deer,
To add the death of you.   *Macbeth*, iv. 3.

To QUARTER.   *To divide into parts.*

I, that with my sword
Quarter'd the world, and o'er green Neptune's back
With ships made cities, condemn myself to lack
The courage of a woman.
                        Antony and Cleopatra, iv. 14.

QUAT.   *A pimple; a pustule.*

I have rubb'd this young *quat* almost to the sense,
And he grows angry.   *Othello*, v. 1.

QUATCH.   *Flat; squat.*

The *quatch* buttock, the brawn buttock, or any
buttock.   *All's well that ends well*, ii. 2.

QUEASINESS.   *Distaste; want of relish.*

And they did fight with *queasiness*, constrain'd,
As men drink potions.   *Henry 4*, P. 2, i. 1.

QUEASY.   *Squeamish; disgusted; sick of; nice; delicate.*

That, in despite of his quick wit and his *queasy*
stomach, he shall fall in love with Beatrice.
                Much Ado about Nothing, ii. 1.

Who, *queasy* with his insolence
Already, will their good thoughts call from him.
                    Antony and Cleopatra, iii. 6.

And I have one thing, of a *queasy* question,
Which I must act.   *King Lear*, i. 2.

To QUEEN.   *To play the queen.*

This dream of mine,
Being now awake, I'll *queen* it no inch further,
But milk my ewes and weep. *Winter's Tale*, iv. 3.

'Tis strange: a three-pence bow'd would hire me,
Old as I am, to *queen* it.   *Henry 8*, ii. 3.

QUELL.   *Assassination.*

What not put upon
His spongy officers, who shall bear the guilt
Of our great *quell*?   *Macbeth*, i. 7.

To QUELL.   *To crush; to subdue.*

O Fates, come, come,
Cut thread and thrum;
Quail, crush, conclude, and *quell*!
                Midsummer-Night's Dream, v. 1.

Remember, lords, your oaths to Henry sworn,
Either to *quell* the Dauphin utterly,
Or bring him in obedience to our yoke.
                              Henry 6, P. 1, i. 1.

To QUENCH.   *To grow cool; to give way; to yield; to bereave.*

Weeps she still, say'st thou? Dost thou think in
    time
She will not *quench*, and let instructions enter
Where folly now possesses? *Cymbeline*, i. 5.

Being thus *quench'd*
Of hope, not longing, mine Italian brain
Gan in your duller Britain operate
Most vilely; for my vantage, excellent.
Cymbeline, v. 5.

QUERN. *A handmill.*

Are you not he
That frights the maidens of the villagery;
Skims milk, and sometimes labours in the *quern?*
Midsummer-Night's Dream, ii. 1.

QUEST. *Suit; courtship; a searcher; an inquirer; a jury.*

What, in the least,
Will you require in present dower with her,
Or cease your *quest* of love?
King Lear, i. 1.
The senate hath sent about three several *quests*
To search you out.
Othello, i. 2.

Volumes of report
Run with these false and most contrarious *quests*
Upon thy doings!
Measure for Measure, iv. 1.
What lawful *quest* have given their verdict up
Unto the frowning judge?
Richard 3, i. 4.

QUESTANT. *A candidate; a competitor.*

When the bravest *questant* shrinks, find what you
seek,
That fame may cry you loud.
All's well that ends well, ii. 1.

QUESTION. *Conversation; discussion; theme; subject; debate; contest.*

I met the duke yesterday, and had much *question* with him.
As you like it, iii. 4.
I am no more mad than you are: make the trial
of it in any constant *question*.
Twelfth-Night, iv. 2.

My liege, this haste was hot in *question*,
And many limits of the charge set down,
But yesternight.
Henry 4, P. 1, i. 1.

'Tis the way
To call hers, exquisite, in *question* more.
Romeo and Juliet, i. 1.

Yet, if you there
Did practise on my state, your being in Egypt
Might be my *question*.
Antony and Cleopatra, ii. 2.

So may he with more facile *question* bear it,
For that it stands not in such warlike brace,
And altogether lacks th' abilities
That Rhodes is dress'd in.
Othello, i. 3.

To QUESTION. *To talk; to converse with; to discuss; to examine; to call in question.*

I pray you, think you *question* with the Jew.
Merchant of Venice, iv. 1.
Stay not to *question*, for the watch is coming.
Romeo and Juliet, v. 3.

Let us meet,
And *question* this most bloody piece of work,
To know it further.
Macbeth, ii. 1.
Therefore, fair Hermia, *question* your desires.
Midsummer-Night's Dream, i. 1.
Question your royal thoughts, make the case yours.
Henry 4, P. 2, v. 2.

Pray, sir, to the army:
I and my brother are not known; yourself
So out of thought, and thereto so o'ergrown,
Cannot be *question'd*.
Cymbeline, iv. 4.

QUESTRIST. *A pursuer; a follower.*

Some five or six and thirty of his knights,
Hot *questrists* after him, met him at gate.
King Lear, iii. 7.

QUICK. *Gay; sprightly; lively; sudden.*

But is there no *quick* recreation granted?
Love's Labour's lost, i. 1.
And cheer his grace with *quick* and merry words.
Richard 3, i. 3.

The *quick* comedians
Extemporally will stage us.
Antony and Cleopatra, v. 2.
A thousand moral paintings I can show,
That shall demonstrate these *quick* blows of Fortune's
More pregnantly than words.
Timon of Athens, i. 1.

To QUICKEN. *To come to life; to revive.*

These hairs, which thou dost ravish from my chin,
Will *quicken* and accuse thee: I'm your host.
King Lear, iii. 7.
Even then this forkèd plague is fated to us
When we do *quicken*.
Othello, iii. 3.
Quicken with kissing: had my lips that power,
Thus would I wear them out.
Antony and Cleopatra, iv. 15.

QUIDDIT. *A cavil; a subtlety.*

Where be his *quiddits* now, his quillets, his
cases, his tenures, and his tricks?
Hamlet, v.1.

QUIDDITY. *Equivocation; quibble.*

How now, mad wag! what, in thy quips and thy *quiddities?*   *Henry 4*, P. 1, i. 2.

QUIETUS. *A final discharge.*

When he himself might his *quietus* make
With a bare bodkin.   *Hamlet*, iii. 1.

QUILLET. *Nicety ; subtlety ; equivocation ; quibble.*

And do not stand on *quillets* how to slay him.
     Henry 6, P. 2, iii. 1.

Some tricks, some *quillets,* how to cheat the devil.
     Love's Labour's lost, iv. 3.

Crack the lawyer's voice,
That he may never more false title plead,
Nor sound his *quillets* shrilly.
     Timon of Athens, iv. 3.

Dost thou hear, my honest friend?—No, I hear
not your honest friend ; I hear you.—Prithee, keep
up thy *quillets.*   *Othello,* iii. 1.

QUINTAIN. *A post ; a thick stake ; a block.*

And that which here stands up
Is but a *quintain,* a mere lifeless block.
     As you like it, i. 2.

QUIP. *A jest; a taunt; a sarcasm.*

How now, mad wag! what, in thy *quips* and
thy quiddities?   *Henry 4*, P. 1, i. 2.

Shall *quips* and sentences, and these paper-bul-
lets of the brain, awe a man from the career of his
humour?   *Much Ado about Nothing,* ii. 3.

To QUIRE. *To sing in concert.*

My throat of war be turn'd,
Which *quir'd* with my drum, into a pipe
Small as an eunuch, or the virgin voice
That babies lulls asleep!   *Coriolanus,* iii. 2.

There's not the smallest orb that thou behold'st,
But in his motion like an angel sings,
Still *quiring* to the young-ey'd cherubins.
     Merchant of Venice, v. 1.

QUIRK. *Taunt ; sarcasm ; fit ; flight of fancy ; sort ; humour.*

I may chance have some odd *quirks* and rem-
nants of wit broken upon me.
     Much Ado about Nothing, ii. 3.

I've felt so many *quirks* of joy and grief,

That the first face of neither, on the start,
Can woman me unto't.
     All's well that ends well, iii. 2.
One that excels the *quirks* of blazoning pens.
     Othello, ii. 1.
Belike this is a man of that *quirk.*
     Twelfth-Night, iii. 4.

QUIT. *Quitted.*

'Twas he inform'd against him;
And *quit* the house on purpose, that their punish-
ment
Might have the freer course.   *King Lear,* iv. 2.
Nor tackle, sail, nor mast; the very rats
Instinctively had *quit* it.   *Tempest,* i. 2.

To QUIT. *To pay ; to recompense ; to requite ; to pardon ; to be even with ; to set free.*

Farewell ; be trusty, and I'll *quit* thy pains.
     Romeo and Juliet, ii. 4.
Is't not perfect conscience,
To *quit* him with this arm?   *Hamlet,* v. 2.
To let a fellow that will take rewards,
And say, " God *quit* you !" be familiar with
My playfellow, your hand !
     Antony and Cleopatra, iii. 13.
Well, Angelo, your evil *quits* you well.
     Measure for Measure, v. 1.
And ere thou bid good-night, to *quit* their grief
Tell thou the lamentable tale of me.
     Richard 2, v. 1.
But, for those earthly faults, I *quit* them all.
     Measure for Measure, v. 1.
To be full *quit* of those my banishers,
Stand I before thee.   *Coriolanus,* iv. 5.
If once I find thee ranging,
Hortensio will be *quit* with thee by changing.
     Taming of the Shrew, iii. 1.
He that dies this year is *quit* for the next.
     Henry 4, P. 2, iii. 2.
Long live so, and so die ! I am *quit.*
     Timon of Athens, iv. 3.

QUITTANCE. *Acquittance ; payment ; return.*

But that's all one ; omittance is no *quittance.*
     As you like it, iii. 5.
But these mine eyes saw him in bloody state,
Rendering faint *quittance,* wearied and outbreath'd,
To Harry Monmouth.   *Henry 4,* P. 2, i. 1.

To QUITTANCE. *To repay ; to requite.*

Embrace we, then, this opportunity,

As fitting best to *quittance* their deceit,
Contriv'd by art and baleful sorcery.
Henry 6, P. 1, ii. 1.

QUIVER. *Active; nimble.*

I remember at Mile-end Green there was a little *quiver* fellow, and he would manage you his piece thus. *Henry 4*, P. 2, iii. 2.

QUOIF. *A cap.*

And hence, thou sickly *quoif!*
Thou art a guard too wanton for the head
Which princes, flesh'd with conquest, aim to hit.
Henry 4, P. 2, i. 1.

To QUOIT. *To throw.*

Quoit him down, Bardolph, like a shove-groat shilling. *Ibid.* ii. 4.

To QUOTE. *To note; to write down.*

A fellow by the hand of nature mark'd,
Quoted, and sign'd to do a deed of shame.
King John, iv. 2.

He's *quoted* for a most perfidious slave,
With all the spots o' the world tax'd and debauch'd;
Whose nature sickens but to speak a truth.
All's well that ends well, v. 3.

I am sorry that with better heed and judgment
I had not *quoted* him. *Hamlet*, ii. 1.

I have with exact view perus'd thee, Hector,
And *quoted* joint by joint.
Troilus and Cressida, iv. 5.

Give me a case to put my visage in :
A visor for a visor !—what care I
What curious eye doth *quote* deformities?
Here are the beetle-brows shall blush for me.
Romeo and Juliet, i. 4.

Her amber hairs for foul have amber *quoted*.
Love's Labour's lost, iv. 3.

QUOTIDIAN. *A quotidian or daily fever.*

If I could meet that fancy-monger, I would give him some good counsel, for he seems to have the *quotidian* of love upon him. *As you like it*, iii. 2.

R.

RABATO. *A kind of ruff.*

I think your other *rabato* were better.
Much Ado about Nothing, iii. 4.

RABBIT-SUCKER. *A young rabbit.*

Do thou stand for me, and I'll play my father.
—Depose me? if thou dost it half so gravely, so majestically, both in word and matter, hang me up by the heels for a *rabbit-sucker* or a poulter's hare.
Henry 4, P. 1, ii. 4.

RABBLEMENT. *The crowd; the multitude.*

And still as he refused it, the *rabblement* hooted, and clapped their chapped hands, and threw up their sweaty night-caps. *Julius Cæsar*, i. 2.

RACE. *Career; taste; flavour; breed; a root; a sprig.*

And now I give my sensual *race* the rein.
Measure for Measure, ii. 4.

No going then ;—
Eternity was in our lips, and eyes ;

Bliss in our brows' bent ; none our parts so poor,
But was a *race* of heaven.
Antony and Cleopatra, i. 3.

Or *race* of youthful and unhandled colts,
Fetching mad bounds. *Merchant of Venice*, v. 1.

I have a gammon of bacon and two *races* of ginger, to be delivered as far as Charing Cross.
Henry 4, P. 1, ii. 1.

A *race* or two of ginger, but that I may beg.
Winter's Tale, iv. 2.

To RACK. *To harass with exactions; to strain; to stretch.*

The commons hast thou *rack'd* ; the clergy's bags
Are lank and lean with thy extortions.
Henry 6, P. 2, i. 3.

But being lack'd and lost,
Why, then we *rack* the value.
Much Ado about Nothing, iv. 1.

Try what my credit can in Venice do :
That shall be *rack'd*, even to the uttermost,
To furnish thee to Belmont.
Merchant of Venice, i. 1.

RACKING. *Flying; fleeting.*

Three glorious suns, each one a perfect sun :
Not separated with the *racking* clouds,
But sever'd in a pale clear-shining sky.
Henry 6, P. 3, ii. 1.

RAG. *A man of low birth; a rogue; a beggar.*

Why shouldst thou hate men?
They never flatter'd thee : what hast thou given?
If thou wilt curse,—thy father, that poor *rag*,
Must be thy subject. *Timon of Athens*, iv. 3.

Lash hence these overweening *rags* of France,
These famish'd beggars, weary of their lives.
Richard 3, v. 3.

To RAGE. *To wanton; to enrage; to chafe; to grow angry.*

But you are more intemperate in your blood
Than Venus, or those pamper'd animals
That *rage* in savage sensuality.
Much Ado about Nothing, iv. 1.

Even where his *raging* eye or savage heart,
Without control, listed to make a prey.
Richard 3, iii. 5.

The king is come : deal mildly with his youth :
For young hot colts being *rag'd* do *rage* the more.
Richard 2, ii. 1.

RAGGED. *Rough; unmusical; mean; beggarly.*

My voice is *ragged* : I know I cannot please you.
As you like it, ii. 5.

And never shall you see that I will beg
A *ragged* and forestall'd remission.
Henry 4, P. 2, v. 2.

To RAKE UP. *To bury; to cover.*

Here, in the sands,
Thee I'll *rake up*, the post unsanctified
Of murderous lechers. *King Lear*, iv. 6.

RAMP. *A romp; a wanton.*

Whiles he is vaulting variable *ramps*,
In your despite, upon your purse. *Cymbeline*, i. 6.

To RAMP. *To rage.*

What a fool art thou,
A *ramping* fool, to brag, and stamp, and swear,
Upon my party! *King John*, iii. 1.
A couching lion and a *ramping* cat,
And such a deal of skimble-skamble stuff
As puts me from my faith. *Henry* 4, P. 1, iii. 1.

Thus yields the cedar to the axe's edge,
Under whose shade the *ramping* lion slept.
Henry 6, P. 3, v. 2.

RAMPALLIAN. *An obsolete term of reproach.*

Away, you scullion, you *rampallian!*
Henry 4, P. 2, ii. 1.

RAMPIRED. *Ramparted; fortified.*

Set but thy foot
Against our *rampir'd* gates, and they shall ope.
Timon of Athens, v. 4.

RANCOUR. *Vexation; bitterness; uneasiness; disquiet.*

For them the gracious Duncan have I murder'd ;
Put *rancours* in the vessel of my peace
Only for them. *Macbeth*, iii. 1.

RANGE. *Rank; order; line.*

What though you fled
From that great face of war, whose several *ranges*
Frighted each other? why should he follow?
Antony and Cleopatra, iii. 13.

To RANGE. *To stand in due rank and order.*

Let Rome in Tiber melt, and the wide arch
Of the *rang'd* empire fall !
Antony and Cleopatra, i. 1.

That is the way to lay the city flat ;
To bring the roof to the foundation,
And bury all, which yet distinctly *ranges*,
In heaps and piles of ruin. *Coriolanus*, iii. 1.

I swear, 'tis better to be lowly born,
And *range* with humble livers in content,
Than to be perk'd up in a glistering grief,
And wear a golden sorrow. *Henry* 8, ii. 3.

RANK. *Thick; exuberant; wanton; rampant.*

In which disguise,
While other jests are something *rank* on foot,
Her father hath commanded her to slip
Away with Slender.
Merry Wives of Windsor, iv. 6.

But, rather, show awhile like fearful war,
To diet *rank* minds sick of happiness.
Henry 4, P. 2, iv. 1.

Ha! what so *rank?* There's mischief in this man.
Henry 8, i. 2.

RANKNESS. *Pride; insolence; redundance; exuberance; excess.*

I will physic your *rankness*, and yet give no thousand crowns neither.   *As you like it*, i. 1.

I am stifled
With the mere *rankness* of their joy.
    Henry 8, iv. 1.

And, like a bated and retirèd flood,
Leaving our *rankness* and irregular course,
Stoop low within those bounds we have o'erlook'd.
    King John, v. 4.

To RANSACK. *To ravish; to carry away; to seize.*

What treason were it to the *ransack'd* queen,
Now to deliver her possession up
On terms of base compulsion!
    Troilus and Cressida, ii. 2.

RANSOM. *Penalty; punishment; requital.*

For me, the *ransom* of my bold attempt
Shall be this cold corpse on the earth's cold face.
    Richard 3, v. 3.

RAPTURE. *Fit; convulsion.*

Your prattling nurse
Into a *rapture* lets her baby cry
While she chats him.   *Coriolanus*, ii. 1.

RARELY. *Strangely; remarkably; egregiously.*

How *rarely* does it meet with this time's guise,
When man was wish'd to love his enemies!
    Timon of Athens, iv. 3.

RASCAL. *A lean deer.*

No, no; the noblest deer hath them as huge as
the *rascal*.   *As you like it*, iii. 3.

To RASE. *To tear away; to strike off.*

Then certifies your lordship, that this night
He dreamt, the boar had *rasèd* off his helm.
    Richard 3, iii. 2.

Stanley did dream the boar did *rase* his helm.
    Ibid. iii. 4.

RASH. *Hasty; precipitate; quick; sudden; urgent.*

O dear father,
Make not too *rash* a trial of him, for
He's gentle and not fearful.   *Tempest*, i. 2.

So will you wish on me,
When the *rash* mood is on.   *King Lear*, ii. 4.

Thou art *rash* as fire, to say
That she was false : O, she was heavenly true !
    Othello, v. 2.

Fear not slander, censure *rash*,
Thou hast finish'd joy and moan.
    Cymbeline, iv. 2.

Though it do work as strong
As aconitum or *rash* gunpowder.
    Henry 4, P. 2, iv. 4.

The best and soundest of his time hath been but
rash.   *King Lear*, i. 1.

I scarce have leisure to salute you,
My matter is so *rash*.   *Troilus and Cressida*, iv. 2.

RASH (adv.). *Hastily; violently; vehemently.*

Why do you speak so startlingly and *rash*?
    Othello, iii. 4.

To RATE. *To assign; to allot; to regulate; to adjust.*

Who does he accuse?—Cæsar : and that, having in
    Sicily
Sextus Pompeius spoil'd, we had not *rated* him
His part o' the isle.   *Antony and Cleopatra*, iii. 6.

Wherefore, ere this time,
Had you not fully laid my state before me ;
That so I might have *rated* my expense,
As I had leave of means?   *Timon of Athens*, ii. 2.

To RATTLE. *To stun; to berattle.*

Sound but another, and another shall,
As loud as thine, *rattle* the welkin's ear.
    King John, v. 2.

RAUGHT. *Reached; extended; grasped at.*

The hand of death hath *raught* him.
    Antony and Cleopatra, iv. 9.

He smiled me in the face, *raught* me his hand,
And with a feeble gripe, says, "Dear my lord,
Commend my service to my sovereign."
    Henry 5, iv. 6.

The moon was a month old when Adam was no
    more,
And *raught* not to five weeks when he came to five-
score.   *Love's Labour's lost*, iv. 2.

This staff of honour *raught*, there let it stand
Where it best fits to be, in Henry's hand.
    Henry 6, P. 2, ii. 3.

Come, make him stand upon this molehill here,
That *raught* at mountains with outstretchèd arms.
    Henry 6, P. 3, i. 4.

To RAVEL OUT.   *To unravel; to disclose.*

Or paddling in your neck with his damn'd fingers,
Make you to *ravel* all this matter *out*,
That I essentially am not in madness,
But mad in craft.   *Hamlet*, iii. 4.

RAVELLED.   *Entangled.*

Sleep that knits up the *ravell'd* sleave of care.
                                      Macbeth, ii. 1.

RAVIN.   *Hungry; voracious; ravenous.*

Better 'twere
I met the *ravin* lion when he roar'd
With sharp constraint of hunger.
                    All's well that ends well, iii. 2.

To RAVIN.   *To devour; to swallow greedily.*

Thriftless ambition that will *ravin* up
Thine own life's means!   *Macbeth*, ii. 2.

Like rats that *ravin* down their proper bane.
                    Measure for Measure, i. 2.

Witches' mummy; maw and 'gulf
Of the *ravin'd* salt-sea shark.   *Macbeth*, iv. 1.

RAW.   *Strange; unusual; new-fangled.*

I've within my mind
A thousand *raw* tricks of these bragging Jacks,
Which I will practise.   *Merchant of Venice*, iii. 4.

The concernancy, sir? Why do we wrap the
gentleman in our more *rawer* breath? *Hamlet*, v. 2.

RAWLY.   *Hastily; precipitately; suddenly.*

Some crying for a surgeon; some upon the debts
they owe; some upon their children *rawly* left.
                                      Henry 5, iv. 1.

RAWNESS.   *Haste; precipitation.*

Why in that *rawness* left you wife and child
Without leave-taking?   *Macbeth*, iv. 3.

To RAY.   *To bemire; to bewray.*

Was ever man so beaten? was ever man so *rayed*?
was ever man so weary?
                    Taming of the Shrew, iv. 1.

RAZED.   *Slashed; striped; streaked.*

Would not this, sir, and a forest of feathers,
with two Provincial roses on my *razed* shoes, get
me a fellowship in a cry of players? *Hamlet*, iii. 2.

RAZORABLE.   *Fit for the razor; requiring the razor.*

Till new-born chins be rough and *razorable*.
                                      Tempest, ii. 1.

RAZURE.   *Erasure; extermination.*

A forted residence 'gainst the tooth of time
And *razure* of oblivion. *Measure for Measure*, v. 1.

To REACH.   *To extend; to spread out; to expand.*

He shall flourish,
And, like a mountain cedar, *reach* his branches
To all the plains about him.   *Henry* 8, v. 4.

READ.   *Counsel; admonition; advice.*

Whilst, like a puff'd and reckless libertine,
Himself the primrose path of dalliance treads,
And recks not his own *read*.   *Hamlet*, i. 3.

To READ.   *To study; to discern; to discover; to learn; to know fully.*

Where is he living
Which calls me pupil, or hath *read* to me?
                                      Henry 4, P. 1, iii. 1.

It were not good; for therein should we *read*
The very bottom and the soul of hope. *Ibid.* iv. 1.

And those about her
From her shall *read* the perfect ways of honour.
                                      Henry 8, v. 4.

O most delicate fiend!
Who is't can *read* a woman? *Cymbeline*, v. 5.

To RE-ANSWER.   *To recompense; to make compensation for.*

Which, in weight to *re-answer*, his pettiness
would bow under.   *Henry* 5, iii. 5.

REARWARD.   *The rear.*

Thought I thy spirits were stronger than thy shames,
Myself would, on the *rearward* of reproaches,
Strike at thy life. *Much Ado about Nothing*, iv. 1.
'A came ever in the *rearward* of the fashion.
                                 Henry 4, P. 2, iii. 2.

To REASON.   *To talk; to question; to converse; to debate; to discuss; to argue.*

How now, sir! what are you *reasoning* with
yourself?   *Two Gentlemen of Verona*, ii. 1.

But *reason* with the fellow,
Before you punish him, where he heard this.
Coriolanus, iv. 6.

Our griefs, and not our manners, *reason* now.
King John, iv. 3.

Let's *reason* with the worst that may befall.
Julius Cæsar, v. 1.

O, *reason* not the need : our basest beggars
Are in the poorest thing.superfluous.
King Lear, ii. 4.

This boy, that cannot tell what he would have,
But kneels and holds up hands for fellowship,
Does *reason* our petition with more strength
Than thou hast to deny't. *Coriolanus,* v. 3.

REASONS. *Discourse; arguments.*

Your *reasons* at dinner have been sharp and sententious. *Love's Labour's lost,* v. 1.

To REAVE. *To bereave; to deprive; to rob.*

To *reave* the orphan of his patrimony.
Henry 6, P. 2, v. 1.

Had you that craft to *reave* her
Of what should stead her most ?
All's well that ends well, v. 3.

To REBATE. *To blunt; to disedge.*

One who never feels
The wanton stings and motions of the sense,
But doth *rebate* and blunt his natural edge
With profits of the mind, study and fast.
Measure for Measure, i. 4.

REBUKABLE. *Reprehensible; shameful; disgraceful.*

Rebukable,
And worthy shameful check it were, to stand
On more mechanic compliment.
Antony and Cleopatra, iv. 4.

To RECANT. *To recall; to retract.*

He shall do this; or else I do *recant*
The pardon that I late pronouncèd here.
Merchant of Venice, iv. 1.

RECANTER. *One who retracts what he has
said or done.*

The public body, which doth seldom
Play the *recanter.* *Timon of Athens,* v. 1.

RECEIPT. *Income; revenue; receptacle; repository.*

It tauntingly replied
To the discontented members, the mutinous parts
That envied his *receipt.* *Coriolanus,* i. 1.

That memory, the warder of the brain
Shall be a fume, and the *receipt* of reason
A limbec only. *Macbeth,* i. 7.

To RECEIVE. *To accept; to allow; to conceive; to understand.*

Will it not be *receiv'd,*
When we have mark'd with blood those sleepy two
Of his own chamber, and us'd their very daggers,
That they have done't ? *Macbeth,* i. 7.

To be *receivèd* plain, I'll speak more gross :
Your brother is to die. *Measure for Measure,* ii. 4.

RECEIVING. *Reception; welcome; understanding; capacity.*

Embrace but my direction, on mine honour
I'll point you where you shall have such *receiving*
As shall become your highness.
Winter's Tale, iv. 3.

To one of your *receiving*
Enough is shown : a cyprus, not a bosom,
Hides my heart. *Twelfth-Night,* iii. 1.

RECHEAT. *The recall; a tune or flourish on
the horn to recall the hounds.*

But that I will have a *recheat* winded in my
forehead, or hang my bugle in an invisible baldrick,
all women shall pardon me.
Much Ado about Nothing, i. 1.

To RECK. *To care; to heed; to mind.*

And little *recks* to find the way to heaven
By doing deeds of hospitality. *As you like it,* ii. 4.

Himself the primrose path of dalliance treads,
And *recks* not his own read. *Hamlet,* i. 3.

RECKLESS. *Scornful; indifferent.*

I'll after, more to be reveng'd on Eglamour
Than for the love of *reckless* Silvia.
Two Gentlemen of Verona, v. 2.

RECKONING. *Estimation; reputation.*

Of honourable *reckoning* are you both.
Romeo and Juliet, i. 2.

NN

RECLUSIVE. *Retired; shut up; secluded.*

In some *reclusive* and religious life.
Much Ado about Nothing, iv. 1.

RECOGNIZANCE. *Security for money; badge; token.*

This fellow might be in's time a great buyer of land, with his statutes, his *recognizances*, his fines, his double vouchers, his recoveries. *Hamlet*, v. 1.

And she did gratify his amorous works
With that *recognizance* and pledge of love
Which I first gave her. *Othello*, v. 2.

To RECOIL. *To shrink; to fail; to degenerate.*

Be reveng'd ;
Or she that bore you was no queen, and you
Recoil from your great stock. *Cymbeline*, i. 6.

A good and virtuous nature may *recoil*
In an imperial charge. *Macbeth*, iv. 3.

RECOMFORTURE. *Consolation; comfort; solace.*

Where, in that nest of spicery, they shall breed
Selves of themselves, to your *recomforture*.
Richard 3, iv. 4.

To RECOMMEND. *To deliver; to commit.*

Denied me mine own purse,
Which I had *recommended* to his use
Not half an hour before. *Twelfth-Night*, v. 1.

RECONCILIATION. *Atonement; expiation.*

Good my lord,
If I have any grace or power to move you,
His present *reconciliation* take. *Othello*, iii. 3.

To RECORD. *To chant; to recite; to register.*

And to the nightingale's complaining notes
Tune my distresses and *record* my woes.
Two Gentlemen of Verona, v. 4.

Let me be *recorded* by the righteous gods,
I am as poor as you. *Timon of Athens*, iv. 2.
The other, that he do *record* a gift,
Here in the court, of all he dies possess'd,
Unto his son Lorenzo and his daughter.
Merchant of Venice, iv. 1.

RECORDATION. *A memorial; a remembrance; a monument.*

And never shall have length of life enough
To rain upon remembrance with mine eyes,

That it may grow and sprout as high as heaven,
For *recordation* to my noble husband.
Henry 4, P. 2, ii. 3.
To make a *recordation* to my soul
Of every syllable that here was spoke.
Troilus and Cressida, v. 2.

RECORDER. *A kind of flagelet.*

Indeed he hath played on his prologue like a child on a *recorder*; a sound, but not in government. *Midsummer-Night's Dream*, v. 1.

O, the *recorders*:—let me see one. *Hamlet*, iii. 2.

RECOURSE. *Access; admission; effusion; overflow.*

Ay, but the doors be lock'd, and keys kept safe,
That no man hath *recourse* to her by night.
Two Gentlemen of Verona, iii. 1.

And to give notice that no manner person
Have any time *recourse* unto the princes.
Richard 3, iii. 5.

Not Priamus and Hecuba on knees,
Their eyes o'er-gallèd with *recourse* of tears;
Nor you, my brother, with your true sword drawn,
Oppos'd to hinder me, should stop my way,
But by my ruin. *Troilus and Cressida*, v. 3.

To RECOVER. *To reach; to attain; to obtain; to get.*

If I cannot *recover* your niece, I am a foul way out. *Twelfth-Night*, ii. 3.

The forest is not three leagues off;
If we *recover* that, we're sure enough.
Two Gentlemen of Verona, v. 1.

Why do you go about to *recover* the wind of me, as if you would drive me into a toil?
Hamlet, iii. 2.

RECREANT. *A traitor.*

Hear me, *recreant*!
On thine allegiance, hear me! *King Lear*, i. 1.
For either thou
Must, as a foreign *recreant*, be led
With manacles thorough our streets, or else
Triumphantly tread on thy country's ruin.
Coriolanus, v. 3.

RECREANT. *Cowardly.*

Thou wear a lion's hide! doff it for shame,
And hang a calf's-skin on those *recreant* limbs.
King John, iii. 1.
Here standeth Thomas Mowbray, Duke of Norfolk,
On pain to be found false and *recreant*.
Richard 2, i. 3.

RECTORSHIP. *Authority; command; power.*

Why, had your bodies
No heart among you ? or had you tongues to cry
Against the *rectorship* of judgment ?
Coriolanus, ii. 3.

To RECURE. *To repair; to remedy.*

Which to *recure,* we heartily solicit
Your gracious self to take on you the charge
And kingly government of this your land.
Richard 3, iii. 7.

To RE-DELIVER. *To return; to report.*

My lord, I have remembrances of yours,
That I have longèd long to *re-deliver ;*
I pray you, now receive them. *Hamlet,* iii. 1.
Shall I *re-deliver* you e'en so ? *Ibid.* v. 2.

RED-LATTICE. *An alehouse.*

And yet you, rogue, will ensconce your rags,
your cat-a-mountain looks, your *red-lattice* phrases,
and your bull-baiting oaths, under the shelter of
your honour ! *Merry Wives of Windsor,* ii. 2.

RED-PLAGUE. *The erysipelas.*

The *red plague* rid you
For learning me your language ! *Tempest,* i. 2.

REDOUBTED. *Dread; formidable.*

So far be mine, my most *redoubted* lord,
As my true service shall deserve your love.
Richard 2, iii. 3.

And these assume but valour's excrement
To render them *redoubted.*
Merchant of Venice, iii. 2.

To REDUCE. *To bring back; to renew.*

Which to *reduce* into our former *favour,*
You are assembled. *Henry* 5, v. 2.

Abate the edge of traitors, gracious Lord,
That would *reduce* these bloody days again,
And make poor England weep in streams of blood !
Richard 3, v. 3.

REECHY. *Smoky; grimy.*

The kitchen malkin pins
Her richest lockram 'bout her *reechy* neck.
Coriolanus, ii. 1.
Like Pharaoh's soldiers in the *reechy* painting.
Much Ado about Nothing, iii. 3.

REED. *An arrow; a dart.*

I had as lief have a *reed* that will do me no service as a partisan I could not heave.
Antony and Cleopatra, ii. 7.

REEK. *Smoke; fume; vapour.*

Thou mightst as well say I love to walk by the
Counter-gate, which is as hateful to me as the *reek*
of a lime-kiln. *Merry Wives of Windsor,* iii. 3.

You common cry of curs ! whose breath I hate
As *reek* o' the rotten fens ! *Coriolanus,* iii. 3.

To REEK. *To emit moisture or vapour of any
kind; to yearn.*

If you bear me hard,
Now, whilst your purpled hands do *reek* and smoke,
Fulfil your pleasure. *Julius Cæsar,* iii. 1.

The violence of action hath made you *reek* as a
sacrifice. *Cymbeline,* i. 2.

You remember
How under my oppression I did *reek,*
When I first mov'd you. *Henry* 8, ii. 4.

REEKING. *Exuberant; overflowing.*

This is Timon's last ;
Who, stuck and spangled with your flattery,
Washes it off, and sprinkles in your faces
Your *reeking* villany. *Timon of Athens,* iii. 6.

REEKY. *Damp; mouldering.*

Or shut me nightly in a charnel-house
O'er-cover'd quite with dead men's rattling bones,
With *reeky* shanks and yellow chapless skulls.
Romeo and Juliet, iv. 1.

To REFEL. *To refute.*

How he *refell'd* me, and how I replied.
Measure for Measure, v. 1.

To REFER. *To betake; to have recourse to.*

Only *refer* yourself to this advantage,—first,
that your stay with him may not be long ; that the
time may have all shadow and silence in it ; and
the place answer to convenience.
Measure for Measure, iii. 1.

Your honours all, I do *refer* me to the oracle.
Winter's Tale, iii. 2.

Hath *referr'd* herself
Unto a poor but worthy gentleman.
Cymbeline, i. 1.

REFERENCE. *Appeal; submission; assignment; grant; allowance.*

Make your full *reference* freely to my lord,
Who is so full of grace, that it flows over
On all that need. *Antony and Cleopatra*, v. 2.
Due *reference* of place and exhibition;
With such accommodation and besort
As levels with her breeding. *Othello*, i. 3.

REFLEX. *Reflection.*

I'll say yon grey is not the morning's eye,
'Tis but the pale *reflex* of Cynthia's brow.
Romeo and Juliet, iii. 5.

To REFLEX. *To reflect.*

May never glorious sun *reflex* his beams
Upon the country where you make abode!
Henry 6, P. 1, v. 4.

To REFUGE. *To shelter; to excuse; to palliate.*

Like silly beggars,
Who, sitting in the stocks, *refuge* their shame,
That many have, and others must sit there.
Richard 2, v. 5.

To REFUSE. *To reject; to renounce; to disown.*

Prove that I yesternight
Maintain'd the change of words with any creature,
Refuse me, hate me, torture me to death!
Much Ado about Nothing, iv. 1.
I may neither choose whom I would, nor *refuse*
whom I dislike. *Merchant of Venice*, i. 2.

REGARD. *Respect; consideration; motive.*

And enterprises of great pith and moment,
With this *regard*, their currents turn awry,
And lose the name of action. *Hamlet*, iii. 1.
Our reasons are so full of good *regard*,
That were you, Antony, the son of Cæsar,
You should be satisfied. *Julius Cæsar*, iii. 1.
Love's not love
When it is mingled with *regards* that stand
Aloof from the entire point. *King Lear*, i. 1.

REGARDFULLY. *Respectfully; reverentially.*

Is this th' Athenian minion, whom the world
Voic'd so *regardfully?* *Timon of Athens*, iv. 3.

REGIMENT. *Rule; government; authority.*

Only th' adulterous Antony, most large

In his abominations, turns you off;
And gives his potent *regiment* to a trull,
That noises it against us.
Antony and Cleopatra, iii. 6.

REGREET. *Salutation; greeting; courtesy.*

From whom he bringeth sensible *regreets.*
Merchant of Venice, ii. 8.
And shall these hands, so lately purg'd of blood,
So newly join'd in love, so strong in both,
Unyoke this seizure, and this kind *regreet?*
King John, iii. 1.

To REGREET. *To salute again; to resalute.*

You, cousin Hereford, upon pain of life,
Till twice five summers have enrich'd our fields,
Shall not *regreet* our fair dominions.
Richard 2, i. 3.

REGUERDON. *Recompense; reward.*

And in *reguerdon* of that duty done,
I girt thee with the valiant sword of York.
Henry 6, P. 1, iii. 1.

To REGUERDON. *To requite; to recompense.*

Yet never have you tasted our regard,
Or been *reguerdon'd* with so much as thanks,
Because till now we never saw your face.
Henry 6, P. 1, iii. 4.

To REIN. *To be obedient to the bridle; to curb; to restrain.*

And, for that I promised you, I'll be as good as
my word: he will bear you easily, and *reins* well.
Twelfth-Night, iii. 5.
Rein up the organs of her fantasy.
Merry Wives of Windsor, v. 5.
Being once chaf'd, he cannot
Be *rein'd* again to temperance. *Coriolanus*, iii. 3.

REJOINDURE. *Rejoinder; reply.*

Where injury of chance
Rudely beguiles our lips of all *rejoindure*
Troilus and Cressida, iv. 4.

To REJOURN. *To adjourn; to put off; to postpone.*

And then *rejourn* the controversy of three-pence
to a second day of audience. *Coriolanus*, ii. 1.

RELAPSE. *New career; renewed course.*

Mark, then, abounding valour in our English;
That, being dead, like to the bullet's grazing,

Break out into a second course of mischief,
Killing in *relapse* of mortality.   *Henry 5*, iv. 3.

RELATION. *History; connection; affinity.*

There is a mystery—with whom *relation*
Durst never meddle—in the soul of state.
                    Troilus and Cressida, iii. 3.
Augurs and understood *relations* have
By magot-pies, and choughs, and rooks, brought
    forth
The secret'st man of blood.   *Macbeth*, iii. 4.

RELATIVE. *Immediate; positive.*

I'll have grounds
More *relative* than this.   *Hamlet*, ii. 2.

RELENTING. *Soft; tender; pitiful; compassionate.*

And Gloster's show
Beguiles him, as the mournful crocodile
With sorrow snares *relenting* passengers.
                    Henry 6, P. 2, iii. 1.

To RELISH. *To taste well; to be approved.*

Had I been the finder-out of this secret, it would
not have *relished* among my other discredits.
                    Winter's Tale, v. 2.

To RELUME. *To rekindle; to renew; to revive.*

But once put out thy light,
Thou cunning'st pattern of excelling nature,
I know not where is that Promethean heat
That can thy light *relume*.   *Othello*, v. 2.

REMAIN. *Sojourn; residence; remainder; rest.*

I know your master's pleasure, and he mine :
All the *remain* is, welcome.   *Cymbeline*, iii. 1.
A most miraculous work in this good king ;
Which often, since my here-*remain* in England,
I've seen him do.   *Macbeth*, iv. 3.

To REMAIN. *To dwell; to inhabit.*

Vouchsafe my prayer
May know if you *remain* upon this island.
                    Tempest, i. 2.

REMEDIATE. *Remedial; restorative; salutary.*

All you unpublish'd virtues of the earth,
Spring with my tears ! be aidant and *remediate*
In the good man's distress !   *King Lear*, iv. 4.

REMEDY. *Help; means; appliance; relief; redress.*

Our *remedies* oft in ourselves do lie,
Which we ascribe to heaven.
                    All's well that ends well, i. 1.
Both suffer under this complaint we bring ;
And both shall cease without your *remedy*.
                    Ibid. v. 3.
His *remedies* are tame i' the present peace
And quietness of the people.   *Coriolanus*, iv. 6:

To REMEMBER. *To remind; to put in mind; to call to mind.*

I'll not *remember* you of my own lord,
Who is lost too.   *Winter's Tale*, iii. 2.
Let me *remember* thee what thou hast promis'd ;
Which is not yet perform'd me.   *Tempest*, i. 2.

REMEMBERED. *Remembering; mindful.*

Though thou the waters warp,
Thy sting is not so sharp
As friend *remember'd* not.   *As you like it*, ii. 7.
Now, by my troth, if I had been *remember'd*,
I could have given my uncle's grace a flout,
To touch his growth nearer than he touch'd mine.
                    Richard 3, ii. 4.

REMEMBRANCE. *Admonition; injunction; caution.*

With this *remembrance*,—that you use the same
With the like bold, just, and impartial spirit
As you have done 'gainst me. *Henry 4*, P. 2, v. 2.

REMEMBRANCER. *Adviser; counsellor; encourager.*

The agent for his master ;
And the *remembrancer* of her to hold
The hand-fast to her lord.   *Cymbeline*, i. 5.

REMONSTRANCE. *Demonstration; display; manifestation; disclosure.*

And you may marvel
Why I obscur'd myself, and would not rather
Make rash *remonstrance* of my hidden power
Than let him so be lost.
                    Measure for Measure, v. 1.

REMORSE. *Pity.*

You, brother mine, that entertain'd ambition,
Expell'd *remorse* and nature.   *Tempest*, v. 1.

REMORSEFUL. *Compassionate; tender; merciful.*

Like a *remorseful* pardon slowly carried.
All's well that ends well, v. 3.

Thou art a gentleman, ...
Valiant, wise, *remorseful*, well-accomplish'd.
Two Gentlemen of Verona, iv. 2.

REMORSELESS. *Without pity; pitiless; relentless.*

Thou stern, obdúrate, flinty, rough, *remorseless*.
Henry 6, P. 3, i. 4.

Even so, *remorseless*, have they borne him hence.
Henry 6, P. 2, iii. 1.

REMOTE. *Distant.*

From Athens is her house *remote* seven leagues.
Midsummer-Night's Dream, i. 1.

REMOTION. *Removal; remoteness.*

All thy safety were *remotion*, and thy defence
absence. *Timon of Athens*, iv. 3.

This act persuades me
That this *remotion* of the duke and her
Is practice only. *King Lear*, ii. 4.

REMOVE. *Removal; change of place; absence; exchange.*

Who hath, for four or five *removes*, come short
To tender it herself. *All's well that ends well*, v. 3.

Hold, therefore, Angelo :
In our *remove* be thou at full ourself.
Measure for Measure, i. 1.

Say, our pleasure,
To such whose place is under us, requires
Our quick *remove* from hence.
Antony and Cleopatra, i. 2.

If they set down before's, for the *remove*
Bring up your army. *Coriolanus*, i. 2.

And change your favours too; so shall your loves
Woo contrary, deceiv'd by these *removes*.
Love's Labour's lost, v. 2.

REMOVED (adj.). *Retired; private; remote; distant.*

None better knows than you
How I have ever lov'd the life *remov'd*.
Measure for Measure, i. 3.

Your accent is something finer than you could
purchase in so *removed* a dwelling.
As you like it, iii. 2.

It waves you to a more *removèd* ground.
Hamlet, i. 4.

REMOVEDNESS. *Absence.*

So far, that I have eyes under my service which
look upon his *removedness*. *Winter's Tale*, iv. 1.

RENDER. *Acknowledgment; confession; account; surrender.*

To satisfy,
If of my freedom 'tis the main part, take
No stricter *render* of me than my all.
Cymbeline, v. 4.

And send forth us to make their sorrow'd *render*,
Together with a recompense more fruitful
Than their offence can weigh down by the dram.
Timon of Athens, v. 1.

Newness
Of Cloten's death . . . .
. . . . may drive us to a *render*
Where we have liv'd. *Cymbeline*, iv. 4.

To RENDER. *To surrender; to give; to afford; to represent; to confess; to declare.*

And I will call him to so strict account,
That he shall *render* every glory up,
Or I will tear the reckoning from his heart.
Henry 4, P. 1, iii. 2.

Not a man
Shall pass his quarter, or offend the stream
Of regular justice in your city's bounds,
But shall be *render'd* to your public laws
At heaviest answer. *Timon of Athens*, v. 4.

Let each man *render* me his bloody hand.
Julius Cæsar, iii. 1.

And public reasons shall be *renderèd*
Of Cæsar's death. *Ibid.* iii. 2.

So nigh at least
That though his actions were not visible, yet
Report should *render* him hourly to your ear
As truly as he moves. *Cymbeline*, iii. 4.

O, I have heard him speak of that same brother,
And he did *render* him the most unnatural
That liv'd 'mongst men. *As you like it*, iv. 3.

My boon is, that this gentleman may *render*
Of whom he had this ring. *Cymbeline*, v. 5.

RENDEZVOUS. *A rallying point; a resource; something to fall back upon.*

A *rendezvous*, a home to fly unto,
If that the devil and mischance look big
Upon the maidenhead of our affairs.
Henry 4, P. 1, iv. 1.

And there my *rendezvous* is quite cut off.
Henry 5, v. 1.

To RENEGE. *To deny; to renounce; to reject.*
Renege, affirm, and turn their halcyon beaks
With every gale and vary of their masters,
Knowing naught, like dogs, but following.
King Lear, ii. 2.
His captain's heart,
Which in the scuffles of great fights hath burst
The buckles on his breast, *reneges* all temper.
Antony and Cleopatra, i. 1.

To RENEW. *To revive; to restore to life; to renovate.*
In such a night
Medea gather'd the enchanted herbs
That did *renew* old Æson. *Merchant of Venice*, v. 1.
Justice, and your father's wrath, should he take
me in his dominion, could not be so cruel to me, as
you, O the dearest of creatures, would even *renew*
me with your eyes. *Cymbeline*, iii. 2.

To RENOWN. *To render famous.*
The blood and courage that *renownèd* them
Runs in your veins. *Henry* 5, i. 2.
With the memorials and the things of fame
That do *renown* this city. *Twelfth-Night*, iii. 3.

To RENT. *To rend; to tear.*
Like one lost in a thorny wood,
That *rents* the thorns, and is rent with the thorns.
Henry 6, P. 3, iii. 2.
And will you *rent* our ancient love asunder?
Midsummer-Night's Dream, iii. 2.
Where sighs, and groans, and shrieks that *rent* the air,
Are made, not mark'd. *Macbeth*, iv. 3.

REPAIR. *Renewal; restoration; abode; resort.*
Before the curing of a strong disease,
Even in the instant of *repair* and health,
The fit is strongest.
*What holier than,—for royalty's *repair*,—
To bless the bed of majesty again
With a sweet fellow to't? *Winter's Tale*, v. 1.
Whose *repair* and franchise
Shall, by the power we hold, be our good deed,
Though Rome be therefore angry. *Cymbeline*, iii. 1.
Where slept our scouts, or how are they seduc'd
That we could hear no news of his *repair?*
Henry 6, P. 3, v. 1.
No, none, but only a *repair* i' the dark.
Measure for Measure, iv. 1.

To REPAIR. *To renovate; to renew.*
It much *repairs* me
To talk of your good father.
All's well that ends well, i. 2.
O disloyal thing,
That shouldst *repair* my youth, thou heapest
A year's age on me! *Cymbeline*, i. 1.

To REPAST. *To feed; to feast.*
To his good friends thus wide I'll ope my arms;
And, like the kind life-rendering pelican,
Repast them with my blood. *Hamlet*, iv. 5.

REPASTURE. *Entertainment; prey.*
Food for his rage, *repasture* for his den.
Love's Labour's lost, iv. 1.

REPEAL. *Recall; return; restoration.*
So, if the time thrust forth
A cause for thy *repeal*, we shall not send
O'er the vast world to seek a single man.
Coriolanus, iv. 1.
I kiss thy hand, but not in flattery, Cæsar;
Desiring thee that Publius Cimber may
Have an immediate freedom of *repeal*.
Julius Cæsar, iii. 1.

To REPEAL. *To recall; to restore.*
Cancel all grudge, *repeal* thee home again.
Two Gentlemen of Verona, v. 4.
And with this healthful hand, whose banish'd sense
Thou hast *repeal'd*, a second time receive
The confirmation of my promis'd gift.
All's well that ends well, ii. 3.

To REPENT. *To regret; to lament; to grieve for.*
Our purposes God justly hath discover'd;
And I *repent* my fault more than my death.
Henry 5, ii. 2.

REPLENISHED. *Consummate; complete; perfect.*
Should a villain say so,
The most *replenish'd* villain in the world,
He were as much more villain. *Winter's Tale*, ii. 1.
We smotherèd
The most *replenishèd* sweet work of nature,
That from the prime creation e'er she fram'd.
Richard 3, iv. 3.

REPLICATION. *Reverberation; reply.*

That Tiber trembled underneath her banks,
To hear the *replication* of your sounds
Made in her concave shores.   *Julius Cæsar,* i. 1.

Besides, to be demanded of a sponge!—what
replication should be made by the son of a king?
Hamlet, iv. 2.

REPORT. *Reputation; a reporter.*

My body's mark'd
With Roman swords; and my *report* was once
First with the best of note.   *Cymbeline,* iii. 3.

I did inquire it,
And have my learning from some true *reports*
That draw their swords with you.
Antony and Cleopatra, ii. 2.

To REPORT. *To expound; to interpret; to unfold.*

Never saw I figures
So likely to *report* themselves.   *Cymbeline,* ii. 4.

REPOSAL. *Belief; confidence; assurance.*

If I would stand against thee, would the *reposal*
Of any trust, virtue, or worth, in thee
Make thy words faith'd?   *King Lear,* ii. 1.

REPRODANCE. *Reprobation; desperation; un-mitigated wickedness.*

Did he live now,
This sight would make him do a desperate turn,
Yea, curse his better angel from his side,
And fall to *reprobance.*   *Othello,* v. 2.

REPROOF. *Disproof; refutation.*

And in the *reproof* of this lies the jest.
Henry 4, P. 1, i. 2.

Yet such extenuation let me beg,
As in *reproof* of many tales devis'd
By smiling pick-thanks and base newsmongers.
Ibid, iii. 2.

In the *reproof* of chance
Lies the true proof of men.
Troilus and Cressida, i. 3.

To REPROVE. *To disprove; to refute; to deny.*

They say the lady is virtuous,—'tis so, I cannot
reprove it.   *Much Ado about Nothing,* ii. 3.
Reprove my allegation, if you can.
Henry 6, P. 2, iii. 1.

To REPUGN. *To deny; to resist; to impugn.*

When stubbornly he did *repugn* the truth
About a certain question in the law
Argu'd betwixt the Duke of York and him
With other vile and ignominious terms.
Henry 6, P. 1, iv. 1.

REPUGNANCY. *Resistance; opposition.*

Why do fond men expose themselves to battle,
And not endure all threats? Sleep upon't,
And let the foes quietly cut their throats,
Without *repugnancy?*   *Timon of Athens,* iii. 5.

REPURED. *Distilled; purified.*

What will it be,
When that the watery palate tastes indeed
Love's thrice-*repured* nectar?
Troilus and Cressida, iii. 2.

REPUTE. *Renown; reputation; credit.*

For here the Trojans taste our dear'st *repute*
With their fin'st palate.   *Troilus and Cressida,* i. 3.

A man of good *repute,* carriage, bearing, and
estimation.   *Love's Labour's lost,* i. 1.

To REPUTE. *To boast; to brag of.*

Yet by *reputing* of his high descent,—
As, next the king, he was successive heir,
And such high vaunts of his nobility,—
Did instigate the bedlam brain-sick duchess
By wicked means to frame our sovereign's fall.
Henry 6, P. 2, iii. 1.

REPUTELESS. *Dishonourable; disgraceful.*

Opinion, that did help me to the crown,
Had still kept loyal to possession,
And left me in *reputeless* banishment,
A fellow of no mark nor likelihood.
Henry 4, P. 1, iii. 2.

To REQUICKEN. *To revive; to renew.*

Then straight his doubled spirit
Requicken'd what in flesh was fatigate,
And to the battle came he.   *Coriolanus,* ii. 2.

To REQUIRE. *To entitle to; to merit; to deserve.*

Sir, be prosperous
In more than this deed does *require!*
Winter's Tale, ii. 3.

For Polixenes,—
. . . .
I lov'd him, as in honour he *requir'd.*   *Ibid.* iii. 2.

REQUIT. *Requited; repaid; recompensed.*
Expos'd unto the sea, which hath *requit* it,
Him and his innocent child. *Tempest,* iii. 3.

RERE-MOUSE. *A bat.*
Some, war with *rere-mice* for their leathern wings.
Midsummer-Night's Dream, ii. 2.

RESEMBLANCE. *Likelihood; probability.*
But what likelihood is in that?
—Not a *resemblance,* but a certainty.
Measure for Measure, iv. 2.

To RE-SEND. *To send back; to return.*
But I sent to her,
By this same coxcomb that we have i' the wind,
Tokens and letters which she did *re-send.*
All's well that ends well, iii. 6.

RESERVATION. *Keeping; custody; care.*
And that he will'd
In heedfull'st *reservation* to bestow them,
As notes, whose faculties inclusive were,
More than they were in note.
All's well that ends well, i. 3.
Till at length
Your ignorance (which finds not till it feels),
Making not *reservation* of yourselves
(Still your own foes), deliver you, as most
Abated captives, to some nation
That won you without blows! *Coriolanus,* iii. 3.

To RESOLVE. *To dissolve; to melt; to certify; to assure; to prepare.*
The sea's a thief, whose liquid surge *resolves*
The moon into salt tears. *Timon of Athens,* iv. 3.
Retaining but a quantity of life,
Which bleeds away, even as a form of wax
Resolveth from his figure 'gainst the fire.
King John, v. 4.
O, that this too-too solid flesh would melt,
Thaw, and *resolve* itself into a dew! *Hamlet,* i. 2.
I am now going to *resolve* him, I had rather
my brother die by the law than my son should be
unlawfully born. *Measure for Measure,* iii. 1.
Right gracious lord, I cannot brook delay:
May't please your highness to *resolve* me now.
Henry 6, P. 3, iii. 2.
Long since we were *resolvèd* of your truth.
Henry 6, P. 1, iii. 4.
Resolve on this,—thou shalt be fortunate,
If thou receive me for thy warlike mate. *Ibid.* i. 2.

Either forbear,
Quit presently the chapel, or *resolve* you
For more amazement. *Winter's Tale,* v. 3.
By him that made us all, I am *resolv'd*
That Clifford's manhood lies upon his tongue.
Henry 6, P. 3, ii. 2.

RESOLVEDLY. *Clearly.*
Of that, and all the progress, more and less,
Resolvedly more leisure shall express.
All's well that ends well, v. 3.

RESOLUTE. *A ruffian; a desperado.*
Now, sir, young Fortinbras
Hath in the skirts of Norway, here and there,
Sharked up a list of landless *resolutes. Hamlet,* i. 1.

RESOLUTION. *Freedom from doubt; assurance; certainty.*
I would unstate myself, to be in a due *resolution.* *King Lear,* i. 2.

RESORT. *Assemblage; number; access; society.*
And what men to-night
Have had *resort* to you. *Julius Cæsar,* ii. 1.
Of all the fair *resort* of gentlemen
That every day with parle encounter me,
In thy opinion which is worthiest love?
Two Gentlemen of Verona, i. 2.
And kept severely from *resort* of men,
That no man hath access by day to her.
Ibid. i. 2.
I prithee, noble lord,
Join with me to forbid him her *resort.*
Timon of Athens, i. 1.

To RESPEAK. *To echo; to resound; to repeat.*
And the king's rouse the heavens shall bruit again,
Re-speaking earthly thunder. *Hamlet,* i. 2.

RESPECT. *Prudence; wisdom; forethought; consideration; motive; reputation; observance.*
Reason and *respect*
Make livers pale and lustihood deject.
Troilus and Cressida, ii. 2.
And never learn'd
The icy precepts of *respect,* but follow'd
The sugar'd game before thee.
Timon of Athens, iv. 3.

That's the *respect*
That makes calamity of so long life. *Hamlet*, iii. 1.

The instances that second marriage move
Are base *respects* of thrift, but none of love.
Ibid. iii. 2.

For my *respects* are better than they seem.
All's well that ends well, ii. 5.

I muse your majesty doth seem so cold,
When such profound *respects* do pull you on.
King John, iii. 1.

Where many of the best *respect* in Rome
Have wish'd that noble Brutus had his eyes.
Julius Cæsar, i. 2.

Nothing is good, I see, without *respect.*
Methinks it sounds much sweeter than by day.
Merchant of Venice, v. 1.

TO RESPECT. *To look upon ; to regard.*

And she *respects* me as her only son.
Midsummer-Night's Dream, i. 1.

RESPECTING. *Considering ; calling to mind.*

Meseemeth, then, it is no policy,
Respecting what a rancorous mind he bears,
And his advantage following your decease,
That he should come about your royal person.
Henry 6, P. 2, iii. 1.

There is none worthy,
Respecting her that's gone. *Winter's Tale*, v. 1.

RESPECTIVE. *Respectful ; reverential ; worthy
of regard ; prudent ; cautious ; considerate.*

For new-made honour doth forget men's names,
'Tis too *respective* and too sociable
For your conversion. *King John*, i. 1.

What should it be that he respects in her,
But I can make *respective* in myself ?
Two Gentlemen of Verona, iv. 2.

Though not for me, yet for your vehement oaths,
You should have been *respective*, and have kept it.
Merchant of Venice, v. 1.

Away to heaven, *respective* lenity,
And fire-ey'd fury be my conduct now !
Romeo and Juliet, iii. 1.

RESPECTIVELY. *Respectfully.*

Flaminius, honest Flaminius ; you are very
respectively welcome, sir. *Timon of Athens*, iii. 1.

RESPITE. *End ; period ; termination.*

This, this All-souls' day to my fearful soul
Is the determin'd *respite* of my wrongs.
Richard 3, v. 1.

TO RESPITE. *To spare ; to leave ; to protract.*

O injurious law,
That *respites* me a life, whose very comfort
Is still a dying horror. *Measure for Measure*, ii. 3.

REST. *Resolution ; determination.*

And when I cannot live any longer, I will die
as I may : that is my *rest*, that is the rendezvous of
it. *Henry 5*, ii. 1.

TO RE-STEM. *To retrace.*

And now they do *re-stem*
Their backward course, bearing with frank appear-
ance
Their purposes towards Cyprus. *Othello*, i. 3.

RESTFUL. *Quiet ; peaceful.*

Is not my arm of length,
That reacheth from the *restful* English court
As far as Calais, to my uncle's head ?
Richard 2, iv. 1.

TO RESTRAIN. *To seize ; to confiscate ; to
keep back ; to withhold ; to deprive.*

You having lands, and bless'd with beauteous wives,
They would *restrain* the one, distain the other.
Richard 3, v. 3.

And the gods will plague thee,
That thou *restrain'st* from me the duty which
To a mother's part belongs. *Coriolanus*, v. 3.

Feeling in itself
A lack of Timon's aid, hath sense withal
Of its own fail, *restraining* aid to Timon.
Timon of Athens, v. 1.

RESTRAINED. *Prohibited ; forbidden.*

'Tis all as easy
Falsely to take away a life true made,
As to put mettle in *restrainèd* means
To make a false one. *Measure for Measure*, ii. 4.

RESTY. *Full of rest ; idle ; lazy.*

Weariness
Can snore upon the flint, when *resty* sloth
Finds the down pillow hard. *Cymbeline*, iii. 6.

TO RETAIL. *To recount ; to repeat ; to report.*

Methinks the truth should live from age to age,
As 'twere *retail'd* to all posterity,
Even to the general all-ending day.
Richard 3, iii. 1.

To whom I will *retail* my conquest won,
And she shall be sole victress, Cæsar's Cæsar.
Richard 3, iv. 4.
And he is furnish'd with no certainties
More than he haply may *retail* from me.
Henry 4, P. 2, i. 1.

RETENTION. *Reservation; restriction; detention.*
His life I gave him, and did thereto add
My love, without *retention* or restraint,
All his in dedication. *Twelfth-Night*, v. 1.
Sir, I thought it fit
To send the old and miserable king
To some *retention* and appointed guard.
King Lear, v. 3.

RETIRE. *Retreat.*
And with a blessèd and unvex'd *retire*,
We will bear home that lusty blood again.
King John, ii. 1.
Why, all his behaviours did make their *retire*
To the court of his eye, peeping thorough desire.
Love's Labour's lost, ii. 1.
And thou hast talk'd of sallies and *retires*.
Henry 4, P. 1, ii. 3.

TO RETIRE. *To bring back.*
Then wherefore dost thou hope he is not shipp'd?—
That he, our hope, might have *retir'd* his power,
And driven into despair an enemy's hope,
Who strongly hath set footing in this land.
Richard 2, ii. 2.

TO RETORT. *To set aside; to reject; to reply.*
The duke's unjust
Thus to *retort* your manifest appeal.
Measure for Measure, v. 1.
Why, then the thing of courage,
As rous'd with rage with rage doth sympathize,
And with an accent tun'd in selfsame key
Retorts to chiding fortune. *Troilus and Cressida*, i. 3.

TO RETURN. *To declare; to announce; to make known to; to inform.*
Withdraw with us :—and let the trumpets sound,
While we *return* these dukes what we decree.
Richard 2, i. 3.

TO REVERB. *To reverberate; to resound.*
Thy youngest daughter does not love thee least;
Nor are those empty-hearted whose low sound
Reverbs no hollowness. *King Lear*, i. 1.

REVERBERATE. *Echoing; resounding.*
Holla your name to the *reverberate* hills,
And make the babbling gossip of the air
Cry out, Olivia ! *Twelfth-Night*, i. 5.

REVOKEMENT. *Revocation; repeal.*
Let it be nois'd
That through our intercession this *revokement*
And pardon comes. *Henry* 8, i. 2.

REVOLT. *Rebellion; mutiny; disobedience; a deserter; a renegade.*
He can report,
As seemeth by his plight, of the *revolt*
The newest state. *Macbeth*, i. 2.
Your daughter,—if you have not given her leave,—
I say again, hath made a gross *revolt*. *Othello*, i. 1.
They are sick? they are weary?
They have travell'd all the night? Mere fetches ;
The images of *revolt* and flying-off. *King Lear*, ii. 4.
Lead me to the *revolts* of England here.
King John, v. 4.
This way, the Romans
Must or for Britons slay us, or receive us
For barbarous and unnatural *revolts*
During their use, and slay us after. *Cymbeline*, iv. 4.

RHEUM. *Humour; moisture.*
Why holds thine eye that lamentable *rheum* ?
King John, iii. 1.
Is he not stupid
With age and altering *rheums* ?
Winter's Tale, iv. 3.
Trust not those cunning waters of his eyes,
For villany is not without such *rheum*.
King John, iv. 3.

RHEUMATIC. *Catarrhal; caused by cold; splenetic; angry.*
Therefore the moon, the governess of floods,
Pale in her anger, washes all the air,
That *rheumatic* diseases do abound.
Midsummer-Night's Dream, ii. 1.
You are both, in good troth, as *rheumatic* as
two dry toasts. *Henry* 4, P. 2, ii. 4.
But then he was *rheumatic*, and talked of the
whore of Babylon. *Henry* 5, ii. 3.

RHEUMY. *Moist; damp.*
What, is Brutus sick,—
And will he steal out of his wholesome bed,
And tempt the *rheumy* and unpurgèd air
To add unto his sickness? *Julius Cæsar*, ii. 1.

To Rid. *To enclose; to surround.*

It were too gross
To *rib* her cerecloth in the obscure grave.
Merchant of Venice, ii. 6.

Your isle, which stands
As Neptune's park, *ribbèd* and palèd in
With rocks unscalable and roaring waters:
Cymbeline, iii. 1.

Ribald. *Unclean; base; mean.*

The busy day,
Wak'd by the lark, hath rous'd the *ribald* crows.
Troilus and Cressida, iv. 2.

Ribaudred. *Licentious; wanton; profligate.*

Yon *ribaudred* nag of Egypt,—
Whom leprosy o'ertake!—i' the midst o' the fight,—
The breeze upon her, like a cow in June,—
Hoists sails and flies. *Antony and Cleopatra*, iii. 10.

To Rich. *To enrich.*

Of all these bounds, even from this line to this,
With shadowy forests and with champains *rich'd*,
With plenteous rivers and wide-skirted meads,
We make thee lady. *King Lear*, i. 1.

To Rid. *To destroy; to kill; to dispatch; to get rid of; to annihilate.*

The red plague *rid* you
For learning me your language! *Tempest*, i. 2.

I am the king's friend, and will *rid* his foe.
Richard 2, v. 4.

Look in his youth to have him so cut off
As, deathsmen, you have *rid* this sweet young prince.
Henry 6, P. 3, v. 5.

We, having now the best at Barnet field,
Will thither straight, for willingness *rids* way.
Ibid. v. 3.

Riddling. *Ambiguous; equivocal.*

Be plain, good son, and homely in thy drift;
Riddling confession finds but *riddling* shrift.
Romeo and Juliet, ii. 3.

This is a *riddling* merchant for the nonce.
Henry 6, P. 1, ii. 3.

To Ride the wild-mare. *To play at see-saw.*

And *rides the wild-mare* with the boys.
Henry 4, P. 2, ii. 4.

To Rift. *To rive; to split.*

Then I'd shriek, that even your ears
Should *rift* to hear me. *Winter's Tale*, v. 1.

Riggish. *Wanton.*

For vilest things
Become themselves in her; that the holy priests
Bless her when she is *riggish*.
Antony and Cleopatra, ii. 2.

Right. *Just; exactly.*

O, do not slander him, for he is kind.—
Right as snow in harvest. *Richard 3*, i. 4.

Came he *right* now to sing a raven's note?
Henry 6, P. 2, iii. 2.

Yet god Achilles still cries, "Excellent!
'Tis Nestor *right*." *Troilus and Cressida*, i. 3.

Rightly. *Directly; straightly; in front.*

Like perspectives, which *rightly* gaz'd upon,
Show nothing but confusion,—ey'd awry,
Distinguish form. *Richard 2*, ii. 2.

Rigol. *A circle; a crown; a diadem.*

This is a sleep,
That from this golden *rigol* hath divorc'd
So many English kings. *Henry 4*, P. 2, iv. 4.

Rigour. *Cruelty; injustice; tyranny.*

If I shall be condemn'd
Upon surmises, all proofs sleeping else,
But what your jealousies awake, I tell you,
'Tis *rigour* and not law. *Winter's Tale*, iii. 2.

Rim. *The lining membrane of the stomach.*

I will have forty moys;
Or I will fetch thy *rim* out at thy throat
In drops of crimson blood. *Henry 5*, iv. 4.

Ripe. *Pressing; urgent; ample.*

Yet, to supply the *ripe* wants of my friend,
I'll break a custom. *Merchant of Venice*, i. 3.

Without *ripe* moving to't, would I do this?
Winter's Tale, i. 2.

To Ripe. *To ripen.*

That yon green boy shall have no sun to *ripe*
The bloom that promiseth a mighty fruit.
King John, ii. 1.

So I, being young, till now *ripe* not to reason.
Midsummer-Night's Dream, ii. 2.

And so, from hour to hour, we *ripe* and *ripe*,
And then, from hour to hour, we rot and rot.
As you like it, ii. 7.

RIPELY. *Fully; amply; duly.*

It fits us therefore *ripely*
Our chariots and our horsemen be in readiness.
Cymbeline, iii. 5.

RIPING. *Ripeness; maturity.*

Slubber not business for my sake, Bassanio,
But stay the very *riping* of the time.
Merchant of Venice, ii. 7.

RIVAGE. *The shore.*

O, do but think
You stand upon the *rivage,* and behold
A city on th' inconstant billows dancing.
Henry 5, iii. Chorus.

RIVAL. *Copartner; associate; companion.*

If you do meet Horatio and Marcellus,
The *rivals* of my watch, bid them make haste.
Hamlet, i. 1.

To RIVAL. *To compete; to contend.*

My lord of Burgundy,
We first address toward you, who with this king
Hath *rivall'd* for our daughter. *King Lear,* i. 1.

RIVALITY. *Equal rank; co-ordinate power; co-partnership.*

Cæsar, having made use of him in the wars
'gainst Pompey, presently denied him *rivality.*
Antony and Cleopatra, iii. 5.

ROAD. *An inroad; an incursion; a journey.*

But lay down our proportions to defend
Against the Scot, who will make *road* upon us
With all advantages. *Henry 5,* i. 2.
Ready, when time shall prompt them, to make *road*
Upon's again. *Coriolanus,* iii. 1.
At last, with easy *roads,* he came to Leicester.
Henry 8, iv. 2.

To ROAR. *To cry out.*

And if the devil come and *roar* for them,
I will not send them. *Henry 4,* P. 1, i. 3.
But I fear they'll *roar* him in again.
Coriolanus, iv. 6.
But at his nurse's tears
He whin'd and *roar'd* away your victory.
Ibid. v. 6.

ROBUSTIOUS. *Boisterous; violent; robust.*

And the men do sympathize with the mastiffs
in *robustious* and rough coming-on. *Henry 5,* iii. 6.

O, it offends me to the soul to hear a *robustious*
periwig-pated fellow tear a passion to tatters, to
very rags. *Hamlet,* iii. 2.

To ROIST. *To bluster; to swagger.*

I have a *roisting* challenge sent amongst
The dull and factious nobles of the Greeks
Will strike amazement to their drowsy spirits.
Troilus and Cressida, ii. 2.

ROMAGE. *Bustle; turmoil.*

And this, I take it,
Is the main motive of our preparations,
The source of this our watch, and the chief head
Of this post-haste and *romage* in the land.
Hamlet, i. 1.

ROMISH. *Roman.*

To mart
As in a *Romish* stew, and to expound
His beastly mind to us. *Cymbeline,* i. 6.

RONDURE. *Circle; circumference.*

But if you fondly pass our proffer'd offer,
'Tis not the *rondure* of your old-fac'd walls
Can hide you from our messengers of war.
King John, ii. 1.

RONYON. *A mangy animal.*

Aroint thee, witch! the rump-fed *ronyon* cries.
Macbeth, i. 3.

You witch, you rag, you baggage, you polecat,
you *ronyon!* *Merry Wives of Windsor,* iv. 2.

To ROOK. *To crouch; to cower; to perch; to lodge.*

The raven *rook'd* her on the chimney's top.
Henry 6, P. 3, v. 6.

ROOKY. *Misty; humid.*

Light thickens; and the crow
Makes wing to the *rooky* wood. *Macbeth,* iii. 2.

ROPERY. *Roguery; rogue's tricks.*

I pray you, sir, what saucy merchant was this,
that was so full of his *ropery?*
Romeo and Juliet, ii. 4.

ROPE-TRICKS. *Ropery ; abusive language ; scurrility.*

An ho begin once, he'll rail in his *rope-tricks.*
Taming of the Shrew, i. 2.

ROPING. *Depending ; hanging ; running down.*

Let us not hang like *roping* icicles
Upon our houses' thatch. *Henry* 5, iii. 4.

Tho gum down-*roping* from their pale-dead eyes.
Ibid. iv. 2.

ROTE. *Practice ; routine ; habit ; memory.*

O, she knew well
Thy love did read by *rote,* and could not spell.
Romeo and Juliet, ii. 3.

All his faults observ'd,
Set in a noto-book, learn'd, and conn'd by *rote,*
To cast into my teeth. *Julius Cæsar,* iv. 3.

First, rehearse your song by *rote,*
To each word a warbling note.
Midsummer-Night's Dream, v. 1.

ROTHER. *An ox.*

It is the pasture lards the *rother's* sides,
The want that makes him lean.
Timon of Athens, iv. 3.

ROUND. *Plain ; unreserved ; free ; explicit ; blunt.*

Your reproof is something too *round.*
Henry 5, iv. 1.

Sir Toby, I must be *round* with you.
Twelfth-Night, ii. 3.

Pray you, be *round* with him. *Hamlet,* iii. 4.

To ROUND. *To surround ; to enclose ; to whisper.*

For within the hollow crown
That *rounds* the mortal temples of a king
Keeps Death his court. *Richard* 2, iii. 2.

And our little life
Is *rounded* with a sleep. *Tempest,* iv. 1.

They're here with me already ; whispering, *rounding,*
" Sicilia is a so-forth." *Winter's Tale,* i. 2.

To ROUND-IN. *To surround ; to encompass ; to environ.*

To weaken and discredit our exposure,

How rank soever *rounded-in* with danger.
Troilus and Cressida, i. 3.

ROUNDEL. *A kind of dance ; a song or tune.*

Come, now a *roundel* and a fairy song.
Midsummer-Night's Dream, ii. 2.

ROUSE. *A bumper ; a full cup.*

The king doth wake to-night, and takes his *rouse.*
Hamlet, i. 4.

And the king's *rouse* the heavens shall bruit again,
Re-speaking earthly thunder. *Ibid.* i. 2.

'Fore heaven, they have given me a *rouse* already.
Othello, ii. 3.

ROUT. *Tumult ; brawl ; disturbance.*

Give me to know
How this foul *rout* began, who set it on.
Othello, ii. 3.

ROYAL. *Loyal.*

'Tis well : the citizens,
I'm sure, have shown at full their *royal* minds.
Henry 8, iv. 1.

That, were our *royal* faiths martyrs in love,
We shall be winnow'd with so rough a wind,
That even our corn shall seem as light as chaff,
And good from bad find no partition.
Henry 4, P. 2, iv. 1.

To ROYALISE. *To make royal.*

To *royalise* his blood I spilt mine own.
Richard 3, i. 3.

ROYALTY. *Nobleness ; superiority ; a crown.*

And in his *royalty* of nature
Reigns that which would be fear'd. *Macbeth,* iii. 1.

Lo, here, this long-usurpèd *royalty*
From the dead temples of this bloody wretch
Have I pluck'd off, to grace thy brows withal.
Richard 3, v. 3.

ROYNISH. *Mean ; base ; paltry.*

My lord, the *roynish* clown, at whom so oft
Your grace was wont to laugh, is also missing.
As you like it, ii. 2.

RUB. *An obstruction ; a hindrance.*

For even the breath of what I mean to speak
Shall blow each dust, each straw, each little *rub,*

Out of the path which shall directly lead
Thy foot to England's throne. *King John*, iii. 4.

We doubt not now
But every *rub* is smoothèd on our way.
Henry 5, ii. 2.

To sleep! perchance to dream:—ay, there's the *rub*.
Hamlet, iii. 1.

Nor has Coriolanus
Deserv'd this so dishonour'd *rub*, laid falsely
I' the plain way of his merit. *Coriolanus*, iii. 1.

To RUB. *To obstruct; to hinder; to restrain.*

I'm sorry for thee, friend; 'tis the duke's pleasure,
Whose disposition, all the world well knows,
Will not be *rubb'd* nor stopp'd. *King Lear*, ii. 2.

RUBIOUS. *Red.*

Diana's lip is not more smooth and *rubious.*
Twelfth-Night, i. 4.

RUDDOCK. *The redbreast.*

The *ruddock* would,
With charitable bill, bring thee all this.
Cymbeline, iv. 2.

RUDESBY. *A ruffian.*

To give my hand, oppos'd against my heart,
Unto a mad-brain'd *rudesby*, full of spleen.
Taming of the Shrew, iii. 2.

Be not offended, dear Cesario.—
Rudesby, begone! *Twelfth-Night*, iv. 1.

RUE. *Grief; sorrow.*

Rue, even for ruth, here shortly shall be seen,
In the remembrance of a weeping queen.
Richard 2, iii. 4.

To RUFFIAN. *To rage; to bluster; to ruffle.*

If it hath *ruffian'd* so upon the sea,
What ribs of oak, when mountains melt on them,
Can hold the mortise? *Othello*, ii. 1.

To RUFFLE. *To stir up; to rouse; to rustle;
to disorder.*

But were I Brutus,
And Brutus Antony, there were an Antony`
Would *ruffle* up your spirits, and put a tongue
In every wound of Cæsar, that should move
The stones of Rome to rise and mutiny.
Julius Cæsar, iii. 2.

Alack, the night comes on, and the high winds
Do sorely *ruffle*. *King Lear*, ii. 4.

The tailor stays thy loisure,
To deck thy body with his *ruffling* treasure.
Taming of the Shrew, iv. 3.

With robbers' hands, my hospitable favours
You should not *ruffle* thus. *King Lear*, iii. 7.

RUIN. *Displeasure; wrath; anger; indignation.*

There is, betwixt that smile we would aspire to,
That sweet aspéct of princes, and their *ruin*,
More pangs and fears than wars or women have.
Henry 8, iii. 2.

To RUINATE. *To demolish; to ruin; to destroy.*

I will not *ruinate* my father's house,
Who gave his blood to lime the stones together.
Henry 6, P. 3, v. 1.

RULE. *Mirth; frolic; revelry.*

How now, mad spirit!
What night-*rule* now about this haunted grove?
Midsummer-Night's Dream, iii. 2.

Mistress Mary, if you prized my lady's favour
at any thing more than contempt, you would not
give means for this uncivil *rule*.
Twelfth-Night, ii. 3.

RUMOURER. *A reporter; a spreader of reports.*

Go see this *rumourer* whipp'd. *Coriolanus*, iv. 6.

RUNAGATE. *A fugitive; a coward.*

White-liver'd *runagate*, what doth he there?
Richard 3, iv. 4.

To RUN WITH. *To keep pace with; accompany.*

Volumes of report
Run with these false and most contrarious quests
Upon thy doings! *Measure for Measure*, iv. 1.

To RUSH. *To break; to dash; to push.*

And I, in such a desperate bay of death,
Like a poor bark of sails and tackling reft,
Rush all to pieces on thy rocky bosom.
Richard 3, iv. 4.

But the kind prince,
Taking thy part, hath *rush'd* aside the law,
And turn'd that black word death to banishment.
Romeo and Juliet, iii. 3.

RUSSET. *Coarse cloth of a reddish colour;*
coarse; home-spun; rustic.

Henceforth my wooing mind shall be express'd
In *russet* yeas, and honest kersey noes.
Love's Labour's lost, v. 2.

RUTH. *Pity; mercy.*

Spur them to ruthful work, rein them from *ruth*.
Troilus and Cressida, v. 3.
Rue, even for *ruth*, here shortly shall be seen,
In the remembrance of a weeping queen.
Richard 2, iii. 4.

RUTHFUL. *Dismal; mournful; full of woe.*

Spur them to *ruthful* work, rein them from ruth.
Troilus and Cressida, v. 3.

S.

SACK. *Sherry.*

You rogue, here's lime in this *sack* too : there is
nothing but roguery to be found in villanous man.
Henry 4, P. 1, ii. 4.

SACRAMENT. *An oath.*

May know wherefore we took the *sacrament*,
And keep our faiths firm and inviolable.
King John, v. 2.

Do : I'll take the *sacrament* on't, how and which
way you will.   *All's well that ends well*, iv. 3.

SACRIFICIAL. *Idolatrous; servile.*

All those which were his fellows but of late,
Follow his strides, his lobbies fill with tendance,
Rain *sacrificial* whisperings in his ear,
Make sacred even his stirrup, and through him
Drink the free air.   *Timon of Athens*, i. 1.

SACRING. *Consecrating; holy; sacred.*

I'll startle you
Worse than the *sacring*-bell, when the brown wench
Lay kissing in your arms, lord cardinal.
Henry 8, iii. 2.

SAD. *Grave; serious.*

My father and the gentleman are in *sad* talk.
Winter's Tale, iv. 3.
Tell me, Panthino, what *sad* talk was that
Wherewith my brother held you in the cloister?
Two Gentlemen of Verona, i. 3.

SADLY. *Gravely; seriously.*

And with his spirit *sadly* I survive,
To mock the expectation of the world.
Henry 4, P. 2, v. 2.
The conference was *sadly* borne.
Much Ado about Nothing, ii. 3.

SADNESS. *Seriousness; gravity.*

But, mighty lord, this merry inclination
Accords not with the *sadness* of my suit.
Henry 6, P. 3, iii. 2.

Tell me in *sadness*, who is that you love.
Romeo and Juliet, i. 1.

SAFE. *Sound; sure; certain.*

Nor do I think the man of *safe* discretion
That does affect it.   *Measure for Measure*, i. 1.

Are his wits *safe* ? is he not light of brain?
Othello, iv. 1.

But who comes here?
The *safer* sense will ne'er accommodate
His master thus.   *King Lear*, iv. 6.

I had thought, by making this well known unto
you,
T' have found a *safe* redress.   *Ibid.* i. 4.

SAFE (adv.). *Safely; surely; certainly; di-*
rectly; without deviation.

Our duties
Are to your throne and state, children and ser-
vants ;
Which do but what they should, by doing every
thing
Safe toward your love and honour.   *Macbeth*, i. 4.

TO SAFE. *To render safe.*

My more particular,
And that which most with you should *safe* my
going,
Is Fulvia's death.   *Antony and Cleopatra*, i. 3.

I tell you true : best you *saf'd* the bringer
Out of the host.   *Ibid.* iv. 6.

SAFE-GUARD. *Safe-conduct; warrant to pass.*

Saw you Aufidius?
On *safe-guard* he came to me. *Coriolanus*, iii. 1.

TO SAFEGUARD. *To protect; to guard; to secure.*

To *safeguard* thine own life,
The best way is to venge my Gloster's death.
Richard 2, i. 2.

We have locks to *safeguard* necessaries,
And pretty traps to catch the petty thieves.
Henry 5, i. 2.

SAFETY. *Safe custody.*

Deliver him to *safety;* and return,
For I must use thee. *King John*, iv. 2.

TO SAG. *To sink; to flag; to droop.*

The mind I sway by and the heart I bear
Shall never *sag* with doubt nor shake with fear.
Macbeth, v. 3.

SAGITTARY. *A centaur.*

The dreadful *Sagittary* appals our numbers.
Troilus and Cressida, v. 5.

That you shall surely find him,
Lead to the *Sagittary* the raisèd search.
Othello, i. 1.

SALE-WORK. *Work for sale; workmanship.*

I see no more in you than in the ordinary
Of nature's *sale-work*. *As you like it*, iii. 5.

SALLET. *A helmet; a salad; ribaldry.*

Many a time, but for a *sallet*, my brain-pan had
been cleft with a brown bill.
Henry 6, P. 2, iv. 10.

I remember, one said there were no *sallets* in
the lines to make the matter savoury.
Hamlet, ii. 2.

SALT. *Brine.*

Why, this would make a man a man of *salt*,
To use his eyes for garden water-pots,
Ay, and laying autumn's dust. *King Lear*, iv. 6.

You lords and heads o' the state, perfidiously
He has betray'd your business, and given up,
For certain drops of *salt*, your city Rome—
I say, your city—to his wife and mother.
Coriolanus, v. 6.

SALT. *Unchaste; wanton; licentious.*

But all the charms of love,
Salt Cleopatra, soften thy wan'd lip!
Antony and Cleopatra, ii. 1.

Make use of thy *salt* hours : season the slaves
For tubs and baths. *Timon of Athens*, iv. 3.

TO SALUTE. *To please; to gratify.*

Would I had no being,
If this *salute* my blood a jot. *Henry 8*, ii. 3.

TO SALVE. *To smooth; to justify; to excuse.*

But lest my liking might too sudden seem,
I would have *salv'd* it with a longer treatise.
Much Ado about Nothing, i. 1.

SANCTIMONY. *A sacred tie; holiness; sanctity.*

If souls guide vows, if vows be *sanctimonies*,
If *sanctimony* be the gods' delight,
If there be rule in unity itself,
This is not she. *Troilus and Cressida*, v. 2.

TO SANCTUARIZE. *To give protection to; to shelter.*

No place, indeed, should murder *sanctuarize*.
Hamlet, iv. 7.

SANDED. *Of a sandy colour.*

My hounds are bred out of the Spartan kind,
So flew'd, so *sanded*.
Midsummer-Night's Dream, iv. 1.

SANGUINE. *Red.*

Guiderius had
Upon his neck a mole, a *sanguine* star,
It was a mark of wonder. *Cymbeline*, v. 5.

This fellow here, with envious carping tongue,
Upbraided me about the rose I wear;
Saying, the *sanguine* colour of the leaves
Did represent my master's blushing cheeks.
Henry 6, P. 1, iv. 1.

SANS. *Without.*

Last scene of all,
That ends this strange eventful history,
Is second childishness and mere oblivion,
Sans teeth, *sans* eyes, *sans* taste, *sans* every thing.
As you like it, ii. 7.

Whose med'cinable eye
Corrects the ill aspècts of planets evil,

And posts, like the commandment of a king,
Sans check, to good and bad.
Troilus and Cressida, i. 3.

SATISFACTION.   *Conviction ; assurance ; certainty ; payment.*

She ceas'd
In heavy *satisfaction*, and would never
Receive the ring again. *All's well that ends well*, v. 3.

O, wilt thou leave mo so unsatisfied ?—
What *satisfaction* canst thou have to-night ?
Romeo and Juliet, ii. 2.

Therefore make present *satisfaction*,
Or I'll attach you by this officer.
Comedy of Errors, iv. 1.

To SATISFY.   *To feed ; to inform ; to instruct ; to certify.*

Do not *satisfy* your resolution with hopes that
are fallible : to-morrow you must die.
Measure for Measure, iii. 1.

It is almost morning,
And yet I'm sure you are not *satisfied*
Of these events at full. *Merchant of Venice*, v. 1.

SAVAGE.   *Churlish ; inhospitable ; uncivilised ; uncultivated.*

Our courtiers say all's *savage* but at court.
Cymbeline, iv. 2.

Ho ! who's here ?
If any thing that's civil, speak ; if *savage*,
Take or lend. *Ibid*. iii. 6.

Our scions, put in wild and *savage* stock.
Henry 5, iii. 4.

SAVAGENESS.   *Wildness ; irregularity.*

A *savageness* in unreclaimèd blood,
Of general assault. *Hamlet*, ii. 1.

SAVAGERY.   *Barbarity ; cruelty ; wildness ; wild growth.*

This is the bloodiest shame,
The wildest *savagery*, the vilest stroke.
King John, iv. 3.

While that the coulter rusts
That should deracinate such *savagery*.
Henry 5, v. 2.

To SAVE.   *To spare.*

If your life be *saved*, will you undertake to betray the Florentine ? *All's well that ends well*, iv. 3.

SAW.   *A saying ; a maxim.*

With oyes severe and beard of formal cut,
Full of wise *saws* and modern instances.
As you like it, ii. 7.

Good king, that must approve the common *saw*.
King Lear, ii. 2.

SAY.   *A taste ; a smack ; a relish ; serge.*

In wisdom I should ask thy name ;
But, since thy outside looks so fair and warlike,
And that thy tongue some *say* of breeding breathes,
What safe and nicely I might well delay
By rule of knighthood, I disdain and spurn.
King Lear, v. 3.

Ah, thou *say*, thou serge, nay, thou buckram lord !
Henry 6, P. 2, iv. 7.

SCAFFOLD.   *The stage of a theatre.*

The flat unraisèd spirits that have dar'd
On this unworthy *scaffold* to bring forth
So great an object. *Henry* 5, i. Chorus.

SCAFFOLDAGE.   *The stage of a theatre.*

Like a strutting player, whose conceit
Lies in his hamstring, and doth think it rich
To hear the wooden dialogue and sound
'Twixt his stretch'd footing and the *scaffoldage*.
Troilus and Cressida, i. 3.

SCALD.   *Scurvy ; paltry ; contemptible.*

Saucy lictors
Will catch at us, like strumpets ; and *scald* rhymers
Ballad us out o' tune. *Antony and Cleopatra*, v. 2.

To SCALE.   *To weigh ; to measure.*

But you have found,
Scaling his present bearing with his past,
That he's your fixèd enemy. *Coriolanus*, ii. 3.

To SCAMBLE.   *To scramble ; to struggle ; to snatch.*

And England now is left to tug and *scamble*.
King John, iv. 3.

Scambling, out-facing, fashion-mongering boys.
Much Ado about Nothing, v. 1.

I get thee with *scambling*, and thou must therefore needs prove a good soldier-breeder.
Henry 5, v. 2.

To SCANDAL. *To calumniate; to defame; to bring shame upon.*

And of late,
Scandal'd the suppliants for the people,—call'd them
Time-pleasers, flatterers, foes to nobleness.
Coriolanus, iii. 1.

If you know
That I do fawn on men, and hug them hard,
And after *scandal* them. *Julius Cæsar*, i. 2.

And Sinon's weeping
Did *scandal* many a holy tear. *Cymbeline*, iii. 4.

SCANT. *Frugal; sparing; deficient; short of.*

From this time
Be somewhat *scanter* of your maiden presence.
Hamlet, i. 3.

Our son shall win.—
He's fat and *scant* of breath. *Ibid.* v. 2.

SCANT (adv.). *Scarcely; hardly.*

And she shall *scant* show well that now shows best.
Romeo and Juliet, i. 2.

To SCANT. *To stint; to fail in; to neglect; to spare; to omit.*

I pray you, sir, take patience : I have hope
You less know how to value her desert
Than she to *scant* her duty. *King Lear*, ii. 4.

And *scants* us with a single famish'd kiss,
Distasted with the salt of broken tears.
Troilus and Cressida, iv. 4.

And what he hath *scanted* men in hair, he hath
given them in wit. *Comedy of Errors*, ii. 2.

Therefore I *scant* this breathing courtesy.
Merchant of Venice, v. 1.

SCANTLING. *A share; a portion; a certain amount.*

For the success,
Although particular, shall give a *scantling*
Of good or bad unto the general.
Troilus and Cressida, i. 3.

SCANTLY. *Sparingly; niggardly.*

Spoke *scantly* of me : when perforce he could not
But pay me terms of honour, cold and sickly
He vented them. *Antony and Cleopatra*, iii. 4.

SCAPE. *Escape; freak; sally; irregularity; immorality.*

Of hair-breadth *scapes* i' the imminent deadly breach.
Othello, i. 3.

Thousand *scapes* of wit
Make thee the father of their idle dreams !
Measure for Measure, iv. 1.

No *scape* of nature, no distemper'd day.
King John, iii. 4.

Mercy on's, a barn ; . . . . . . a pretty one ; a
very pretty one : sure, some *scape* : though I am not
bookish, yet I can read waiting-gentlewoman in the
scape. *Winter's Tale*, iii. 3.

To SCAPE. *To escape.*

How *scap'd* I killing when I cross'd you so ?
Julius Cæsar, iv. 3.

To SCARF. *To close; to bandage; to clothe in any loose vesture; to cover loosely.*

Come, seeling night,
Scarf up the tender eye of pitiful day !
Macbeth, iii. 2.

How like a younker or a prodigal
The *scarfèd* bark puts from her native bay !
Merchant of Venice, ii. 5.

Up from my cabin,
My sea-gown *scarf'd* about me, in the dark
Grop'd I to find out them. *Hamlet*, v. 2.

SCATHE. *Destruction; damage; harm.*

All these could not procure me any *scathe*,
So long as I am loyal, true, and crimeless.
Henry 6, P. 2, ii. 4.

In brief, a braver choice of dauntless spirits
Did never float upon the swelling tide
To do offence and *scathe* in Christendom.
King John, ii. 1.

To SCATHE. *To harm; to hurt; to injure.*

This trick may chance to *scathe* you.
Romeo and Juliet, i. 5.

SCATHEFUL. *Destructive.*

With which such *scatheful* grapple did he make
With the most noble bottom of our fleet,
That very envy and the tongue of loss
Cried fame and honour on him.
Twelfth-Night, v. 1.

SCATTERED. *Distracted; divided; disunited.*

But, true it is, from France there comes a power
Into this *scatter'd* kingdom. *King Lear*, iii. 1.

SCOFF. *Ridicule; raillery; banter.*

By heaven, all dry-beaten with pure *scoff* !
Love's Labour's lost, v. 2.

SCONCE. *The head; a fort.*

Must I go show them my unbarb'd *sconce?*
       Coriolanus, iii. 2.
Or I shall break that merry *sconce* of yours,
That stands on tricks when I am undispos'd.
      Comedy of Errors, i. 2.
An you use these blows long, I must get a *sconce*
for my head, and ensconce it too. *Ibid.* ii. 2.

To SCONCE. *To ensconce.*

I'll *sconce* me even here.
Pray you, be round with him. *Hamlet,* iii. 4.

SCOPE. *Liberty; license; wildness; freak; irregularity.*

Sith 'twas my fault to give the people *scope,*
'Twould be my tyranny to strike and gall them
For what I bid them do.
     Measure for Measure, i. 3.
   The fated sky
Gives us free *scope;* only doth backward pull
Our slow designs when we ourselves are dull.
     All's well that ends well, i. 1.
As surfeit is the father of much fast,
So every *scope* by the immoderate use
Turns to restraint. *Measure for Measure,* i. 2.

To SCORE. *To mark; to brand.*

Have you *scored* me? Well. *Othello,* iv. 1.
   Let us *score* their backs,
And snatch 'em up, as we take hares, behind.
     Antony and Cleopatra, iv. 7.

To SCREW. *To wrest; to wrench; to force.*

And that I partly know the instrument
That *screws* me from my true place in your favour,
Live you, the marble-breasted tyrant, still.
     Twelfth-Night, v. 1.

SCRIMER. *A fencer.*

   The *scrimers* of their nation,
He swore, had neither motion, guard, nor eye,
If you oppos'd them. *Hamlet,* iv. 7.

SCRIP. *A list; a schedule; a small bag; a satchel.*

You were best to call them generally, man by
man, according to the *scrip.*
     Midsummer-Night's Dream, i. 2.
Though not with bag and baggage, yet with
scrip and scrippage. *As you like it,* iii. 2.

SCRIPPAGE. *The contents of a scrip.*

Though not with bag and baggage, yet with
scrip and *scrippage.* *As you like it,* iii. 2.

SCROYLE. *A mean fellow; a rogue; a rascal.*

By heaven, these *scroyles* of Angiers flout you, kings.
     King John, ii. 1.

SCRUBBED. *Mean; shabby; stunted.*

A kind of boy; a little *scrubbed* boy,
No higher than thyself, the judge's clerk.
     Merchant of Venice, v. 1.

SCRUPULOUS. *Uncertain; doubtful.*

Equality of two domestic powers
Breed *scrupulous* faction. *Antony and Cleopatra,* i. 3.

SCULL. *A shoal of fish.*

   Anon he's there afoot,
And there they fly or die, like scaled *sculls*
Before the belching whale.
     Troilus and Cressida, v. 5.

SCURRIL. *Scurrilous; mean; low; contemptible.*

   With him, Patroclus,
Upon a lazy bed, the livelong day,
Breaks *scurril* jests. *Troilus and Cressida,* i. 3.

'SCUSE. *Excuse.*

That *'scuse* serves many men to save their gifts.
     Merchant of Venice, iv. 1.

SCUTCHEON. *An armorial shield; a coat of arms.*

Therefore I'll none of it: honour is a mere *scutcheon:*—and so ends my catechism.
     Henry 4, P. 1, v. 1.
   And we,
Your *scutcheons* and your signs of conquest, shall
Hang in what place you please.
     Antony and Cleopatra, v. 2.

SEA OF WAX. *An allusion to the ancient practice of writing upon waxen tablets.*

   My free drift
Halts not particularly, but moves itself
In a wide *sea of wax.* *Timon of Athens,* i. 1.

SEA-BANK. *The sea-coast.*

   In such a night
Stood Dido with a willow in her hand

Upon the wild *sea-banks*, and wav'd her love
To come again to Carthage.
Merchant of Venice, v. 1.
I was, the other day, talking on the *sea-bank*
with certain Venetians. *Othello*, iv. 1.

SEA-MAID. *A mermaid; a siren.*

Some report a *sea-maid* spawned him.
Measure for Measure, iii. 2.
And certain stars shot madly from their spheres,
To hear the *sea-maid's* music.
Midsummer-Night's Dream, ii. 1.

SEA-MONSTER. *The hippopotamus.*

Ingratitude, thou marble-hearted fiend,
More hideous when thou show'st thee in a child
Than the *sea-monster!* *King Lear*, i. 4.

TO SEAL. *To ratify; to confirm.*

My soul is purg'd from grudging hate;
And with my hand I *seal* my true heart's love.
Richard 3, ii. 1.
Thou hast stol'n that which, after some few hours,
Were thine without offence; and at my death
Thou hast *seal'd* up my expectation.
Henry 4, P. 2, iv. 4.

SEAM. *Lard; grease.*

The proud lord,
That bastes his arrogance with his own *seam*.
Troilus and Cressida, ii. 3.

TO SEAR. *To brand; to stigmatize; to dry
up; to burn; to wither.*

These petty brands
That calumny doth use:—O, I am out,
That mercy does; for calumny will *sear*
Virtue itself. *Winter's Tale*, ii. 1.
Thou art too like the spirit of Banquo; down!
Thy crown does *sear* mine eye-balls.
Macbeth, iv. 1.

TO SEAR UP. *To close up; to prevent; to
hinder.*

You gentle gods, give me but this I have,
And *sear up* my embracements from a next
With bonds of death! *Cymbeline*, i. 1.

TO SEARCH. *To probe; to tent.*

Alas, poor shepherd! *searching* of thy wound,
I have by hard adventure found mine own.
As you like it, ii. 4.

And thus I *search* it with a sovereign kiss.
Two Gentlemen of Verona, i. 2.

SEASON. *Seasoning; that which gives a high
relish; time; occasion.*

And salt too little which may *season* give
To her foul-tainted flesh.
Much Ado about Nothing, iv. 1.
You lack the *season* of all natures, sleep.
Macbeth, iii. 4.
He's noble, wise, judicious, and best knows
The fits o' the *season*. *Ibid.* iv. 2.
In brief,—for so the *season* bids us be,—
Prepare thy battle early in the morning.
Richard 3, v. 3.

TO SEASON. *To flavour; to preserve; to
temper; to qualify; to ripen; to fix; to
confirm.*

Bless'd be those
How mean soe'er, that have their honest wills,
Which *seasons* comfort. *Cymbeline*, i. 6.
How much salt water thrown away in waste,
To *season* love, that of it doth not taste!
Romeo and Juliet, ii. 3.
All this to *season*
A brother's dead love, which she would keep fresh
And lasting in her sad remembrance.
Twelfth-Night, i. 1.
And earthly power doth then show likest God's
When mercy *seasons* justice.
Merchant of Venice, iv. 1.
Season your admiration for a while
With an attent ear. *Hamlet*, i. 2.
Farewell: my blessing *season* this in thee. *Ibid.* i. 3.
And who in want a hollow friend doth try,
Directly *seasons* him an enemy. *Ibid.* iii. 2.

SEASONED. *Established; customary.*

We charge you, that you have contriv'd to take
From Rome all *season'd* office, and to wind
Yourself into a power tyrannical. *Coriolanus*, iii. 3.

SEAT. *Site; situation.*

This castle hath a pleasant *seat*. *Macbeth*, i. 6.

SECOND. *A seconder; an assistant; a sup-
porter.*

Stand! who's there?—A Roman;
Who had not now been drooping here, if *seconds*
Had answer'd him. *Cymbeline*, v. 3.

So, now the gates are ope : now prove good *seconds.*
Coriolanus, i. 4.

You have sham'd me
In your condemnèd *seconds.*   *Ibid.* i. 8.

SECONDARY.   *A delegate ; a deputy.*

I am too high-born to be propertied,
To be a *secondary* at control.   *King John,* v. 2.

Old Escalus,
Though first in question, is thy *secondary.*
Measure for Measure, i. 1.

SECRET.   *Close ; faithful ; honourable ; occult.*

What other bond
Than *secret* Romans, that have spoke the word,
And will not palter ?   *Julius Cæsar,* ii. 1.

The government I cast upon my brother,
And to my state grew stranger, being transported
And rapt in *secret* studies.   *Tempest,* i. 2.

SECT.   *Class ; party ; sex ; a twig ; a cutting ; a scion.*

All *sects,* all ages smack of this vice ; and he
To die for it !   *Measure for Measure,* ii. 2.

And we'll wear out,
In a wall'd prison, packs and *sects* of great ones,
That ebb and flow by the moon.   *King Lear,* v. 3.

So is all her *sect ;* an they be once in a calm,
they are sick.   *Henry* 4, P. 2, ii. 4.

Our unbitted lusts ; whereof I take this, that
you call love, to be a *sect* or scion.   *Othello,* i. 3.

SECURE.   *Careless ; unsuspecting ; confident.*

Upon my *secure* hour thy uncle stole. *Hamlet,* i. 5.

Though Page be a *secure* fool, and stands so
firmly on his wife's frailty, yet I cannot put off my
opinion so easily.   *Merry Wives of Windsor,* ii. 1.

Open the door, *secure,* foolhardy king.
Richard 2, v. 3.

SECURELY.   *Confidently ; boldly.*

'Tis done like Hector ; but *securely* done.
Troilus and Cressida, iv. 5.

We see the wind sit sore upon our sails,
And yet we strike not, but *securely* perish.
Richard 2, ii. 1.

She dwells so *securely* on the excellency of her
honour, that the folly of my soul dares not present
itself.   *Merry Wives of Windsor,* ii. 2.

SECURITY.   *Suretyship ; carelessness ; want of caution ; blind confidence.*

There is scarce truth enough alive to make societies secure, but *security* enough to make fellow-
ships accursed.   *Measure for Measure,* iii. 2.

Whilst Bolingbroke, through our *security,*
Grows strong and great in substance and in friends.
Richard 2, iii. 2.

That's mercy but too much *security.*
Henry 5, ii. 2.

SEEDED.   *Seedy ; abounding with seeds ; ma-tured ; ripened.*

The *seeded* pride
That hath to this maturity blown up
In rank Achilles must be cropp'd.
Troilus and Cressida, i. 3.

SEEDNESS.   *Seed-time ; time of sowing.*

As blossoming time,
That from the *seedness* the bare fallow brings
To teeming foison.   *Measure for Measure,* i. 4.

SEEKING.   *Suit ; petition ; demand.*

What's their *seeking* ?   *Coriolanus,* i. 1.

To SEEL.   *To close up the eyes ; to blind.*

Come, *seeling* night,
Scarf up the tender eye of pitiful day !
Macbeth, iii. 2.

But when we in our viciousness grow hard,
O misery on't ! the wise gods *seel* our eyes.
Antony and Cleopatra, iii. 13.

To SEEM.   *To play ; to pass for ; to personate.*

I would not, though 'tis my familiar sin
With maids to *seem* the lapwing, and to jest,
Tongue far from heart, play with all virgins so.
Measure for Measure, i. 4.

If he be credulous and trust my tale,
I'll make him glad to *seem* Vincentio.
Taming of the Shrew, iv. 2.

SEEMING.   *Fair looks ; appearance.*

For you there's rosemary and rue ; these keep
Seeming and savour all the winter long.
Winter's Tale, iv. 3.

And, as you can, disliken
The truth of your own *seeming.*   *Ibid.* iv. 3.

SEEMING (adj.). *Specious.*

I will pluck the borrowed veil of modesty from the so *seeming* Mistress Page.
Merry Wives of Windsor, iii. 2.

If aught within that little *seeming* substance
. . . . . . may fitly like your grace,
She's there, and she is yours. *King Lear*, i. 1.

SEEMING (adv.). *Seemly; becomingly.*

Bear your body more *seeming*, Audrey.
As you like it, v. 4.

SEEN. *Skilled; versed.*

And offer me, disguis'd in sober robes,
To old Baptista as a schoolmaster
Well *seen* in music, to instruct Bianca.
Taming of the Shrew, i. 2.

To SEETHE. *To boil; to be hot.*

I will make a complimental assault upon him,
for my business *seethes*. *Troilus and Cressida*, ii. 3.

Lovers and madmen have such *seething* brains.
Midsummer-Night's Dream, v. 1.

Go, suck the subtle blood o' the grape,
Till the high fever *seethe* your blood to froth,
And so scape hanging. *Timon of Athens*, iv. 3.

SEGREGATION. *Separation; dispersion.*

What shall we hear of this?—
A *segregation* of the Turkish fleet. *Othello*, ii. 1.

SEIZURE. *Grasp; clasp.*

And shall these hands so lately purg'd of blood,
So newly join'd in love, so strong in both,
Unyoke this *seizure* and this kind regreet?
King John, iii. 1.

To whose soft *seizure*
The cygnet's down is harsh, and spirit of sense
Hard as the palm of ploughman !
Troilus and Cressida, i. 1.

SELD. *Seldom.*

Seld-shown flamens
Do press among the popular throngs, and puff
To win a vulgar station. *Coriolanus*, ii. 1.

If I might in entreaties find success—
As *seld* I have the chance—I would desire
My famous cousin to our Grecian tents.
Troilus and Cressida, iv. 5.

SELDOM (adj.). *Rare; not frequent.*

And so my state,
Seldom but sumptuous, showèd like a feast,
And won by rareness such solemnity.
Henry 4, P. 1, iii. 2.

SELDOM-WHEN. *Seldom that.*

'Tis *seldom-when* the bee doth leave her comb
In the dead carrion. *Henry 4*, P. 2, iv. 4.

SELF. *Same; self-same.*

The stars above us govern our conditions ;
Else one *self* mate and mate could not beget
Such different issues. *King Lear*, iv. 3.

I'm made of that *self* metal as my sister,
And prize me at her worth. *Ibid.* i. 1.

But that *self* hand,
Which writ his honour in the acts it did,
Hath, with the courage which the heart did lend it,
Splitted the heart. *Antony and Cleopatra*, v. 1.

SELF-ADMISSION. *Self-approbation.*

But carries on the stream of his dispose,
Without observance or respect of any,
In will peculiar and in *self-admission*.
Troilus and Cressida, ii. 3.

SELF-CHARITY. *Self-defence; self-preservation.*

Unless *self-charity* be sometimes a vice,
And to defend ourselves it be a sin
When violence assails us. *Othello*, ii. 3.

SELF-COVERED. *Self-shielded; self-protected; sex-protected.*

Thou changèd and *self-cover'd* thing, for shame,
Be-monster not thy feature. *King Lear*, iv. 2.

SELF-FIGURED. *Self-formed; self-tied.*

Though it be allow'd in meaner parties,—
Yet who than he more mean?—to knit their souls—
On whom there is no more dependency
But brats and beggary—in *self-figur'd* knot.
Cymbeline, ii. 3.

SEMBLABLE. *Like; semblative; resembling; equal.*

Nay, nay, Octavia, not only that,—
That were excusable, that, and thousands more
Of *semblable* import. *Antony and Cleopatra*, iii. 4.

It is a wonderful thing to see the *semblable* coherence of his men's spirits and his.
Henry 4, P. 2, v. 1.

His *semblable*, yea, himself, Timon disdains.
Timon of Athens, iv. 3.

SEMBLABLY.   *In appearance; in the same manner.*

A gallant knight he was, his name was Blunt;
Semblably furnish'd like the king himself.
Henry 4, P. 1, v. 3.

SEMBLANCE.   *Likeness; figure; show.*

Which if granted,
As he made *semblance* of his duty, would
Have put his knife into him.   *Henry* 8, i. 2.

If you go out in your own *semblance*, you die.
Merry Wives of Windsor, iv. 2.

But now two mirrors of his princely *semblance*
Are crack'd in pieces by malignant death.
Richard 3, ii. 2.

For if thou put thy native *semblance* on,
Not Erebus itself were dim enough
To hide thee from prevention.   *Julius Cæsar*, ii. 1.

SEMBLATIVE.   *Resembling; like; suited to; semblable.*

And all is *semblative* a woman's part.
Twelfth-Night, i. 4.

SENIORY.   *Seniority.*

If ancient sorrow be most reverent,
Give mine the benefit of *seniory*. *Richard* 3, iv. 4.

SE'NNIGHT.   *A week.*

Whose footing here anticipates our thoughts
A *se'nnight's* speed.   *Othello*, ii. 1.

If the interim be but a *se'nnight*, Time's pace is
so hard that it seems the length of seven year.
As you like it, iii. 2.

SENOYS.   *The people of Sienna.*

The Florentines and *Senoys* are by the ears.
All's well that ends well, i. 2.

SENSE.   *Touch; feeling; sensation; sensibility; the quick.*

To whose soft seizure
The cygnet's down is harsh, and spirit of *sense*
Hard as the palm of ploughman!
Troilus and Cressida, i. 1.

Nor doth the eye itself,
That most pure spirit of *sense*, behold itself,
Not going from itself. *Troilus and Cressida*, iii. 3.

He should have liv'd,
Save that his riotous youth, with dangerous *sense*,
Might in the times to come have ta'en revenge.
Measure for Measure, iv. 4.

I've rubb'd this young quat almost to the *sense*,
And he grows angry.   *Othello*, v. 1.

SENSELESS.   *Insensible.*

The ears are *senseless* that should give us hearing.
Hamlet, v. 2.

You might have pinched a placket,—it was *senseless*.
Winter's Tale, iv. 3.

He that a fool doth very wisely hit
Doth very foolishly, although he smart,
But to seem *senseless* of the bob.
As you like it, ii. 7.

Harm not yourself with your vexation :
I'm *senseless* of your wrath.   *Cymbeline*, i. 1.

SENSIBLE.   *Substantial; tangible; sensitive.*

From whom he bringeth *sensible* regreets,
To wit, besides commends and courteous breath,
Gifts of rich value.   *Merchant of Venice*, ii. 8.

Love's feeling is more soft and *sensible*
Than are the tender horns of cockled snails.
Love's Labour's lost, iv. 3.

SENTENCE.   *A maxim; an axiom.*

Shall quips and *sentences* awe a man from the
career of his humour?
Much Ado about Nothing, ii. 3.

SEPTENTRION.   *The north.*

Thou art as opposite to every good
As the Antipodes are unto us,
Or as the south to the *septentrion*.
Henry 6, P. 3, i. 4.

TO SEPULCHRE.   *To entomb; to inurn; to enfold.*

If thou shouldst not be glad,
I would divorce me from thy mother's tomb,
Sepulchring an adultress.   *King Lear*, ii. 4.

SEQUEL.   *Succession; order.*

His daughter first; and, in *sequel*, all,
According to their firm proposèd natures.
Henry 5, v. 2.

SEQUENCE. *Order of succession.*

For how art thou a king
But by fair *sequence* and succession?
Richard 2, ii. 1.
Cut off the *sequence* of posterity. *King John*, ii. 1.
Tell Athens, in the *sequence* of degree,
From high to low throughout, that whoso please
To stop affliction, let him take his haste,
Come hither, ere my tree hath felt the axe,
And hang himself. *Timon of Athens*, v. 1.

SEQUENT. *A follower.*

And here he hath framed a letter to a *sequent* of
the stranger queen's. *Love's Labour's lost*, iv. 2.

SEQUENT (adj.). *Following; consequent; successive.*

Immediate sentence then, and *sequent* death,
Is all the grace I beg. *Measure for Measure*, v. 1.
Now, the next day
Was our sea-fight; and what to this was *sequent*
Thou know'st already. *Hamlet*, v. 2.
The galleys
Have sent a dozen *sequent* messengers
This very night at one another's heels. *Othello*, j. 2.
Indeed, your "O Lord, sir!" is very *sequent* to
your whipping. *All's well that ends well*, ii. 2.

SEQUESTER. *Separation; retirement.*

This hand of yours requires
A *sequester* from liberty, fasting and prayer,
Much castigation, exercise devout. *Othello*, iii. 4.

TO SEQUESTER. *To separate.*

Sequestering from me all
That time, acquaintance, custom, and condition,
Made tame and most familiar to my nature.
Troilus and Cressida, iii. 3.
To the which place a poor *sequester'd* stag,
That from the hunter's aim had ta'en a hurt,
Did come to languish. *As you like it*, ii. 1.

SEQUESTRATION. *Seclusion; separation; rupture.*

Since Henry Monmouth first began to reign
This loathsome *sequestration* have I had.
Henry 6, P₁ 1, ii. 5.
And never noted in him any study,
Any retirement, any *sequestration*
From open haunts and popularity. *Henry 5*, i. 1.
It was a violent commencement, and thou shalt
see an answerable *sequestration*. *Othello*, i. 3.

SERGEANT. *A sheriff's officer; a bailiff.*

If Time be in debt and theft, and a *sergeant* in the
way,
Hath he not reason to turn back an hour in a day?
Comedy of Errors, iv. 2.
Had I but time,—as this fell *sergeant*, death,
Is strict in his arrest,—O, I could tell you;
But let it be. *Hamlet*, v. 2.

TO SERMON. *To lecture; to admonish; to dogmatize.*

Come, *sermon* me no further:
No villanous bounty yet hath pass'd my heart.
Timon of Athens, ii. 2.

SERPIGO. *An eruption on the skin; a scab; a tetter.*

Now, the dry *serpigo* on the subject!
Troilus and Cressida, ii. 3.
For thine own bowels, which do call thee sire,
Do curse the gout, *serpigo*, and the rheum,
For ending thee no sooner.
Measure for Measure, iii. 1.

SERVANT. *Lover.*

Too low a mistress for so high a *servant*.
Two Gentlemen of Verona, ii. 4.

SERVANTED. *Subjected; resigned; abandoned; given up.*

My affairs are *servanted* to others. *Coriolanus*, v. 2.

TO SERVE. *To serve for; to satisfy.*

Show me a mistress that is passing fair,
What doth her beauty *serve*, but as a note
Where I may read who pass'd that passing fair?
Romeo and Juliet, i. 1.
Vincentio's son, brought up in Florence,
It shall become, to *serve* all hopes conceiv'd,
To deck his fortune with his virtuous deeds.
Taming of the Shrew, i. 1.

SERVICE. *Homage; deed; action.*

I'll do thee *service* for so good a gift.
Henry 6, P. 3, v. 1.
I know not whether God will have it so,
For some displeasing *service* I have done,
· That, in his secret doom, out of my blood
He'll breed revengement and a scourge for me.
Henry 4, P. 1, iii. 2.

SERVICEABLE. *Obsequious; diligent; officious; useful.*

You must lay lime to tangle her desires
By wailful sonnets, whose composèd rhymes
Should be full-fraught with *serviceable* vows.
Two Gentlemen of Verona, iii. 2.

I know thee well : a *serviceable* villain.
King Lear, iv. 6.

SERVING. *Service; use; employment.*

In their *serving,*
And with what imitation you can borrow
From youth of such a season, fore noble Lucius
Present yourself. *Cymbeline*, iii. 4.

SERVITOR. *Servant; retainer; adherent; follower.*

Come,—I have learn'd that fearful commenting
Is leaden *servitor* to dull delay. *Richard 3*, iv. 3.

My noble queen, let former grudges pass,
And henceforth I am thy true *servitor*.
Henry 6, P. 3, iii. 3.

Signior Montano,
Your trusty and most valiant *servitor*,
With his free duty recommends you thus,
And prays you to believe him. *Othello*, i. 3.

SET. *A game; a bout.*

Well bandied both ; a *set* of wit well play'd.
Love's Labour's lost, v. 2.

To SET. *To set out; to set on; to close; to set aside.*

The king is *set* from London ; and the scene
Is now transported, gentles, to Southampton.
Henry 5, ii. Chorus.

O cousin, thou art come to *set* mine eye.
King John, v. 7.

And, England, if my love thou hold'st at aught,
Thou mayst not coldly *set* our sovereign process.
Hamlet, iv. 3.

To SET ABROACH. *To diffuse; to disseminate.*

Would he abuse the countenance of the king,
Alack, what mischiefs might he *set abroach*,
In shadow of such greatness ! *Henry 4*, P. 2, iv. 2.

To SET COCK-A-HOOP. *To swagger; to bully.*

You will *set cock-a-hoop !* you'll be the man !
Romeo and Juliet, i. 5.

To SET DOWN. *To let down; to lower.*

O, you are well tun'd now !
But I'll *set down* the pegs that make this music,
As honest as I am. *Othello*, ii. 1.

To SET ON. *To begin; to proceed; to go forward; to set out.*

Set on ; and leave no ceremony out.
Julius Cæsar, i. 2.

Be it your charge, my lord,
To see perform'd the tenour of our word.—
Set on. *Henry 4*, P. 2, v. 5.

Therefore your best appointment make with speed ;
To-morrow you *set on. Measure for Measure*, iii. 1.

To SET UP. *To cause; to be the cause of.*

And thou, Posthumus, thou that didst *set up*
My disobedience 'gainst the king my father,
And make me put into contempt the suits
Of princely fellows, shalt hereafter find
It is no act of common passage, but
A strain of rareness. *Cymbeline*, iii. 4.

SETTER. *A jackal; a provider; a spy.*

O, 'tis our *setter :* I know his voice.
Henry 4, P. 1, ii. 2.

SETTLING. *Restoration; return of reason.*

Desire him to go in ; trouble him no more
Till further *settling.* *King Lear*, iv. 7.

SEVEN-NIGHT. *A week.*

Weary *seven-nights* nine times nine
Shall he dwindle, peak, and pine. *Macbeth*, i. 3.

SEVERAL. *An individual.*

Not noted, is't, but by some *severals*
Of head-piece extraordinary ? *Winter's Tale*, i. 2.

SEVERAL. *Distinct; separate; divided; individual.*

To every *several* man seventy-five drachmas.
Julius Cæsar, iii. 2.

You may jest on, but, by the rood,
I do not like these *several* councils, I.
Richard 3, iii. 2.

Larded with many *several* sorts of reasons.
Hamlet, v. 2.

He shall have every day a *several* greeting,
Or I'll unpeople Egypt.
Antony and Cleopatra, i. 5.

Twinn'd brothers of one womb,—
Whose procreation, residence, and birth,
Scarce is dividant,—touch them with *several* for-
    tunes ;
The greater scorns the lesser.
                                    Timon of Athens, iv. 3.

SHADOW.   *A ghost ; a corpse.*

Haply you shall not see me more ; or if,
A mangled *shadow.*   *Antony and Cleopatra,* iv. 2.

TO SHAKE UP.   *To deal with ; to handle.*

Go apart, Adam, and thou shalt hear how he
will *shake me up.*   *As you like it,* i. 1.

SHALE.   *A husk ; a shell.*

And your fair show shall suck away their souls,
Leaving them but the *shales* and husks of men.
                                        Henry 5, iv. 2.

SHALLOW.   *Unskilled ; inexperienced.*

You are *shallow,* madam ; e'en great friends.
                                All's well that ends well, i. 3.

SHAME.   *Modesty.*

            He, with two striplings,—
With faces fit for masks, or rather fairer
Than those for preservation cas'd, or *shame,*—
Made good the passage.   *Cymbeline,* v. 3.

TO SHAME.   *To blush ; to be ashamed.*

            And one that knows
What she should *shame* to know herself
But with her most vile principal.
                                    Winter's Tale, ii. 1.
My hands are of your colour ; but I *shame*
To wear a heart so white.   *Macbeth,* ii. 1.

SHAPE.   *Conceit ; invention ; plan ; scheme ;
contrivance ; device.*

So full of *shapes* is fancy,
That it alone is high-fantastical. *Twelfth-Night,* i. 1.
        Let's further think of this ;
Weigh what convenience both of time and means
May fit us to our *shape.*   *Hamlet,* iv. 7.

SHAPELESS.   *Strange ; uncouth ; diffused.*

Disguis'd like Muscovites, in *shapeless* gear.
                                Love's Labour's lost, v. 2.

SHARDED.   *Covered with shards ; sheathed.*

And often, to our comfort, shall we find

The *sharded* beetle in a safer hold
Than is the full-wing'd eagle.   *Cymbeline,* iii. 3.

SHARD.   *The winged integument of a chafer
or beetle ; a fragment of pottery, or other
brittle substance.*

            Ere to black Hecate's summons,
The *shard*-borne beetle, with his drowsy hums,
Hath rung night's yawning peal, there shall be done
A deed of dreadful note.   *Macbeth,* iii. 2.
They are his *shards,* and he their beetle.
                                Antony and Cleopatra, iii. 2.
And, but that great command o'ersways the order,
She should in ground unsanctified have lodg'd
Till.the last trumpet ; for charitable prayers,
Shards, flints, and pebbles, should be thrown on her.
                                        Hamlet, v. 1.

TO SHARE.   *To shear ; to cut ; to separate.*

What glory our Achilles *shares* from Hector,
Were he not proud, we all should share with him.
                                Troilus and Cressida, i. 3.

TO SHARK.   *To pick up ; to collect together ;
to enrol.*

            Now, sir, young Fortinbras,
Of unimprovèd mettle hot and full,
Hath in the skirts of Norway, here and there,
Shark'd up a list of landless resolutes. *Hamlet,* i. 1.

SHE.   *A woman.*

That *she* was never yet that ever knew
Love got so sweet as when desire did sue.
                                Troilus and Cressida, i. 2.
Run, run, Orlando ; carve on every tree
The fair, the chaste, and unexpressive *she.*
                                        As you like it, iii. 1.
        Or I could make him swear
The *shes* of Italy should not betray
Mine interest and his honour.   *Cymbeline,* i. 3.

TO SHEAL.   *To shell.*

That's a *shealed* peascod.   *King Lear,* i. 4.

SHEARMAN.   *A cloth-worker ; a shearer.*

Villain, thy father was a plasterer ;
And thou thyself a *shearman,*—art thou not ?
                                        Henry 6, P. 2, iv. 2.

SHEEN.   *Lustre.*

And thirty dozen moons with borrow'd *sheen*
About the world have times twelve thirties been.
                                        Hamlet, iii. 2.

SHEEN. *Bright; glittering.*

By fountain clear, or spangled starlight *sheen*,
But they do square. *Midsum.-Night's Dream*, ii. 1.

SHEER. *Clear; pure; transparent.*

Thou *sheer*, immaculate, and silver fountain,
Thy overflow of good converts to bad.
Richard 2, v. 3.

To SHEND. *To blame; to chide; to reprimand.*

I am *shent* for speaking to you.
Twelfth-Night, iv. 2.
We shall all be *shent*. *Merry W. of Windsor*, i. 4.
He *shent* our messengers. *Troilus and Cressida*, ii. 3.
Do you hear how we are *shent* for keeping your
greatness back?   *Coriolanus*, v. 2.
How in my words soever she be *shent*,
To give them seals never my soul consent!
Hamlet, iii. 2.

To SHINE. *To succeed; to thrive; to prosper;
to come to pass.*

If there come truth from them,—
As upon thee, Macbeth, their speeches *shine*,—
Why, by the verities on thee made good,
May they not be my oracles as well,
And set me up in hope?   *Macbeth*, iii. 1.

SHINY. *Bright.*

The night is *shiny*. *Antony and Cleopatra*, iv. 9.

To SHOCK. *To oppose; to encounter.*

Now these her princes are come home again,
Come the three corners of the world in arms,
And we shall *shock* them.   *King John*, v. 7.

To SHOG. *To move off; to go.*

Will you *shog* off?   I would have you solus.
Henry 5, ii. 1.

SHOON. *Shoes.*

Spare none but such as go in clouted *shoon*.
Henry 6, P. 2, iv. 2.

How should I your true love know
From another one?
By his cockle hat and staff,
And his sandal *shoon*.   *Hamlet*, iv. 5.

SHOOT. *A shot; the act of shooting.*

Thus will I save my credit in the *shoot*:
Not wounding, pity would not let me do't.
Love's Labour's lost, iv. 1.

The noise of thy cross-bow
Will scare the herd, and so my *shoot* is lost.
Henry 6, P. 3, iii. 1.

To SHORE. *To set on shore; to dismiss.*

If he think it fit to *shore* them again, and that
the complaint they have to the king concerns him
nothing, let him call me rogue for being so far
officious.   *Winter's Tale*, iv. 3.

To SHORT. *To come short of; to fail in; to
forfeit.*

Yes, I beseech; or I shall *short* my word
By lengthening my return.   *Cymbeline*, i. 6.

SHOT. *A reckoning.*

So, if I prove a good repast to the spectators,
the dish pays the *shot*.   *Cymbeline*, v. 4.

Nor never welcome to a place till some certain
shot be paid, and the hostess say, "Welcome."
Two Gentlemen of Verona, ii. 5.

SHOW. *Appearance; pretence; semblance.*

It is not so with Him that all things knows,
As 'tis with us that square our guess by *shows*.
All's well that ends well, ii. 1.

In which time she purpos'd,
By watching, weeping, tendance, kissing, to
O'ercome you with her *show*.   *Cymbeline*, v. 5.

To SHOW. *To appear; to seem.*

Show men dutiful? why, so didst thou.
Henry 5, ii. 2.

Though thy tackle's torn,
Thou *show'st* a noble vessel: what's thy name?
Coriolanus, iv. 5.

To SHREW. *To beshrew; to curse.*

Search for a jewel, that too casually
Hath left mine arm: it was thy master's; *shrew* me
If I would lose it for a revenue
Of any king's in Europe.   *Cymbeline*, ii. 3.

SHREWD. *Bad; unfavourable; malicious;
severe; pinching.*

To lift *shrewd* steel against our golden crown.
Richard 2, iii. 2.

She enlargeth her mirth so far that there is
shrewd construction made of her.
Merry Wives of Windsor, ii. 2.

And after, every of this happy number,

That have endur'd *shrewd* days and nights with us,
Shall share the good of our returnèd fortunes.
As you like it, v. 4.

SHREWISH. *Peevish; cross; froward.*

My wife is *shrewish* when I keep not hours.
Comedy of Errors, iii. 1.

SHREWISHLY. *Petulantly; peevishly.*

He is very well-favoured, and he speaks very
shrewishly. *Twelfth-Night*, i. 5.

SHRIEVE. *A sheriff.*

The Earl Northumberland and the Lord Bardolph,
With a great power of English and of Scots,
Are by the *shrieve* of Yorkshire overthrown.
Henry 4, P. 2, iv. 4.

SHRIFT. *Confession of sins to a priest; ab-
solution.*

I will give him a present *shrift*, and advise him
for a better place. ' *Measure for Measure*, iv. 2.
The ghostly father now hath done his *shrift*.
Henry 6, P. 3, iii. 2.

To SHRILL. *To shriek; to scream; to utter
vociferously.*

How poor Andromache *shrills* her dolours forth!
Troilus and Cressida, v. 3.

SHRILL-GORGED. *Shrill-throated; shrill-voiced.*

Look up a-height;—the *shrill-gorg'd* lark so far
Cannot be seen or heard. *King Lear*, iv. 6.

To SHRIVE. *To hear at confession; to confess.*

Not *shriving*-time allow'd. *Hamlet*, v. 2.
Your honour hath no *shriving*-work in hand.
Richard 3, iii. 2.
Husband, I'll dine above with you to-day,
And *shrive* you of a thousand idle pranks.
Comedy of Errors, ii. 2.

SHRIVER. *A confessor.*

When he was made a *shriver*, 'twas for shift.
Henry 6, P. 3, iii. 2.

SHROUD. *Mantle; protection.*

But it would warm his spirits, '
To hear from me you had left Antony,
And put yourself under his *shroud*,
The universal landlord.
Antony and Cleopatra, iii. 13.

To SHROUD. *To take shelter.*

I will here *shroud* till the dregs of the storm be past.
Tempest, ii. 2.

SHROW. *A shrew.*

And I beshrew all *shrows*. *Love's Labour's lost*, v. 2.
Now, go thy ways; thou hast tam'd a curst *shrow*.
'Tis a wonder, by your leave, she will be tam'd so.
Taming of the Shrew, v. 2.

To SHUFFLE. *To shift; to struggle; to depend upon.*

I see a thing
Bitter to me as death : your life, good master,
Must *shuffle* for itself. *Cymbeline*, v. 5.

To SHUN. *To lose; to forfeit.*

Make choice ; and, see,
Who shuns thy love *shuns* all his love in me.
All's well that ends well, ii. 3.

SHUNLESS. *Unavoidable.*

Alone he enter'd
The mortal gate of the city, which he painted
With *shunless* destiny. *Coriolanus*, ii. 2.

To SHUT UP. *To close; to finish; to conclude.*

This diamond he greets your wife withal,
By the name of most kind hostess; and *shut up*
In measureless content. *Macbeth*, ii. 1.

To SICK. *To sicken; to grow sick.*

And the old folk, time's doting chronicles,
Say it did so a little time before
That our great-grandsire, Edward, *sick'd* and died.
Henry 4, P. 2, iv. 4.

To SICKEN. *To impair; to injure.*

Kinsmen of mine, three at the least, that have
By this so *sicken'd* their estates, that never
They shall abound as formerly. *Henry 8*, i. 1.

SICKLIED OVER. *Infected; tainted; imbued.*

And thus the native hue of resolution
Is *sicklied* o'er with the pale cast of thought.
Hamlet, iii. 1.

SIDE. *Game; object; purpose; faction; party.*

To take the widow
Exasperates and makes mad her sister Goneril ;
And hardly shall I carry out my *side*,
Her husband being alive. *King Lear*, v. 1.

These are a *side* that would be glad to have
This true which they so seem to fear.
Coriolanus, iv. 6.

SIDE SLEEVES. *Hanging sleeves.*

Set with pearls down sleeves, *side sleeves*, and
skirts round underborne with a bluish tinsel.
Much Ado about Nothing, iii. 4.

SIEGE. *Seat; bench; chair; rank; sort; kind.*

Besides, upon the very *siege* of justice
Lord Angelo hath to the public ear
Profess'd the contrary. *Measure for Measure*, iv. 2.
'Tis yet to know,—
Which, when I know that boasting is an honour,
I shall promulgate,—I fetch my life and being
From men of royal *siege*. *Othello*, i. 2.
Your sum of parts
Did not together pluck such envy from him,
As did that one; and that, in my regard,
Of the unworthiest *siege*. *Hamlet*, iv. 7.

SIEVE. *A basket; a voider; a receptacle for broken meat.*

Nor the remainder viands
We do not throw in unrespective *sieve*,
Because we now are full. *Troilus and Cressida*, ii. 2.

SIGHTLESS. *Unsightly; invisible.*

Full of unpleasing blots and *sightless* stains,
Lame, foolish, crookèd, swart, prodigious.
King John, iii. 1.
Wherever in your *sightless* substances
You wait on nature's mischief. *Macbeth*, i. 5.
And pity . . . .
. . . . hors'd
Upon the *sightless* couriers of the air,
Shall blow the horrid deed in every eye,
That tears shall drown the wind. *Macbeth*, i. 7.

SIGHTS. *Apertures for the eyes.*

Their eyes of fire sparkling through *sights* of steel.
Henry 4, P. 2, iv. 1.

To SIGN. *To mark; to denote; to show; to bode; to portend.*

A fellow by the hand of nature mark'd,
Quoted and *sign'd*, to do a deed of shame.
King John, iv. 2.
Hark! music i' the air: under the earth.—
It *signs* well, does it not?
Antony and Cleopatra, iv. 3.

You *sign* your place and calling, in full seeming,
With meekness and humility; but your heart
Is cramm'd with arrogancy, spleen, and pride.
Henry 8, ii. 4.
Here didst thou fall; and here thy hunters stand,
Sign'd in thy spoil, and crimson'd in thy lethe.
Julius Cæsar, iii. 1.

SIGNIFICANT. *A sign; a token.*

Bear this *significant* to the country maid Jaquenetta.
Love's Labour's lost, iii. 1.
Since you are tongue-tied and so loth to speak,
In dumb *significants* proclaim your thoughts.
Henry 6, P. 1, ii. 4.

SIGNIORY. *A domain; a lordship; state; government.*

Through all the *signiories* it was the first,
And Prospero the prime duke. *Tempest*, i. 2.
Whilst you have fed upon my *signiories*.
Richard 2, iii. 1.
My services, which I have done the *signiory*.
Othello, i. 2.

SILENT. *Silence.*

Deep night, dark night, the *silent* of the night,
The time of night when Troy was set on fire.
Henry 6, P. 2, i. 4.

SILLY. *Weak; helpless; plain; simple; slight; rustic.*

I take your offer, and will live with you,
Provided that you do no outrages
On *silly* women or poor passengers.
Two Gentlemen of Verona, iv. 1.
It is *silly* sooth,
And dallies with the innocence of love,
Like the old age. *Twelfth-Night*, ii. 4.
But for the rest,—you tell a pedigree
Of threescore and two years; a *silly* time
To make prescription for a kingdom's worth.
Henry 6, P. 3, iii. 3.
These kind of knaves I know, which in this plainness
Harbour more craft and more corrupter ends
Than twenty *silly* ducking observants
That stretch their duties nicely. *King Lear*, ii. 2.
There was a fourth man, in a *silly* habit,
That gave th' affront with them. *Cymbeline*, v. 3.

SILLY-CHEAT. *Fraud; cozenage; filching; petty thievery.*

With die and drab I purchased this caparison; and my revenue is the *silly-cheat.*
Winter's Tale, iv. 2.

SIMPLE. *Plain; straightforward; direct.*

Be *simple*-answer'd, for we know the truth.
King Lear, iii. 7.

SIMPLICITY. *Weakness; folly; silliness.*

The shape of Love's Tyburn that hangs up *simplicity.*
Love's Labour's lost, iv. 3.

Since all the power thereof it doth apply
To prove, by wit, worth in *simplicity.*
Ibid. v. 2.

SIMULAR. *Pretender; simulator.*

Hide thee, thou bloody hand;
Thou perjur'd, and thou *simular* of virtue
That art incestuous.
King Lear, iii. 2.

SIMULAR (adj.). *Pretended; simulated; forged.*

And, to be brief, my practice so prevail'd,
That I return'd with *simular* proof enough
To make the noble Leonatus mad,
By wounding his belief in her renown
With tokens thus, and thus.
Cymbeline, v. 5.

SIMULATION. *Semblance; symbolical representation.*

M, O, A, I;—this *simulation* is not as the former.
Twelfth-Night, ii. 5.

To SINEW. *To knit together; to unite.*

From whence shall Warwick cut the sea to France,
To ask the Lady Bona for thy queen:
So shalt thou *sinew* both these lands together.
Henry 6, P. 3, ii. 6.

SINEWED. *Firm; resolute; determined.*

He will the rather do it when he sees
Ourselves well *sinewèd* to our defence.
King John, v. 7.

SINGLE. *Pure; sincere; weak; foolish; particular; individual.*

Nor is there living—
I speak it with a *single* heart, my lords—
A man that more detests, more stirs against,
Defacers of a public peace, than I do.
Henry 8, v. 2.

Is not your voice broken? your wind short? your chin double? your wit *single*? and every part of you blasted with antiquity? and will you yet call yourself young?
Henry 4, P. 2, i. 2.

Trust to thy *single* virtue; for thy soldiers,
All levied in my name, have in my name
Took their discharge.
King Lear, v. 3.

SINGLE-SOLED. *Slight; flimsy; also mean, contemptible.*

O *single-soled* jest, solely singular for the singleness!
Romeo and Juliet, ii. 4.

SINGULARITY. *Rarity; curiosity.*

Your gallery
Have we pass'd through, not without much content
In many *singularities.*
Winter's Tale, v. 3.

SIR. *A man; a gentleman.*

Sole *sir* o' the world,
I cannot project mine own cause so well
To make it clear.
Antony and Cleopatra, v. 2.

My true preserver, and a loyal *sir*
To him thou follow'st!
Tempest, v. 1.

Honour'd with confirmation your great judgment
In the election of a *sir* so rare,
Which you know cannot err.
Cymbeline, i. 6.

Which now again you are most apt to play the *sir* in.
Othello, ii. 1.

SIR-REVERENCE. *Save reverence; salvâ reverentiâ; with all due respect.*

If thou art dun, we'll draw thee from the mire
Of this (*sir-reverence*) love, wherein thou stick'st
Up to the ears.
Romeo and Juliet, i. 4.

Such a one as a man may not speak of, without he say *sir-reverence.*
Comedy of Errors, iii. 2.

To SIRE. *To father; to beget.*

Cowards father cowards, and base things *sire* base.
Cymbeline, iv. 2.

SITH. *Since; seeing that.*

And yet I will not, *sith* so prettily
He couples it to his complaining names.
Two Gentlemen of Verona, i. 2.

Sith I have cause, and will, and strength, and means.
Hamlet, iv. 4.

Talk not of France, *sith* thou hast lost it all.
Henry 6, P. 3, i. 1.

SITHENCE. *Since.*

Have you inform'd them *sithence?*
                    Coriolanus, iii. 1.
Sithence, in the loss that may happen, it concerns you something to know it.
                    All's well that ends well, i. 3.

SIZES. *Entertainment; allowance; pension.*

'Tis not in thee
To grudge my pleasures, to cut off my train,
To bandy hasty words, to scant my *sizes,*
And, in conclusion, to oppose the bolt
Against my coming in.   *King Lear,* ii. 4.

SKILL. *Cunning; cause; reason; a science; an art.*

If you—or stupefied,
Or seeming so in *skill*—cannot or will not
Relish a truth, like us, inform yourselves
We need no more of your advice.
                    Winter's Tale, ii. 1.
I think you have
As little *skill* to fear as I have purpose
To put you to't.   *Ibid.* iv. 3.
I'll so offend, to make offence a *skill;*
Redeeming time, when men think least I will.
                    Henry 4, P. 1, i. 2.

To SKILL. *To matter; to import; to signify.*

And now we three have spoke it,
It *skills* not greatly who impugns our doom.
                    Henry 6, P. 2, iii. 1.
I am to get a man,—whate'er he be,
It *skills* not much, we'll fit him to our turn,—
And he shall be Vincentio of Pisa.
                    Taming of the Shrew, iii. 2.
But as a madman's epistles are no gospels, so it *skills* not much when they are delivered.
                    Twelfth-Night, v. 1.

SKILLESS. *Ignorant; unacquainted with; unskilful.*

But jealousy what might befall your travel,
Being *skilless* in these parts. *Twelfth-Night,* iii. 3.
Like powder in a *skilless* soldier's flask.
                    Romeo and Juliet, iii. 3.

SKILLET. *A boiler; a kettle.*

When my disports corrupt and taint my business,
Let housewives make a *skillet* of my helm.
                    Othello, i. 3.

SKIMBLE-SKAMBLE. *Incoherent; rambling.*

And such a deal of *skimble-skamble* stuff
As puts me from my faith. *Henry* 4, P. 1, iii. 1.

SKINKER. *A drawer; a tapster.*

To sweeten which name of Ned, I give thee this pennyworth of sugar, clapped even now into my hand by an under-*skinker.* *Henry* 4, P. 1, ii. 4.

SKIPPER. *A younker; a youngster.*

Skipper, stand back ; 'tis age that nourisheth.
                    Taming of the Shrew, ii. 1.

SKIPPING. *Flighty.*

The *skipping* king, he ambled up and down
With shallow jesters and rash bavin wits.
                    Henry 4, P. 1, iii. 2.
'Tis not that time of moon with me to make one in so *skipping* a dialogue. *Twelfth-Night,* i. 5.

To SKIRR. *To scour; to scud.*

If they'll do neither, we will come to them,
And make them *skirr* away, as swift as stones
Enforcèd from the old Assyrian slings.
                    Henry 5, iv. 7.
Send out more horses, *skirr* the country round.
                    Macbeth, v. 3.

SKITTISH. *Fickle; changeable; volatile.*

Now expectation, tickling *skittish* spirits,
Sets all on hazard.
                    Troilus and Cressida, Prologue.
How some men creep in *skittish* fortune's hall,
While others play the idiots in her eyes !
                    Ibid. iii. 3.

SKYEY. *Ethereal.*

A breath thou art,
Servile to all the *skyey* influences
That do this habitation, where thou keep'st,
Hourly afflict.   *Measure for Measure,* iii. 1.

SKYISH. *Reaching to the skies.*

Now pile your dust upon the quick and dead,
Till of this flat a mountain you have made,
T' o'ertop old Pelion or the *skyish* head
Of blue Olympus.   *Hamlet,* v. 1.

SLAB. *Adhesive; glutinous.*

Make the gruel thick and *slab.* *Macbeth,* iv. 1.

SLACK.   *Slow; remiss; negligent; short.*

If you come *slack* of former services,
You shall do well; the fault of it I'll answer.
             King Lear, i. 3.
And, being a woman, I will not be *slack*
To play my part in Fortune's pageant.
             Henry 6, P. 2, i. 2.
Sir, I shall not be *slack. Taming of the Shrew,* i. 2.

To SLACK.   *To neglect; to abate; to lessen.*

My father Capulet will have it so;
And I am nothing slow to *slack* his haste.
             Romeo and Juliet, iv. 1.
What a beast am I to *slack* it !
           Merry Wives of Windsor, iii. 4.
If then they chanc'd to *slack* you, we could control them.   *King Lear,* ii. 4.

SLACKLY.   *Negligently; carelessly.*

That a king's children should be so convey'd !
So *slackly* guarded !   *Cymbeline,* i. 1.

SLACKNESS.   *Negligence; remissness.*

        And these thy offices,
So rarely kind, are as interpreters
Of my behind-hand *slackness!* *Winter's Tale,* v. 1.
        A good rebuke,
Which might have well becom'd the best of men,
To taunt at *slackness. Antony and Cleopatra,* iii. 7.

SLANDER.   *Disgrace; reproach; shame.*

A partial *slander* sought I to avoid,
And in the sentence my own life destroy'd.
             Richard 2, i. 3.
No, be assur'd, you shall not find me, daughter,
After the *slander* of most stepmothers,
Evil-ey'd unto you.   *Cymbeline,* i. 1.
Thou *slander* of thy heavy mother's womb !
             Richard 3, i. 3.
And bid his ears a little while be deaf
Till I have told this *slander* of his blood,
How God and good men hate so foul a liar.
             Richard 2, i. 1.

SLAUGHTER-MAN.   *A slayer; a destroyer.*

        Ten, chas'd by one,
Are now each one the *slaughter-man* of twenty.
             Cymbeline, v. 3.

To SLAVE.   *To enslave.*

Heavens, deal so still !
Let the superfluous and lust-dieted man,

That *slaves* your ordinance, that will not see
Because he doth not feel, feel your power quickly.
             King Lear, iv. 1.

SLEAVE.   *Floss or raw silk.*

Why art thou, then, exasperate, thou idle immaterial skein of *sleave*-silk ?
         Troilus and Cressida, v. 1.
Sleep that knits up the ravell'd *sleave* of care.
             Macbeth, ii. 1.

SLEDDED.   *Sledged; sledge-borne; mounted on sledges.*

So frown'd he once, when, in an angry parle,
He smote the *sledded* Polacks on the ice.
             Hamlet, i. 1.

SLEEVE-HAND.   *A cuff; a wristband.*

You would think, a smock were a she-angel, he
so chants to the *sleeve-hand,* and the work about
the square on't.   *Winter's Tale,* iv. 3.

SLEEVELESS.   *Unprofitable; bootless.*

That that same young Trojan ass might send
that Greekish whoremasterly villain, with the sleeve,
back to the dissembling luxurious drab, of a *sleeveless* errand.   *Troilus and Cressida,* v. 4.

SLEIGHT.   *Deceit; trick; cunning; artifice.*

        As Ulysses and stout Diomede
With *sleight* and manhood stole to Rhesus' tents,
And brought from thence the Thracian fatal steeds.
             Henry 6, P. 3, iv. 2.
And that, distill'd by magic *sleights,*
Shall raise such artificial sprites,
As by the strength of their illusion
Shall draw him on to his confusion.
             Macbeth, iii. 5.

SLIGHT.   *Insignificant; remiss; negligent; easy.*

For such things as you, I can scarce think there's
any, ye're so *slight.*   *Coriolanus,* v. 2.
Away, *slight* man !   *Julius Cæsar,* iv. 3.
        Call her before us ; for
We have been too *slight* in sufferance.
             Cymbeline, iii. 5.
The more degenerate and base art thou,
To make such means for her as thou hast done,
And leave her on such *slight* conditions.
        Two Gentlemen of Verona, iv. 5.

To **Slight.** *To pitch; to throw carelessly; to disregard.*

The rogues *slighted* me into the river with as little remorse as they would have drowned a bitch's blind puppies. *Merry Wives of Windsor,* iii. 5.
Wherein my letters, praying on his side,
Were *slighted* off. *Julius Cæsar,* iv. 3.

Slightly. *Easily; readily.*

You were to blame,
To part so *slightly* with your wife's first gift.
Merchant of Venice, v. 1.
You have, by fortune and his highness' favours,
Gone *slightly* o'er low steps. *Henry 8,* ii. 4.

Slip. *A leash; a string with a noose to it; a counterfeit coin.*

I see you stand like greyhounds in the *slips,*
Straining upon the start. *Henry 5,* iii. 1.
The *slip,* sir, the *slip;* can you not conceive?
Romeo and Juliet, ii. 4.

To **Slip.** *To let loose; to pass over.*

And Cæsar's spirit, ranging for revenge,
Shall in these confines with a monarch's voice
Cry " Havoc," and let *slip* the dogs of war.
Julius Cæsar, iii. 1.
Holding Corioli in the name of Rome,
Even like a fawning greyhound in the leash,
To let him *slip* at will. *Coriolanus,* i. 6.
The time is troublesome,—
We'll *slip* you for a season; but our jealousy
Does yet depend. *Cymbeline,* iv. 3.

Slipper. *Slippery.*

A *slipper* and subtle knave; a finder of occasions.
Othello, ii. 1.

Sliver. *A branch.*

There, on the pendent boughs her coronet weeds
Clambering to hang, an envious *sliver* broke.
Hamlet, iv. 7.

To **Sliver.** *To cut; to sever.*

She that herself will *sliver* and disbranch
From her material sap, perforce must wither,
And come to deadly use. *King Lear,* iv. 2.
Gall of goat; and slips of yew
Sliver'd in the moon's eclipse. *Macbeth,* iv. 1.

Slobbery. *Moist; wet.*

If they march along
Unfought withal, but I will sell my dukedom,

To buy a *slobbery* and a dirty farm
In that nook-shotten isle of Albion. *Henry 5,* iii. 4.

Slops. *Wide breeches.*

A German from the waist downward, all *slops.*
Much Ado about Nothing, iii. 2.
What said Master Dumbleton about the satin
for my short cloak and my *slops?*
Henry 4, P. 2, i. 2.

Slovenry. *Slovenliness; want of neatness.*

There's not a piece of feather in our host,
And time hath worn us into *slovenry.*
Henry 5, iv. 3.

Slow. *Sad; heavy; serious.*

Ay, I would I were deaf; it makes me have a
slow heart. *Two Gentlemen of Verona,* iv. 2.
But, gentle Lady Anne,—
To leave this keen encounter of our wits,
And fall somewhat into a *slower* method.
Richard 3, i. 2.

To **Slow.** *To delay; to defer.*

I would I knew not why it should be *slow'd.*
Romeo and Juliet, iv. 1.

To **Slubber.** *To execute imperfectly; to smear; to sully.*

Slubber not business for my sake, Bassanio.
Merchant of Venice, ii. 7.
You must therefore be content to *slubber* the
gloss of your new fortunes with this more stubborn
and boisterous expedition. *Othello,* i. 3.

Sluttery. *Sluttishness; want of cleanliness.*

Sluttery, to such neat excellence oppos'd,
Should make desire vomit emptiness,
Not so allur'd to feed. *Cymbeline,* i. 6.

Smack. *A smattering; a relish.*

Now he hath a *smack* of all neighbouring languages.
All's well that ends well, iv. 1.

To **Smack.** *To have a taste of; to be flavoured with.*

How like you this wild counsel, mighty states?
Smacks it not something of the policy?
King John, ii. 1.
All sects, all ages *smack* of this vice; and he
To die for it! *Measure for Measure,* ii. 2.

So well thy words become thee as thy wounds;
They *smack* of honour both. *Macbeth*, i. 2.

SMALL. *Little; not much.*

I play tho torturer, by *small* and *small*
To lengthen out tho worst that must be spoken.
Richard 2, iii. 2.

Small have continual plodders ever won.
Love's Labour's lost, i. 1.

SMART. *Sharp; keen.*

Their softest touch as *smart* as lizards' stings.
Henry 6, P. 2, iii. 2.

SMATCH. *Smack; taste; relish.*

Thy life hath had some *smatch* of honour in it.
Julius Cæsar, v. 5.

SMEARED. *Stained; dishonoured; shamed.*

Triumphant death, *smear'd* with captivity,
Young Talbot's valour makes me smile at thee.
Henry 6, P. 1, iv. 7.

SMILET. *A smile.*

Those happy *smilets*
That play'd on her ripe lip seem'd not to know
What guests were in her eyes. *King Lear*, iv. 3.

To **SMIRCH.** *To stain; to soil; to sully.*

Sometime like tho shaven Hercules in the
smirched worm-eaten tapestry.
Much Ado about Nothing, iii. 3.

To **SMOKE.** *To find out; to see through.*

They begin to *smoke* me.
All's well that ends well, iv. 1.

He was first *smoked* by the old Lord Lafeu.
Ibid. iii. 6.

To **SMOOTH.** *To soothe; to fondle; to caress; to flatter.*

Ah, my poor lord, what tongue shall *smooth* thy
name,
When I, thy three-hours wife, have mangled it?
Romeo and Juliet, iii. 2.

Look to it, lords; let not his *smoothing* words
Bewitch your hearts. *Henry 6, P. 2*, i. 1.

For every grise of fortune
Is *smooth'd* by that below. *Timon of Athens*, iv. 3.

My tongue could never learn sweet *smoothing* word.
Richard 3, i. 2.

SMUG. *Trim; spruce; gay; gaudy.*

And here the *smug* and silver Trent shall run
In a new channel, fair and evenly.
Henry 4, P. 1, iii. 1.

A beggar, that was used to come so *smug* upon
the mart; let him look to his bond.
Merchant of Venice, iii. 1.

I will die bravely, like a *smug* bridegroom.
King Lear, iv. 6.

To **SMUTCH.** *To black; to stain; to smirch.*

What, hast *smutch'd* thy nose?
Winter's Tale, i. 2.

SNATCH. *Quibble; break; short fit; scrap; fragment.*

Come, sir, leave me your *snatches*, and yield me
a direct answer. *Measure for Measure*, iv. 2.

The *snatches* in his voice,
And burst of speaking, were as his.
Cymbeline, iv. 2.

Which time she chanted *snatches* of old tunes,
As one incapable of her own distress.
Hamlet, iv. 7.

To **SNATCH.** *To bite; to snap.*

And, like a dog that is compell'd to fight,
Snatch at his master that doth tarre him on.
King John, iv. 1.

SNATCHER. *A robber; a freebooter; a pilferer.*

We do not mean the coursing *snatchers* only,
But fear the main intendment of the Scot.
Henry 5, i. 2.

SNEAK-CUP. *A paltry sneaking fellow; a milk-sop.*

How! the prince is a Jack, a *sneak-cup*: 'sblood,
an he were here, I would cudgel him like a dog, if
he would say so. *Henry 4, P. 1*, iii. 3.

SNEAP. *A check; a reprimand; a rebuke; a taunt; a reproach.*

My lord, I will not undergo this *sneap* without
reply. *Henry 4, P. 2*, ii. 1.

To **SNEAP.** *To nip.*

Biron is like an envious *sneaping* frost.
Love's Labour's lost, i. 1.

SNIPE. *A fool; a simpleton.*

For I mine own gain'd knowledge should profane,
If I would time expend with such a *snipe*,
But for my sport and profit.   *Othello*, i. 3.

SNUFF. *Anger; spleen; scorn; the expiring wick of a candle.*

Who therewith angry, when it next came there,
Took it in *snuff*.   *Henry* 4, P. 1, i. 3.

You'll mar the light by taking it in *snuff*.
        Love's Labour's lost, v. 2.

What hath been seen,
Either in *snuffs* and packings of the dukes;
Or the hard rein which both of them have borne
Against the old kind king.   *King Lear*, iii. 1.

Let me not live, after my flame lacks oil,
To be the *snuff* of younger spirits.
        All's well that ends well, i. 2.

What,
To hide me from the radiant sun, and solace .
I' the dungeon by a *snuff*?   *Cymbeline*, i. 6.

SOIL. *Stain; shame; disgrace.*

For all the *soil* of the achievement goes
With me into the earth.   *Henry* 4, P. 2, iv. 4.

SOILED. *High-fed; pampered.*

The fitchew, nor the *soilèd* horse, goes to't
With a more riotous appetite.   *King Lear*, iv. 6.

SOILURE. *Pollution; stain.*

He merits well to have her, that doth seek her—
Not making any scruple of her *soilure*—
With such a hell of pain and world of charge.
        Troilus and Cressida, iv. 1.

To SOLACE. *To take delight in; to rejoice.*

But one, poor one, one poor and loving child,
But one thing to rejoice and *solace* in,
And cruel death hath catch'd it from my sight !
        Romeo and Juliet, iv. 5.

What,
To hide me from the radiant sun, and *solace*
I' the dungeon with a snuff?   *Cymbeline*, i. 6.

And were they to be rul'd, and not to rule,
This sickly land might *solace* as before.
        Richard 3, ii. 3.

SOLELY. *Altogether; wholly; entirely.*

Think him a great way fool, *solely* a coward.
        All's well that ends well, i. 1.

SOLEMN. *Set; formal; ceremonious; grave; serious.*

To-night we hold a *solemn* supper, sir,
And I'll request your presence.   *Macbeth*, iii. 1.

Look you, who comes here;
A young man and an old in *solemn* talk.
        As you like it, ii. 4.

SOLEMNESS. *Gravity; seriousness.*

Prithee, Virgilia, turn thy *solemness* out o' door,
and go along with us.   *Coriolanus*, i. 3.

SOLEMNITY. *Festivity.*

Uncomfortable time, why cam'st thou now
To murder, murder our *solemnity*?
        Romeo and Juliet, iv. 5.

What, dares the slave
Come hither, cover'd with an antic face,
To fleer and scorn at our *solemnity*?   *Ibid.* i. 5.

A fortnight hold we this *solemnity*,
In nightly revels and new jollity.
        Midsummer-Night's Dream, v. 1.

To SOLICIT. *To rouse; to excite; to stimulate.*

Solicit Henry with her wondrous praise.
        Henry 6, P. 1, v. 3.

SOLICITING. *Incitement; encouragement; solicitation.*

This supernatural *soliciting*
Cannot be ill; cannot be good.   *Macbeth*, i. 3.

This, in obedience, hath my daughter show'd me :
And more above, hath his *solicitings*,
As they fell out by time, by means, and place,
All given to mine ear.   *Hamlet*, ii. 2.

SOLICITS. *Solicitation; courtship.*

Frame yourself
To orderly *solicits*, and be friended
With aptness of the season.   *Cymbeline*, ii. 3.

SOLIDARE. *A piece of money.* The daily pay of a common soldier is called, in low Latin, *solidata*. Hence the modern word *soldier.* (Nares.)

Here's three *solidares* for thee.
        Timon of Athens, iii. 1.

SOMETHING. *Somewhat.*

For thy part, I do wish thou wert a dog,
That I might love thee *something.*
Timon of Athens, iv. 3.

Which hath *something* emboldened me to this
unseasoned intrusion. *Merry Wives of Windsor,* ii. 2.

Here, on her breast,
There is a vent of blood, and *something* blown.
Antony and Cleopatra, v. 2.

SOMETIME. *Formerly.*

I will disease me, and myself present
As I was *sometime* Milan.   *Tempest,* v. 1.

Herne the hunter,
Sometime a keeper here in Windsor Forest.
Merry Wives of Windsor, iv. 4.

SONNETIST. *A sonneteer; a writer of sonnets.*

Assist me some extemporal god of rhyme, for I
am sure I shall turn *sonnetist.*
Love's Labour's lost, i. 2.

SOON. *Quick; speedy.*

For when lenity and cruelty play for a kingdom, the gentler gamester is the *soonest* winner.
Henry 5, iii. 5.

Make your *soonest* haste. *Antony and Cleop.,* iii. 4.

SOOTH. *Sweetness; mildness; gentleness.*

O God, O God! that e'er this tongue of mine,
That laid the sentence of dread banishment
On yond proud man, should take it off again
With words of *sooth!*   *Richard* 2, iii. 3.

To SOOTHE. *To flatter.*

You *sooth'd* not, therefore hurt not.
Coriolanus, ii. 2.

Thou art perjur'd too,
And *sooth'st* up greatness.   *King John,* iii. 1.

SOOTHER. *A flatterer.*

By heaven, I cannot flatter; I defy
The tongues of *soothers.*   *Henry* 4, P. 1, iv. 1.

SOOTHING. *Flattery.*

When drums and trumpets shall
I' the field prove flatterers, let courts and cities be
Made all of false-fac'd *soothing!*   *Coriolanus,* i. 9.

To SOOTHSAY. *To predict; to prophesy.*

Go, you wild bedfellow, you cannot *soothsay.*
Antony and Cleopatra, i. 2.

SOPHISTER. *A fallacious reasoner; a sophist.*

A subtle traitor needs no *sophister.*
Henry 6, P. 2, v. 1.

SORE. *Severe; grievous; heavy; fearful.*

I must remove
Some thousands of these logs, and pile them up
Upon a *sore* injunction.   *Tempest,* iii. 1.

But this *sore* night
Hath trifled former knowings.   *Macbeth,* ii. 2.

Why such impress of shipwrights, whose *sore* task
Does not divide the Sunday from the week?
Hamlet, i. 1.

SORE. *Intensely; in a great degree.*

Well, while I live I'll fear no other thing
So *sore* as keeping safe Nerissa's ring.
Merchant of Venice, v. 1.

SORROWED. *Regretful; penitent; remorseful.*

And send forth us, to make their *sorrow'd* render.
Timon of Athens, v. 1.

SORRY. *Dismal; sad; mournful; trouble-some.*

The place of death and *sorry* execution,
Behind the ditches of the abbey here.
Comedy of Errors, v. 1.

This is a *sorry* sight.   *Macbeth,* ii. 1.

How now, my lord! why do you keep alone,
Of *sorriest* fancies your companions making?
Ibid. iii. 2.

I have a salt and *sorry* rheum offends me;
Lend me thy handkerchief.   *Othello,* iii. 4.

SORT. *Rank; dignity; a pack; a crew; manner; method; lot.*

What prisoners of good *sort* are taken, uncle?
Henry 5, iv. 8.

It may be his enemy is a gentleman of great
sort, quite from the answer of his degree.
Ibid. iv. 7.

And yet salt water blinds them not so much
But they can see a *sort* of traitors here.
Richard 2, iv. 1.

The shallowest thickskin of that barren *sort,*
Who Pyramus presented in their sport,
Forsook his scene, and enter'd in a brake.
Midsummer-Night's Dream, iii. 2.

Seldom he smiles; and smiles in such a *sort*
As if he mock'd himself, and scorn'd his spirit

That could be mov'd to smile at any thing.
Julius Cæsar, i. 2.
Unless you can be won by some other *sort* than
your father's imposition, depending on the caskets.
Merchant of Venice, i. 2.
No, make a lottery ;
And, by device, let blockish Ajax draw
The *sort* to fight with Hector.
Troilus and Cressida, i. 3.

To SORT. *To terminate ; to fall out ; to happen ; to choose ; to select ; to suit ; to fit ;
to rank ; to order ; to ordain.*

Sort how it will,. I shall have gold for all.
Henry 6, P. 2, i. 2.
Nay, then thou lov'st it not ;
And all my pains is *sorted* to no proof.
Taming of the Shrew, iv. 3.
And so far am I glad it so did *sort,*
As this their jangling I esteem a sport.
Midsummer-Night's Dream, iii. 2.
And if it *sort* not well, you may conceal her
In some reclusive and religious life,
Out of all eyes, tongues, minds, and injuries.
Much Ado about Nothing, iv. 1.
Well may it *sort,* that this portentous figure
Comes armèd through our watch. *Hamlet,* i. 1.
Let us into the city presently,
To *sort* some gentlemen well skill'd in music.
Two Gentlemen of Verona, iii. 2.
I pray thee, *sort* thy heart to patience.¹
Henry 6, P.·2, ii. 4.
I will not *sort* you with the rest of my servants;
for, to speak to you like an honest man, I am most
dreadfully attended. *Hamlet,* ii. 2.
But if God *sort* it so,
'Tis more than we deserve, or I expect.
Richard 3, ii. 3.

SORTANCE. *Fitness.*
Here doth he wish his person, with such powers
As might hold *sortance* with his quality.
Henry 4, P. 2, iv. 1.

SOT. *A fool ; a dolt ; a blockhead.*
Remember,
First to possess his books ; for without them
He's but a *sot,* as I am, nor hath not
One spirit to command. *Tempest,* iii. 2.
When I inform'd him, then he call'd me *sot,*
And told me I had turn'd the wrong side out.
King Lear, iv. 2.

Either our brags
Were crack'd of kitchen-trulls, or his description
Prov'd us unspeaking *sots.* *Cymbeline,* v. 5.

SOUL-FEARING. *Terrific ; fear-inspiring.*
Till their *soul-fearing* clamours have brawl'd down
The flinty ribs of this contemptuous city.
King John, ii. 1.

SOUND. *Soundly.*
And till he tell the truth,
Let the supposèd fairies pinch him *sound.*
Merry Wives of Windsor, iv. 4.

To SOUND. *To declare ; to make known ; to
publish.*
Pray heaven, he *sound* not my disgrace !
Henry 8, .v. 2.
Then I, as one that am the tongue of these,
To *sound* the purposes of all their hearts,
. . . . heartily request
Th' enfranchisement of Arthur. *King John,* iv. 2.

SOUNDLY. *Thoroughly ; perfectly ; entirely.*
O fair Katharine, if you will love me *soundly*
with your French heart, I will be glad to hear you
confess it brokenly with your French tongue.
Henry 5, v. 2.
Good Catesby, go, effect this business *soundly.*
Richard 3, iii. 1.

SOUR. *Morose ; peevish ; crabbed.*
This week he hath been heavy, *sour,* sad.
Comedy of Errors, v. 1.

To SOUSE. *To pounce upon ; to seize.*
And like an eagle o'er his aery towers,
To *souse* annoyance that comes near his nest.
King John, v. 2.

SOUSED. *Pickled.*
If I be not ashamed of my soldiers, I am a *soused*
gurnet. *Henry 4,* P. 1, iv. 2.

SOVEREIGNTY. *Excellence ; superiority ; pre-
eminence.*
My father left me some prescriptions
Of rare and prov'd effects, such as his reading
And manifold experience had collected,
For general *sovereignty.*
All's well that ends well, i. 3.

To SOWL. *To seize; to pull; to drag.*

He'll go, he says, and *sowl* the porter of Rome gates by the ears. *Coriolanus,* iv. 5.

SPACE. *A length of time.*

Since he went from Egypt 'tis
A *space* for further travel.
Antony and Cleopatra, ii. 1.

SPAN-COUNTER. *A game.*

Tell the king from me, that, for his father's sake,
Henry the fifth, in whose time boys went to *span-counter* for French crowns, I am content he shall reign. *Henry 6, P. 2, iv. 2.*

To SPANIEL. *To follow like a spaniel.*

The hearts
That *spaniel'd* me at heels, to whom I gave
Their wishes, do discandy, melt their sweets
On blossoming Cæsar.
Antony and Cleopatra, iv. 12.

SPARE. *Parsimony; saving; stint.*

Alas, I know not; how gets the tide in?
As much as one sound cudgel of four foot—
You see the poor remainder—could distribute,
I made no *spare,* sir. *Henry 5, v. 3.*

To SPARE. *To do without; to part with; to save.*

For life, I prize it
As I weigh grief, which I would *spare.*
Winter's Tale, iii. 2.

Poor Jack, farewell!
I could have better *spar'd* a better man.
Henry 4, P. 1, v. 4.

Come, come, my lord, you'd *spare* your spoons.
Henry 8, v. 2.

SPECIALTY. *Peculiarity; principle; terms; stipulations; particulars.*

The *specialty* of rule hath been neglected.
Troilus and Cressida, i. 3.

Let *specialties* be therefore drawn between us,
That covenants may be kept on either hand.
Taming of the Shrew, ii. 1.

So please your grace, the packet is not come,
Where that and other *specialties* are bound.
Love's Labour's lost, ii. 1.

SPECTATORSHIP. *Representation; exhibition.*

Guess if thou standest not i' the state of hanging, or of some death more long in *spectatorship* and crueller in suffering. *Coriolanus,* v. 2.

SPECULATION. *Observation; an observer; a spy; sight; the sense of seeing.*

Though we upon this mountain's basis by
Took stand for idle *speculation.* *Henry 5,* iv. 2.
Servants, who seem no less,
Which are to France the spies and *speculations*
Intelligent of our state. *King Lear,* iii. 1.
Thou hast no *speculation* in those eyes
Which thou dost glare with. *Macbeth,* iii. 4.

SPECULATIVE. *Visual.*

When light-wing'd toys
Of feather'd Cupid seel with wanton dullness
My *speculative* and offic'd instruments. *Othello,* i. 3.

SPED. *Undone; ruined; dispatched; killed.*

A plague o' both your houses! I am *sped.*
Romeo and Juliet, iii. 1.
We three are married, but you two are *sped.*
Taming of the Shrew, v. 2.

SPEED. *The event of any incident or undertaking.*

The prince your son, with mere conceit and fear
Of the queen's *speed,* is gone. *Winter's Tale,* iii. 2.
Well mayst thou woo, and happy be thy *speed!*
Taming of the Shrew, ii. 1.

To SPEED. *To prosper; to have good success.*

Lucentio shall make one,
Though Paris came in hope to *speed* alone.
Taming of the Shrew, i. 2.

SPEEDING. *Success, whether good or ill.*

Is this your *speeding?* nay, then, good night our pact! *Taming of the Shrew,* ii. 1.

To SPELL. *To interpret; to explain; to construe; to read.*

O, she knew well
Thy love did read by rote, and could not *spell.*
Romeo and Juliet, ii. 3.
I never yet saw man,
How wise, how noble, young, how rarely featur'd,
But she would *spell* him backward.
Much Ado about Nothing, iii. 1.

SPELLING. *Secret; occult; magical.*
Unchain your spirits now with *spelling* charms,
And try if they can gain your liberty.
Henry 6, P. 1, v. 3.

To SPERR. *To shut; to close; to bar.*
With massy staples,
And corresponsive and fulfilling bolts,
Sperr up the sons of Troy.
Troilus and Cressida, Prologue.

SPHERE. *Orbit; socket.*
Make thy two eyes, like stars, start from their
spheres.   *Hamlet*, i. 5.

To SPHERE. *To round; to make round.*
Blow, villain, till thy *spherèd* bias cheek
Outswell the colic of puff'd Aquilon.
Troilus and Cressida, iv. 5.

SPILTH. *Waste; effusion.*
When our vaults have wept
With drunken *spilth* of wine; when every room
Hath blaz'd with lights, and bray'd with minstrelsy.
Timon of Athens, ii. 2.

SPIRIT. *Anticipation; presentiment.*
You are too great to be by me gainsaid :
Your *spirit* is too true, your fears too certain.
Henry 4, P. 2, i. 1.

SPIRITUALTY. *The clergy; the ecclesiastical body.*
In aid whereof we of the *spiritualty*
Will raise your highness such a mighty sum
As never did the clergy at one time
Bring in to any of your ancestors. *Henry* 5, i. 2.

To SPIT. *To pierce.*
Methinks I see my cousin's ghost
Seeking out Romeo, that did *spit* his body
Upon a rapier's point :—stay, Tybalt, stay !
Romeo and Juliet, iv. 3.

SPITAL-HOUSE. *Hospital.*
She, whom the *spital-house* and ulcerous sores
Would cast the gorge at, this embalms and spices
To th' April day again. *Timon of Athens*, iv. 3.

SPITE. *Torment; vexation.*
This is the deadly *spite* that angers me,—

My wife can speak no English, I no Welsh.
Henry 4, P. 1, iii. 1.
He meant he did me none; the more my *spite.*
Comedy of Errors, iv. 2.

To SPITE. *To vex; to torment.*
But that which *spites* me more than all these wants,
He does it under name of perfect love.
Taming of the Shrew, iv. 3.

SPLEEN. *Mirth; merriment; caprice; humour; haste.*
Or give me ribs of steel ! I shall split all
In pleasure of my *spleen.*   •
Troilus and Cressida, i. 3.
That in this *spleen* ridiculous appears,
To check their folly, passion's solemn tears.
Love's Labour's lost, v. 2.
A hare-brain'd Hotspur, govern'd by a *spleen.*
Henry 4, P. 1, v. 2.
A mad-brain rudesby, full of *spleen.*
Taming of the Shrew, iii. 2.
For, at this match,
With swifter *spleen* than powder can enforce,
The mouth of passage shall we fling wide ope,
And give you entrance.   *King John*, ii. 1.
Brief as the lightning in the collied night,
That, in a *spleen*, unfolds both heaven and earth,
And ere a man hath power to say, " Behold !"
The jaws of darkness do devour it up.
Midsummer-Night's Dream, i. 1.

SPLEENFUL. *Angry; furious.*
Myself have calm'd their *spleenful* mutiny.
Henry 6, P. 2, iii. 2.

SPLEENY. *Peevish; fretful.*
What though I know her virtuous
And well deserving? yet I know her for
A *spleeny* Lutheran.   *Henry* 8, iii. 2.

SPLENITIVE. *Hot; fiery; passionate.*
For, though I am not *splenitive* and rash,
Yet I have something in me dangerous,
Which let thy wiseness fear.   *Hamlet*, v. 1.

To SPLINTER. *To splint; to unite with splints.*
The broken rancour of your high-swoln hearts,
But lately *splinter'd*, knit, and join'd together,
Must gently be preserv'd, cherish'd, and kept.
Richard 3, ii. 2.

This broken joint between you and her husband entreat her to *splinter*. *Othello*, ii. 3.

SPOIL. *Waste ; havoc ; destruction ; spoliation.*

The man that hath no music in himself,
Nor is not mov'd with concord of sweet sounds,
Is fit for treasons, stratagems, and *spoils*.
Merchant of Venice, v. 1.

Nay, then indeed she cannot choose but hate thee,
Having bought love with such a bloody *spoil*.
Richard 3, iv. 4.

My comfort is, that old age, that ill layer-up of beauty, can do no more *spoil* upon my face.
Henry 5, v. 2.

Company, villanous company, hath been the *spoil* of me. *Henry 4*, P. 1, iii. 3.

To SPOIL. *To be undone; to hurt; to wound.*

O, we are *spoiled!* and yonder he is.
Taming of the Shrew, v. 1.

This is some priory : in, or we are *spoil'd*.
Comedy of Errors, v. 1.

O, I am *spoil'd*, undone by villains! *Othello*, v. 1.

SPONGY. *Drenched; stupefied with drink.*

What not put upon
His *spongy* officers, who shall bear the guilt
Of our great quell? *Macbeth*, i. 7.

SPOT. *Crime; shame; reproach; scandal; stain; mark; blot; a raised sprig or other figure in needle-work.*

Wert thou a leopard, thou wert german to the lion, and the *spots* of thy kindred were jurors on thy life. *Timon of Athens*, iv. 3.

Follow his chariot, like the greatest *spot*
Of all thy sex. *Antony and Cleopatra*, iv. 12.

And the like tender of our love we make,
To rest without a *spot* for evermore.
King John, v. 7.

Out, damnèd *spot!* out, I say! *Macbeth*, v. 1.

He shall not live ; look, with a *spot* I damn him.
Julius Cæsar, iv. 1.

What are you sewing here? A fine *spot*, in good faith. *Coriolanus*, i. 3.

SPOTTED. *Marked; figured; embroidered.*

Have you not sometimes seen a handkerchief
Spotted with strawberries in your wife's hand?
Othello, iii. 3.

SPRAG. *Retentive ; vigorous ; sprightly.*

He is a good *sprag* memory.
Merry Wives of Windsor, iv. 1.

SPRITED. *Haunted ; plagued ; tormented ; harassed.*

I am *sprited* with a fool ;
Frighted, and anger'd worse. *Cymbeline*, ii. 3.

SPRITEFUL. *Spritely; spirited.*

Spoke like a *spriteful* noble gentleman.
King John, iv. 2.

SPRITELY. *Spirited ; courageous ; spiritual ; ghostly.*

Hector's opinion
Is this in way of truth : yet, ne'ertheless,
My *spritely* brethren, I propend to you
In resolution to keep Helen still.
Troilus and Cressida, ii. 2.

As I slept, methought
Great Jupiter, upon his eagle back'd,
Appear'd to me, with other *spritely* shows
Of mine own kindred. *Cymbeline*, v. 5.

SPRITES. *Spirits.*

Come, sisters, cheer we up his *sprites*,
And show the best of our delights. *Macbeth*, iv. 1.

SPRITING. *Spiriting ; ministering ; service.*

I will be correspondent to command,
And do my *spriting* gently. *Tempest*, i. 2.

SPUR. *A root.*

And by the *spurs* pluck'd up the pine and cedar.
Tempest, v. 1.

Grief and patience, rooted in him both,
Mingle their *spurs* together. *Cymbeline*, iv. 2.

SPURN. *Insult.*

Who dies, that bears not one *spurn* to their graves
Of their friends' gift? *Timon of Athens*, i. 2.

The insolence of office, and the *spurns*
That patient merit of th' unworthy takes.
Hamlet, iii. 1.

SQUANDERING. *Random ; uncertain.*

The wise man's folly is anatomiz'd
Even by the *squandering* glances of the fool.
As you like it, ii. 7.

SQUARE. *Extent; range; compass.*

Only she comes too short,—that I profess
Myself an enemy to all other joys,
Which the most precious *square* of sense possesses;
And find I am alone felicitate
In your dear highness' love. *King Lear*, i. 1.

SQUARE (adj.). *Fair; just; equitable.*

She's a most triumphant lady, if report be *square*
to her. *Antony and Cleopatra*, ii. 2.

All have not offended ;
For those that were, it is not *square* to take,
On those that are, revenges. *Timon of Athens*, v. 4.

To SQUARE. *To quarrel; to shape; to regulate.*

They never meet in grove or green,
By fountain clear, or spangled starlight sheen,
But they do *square*.
Midsummer-Night's Dream, ii. 1.

Were't not that we stand up against them all,
'Twere pregnant they should *square* between themselves. *Antony and Cleopatra*, ii. 1.

Dreams are toys ;
Yet, for this once, yea, superstitiously,
I will be *squar'd* by this. *Winter's Tale*, iii. 3.

SQUARER. *A quarreller ; a brawler.*

Is there no young *squarer* now that will make
a voyage with him to the devil ?
Much Ado about Nothing, i. 1.

To SQUINY. *To look obliquely ; to squint.*

I remember thine eyes well enough. Dost thou
squiny at me ? *King Lear*, iv. 6.

SQUIRE. *A pander ; a rascal ; rule ; measure.*

Some such *squire* he was
That turn'd your wit the seamy side without,
And made you to suspect me with the Moor.
Othello, iv. 2.

If I travel but four foot by the *squire* further, I
shall break my wind. *Henry 4*, P. 1, ii. 2.

Do not you know my lady's foot by the *squire* ?
Love's Labour's lost, v. 2.

And not the worst of the three but jumps twelve
foot and a half by the *squire*. *Winter's Tale*, iv. 3.

STABLISHMENT. *Establishment; inheritance; kingdom.*

Unto her
He gave the *stablishment* of Egypt ; made her

Of lower Syria, Cyprus, Lydia,
Absolute queen. *Antony and Cleopatra*, iii. 6.

STAFF. *A lance.*

Their armèd *staves* in charge, their beavers down.
Henry 4, P. 2, iv. 1.

To STAGE. *To represent on the stage ; to exhibit in public.*

The quick comedians
Extemporally will *stage* us, and present
Our Alexandrian revels.
Antony and Cleopatra, v. 2.

But do not like to *stage* me to their eyes.
Measure for Measure, i. 1.

Yes, like enough, high-battled Cæsar will
Unstate his happiness, and be *stag'd* to the show,
Against a sworder ! *Antony and Cleopatra*, iii. 13.

To STAGGER. *To hesitate; to be in doubt; to assail with violence ; to assault.*

Whether the tyranny be in his place,
Or in his eminence that fills it up,
I *stagger* in. *Measure for Measure*, i. 2.

A man may, if he were of a fearful heart, *stagger*
in this attempt. *As you like it*, iii. 3.

That hand shall burn in never-quenching fire
That *staggers* thus my person. *Richard 2*, v. 5.

STAGGERS. *Wildness ; violence ; perturbation ; vehement emotion.*

Or I will throw thee from my care for ever,
Into the *staggers*, and the cureless lapse
Of youth and ignorance.
All's well that ends well, ii. 3.

How come these *staggers* on me ? *Cymbeline*, v. 5.

STALE. *A decoy ; a bait ; a stalking-horse ; a pretence ; a wanton ; a drab.*

The trumpery in my house, go bring it hither,
For *stale* to catch these thieves. *Tempest*, iv. 1.

Poor I am but his *stale*. *Comedy of Errors*, ii. 1.

I stand dishonour'd, that have gone about
To link my dear friend to a common *stale*.
Much Ado about Nothing, iv. 1.

To STALE. *To wear out; to make common.*

Age cannot wither her, nor custom *stale*
Her infinite variety. *Antony and Cleopatra*, ii. 2.

I shall tell you
A pretty tale : it may be you have heard it ;

But, since it serves my purpose, I will venture
To *stale* 't a little more. *Coriolanus*, i. 1.

Were I a common laugher, or did use
To *stale* with ordinary oaths my love
To every new protester. *Julius Cæsar*, i. 2.

Which, out of use and *stal'd* by other men,
Begin his fashion. *Ibid.* iv. 1.

To STALL. *To install; to invest; to dwell; to
live.*

And see another, as I see thee now,
Deck'd in thy rights, as thou art *stall'd* in mine.
Richard 3, i. 3.

We could not *stall* together
In the whole world. *Antony and Cleopatra*, v. 1.

STAMP. *A coin.*

Hanging a golden *stamp* about their necks,
Put on with holy prayers. *Macbeth*, iv. 3.

STANCH. *United; firm.*

Yet, if I knew
What hoop should hold us *stanch*, from edge to
edge
O' the world I would pursue it.
Antony and Cleopatra, ii. 2.

STANCHLESS. *Insatiable.*

With this, there grows,
In my most ill-compos'd affection, such
A *stanchless* avarice, that, were I king,
I should cut off the nobles for their lands.
Macbeth, iv. 3.

To STAND FOR. *To protect; to fight for; to
defend.*

Thrusts forth his horns again into the world;
Which were inshell'd when Marcius *stood for* Rome.
Coriolanus, iv. 6.

Pisanio, thou that *stand'st so for* Posthumus!
Cymbeline, iii. 5.

It remains,
As the main point of this our after-meeting,
To gratify his noble service that
Hath thus *stood for* his country. *Coriolanus*, ii. 2.

To STAND UPON. *To concern; to affect; to
touch nearly; to depend upon.*

It *stands* your grace *upon* to do him right.
Richard 2, ii. 3.

You wrong me more, sir, in denying it:
Consider how it *stands upon* my credit.
Comedy of Errors, iv. 1.

Does it not, thinks't thee, *stand me now upon,*—
. . . . . . Is't not perfect conscience
To quit him with this arm? *Hamlet*, v. 2.
For my state
Stands on me to defend, not to debate.
King Lear, v. 1.

O, let us hence; I *stand on* sudden haste.
Romeo and Juliet, ii. 3.

STANDING. *Continuance; duration.*

As, or by oath remove, or counsel shake
The fabric of his folly, whose foundation
Is pil'd upon his faith, and will continue
The *standing* of his body. *Winter's Tale*, i. 2.

STANIEL. *A kind of hawk.*

And with what wing the *staniel* checks at it!
Twelfth-Night, ii. 5.

STAR. *The Polestar.*

Well, an you be not turned Turk, there's no
more sailing by the *star.*
Much Ado about Nothing, iii. 4.

To STARE. *To stand on end.*

Art thou some god, some angel, or some devil,
That mak'st my blood cold, and my hair to *stare*?
Julius Cæsar, iv. 3.

STARK. *Straight; unbending.*

Many a nobleman lies *stark* and stiff
Under the hoofs of vaunting enemies.
Henry 4, P. 1, v. 3.

STARKLY. *Stiffly.*

As fast lock'd up in sleep as guiltless labour
When it lies *starkly* in the traveller's bones.
Measure for Measure, iv. 2.

START. *A snatch; a hasty fit.*

In little room confining mighty men,
Mangling by *starts* the full course of their glory.
Henry 5, v. Chorus.

That, as methought, her eyes had lost her tongue,
For she did speak in *starts* distractedly.
Twelfth-Night, ii. 2.

To START. *To startle; to disturb; to call up;
to raise.*

Direness, familiar to my slaughterous thoughts,
Cannot once *start* me. *Macbeth*, v. 5.

Being full of supper and distempering draughts,
Upon malicious bravery, dost thou come
To *start* my quiet.　　　　　　*Othello*, i. 1.

Weigh them, it is as heavy; conjure with 'em,
Brutus will *start* a spirit as soon as Cæsar.
　　　　　　　　　　　　Julius Cæsar, i. 2.

STARTING-HOLE. *Hiding-place.*
　　What trick, what device, what *starting-hole*,
canst thou now find out to hide thee from this
open and apparent shame?　*Henry* 4, P. 1, ii. 4.

START-UP. *An upstart; one newly come into
notice.*
　　That young *start-up* hath all the glory of my
overthrow.　　　*Much Ado about Nothing*, i. 3.

To STARVE. *To perish ; to come to nothing.*
　　We will have these things set down by lawful
counsel, and straight away for Britain, lest the bargain should catch cold and *starve. Cymbeline*, i. 4.

STATE. *Congress ; assembly ; nobility; a
noble; a seat of dignity; mode of standing.*
Now doth it turn, and ebb back to the sea,
Where it shall mingle with the *state* of floods,
And flow henceforth in formal majesty.
　　　　　　　　　　Henry 4, P. 2, v. 2.

Our coronation done, we will accite,
As I before remember'd, all our *state.*　*Ibid.* v. 2.

　　　　Kings, queens, and *states,*
Maids, matrons, nay, the secrets of the grave
This viperous slander enters.　*Cymbeline*, iii. 4.

　　This chair shall be my *state*, this dagger my
sceptre, and this cushion my crown.
　　　　　　　　　　Henry 4, P. 1, ii. 4.

He sits in his *state*, as a thing made for Alexander.
　　　　　　　　　　　　Coriolanus, v. 4.

Our hostess keeps her *state ;* but, in best time,
We will require her welcome.　*Macbeth*, iii. 4.

And in this *state* she gallops night by night
Through lovers' brains, and then they dream of love.
　　　　　　　　　Romeo and Juliet, i. 4.

　　When shall you hear that I
Will praise a hand, a foot, a face, an eye,
A gait, a *state*, a brow, a breast, a waist?
　　　　　　　Love's Labour's lost, iv. 3.

STATION. *Mode of standing.*
　A *station* like the herald Mercury
New-lighted on a heaven-kissing hill. *Hamlet*, iii. 4.

　　　　She creeps,—
Her motion and her *station* are as one.
　　　　　　Antony and Cleopatra, iii. 3.

STATIST. *A statesman ; a politician.*
　　I once did hold it, as our *statists* do,
A baseness to write fair, and labour'd much
How to forget that learning.　　*Hamlet*, v. 2.
　　　　　　I do believe,—
Statist though I am none, nor like to be,—
That this will prove a war.　*Cymbeline*, ii. 4.

STATUA. *A statue.*
　She dreamt to-night she saw my *statua,*
Which, like a fountain with a hundred spouts,
Did run pure blood.　　*Julius Cæsar*, ii. 2.
And, in his mantle muffling up his face,
Even at the base of Pompey's *statua,*
Which all the while ran blood, great Cæsar fell.
　　　　　　　　　　Ibid. iii. 2.

　　　　Erect his *statua*, and worship it,
And make my image but an alehouse sign.
　　　　　　　　　　Henry 6, P. 2, iii. 2.

But, like dumb *statuas* or breathing stones,
Star'd each on other, and look'd deadly pale.
　　　　　　　　　　Richard 3, iii. 7.

STATUE. *A portrait ; a picture.*
　And, were there sense in his idolatry,
My substance should be *statue* in thy stead.
　　　　　　Two Gentlemen of Verona, iv. 2.

STATUTE. *A mortgage.*
　This fellow might be in's time a great buyer of
land, with his *statutes*, his recognizances, his fines,
his double vouchers, his recoveries.　*Hamlet*, v. 1.

STATUTE-CAPS. *Woollen caps, the wearing of
which was enforced by Act of Parliament
in 1571.*
　Well, better wits have worn plain *statute-caps.*
　　　　　　　　　Love's Labour's lost, v. 2.

STAY. *A stop; an impediment ; an obstruc-
tion ; an obstacle.*
　　　　　Here's a *stay,*
That shakes the rotten carcass of old Death
Out of his rags !　　　　*King John*, ii. 1.

To STAY UPON. *To wait upon.*
　　　　Worthy Macbeth,
We *stay upon* your leisure.　*Macbeth*, i. 3.

I have a servant comes with me along,
That *stays upon* me.   *Measure for Measure*, iv. 1.
He *stays upon* your will.
                              Antony and Cleopatra, i. 2.

STEAD.   *Use; help; advantage.*
Fly, to revenge my death when I am dead :
The help of one stands me in little *stead.*
                              Henry 6, P. 1, iv. 6.

TO STEAD.   *To help; to assist; to advantage.*
I bear no hatred, blessèd man; for, lo,
My intercession likewise *steads* my foe.
                              Romeo and Juliet, ii. 3.
                  With
Rich garments, linens, stuffs, and necessaries,
Which since have *steaded* much.   *Tempest*, i. 2.
                  It nothing *steads* us
To chide him from our eaves ; for he persists,
As if his life lay on't.
                              All's well that ends well, iii. 7.
May you *stead* me ? will you pleasure me ? shall
I know your answer ?   *Merchant of Venice*, i. 3.

TO STEAD UP.   *To keep; to fulfil; to make good.*
We shall advise this wronged maid to *stead up*
your appointment, go in your place.
                              Measure for Measure, iii. 1.

TO STEAL.   *To assume; to put on; to adopt.*
Ah, that deceit should *steal* such gentle shape,
And with a virtuous visor hide deep vice !
                              Richard 3, ii. 2.

STEALTH.   *Theft; robbery; stealing.*
I know my lord hath spent of Timon's wealth,
And now ingratitude makes it worse than *stealth.*
                              Timon of Athens, iii. 4.

STEELY.   *Firm; unyielding; uncomplying; made of steel.*
Yet these fix'd evils sit so fit in him,
That they take place, when virtue's *steely* bones
Look bleak i' the cold wind.
                              All's well that ends well, i. 1.
Thy brother's blood the thirsty earth hath drunk,
Broach'd with the *steely* point of Clifford's lance.
                              Henry 6, P. 3, ii. 3.

STELLED.   *Fixed.*
The sea, with such a storm as his bare head

In hell-black night endur'd, would have buoy'd up,
And quench'd the *stellèd* fires.   *King Lear*, iii. 7.

STERNAGE.   *Steerage; the stern.*
Grapple your minds to *sternage* of this navy.
                              Henry 5, iii. Chorus.

STICKLER.   *An arbitrator; an umpire; a judge.*
The dragon wing of night o'erspreads the earth,
And, *stickler*-like, the armies separates.
                              Troilus and Cressida, v. 8.

STIFF.   *Hard; unpleasant.*
                  Labienus—
This is *stiff* news—hath, with his Parthian force,
Extended Asia from Euphrates.
                              Antony and Cleopatra, i. 2.

STIGMATIC.   *A deformed person.*
Foul *stigmatic*, that's more than thou canst tell.
                              Henry 6, P. 2, v. 1.
But like a foul mis-shapen *stigmatic*,
Mark'd by the destinies to be avoided.
                              Henry 6, P. 3, ii. 2.

STIGMATICAL.   *Branded with shame or deformity.*
Stigmatical in making, worse in mind.
                              Comedy of Errors, iv. 2.

STILL.   *Continual; unceasing.*
But that *still* use of grief makes wild grief tame,
My tongue should to thy ears not name my boys
Till that my nails were anchor'd in thine eyes.
                              Richard 3, iv. 4.

STILL.   *Ever; always.*
And nothing is at a like goodness *still.*
                              Hamlet, iv. 7.

STILL AN END.   *Continually.*
A slave, that *still an end* turns me to shame.
                              Two Gentlemen of Verona, iv. 2.

STILLY.   *Softly.*
From camp to camp, through the foul womb of night,
The hum of either army *stilly* sounds.
                              Henry 5, iv. Chorus.

To STINT.   *To check; to restrain; to cease; to stop.*

Make war breed peace; make peace *stint* war.
Timon of Athens, v. 4.

We must not *stint*
Our necessary actions, in the fear
To cope malicious censurers.   *Henry* 8, i. 2.

Wilt thou not, Jule? it *stinted*, and said "Ay."—
And *stint* thou too, I pray thee, nurse, say I.
Romeo and Juliet, i. 3.

STITCHERY.   *Needlework.*

Come, lay aside your *stitchery*.   *Coriolanus*, i. 3.

STITHY.   *A smithy.*

And my imaginations are as foul
As Vulcan's *stithy*.   *Hamlet*, iii. 2.

To STITHY.   *To shape on the anvil; to forge; to fabricate.*

But by the forge that *stithied* Mars his helm,
I'll kill thee everywhere.
Troilus and Cressida, iv. 5.

STOCK.   *A stocking; a thrust.*

Ay, 'tis strong, and it does indifferent well in a
flame-coloured *stock*.   *Twelfth-Night*, i. 3.

What need a man care for a stock with a wench,
when she can knit him a *stock*?
Two Gentlemen of Verona, iii. 1.

With a linen *stock* on one leg, and a kersey
boot-hose on the other. *Taming of the Shrew*, iii. 2.

To see thee pass thy punto, thy *stock*, thy reverse,
thy distance, thy montant.
Merry Wives of Windsor, ii. 3.

To STOCK.   *To put in the stocks.*

You shall do small respect, show too bold malice
Against the grace and person of my master,
Stocking his messenger.   *King Lear*, ii. 2.

STOCK-FISH.   *A dried cod.*

I'll turn my mercy out o' doors, and make a
stock-fish of thee.   *Tempest*, iii. 2.

STOMACH.   *Resolution; firmness; resentment; anger; pride; haughtiness.*

Which rais'd in me
An undergoing *stomach*, to bear up
Against what should ensue.   *Tempest*, i. 2.

I would it were,
That you might kill your *stomach* on your meat,
And not upon your maid.
Two Gentlemen of Verona, i. 2.

He was a man
Of an unbounded *stomach*, ever ranking
Himself with princes.   *Henry* 8, iv. 2.

To STOMACH.   *To resent.*

O my good lord,
Believe not all; or, if you must believe,
Stomach not all.   *Antony and Cleopatra*, iii. 4.

STOMACHING.   *Resentment; anger.*

'Tis not a time for private *stomaching*.
Antony and Cleopatra, ii. 2.

To STONE.   *To harden.*

O perjur'd woman! thou dost *stone* my heart,
And mak'st me call what I intend to do
A murder, which I thought a sacrifice.
Othello, v. 2.

STONE-BOW.   *A cross-bow for shooting stones.*

O, for a *stone-bow*, to hit him in the eye!
Twelfth-Night, ii. 5.

STOOP.   *A drinking vessel; a flagon.*

Set me the *stoops* of wine upon that table.
Hamlet, v. 2.

A *stoop* of wine, Maria!   ,   *Twelfth-Night*, ii. 3.

Go, fetch me a *stoop* of liquor.   *Hamlet*, v. 1.

To STOOP.   *To pounce upon; to seize.*

And though his affections are higher mounted
than ours, yet, when they *stoop*, they *stoop* with
the like wing.   *Henry* 5, iv. 1.

STORE.   *Stuff; material.*

And here's another, whose warp'd looks proclaim
What *store* her heart is made on. *King Lear*, iii. 6.

To STORY.   *To describe; to unfold.*

How worthy he is I will leave to appear hereafter, rather than *story* him in his own hearing.
Cymbeline, i. 4.

STOUT.   *Proud; resolute; unbending; firm.*

For grief is proud, and makes his owner *stout*.
King John, iii. 1.

I will be strange, *stout*, in yellow stockings, and
cross-gartered, even with the swiftness of putting on.
Twelfth-Night, ii. 5.

STOUTNESS.   *Stubbornness ; obstinacy ; inflexibility.*

Come all to ruin : let
Thy mother rather feel thy pride than fear
Thy dangerous *stoutness.*   *Coriolanus,* iii. 2.

STOVER.   *Fodder ; food for cattle.*

And flat meads thatch'd with *stover,* them to keep.
Tempest, iv. 1.

STRAIGHT (adv.).   *Straightway ; immediately.*

I tell thee she is; and therefore make her grave
straight.   *Hamlet,* v. 1.
And if the devil come and roar for them,
I will not send them :—I will after *straight,*
And tell him so.   *Henry 4,* P. 1, i. 3.

STRAIN.   *Defect ; taint ; weakness ; race ;
disposition ; doubt ; quality.*

For, sure, unless he know some *strain* in me,
that I know not myself, he would never have
boarded me in this fury.
Merry Wives of Windsor, ii. 1.

Can it be
That so degenerate a *strain* as this
Should once set footing in your generous bosoms ?
Troilus and Cressida, ii. 2.

The *strain* of man's bred out
Into baboon and monkey.   *Timon of Athens,* i. 1.
And he is bred out of that bloody *strain*
That haunted us in our familiar paths.
Henry 5, ii. 4.
Sir, you have show'd to-day your valiant *strain,*
And fortune led you well.   *King Lear,* v. 3.

And, in the publication, make no *strain,*
But that Achilles will find Hector's purpose
Pointing on him.   *Troilus and Cressida,* i. 3.

Speak to me, son :
Thou hast affected the fine *strains* of honour,
To imitate the graces of the gods. *Coriolanus,* v. 3.

TO STRAIN.   *To wry ; to swerve ; to slip ; to
blench ; to embrace ; to hug.*

Since he came,
With what encounter so uncurrent I
Have *strain'd,* to appear thus. *Winter's Tale,* iii. 2.

Our king has all the Indies in his arms,
And more and richer, when he *strains* that lady.
Henry 8, iv. 1.

STRAIT.   *Narrow-minded ; avaricious ; mean ;
strict ; rigorous.*

His means most short, his creditors most *strait.*
Timon of Athens, i. 1.
I do not ask you much,
I beg cold comfort ; and you are so *strait,*
And so ingrateful, you deny me that.
King John, v. 7.
Proceed no *straiter* 'gainst our uncle Gloster
Than from true evidence, of good esteem,
He be approv'd in practice culpable.
Henry 6, P. 2, iii. 2.

TO STRAIT.   *To puzzle ; to pose ; to be at a
loss.*

If your lass
Interpretation should abuse, and call this
Your lack of love or bounty, you were *straited*
For a reply.   *Winter's Tale,* iv. 3.

STRANGE.   *Unwelcome; coy; reserved; new;
ignorant ; unacquainted.*

She makes it *strange,* but she would be best pleas'd
To be so anger'd with another letter.
Two Gentlemen of Verona, i. 2.
But trust me, gentleman, I'll prove more true
Than those that have more cunning to be *strange.*
Romeo and Juliet, ii. 2.

You make me *strange*
Even to the disposition that I owe,
When now I think you can behold such sights
And keep the natural ruby of your cheeks,
When mine are blanch'd with fear. *Macbeth,* iii. 4.

Beseech you, sir, desire
My man's abode where I did leave him : he
Is *strange* and peevish.   *Cymbeline,* i. 6.

STRANGELY.   *As a stranger, an alien.*

As by strange fortune
It came to us, I do in practice charge thee,
That thou commend it *strangely* to some place,
Where chance may nurse or end it.
Winter's Tale, ii. 3.

STRANGENESS.   *Uncouthness ; oddness ; singularity.*

And worthier than himself
Here tend the savage *strangeness* he puts on.
Troilus and Cressida, ii. 3.

STRANGERED. *Estranged ; alienated.*

Will you, with those infirmities she owes,
Unfriended, now-adopted to our hate,
Dower'd with our curse, and *stranger'd* with our
oath,
Take her, or leave her? *King Lear,* i. 1.

TO STRANGLE. *To disown ; to renounce ; to
extinguish.*

Alas, it is the baseness of thy fear
That makes thee *strangle* thy propriety.
Twelfth-Night, v. 1.
By the clock, 'tis day,
And yet dark night *strangles* the travelling lamp.
Macbeth, ii. 2.

STRAPPADO. *A species of torture formerly
practised.*

No; were I at the *strappado,* or all the racks in
the world, I would not tell you on compulsion.
Henry 4, P. 1, ii. 4.

STRATAGEM. *Calamity ; mischance ; direful
event ; distress ; extremity.*

What news, Lord Bardolph? every minute now
Should be the father of some *stratagem.*
Henry 4, P. 2, i. 1.
What *stratagems,* how fell, how butcherly,
Erroneous, mutinous, and unnatural,
This deadly quarrel daily doth beget!
Henry 6, P. 3, ii. 5.
Alack, alack, that heaven should practise *stratagems*
Upon so soft a subject as myself!
Romeo and Juliet, iii. 5.

STRAWY. *Strawlike.*

And there the *strawy* Greeks, ripe for his edge,
Fall down before him like the mower's swath.
Troilus and Cressida, v. 5.

STRAT. *Dereliction ; deviation ; a straggler.*

I would not from your love make such a *stray,*
To match you where I hate. *King Lear,* i. 1.
Strike up our drums, pursue the scatter'd *stray.*
Henry 4, P. 2, iv. 2.

TO STRAY. *To mislead ; to cause to stray.*

Hath not else his eye
Stray'd his affection in unlawful love?
Comedy of Errors, v. 1.

STREWMENT. *Anything scattered loosely.*

Her maiden *strewments,* and the bringing home
Of bell and burial. *Hamlet,* v. 1.

STRICKEN, STRUCKEN. *Struck.*

The clock hath *stricken* three. *Julius Cæsar,* ii. 1.
Why, let the *strucken* deer go weep,
The hart ungallèd play ;
For some must watch, while some must sleep :
So runs the world away. *Hamlet,* iii. 2.

STRICTURE. *Strictness ; austerity.*

A man of *stricture* and firm abstinence.
Measure for Measure, i. 3.

TO STRIDE. *To overpass ; to cross.*

A prison for a debtor, that not dares
To *stride* a limit. *Cymbeline,* iii. 3.

STRIFE. *Endeavour.*

Which we will pay,
With *strife* to please you, day exceeding day.
All's well that ends well, v. 3.

STROSSERS. *Tight drawers or breeches.*

And you rode, like a kern of Ireland, your
French hose off, and in your strait *strossers.*
Henry 5, iii. 6.

TO STROW. *To strew.*

You were as flowers, now wither'd : even so
These herb'lets shall, which we upon you *strow.*
Cymbeline, iv. 2.

TO STROY. *To destroy.*

See,
How I convey my shame out of thine eyes
By looking back what I have left behind
Stroy'd in dishonour. *Antony and Cleopatra,* iii. 11.

STRUCK. *Stricken ; advanced.*

And his noble queen
Well *struck* in years, fair, and not jealous.
Richard 3, i. 1.

STUCK. *A thrust.*

Whereon but sipping,
If he by chance escape your venom'd *stuck,*
Our purpose may hold there. *Hamlet,* iv. 7.
I had a pass with him, rapier, scabbard, and all,
and he gives me the *stuck* in with such a mortal
motion, that it is inevitable. *Twelfth-Night,* iii. 5.

STUDIED. *Experienced; practised.*

Like one well *studied* in a sad ostent
To please his grandam.   *Merchant of Venice,* ii. 2.
  He died
As one that had been *studied* in his death.
  Macbeth, i. 4.

STUFF. *Goods; baggage; necessaries.*

Therefore away, to get our *stuff* aboard.
  Comedy of Errors, iv. 4.

STYLE. *Title; appellation.*

Ford's a knave, and I will aggravate his *style.*
  Merry Wives of Windsor, ii. 2.

SUB-CONTRACTED. *Engaged; plighted; under a contract.*

'Tis she is *sub-contracted* to this lord,
And I, her husband, contradict your bans.
  King Lear, v. 3.

SUBDUEMENT. *Conquest.*

And I have seen thee,
As hot as Perseus, spur thy Phrygian steed,
Despising many forfeits and *subduements.*
  Troilus and Cressida, iv. 5.

SUBJECT. *An inferior; a subordinate.*

Sir, by your patience,
I hold you but a *subject* of this war,
Not as a brother.   *King Lear,* v. 3.

SUBJECTED. *Subdued; enslaved; obedient; submissive.*

Subjected thus,
How can you say to me, I am a king?
  Richard 2, iii. 2.
Needs must you lay your heart at his dispose,
Subjected tribute to commanding love.
  King John, i. 1.

SUBJECTION. *Service; duty.*

I dare be bound he's true, and shall perform
All parts of his *subjection* loyally. *Cymbeline,* iv. 3.

To SUBSCRIBE. *To give up; to renounce; to yield; to submit; to proclaim; to protest.*

And the king gone to-night! *subscrib'd* his power!
Confin'd to exhibition! All this done
Upon the gad!   *King Lear,* i. 2.
All cruels else *subscrib'd.*   *Ibid.* iii. 7.

For Hector, in his blaze of wrath, *subscribes*
To tender objects.   *Troilus and Cressida,* iv. 5.
As I *subscribe* not that, nor any other,
But in the loss of question.
  Measure for Measure, ii. 4.
Claudio undergoes my challenge; and either I must shortly hear from him, or I will *subscribe* him a coward.   *Much Ado about Nothing,* v. 2.
I know thou art valiant; and, to the possibility of thy soldiership, will *subscribe* for thee.
  All's well that ends well, iii. 6.
I will *subscribe* for thee, thou art both knave and fool.   *Ibid.* iv. 5.

SUBSCRIPTION. *Submission; obedience; subjection.*

I never gave you kingdom, call'd you children,
You owe me no *subscription.*   *King Lear,* iii. 2.

To SUBSIST. *To remain; to continue.*

No more infected with my country's love
Than when I parted hence, but still *subsisting*
Under your great command.   *Coriolanus,* v. 6.

SUBSTANCE. *Wealth; treasure.*

The purpose is perspicuous even as *substance,*
Whose grossness little characters sum up.
  Troilus and Cressida, i. 3.
Then, that you've sent innumerable *substance*
. . . .
To furnish Rome, and to prepare the ways
You have for dignities.   *Henry 8,* iii. 2.

SUBSTITUTE. *A deputy; a delegate.*

And though we have there a *substitute* of most allowed sufficiency, yet opinion throws a more safer voice on you.   *Othello,* i. 3.
And to set on this wretched woman here
Against our *substitute!*   *Measure for Measure,* v. 1.
This devil here shall be my *substitute.*
  Henry 6, P. 2, iii. 1.

To SUBSTITUTE. *To delegate; to appoint in the place of another.*

But who is *substituted* 'gainst the French,
I have no certain notice.   *Henry 4, P. 2,* i. 3.

SUBSTRACTOR. *A detractor.*

By this hand, they are scoundrels and *substractors* that say so of him.   *Twelfth-Night,* i. 3.

TT

SUBTILTY. *Enchantment; spell.*

You do yet taste
Some *subtilties* o' the isle, that will not let you
Believe things certain. *Tempest*, v. 1.

SUBTLE. *Uneven; treacherous.*

Nay, sometimes,
Like to a bowl upon a *subtle* ground,
I've tumbled past the throw. *Coriolanus*, v. 2.

To SUCCEED. *To descend; to devolve; to follow; to succeed to; to inherit.*

Gratiano, keep the house,
And seize upon the fortunes of the Moor,
For they *succeed* on you. *Othello*, v. 2.

I promise you, the effects he writes of *succeed*
unhappily. *King Lear*, i. 2.

Else let my brother die,
If not a fedary, but only he
Owe, and *succeed* this weakness.
Measure for Measure, ii. 4.

SUCCEEDER. *Successor; heir; inheritor.*

Windy attorneys to their client woes,
Airy *succeeders* of intestate joys,
Poor breathing orators of miseries!
Let them have scope: though what they do impart
Help nothing else, yet do they ease the heart.
Richard 3, iv. 4.

O, now, let Richmond and Elizabeth,
The true *succeeders* of each royal house,
By God's fair ordinance conjoin together!
Ibid. v. 5.

SUCCEEDING. *Consequence.*

A most harsh one, and not to be understood
without bloody *succeeding*.
All's well that ends well, ii. 3.

SUCCESS. *Descent; succession; issue; result; event.*

Thereto
Clerk-like, experienc'd, which no less adorns
Our gentry than our parents' noble names,
In whose *success* we are gentle. *Winter's Tale*, i. 2.

And so *success* of mischief shall be born,
And heir from heir shall hold this quarrel up,
Whiles England shall have generation.
Henry 4, P. 2, iv. 2.

If the assassination
Could trammel up the consequence, and catch,
With his surcease, *success*. *Macbeth*, i. 7.

Madam, so thrive I in my enterprise
And dangerous *success* of bloody wars.
Richard 3, iv. 4.

Our imputation shall be oddly pois'd
In this wild action; for the *success*,
Although particular, shall give a scantling
Of good or bad unto the general.
Troilus and Cressida, i. 3.

Should you do so, my lord,
My speech should fall into such vile *success*,
Which my thoughts aim'd not. *Othello*, iii. 3.

SUCCESSION. *Successors; heirs; inheritance.*

Cassibelan, thine uncle, for him
And his *succession* granted Rome a tribute,
Yearly three thousand pounds; which by thee lately
Is left untender'd. *Cymbeline*, iii. 1.

Thinking to bar thee of *succession*, as
Thou reft'st me of my lands. *Ibid.* iii. 3.

Will they not say afterwards, if they should
grow themselves to common players, their writers
do them wrong, to make them exclaim against their
own *succession?* *Hamlet*, ii. 2.

SUCCESSIVE. *Following in order; sequent; consequential.*

And, like a prophet,
Looks in a glass, that shows what future evils,
Either new, or by remissness new-conceiv'd,
And so in progress to be hatch'd and born,
Are now to have no *successive* degrees,
But, ere they live, to end.
Measure for Measure, ii. 2.

SUCCESSIVELY. *In due order; in succession; by descent.*

So thou the garland wear'st *successively*.
Henry 4, P. 2, iv. 4.

Not as protector, steward, substitute,
Or lowly factor for another's gain;
But as *successively*, from blood to blood,
Your right of birth, your empery, your own.
Richard 3, iii. 7.

SUCH. *So much; so great.*

Your daughter, whom she bore in hand to love
With *such* integrity, she did confess
Was as a scorpion to her sight. *Cymbeline*, v. 5.

And frame some feeling line
That may discover *such* integrity.
Two Gentlemen of Verona, iii. 2.

SUDDEN. *Quick; violent; hasty.*

Casca, be *sudden*, for we fear prevention.
Julius Cæsar, iii. 1.

Small showers last long, but *sudden* storms are
short. *Richard* 2, ii. 1.

I grant him bloody,
Luxurious, avaricious, false, deceitful,
Sudden, malicious, smacking of every sin
That has a name. *Macbeth,* iv. 3.

Jealous in honour, *sudden* and quick in quarrel.
As you like it, ii. 7.

SUDDENLY. *Quickly; immediately.*

When time is ripe (which will be *suddenly*),
I'll steal to Glendower and Lord Mortimer.
Henry 4, P. 1, i. 3.

I'll make him find him : do this *suddenly*.
As you like it, ii. 2.

I will leave him, and *suddenly* contrive the
means of meeting between him and my daughter.
Hamlet, ii. 2.

SUFFERANCE. *Suffering; patience; moderation; connivance.*

Mistress Ford, hath eaten up my *sufferance*.
Merry Wives of Windsor, iv. 2.

For *sufferance* is the badge of all our tribe.
Merchant of Venice, i. 3.

Thy nature did commence in *sufferance*, time
Hath made thee hard in't. *Timon of Athens,* iv. 3.

England shall repent his folly, see his weakness,
and admire our *sufferance*. *Henry* 5, iii. 5.

It cannot be : some villains of my court
Are of consent and *sufferance* in this.
As you like it, ii. 2.

SUFFICIENCY. *Fitness; competence; capability.*

Though we have there a substitute of most allowed *sufficiency*, yet opinion, a sovereign mistress
of effects, throws a more safer voice on you.
Othello, i. 3.

Then no more remains,
But that to your *sufficiency*, as your worth is able,
And let them work. *Measure for Measure,* i. 1.

Cleomenes and Dion, whom you know
Of stuff'd *sufficiency*. *Winter's Tale,* ii. 1.

SUFFOCATE. *Choked; suffocated.*

For Suffolk's duke may he be *suffocate*,
That dims the honour of this warlike isle !
Henry 6, P. 2, i. 1.

This chaos, when degree is *suffocate*,
Follows the choking. *Troilus and Cressida,* i. 3.

To SUGGEST. *To tempt; to seduce; to persuade; to prompt; to instigate.*

When devils will the blackest sins put on,
They do *suggest* at first with heavenly shows.
Othello, ii. 3.

Knowing that tender youth is soon *suggested*,
I nightly lodge her in an upper tower.
Two Gentlemen of Verona, iii. 1.

We must *suggest* the people in what hatred
He still hath hold them. *Coriolanus,* ii. 1.

SUGGESTION. *Intimation; instigation; prompting; temptation; underhand means.*

For all the rest,
They'll take *suggestion* as a cat laps milk.
Tempest, ii. 1.

A filthy officer he is in those *suggestions* for the
young earl. *All's well that ends well,* iii. 5.

And others more, going to seek the grave
Of Arthur, who, they say, is kill'd to-night
On your *suggestion*. *King John,* iv. 2.

One that by *suggestion*
Tith'd all the kingdom. *Henry* 8, iv. 2.

And pardon absolute for yourself, and these
Herein misled by your *suggestion*.
Henry 4, P. 1, iv. 3.

SUIT. *Service due to a superior lord; a petition.*

Mine ears against your *suits* are stronger than
Your gates against my force. *Coriolanus,* v. 2.

Give notice to such men of sort and *suit*
As are to meet him. *Measure for Measure,* iv. 4.

Sometimes she gallops o'er a courtier's nose,
And then dreams he of smelling out a *suit*.
Romeo and Juliet, i. 4.

To SUIT. *To clothe; to dress; to be consistent with; to accord with.*

So went he *suited* to his watery tomb.
Twelfth-Night, v. 1.

Description cannot *suit* itself in words
To démonstrate the life of such a battle.
Henry 5, iv. 2.

I'll disrobe me
Of these Italian weeds, and *suit* myself
As does a Briton peasant. *Cymbeline,* v. 1.

A prologue arm'd,—but not in confidence
Of author's pen or actor's voice; but *suited*
In like conditions as our argument.
Troilus and Cressida, Prologue.
How oddly he is *suited! Merchant of Venice*, i. 2.
My master is awak'd by great occasion,
To call upon his own; and humbly prays you,
That with your other noble parts you'll *suit*,
In giving him his right.   *Timon of Athens*, ii. 2.

SULLEN.   *Heavy; dull; dark.*
Shorten my days thou canst with *sullen* sorrow,
And pluck nights from me, but not lend a morrow.
Richard 2, i. 3.
Be thou the trumpet of our wrath,
And *sullen* presage of your own decay.
King John, i. 1.
Like bright metal on a *sullen* ground.
Henry 4, P. 1, i. 2.

SULLY.   *Stain; spot; blemish.*
You laying these slight *sullies* on my son,
As 'twere a thing a little soil'd i' the working.
Hamlet, ii. 1.

SUMLESS.   *Incalculable; inestimable.*
And make her chronicle as rich with praise
As is the ooze and bottom of the sea.
With sunken wreck and *sumless* treasuries.
Henry 5, i. 2.

SUMPTER.   *A horse that carried provisions or other necessaries.*
Persuade me rather to be slave and *sumpter*
To this detested groom.   *King Lear*, ii. 4.

SUPERFLUOUS.   *Rich; wealthy; having more than enough; affluent; exuberant.*
Let the *superfluous* and lust-dieted man,
That slaves your ordinance, that will not see
Because he doth not feel, feel your power quickly.
King Lear, iv. 1.
Withal, full oft we see
Cold wisdom waiting on *superfluous* folly.
All's well that ends well, i. 1.
O, reason not the need: our basest beggars
Are in the poorest thing *superfluous*.
King Lear, ii. 4.

SUPERFLUX.   *Superfluity; superabundance.*
Take physic, pomp,
Expose thyself to feel what wretches feel,

That thou mayst shake the *superflux* to them,
And show the heavens more just. *King Lear*, iii. 4.

TO SUPERPRAISE.   *To overpraise.*
To vow, and swear, and *superpraise* my parts.
Midsummer-Night's Dream, iii. 2.

SUPERSERVICEABLE.   *Officious; overforward.*
A lily-livered, action-taking, whoreson, glass-gazing, *superserviceable*, finical rogue.
King Lear, ii. 2.

SUPERSTITIOUS.   *Reverential; idolatrous; devoted.*
Have I with all my full affections
Still met the king? lov'd him next heaven? obey'd him?
Been, out of fondness, *superstitious* to him?
And am I thus rewarded?   *Henry 8*, iii. 1.

SUPERSTITIOUSLY.   *Reverently.*
Dreams are toys;
Yet, for this once, yea, *superstitiously*,
I will be squar'd by this.   *Winter's Tale*, iii. 3.

SUPERVISE.   *Inspection; sight.*
That, on the *supervise*, no leisure bated,
No, not to stay the grinding of the axe,
My head should be struck off.   *Hamlet*, v. 2.

TO SUPPLANT.   *To displace; to force away; to expel.*
That you three
From Milan did *supplant* good Prospero.
Tempest, iii. 3.
Now for our Irish wars:
We must *supplant* those rough rug-headed kerns.
Richard 2, ii. 1.

SUPPLIANCE.   *Duration; continuance.*
A violet in the youth of primy nature,
Forward, not permanent, sweet, not lasting,
The perfume and *suppliance* of a minute.
Hamlet, i. 3.

SUPPLY.   *Help; support; re-enforcement.*
If it will please you
. . . . to expend your time with us awhile,
For the *supply* and profit of our hope,
Your visitation shall receive such thanks
As fits a king's remembrance.   *Hamlet*, ii. 2.

Be of good comfort; for the great *supply*,
That was expected by the Dauphin here,
Are wreck'd three nights ago on Goodwin sands.
King John, v. 3.
And our *supplies* live largely in the hope
Of great Northumberland.   *Henry 4*, P. 2, i. 3.

To SUPPLY.   *To fill.*

Though bride and bridegroom wants
For to *supply* the places at the table,
You know there wants no junkets at the feast.
Taming of the Shrew, iii. 2.
Faith, nothing but an empty box, sir; which in
my lord's behalf, I come to entreat your honour to
supply.   *Timon of Athens*, iii. 1.

SUPPLYANT.   *Supplementary; additional.*

With those legions
Which I have spoke of, whereunto your levy
Must be *supplyant*.   *Cymbeline*, iii. 7.

SUPPLYMENT.   *Supply; continuance.*

Your means abroad,
You have me, rich; and I will never fail
Beginning nor *supplyment*.   *Cymbeline*, iii. 4.

SUPPORTANCE.   *Justification; fulfilment; support.*

Therefore draw, for the *supportance* of his vow.
Twelfth-Night, iii. 5.
Give some *supportance* to the bending twigs.
Richard 2, iii. 4.

SUPPOSAL.   *Opinion; belief; notion.*

Now follows, that you know, young Fortinbras,
Holding a weak *supposal* of our worth,
Or thinking by our late dear brother's death
Our state to be disjoint and out of frame,
Colleagued with the dream of his advantage.
Hamlet, i. 2.

SUPPOSE.   *Pretence; appearance; supposition; expectation.*

That have by marriage made thy daughter mine,
While counterfeit *supposes* blear'd thine eyne.
Taming of the Shrew, v. 1.
Nor, princes, is it matter new to us,
That we come short of our *suppose* so far,
That, after seven years' siege, yet Troy walls stand.
Troilus and Cressida, i. 3.

SUPPOSED.   *Supposititious; false; counterfeit; imaginary.*

And, till he tell the truth,
Let the *supposèd* fairies pinch him round.
Merry Wives of Windsor, iv. 4.
So are those crispèd snaky golden locks,
Which make such wanton gambols with the wind,
Upon *supposèd* fairness. *Merchant of Venice*, iii. 2.
Which daily grow to quarrel and to bloodshed,
Wounding *supposèd* peace.   *Henry 4*, P. 2, iv. 4.

SUPPOSITION.   *Imagination; fancy; idea; notion.*

And, in that glorious *supposition*, think
He gains by death that hath such means to die.
Comedy of Errors, iii. 2.
Yet his means are in *supposition*.
Merchant of Venice, i. 3.
Only to seem to deserve well, and to beguile the
supposition of that lascivious young boy the count,
have I run into this danger.
All's well that ends well, iv. 3.

SUR-ADDITION.   *Surname; additional name; title.*

But had his titles by Tenantius, whom
He serv'd with glory and admir'd success,—
So gain'd the *sur-addition* Leonatus.
Cymbeline, i. 1.

SUR-REINED.   *Overworked.*

Can sodden water,
A drench for *sur-rein'd* jades, their barley broth,
Decoct their cold blood to such valiant heat?
Henry 5, iii. 4.

SURCEASE.   *Cessation; completion; accomplishment.*

If the assassination
Could trammel up the consequence, and catch,
With his *surcease*, success.   *Macbeth*, i. 7.

To SURCEASE.   *To cease.*

For no pulse
Shall keep his native progress, but *surcease*.
Romeo and Juliet, iv. 1.
I will not do't;
Lest I *surcease* to honour mine own truth,
And, by my body's action, teach my mind
A most inherent baseness.   *Coriolanus*, iii. 2.

SURE. *Safe; out of danger; faithful; trustworthy.*

You are both *sure*, and will assist me?
Much Ado about Nothing, i. 3.

The forest is not three leagues off;
If we recover that, we're *sure* enough.
Two Gentlemen of Verona, v. 1.

TO SURETY. *To bail.*

The jeweller that owes the ring is sent for,
And he shall *surety* me.
All's well that ends well, v. 3.

We'll *surety* him. Agèd sir, hands off.
Coriolanus, iii. 1.

SURFEITER. *A feaster; a reveller; an epicure.*

Menas, I did not think
This amorous *surfeiter* would have donn'd his helm
For such a petty war. *Antony and Cleopatra*, ii. 1.

TO SURMOUNT. *To surpass; to exceed.*

Bethink thee on her virtues that *surmount*
And natural graces that extinguish art.
Henry 6, P. 1, v. 3.

SUSPECT. *Suspicion.*

My Lord of Gloster, 'tis my special hope
That you will clear yourself from all *suspect*.
Henry 6, P. 2, iii. 1.

And draw within the compass of *suspect*
Th' unviolated honour of your wife.
Comedy of Errors, iii. 1.

No, my most worthy master; in whose breast
Doubt and *suspect*, alas, are plac'd too late.
Timon of Athens, iv. 3.

Suspect still comes where an estate is least.
Ibid. iv. 3.

SUSPICION. *Doubt; uncertainty; apprehension of evil.*

Hath not the world one man but he will wear his
cap with *suspicion*? *Much Ado about Nothing*, i. 1.

See what a ready tongue *suspicion* hath!
Henry 4, P. 2, i. 1.

Suspicion always haunts the guilty mind;
The thief doth fear each bush an officer.
Henry 6, P. 3, v. 6.

SUSPIRATION. *Expiration.*

'Tis not alone my inky cloak, good mother,
Nor customary suits of solemn black,

Nor windy *suspiration* of forc'd breath
That can denote me truly. *Hamlet*, i. 2.

TO SUSPIRE. *To breathe.*

For since the birth of Cain, the first male child,
To him that did but yesterday *suspire*,
There was not such a gracious creature born.
King John, iii. 4.

Did he *suspire*, that light and weightless down
Perforce must move. *Henry 4, P. 2*, iv. 4.

SWABBER. *Deck-cleaner, a sea term.*

The master, the *swabber*, the boatswain, and I.
Tempest, ii. 1.

No, good *swabber;* I am to hull here a little longer.
Twelfth-Night, i. 5.

SWAG-BELLIED. *Gor-bellied; having a large stomach.*

Your Dane, your German, and your *swag-bellied*
Hollander, are nothing to your English.
Othello, ii. 3.

SWART. *Swarthy; black.*

Lame, foolish, crookèd, *swart*, prodigious,
Patch'd with foul moles and eye-offending marks.
King John, iii. 1.

Swart, like my shoe, but her face nothing like
so clean kept. *Comedy of Errors*, iii. 2.

SWASHER. *A boaster; a braggart.*

As young as I am, I have observed these three
swashers. *Henry 5*, iii. 1.

SWASHING. *Showy; dashing; slashing.*

Gregory, remember thy *swashing* blow.
Romeo and Juliet, i. 1.

We'll have a *swashing* and a martial outside.
As you like it, i. 3.

SWATH. *A swaddling cloth or band.*

Hadst thou, like us from our first *swath*, proceeded
The sweet degrees that this brief world affords
To such as may the passive drugs of it
Freely command; thou wouldst have plung'd thyself
In general riot. *Timon of Athens*, iv. 3.

SWATHING-CLOUTS. *Swaddling-clothes.*

That great baby you see there is not yet out of
his *swathing-clouts*. *Hamlet*, ii. 2.

SWAY. *Bulk; fabric.*

Are not you mov'd, when all the *sway* of earth
Shakes like a thing infirm?   *Julius Cæsar*, i. 3.

To SWAY. *To bias; to turn aside.*

And God forgive them that so much have *sway'd*
Your majesty's thoughts away from me!
Henry 4, P. 1, iii. 2.

To SWAY ON. *To march on; to go forward.*

Let us *sway on*, and face them in the field.
Henry 4, P. 2, iv. 1.

To SWEAR-OUT. *To forswear; to renounce.*

I hear your grace hath *sworn-out* house-keeping.
Love's Labour's lost, ii. 1.

SWEET-FACED. *Handsome; well-favoured.*

I see by you I am a *sweet-fac'd* youth.
Comedy of Errors, v. 1.
For Pyramus is a *sweet-faced* man.
Midsummer-Night's Dream, i. 2.

SWEETING. *A kind of apple; a term of endearment.*

Thy wit is a very bitter *sweeting*; it is a most
sharp sauce.   *Romeo and Juliet*, ii. 4.

Trip no further, pretty *sweeting*.
Twelfth-Night, ii. 3.
How fares my Kate? What, *sweeting*, all amort?
Taming of the Shrew, iv. 3.
All's well now, *sweeting*; come away to bed.
Othello, ii. 3.

SWEETMEATS. *Kissing-comfits.*

Which oft the angry Mab with blisters plagues,
Because their breaths with *sweetmeats* tainted are.
Romeo and Juliet, i. 4.
And stolen the impression of her fantasy
With bracelets of thy hair, rings, gauds, conceits,
Knacks, trifles, nosegays, *sweetmeats*, messengers
Of strong prevailment in unharden'd youth.
Midsummer-Night's Dream, i. 1.

SWELLING. *Grand; important; eventful.*

A kingdom for a stage, princes to act,
And monarchs to behold the *swelling* scene.
Henry 5, i. Chorus.
Two truths are told,
As happy prologues to the *swelling* act
Of the imperial theme.   *Macbeth*, i. 5.

SWET. *Sweated.*

O good old man, how well in thee appears
The constant service of the antique world,
When service *swet* for duty, not for meed!
As you like it, ii. 3.

SWIFT. *Prompt; ready.*

By my faith, he is very *swift* and sententious.
As you like it, v. 4.
She cannot be so much without true judgment,—
Having so *swift* and excellent a wit
As she is priz'd to have.
Much Ado about Nothing, iii. 1.
O mischief, thou art *swift*
To enter in the thoughts of desperate men!
Romeo and Juliet, v. 1.

To SWINGE. *To whip; to chastise; to punish.*

I thank you, you *swinged* me for my love, which
makes me the bolder to chide you for yours.
Two Gentlemen of Verona, ii. 1.
Now will he be *swinged* for reading my letter.
Ibid. iii. 1.

SWINGE-BUCKLER. *A roisterer; a noisy turbulent fellow; a rake.*

You had not four such *swinge-bucklers* in all the
inns of court again.   *Henry 4*, P. 2, iii. 2.

SWOOP. *Sweep; souse; stroke.*

What, all my pretty chickens and their dam
At one fell *swoop*?   *Macbeth*, iv. 3.

SWOOPSTAKE. *Indiscriminately; indifferently; without distinction.*

Is't writ in your revenge,
That *swoopstake* you will draw both friend and foe,
Winner and loser?   *Hamlet*, iv. 5.

SWORDER. *A swordman; a gladiator; a cutthroat.*

Yes, like enough, high-battled Cæsar will
Unstate his happiness, and be stag'd to the show,
Against a *sworder!*   *Antony and Cleopatra*, iii. 13.
A Roman *sworder* and banditto slave
Murder'd sweet Tully.   *Henry 6*, P. 2, iv. 1.

SYMPATHIZED. *Mutually felt.*

And all that are assembled in this place,
That by this *sympathiz'd* one day's error

Have suffer'd wrong, go keep us company,
And we shall make full satisfaction.
Comedy of Errors, v. 1.

SYMPATHY. *Equality.*

If that thy valour stand on *sympathy*,

There is my gage, Aumerle, in gage to thine.
Richard 2, iv. 1.

Or if there were a *sympathy* in choice,
War, death, or sickness, did lay siege to it.
Midsummer-Night's Dream, i. 1.

T.

TABLE. *A note-book; a memorandum-book; a pocket-book; the palm of the hand.*

'Twas pretty, though a plague,
To see him every hour; to sit and draw
His archèd brows, his hawking eye, his curls,
In our heart's *table*. *All's well that ends well*, i. 1.

Yea, from the *table* of my memory
I'll wipe away all trivial fond records. *Hamlet*, i. 5.

I do cónjure thee,
Who art the *table* wherein all my thoughts
Are visibly charácter'd and engrav'd.
Two Gentlemen of Verona, ii. 7.

Well, if any man in Italy have a fairer *table*
which doth offer to swear upon a book, I shall have
good fortune! *Merchant of Venice*, ii. 2.

To TABLE. *To set down; to inscribe.*

Though the catalogue of his endowments had
been *tabled* by his side, and I to peruse him by
items. *Cymbeline*, i. 4.

TABLES. *Backgammon.*

That, when he plays at *tables*, chides the dice
In honourable terms. *Love's Labour's lost*, v. 2.

TABORER. *One who beats the tabour.*

I would I could see this *taborer* ! he lays it on.
Tempest, iii. 2.

TABOURINE. *A drum.*

Beat loud the *tabourines*, let the trumpets blow.
Troilus and Cressida, iv. 5.

Trumpeters,
With brazen din blast you the city's ear;
Make mingle with our rattling *tabourines*.
Antony and Cleopatra, iv. 8.

TACKLED. *Made of ropes fastened together.*

Within this hour my man shall be with thee,
And bring thee cords made like a *tackled* stair.
Romeo and Juliet, ii. 4.

TACKLING. *Sails and ropes.*

Like a poor bark, of sails and *tackling* reft,
Rush all to pieces on thy rocky bosom.
Richard 3, iv. 4.

The friends of France our shrouds and *tacklings*?
Henry 6, P. 3, v. 4.

TAG. *The rabble; the crowd.*

Will you hence, before the *tag* return?
Coriolanus, iii. 1.

TAG-RAG. *Common; vulgar; mean.*

If the *tag-rag* people did not clap him and hiss
him, as he pleased and displeased them, as they use
to do the players in the theatre, I am no true man.
Julius Cæsar, i. 2.

TAINT. *Stain; discredit; reproach; censure.*

Here abjure
The *taints* and blames I laid upon myself,
For strangers to my nature. *Macbeth*, iv. 3.

If he were foil'd,
Why, then we did our main opinion crush
In *taint* of our best man.
Troilus and Cressida, i. 3.

His *taints* and honours
Wag'd equal with him. *Antony and Cleopatra*, v. 1.

TAINT. *Tainted; imbued.*

Yes, my good lord,—a pure unspotted heart,
Never yet *taint* with love, I send the king.
Henry 6, P. 1, v. 3.

To TAINT. *To be infected; to stain; to sully; to blame; to censure.*

Till Birnam Wood remove to Dunsinane,
I cannot *taint* with fear. *Macbeth*, v. 3.

Sure, the man is *tainted* in 's wits.
Twelfth-Night, iii. 4.

We come not by the way of accusation,
To *taint* that honour every good tongue blesses.
                                    Henry 8, iii. 1.

Do you find some occasion to anger Cassio,
either by speaking too loud, or *tainting* his discipline.   *Othello*, ii. 1.

TAINTURE. *Defilement; soilure.*

Gloster, see here the *tainture* of thy nest.
                                Henry 6, P. 2; ii. 1.

To TAKE. *To blast; to bewitch; to go into;
to leap; to strike; to captivate; to believe;
to be convinced.*

Then no planets strike,
No fairy *takes*, no witch hath power to charm.
                                    Hamlet, i. 1.

Strike her young bones,
You *taking* airs, with lameness ! *King Lear*, ii. 4.

And *takes* the cattle,
And makes milch-kine yield blood.
                        Merry Wives of Windsor, iv. 4.

Run, master, run ; for God's sake, *take* a house !
                            Comedy of Errors, v. 1.

That hand which had the strength, even at your
door,
To cudgel you, and make you *take* the hatch.
                                King John, v. 2.

Take him over the costard with the hilts of thy
sword.   *Richard* 3, i. 4.

And does not Toby *take* you a blow o' the lips
then ?   *Twelfth-Night*, ii. 5.

Which is more
Than history can pattern, though devis'd
And play'd to *take* spectators. *Winter's Tale*, iii. 2.

Daffodils, that come before the swallow dares,
And *take* the winds of March with beauty.
                                    Ibid. iv. 3.

Upon his death-bed he by will bequeath'd
His lands to me ; and *took* it, on his death,
That this, my mother's son, was none of his.
                                King John, i. 1.

To TAKE ALONG WITH. *To make to understand.*

Soft ! *take me with* you, *take me with* you, wife.
                            Romeo and Juliet, iii. 5.

I would your grace would *take me with* you :
whom means your grace ?   *Henry* 4, P. 1, ii. 4.

To TAKE AWAY. *To push aside; to remove;
to destroy.*

Safer than trust too far :
Let me still *take away* the harms I fear,
Not fear still to be taken.   *King Lear*, i. 4.

To TAKE HASTE. *To make haste; to hasten;
to lose no time.*

That whoso please
To stop affliction, let him *take his haste*,
Come hither, ere my tree hath felt the axe,
And hang himself.   *Timon of Athens*, v. 1.

To TAKE IN. *To capture; to subdue.*

Take in that kingdom, and enfranchise that.
                        Antony and Cleopatra, i. 1.

By the discovery,
We shall be shorten'd in our aim ; which was,
To *take in* many towns, ere, almost, Rome
Should know we were a-foot.   *Coriolanus*, i. 2.

Is it not strange, Canidius, ...
He could so quickly cut th' Ionian sea,
And *take in* Toryne ? *Antony and Cleopatra*, iii. 7.

I think affliction may subdue the cheek,
But not *take in* the mind.   *Winter's Tale*, iv. 3.

Now, this no more dishonours you at all
Than to *take in* a town with gentle words,
Which else would put you to your fortune, and
The hazard of much blood.   *Coriolanus*, iii. 2.

And swore,
With his own single hand he'd *take us in*.
                                Cymbeline, iv. 2.

To TAKE NOTE. *To notice; to observe.*

Therefore I do advise you, *take this note :*
My lord is dead ; Edmund and I have talk'd ;
And more convenient is he for my hand
Than for your lady's.   *King Lear*, iv. 5.

The law hath not been dead, though it hath slept :
Now 'tis awake, *takes note* of what is done.
                        Measure for Measure, ii. 2.

To TAKE ON. *To come on; to advance.*

Take on as you would follow,
But yet come not.
                    Midsummer-Night's Dream, iii. 2.

To TAKE ORDER FOR. *To provide for or against
any contingency; to take measures.*

No, his mouth is stopp'd ;
Honest Iago hath *ta'en order for't*. *Othello*, v. 2.
                                                UU

We will have away thy cold; and I will *take
such order*, that thy friends shall ring for thee.
Henry 4, P. 2, iii. 2.

And, madam, there is *order ta'en for* you.
Richard .2, v. 1.

Some one *take order* Buckingham be brought
To Salisbury.   *Richard* 3, iv. 4.

Now will I in, to *take* some privy *order*,
To draw the brats of Clarence out of sight.
Ibid. iii. 5.

Therefore this *order* hath Baptista ta'en.
Taming of the Shrew, i. 2.

If your worship will *take order for* the drabs
and the knaves, you need not fear the bawds.
Measure for Measure, ii. 1.

To TAKE OUT.   *To copy.*
I'll have the work *ta'en out*,
And give 't Iago.   *Othello*, iii. 3.
Sweet Bianca, *take me* this work *out.*   *Ibid.* iii. 4.
I must *take out* the work?   *Ibid.* iv. 1.

To TAKE PEACE WITH.   *To pardon; to for-
give.*
There cannot be those numberless offences
'Gainst me, that I cannot *take peace with.*
Henry 8, ii. 1.

To TAKE SCORN.   *To disdain.*
I owe him little duty, and less love,
And *take* foul *scorn* to fawn on him by sending.
Henry 6, P. 1, iv. 4.

Take thou no *scorn* to wear the horn;
It was a crest ere thou wast born.
As you like it, iv. 2.

To TAKE THE HEAD.   *To take liberties; to
presume.*
The time hath been,
Would you have been so brief with him, he would
Have been so brief with you, to shorten you,
For *taking so the head*, your whole head's length.
Richard 2, iii. 3.

To TAKE THOUGHT.   *To turn melancholy.*
If he love Cæsar, all that he can do
Is to himself,—*take thought*, and die for Cæsar.
Julius Cæsar, ii. 1.

To TAKE UP.   *To borrow; to buy upon trust;
to make up; to compose; to raise; to levy.*
And if a man is thorough with them in honest
taking-up, then they must stand upon security.
Henry 4, P. 2, i. 2.

I knew when seven justices could not *take up* a
quarrel.   *As you like it*, v. 4.

You have *ta'en up*,
Under the counterfeited seal of God,
The subjects of his substitute, my father,
And both against the peace of heaven and him
Have here *up-swarm'd* them.   *Henry* 4, P. 2, iv. 2.

To TAKE UPON.   *To assume an air of author-
ity or importance.*
Look that you *take upon* you as you should;
You understand me, sir.   *Taming of the Shrew*, iv. 3.

She *takes upon* her bravely at first dash.
Henry 6, P. 1, i. 2.

TALE.   *A lie; a fiction; a fable.*
Your vows to her and me, put in two scales,
Will even weigh; and both as light as *tales*.
Midsummer-Night's Dream, iii. 2.

Truths would be but *tales*,
Where now half *tales* be truths.
Antony and Cleopatra, ii. 2.

TALL.   *Bold; spirited; courageous; valiant.*
I'll swear to the prince thou art a *tall* fellow of
thy hands, and that thou wilt not be drunk.
Winter's Tale, v. 2.

Which many a good *tall* fellow had destroy'd
So cowardly.   *Henry* 4, P. 1, i. 3.

TAME.   *Feeble; ineffectual; impotent; harm-
less.*
His remedies are *tame* i' the present peace
And quietness of the people.   *Coriolanus*, iv. 6.

To TANG.   *To twang; to resound.*
Let thy tongue *tang* arguments of state.
Twelfth-Night, ii. 5.

To TANGLE.   *To ensnare.*
'Od's my little life,
I think she means to *tangle* my eyes too!
As you like it, iii. 5.

TANLING.   *One who is sunburnt.*
Aye hopeless
To have the courtesy your cradle promis'd,

But to be still hot summer's *tanlings*, and
The shrinking slaves of winter.　*Cymbeline*, iv. 4.

To TARDY.　*To delay; to hinder.*

Which had been done,　·
But that the good mind of Camillo *tardied*
My swift command.　*Winter's Tale*, iii. 2.

TARGE.　*A shield.*

This 'greed upon,
To part with unhack'd edges, and bear back
Our *targes* undinted.　*Antony and Cleopatra*, ii. 6.

Pompey surnam'd the Great ;
That oft in field, with *targe* and shield, did make my
foe to sweat.　*Love's Labour's lost*, v. 2.

Woe is my heart,
That the poor soldier, that so richly fought,
Whose rags sham'd gilded arms, whose naked breast
Stepp'd before *targes* of proof, cannot be found.
Cymbeline, v. 5.

TARGET.　*A shield.*

Bear our hack'd *targets* like the men that owe them.
Antony and Cleopatra, iv. 8.

And I had purpose
Once more to hew thy *target* from thy brawn,
Or lose mine arm for 't.　*Coriolanus*, iv. 5.

To TARRE.　*To urge; to incite; to encourage;
to provoke.*

And, like a dog that is compell'd to fight,
Snatch at his master that doth *tarre* him on.
King John, iv. 1.

And the nation holds it no sin to *tarre* them to
controversy.　*Hamlet*, ii. 2.

Pride alone
Must *tarre* the mastiffs on, as 'twere a bone.
Troilus and Cressida, i. 3.

TARRIANCE.　*Delay.*

I am impatient of my *tarriance*.
Two Gentlemen of Verona, ii. 7.

TARTAR.　*Tartarus.*

To the gates of *Tartar*, thou most excellent devil
of wit !　*Twelfth-Night*, ii. 5.

He might return to vasty *Tartar* back,
And tell the legions, "I can never win
A soul so easy as that Englishman's."
Henry 5, ii. 2.

To TASK.　*To tax.*

And, in the neck of that, *task'd* the whole state.
Henry 4, P. 1, iv. 3.

TASKING.　*Blame; censure; reproach.*

Tell me, tell me,
How show'd his *tasking* ? seem'd it in contempt ?
Henry 4, P. 1, v. 2.

TASSEL-GENTLE.　*The male goshawk.*

O, for a falconer's voice,
To lure this *tassel-gentle* back again !
Romeo and Juliet, ii. 2.

TASTE.　*Sort; degree.*

And, in some *taste*, is Lepidus but so.
Julius Cæsar, iv. 1.

TATTERING.　*Tattered; torn.*

And wound our *tattering* colours clearly up,
Last in the field, and almost lords of it !
King John, v. 5.

TAX.　*Imputation; charge; accusation.*

Tax of impudence,
A strumpet's boldness, a divulgèd shame.
All's well that ends well, ii. 1.

To TAX.　*To blame; to censure.*

Why, who cries out on pride,
That can therein *tax* any private party ?
As you like it, ii. 7.

TAXATION.　*Scandal; censure; satire.*

You'll be whipped for *taxation* one of these days.
As you like it, i. 2.

TAWDRY-LACE.　*A kind of necklace.*

Come, you promised me a *tawdry-lace* and a pair
of sweet gloves.　*Winter's Tale*, iv. 3.

TEDIOUS.　*Artful; complicated; intricate;
laborious.*

My brain, more busy than the labouring spider,
Weaves *tedious* snares to trap mine enemies.
Henry 6, P. 2, iii. 1.

And bring him out that is but woman's son
Can trace me in the *tedious* ways of art.
Henry 4, P. 1, iii. 1.

To TEEM. *To breed ; to bear children.*

Is not my *teeming* date drunk up with time ?
Richard 2, v. 2.

If she must *teem,*
Create her child of spleen ; that it may live,
And be a thwart disnatur'd torment to her !
King Lear, v. 2.

TEEN. *Trouble ; sorrow.*

Eighty odd years of sorrow have I seen,
And each hour's joy wreck'd with a week of *teen.*
Richard 3, iv. 1.

To think o' the *teen* that I have turn'd you to.
Tempest, i. 2.

To TELL. *To count ; to sum up ; to go in a
reckoning ; to pass current.*

But for the rest,—you *tell* a pedigree
Of threescore and two years ; a silly time
To make prescription for a kingdom's worth.
Henry 6, P. 3, iii. 3.

And yet in some respects, I grant, I cannot go ; I
cannot tell.   *Henry 4,* P. 2, i. 2.

TEMPER. *Temperament ; constitution of mind
or body ; disposition.*

Ye gods, it doth amaze me,
A man of such a feeble *temper* should
So get the start of the majestic world,
And bear the palm alone.   *Julius Cæsar,* i. 2.

The brain may devise laws for the blood ; but
a hot *temper* leaps o'er a cold decree.
Merchant of Venice, i. 2.

To TEMPER. *To soften; to incline; to dispose;
to mix ; to compound ; to comply.*

Old fond eyes,
Beweep this cause again, I'll pluck you out,
And cast you, with the waters that you lose,
To *temper* clay.   *King Lear,* i. 4.

There will I visit Master Robert Shallow, esquire ;
I have him already *tempering* between my finger
and my thumb, and shortly will I seal with him.
Henry 4, P. 2, iv. 3.

Where you may *temper* her, by your persuasion,
To hate young Valentine, and love my friend.
Two Gentlemen of Verona, iii. 2.

I will talk to you
When you are better *temper'd* to attend.
Henry 4, P. 1, i. 3.

Madam, if you could find out but a man
To bear a poison, I would *temper* it.
Romeo and Juliet, iii. 5.

The queen, sir, very oft impórtun'd me
To *temper* poisons for her.   *Cymbeline,* v. 5.

The poison of that lies in you to *temper.*
Much Ado about Nothing, ii. 2.

He is justly serv'd ;
It is a poison *temper'd* by himself.   *Hamlet,* v. 2.

For few men rightly *temper* with the stars.
Henry 6, P. 3, iv. 6.

TEMPERANCE. *Temperature ; calmness ; moderation ; patience.*

It must needs be of subtle, tender, and delicate
temperance.   *Tempest,* ii. 1.

Be by, good madam, when we do awake him ;
I doubt not of his *temperance.*   *King Lear,* iv. 7.

Being once chaf'd, he cannot
Be rein'd again to *temperance.*   *Coriolanus,* iii. 3.

Ask God for *temperance ;* that's th' appliance only
Which your disease requires.   *Henry 8,* i. 1.

TEMPORAL. *Temporary.*

Though 't be *temporal,*
Yet, if that quarrel, fortune, do divorce
It from the bearer, 'tis a sufferance panging
As soul and body's severing.   *Henry 8,* ii. 3.

TEMPORARY. *Temporal.*

Not scurvy, nor a *temporary* meddler,
As he's reported by this gentleman.
Measure for Measure, v. 1.

To TEMPORIZE. *To comply ; to yield ; to delay ; to procrastinate.*

The Dauphin is too wilful-opposite,
And will not *temporize* with my entreaties.
King John, v. 2.

All's well ; and might have been much better, if
He could have *temporiz'd.*   *Coriolanus,* iv. 6.

Well, you will *temporize* with the hours.
Much Ado about Nothing, i. 1.

TEMPORIZER. *A trimmer ; a time-pleaser ; a
waverer.*

Or else a hovering *temporizer,* that
Canst with thine eyes at once see good and evil,
Inclining to them both.   *Winter's Tale,* i. 2.

To TEMPT. *To provoke; to try; to defy.*

But wherefore did you so much *tempt* the heavens?
Julius Cæsar, i. 3.

Have mind upon your health, *tempt* me no further.
Ibid. iv. 3.

That man is not alive
Might so have *tempted* him as you have done,
Without the taste of danger and reproof.
Henry 4, P. 1, iii. 1.

I am much too venturous
In *tempting* of your patience.
Henry 8, i. 2.

And *tempt* not yet the brushes of the war.
Troilus and Cressida, v. 3.

And sometimes we are devils to ourselves,
When we will *tempt* the frailty of our powers,
Presuming on their changeful potency. *Ibid.* iv. 4.

To TEND. *To attend; to wait upon; to follow.*

Th' associates *tend,* and every thing is bent
For England. *Hamlet,* iv. 3.

And worthier than himself
Here *tend* the savage strangeness he puts on.
Troilus and Cressida, ii. 3.

Let us address to *tend* on Hector's heels.
Ibid. iv. 4.

Was he not companion with the riotous knights
That *tend* upon my father? *King Lear,* ii. 1.

TENDANCE. *Attention; care; attendance; waiting on.*

Nature does require
Her times of preservation, which perforce
I, her frail son, amongst my brethren mortal,
Must give my *tendance* to. *Henry* 8, iii. 2.

In which time she purpos'd
By watching, weeping, *tendance,* kissing, to
O'ercome you with her show. *Cymbeline,* v. 5.

All those which were his fellows but of late,—
Some better than his value,—on the moment
Follow his strides, his lobbies fill with *tendance.*
Timon of Athens, i. 1.

TENDER. *Regard; kind concern; care.*

Which, in the *tender* of a wholesome weal,
Might in their working do you that offence
Which else were shame. *King Lear,* i. 4.

And show'd thou mak'st some *tender* of my life,
In this fair rescue thou hast brought to me.
Henry 4, P. 1, v. 4.

TENDER. *Dear; precious; young.*

Now, for my life, she's wandering to the Tower,
On pure heart's love, to greet the *tender* princes.
Richard 3, iv. 1.

O, Heaven be judge how I love Valentine,
Whose life's as *tender* to me as my soul.
Two Gentlemen of Verona, v. 4.

To TENDER. *To esteem; to value; to watch over; to protect; to pity; to regard with kindness.*

But we our kingdom's safety must so *tender,*
Whose ruin you have sought, that to her laws
We do deliver you. *Henry* 5, ii. 2.

By my life, I do; which I *tender* dearly, though
I say I am a magician. *As you like it,* v. 2.

Tender yourself more dearly;
Or—not to crack the wind of the poor phrase,
Running it thus—you'll *tender* me a fool.
Hamlet, i. 3.

Tendering my ruin, and assail'd of none.
Henry 6, P. 1, iv. 7.

I thank you, madam, that you *tender* her.
Two Gentlemen of Verona, iv. 2.

TENDER-HEFTED. *Tender-hearted; compassionate.*

No, Regan, thou shalt never have my curse:
Thy *tender-hefted* nature shall not give
Thee o'er to harshness. *King Lear,* ii. 4.

TENT. *Lint or other material employed in examining a wound; a probe.*

But modest doubt is call'd
The beacon of the wise, the *tent* that searches
To the bottom of the worst.
Troilus and Cressida, ii. 2.

I've heard I am a strumpet; and mine ear,
Therein false struck, can take no greater wound,
Nor *tent* to bottom that. *Cymbeline,* iii. 4.

To TENT. *To search; to probe; to heal; to lodge as in a tent; to dwell.*

Should they not,
Well might they foster 'gainst ingratitude,
And *tent* themselves with death. *Coriolanus,* i. 9.

I'll observe his looks;
I'll *tent* him to the quick: if he but blench,
I know my course. *Hamlet,* ii. 2.

For 'tis a sore upon us,
You cannot *tent* yourself; be gone, beseech you.
Coriolanus, iii. 1.
The smiles of knaves *tent* in my cheeks !
Ibid. iii. 2.

TERCEL. *The male of the goshawk.*

The falcon as the *tercel,* for all the ducks i' the river.
Troilus and Cressida, iii. 2.

TERMINATION. *A sentence ; a phrase.*

If her breath were as terrible as her *terminations,*
there were no living near her.
Much Ado about Nothing, ii. 1.

TERRENE. *Earthly.*

Alack, our *terrene* moon
Is now eclips'd ; and it portends alone
The fall of Antony. *Antony and Cleopatra,* iii. 13.

TEST. *Testimony ; proof ; evidence.*

To vouch this, is no proof,
Without more wider and more overt *test*
Than these thin habits and poor likelihoods
Of modern seeming do prefer against him.
Othello, i. 3.

TESTER. *A sixpence.*

Hold, there's a *tester* for thee. *Henry* 4, P. 2, iii. 2.

TO TESTERN. *To present with sixpence.*

To testify your bounty, I thank you, you have
testerned me. *Two Gentlemen of Verona,* i. 1.

TO TESTIMONY. *To try ; to test ; to judge ; to
witness.*

Let him be but *testimonied* in his own bringings-
forth, and he shall appear to the envious a scholar,
a statesman, and a soldier.
Measure for Measure, iii. 2.

TESTRIL. *A sixpence.*

There's a *testril* of me too. *Twelfth-Night,* ii. 3.

TETCHY. *Peevish ; froward.*

And he's as *tetchy* to be woo'd to woo,
As she is stubborn-chaste against all suit.
Troilus and Cressida, i. 1.
Tetchy and wayward was thy infancy.
Richard 3, iv. 4.
To see it *tetchy,* and fall out with the dug !
Romeo and Juliet, i. 3.

TETTER. *An eruption of the skin ; a scab or
scurf.*

And a most instant *tetter* bark'd about,
Most lazar-like, with vile and loathsome crust,
All my smooth body. *Hamlet,* i. 5.

To TETTER. *To infect with scabs ; to taint.*

So shall my lungs
Coin words till their decay against those measles
Which we disdain should *tetter* us.
Coriolanus, iii. 1.

THANKINGS. *Thanks ; gratitude.*

The forlorn soldier, that so nobly fought,
He would have well becom'd this place, and grac'd
The *thankings* of a king. *Cymbeline,* v. 5.

THARBOROUGH. *Constable ; thirdborough.*

For I am his grace's *tharborough.*
Love's Labour's lost, i. 1.

THAT. *So that.*

Yet, since I see you fearful, *that* neither my
coat, integrity, nor persuasion can with ease attempt
you, I will go further than I meant.
Measure for Measure, iv. 1.
But, if yourself,
Whose aged honour cites a virtuous youth,
Did ever, in so true a flame of liking,
Wish chastely, and love dearly, *that* your Dian
Was both herself and love ; O, then, give pity
To her, whose state is such, that cannot choose
But lend and give, where she is sure to lose.
All's well that ends well, i. 3.
One touch of nature makes the whole world kin,—
That all, with one consent, praise new-born gauds,
Though they are made and moulded of things past,
And give to dust, that is a little gilt,
More laud than gilt o'er-dusted.
Troilus and Cressida, iii. 3.

THEME. *Discourse ; contest ; conflict ; controversy.*

Alone, it was the subject of my *theme.*
Comedy of Errors, v. 1.
For in a *theme* so bloody-fac'd as this,
Conjecture, expectation, and surmise
Of aids incertain, should not be admitted.
Henry 4, P. 2, i. 3.

THEORIC. *Theory.*

So that the art and practice part of life
Must be the mistress to this *theoric.* *Henry* 5, i. 1.

That had the whole *theoric* of war in the knot of his scarf. *All's well that ends well*, iv. 3.
Unless the bookish *theoric*,
Wherein the togèd consuls can propose
As masterly as he. *Othello*, i. 1.

THEREFORE. *For that purpose.*

Therefore we meet not now. *Henry* 4, P. 1, i. 1.

THEW. *Brawn; muscle.*

Care I for the limb, the *thews*, the stature, bulk, and big assemblance of a man! Give me the spirit, Master Shallow. *Henry* 4, P. 2, iii. 2.
For nature, crescent, does not grow alone
In *thews* and bulk. *Hamlet*, i. 3.
Let it be who it is : for Romans now
Have *thews* and limbs like to their ancestors.
Julius Cæsar, i. 3.

THICK. *Fast; quick; dull; dim.*

My heart beats *thicker* than a feverous pulse.
Troilus and Cressida, iii. 2.
And speaking *thick*, which nature made his blemish,
Became the accents of the valiant.
Henry 4, P. 2, ii. 3.
As *thick* as hail came post with post. *Macbeth*, i. 3.
Ay, madam, twenty several messengers :
Why do you send so *thick* ?
Antony and Cleopatra, i. 5.
Say, and speak *thick*,—
Love's counsellor should fill the bores of hearing,
To the smothering of the sense,—how far it is
To this same blessèd Milford. *Cymbeline*, iii. 2.
Go, Pindarus, get higher on that hill ;
My sight was over *thick*; regard Titinius,
And tell me what thou not'st about the field.
Julius Cæsar, v. 3.

TO THICKEN. *To grow dim; to wane; to be obscured.*

Light *thickens*; and the crow
Makes wing to the rooky wood. *Macbeth*, iii. 2.
Thy lustre *thickens*, when he shines by.
Antony and Cleopatra, ii. 3.

THICKSKIN. *A dolt; a blockhead; a lout.*

What wouldst thou have, boor? what, *thickskin* ?
Merry Wives of Windsor, iv. 5.
The shallowest *thickskin* of that barren sort,
Who Pyramus presented in their sport,
Forsook his scene, and enter'd in a brake.
Midsummer-Night's Dream, iii. 2.

THIEVERY. *Booty; plunder.*

Injurious time now, with a robber's haste,
Crams his rich *thievery* up, he knows not how.
Troilus and Cressida, iv. 4.

TO THINK. *To hope; to expect.*

Cromwell, I did not *think* to shed a tear
In all my miseries. *Henry* 8, iii. 2.
He that will *think* to live till he be old,
Give me some help !—O cruel !—O you gods !
King Lear, iii. 7.

TO THINK SCORN. *To disdain; to feel shame.*

The time seems long ; their blood *thinks* scorn,
Till it fly out, and show them princes born.
Cymbeline, iv. 4.
The nobility *think* scorn to go in leather aprons.
Henry 6, P. 2, iv. 2.

THITHERWARD. *Thither; in that direction.*

Madam, he's gone to serve the Duke of Florence :
We met him *thitherward*.
All's well that ends well, iii. 2.

THOROUGH. *Through; by means of.*

These words become your lips as they pass *thorough* them. *Timon of Athens*, v. 1.
The false revolting Normans *thorough* thee
Disdain to call us lord. *Henry* 6, P. 2, iv. 1.

THOUGHT. *Melancholy; grief; sadness; opinion; expectation; hope.*

Thought and affliction, passion, hell itself,
She turns to favour and to prettiness.
Hamlet, iv. 5.
This blows my heart,
If swift *thought* break it not, a swifter mean
Shall outstrike *thought*; but *thought* will do't, I feel.
Antony and Cleopatra, iv. 6.
That same wicked bastard of Venus, that was
begot of *thought*, conceived of spleen, and born of madness. *As you like it*, iv. 1.
Let your highness
Lay a more noble *thought* upon mine honour
Than for to think that I would sink it here.
All's well that ends well, v. 3.
Flattering himself with project of a power
Much smaller than the smallest of his *thoughts*.
Henry 4, P. 2, i. 3.
The main descry
Stands on the hourly *thought*. *King Lear*, iv. 6.

THOUGHTFUL. *Anxious ; solicitous.*

For this they have been *thoughtful* to invest
Their sons with arts and martial exercises.
Henry 4, P. 2, iv. 4.

THRALL. *A slave.*

How it did grieve Macbeth! did he not straight,
In pious rage, the two delinquents tear,
That were the slaves of drink and *thralls* of sleep?
Macbeth, iii. 6.

Go, hie thee, hie thee from this slaughter-house,
Lest thou increase the number of the dead ;
And make me die the *thrall* of Margaret's curse.
Richard 3, iv. 1.

THREE-NOOKED. *Having three angles or corners.*

Prove this a prosperous day, the *three-nook'd* world
Shall bear the olive freely.
Antony and Cleopatra, iv. 6.

THREE-PILE. *The richest velvet.*

I have served Prince Florizel, and, in my time,
wore *three-pile;* but now I am out of service.
Winter's Tale, iv. 2.

THREE-PILED. *Superfine.*

Three-pil'd hyperboles, spruce affectation.
Love's Labour's lost, v. 2.

To THRIVE. *To help; to speed; to advantage.*

Mine innocency and Saint George to *thrive!*
Richard 2, i. 3.

THROE. *A pang.*

And that gave to me
Many a groaning *throe.*   *Henry* 8, ii. 4.

And tell them that, to ease them of their griefs, . . .
Their pangs of love, with other incident *throes*
That nature's fragile vessel doth sustain
In life's uncertain voyage, I will
Some kindness do them.   *Timon of Athens*, v. 1.

To THROE. *To cause pain ; to bring forth.*

The setting of thine eye and cheek proclaim
A birth, indeed, which *throes* thee much to yield.
Tempest, ii. 1.

With news the time's in labour, and *throes* forth,
Each minute, some.   *Antony and Cleopatra*, iii. 7.

THROUGHFARE. *A thoroughfare.*

His body's a passable carcass, if he be not hurt:
it is a *throughfare* for steel, if it be not hurt.
Cymbeline, i. 2.

Th' Hyrcanian deserts, and the vasty wilds
Of wide Arabia are as *throughfares* now.
Merchant of Venice, ii. 6.

THROUGHLY. *Thoroughly ; amply.*

Only I'll be reveng'd
Most *throughly* for my father.   *Hamlet*, iv. 5.
The next advantage will we take *throughly.*
.   *Tempest*, iii. 3.

My point and period will be *throughly* wrought,
Or well or ill, as this day's battle's fought.
King Lear, iv. 7.

THRUM. *A coarse sort of yarn.*

O Fates, come, come,
Cut thread and *thrum;*
Quail, crush, conclude, and quell!
Midsummer-Night's Dream, v. 1.

THRUMMED. *Made of coarse woollen cloth or thrum.*

And there's her *thrummed* hat, and her muffler
too.   *Merry Wives of Windsor*, iv. 2.

THUNDER-STONE. *A thunderbolt; lightning.*

And, thus unbracèd, Casca, as you see,
Have bar'd my bosom to the *thunder-stone.*
Julius Cæsar, i. 3.

Fear no more the lightning-flash,
Nor th' all-dreaded *thunder-stone.*   *Cymbeline*, iv. 2.

THWART. *Perverse; spiteful; malicious.*

If she must teem,
Create her child of spleen ; that it may live
And be a *thwart* disnatur'd torment to her!
King Lear, i. 4.

To TICE. *To entice.*

He thinks, nay, with all confidence he swears,
As he had seen't, or been an instrument
To *tice* you to't, that you have touch'd his queen
Forbiddenly.   *Winter's Tale*, i. 2.

TICKLE. *Tottering; uncertain ; unsteady.*

The state of Normandy
Stands on a *tickle* point, now they are gone.
Henry 6, P. 2, i. 1.

And thy head stands so *tickle* on thy shoulders,
that a milkmaid, if she be in love, may sigh it off.
Measure for Measure, i. 2.

To Tickle. *To please ; to gratify ; to excite ;
to stir up.*

Nay, I'll *tickle* ye for a young prince, i' faith.
Henry 4, P. 1, ii. 4.

She's *tickled* now ; her fury needs no spurs.
Henry 6, P. 2, i. 3.

That smooth-fac'd gentleman, *tickling* commodity.
King John, ii. 1.

Now expectation, *tickling* skittish spirits,
Sets all on hazard. *Troilus and Cressida*, Prologue.

Such a nature,
Tickled with good success, disdains the shadow
Which he treads on at noon. *Coriolanus*, i. 2.

Tickled o' the sere. *Moved by coarse mirth
and ribaldry.*

The clown shall make those laugh whose lungs
are *tickled o' the sere.* *Hamlet*, ii. 2.

Tick-tack. *Backgammon.*

Who I would be sorry should be thus foolishly
lost at a game of *tick-tack*. *Measure for Measure*, i. 2.

Tide. *Time ; season ; festival ; holiday.*

I have important business,
The *tide* whereof is now.
Troilus and Cressida, v. 1.

What hath this day deserv'd ? what hath it done,
That it in golden letters should be set
Among the high *tides* in the calendar ?
King John, iii. 1.

A brave fellow ! he keeps his *tides* well.
Timon of Athens, i. 2.

Tight. *Handy ; quick ; clever.*

Thou fumblest, Eros ; and my queen's a squire
More *tight* at this than thou : dispatch.
Antony and Cleopatra, iv. 4.

Tightly. *Neatly ; cleverly ; briskly ; adroitly.*

Hold, sirrah, bear you these letters *tightly.*
Merry Wives of Windsor, i. 3.

Tike. *A cur ; a dog.*

Or bobtail *tike* or trundle-tail. *King Lear*, iii. 6.

Till. *To.*

That sleep and feeding may prorogue his honour
Even *till* a lethe'd dulness !
Antony and Cleopatra, ii. 1.

Tilth. *Tillage ; arable land.*

Our corn's to reap, for yet our *tilth*'s to sow.
Measure for Measure, iv. 1.

Timbered. *Shaped ; formed ; built.*

So that my arrows,
Too slightly *timber'd* for so loud a wind,
Would have reverted to my bow again,
And not where I had aim'd them. *Hamlet*, iv. 7.

His bark is stoutly *timber'd*, and his pilot .
Of very expert and approv'd allowance.
Othello, ii. 1.

Time. *Season of the year ; time of life ; age ;
termination ; end.*

For, ere the six years that he hath to spend
Can change their moons and bring their *times* about,
My oil-dried lamp and time-bewasted light
Shall be extinct with age and endless night.
Richard 2, i. 3.

To be fantastic may become a youth
Of greater *time* than I shall show to be.
Two Gentlemen of Verona, ii. 7.

But I do find it cowardly and vile,
For fear of what might fall, so to prevent
The *time* of life. *Julius Cæsar*, v. 1.

Timeless. *Untimely ; premature.*

Who wrought it with the king, and who perform'd
The bloody office of his *timeless* end.
Richard 2, iv. 1.

Poison, I see, hath been his *timeless* end.
Romeo and Juliet, v. 3.

Timely (adj.). *Early ; opportune ; seasonable.*

Now spurs the lated traveller apace
To gain the *timely* inn. *Macbeth*, iii. 3.

And happy were I in my *timely* death,
Could all my travels warrant me they live.
Comedy of Errors, i. 1.

Timely (adv.). *Early ; betimes ; soon.*

He did command me to call *timely* on him.
Macbeth, ii. 1.

The beds i' th' east are soft ; and thanks to you

xx

That call'd me, *timelier* than my purpose, hither;
For I have gain'd by't.
Antony and Cleopatra, ii. 6.

TIMELY-PARTED. *Newly-parted ; just dead.*

Oft have I seen a *timely-parted* ghost,
Of ashy semblance, meagre, pale, and bloodless,
Being all descended to the labouring heart.
Henry 6, P. 2, iii. 2.

TIME-PLEASER. *A flatterer ; a parasite.*

The devil a puritan that he is, or any thing
constantly, but a *time-pleaser*. *Twelfth-Night*, ii. 3.

TINCT. *Tincture ; colour ; hue ; tint.*

Plutus himself,
That knows the *tinct* and multiplying medicine,
Hath not in nature's mystery more science
Than I have in this ring.
All's well that ends well, v. 3.

Yet, coming from him, that great medicine hath
With his *tinct* gilded thee.
Antony and Cleopatra, i. 5.

Lac'd
With blue of heaven's own *tinct*. *Cymbeline*, ii. 2.

And there I see such black and grainèd spots
As will not leave their *tinct*. *Hamlet*, iii. 4.

TINCTURE. *Colour ; hue ; tint.*

And that great men shall press
For *tinctures*, stains, relics, and cognizance'.
Julius Cæsar, ii. 2.

The air hath starv'd the roses in her cheeks,
And pinch'd the lily *tincture* of her face,
That now she is become as black as I.
Two Gentlemen of Verona, iv. 2.

If you can bring
Tincture or lustre in her lip, her eye,
Heat outwardly, or breath within, I'll serve you
As I would do the gods. *Winter's Tale*, iii. 2.

TIRE. *A head-dress.*

And in that *tire*
Shall Master Slender steal my Nan away.
Merry Wives of Windsor, iv. 4.

If I had such a *tire*, this face of mine
Were full as lovely as is this of hers.
Two Gentlemen of Verona, iv. 2.

Then put my *tires* and mantles on him, whilst
I wore his sword Philippan.
Antony and Cleopatra, ii. 5.

To TIRE. *To prey upon ; to feed ; to dress up ; to deck.*

Whose haughty spirit, wingèd with desire,
Will cost my crown, and like an empty eagle
Tire on the flesh of me and of my son.
Henry 6, P. 3, i. 1.

Disedg'd by her
That now thou *tir'st* on. *Cymbeline*, iii. 4.

Upon that were my thoughts *tiring* when we
encountered. *Timon of Athens*, iii. 6.

Imitari is nothing : so doth the hound his master, the ape his keeper, and the *tired* horse his rider.
Love's Labour's lost, iv. 2.

To. *Equal to ; compared to ; according to ; in addition to ; with respect to.*

There is no woe *to* his correction,
Nor *to* his service no such joy on earth !
Two Gentlemen of Verona, ii. 4.

War is no strife
To the dark house and the detested wife.
All's well that ends well, ii. 3.

And, *to* this preservative, of no better report
than a horse-drench. *Coriolanus*, ii. 1.

O, these flaws and starts,
Impostors *to* true fear, would well become
A woman's story at a winter's fire. *Macbeth*, iii. 4.

Construe the times *to* their necessities,
And you shall say indeed, it is the time,
And not the king, that doth you injuries.
Henry P. 2, iv. 1.

The Greeks are strong, and skilful *to* their strength,
Fierce *to* their skill, and *to* their fierceness valiant.
Troilus and Cressida, i. 1.

'Tis much he dares ;
And, *to* that dauntless temper of his mind,
He hath a wisdom that doth guide his valour
To act in safety. *Macbeth*, iii. 1.

To his mistress,
For whom he now is banish'd, her own price
Proclaims how she esteem'd him and his virtue.
Cymbeline, i. 1.

To POINT. *Exactly.*

Hast thou, spirit,
Perform'd *to point* the tempest that I bade thee?
Tempest, i. 2.

TOAST. *A sop.*

Where's then the saucy boat?
. . . . either to harbour fled,
Or made a *toast* for Neptune.
Troilus and Cressida, i. 3.

TOD. *Twenty-eight pounds of wool.*

Let me see :—every 'leven wether tods; every
tod yields pound and odd shilling.
Winter's Tale, iv. 2.

To TOD. *To yield a tod, or twenty-eight pounds
of wool.*

Let me see :—every 'leven wether tods.
Winter's Tale, iv. 2.

TOGE. *A toga; a gown; a garment.*

Why in this woolless *toge* should I stand here,
To beg of Hob and Dick their needless vouches ?
Coriolanus, ii. 3.

TOGED. *Drest in a toga; gowned.*

Unless the bookish theoric,
Wherein the *togèd* consuls can propose
As masterly as he. *Othello,* i. 1.

To TOIL. *To weary; to overlabour.*

And tell me, he that knows,
Why this same strict and most observant watch
So nightly *toils* the subject of the land. *Hamlet,* i. 1.

And now have *toil'd* their unbreath'd memories
With this same play, against your nuptial.
Midsummer-Night's Dream, v. 1.

To TOKEN. *To make known; to declare.*

That, what in time proceeds
May *token* to the future our past deeds.
All's well that ends well, iv. 2.

TOKENED. *Spotted; marked.*

On our side like the *token'd* pestilence,
Where death is sure. *Antony and Cleopatra,* iii. 10.

To TOLL. *To take tribute; to glean; to collect.*

Add thus much more,—That no Italian priest
Shall tithe or *toll* in our dominions.
King John, iii. 1.

When, like the bee, *tolling* from every flower
The virtuous sweets,
Our thighs with wax, our mouths with honey pack'd,
We bring it to the hive ; and, like the bees,
Are murder'd for our pains. *Henry 4, P. 2,* iv. 4.

TOMBOY. *A courtezan; a wanton; a drab.*

To be partner'd
With *tomboys,* hir'd with that self-exhibition
Which your own coffers yield ! *Cymbeline,* i. 6.

TONGUE. *Talk; language.*

No, my good lord ; he speaks the common *tongue,*
Which all men speak with him.
Timon of Athens, i. 1.

To TONGUE. *To denounce; to publish; to
utter; to prate.*

But that her tender shame
Will not proclaim against her maiden loss,
How might she *tongue* me !
Measure for Measure, iv. 4.

'Tis still a dream ; or else such stuff as madmen
Tongue, and brain not. *Cymbeline,* v. 4.

TOO-MUCH. *Excess; exuberance.*

For goodness, growing to a plurisy,
Dies in his own *too-much.* *Hamlet,* iv. 7.

This would have seem'd a period
To such as love not sorrow ; but another,
To amplify *too-much,* would make much more,
And top extremity. *King Lear,* v. 3.

To TOP. *To surpass; to outgo; to rise above;
to overtop.*

So far he *topp'd* my thought,
That I, in forgery of shapes and tricks,
Come short of what he did. *Hamlet,* iv. 7.

Well, my legitimate, if this letter speed,
And my invention thrive, Edmund the base
Shall *top* the legitimate. *King Lear,* i. 2.

TOPLESS. *Supreme; sovereign; without a
superior.*

Sometime, great Agamemnon,
Thy *topless* deputation he puts on.
Troilus and Cressida, i. 3.

To TOPPLE. *To tumble; to fall down; to
overthrow.*

Though castles *topple* on their warders' heads.
Macbeth, iv. 1.

I'll look no more :
Lest my brain turn, and the deficient sight
Topple down headlong. *King Lear,* iv. 6.

Which, for enlargement striving,
Shakes the old beldame earth, and *topples* down
Steeples and moss-grown towers.
Henry 4, P. 1, ii. 4.

TORCHER. *A torch-bearer.*

Ere twice the horses of the sun shall bring
Their fiery *torcher* his diurnal ring.
All's well that ends well, ii. 1.

TORTIVE. *Twisted.*

As knots, by the conflux of meeting sap,
Infect the sound pine, and divert his grain
Tortive and errant from his course of growth.
Troilus and Cressida, i. 3.

TOUCH. *Stroke; grace; smack; sensibility; proof; touchstone; hint; stain.*

One *touch* of nature makes the whole world kin.
Troilus and Cressida, iii. 3.

I'm senseless of your wrath; a *touch* more rare
Subdues all pangs, all fears. *Cymbeline,* i. 1.

O brave *touch!*
Could not a worm, an adder, do so much?
Midsummer-Night's Dream, iii. 2.

Thus Rosalind of many parts
By heavenly synod was devis'd;
Of many faces, eyes, and hearts,
To have the *touches* dearest priz'd.
As you like it, iii. 2.

Madam, I have a *touch* of your condition,
That cannot brook the accent of reproof.
Richard 3, iv. 4.

He loves us not; he wants the natural *touch.*
Macbeth, iv. 2.

Come, my sweet wife, my dearest mother, and
My friends of noble *touch.* *Coriolanus,* iv. 1.

Ah, Buckingham, now do I play the *touch,*
To try if thou be current gold indeed.
Richard 3, iv. 2.

An if there be
No great offence belongs to't, give your friend
Some *touch* of your late business. *Henry 8,* v. 1.

Or ever spoke one the least word that might
Be to the prejudice of her present state,
Or *touch* of her good person. *Ibid.* ii. 4.

Who is as free from *touch* or soil with her,
As she from one ungot. *Measure for Measure,* v. 1.

To TOUCH. *To test; to try; to seize; to arrest.*

You have beguil'd me with a counterfeit
Resembling majesty; which, being *touch'd* and tried,
Proves valueless. *King John,* iii. 1.

Nay, when I have a suit
Wherein I mean to *touch* your love indeed,

It shall be full of poise, and difficult
And fearful to be granted. *Othello,* iii. 3.

No, they cannot *touch* me for coining; I am the
king himself. *King Lear,* iv. 6.

TOUCHED. *Afflicted; tainted; implicated; stained; sullied.*

And, hearing your high majesty is *touch'd*
With that malignant cause, wherein the honour
Of my dear father's gift stands chief in power,
I come to tender it, and my appliance,
With all bound humbleness.
All's well that ends well, ii. 1.

If by direct or by collateral hand
They find us *touch'd,* we will our kingdom give,
Our crown, our life, and all that we call ours,
To you in satisfaction. *Hamlet,* iv. 5.

But with a noble fury and fair spirit,
Seeing his reputation *touch'd* to death,
He did oppose his foe. *Timon of Athens,* iii. 5.

To TOUSE. *To tear; to rend.*

Thinkest thou, for that I insinuate or *touse*
from thee thy business, I am therefore no courtier?
Winter's Tale, iv. 3.

We'll *touse* you
Joint by joint, but we will know your purpose.
Measure for Measure, v. 1.

TOWARD (adj.). *Ready; forward.*

Why, that is spoken like a *toward* prince.
Henry 6, P. 3, ii. 2.

'Tis a good hearing, when children are *toward.*
Taming of the Shrew, v. 2.

TOWARD. *At hand; near; in preparation.*

What, a play *toward!* I'll be an auditor;
An actor too perhaps, if I see cause.
Midsummer-Night's Dream, iii. 1.

What might be *toward,* that this sweaty haste
Doth make the night joint-labourer with the day?
Hamlet, i. 1.

O proud death,
What feast is *toward* in thine eternal cell,
That thou so many princes at a shot
So bloodily hast struck? *Ibid.* v. 2.

TOWARDLY. *Civil; docile; complaisant; tractable.*

I have observed thee always for a *towardly*
prompt spirit,—and one that knows what belongs
to reason. *Timon of Athens,* iii. 1.

TOY. *An idle tale; whim; freak; fancy; caprice; trifle.*

I never may believe
These antique fables, nor these fairy toys.
Midsummer-Night's Dream, v. 1.

There's *toys* abroad : anon I'll tell thee more.
King John, i. 1.

These, as I learn, and such-like *toys* as these
Have mov'd his highness to commit me now.
Richard 3, i. 1.

And this shall free thee from this present shame;
If no inconstant *toy*, nor womanish fear,
Abate thy valour in the acting it.
Romeo and Juliet, iv. 1.

The very place puts *toys* of desperation,
Without more motive, into every brain.
Hamlet, i. 4.

Immoment *toys*, things of such dignity
As we greet modern friends withal.
Antony and Cleopatra, v. 2.

To TRACE. *To pace; to follow; to succeed; to follow in succession.*

As we do *trace* this alley up and down,
Our talk must only be of Benedick.
Much Ado about Nothing, iii. 1.

And bring him out that is but woman's son
Can *trace* me in the tedious ways of art.
Henry 4, P. 1, iii. 1.

Now all my joy
Trace the conjunction !
Henry 8, iii. 2.

The castle of Macduff I will surprise;
Seize upon Fife; give to the edge o' the sword
His wife, his babes, and all unfortunate souls
That *trace* him in his line.
Macbeth, iv. 1.

TRACT. *Relation; narrative; description.*

The *tract* of every thing
Would by a good discourser lose some life,
Which action's self was tongue to.
Henry 8, i. 1.

TRACTABLE. *Inclinable; favourably disposed.*

If thou dost find him *tractable* to us,
Encourage him, and tell him all our reasons.
Richard 3, iii. 1.

TRADE. *Passage; traffic; custom; habit; business.*

Further, sir,
Stands in the gap and *trade* of more preferments,
With which the time will load him.
Henry 8, v. 1.

O, fie, fie, fie !
Thy sin's not accidental, but a *trade*.
Measure for Measure, iii. 1.

Have you any further *trade* with us?
Hamlet, iii. 2.

My niece is desirous you should enter, if your
trade be to her.
Twelfth-Night, iii. 1.

TRADED. *Practised; versed; experienced.*

My will enkindled by mine eyes and ears,
Two *traded* pilots 'twixt the dangerous shores
Of will and judgment.
Troilus and Cressida, ii. 2.

TRADITION. *Usage; old custom.*

Throw away respect,
Tradition, form, and ceremonious duty.
Richard 2, iii. 2.

TRADITIONAL. *Governed by prescriptive rules and practices.*

You are too senseless-obstinate, my lord,
Too ceremonious and *traditional*.
Richard 3, iii. 1.

TRADUCEMENT. *Slander; calumny.*

'Twere a concealment
Worse than a theft, no less than a *traducement*,
To hide your doings.
Coriolanus, i. 9.

TRAGICAL. *Terrible.*

Why look you still so stern and *tragical* ?
Henry 6, P. 1, iii. 1.

TRAIL. *Track; scent.*

This is an aspic's *trail* : and these fig-leaves
Have slime upon them, such as th' aspic leaves
Upon the caves of Nile.
Antony and Cleopatra, v. 2.

How cheerfully on the false *trail* they cry !
O, this is counter, you false Danish dogs !
Hamlet, iv. 5.

TRAIN. *A trained force; an army; trick; artifice; device.*

And, good my lord, so please you, let our *trains*
March by us, that we may peruse the men
We should have cop'd withal.
Henry 4, P. 2, iv. 2.

Devilish Macbeth
By many of these *trains* hath sought to win me
Into his power.
Macbeth, iv. 3.

To TRAIN. *To entice; to allure; to invite.*

You *train* me to offend you; get you in.
By all the everlasting gods, I'll go !
Troilus and Cressida, v. 3.

O, *train* me not, sweet mermaid, with thy note
To drown me in thy sister flood of tears!
        Comedy of Errors, iii. 2.
And for that cause I *train'd* thee to my house.
        Henry 6, P. 1, ii. 3.

To TRAMMEL UP. *To intercept; to catch.*
    If the assassination
Could *trammel up* the consequence, and catch,
With his surcease, success.   *Macbeth*, i. 7.

TRANCED. *Insensible; in a trance.*
    Twice then the trumpet sounded,
And there I left him *tranc'd*.   *King Lear*, v. 3.

TRANSCENDENCE. *Excellence.*
    In a most weak and debile minister great power,
great *transcendence*. *All's well that ends well*, ii. 3.

To TRANSFORM. *To transport; to transfer.*
    And there were drawn
Upon a heap a hundred ghastly women,
Transformèd with their fear.   *Julius Cæsar*, i. 3.
And, gentle Puck, take this *transformèd* scalp
From off the head of this Athenian swain.
        Midsummer-Night's Dream, iv. 1.

To TRANSLATE. *To transform; to change.*
    The rest I'll give to be to you *translated*.
        Midsummer-Night's Dream, i. 1.
One do I personate of Lord Timon's frame,
Whom Fortune with her ivory hand wafts to her;
Whose present grace to present slaves and servants
Translates his rivals.   *Timon of Athens*, i. 1.
Bless thee, Bottom! bless thee! thou art *translated*.
        Midsummer-Night's Dream, iii. 1.

To TRANSPORT. *To put to death; to remove
from this world to the next.*
And to *transport* him in the mind he is
Were damnable.   *Measure for Measure*, iv. 3.
He cannot be heard of. Out of doubt he is
transported.   *Midsummer-Night's Dream*, iv. 2.

TRANSPORTANCE. *Conveyance; passage; waft-
age.*
And give me swift *transportance* to those fields
Where I may wallow in the lily-beds
Propos'd for the deserver!
        Troilus and Cressida, iii. 2.

To TRANSPOSE. *To change; to transform;
to convert.*
That which you are, my thoughts cannot *transpose*.
        Macbeth, iv. 3.
Things base and vile, holding no quantity,
Love can *transpose* to form and dignity.
        Midsummer-Night's Dream, i. 1.

To TRANS-SHAPE. *To transform; to meta-
morphose.*
    Thus did she, an hour together, *trans-shape* thy
particular virtues. *Much Ado about Nothing*, v. 1.

TRASH. *A mean worthless person; a simple-
ton.*
I do suspect this *trash* to be a party in this injury.
        Othello, v. 1.
If this poor *trash* of Venice, whom I trash
For his quick hunting, stand the putting on.
        Ibid. ii. 1.

To TRASH. *To check; to restrain; to clog.*
    Being once perfected how to grant suits,
How to deny them, who to advance, and who
To *trash* for over-topping.   *Tempest*, i. 2.
    Trash Merriman,—the poor cur is emboss'd.
        Taming of the Shrew, Induction, 1.
If this poor trash of Venice, whom I *trash*
For his quick hunting, stand the putting on.
        Othello, ii. 1.

TRAVAIL. *Pains; trouble.*
As honour, loss of time, *travail*, expense.
        Troilus and Cressida, ii. 1.
I have had my labour for my *travail*.   *Ibid.* i. 2.

To TRAVEL. *To stroll; to go from town to
town.*
    How chances it they *travel?* their residence,
both in reputation and profit, was better both ways.
        Hamlet, ii. 2.

TRAVEL-TAINTED. *Fatigued with travel; weary;
harassed.*
    And here, *travel-tainted* as I am, have, in my
pure and immaculate valour, taken Sir John Colevile of the dale, a most furious knight and valorous
enemy.   *Henry 4*, P. 2, iv. 3.

TRAVERSE. *Across.*
    He writes brave verses, speaks brave words,

swears brave oaths, and breaks them bravely, quite *traverse*, athwart the heart of his lover.

    As you like it, iii. 4.

To TRAVERSE. *An ancient term in military exercise; to move about, to encounter, in fencing.*

Hold, Wart, *traverse;* thus, thus, thus.

    Henry 4, P. 2, iii. 2.

Traverse; go; provide thy money.   *Othello*, i. 1.

To see thee fight, to see thee foin, to see thee *traverse*.

    Merry Wives of Windsor, ii. 3.

TRAVERSED. *Crossed; folded.*

Till now, myself, and such
As slept within the shadow of your power,
Have wander'd with our *travers'd* arms, and breath'd
Our sufferance vainly.   *Timon of Athens*, v. 4.

TRAY-TRIP. *A game at dice.*

Shall I play my freedom at *tray-trip*, and become thy bond-slave ?   *Twelfth-Night*, ii. 5.

TREACHER. *A traitor.*

Knaves, thieves, and *treachers*, by spherical predominance.   *King Lear*, i. 2.

TREASURY. *Treasure.*

Thy sumptuous buildings, and thy wife's attire,
Have cost a mass of public *treasury*.

    Henry 6, P. 2, i. 3.

And make her chronicle as rich with praise
As is the ooze and bottom of the sea
With sunken wreck and sumless *treasuries*.

    Henry 5, i. 2.

TREATY. *Entreaty; supplication; petition.*

Now I must
To the young man send humble *treaties*, dodge
And palter in the shifts of lowness.

    Antony and Cleopatra, iii. 11.

To TRENCH. *To cut; to carve; to wound; to damage.*

No more shall *trenching* war channel her fields.

    Henry 4, P. 1, i. 1.

This weak impress of love is as a figure
Trench'd in ice.   *Two Gentlemen of Verona*, iii. 2.

Safe in a ditch he bides,
With twenty *trenchèd* gashes on his head.

    Macbeth, iii. 4.

TRENCHANT. *Sharp; cutting.*

Let not the virgin's cheek
Make soft thy *trenchant* sword.

    Timon of Athens, iv. 3.

TRENCHER-KNIGHT. *One who holds a trencher; a serving-man.*

Some mumble-news, some *trencher-knight*, some
Dick.   *Love's Labour's lost*, v. 2.

TRIAL. *Endurance.*

It is to be all made of fantasy,
All made of passion, and all made of wishes ;
All adoration, duty, and obedience,
All humbleness, all patience, and impatience,
All purity, all *trial*, all observance.

    As you like it, v. 2.

TRICK. *A toy; a plaything; a puppet; a trifle.*

He has discover'd my design, and I
Remain a pinch'd thing; yea, a very *trick*
For them to play at will.   *Winter's Tale*, ii. 1.

Why, 'tis a cockle or a walnut-shell,
A knack, a toy, a *trick*, a baby's cap.

    Taming of the Shrew, iv. 3.

So, fellest foes,
Whose passions and whose plots have broke their
    sleep
To take the one the other, by some chance,
Some *trick* not worth an egg, shall grow dear friends.

    Coriolanus, iv. 4.

To TRICK. *To deck; to adorn.*

Horribly *trick'd*
With blood of fathers, mothers, daughters, sons.

    Hamlet, ii. 2.

TRICKING. *Dresses; decoration.*

And *tricking* for our fairies.

    Merry Wives of Windsor, iv. 4.

TRICKSY. *Quick; lively; merry; playful.*

My *tricksy* spirit !   *Tempest*, v. 1.

Garnish'd like him, that for a *tricksy* word
Defy the matter.   *Merchant of Venice*, iii. 5.

To TRIFLE. *To dwarf; to make of no importance.*

But this sore night
Hath *trifled* former knowings.   *Macbeth*, ii. 2.

To **Trill**. *To trickle; to fall in drops.*

Ay, sir; she took them, read them in my presence;
And now and then an ample tear *trill'd* down
Her delicate cheek. *King Lear,* iv. 3.

Trim. *Dress; decoration; equipment; caparison.*

They come like sacrifices in their *trim,*
And to the fire-ey'd maid of smoky war,
All hot and bleeding, will we offer them.
Henry 4, P. 1, iv. 1.

When we, in all her *trim,* freshly beheld
Our royal, good, and gallant ship. *Tempest,* v. 1.

A thousand, sir, have on their riveted *trim,*
And at the port expect you.
Antony and Cleopatra, iv. 4.

Trim. *Smooth; plausible; specious; gay; delicate; nice.*

What is that word, honour? air. A *trim* reckoning! *Henry 4, P. 1,* v. 1.

And men are only turned into tongue, and *trim*
ones too. *Much Ado about Nothing,* iv. 1.

Trim gallants, full of courtship and of state.
Love's Labour's lost, v. 2.

A *trim* exploit, a manly enterprise !
Midsummer-Night's Dream, iii. 2.

Trim (adv.). *Trimly; nicely; neatly.*

Young Adam Cupid, he that shot so *trim,*
When King Cophetua lov'd the beggar-maid.
Romeo and Juliet, ii. 1.

To **Trim.** *To clothe; to dress; to decorate; to equip.*

Is supper ready, the house *trimmed,* rushes
strowed, cobwebs swept? *Taming of the Shrew,* iv. 1.

Our youth got me to play the woman's part,
And I was *trimm'd* in Madam Julia's gown.
Two Gentlemen of Verona, iv. 2.

Trimly. *Nicely; sprucely.*

Came there a certain lord, neat, *trimly* dress'd.
Henry 4, P. 1, i. 3.

Trinkets. *Tools; tackle; implements.*

We'll see your *trinkets* here all forthcoming.
Henry 6, P. 2, i. 4.

To **Trip**. *To find out; to detect.*

What she confess'd
I will report, so please you : these her women
Can *trip* me, if I err. *Cymbeline,* v. 5.

Triple. *Third.*

Chiefly one
He bade me store up as a *triple* eye.
All's well that ends well, ii. 1.

Take but good note, and you shall see in him
The *triple* pillar of the world transform'd
Into a strumpet's fool. *Antony and Cleopatra,* i. 1.

Tristful. *Sad; gloomy; melancholy.*

For God's sake, lords, convey my *tristful* queen.
Henry 4, P. 1, ii. 4.

Yea, this solidity and compound mass,
With *tristful* visage, as against the doom,
Is thought-sick at the act. *Hamlet,* iii. 4.

Triumph. *A show; a pageant; a procession.*

Thou art a perpetual *triumph,* an everlasting
bonfire-light. *Henry 4, P. 1,* iii. 3.

But I will wed thee in another key,
With pomp, with *triumph,* and with revelling.
Midsummer-Night's Dream, i. 1.

We have not yet set down this day of *triumph.*
Richard 3, iii. 4.

What news from Oxford? hold these justs and *triumphs* ? *Richard 2,* v. 2.

Triumpher. *One who triumphs; a conqueror.*

And enter in our ears, like great *triúmphers*
In their applauding gates. *Timon of Athens,* v. 1.

Triumviry. *A triumvirate.*

Thou mak'st the *triumviry,* the corner-cap of society.
Love's Labour's lost, iv. 3.

To **Troll.** *To sing.*

Will you *troll* the catch
You taught me but while-ere? *Tempest,* iii. 2.

Troll-my-dames. *A game, the same as Troumadame.*

A fellow, sir, that I have known to go about
with *troll-my-dames.* *Winter's Tale,* iv. 2.

Tropically. *Figuratively.*

The Mouse-trap. Marry, how? *Tropically.*
Hamlet, iii. 2.

TROT. *An old woman.*

Or an old *trot* with ne'er a tooth in her head.
Taming of the Shrew, i. 2.

TROTH. *Faith; truth.*

My lord, now fear is from me, I'll speak *troth.*
Cymbeline, v. 5.

Now, by mine honour, by my life, my *troth,*
I will appeach the villain. *Richard 2,* v. 2.

Bid her alight,
And her *troth* plight,
And, aroint thee, witch, aroint thee!
King Lear, iii. 4.

TROTH-PLIGHT. *Betrothment; affiance.*

As rank as any flax-wench that puts to
Before her *troth-plight.* *Winter's Tale,* i. 2.

To TROTH-PLIGHT. *To betroth; to affiance.*

And certainly she did you wrong; for you were
troth-plight to her. *Henry 5,* ii. 1.

This' your son-in-law,
And son unto the king, whom heavens directing,
Is *troth-plight* to your daughter.
Winter's Tale, i. 2.

TROUBLOUS. *Uneasy; painful; troublesome.*

My *troublous* dream this night doth make me sad.
Henry 6, P. 2, i. 2.

But in this *troublous* time what's to be done?
Henry 6, P. 3, ii. 1.

So part we sadly in this *troublous* world.
Ibid. v. 5.

TROW. I TROW. *An exclamation of surprise or inquiry.*

What is the matter, *trow?* *Cymbeline,* i. 6.

What means the fool, *trow?*
Much Ado about Nothing, iii. 4.

What tempest, *I trow,* threw this whale, with
so many tons of oil in his belly, ashore at Windsor?
Merry Wives of Windsor, ii. 1.

Who's there, *I trow?* *Ibid.* i. 4.

To TROW. *To believe; to think.*

'Twas no need, *I trow,*
To bid me trudge. *Romeo and Juliet,* i. 3.

Trow you who hath done this? *As you like it,* iii. 2.

Learn more than thou *trowest,*
Set less than thou throwest. *King Lear,* i. 4.

To TRUANT. *To play the truant; to be absent from.*

'Tis double wrong, to *truant* with your bed,
And let her read it in thy looks at board.
Comedy of Errors, iii. 2.

TRUE. *Honest; just; equitable.*

Thou shalt have a share in our purchase, as I
am a *true* man. *Henry 4,* P. 1, ii. 1.

Mark but the badges of these men, my lords,
Then say if they be *true.* *Tempest,* v. 1.

Prince, as thou art *true,*
For blood of ours, shed blood of Montague.
Romeo and Juliet, iii. 1.

TRUE-PENNY. *An honest fellow.*

Ah, ha, boy! say'st thou so? art thou there, *true-penny?* *Hamlet,* i. 5.

TRULL. *A wanton; a drab.*

And gives his potent regiment to a *trull,*
That noises it against us.
Antony and Cleopatra, iii. 6.

TRULY. *Honestly; faithfully.*

We cannot all be masters, nor all masters
Cannot be *truly* follow'd. *Othello,* i. 1.

TRUNCHEON. *A club; a cudgel; a staff.*

Thy leg a stick compared to this *truncheon.*
Henry 6, P. 2, iv. 10.

To TRUNCHEON. *To beat; to cudgel.*

An captains were of my mind, they would *truncheon* you out, for taking their names upon you before you have earned them. *Henry 4,* P. 2, ii. 4.

TRUNCHEONER. *One armed with a cudgel.*

When I might see from far some forty *truncheoners* draw to her succour. *Henry 8,* v. 3.

TRUNDLE-TAIL. *A curly-tailed dog.*

Or bobtail tike or *trundle-tail.* *King Lear,* iii. 6.

TRUNK SLEEVE. *A wide sleeve.*

With a *trunk sleeve.* *Taming of the Shrew,* iv. 4.

TRUST. *Belief; opinion.*

That I am ready to distrust mine eyes,
And wrangle with my reason, that persuades me

YY

To any other *trust* but that I am mad,—
Or else the lady's mad. *Twelfth-Night*, iv. 3.

TRUTH. *Honesty; fidelity; loyalty.*

There is scarce *truth* enough alive to make societies secure. *Measure for Measure*, iii. 2.
She's punish'd for her *truth;* and undergoes,
More goddess-like than wife-like, such assaults
As would take in some virtue. *Cymbeline*, iii. 2.
I am in parliament pledge for his *truth*
And lasting fealty to the new-made king.
Richard 2, v. 2.

TRY. *Trial; assay; test.*

Then this breaking of his has been but a *try* for
his friends. *Timon of Athens*, v. 1.

To TRY. *To test; to prove.*

I fear it is : and yet, methinks, it should not,
For he hath still been *tried* a holy man.
Romeo and Juliet, iv. 3.

TUB-FAST. *Cure of diseases by means of salivation.*

Bring down rose-cheek'd youth to
The *tub-fast* and the diet. *Timon of Athens*, iv. 3.

TUCK. *A rapier.*

Dismount thy *tuck*, be yare in thy preparation.
Twelfth-Night, iii. 4.
You sheath, you bow-case, you vile standing *tuck*.
Henry 4, P. 1, ii. 4.

TUCKET-SONANCE. *A flourish on the trumpet.*

Then let the trumpets sound
The *tucket-sonance* and the note to mount.
Henry 5, iv. 2.

TUGGED. *Harassed; tormented; plagued.*

And I another
So weary with disasters, *tugg'd* with fortune,
That I would set my life on any chance,
To mend it, or be rid on't. *Macbeth*, iii. 1.

TUITION. *Protection.*

And so I commit you,—
To the *tuition* of God.
Much Ado about Nothing, i. 1.

TUN-DISH. *A funnel.*

Why, for filling a bottle with a *tun-dish*.
Measure for Measure, iii. 2.

TUNE. *State of mind; mood; tone; voice.*

Well, sir, the poor distressèd Lear's i' the town ;
Who sometime, in his better *tune*, remembers
What we are come about, and by no means
Will yield to see his daughter. *King Lear*, iv. 3.
The *tune* of Imogen ! *Cymbeline*, v. 5.

To TURN. *To change; to alter.*

Some news is come
That *turns* their countenances. *Coriolanus*, iv. 6.
Some dear friend dead ; else nothing in the world
Could *turn* so much the constitution
Of any constant man. *Merchant of Venice*, iii. 2.
Look, where he has not *turned* his colour, and
has tears in's eyes.—Pray you, no more.
Hamlet, ii. 2.

To TURN TO. *To cause; to occasion.*

If he be chaste, the flame will back descend,
And *turn* him to no pain.
Merry Wives of Windsor, v. 5.
O, my heart bleeds
To think o' the teen that I have *turn'd you* to.
Tempest, i. 2.

TWANGLING. *Shrill-sounding.*

Sometimes a thousand *twangling* instruments
Will hum about mine ears. *Tempest*, iii. 2.
While she did call me rascal fiddler
And *twangling* Jack. *Taming of the Shrew*, ii. 1.

TWIGGEN. *Made of twigs; wicker.*

I'll beat the knave into a *twiggen* bottle.
Othello, ii. 3.

To TWIN. *To be born at the same time; to join; to be united.*

Twinn'd brothers of one womb,
Whose procreation, residence, and birth,
Scarce is dividant,—touch them with several fortunes,
The greater scorns the lesser.
Timon of Athens, iv. 3.
And he that is approv'd in this offence,
Though he had *twinn'd* with me, both at a birth,
Shall lose me. *Othello*, ii. 3.
Friends now fast sworn, who *twin*, as 'twere, in love
Unseparable, shall within this hour,

On a dissension of a doit break out
To bitterest enmity.   *Coriolanus*, iv. 4.

TWINNED.   *Twinlike; like; similar.*

Which can distinguish 'twixt
The fiery orbs above, and the *twinn'd* stones
Upon the number'd beach.   *Cymbeline*, i. 6.

TWINK.   *A wink; a twinkling of the eye.*

Ay, with a *twink*.   *Tempest*, iv. 1.

That in a *twink* she won me to her love.
    Taming of the Shrew, ii. 1.

TWIT.   *Twitted; reproached; blamed; censured.*

Hath he not *twit* our sovereign lady here
With ignominious words, though clerkly couch'd?
    Henry 6, P. 2, iii. 1.

TYPE.   *Distinguishing mark; badge.*

Thy father bears the *type* of king of Naples,
Of both the Sicils and Jerusalem.
    Henry 6, P. 3, i. 4.

No, to the dignity and height of honour,
The high imperial *type* of this earth's glory.
    Richard 3, iv. 4.

U.

UMBER.   *A species of ochre of a brown colour.*

And with a kind of *umber* smirch my face.
    As you like it, i. 3.

UMBERED.   *Embrowned.*

Fire answers fire; and through their paly flames
Each battle sees the other's *umber'd* face.
    Henry 5, iii. Chorus.

UNABLE.   *Weak; impotent.*

Come, come, you froward and *unable* worms!
    Taming of the Shrew, v. 2.

A love that makes breath poor, and speech *unable*;
Beyond all manner of so much I love you.
    King Lear, i. 1.

Why does my blood thus muster to my heart,
Making both it *unable* for itself,
And dispossessing all my other parts
Of necessary fitness?   *Measure for Measure*, ii. 4.

UNACCOMMODATED.   *Unsupplied with the conveniences of life; in a state of nature.*

Unaccommodated man is no more but such a
poor, bare, forked animal as thou art.
    King Lear, iii. 4.

UNACCUSTOMED.   *Strange; unusual.*

You of my household, leave this peevish broil,
And set this *unaccustom'd* fight aside.
    Henry 6, P. 1, iii. 1.

I'll send to one in Mantua, ...
Shall give him such an *unaccustom'd* dram,
That he shall soon keep Tybalt company.
    Romeo and Juliet, iii. 5.

UNACQUAINTED.   *Strange; foreign.*

To grace the gentry of a land remote,
And follow *unacquainted* colours here.
    King John, v. 2.

UNADVISED.   *Imprudent; rash; inconsiderate.*

This harness'd masque and *unadvisèd* revel,
This unhair'd sauciness and boyish troop,
The king doth smile at.   *King John*, v. 2.

UNAGREEABLE.   *Unsuitable; unfitted.*

Please you, gentlemen,
The time is *unagreeable* to this business.
    Timon of Athens, ii. 2.

UNANELED.   *Unanointed.*

Unhousell'd, disappointed, *unanel'd*.   *Hamlet*, i. 5.

UNATTAINTED.   *Unprejudiced.*

Go thither; and, with *unattainted* eye,
Compare her face with some that I shall show,
And I will make thee think thy swan a crow.
    Romeo and Juliet, i. 2.

UNAVOIDED.   *Inevitable; not to be avoided.*

All *unavoided* is the doom of destiny.
    Richard 3, iv. 4.

And *unavoided* is the danger now. *Richard* 2, ii. 1.
A terrible and *unavoided* danger.
Henry 6, P. 1, iv. 5.

UNBARBED. *Untrimmed ; unclipped.*

Must I go show them my *unbarb'd* sconce?
Coriolanus, iii. 2.

UNBATED. *Not blunted ; unabated ; undiminished.*

The treacherous instrument is in thy hand,
Unbated and envenom'd.   *Hamlet*, v. 2.
So that, with ease,
Or with a little shuffling, you may choose
A sword *unbated*, and, in a pass of practice,
Requite him for your father.   *Ibid.* iv. 7.
Where is the horse that doth untread again
His tedious measures with th' *unbated* fire
That he did pace them first?
Merchant of Venice, ii. 5.

UNDID. *Unexpected.*

O *unbid* spite! is sportful Edward come?
Henry 6, P. 3, v. 1.

UNBITTED. *Unrestrained ; uncurbed.*

But we have reason to cool our raging motions,
our carnal stings, our *unbitted* lusts. *Othello*, i. 3.

UNBOLTED. *Coarse.*

My lord, if you will give me leave, I will tread
this *unbolted* villain into mortar. *King Lear*, ii. 2.

UNBONNETED. *Undignified with rank or power.*
And my demerits
May speak, *unbonneted*, to as proud a fortune
As this that I have reach'd.   *Othello*, i. 2.

UNBOOKISH. *Ignorant; uninformed; unskilled.*

And his *unbookish* jealousy must construe
Poor Cassio's smiles, gestures, and light behaviour,
Quite in the wrong.   *Othello*, iv. 1.

UNBRACED. *Having the vesture loosened.*

And, thus *unbrac'd*, Casca, as you see,
Have bar'd my bosom to the thunder-stone.
Julius Cæsar, i. 3.

UNBRAIDED. *Embroidered.* (Evidently an intentional blunder.)

Believe me, thou talkest of an admirable-conceited fellow. Has he any *unbraided* wares?
Winter's Tale, iv. 3.

UNBREATHED. *Unexercised; unpractised.*

And now have toil'd their *unbreath'd* memories
With this same play, against your nuptial.
Midsummer-Night's Dream, v. 1.

UNCAPABLE. *Incapable.*

A stony adversary, an inhuman wretch,
Uncapable of pity.   *Merchant of Venice*, iv. 1.
Why, by making him *uncapable* of Othello's
place,—knocking out his brains.   *Othello*, iv. 2.

To UNCASE. *To undress.*

Tranio, at once
Uncase thee ; take my colour'd hat and cloak.
Taming of the Shrew, i. 1.

UNCERTAIN. *Incredulous ; doubtful.*

Be not *uncertain* ;
For, by the honour of my parents, I
Have utter'd truth.   *Winter's Tale*, i. 2.

To UNCHARGE. *To retract an accusation.*

And for his death no wind of blame shall breathe ;
But even his mother shall *uncharge* the practice,
And call it accident.   *Hamlet*, iv. 7.

UNCHARGED. *Unassailed.*

Descend, and open your *uncharged* ports.
Timon of Athens, v. 4.

UNCHARY. *Incautious ; not wary ; imprudent.*

I've said too much unto a heart of stone,
And laid mine honour too *unchary* out.
Twelfth-Night, iii. 4.

UNCHECKED. *Uncontradicted.*

It lives there *unchecked*, that Antonio hath a
ship of rich lading wrecked on the narrow seas.
Merchant of Venice, iii. 1.

To UNCHILD. *To deprive of children.*

Though in this city he
Hath widow'd and *unchilded* many a one,
Which to this hour bewail the injury,
Yet he shall have a noble memory. *Coriolanus*, v. 6.

UNCIVIL. *Unbecoming ; rude ; boisterous ; uncivilised.*

Th' *uncivil* kerns of Ireland are in arms.
Henry 6, P. 2, iii. 1.

If you prized my lady's favour at anything more than contempt, you would not give means for this uncivil rule. *Twelfth-Night*, ii. 3.

To UNCLEW. *To undo; to ruin.*

If I should pay you for't as 'tis extoll'd, It would *unclew* me quite. *Timon of Athens*, i. 1.

To UNCLOG. *To disencumber; to relieve.*

Could I meet 'em But once a-day, it would *unclog* my heart Of what lies heavy to 't. *Coriolanus*, iv. 3.

UNCOINED. *Unstamped; not current.*

And while thou livest, dear Kate, take a fellow of plain and *uncoined* constancy; for he perforce must do thee right, because he hath not the gift to woo in other places. *Henry 5*, v. 2.

UNCOMFORTABLE. *Unhappy; gloomy; dismal.*

Uncomfortable time, why cam'st thou now To murder, murder our solemnity? *Romeo and Juliet*, iv. 5.

UNCOMPREHENSIVE. *Unknown; unexplored; mysterious.*

The providence that's in a watchful state Knows almost every grain of Plutus' gold; Finds bottom in th' *uncomprehensive* deeps. *Troilus and Cressida*, iii. 3.

UNCONFINABLE. *Unbounded; unlimited.*

Why, thou *unconfinable* baseness, it is as much as I can do to keep the terms of my honour precise. *Merry Wives of Windsor*, ii. 2.

UNCONFIRMED. *Raw; inexperienced.*

That shows thou art *unconfirmed*. *Much Ado about Nothing*, iii. 3.

UNCURRENT. *Forbidden; irregular; unlawful.*

Since he came, With what encounter so *uncurrent* I Have strain'd, to appear thus. *Winter's Tale*, iii. 2.

To UNDEAF. *To free from deafness.*

Though Richard my life's counsel would not hear, My death's sad tale may still *undeaf* his ear. *Richard 2*, ii. 1.

UNDEEDED. *Unsignalized with deeds of prowess.*

Either thou, Macbeth, Or else my sword, with an unbatter'd edge, I sheathe again *undeeded*. *Macbeth*, v. 7.

To UNDERBEAR. *To line; to guard; to support; to endure.*

Side sleeves and skirts round *underborne* with a bluish tinsel. *Much Ado about Nothing*, iii. 4.

And leave those woes alone which I alone Am bound to *underbear*. *King John*, iii. 1.

Wooing poor craftsmen with the craft of smiles, And patient *underbearing* of his fortune As 'twere to banish their affects with him. *Richard 2*, i. 4.

To UNDERCREST. *To support; to wear.*

I mean to stride your steed; and at all times To *undercrest* your good addition To the fairness of my power. *Coriolanus*, i. 9.

UNDER GENERATION. *The antipodes.*

Ere twice the sun hath made his journal greeting To th' *under generation*, you shall find Your safety manifested. *Measure for Measure*, iv. 3.

To UNDERGO. *To support; to bear; to maintain; to undertake; to hazard; to be subject to.*

Which mis'd in me An *undergoing* stomach, to bear up Against what should ensue. *Tempest*, i. 2.

If any in Vienna be of worth To *undergo* such ample grace and honour, It is Lord Angelo. *Measure for Measure*, i. 1.

Is't not I that *undergo* this charge? *King John*, v. 2.

Their virtues else—be they as pure as grace, As infinite as man may *undergo*— Shall in the general censure take corruption From that particular fault. *Hamlet*, i. 4.

You *undergo* too strict a paradox, Striving to make an ugly deed look fair. *Timon of Athens*, iii. 5.

I am the master of my speeches, and would *undergo* what's spoken, I swear. *Cymbeline*, i. 4.

I have mov'd already Some certain of the noblest-minded Romans

To *undergo* with mo an enterprise
Of honourable-dangerous consequence.
                    Julius Cæsar, i. 3.
This follows,—if you will not change your purpose,
But *undergo* this flight,—make for Sicilia.
                    Winter's Tale, iv. 3.

I must tell thee plainly, Claudio *undergoes* my
challenge ; and either I must shortly hear from
him, or I will subscribe him a coward.
            Much Ado about Nothing, v. 2.

UNDERHAND. *Secret.*

I had myself notice of my brother's purpose
herein, and have by *underhand* means laboured to
dissuade him from it.   *As you like it*, i. 1.

To UNDERPRIZE. *To undervalue ; to under-
rate.*

Yet look, how far
The substance of my praise doth wrong this shadow
In *underprizing* it, so far this shadow
Doth limp behind the substance.
           Merchant of Venice, iii. 2.

To UNDERPROP. *To support ; to sustain.*

What penny hath Rome borne,
What men provided, what munition sent,
To *underprop* this action ?   *King John*, v. 2.
Here am I left to *underprop* his land,
Who, weak with age, cannot support myself.
           Richard 2, ii. 2.

UNDERSTANDING. *Knowledge ; information.*

Believe me, I speak as my *understanding* instructs
me, and as mine honesty puts it to utterance.
           Winter's Tale, i. 1.
I know you are of her bosom.—I, madam ?—
I speak in *understanding* ; you are, I know't.
           King Lear, iv. 5.

To UNDERTAKE. *To engage with ; to attack ;
to assume ; to take charge of ; to venture ;
to oppose.*

My suit, then, is desperate ; you'll *undertake* her
no more ?   *Merry Wives of Windsor*, iii. 5.
It is not fit your lordship should *undertake*
every companion that you give offence to.
           Cymbeline, ii. 1.
His name and credit shall you *undertake*,
And in my house you shall be friendly lodg'd.
        Taming of the Shrew, iv. 3.

To tho water side I must conduct your grace ;
Then give my charge up to Sir Nicholas Vaux,
Who *undertakes* you to your end. *Henry 8*, ii. 1.
It is the cowish terror of his spirit,
That dares not *undertake*.   *King Lear*, iv. 2.

UNDERTAKER. *An opponent ; an encounterer ;
an assailant ; a challenger.*

And for Cassio,—let me be his *undertaker*.
            Othello, iv. 1.
Nay, if you be an *undertaker*, I am for you.
          Twelfth-Night, iii. 5.

UNDERVALUED. *Inferior ; unworthy to be
compared.*

Her name is Portia ; nothing *undervalu'd*
To Cato's daughter, Brutus' Portia.
          Merchant of Venice, i. 1.

To UNDERWORK. *To undermine ; to destroy
clandestinely.*

But thou from loving England art so far,
That thou hast *under-wrought* his lawful king.
           King John, ii. 1.

To UNDERWRITE. *To subscribe ; to obey.*

Disguise the holy strength of their command,
And *underwrite* in an observing kind
His humorous predominance.
         Troilus and Cressida, ii. 3.

UNDESERVER. *An undeserving and worthless
person.*

And let me tell you, Cassius, you yourself
Are much condemn'd to have an itching palm ;
To sell and mart your offices for gold
To *undeservers*.   *Julius Cæsar*, iv. 3.

UNDESERVING. *Undeserved.*

My lady, to the manner of the days,
In courtesy gives *undeserving* praise.
         Love's Labour's lost, v. 2.

UNDINTED. *Unmarked ; unbruised.*

This 'greed upon,
To part with unhack'd edges, and bear back
Our targes *undinted*. *Antony and Cleopatra*, ii. 6.

UNDISCERNIBLE. *Undiscovered ; not seen through.*

I should be guiltier than my guiltiness,
To think I can be *undiscernible*
When I perceive your grace, like power divine,
Hath look'd upon my passes.
Measure for Measure, v. 1.

UNDISTINGUISHED. *Undistinguishable; boundless ; unlimited.*

O *undistinguish'd* space of woman's will !
King Lear, iv. 6.

UNDIVULGED. *Clandestine; secret ; hidden.*

And thence
Against the *undivulg'd* pretence I fight
Of treasonous malice. *Macbeth*, i. 2.

Tremble, thou wretch,
That hast within thee *undivulgèd* crimes,
Unwhipp'd of justice. *King Lear*, iii. 2.

To UNDO. *To lose ; to miss.*

How unluckily it happened, that I should purchase the day before for a little part, and *undo* a great deal of honour! *Timon of Athens*, iii. 2.

UNEARNED. *Undeserved ; unmerited.*

If we have *unearnèd* luck
Now to scape the serpent's tongue,
We will make amends ere long.
Midsummer-Night's Dream, v. 1.

UNEATH. *Not easily ; scarcely.*

Uneath may she endure the flinty streets.
Henry 6, P. 2, ii. 4.

UNEQUAL. *Unjust.*

.To punish me for what you make me do
Seems much *unequal*. *Antony and Cleopatra*, ii. 5.

UNEXPRESSIVE. *Ineffable ; not to be described.*

Run, run, Orlando ; carve on every tree
The fair, the chaste, and *unexpressive* she.
As you like it, iii. 2.

UNFAMED. *Inglorious.*

Nor none so noble,
Whose life were ill bestow'd, or death *unfam'd*,
Where Helen is the subject.
Troilus and Cressida, ii. 2.

To UNFOLD. *To undo; to lay bare; to declare; to make known.*

I, that please some, try all ; both joy and terror
Of good and bad ; that make and *unfold* error,
Now take upon me, in the name of Time,
To use my wings. *Winter's Tale*, Chorus to act iv.

Time shall *unfold* what plighted cunning hides.
King Lear, i. 1.

*Must I be *unfolded*
With one that I have bred ?
Antony and Cleopatra, v. 2.

Nay, answer me : stand and *unfold* yourself.
Hamlet, i. 1.

To UNFURNISH. *To deprive ; to divest.*

When I shall see this gentleman, thy speeches
Will bring me to consider that which may
Unfurnish me of reason. *Winter's Tale*, v. 1.

UNFURNISHED. *Unprepared ; untapestried ; unprovided with a fellow.*

My great-grandfather
Never went with his forces into France,
But that the Scot on his *unfurnish'd* kingdom
Came pouring, like the tide into a breach.
Henry 5, i. 2.
Go, be gone.—
We shall be much *unfurnish'd* for this time.
Romeo and Juliet, iv. 2.

Alack, and what shall good old York there see,
But empty lodgings and *unfurnish'd* walls,
Unpeopled offices, untrodden stones ?
Richard 2, i. 2.

Methinks it should have power to steal both his,
And leave itself *unfurnish'd*.
Merchant of Venice, iii. 2.

To UNGIRD. *To lay aside.*

I prithee, now, *ungird* thy strangeness, and tell me what I shall vent to my lady.
Twelfth-Night, iv. 1.

UNGOVERNED. *Having no ruler.*

Which would be so much the more dangerous,
By how much the state's green and yet *ungovern'd*.
Richard 3, ii. 2.

Even that, I hope, which pleaseth God above,
And all good men of this *ungovern'd* isle. *Ibid*. iii. 7.

To UNHAIR. *To deprive of hair.*

Hence,
Horrible villain ! or I'll spurn thine eyes

Like balls before me; I'll *unhair* thy head.
Antony and Cleopatra, ii. 5.

UNHAPPIED. *Made wretched; degraded.*

A happy gentleman in blood and lineaments,
By you *unhappied* and disfigur'd clean.
Richard 2, iii. 1.

UNHAPPILY. *Mischievously; unfavourably; censoriously.*

Which, as her winks, and nods, and gestures yield them,
Indeed would make one think there might be thought,
Though nothing sure, yet much *unhappily.*
Hamlet, iv. 5.

You are a churchman, or, I'll tell you, cardinal,
I should judge now *unhappily.* *Henry 8*, i. 4.

UNHAPPINESS. *A mischievous prank; a wild frolic; malevolence; evil qualities.*

She hath often dreamed of *unhappiness*, and waked herself with laughing.
Much Ado about Nothing, ii. 1.

UNHAPPY. *Unlucky; mischievous.*

Sure, there's some wonder in this handkerchief:
I'm most *unhappy* in the loss of it. *Othello*, iii. 4.
A shrewd knave and an *unhappy.*
All's well that ends well, iv. 5.
Ay, and a shrewd *unhappy* gallows too.
Love's Labour's lost, v. 2.

To UNHEART. *To discourage; to dishearten.*

I think he'll hear me. Yet, to bite his lip
And hum at good Cominius, much *unhearts* me.
Coriolanus, v. 1.

UNHOUSED. *Having no settled habitation; homeless.*

But that I love the gentle Desdemona,
I would not my *unhoused* free condition
Put into circumscription and confine
For the sea's worth. *Othello*, i. 2.
Call the creatures,—whose bare *unhoused* trunks,
To the conflicting elements expos'd,
Answer mere nature,—bid them flatter thee.
Timon of Athens, iv. 3.

UNHOUSELLED. *Without receiving the sacrament.*

Unhousell'd, disappointed, unanel'd. *Hamlet*, i. 5.

UNIMPROVED. *Untried; unproved.*

Now, sir, young Fortinbras,
Of *unimproved* mettle hot and full,
Hath in the skirts of Norway, here and there,
Shark'd up a list of landless resolutes. *Hamlet*, i. 1.

UNION. *A pearl.*

And in the cup a *union* shall he throw
Richer than that which four successive kings
In Denmark's crown have worn. *Hamlet*, v. 2.

UNKIND. *Unnatural.*

'Tis much when sceptres are in children's hands;
But more when envy breeds *unkind* division.
Henry 6, P. 1, iv. 1.
Blow, blow, thou winter wind,
Thou art not so *unkind*
As man's ingratitude. *As you like it*, ii. 7.

To UNKING. *To deprive of kingship; to depose.*

God save King Henry, *unking'd* Richard says,
And send him many years of sunshine days!
Richard 2, iv. 1.
Then am I king'd again: and by and by
Think that I am *unking'd* by Bolingbroke,
And straight am nothing. *Ibid. 2*, v. 5.

To UNKNIT. *To untie; to loose.*

I would he had continu'd to his country
As he began, and not *unknit* himself
The noble knot he had made. *Coriolanus*, iv. 3.

UNLESS. *Except; save.*

So that all hope is vain,
Unless in 's noble mother, and his wife.
Coriolanus, v. 2.
That never set a squadron in the field,
Nor the division of a battle knows
More than a spinster; *unless* the bookish theoric,
Wherein the toged consuls can propose
As masterly as he. *Othello*, i. 1.

UNLESSONED. *Untaught.*

But the full sum of me
Is sum of nothing; which, to term in gross,
Is an *unlesson'd* girl, unschool'd, unpractis'd.
Merchant of Venice, iii. 2.

UNLIKE. *Unlikely; improbable.*

The service that you three have done is more
Unlike than this thou tell'st. *Cymbeline*, v. 5.

Make not impossible
That which but seems *unlike*.
Measure for Measure, v. 1.

UNLINEAL. *Indirect; collateral.*

And put a barren sceptre in my gripe,
Thence to be wrench'd with an *unlineal* hand,
No son of mine succeeding. *Macbeth*, iii. 1.

UNLUSTROUS. *Dull; wanting brightness.*

Then lie peeping in an eye
Base and *unlustrous* as the smoky light
That's fed with stinking tallow. *Cymbeline*, i. 6.

UNMANNED. *Untamed.*

Hood my *unmann'd* blood, bating in my cheeks,
With thy black mantle. *Romeo and Juliet*, iii. 2.

UNMASTERED. *Unbridled; unlicensed; un-
controlled.*

Or your chaste treasure open
To his *unmaster'd* importunity. *Hamlet*, i. 3.

UNMERITABLE. *Without merit; unworthy.*

This is a slight *unmeritable* man,
Meet to be sent on errands. *Julius Cæsar*, iv. 1.
Unmeritable shuns your high request.
Richard 3, iii. 7.

UNMERITING. *Undeserving; unworthy.*

Why, then you should discover a brace of *unmeriting*, proud, violent, testy magistrates (alias
fools), as any in Rome. *Coriolanus*, ii. 1.

UNMINDED. *Disregarded; despised; unno-
ticed.*

A poor *unminded* outlaw sneaking home.
Henry 4, P. 1, iv. 3.

UNNECESSARY. *Of no use; useless.*

Do you but mark how this becomes the house :
"Dear daughter, I confess that I am old ;
Age is *unnecessary*: on my knees I beg ·
That you'll vouchsafe me raiment, bed, and food."
King Lear, ii. 4.

UNNOBLE. *Ignoble; base; ignominious.*

I have offended reputation,—
A most *unnoble* swerving.
Antony and Cleopatra, iii. 11.

UNPERFECTNESS. *Imperfection.*

One *unperfectness* shows me another, to make
me frankly despise myself. *Othello*, ii. 3.

UNPINKED. *Not pierced with holes.*

And Gabriel's pumps were all *unpink'd* i' the heel.
Taming of the Shrew, iv. 1.

UNPITIED. *Unmerciful.*

If not, you shall have your full time of impri-
sonment, and your deliverance with an *unpitied*
whipping. *Measure for Measure*, iv. 2.

UNPLAUSIVE. *Disapproving; neglectful; contemptuous.*

'Tis like he'll question me
Why such *unplausive* eyes are bent on him.
Troilus and Cressida, iii. 3.

UNPOLICIED. *Without policy; dull; stupid.*

O, couldst thou speak,
That I might hear thee call great Cæsar ass
Unpolicied ! *Antony and Cleopatra*, v. 2.

UNPOSSESSING. *Incapable of inheriting land.*

Thou *unpossessing* bastard ! *King Lear*, ii. 1.

UNPREGNANT. *Insensible; unmindful; un-
ready.*

This deed unshapes me quite, makes me *unpregnant*,
And dull to all proceedings.
Measure for Measure, iv. 4.

Yet I,
A dull and muddy-mettled rascal, peak,
Like John-a-dreams, *unpregnant* of my cause,
And can say nothing. *Hamlet*, ii. 2.

UNPREVAILING. *Unavailing; vain ; useless.*

We pray you, throw to earth
This *unprevailing* woe. *Hamlet*, i. 2.

UNPRIZABLE. *Invaluable; priceless; of small
account; inconsiderable.*

Your ring may be stolen too : so, your brace of
unprizable estimations, the one is but frail, and the
other casual. *Cymbeline*, i. 4.
A bawbling vessel was he captain of,
For shallow draught and bulk *unprizable*.
Twelfth-Night, v. 1.

zz

UNPRIZED. *Not valued; underrated.*

Not all the dukes of waterish Burgundy
Can buy this *unpriz'd* precious maid of me.
King Lear, i. 1.

UNPROFITED. *Profitless; unprofitable.*

Be clamorous, and leap all civil bounds,
Rather than make *unprofited* return.
Twelfth-Night, i. 4.

UNPROPER. *Common; not peculiar; not exclusive.*

There's millions now alive
That nightly lie in those *unproper* beds,
Which they dare swear peculiar.   *Othello,* iv. 1.

UNPROPORTIONED. *Unbecoming; unworthy.*

Give thy thoughts no tongue,
Nor any *unproportion'd* thought his act.
Hamlet, i. 3.

To UNPROVIDE. *To disqualify; to deprive of resolution.*

I'll not expostulate with her, lest her body and
beauty *unprovide* my mind again.   *Othello,* iv. 1.

UNPROVIDED. *Unprepared; unprotected; unarmed.*

Then if they die *unprovided,* no more is the king
guilty of their damnation.   *Henry 5,* iv. 1.

In fine,
Seeing how loathly opposite I stood
To his unnatural purpose, in fell motion,
With his preparèd sword he charges home
My *unprovided* body, lanc'd mine arm.
King Lear, ii. 1.

UNPURGED. *Unwholesome; noxious.*

What, is Brutus sick,—
And will he steal out of his wholesome bed,
And tempt the rheumy and *unpurgèd* air
To add unto his sickness?   *Julius Cæsar,* ii. 1.

UNQUALITIED. *Dejected; overwhelmed; crushed.*

Go to him, madam, speak to him:
He is *unqualitied* with very shame.
Antony and Cleopatra, iii. 11.

UNQUEENED. *Deprived of the dignity of queen.*

Although *unqueen'd,* yet like
A queen, and daughter to a king, inter me.
Henry 8, iv. 2.

UNQUESTIONABLE. *Averse to conversation.*

An *unquestionable* spirit,—which you have not.
As you like it, iii. 2.

UNRAKED. *Not raked together; not covered.*

Where fires thou find'st *unrak'd* and hearths unswep,
There pinch the maids as blue as bilberry.
Merry Wives of Windsor, v. 5.

UNRECONCILED. *Unrepented; unatoned for.*

If you bethink yourself of any crime
Unreconcil'd as yet to heaven and grace,
Solicit for it straight.   *Othello,* v. 2.

UNRECONCILIABLE. *Implacable; unappeasable.*

That our stars,
Unreconciliable, should divide
Our equalness to this. *Antony and Cleopatra,* v. 1.

UNRESPECTIVE. *Unthinking; unreflecting; mean; common; disregarded.*

I will converse with iron-witted fools
And *unrespective* boys.   *Richard 3,* iv. 2.

Nor the remainder viands
We do not throw in *unrespective* sieve,
Because we now are full.
Troilus and Cressida, ii. 2.

UNREST. *Disquiet; uneasiness.*

Ay, so I fear; the more is my *unrest.*
Romeo and Juliet, i. 5.

The sun sets weeping in the lowly west,
Witnessing storms to come, woe, and *unrest.*
Richard 2, ii. 4.

UNRESTRAINED. *Licentious; dissolute.*

For there, they say, he daily doth frequent,
With *unrestrainèd* loose companions.
Richard 2, v. 3.

UNROLLED. *Struck off the roll or register.*

If I make not this cheat bring out another, let

me be *unrolled*, and my name put in the book of virtue ! *Winter's Tale*, iv. 2.

UNROUGH. *Unbearded; smoothfaced.*

There is Siward's son,
And many *unrough* youths, that even now
Protest their first of manhood.   *Macbeth*, v. 2.

UNSCALABLE. *Not to be scaled; inaccessible.*

Together with
The natural bravery of your isle, which stands
As Neptune's park, ribbèd and palèd in
With rocks *unscalable* and roaring waters.
Cymbeline, iii. 1.

UNSCOURED. *Rusty.*

Which have, like *unscour'd* armour, hung by the
wall
So long.   *Measure for Measure*, i. 2.

UNSEALED. *Unratified; unconfirmed; imperfect.*

Therefore your oaths
Are words and poor conditions; but *unseal'd*,—
At least in my opinion.
All's well that ends well, iv. 2.

To UNSEAM. *To rip; to cut open.*

And ne'er shook hands, nor bade farewell to him,
Till he *unseam'd* him from the nave to the chaps,
And fix'd his head upon our battlements.
Macbeth, i. 2.

UNSEASONABLE. *Changeable; variable; unsettled.*

Like an *unseasonable* stormy day,
Which makes the silver rivers drown their shores,
As if the world were all dissolv'd to tears.
Richard 2, iii. 2.

UNSEASONED. *Unseasonable; untimely.*

And these *unseason'd* hours perforce must add
Unto your sickness.   *Henry 4*, P. 2, iii. 1.

The which hath something emboldened me to
this *unseasoned* intrusion.
Merry Wives of Windsor, ii. 2.

UNSEEMING. *Hesitating; scrupling.*

You wrong the reputation of your name,
In so *unseeming* to confess receipt
Of that which hath so faithfully been paid.
Love's Labour's lost, ii. 1.

To UNSETTLE. *To give way; to be disordered.*

His wits begin t' *unsettle*.   *King Lear*, iii. 4.

UNSETTLED. *Weak; dull.*

And all th' *unsettled* humours of the land.
King John, ii. 1.

Dost think I am so muddy, so *unsettled*,
T' appoint myself in this vexation ?
Winter's Tale, i. 2.

To UNSHAPE. *To confound; to distract.*

This deed *unshapes* me quite.
Measure for Measure, iv. 4.

To UNSHOUT. *To recall a shout.*

Unshout the noise that banish'd Marcius,
Repeal him with the welcome of his mother.
Coriolanus, v. 5.

UNSHUNNED. *Inevitable.*

An *unshunned* consequence ; it must be so.
Measure for Measure, iii. 2.

UNSIFTED. *Unversed; inexperienced.*

Affection ! pooh ! you speak like a green girl,
Unsifted in such perilous circumstance.
Hamlet, i. 3.

UNSINEWED. *Weak; slight; not cogent.*

O, for two special reasons ;
Which may to you, perhaps, seem much *unsinew'd*,
But yet to me they're strong.   *Hamlet*, iv. 7.

UNSISTING. *Unceasing.*

That spirit's possess'd with haste
That wounds th' *unsisting* postern with these strokes.
Measure for Measure, iv. 2.

UNSMIRCHED. *Unstained; unpolluted.*

Cries cuckold to my father ; brands the harlot
Even here, between the chaste *unsmirchèd* brow
Of my true mother.   *Hamlet*, iv. 5.

UNSORTED. *Unsuitable; ill chosen.*

The time itself *unsorted* ; and your whole plot
too light for the counterpoise of so great an opposition.   *Henry 4*, P. 1, ii. 3.

UNSQUARED. *Overstrained; exaggerated; hyperbolical.*

With terms *unsquar'd,*
Which, from the tongue of roaring Typhon dropp'd,
Would seem hyperboles. *Troilus and Cressida, i. 3.*

UNSTAID. *Unsteady; mutable; indiscreet.*

Will the king come, that I may breathe my last
In wholesome counsel to his *unstaid* youth?
Richard 2, ii. 1.

UNSTANCHED. *Insatiable.*

And with the issuing blood
Stifle the villain, whose *unstanchèd* thirst
York and young Rutland could not satisfy.
Henry 6, P. 3, ii. 6.

To UNSTATE. *To resign rank or dignity; to lay aside.*

I would *unstate* myself to be in a due resolution.
King Lear, i. 2.
Yes, like enough, high-battled Cæsar will
Unstate his happiness, and be stag'd to the show,
Against a sworder! *Antony and Cleopatra, iii. 13.*

UNSTUFFED. *Free from cares; thoughtless.*

But where unbruisèd youth with *unstuff'd* brain
Doth couch his limbs, there golden sleep doth reign.
Romeo and Juliet, ii. 3.

To UNSWEAR. *To recant what has been sworn to.*

He hath, my lord; but be you well assur'd,
No more than he'll *unswear.* *Othello, iv. 1.*

UNTAUGHT. *Rude; churlish; unmannerly.*

O thou *untaught!* what manners is in this,
To press before thy father to a grave?
Romeo and Juliet, v. 3.

UNTENDER. *Void of affection.*

So young, and so *untender?*—
So young, my lord, and true. *King Lear, i. 1.*

To UNTENT. *To remove from a tent; to expose; to air; to make public.*

Why will he not, upon our fair request,
Untent his person, and share the air with us?
Troilus and Cressida, ii. 3.

UNTENTED. *Unsoothed; unmitigated; unrelieved.*

Th' *untented* woundings of a father's curse
Pierce every sense about thee! *King Lear, i. 4.*

UNTHRIFT. *A prodigal; a spendthrift.*

My rights and royalties
Pluck'd from my arms perforce, and given away
To upstart *unthrifts.* *Richard 2, ii. 3.*

UNTHRIFT. *Unthrifty; prodigal.*

What man didst thou ever know *unthrift* that
was beloved after his means?
Timon of Athens, iv. 3.
In such a night
Did Jessica steal from the wealthy Jew,
And with an *unthrift* love did run from Venice
As far as Belmont. *Merchant of Venice, v. 1.*

UNTIMEABLE. *Not in good time; inharmonious.*

Truly, young gentlemen, though there was no
great matter in the ditty, yet the note was very *untimeable.* *As you like it, v. 3.*

UNTITLED. *Unrightful; usurping.*

O nation miserable,
With an *untitled* tyrant bloody-sceptred!
Macbeth, iv. 3.

UNTRADED. *Strange; unusual.*

Mock not, that I affect th' *untraded* oath.
Troilus and Cressida, iv. 5.

UNTRUTH. *Treachery; disloyalty.*

I would to God—
So my *untruth* had not provok'd him to it—
The king had cut off my head with my brother's.
Richard 2, ii. 2.

To UNTWINE. *To cease to entwine.*

Grow, patience!
And let the stinking elder, grief, *untwine*
His perishing root with the increasing vine!
Cymbeline, iv. 2.

UNVALUED. *Invaluable; not to be estimated; inferior; ordinary.*

Inestimable stones, *unvalu'd* jewels,
All scatter'd in the bottom of the sea.
Richard 3, i. 4.

He may not, as *unvalu'd* persons do,
Carve for himself. *Hamlet*, i. 3.

UNWARES. *Unknowingly; without premeditation.*

O God! it is my father's face,
Whom in this conflict I *unwares* have kill'd.
Henry 6, P. 3, ii. 5.

UNWED. *Unwedded.*

This servitude makes you to keep *unwed*.
Comedy of Errors, ii. 1.

UNWHOLESOME. *Infected; tainted.*

Prithee, bear some charity to my wit; do not
think it so *unwholesome*. *Othello*, iv. 1.
Yea, like fair fruit in an *unwholesome* dish,
Are like to rot untasted. *Troilus and Cressida*, i. 3.
Go to, then : we'll use this *unwholesome* humidity, this gross watery pumpion.
Merry Wives of Windsor, iii. 3.

TO UNWISH. *To reverse a wish.*

Why, now thou hast *unwish'd* five thousand men;
Which likes me better than to wish us one.
Henry 5, iv. 3.

TO UNWIT. *To deprive of understanding.*

As if some planet had *unwitted* men. *Othello*, ii. 3.

UP. *Shut up; in prison.*

So the poor third is *up*, till death enlarge his
confine. *Antony and Cleopatra*, iii. 5.

UP-CAST; a term peculiar to the game of
bowls. *A throw; a cast.*

Was there ever man had such luck! when I
kissed the jack, upon an *up-cast* to be hit away!
Cymbeline, ii. 1.

UP-SPRING. *Upstart.*

The king doth wake to-night, and takes his rouse,
Keeps wassail, and the swaggering *up-spring* reels.
Hamlet, i. 4.

UPTRIMMED. *Adorned; decorated.*

The devil tempts thee here ,
In likeness of a new-*uptrimmèd* bride.
King John, iii. 1.

UPMOST. *Topmost; highest.*

But when he once attains the *upmost* round,

He then unto the ladder turns his back,
Looks in the clouds, scorning the base degrees
By which he did ascend. *Julius Cæsar*, ii. 1.

UPON THE GAD. *Suddenly; precipitately; on
the spur.*

Kent banish'd thus! and France in choler parted!
And the king gone to-night! subscrib'd his power!
Confin'd to exhibition! All this done
Upon the *gad*! *King Lear*, i. 2.

UPRIGHT. *Upward.*

Give me your hand :—you are now within a foot
Of the extreme verge : for all beneath the moon
Would I not leap *upright*. *King Lear*, iv. 6.

TO UPROAR. *To disorder; to throw into confusion.*

Nay, had I power, I should
Pour the sweet milk of concord into hell,
Uproar the universal peace, confound
All unity on earth. *Macbeth*, iv. 3.

TO UP-SWARM. *To assemble; to muster.*

You have ta'en up . . . . .
The subjects of his substitute, my father,
And both against the peace of heaven and him
Have here *up-swarm'd* them. *Henry* 4, P. 2, iv. 2.

UPWARD. *The top; the crown.*

Conspirant 'gainst this high illustrious prince;
And, from th' extremest *upward* of thy head
To the descent and dust below thy foot,
A most toad-spotted traitor. *King Lear*, v. 3.

URCHIN. *A fairy.*

Urchins
Shall, for that vast of night that they may work,
All exercise on thee. *Tempest*, i. 2.

URCHIN-SHOWS. *Fairy-shows.*

But they'll nor pinch,
Fright me with *urchin-shows*, pitch me i' the mire,
Nor lead me, like a firebrand in the dark,
Out of my way, unless he bid 'em. *Tempest*, ii. 2.

USANCE. *Interest paid for money; usury.*

He lends out money gratis, and brings down
The rate of *usance* here with us in Venice.
Merchant of Venice, i. 3.

USE. *Advantage ; interest ; usage ; custom ; want ; necessity.*

Wouldst thou havo practis'd on mo for thy *use* ?
Henry 5, ii. 2.

Mako *use* now, and provido
For thino own future safety. *Henry* 8, iii. 2.

She determines
Herself tho glory of a creditor,
Both thanks and *use*. *Measure for Measure,* i. 1.

No gift to him
But breeds tho giver a return exceeding
All *use* of quittance. *Timon of Athens,* i. 1.

Heaven mo such *uses* send,
Not to pick bad from bad, but by bad mend !
Othello, iv. 3.

My *uses* cry to me, I must servo my turn
Out of mino own. *Timon of Athens,* ii. 1.

Requesting your lordship to supply his instant
use with so many talents. *Ibid.* iii. 2.

To USE. *To persist ; to continue ; to behave ; to be accustomed.*

If thou *use* to boat me, I will begin at thy heel,
and tell what thou art by inches.
Troilus and Cressida, ii. 1.

Do what ye will, my lords : and, pray, forgive me
If I have *us'd* myself unmannerly. *Henry* 8, iii. 1.

But, sirrah, mark, wo *use*
To say tho dead are well.
Antony and Cleopatra, ii. 6.

USURING. *Usurious.*

Is this tho balsam that the *usuring* senate
Pours into captains' wounds ?
Timon of Athens, iii. 6.

Is not thy kindness subtle-covetous,
If not a *usuring* kindness, and, as rich men deal gifts,
Expecting in return twenty for one ? *Ibid.* iv. 3.

To USURP. *To assume ; to adopt ; to borrow ; to encroach ; to seize upon ; to destroy.*

It was a mad fantastical trick of him to steal
from his state, and *usurp* tho beggary he was never
born to. *Measure for Measure,* iii. 2.

Defeat thy favour with a *usurped* beard.
Othello, i. 3.

It mourns that painting and *usurping* hair
Should ravish doters with a falso aspéct.
Love's Labour's lost, iv. 3.

Thy natural magic and dire property
On wholesome lifo *usurp* immediately.
Hamlet, iii. 2.

USURPATION. *Incursion ; devastation ; ravage.*

So looks tho strand, whereon th' imperious flood
Hath left a witness'd *usurpation.*
Henry 4, P. 2, i. 1.

To UTTER. *To sell ; to vend ; to disclose.*

Such mortal drugs I have ; but Mantua's law
Is death to any ho that *utters* them.
Romeo and Juliet, v. 1.

Come to the pedler ;
Money's a meddler,
That doth *utter* all men's ware-a.
Winter's Tale, iv. 3.

This must bo known ; which, being kept closo, might
move
Moro grief to hide than hate to *utter* love.
Hamlet, ii. 1.

UTTERANCE. *The highest degree ; the last extremity ; eloquence.*

But he has a merit,
To choke it in tho *utterance.* *Coriolanus,* iv. 7.

Rather than so, come, fate, into tho list,
And champion mo to the *utterance* ! *Macbeth,* iii. 1.

Which ho to seek of me again, perforce,
Behoves me koop at *utterance.* *Cymbeline,* iii. 1.

For I have neither wit, nor words, nor worth,
Action, nor *utterance,* nor the power of speech,
To stir men's blood. *Julius Cæsar,* iii. 2.

UTIS. *The eight days following a religious festival, which were formerly devoted to feasting and merriment.*

By tho mass, hero will be old *utis :* it will bo
an excellent stratagem. *Henry* 4, P. 2, ii. 4.

V.

VAIL. *Descent; sinking.*
Even with the *vail* and darkening of the sun,
To close the day up, Hector's day is done.
Troilus and Cressida, v. 8.

To VAIL. *To lower; to let fall; to disperse.*
Do not for ever with thy *vailèd* lids
Seek for thy noble father in the dust. *Hamlet,* i. 2.
If he have power,
Then *vail* your ignorance. *Coriolanus,* iii. 1.
And see my wealthy Andrew dock'd in sand,
Vailing her high-top lower than her ribs.
Merchant of Venice, i. 1.
Fair ladies mask'd are roses in their bud,
Dismask'd, their damask sweet commixture shown,
Are angels *vailing* clouds, or roses blown.
Love's Labour's lost, v. 2.

VAILFUL. *Availful; advantageous; beneficial.*
I'm advis'd to do it;
He says, to *vailful* purpose.
Measure for Measure, iv. 6.

VAIN. *False; not true; deceitful.*
'Tis holy sport, to be a little *vain,*
When the sweet breath of flattery conquers strife.
Comedy of Errors, iii. 2.

VALANCE. *Fringe.*
Valance of Venice gold in needlework.
Taming of the Shrew, ii. 1.

VALANCED. *Fringed; bearded.*
O, my old friend! Thy face is *valanced* since
I saw thee last. *Hamlet,* ii. 2.

VALIDITY. *Worth; value; privilege.*
More *validity,*
More honourable state, more courtship lives
In carrion-flies than Romeo.
Romeo and Juliet, iii. 3.
Behold this ring,
Whose high respect and rich *validity*
Did lack a parallel. *All's well that ends well,* v. 3.

No less in space, *validity,* and pleasure,
Than that conferr'd on Goneril. *King Lear,* i. 1.
Naught enters there
Of what *validity* and pitch soe'er,
But falls into abatement and low price,
Even in a minute. *Twelfth-Night,* i. 1.

VALUATION. *Reputation; credit.*
Ay, but our *valuation* shall be such,
That every slight and false-devised cause,
Yea, every idle, nice, and wanton reason,
Shall to the king taste of this action.
Henry 4, P. 2, iv. 1.

To VALUE. *To weigh; to take account of; to consider.*
By which account,
Our business *valuèd,* some twelve days hence
Our general forces at Bridgenorth shall meet.
Henry 4, P. 1, iii. 2.

VALUED. *Superior.*
The *valu'd* file
Distinguishes the swift, the slow, the subtle,
The housekeeper, the hunter. *Macbeth,* iii. 1.

VANITY. *Display; show; exhibition.*
For I must
Bestow upon the eyes of this young couple
Some *vanity* of mine art. *Tempest,* iv. 1.

VANTAGE. *Advantage; opportunity; policy.*
And with the *vantage* of mine own excuse
Hath he excepted most against my love.
Two Gentlemen of Verona, i. 3.
Therefore, at your *vantage*
. . . . . . let him feel your sword,
Which we will second. *Coriolanus,* v. 6.
I have some rights of memory in this kingdom,
Which now to claim my *vantage* doth invite me.
Hamlet, v. 2.
Though 'tis no wisdom to confess so much
Unto an enemy of craft and *vantage.* *Hen. 5,* iii. 5.
You fled for *vantage* every one will swear.
Henry 6, P. 1, iv. 5.

VANTBRACE. *Armour for the arm.*

I'll hide my silver beard in a gold beaver,
And in my *vantbrace* put this wither'd brawn.
Troilus and Cressida, i. 3.

VARIABLE. *Various; different.*

Stalls, bulks, windows,
Are smother'd up, leads fill'd, and ridges hors'd
With *variable* complexions. *Coriolanus*, ii. 1.

While he is vaulting *variable* ramps,
In your despite, upon your purse. *Cymbeline*, i. 6.

Haply, the seas, and countries different,
With *variable* objects, shall expel
This something-settled matter in his heart.
Hamlet, iii. 1.

VARLET. *A servant; an attendant; a rascal; a scoundrel.*

Thou precious *varlet*,
My tailor made them not. *Cymbeline*, iv. 2.

A good *varlet*, a very good *varlet*, Sir John.
Henry 4, P. 2, v. 3.

Call here my *varlet*; I'll unarm again.
Troilus and Cressida, i. 1.

Say again, where didst thou leave these *varlets*?
Tempest, iv. 1.

And tell me now, thou naughty *varlet*, tell me,
where hast thou been this month?
Henry 4, P. 1, ii. 4.

VARLETRY. *The crowd; the rabble; the populace.*

Shall they hoist me up,
And show me to the shouting *varletry*
Of censuring Rome? *Antony and Cleopatra*, v. 2.

VARY. *Variation; turn; caprice; humour.*

Renege, affirm, and turn their halcyon beaks
With every gale and *vary* of their masters.
King Lear, ii. 2.

VAST. *An empty space; a waste; a wilderness; a void.*

Shook hands as over a *vast*; and embraced, as it
were, from the ends of opposed winds.
Winter's Tale, i. 1.

Urchins
Shall, for that *vast* of night that they may work,
All exercise on thee. *Tempest*, i. 2.

In the dead *vast* and middle of the night.
Hamlet, i. 2.

VAST (adj.). *Waste; desolate.*

But still the envious flood
Stopp'd-in my soul, and would not let it forth
To find the empty, *vast*, and wandering air.
Richard 3, i. 4.

VASTIDITY. *Vastness; immensity.*

A restraint,
Though all the world's *vastidity* you had,
To a determin'd scope. *Measure for Measure*, iii. 1.

VAULTAGE. *An arched cellar.*

He'll call you to so hot an answer of it,
That caves and womby *vaultages* of France
Shall chide your trespass. *Henry 5*, ii. 4.

VAULTY. *Arched; concave.*

And I will kiss thy detestable bones,
And put my eyeballs in thy *vaulty* brows.
King John, iii. 4.

Nor that is not the lark, whose notes do beat
The *vaulty* heaven so high above our heads.
Romeo and Juliet, iii. 5.

VAUNT. *Commencement; opening.*

To tell you, fair beholders, that our play
Leaps o'er the *vaunt* and firstlings of those broils,
Beginning in the middle.
Troilus and Cressida, Prologue.

VAUNT-COURIER. *Precursor; forerunner.*

You sulphurous and thought-executing fires,
Vaunt-couriers of oak-cleaving thunderbolts,
Singe my white head! *King Lear*, iii. 2.

VAWARD. *Front; vanguard.*

Their bands i' the *vaward* are the Antiates.
Coriolanus, i. 6.

And we that are in the *vaward* of our youth, I
must confess, are wags too. *Henry 4, P. 2*, i. 2.

And since we have the *vaward* of the day,
My love shall hear the music of my hounds.
Midsummer-Night's Dream, iv. 1.

VELURE. *Velvet.*

One girth six times pieced, and a woman's
crupper of *velure*. *Taming of the Shrew*, iii. 2.

VENEY. *A hit in fencing; a bout; a venue.*

Three *veneys* for a dish of stewed prunes.
Merry Wives of Windsor, i. 1.

To **Venge.** *To punish; to avenge.*

Tell you the Dauphin, I am coming on,
To *venge* me as I may. *Henry* 5, i. 2.
To safeguard thine own life,
The best way is to *venge* my Gloster's death.
Richard 2, i. 2.
This shows you are above,
You justicers, that these our nether crimes
So speedily can *venge !* *King Lear*, iv. 2.
It is an office of the gods to *venge* it,
Not mine to speak on't. *Cymbeline*, i. 6.

Vengeance. *Mischief; harm; correction; punishment.*

Whiles the eye of man did woo me,
That could no *vengeance* to me.
As you like it, iv. 3.
That lie shall lie so heavy on my sword
That it shall render *vengeance* and revenge.
Richard 2, iv. 1.

Venomous. *Sorcerous; malignant; noxious; hurtful; pernicious.*

Beshrew the witch! with *venomous* wights she stays
As tediously as hell. *Troilus and Cressida*, iv. 2.
Thou old and true Menenius,
Thy tears are salter than a younger man's,
And *venomous* to thine eyes. *Coriolanus*, iv. 1.

Venomously. *Grievously; sorely; poignantly.*

These things sting
His mind so *venomously*, that burning shame
Detains him from Cordelia. *King Lear*, iv. 3.

Vent. *Report; rumour.*

Let me have war, say I ; it exceeds peace as far
as day does night ; it's spritely, waking, audible,
and full of *vent*. *Coriolanus*, iv. 5.

Ventage. *A small hole or aperture.*

'Tis as easy as lying : govern these *ventages* with
your finger and thumb, give it breath with your
mouth, and it will discourse most eloquent music.
Hamlet, iii. 2.

Venture. *Something hazarded with a view to ultimate profit.*

Had I such *venture* forth,
The better part of my affections would
Be with my hopes abroad.
Merchant of Venice, i. 1.

Venue. *A hit in fencing; a bout.*

A sweet touch, a quick *venue* of wit.
Love's Labour's lost, v. 1.

Verbal. *Verbose; full of words; talkative.*

I am much sorry, sir,
You put me to forget a lady's manners,
By being so *verbal*. *Cymbeline*, ii. 3.

Versal. *Universal; whole.*

But, I'll warrant you, when I say so, she looks
as pale as any clout in the *versal* world.
Romeo and Juliet, ii. 4.

To **Verse.** *To tell in verse.*

Playing on pipes of corn, and *versing* love
To amorous Phillida.
Midsummer-Night's Dream, ii. 1.

Very. *Real; mere; empty.*

Or may we cram
Within this wooden O the *very* casques
That did affright the air at Agincourt ?
Henry 5, first Chorus.
Go, get thee gone, thou false deluding slave,
That feed'st me with the *very* name of meat.
Taming of the Shrew, iv. 4.

Vice. *The buffoon of our ancient drama; an antic; grasp; defect.*

Thus, like the formal *vice*, Iniquity,
I moralize two meanings in one word.
Richard 3, iii. 1.
I'll be with you again,
In a trice,
Like to the old *vice*,
Your need to sustain. *Twelfth-Night*, iv. 2.
A *vice* of kings ;
A cutpurse of the empire and the rule.
Hamlet, iii. 4.
An I but fist him once ; an he come but within
my *vice*. *Henry* 4, P. 2, ii. 1.
If it do not, it is a *vice* in her ears, which horse-
hairs and calves-guts can never amend.
Cymbeline, ii. 3.

Vicious. *Wrong; faulty; blameable.*

Vicious in my guess. *Othello*, iii. 3.
It had been *vicious*
To have mistrusted her. *Cymbeline*, v. 5.

3 A

To **Vie.** *To wager; to stake; to risk.*
Nature wants stuff
To *vie* strange forms 'gainst fancy.
Antony and Cleopatra, v. 2.
And kiss on kiss
She *vied* so fast, protesting oath on oath,
That in a twink she won me to her love.
Taming of the Shrew, ii. 1.

Vigil. *The eve of a holiday.*
He that shall live this day, and see old age,
Will yearly on the *vigil* feast his neighbours,
And say, To-morrow is Saint Crispian.
Henry 5, iv. 3.

Viliaco. *Rascal; coward.*
I see them lording it in London streets,
Crying " *Viliaco !*" unto all they meet.
Henry 6, P. 2, iv. 7.

Villagery. *Villages.*
Are you not he
That frights the maidens of the *villagery?*
Midsummer-Night's Dream, ii. 1.

Villain. *A servant; a slave.*
A trusty *villain*, sir; that very oft,
When I am dull with care and melancholy,
Lightens my humour with his merry jests.
Comedy of Errors, i. 2.

Vindicative. *Revengeful; vindictive.*
But he, in heat of action,
Is more *vindicative* than jealous love.
Troilus and Cressida, iv. 5.

Vinewed. *Mouldy.*
Speak, then, thou *vinewedst* leaven, speak : I
will beat thee into handsomeness.
Troilus and Cressida, ii. 1.

Viol-de-gamboys. *The viol-de-gambo, a six-stringed violin.*
He plays o' the *viol-de-gamboys*, and speaks
three or four languages word for word without book.
Twelfth-Night, i. 3.

To **Violent.** *To rage; to be violent.*
The grief is fine, full, perfect, that I taste,

And *violenteth* in a sense as strong
As that which causeth it.
Troilus and Cressida, iv. 4.

Viperous. *Venomous; noxious.*
Kings, queens, and states,
Maids, matrons, nay, the secrets of the grave
This *viperous* slander enters. *Cymbeline*, iii. 4.

To **Virgin.** *To play the virgin.*
Now, by the jealous queen of heaven, that kiss
I carried from thee, dear ; and my true lip
Hath *virgin'd* it e'er since. *Coriolanus*, v. 3.

Virginal. *Maidenly.*
Can you think to front his revenges with the
virginal palms of your daughters, or with the palsied
intercession of such a decayed dotant as you seem
to be? *Coriolanus*, v. 2.
Tears *virginal*
Shall be to me even as the dew to fire.
Henry 6, P. 2, v. 2.

To **Virginal.** *To finger; to play upon.*
Still *virginalling* upon his palm? *Winter's Tale*, i. 2.

Virtue. *Power; valour; forgiveness.*
The *virtue* of your eye must break my oath.
Love's Labour's lost, v. 2.
Trust to thy single *virtue*; for thy soldiers,
All levied in my name, have in my name
Took their discharge. *King Lear*, v. 3.
The rarer action is
In *virtue* than in vengeance. *Tempest*, v. 1.
Think, thy slave man rebels : and by thy *virtue*
Set them into confounding odds, that boasts
. May have the world in empire.
Timon of Athens, iv. 3.

Virtuous. *Benign ; wholesome ; salutary ;
eminent; superior.*
But it is I
That lying by the violet in the sun,
Do as the carrion does, not as the flower,
Corrupt with *virtuous* season.
Measure for Measure, ii. 2.
Whose liquor hath this *virtuous* property,
To take from thence all error with his might.
Midsummer-Night's Dream, iii. 2.
For where an unclean mind carries *virtuous*
qualities, there commendations go with pity.
All's well that ends well, i. 1.

VISITATION. *Visit.*

What have you now to present unto him?—
Nothing at this time but my *visitation.*
Timon of Athens, v. 1.

His approach,
So out of circumstance and sudden, tells us
'Tis not a *visitation* fram'd, but forc'd
By need and accident. *Winter's Tale,* v. 1.

VISITOR. *A comforter; one who gives consolation.*

The *visitor* will not give him o'er so. *Tempest,* ii. 1.

TO VIZARD. *To mask; to disguise.*

Degree being *vizarded,*
Th' unworthiest shows as fairly in the mask.
Troilus and Cressida, i. 3.

VOICE. *Report; public opinion; vote; suffrage.*

In *voices* well divulg'd, free, learn'd, and valiant.
Twelfth-Night, i. 5.

Well, the *voice* goes, madam. *Henry* 8, iv. 2.
The common *voice,* I see, is verified
Of thee. *Ibid.* v. 2.

Are you all resolved to give your *voices?* But
that's no matter, the greater part carries it.
Coriolanus, ii. 3.

Of that I shall have also cause to speak,
And from his mouth whose *voice* will draw on more.
Hamlet, v. 2.

If the dull brainless Ajax come safe off,
We'll dress him up in *voices.*
Troilus and Cressida, i. 3.

TO VOICE. *To nominate; to elect; to report;
to proclaim.*

And that your minds,
Pre-occupied with what you rather must do
Than what you should, made you against the grain
To *voice* him consul. *Coriolanus,* ii. 3.

Is this th' Athenian minion, whom the world
Voic'd so regardfully? *Timon of Athens,* iv. 3.

VOID. *Unoccupied; uncrowded.*

I'll get me to a place more *void,* and there
Speak to great Cæsar as he comes along.
Julius Cæsar, ii. 4.

TO VOID. *To quit; to leave; to depart.*

If they will fight with us, bid them come down,
Or *void* the field. *Henry* 5, iv. 7.

How in our *voiding*-lobby hast thou stood,
And duly waited for my coming forth!
Henry 6, P. 2, iv. 1.

TO VOLLEY. *To shout; to vociferate.*

The holding every man shall bear as loud
As his strong sides can *volley.*
Antony and Cleopatra, ii. 7.

VOTARIST. *Votary.*

The jewels you have had from me to deliver to
Desdemona would half have corrupted a *votarist.*
Othello, iv. 2.

Gold? yellow, glittering, precious gold? No, gods,
I am no idle *votarist:* roots, you clear heavens!
Timon of Athens, iv. 3.

VOLUNTARY. *A volunteer.*

Rash, inconsiderate, fiery *voluntaries.*
King John, ii. 1.

VOUCH. *Testimony; attestation; warrant.*

To the king I'll say't; and make my *vouch* as strong
As shore of rock. *Henry* 8, i. 1.

My *vouch* against you, and my place i' the state,
Will so your accusation overweigh,
That you shall stifle in your own report.
Measure for Measure, ii. 4.

What praise couldst thou bestow on a deserving
woman indeed, one that, in the authority of her
merit, did justly put on the *vouch* of very malice
itself. *Othello,* ii. 1.

Why in this woolless toge should I stand here,
To beg of Hob and Dick, that do appear,
Their needless *vouches?* *Coriolanus,* ii. 3.

TO VOUCH. *To declare; to affirm; to warrant.*

To *vouch* this, is no proof. *Othello,* i. 3.
What can you *vouch* against him, Signior Lucio?
Measure for Measure, v. 1.

The feast is sold
That is not often *vouch'd,* while 'tis a-making,
'Tis given with welcome. *Macbeth,* iii. 4.

TO VOUCHSAFE. *To condescend to; to accept.*

If your back
Cannot *vouchsafe* this burden, 'tis too weak
Ever to get a boy. *Henry* 8, ii. 3.

Vouchsafe my labour, and long live your lordship!
Timon of Athens, i. 1.

Vouchsafe good morrow from a feeble tongue.
Julius Cæsar, ii. 1.

VOYAGE. *Attack; enterprise; assault.*

If he should intend this *voyage* toward my wife,
I would turn her loose to him; and what he gets
more of her than sharp words, let it lie on my head.
Merry Wives of Windsor, ii. 1.

If you make your *voyage* upon her, and give me
directly to understand you have prevailed, I am no
further your enemy; she is not worth our debate.
Cymbeline, i. 4.

VULGARLY. *Openly; publicly.*

To justify this worthy nobleman,
So *vulgarly* and personally accus'd.
Measure for Measure, v. 1.

W.

WAFT. *Wafted; waved.*

In such a night
Stood Dido with a willow in her hand
Upon the wild sea-banks, and *waft* her love
To come again to Carthage.
Merchant of Venice, v. 1.

In brief, a braver choice of dauntless spirits,
Than now the English bottoms have *waft* o'er,
Did never float upon the swelling tide
To do offence and scathe in Christendom.
King John, ii. 1.

To WAFT. *To wave; to beckon; to convey; to carry; to turn; to direct.*

In such a night
Stood Dido with a willow in her hand
Upon the wild sea-banks, and *waft* her love
To come again to Carthage.
Merchant of Venice, v. 1.

But, soft! who *wafts* us yonder?
Comedy of Errors, ii. 2.

One do I personate of Lord Timon's frame,
Whom Fortune with her ivory hand *wafts* to her.
Timon of Athens, i. 1.

I charge thee *waft* me safely cross the Channel.
Henry 6, P. 2, iv. 1.

When he,
Wafting his eyes to the contrary, and falling
A lip of much contempt, speeds from me.
Winter's Tale, i. 2.

WAFTAGE. *Passage.*

Like a strange soul upon the Stygian banks
Staying for *waftage.* *Troilus and Cressida,* iii. 2.

What ship of Epidamnum stays for me?—
A ship you sent me to, to hire *waftage.*
Comedy of Errors, iv. 1.

WAFTURE. *The act of waving; gesture; movement.*

Yet I insisted, yet you answer'd not;
But with an angry *wafture* of your hand
Gave sign for me to leave you. *Julius Cæsar,* ii. 1.

To WAG. *To go.*

Bid sorrow *wag,* cry "hem" when he should groan.
Much Ado about Nothing, v. 1.

Let us *wag,* then. *Merry Wives of Windsor,* ii. 3.

To WAGE. *To stake; to wager; to make; to carry on; to hire for pay.*

My life I never held but as a pawn
To *wage* against thine enemies; nor fear to lose it,
Thy safety being the motive. *King Lear,* i. 1.

Return to her, and fifty men dismiss'd?
No, rather I abjure all roofs, and choose
To *wage* against the enmity o' th' air;
To be a comrade with the wolf and owl,—
Necessity's sharp pinch! *Ibid.* ii. 4.

His taints and honours
Wag'd equal with him.
Antony and Cleopatra, v. 1.

I will *wage* against your gold, gold to it.
Cymbeline, i. 4.

Neglecting an attempt of ease and gain,
To wake and *wage* a danger profitless. *Othello,* i. 3.

Till at the last,
I seem'd his follower, not partner; and
He *wag'd* me with his countenance, as if
I had been mercenary. *Coriolanus,* v. 6.

WAIST. *The middle deck of a ship.*

Now in the *waist,* the deck, in every cabin,
I flam'd amazement. *Tempest,* i. 2.

WAKE. *Waking.*

The man that makes his toe
  What he his heart should make,
Shall of a corn cry woe,
  And turn his sleep to *wake*. *King Lear*, iii. 2.

To WAKE. *To watch; to remain awake; to abstain from sleep.*

I'll *wake* mine eye-balls blind first.
                        Cymbeline, iii. 4.

To WALK. *To go; to act; to behave; to conduct one's self.*

              What! mother dead!
How wildly, then, *walks* my estate in France!
                  King John, iv. 2.
But, gentle sir, methinks you *walk* like a stranger.
            Taming of the Shrew, ii. 1.

To WALL. *To wall in; to enclose; to surround.*

On either hand thee there are squadrons pitch'd,
To *wall* thee from the liberty of flight.
             Henry 6, P. 1, iv. 2.

WALL-EYED. *Fierce-eyed; glaring.*

          The vilest stroke
That ever *wall-eyed* wrath or staring rage
Presented to the tears of soft remorse.
              King John, iv. 3.

To WAN. *To turn pale.*

Is it not monstrous, that this player here,
But in a fiction, in a dream of passion,
Could force his soul so to his own conceit,
That, from her working, all his visage *wann'd* ?
               Hamlet, ii. 2.

WANED. *Wasted; shrunk; withered; diminished.*

       But all the charms of love,
Salt Cleopatra, soften thy *wan'd* lip !
         Antony and Cleopatra, ii. 1.
Yet thus far fortune maketh us amends,
And says, that once more I shall interchange
My *waned* state for Henry's regal crown.
           Henry 6, P. 3, iv. 7.

WANT. *Absence.*

         His present *want*
Seems more than we shall find it.
           Henry 4, P. 1, iv. 1.

To WANT. *To lack; to be without.*

You are dull, Casca; and those sparks of life
That should be in a Roman you do *want*,
Or else you use not. *Julius Cæsar*, i. 3.
     You have obedience scanted,
And well are worth the want that you have *wanted* ?
             King Lear, i. 1.
And what does else *want* credit, come to me,
And I'll be sworn 'tis true. *Tempest*, iii. 3.
Down, down I come; like glistering Phaëthon,
Wanting the manage of unruly jades.'
             Richard 2, iii. 3.

WANTON. *An effeminate person; a trifler.*

I pray you, pass with your best violence;
I am afeard you make a *wanton* of me.
               Hamlet, v. 2.
      Shall a beardless boy,
A cocker'd silken *wanton*, brave our fields,
And flesh his spirit in a warlike soil,
Mocking the air with colours idly spread,
And find no check ? *King John*, v. 1.
      I am not well ;
But not so citizen a *wanton* as
To seem to die ere sick. *Cymbeline*, iv. 2.

WANTON (adj.). *Irregular; frivolous; licentious; slight; fantastic.*

What with the injuries of a *wanton* time,
And from this swarm of fair advantages,
You took occasion to be quickly woo'd,
To gripe the general sway into your hand.
         Henry 4, P. 1, v. 1.
     And hence, thou sickly quoif !
Thou art a guard too *wanton* for the head
Which princes, flesh'd with conquest, aim to hit.
         Henry 4, P. 2, i. 1.

WAPPENED. *Stale; over-worn; worn out.*

          This is it
That makes the *wappen'd* widow wed again.
        Timon of Athens, iv. 3.

WARD. *Custody; confinement; guard; attitude of defence.*

I know, ere they will have me go to *ward*,
They'll pawn their swords for my enfranchisement.
         Henry 6, P. 2, v. 1.
Say this to him, he's beat from his best *ward*.
         Winter's Tale, i. 2.
Come from thy *ward*. *Tempest*, i. 2.

To WARD.   *To defend; to protect; to guard.*

Then, if you fight against God's enemy,
God will, in justice, *ward* you as his soldiers.
Richard 3, v. 3.

WARDEN.   *A species of pear so called.*

I must have saffron, to colour the *warden*-pies.
Winter's Tale, iv. 2.

WARDER.   *A staff; a truncheon.*

Stay, the king hath thrown his *warder* down.
Richard 2, i. 3.

WARE.   *Wore.*

And, if we thrive, promise them such rewards
As victors *ware* at the Olympian games.
Henry 6, P. 3, ii. 3.

WARE.   *Aware of; sensible of; conscious of.*

Come, come, you'll do him wrong ere you're *ware*.
Troilus and Cressida, iv. 2.

Nay, I shall ne'er be *ware* of mine own wit till
I break my shins against it.   *As you like it*, ii. 4.

Towards him I made; but he was *ware* of me,
And stole into the covert of the wood.
Romeo and Juliet, i. 1.

To WARN.   *To summon.*

They mean to *warn* us at Philippi here,
Answering before we do demand of them.
Julius Cæsar, v. 1.

Who is it that hath *warn'd* us to the walls?
King John, ii. 1.

And sent to *warn* them to his royal presence.
Richard 3, i. 3.

O me! this sight of death is as a bell,
That *warns* my old age to a sepulchre.
Romeo and Juliet, v. 3.

To WARP.   *To swell; to raise; to upheave.*

Though thou the waters *warp*,
Thy sting is not so sharp
As friend remember'd not.   *As you like it*, ii. 7.

WARRANT.   *Legality; right; law; canon.*

There's *warrant* in that theft
Which steals itself, when there's no mercy left.
Macbeth, ii. 1.

I therefore apprehend and do attach thee
For an abuser of the world, a practiser
Of arts inhibited and out of *warrant*.   *Othello*, i. 2.

WARRANTISE.   *Authority; warrant.*

Break up the gates, I'll be your *warrantise*.
Henry 6, P. 1, i. 3.

Her obsequies have been as far enlarg'd
As we have *warrantise*.   *Hamlet*, v. 1.

WARRANTY.   *' Warrant; allowance.*

I never did
Offend you in my life; never lov'd Cassio
But with such general *warranty* of heaven
As I might love.   *Othello*, v. 2.

WASH.   *The sea-shore; the coast.*

Full thirty times hath Phœbus' cart gone round
Neptune's salt *wash* and Tellus' orbèd ground.
Hamlet, iii. 2.

I'll tell thee, Hubert, half my power this night,
Passing these flats, are taken by the tide,—
These Lincoln *washes* have devourèd them.
King John, v. 6.

WASSAIL.   *A carouse; a drinking bout; a revel; an orgy.*

Antony, leave thy lascivious *wassails*.
Antony and Cleopatra, i. 4.

His two chamberlains
Will I with wine and *wassail* so convince,
That memory, the warder of the brain,
Shall be a fume.   *Macbeth*, i. 7.

At wakes and *wassails*, meetings, markets, fairs.
Love's Labour's lost, v. 2.

The king doth wake to-night, and takes his rouse,
Keeps *wassail*, and the swaggering up-spring reels.
Hamlet, i. 4.

A *wassail* candle, my lord; all tallow.
Henry 4, P. 2, i. 2.

WATCH.   *Abstinence from sleep; a watch-light.*

False to his bed! What is it to be false?
To lie in *watch* there, and to think on him?
To weep 'twixt clock and clock? *Cymbeline*, iii. 4.
Fill me a bowl of wine.—Give me a *watch*.
Richard 3, v. 2.

To WATCH.   *To hinder from sleeping; to be awake.*

That is to *watch* her, as we *watch* these kites
That bate, and beat, and will not be obedient.
Taming of the Shrew, iv. 1.

You must be *watched* ere you be made tame,
must you?   *Troilus and Cressida*, iii. 2.

A great perturbation in nature,—to receive at once the benefit of sleep, and do the effects of watching! *Macbeth*, v. 1.

WATCHING. *Voluntary abstinence from sleep.*

First her bedchamber,—
Where, I confess, I slept not; but profess
Had that was well worth *watching*.
Cymbeline, ii. 4.

WATERISH. *Watery; moist; marshy.*

Not all the dukes of *waterish* Burgundy
Can buy this unpriz'd precious maid of me.
King Lear, i. 1.

WATER-WORK. *A sort of painted cloth.*

A pretty slight drollery, or the story of the Prodigal, or the German hunting in *water-work*, is worth a thousand of these bed-hangings, and these fly-bitten tapestries. *Henry 4*, P. 2, ii. 1.

To **WAVE.** *To fluctuate; to lean; to incline; to waft; to beckon.*

If he did not care whether he had their love or no, he *waved* indifferently 'twixt doing them neither good nor harm. *Coriolanus*, ii. 2.

Look, with what courteous action
It *waves* you to a more removèd ground.
Hamlet, i. 4.

To **WAWL.** *To scream; to shriek.*

Thou know'st, the first time that we smell the air,
We *wawl* and cry. *King Lear*, iv. 6.

WAXEN. *Soft; penetrable; waxlike.*

And with thy blessings steel my lance's point,
That it may enter Mowbray's *waxen* coat.
Richard 2, i. 3.

To **WAXEN.** *To wax; to increase; to grow.*

And *waxen* in their mirth, and neeze.
Midsummer-Night's Dream, ii. 1.

WAY. *Creed; religious opinion.*

Hear me, Sir Thomas: you are a gentleman
Of mine own *way*. *Henry 8*, v. 1.

WEAK. *Foolish; worthless.*

And her wit
Values itself so highly, that to her
All matter else seems *weak*.
Much Ado about Nothing, iii. 1.

WEAKLING. *A feeble creature; a weak person.*

And, *weakling*, Warwick takes his gift again.
Henry 6, P. 3, v. 1.

WEAL. *State; commonwealth.*

Which, in the tender of a wholesome *weal*,
Might in their working do you that offence,
Which else were shame. *King Lear*, i. 4.

Ever spake against
Your liberties, and the charters that you bear
I' the body of the *weal*. *Coriolanus*, ii. 3.

WEALSMAN. *A statesman; a politician.*

Meeting two such *wealsmen* as you are, if the drink you give me touch my palate adversely, I make a crooked face at it. *Coriolanus*, ii. 1.

WEALTH. *Weal; advantage; prosperity.*

I once did lend my body for his *wealth*.
Merchant of Venice, v. 1.

WEAPONED. *Armed.*

Be not afraid, though you do see me weapon'd.
Othello, v. 2.

WEAR. *Custom; practice; mode; fashion; vogue.*

No, indeed, will I not, Pompey; it is not the *wear*.
Measure for Measure, iii. 2.
A worthy fool!—Motley's the only *wear*.
As you like it, ii. 7.

To **WEAR.** *To harass; to weary; to be in vogue; to be worn.*

Just like the brooch and the tooth-pick, which *wear* not now. *All's well that ends well*, i. 1.
Or if thou hast not sat as I do now,
Wearing thy hearer in thy mistress' praise,
Thou hast not lov'd. *As you like it*, ii. 4.

WEARING. *Apparel; dress; clothes.*

Your high self,
The gracious mark o' the land, you have obscur'd
With a swain's *wearing*. *Winter's Tale*, iv. 3.
Give me my nightly *wearing*, and adieu:
We must not now displease him. *Othello*, iv. 3.

WEATHER. *The weather-gage.* *A sea term.*

Mine honour keeps the *weather* of my fate.
Troilus and Cressida, v. 3.

To **WEATHER-FEND.** *To shelter.*

In the line-grove which *weather-fends* your cell.
Tempest, v. 1.

WED. *Wedded; married.*

You've show'd a tender fatherly regard,
To wish me *wed* to one half-lunatic.
         Taming of the Shrew, ii. 1.

And *wed*
Unto a woman, happy but for me.
         Comedy of Errors, i. 1.

This is it
That makes the wappen'd widow *wed* again.
         Timon of Athens, iv. 3.

WEE. *Very small; tiny.*

He hath but a little *wee* face.
         Merry Wives of Windsor, i. 4.

WEED. *Garment; clothes; apparel.*

Give me thy hand;
And let me see thee in thy woman's *weeds.*
         Twelfth-Night, v. 1.

And there the snake throws her enamell'd skin,
Weed wide enough to wrap a fairy in.
         Midsummer-Night's Dream, ii. 1.

Which to confirm,
I'll bring you to a captain's in this town,|
Where lie my maid's *weeds.*   *Twelfth-Night,* v. 1.

With a proud heart he wore his humble *weeds.*
         Coriolanus, ii. 3.

WEEK. *A short period; time indefinitely.*

Thou old traitor,
I'm sorry that, by hanging thee, I can but
Shorten thy life one *week.*   *Winter's Tale,* iv. 3.

At seventeen years many their fortunes seek;
But at fourscore it is too late a *week.*
         As you like it, ii. 3.

To **WEEN.** *To think; to suppose; to look for; to expect.*

Ween you of better luck,
I mean, in perjur'd witness, than your master,
Whose minister you are?   *Henry* 8, v. 1.

To **WEET.** *To know; to be informed.*

When such a mutual pair
And such a twain can do't, in which I bind,
On pain of punishment, the world to *weet*
We stand up peerless. *Antony and Cleopatra,* i. 1.

To **WEIGH.** *To value; to esteem; to regard; to care for; to hesitate.*

Which I *weigh* not,
Being of those virtues vacant.   *Henry* 8, v. 1.

Let every word weigh heavy of her worth,
That he does *weigh* too light.
     All's well that ends well, iii. 4.

You *weigh* me not,—O, that's you care not for me.
         Love's Labour's lost, v. 2.

They that must *weigh* out my afflictions,
They that my trust must grow to, live not here.
         Henry 8, iii. 1.

And the fair soul herself
Weigh'd, between loathness and obedience, at
Which end o' the beam she'd bow. *Tempest,* ii. 1.

WEIRD SISTERS. *The Fates.*

The *weird sisters,* hand in hand,
Posters of the sea and land,
Thus do go about, about.   *Macbeth,* i. 3.

WELSH HOOK. *A kind of bill or axe with two edges.*

He of Wales, that made Lucifer cuckold, and
swore the devil his true liegeman upon the cross of
a *Welsh hook.*   *Henry* 4, P. 1, ii. 4.

WELL. *Happy.*

O, in this love, you love your child so ill,
That you run mad, seeing that she is *well.*
         Romeo and Juliet, iv. 5.

Why, there's more gold.
But, sirrah, mark, we use
To say the dead are *well.*
         Antony and Cleopatra, ii. 5.

WELL-ADVISED. *Sane; in possession of reason.*

Am I in earth, in heaven, or in hell?
Sleeping or waking? mad or *well-advis'd?*
         Comedy of Errors, ii. 2.

WELL-FITTED. *Well-versed; well-skilled.*

Well-fitted in the arts, glorious in arms.
         Love's Labour's lost, ii. 1.

WELL-POSSESSED. *Wealthy.*

I am, my lord, as well-deriv'd as he,
As *well-possess'd.* *Midsummer-Night's Dream,* i. 1.

WELL BE-MET. *Well met; welcome.*

Our very loving sister, *well be-met. King Lear,* v. 1.

WELL-DIVULGED. *Well-proclaimed; well-reported.*

In voices *well-divulg'd*, free, learn'd, and valiant.
Twelfth-Night, i. 5.

Ay, Greek; and that shall be *divulgèd well*
In characters as red as Mars his heart
Inflam'd with Venus. *Troilus and Cressida*, v. 2.

WELL FOUND. *Well skilled; skilful; well seen.*

Gerard de Narbon was my father; one
In what he did profess *well found*.
All's well that ends well, ii. 1.

TO WEND. *To go.*

Wend you with this letter.
Measure for Measure, iv. 3.

Hopeless and helpless doth Ægeon *wend*.
Comedy of Errors, i. 1.

WESAND. *Throat; windpipe.*

Or cut his *wesand* with thy knife. *Tempest*, iii. 2.

WHALESBONE. *Ivory.*

This is the flower that smiles on every one,
To show his teeth as white as *whalesbone*.
Love's Labour's lost, v. 2.

WHAT. *Which; who.*

Madam, your mother craves a word with you.—
What is her mother? *Romeo and Juliet*, i. 5.

What should he be?—
It is myself I mean. *Macbeth*, iv. 3.

WHAT THOUGH. *What then.*

Madam, by chance, but not by truth: *what though?*
Something about, a little from the right.
King John, i. 1.

But *what though?* Courage! As horns are
odious, they are necessary. *As you like it*, iii. 3.

It is a simple one; but *what though?* it will
toast cheese, and it will endure cold as another
man's sword will. *Henry 5*, ii. 1.

WHELK. *A protuberance; a bump; a swelling.*

His face is all bubuckles, and *whelks*, and knobs,
and flames o' fire. *Henry 5*, iii. 5.

WHELKED. *Embossed; full of protuberances.*

He had a thousand noses,
Horns *whelk'd* and wav'd like the enridgèd sea.
King Lear, iv. 6.

WHEN. *An expression of impatience.*

When, Harry? *when?* *Richard 2*, i. 1.
Come, thou tortoise! *when?* *Tempest*, i. 2.
When, Lucius, *when?* awake, I say!
Julius Cæsar, ii. 1.

WHENAS. *When.*

Many a battle have I won in France,
Whenas the enemy hath been ten to one.
Henry 6, P. 3, i. 2.

Whenas your husband, all in rage, to-day
Came to my house, and took away my ring.
Comedy of Errors, iv. 4.

WHER. *Whether.*

See, *whér* their basest metal be not mov'd.
Julius Cæsar, i. 1.

Whér thou beest he or no,
Or some enchanted trifle to abuse me.
Tempest, v. 1.

WHERE. *Whereas; whereby; by whom.*

Where now his knowledge must prove ignorance.
Love's Labour's lost, ii. 1.

And *where* I thought the remnant of mine age
Should have been cherish'd by her child-like duty,
I now am full resolv'd to take a wife,
And turn her out to who will take her in.
Two Gentlemen of Verona, iii. 1.

Where now remains a sweet reversion.
Henry 4, P. 1, iv. 1.

Where, from thy sight, I should be raging mad.
Henry 6, P. 2, iii. 2.

And I, the hapless mate to one sweet bird,
Have now the fatal object in my eye
Where my poor young was lim'd, was caught, and
kill'd. *Henry 6*, P. 3, v. 6.

WHEREAS. *Where.*

'Tis his highness' pleasure
You do prepare to ride unto Saint Alban's,
Whereas the king and queen do mean to hawk.
Henry 6, P. 2, i. 2.

WHEREFORE. *For that purpose.*

Rouse him, and give him note of our approach,
With the whole quality *wherefore*.
Troilus and Cressida, iv. 2.

3 B

WHERE THAT. *Whereas.*

And *where that* you have vow'd to study, lords,
In that each of you have forsworn his book.
Love's Labour's lost, iv. 3.

WHEREUPON. *For what reason; wherefore.*

And *whereupon*
You cónjure from the breast of civil peace
Such bold hostility. *Henry 4,* P. 1, iv. 3.

WHIFFLER. *A harbinger; the leader of a procession.*

Whose shouts and claps out-voice the deep-mouth'd sea,
Which like a mighty *whiffler* 'fore the king
Seems to prepare his way.
Henry 5, Chorus to act v.

WHILE-ERE. *Ere-while; some time ago.*

Will you troll the catch
You taught me but *while-ere?* *Tempest,* iii. 2.

WHILES, WHILE. *Till.*

And let the trumpets sound
While we return these dukes what we decree.
Richard 2, i. 3.

He shall conceal it,
Whiles you are willing it shall come to note
What time we will our celebration keep,
According to my birth. *Twelfth-Night,* iv. 3.

To make society
The sweeter welcome, we will keep ourself
Till supper-time alone: *while* then, God b' wi' you!
Macbeth, iii. 1.

WHIP. *The sword; the right hand.*

Wert thou the Hector
That was the *whip* of your bragg'd progeny,
Thou shouldst not scape me here.
Coriolanus, i. 8.

WHIPSTER. *A sharp nimble fellow.*

I am not valiant neither,
But every puny *whipster* gets my sword.
Othello, v. 2.

WHIPSTOCK. *The handle of a whip; the whip itself.*

For Malvolio's nose is no *whipstock.*
Twelfth-Night, ii. 3.

WHIST. *Hushed; silenced.*

Court'sied when you have and kiss'd,—
The wild waves *whist.* *Tempest,* i. 2.

WHITE. *The white mark on a target; the centre.*

'Twas I won the wager, but you hit the *white.*
Taming of the Shrew, v. 2.

To WHISTLE OFF. *To discard; to dismiss.*

Though that her jesses were my dear heart-strings,
I'd *whistle her off,* and let her down the wind,
To prey at fortune. *Othello,* iii. 3.

WHITE HERRING. *A pickled herring.*

Hopdance cries in Tom's belly for two *white herring.* *King Lear,* iii. 6.

WHITELY. *Whitish; pale.*

A *whitely* wanton with a velvet brow.
Love's Labour's lost, iii. 1.

WHITHER. *Whithersoever.*

A fool go with thy soul, *whither* it goes!
Henry 4, P. 1, v. 3.

WHITING-TIME. *Bleaching-time.*

Or, it is *whiting-time,* send him by your two men to Datchet-mead.
Merry Wives of Windsor, iii. 3.

WHITSTER. *A whitener; a bleacher.*

And carry it among the *whitsters* in Datchet-mead.
Merry Wives of Windsor, iii. 3.

WHITTLE. *A knife.*

For myself,
There's not a *whittle* in th' unruly camp,
But I do prize it at my love, before
The reverend'st throat in Athens.
Timon of Athens, v. 1.

WHOLESOME. *Entire; perfect; unimpaired; suitable; reasonable; salutary.*

That it may stand till the perpetual doom,
In state as *wholesome* as in state 'tis fit,
Worthy the owner, and the owner it.
Merry Wives of Windsor, v. 5.

If it shall please you to make me a *wholesome* answer, I will do your mother's commandment.
Hamlet, iii. 2.

Speak to 'em, I pray you, in *wholesome* manner.
Coriolanus, ii. 3.
If, sir, perchance,
She have restrain'd the riots of your followers,
'Tis on such ground, and to such *wholesome* end,
As clears her from all blame. *King Lear*, ii. 4.

WHOOBUB. *A hubbub ; a bustle ; a loud noise.*

And had not the old man come in with a *whoobub* against his daughter and the king's son, I had not left a purse alive in the whole army.
Winter's Tale, iv. 3.

WICKED. *Baneful ; poisonous ; noxious.*

As *wicked* dew as e'er my mother brush'd
With raven's feather from unwholesome fen,
Drop on you both ! *Tempest*, i. 2.

WIDE. *Wild ; unsettled in mind ; wide of the mark.*

Is my lord well, that he doth speak so *wide* ?
Much Ado about Nothing, iv. 1.

Still, still, far *wide* ! *King Lear*, iv. 7.

No, no, no such matter ; you are *wide*.
Troilus and Cressida, iii. 1.

To **WIDOW.** *To endow with a widow's right ; to jointure.*

For his possessions,
We do instate and *widow* you withal,
To buy you a better husband.
Measure for Measure, v. 1.

WIGHT. *A person ; a being.*

She was a *wight*, if ever such *wight* were,—
To suckle fools, and chronicle small beer.
Othello, ii. 1.

He was a *wight* of high renown,
And thou art but of low degree. *Ibid.* ii. 3.

WILD. *Rash ; unadvised ; precipitate.*

For, in an act of this importance 'twere
Most piteous to be *wild*. *Winter's Tale*, ii. 1.

WILDERNESS. *Wildness ; wild growth ; savagery.*

For such a warped slip of *wilderness*
Ne'er issu'd from his blood.
Measure for Measure, iii. 1.

WILDLY. *Rashly ; heedlessly ; without control.*

But as the unthought-on accident is guilty
To what we *wildly* do, so we profess
Ourselves to be the slaves of chance, and flies
Of every wind that blows. *Winter's Tale*, iv. 3.

What ! mother dead !
How *wildly* then walks my estate in France !
King John, iv. 2.

WIMPLED. *Muffled ; hoodwinked.*

This *wimpled*, whining, purblind, wayward boy.
Love's Labour's lost, iii. 1.

WINDOWED. *Placed in a window ; full of openings.*

Wouldst thou be *window'd* in great Rome, and see
Thy master thus with pleach'd arms, bending down
His corrigible neck ? *Antony and Cleopatra*, iv. 14.

How shall your houseless heads and unfed sides,
Your loop'd and *window'd* raggedness, defend you
From seasons such as these ? *King Lear*, iii. 4.

To **WINTER-GROUND.** *To winter-strew ; to strew in winter-time.*

Yea, and furr'd moss besides, when flowers are none,
To *winter-ground* thy corse. *Cymbeline*, iv. 2.

To **WIS.** *To know ; to think.*

I *wis* your grandam had a worser match.
Richard 3, i. 3.

An if I *wist* he did,—but let it rest ;
Other affairs must now be managèd.
Henry 6, P. 1, iv. 1.

There be fools alive, I *wis*,
Silver'd o'er ; and so was this.
Merchant of Venice, ii. 8.

WISDOM. *Study ; knowledge ; observation ; philosophy.*

Though the *wisdom* of nature can reason it thus
and thus, yet nature finds itself scourged by the
sequent effects. *King Lear*, i. 2.

To **WISH.** *To recommend ; to persuade ; to imprecate.*

Marry, 'tis not monstrous in you ; neither *wish* I,
You take much pains to mend.
Timon of Athens, v. 1.

Petruchio, shall I, then, come roundly to thee,
And *wish* thee to a shrewd ill-favour'd wife?
Taming of the Shrew, i. 2.

If I can by any means light on a fit man to
teach her that wherein she delights, I will *wish*
him to her father. *Ibid.* i. 1.

But I persuaded them, if they lov'd Benedick,
To *wish* him wrestle with affection.
Much Ado about Nothing, iii. 1.

How rarely does it meet with this time's guise,
When man was *wish'd* to love his enemies!
Timon of Athens, iv. 3.

Her hair, what colour?—
Brown, madam: and her forehead
As low as she could *wish* it.
Antony and Cleopatra, iii. 3.

WISHFUL. *Longing.*

From Scotland am I stol'n, even of pure love,
To greet mine own land with my *wishful* sight.
Henry 6, P. 3, iii. 1.

WISTLY. *Wistfully; earnestly.*

And speaking it, he *wistly* look'd on me.
Richard 2, v. 4.

WIT. *Sense; judgment; contrivance; stratagem.*

Hath the fellow any *wit* that told you this?
Much Ado about Nothing, i. 2.

Hector shall not have his *wit* this year.
Troilus and Cressida, i. 2.

But that my admirable dexterity of *wit*, my
counterfeiting the action of an old woman, delivered me, the knave constable had set me i' the
stocks, i' the common stocks, for a witch.
Merry Wives of Windsor, iv. 5.

Let me, if not by birth, have lands by *wit*.
King Lear, i. 2.

To WIT. *To know.*

Yet are these feet, whose strengthless stay is numb,
Swift-wingèd with desire to get a grave,
As *witting* I no other comfort have.
Henry 6, P. 1, ii. 5.

WITCH. *A wizard; a charmer; a sorcerer.*

Such a holy *witch*,
That he enchants societies into him.
Cymbeline, i. 6.

WITHAL. *Therewith; likewise.*

Romeo that spoke him fair, bade him bethink
How nice the quarrel was, and urg'd *withal*
Your high displeasure. *Romeo and Juliet*, iii. 2.

WITHIN. *Under; beneath.*

Come not within those doors! *within* this roof
The enemy of all your graces lives.
As you like it, ii. 3.

WITHOUT (adv.). *Outwardly; externally.*

Senseless bauble,
Art thou a fedary for this act, and look'st
So virgin-like *without*? *Cymbeline*, iii. 2.

WITHOUT (prep.). *Beyond; out of the reach of; but with; except with.*

Our intent
Was to be gone from Athens, where we might,
Without the peril of th' Athenian law,—
Midsummer-Night's Dream, iv. 1.

A thing
More slavish did I ne'er than answering
A slave *without* a knock. *Cymbeline*, iv. 2.

WITHOUT BOOK. *By heart; by memory.*

An affectioned ass, that cons state *without book*,
and utters it by great swaths. *Twelfth-Night*, ii. 3.

WITHOUT CONTRADICTION. *Unquestionably; without doubt.*

'Twas a contention in public, which may, *without
contradiction*, suffer the report. *Cymbeline*, i. 4.

WITH THE MANNER. *In the fact.*

The manner of it is, I was taken *with the manner*.
Love's Labour's lost, i. 1.

Thou stolest a cup of sack eighteen years ago,
and wert taken *with the manner*.
Henry 4, P. 1, ii. 4.

WITNESS. *Testimony; evidence.*

Ween you of better luck,
I mean, in perjur'd *witness*, than your master,
Whose minister you are? *Henry* 8, v. 1.

WIT-SNAPPER. *A witling; a pretender to wit.*

Goodly lord, what a *wit-snapper* are you!
Merchant of Venice, iii. 5.

WITTOLLY. *Cuckoldly; contemptible.*

They say the jealous *wittolly* knave hath masses
of money. *Merry Wives of Windsor*, ii. 2.

WITTY. *Sagacious; penetrating; shrewd;
judicious; reasonable.*

You must be *witty* now. *Troilus and Cressida*, iii. 2.
The deep-revolving *witty* Buckingham
No more shall be the neighbour to my counsels.
Richard 3, iv. 2.

WOE. *Sorry; sad; grieved.*

I am *woe* for 't, sir. *Tempest*, v. 1.
Woe, woe are we, sir, you may not live to wear
All your true followers out.
Antony and Cleopatra, iv. 14.
Be *woe* for me, more wretched than he is.
Henry 6, P. 2, iii. 2.

To WOMAN. *To make womanish; to soften;
to womanize.*

I've felt so many quirks of joy and grief,
That the first face of neither, on the start,
Can *woman* me unto 't. *All's well that ends well*, iii. 2.

WOMAN-TIRED. *Henpecked.*

Thou dotard, thou art *woman-tir'd*, unroosted
By thy dame Partlet here. *Winter's Tale*, ii. 3.

WOMANED. *Associated with a woman; ac-
companied by a woman.*

I do attend here on the general;
And think it no addition, nor my wish,
To have him see me *woman'd*. *Othello*, iii. 4.

WOMB. *The stomach.*

An I had but a belly of any indifferency, I were
simply the most active fellow in Europe : my *womb*,
my *womb*, my *womb*, undoes me. *Henry 4*, P. 2, iv. 3.

To WOMB. *To enclose; to contain.*

Not . . . .
. . . . for all the sun sees, or
The close earth *wombs*, or the profound seas hide
In unknown fathoms, will I break my oath
To this my fair belov'd. *Winter's Tale*, iv. 3.

WOMBY. *Hollow; capacious.*

He'll call you to so hot an answer of it,
That caves and *womby* vaultages of France
Shall chide your trespass. *Henry 5*, ii. 4.

WOOD. *Frantic; distracted; mad.*

O, that she could speak now like a *wood* woman !
Two Gentlemen of Verona, ii. 3.
And *wood* within this wood.
Midsummer-Night's Dream, ii. 1.
How the young whelp of Talbot's, raging-*wood*,
Did flesh his puny sword in Frenchmen's blood !
Henry 6, P. 1, iv. 7.

WOODBINE. *The bindweed, or wild convol-
vulus.*

So doth the *woodbine* the sweet honeysuckle
Gently entwist. *Midsummer-Night's Dream*, iv. 1.

WOODCOCK. *A fool; a simpleton.*

O this *woodcock* ! what an ass it is !
Taming of the Shrew, i. 2.

WOODEN. *Dull; stupid; foolish; clumsy.*

I'll win this Lady Margaret. For whom ?
Why, for my king : tush, that's a *wooden* thing !
Henry 6, P. 1, v. 3.

WOODMAN. *A hunter; a sportsman.*

You, Polydore, have prov'd best *woodman*, and
Are master of the feast. *Cymbeline*, iii. 6.
Am I a *woodman*, ha ? Speak I like Herne the
hunter ? *Merry Wives of Windsor*, v. 5.

WOOLWARD. *Without linen.*

The naked truth of it is, I have no shirt ; I go
woolward for penance. *Love's Labour's lost*, v. 2.

WOO'T. *Wilt.*

Noblest of men, *woo't* die ?
Antony and Cleopatra, iv. 15.
Woo't weep ? *woo't* fight ? *woo't* fast ? *woo't* tear
thyself ?
Woo't drink up eisel ? eat a crocodile ?
Hamlet, v. 1.

WORD. *A saying; a saw; a proverb; a
watch-word; a pass-word.*

Thus, like the formal vice, Iniquity,
I moralize two meanings in one *word*.
Richard 3, iii. 1.
Give the *word*.—Sweet marjoram.—Pass.
King Lear, iv. 6.
Now to my *word* :
It is, " Adieu, adieu ! remember me." *Hamlet*, i. 5.

To WORD. *To overpower with words.*

He *words* me, girls, he *words* me, that I should not
Be noble to myself.   *Antony and Cleopatra*, v. 2.

WORDS. *Strife; contention.*

Why should she live, to fill the world with words?
                                        Henry 6, P. 3, v. 5.
This day, in argument upon a case,
Some *words* there grew 'twixt Somerset and me.
                                        Henry 6, P. 1, ii. 5.

To WORK. *To move; to induce; to prevail
upon.*

Doth she not count her bless'd,
Unworthy as she is, that we have *wrought*
So worthy a gentleman to be her bridegroom?
                                        Romeo and Juliet, iii. 5.

A WORLD TO SEE. *A wonder; a marvel.*

'Tis *a world to see,* how tame, when men and
women are alone, a meacock wretch can make the
curstest shrew.   *Taming of the Shrew*, ii. 1.

WORM. *A snake.*

Hast thou the pretty *worm* of Nilus there,
That kills and pains not?
                                        Antony and Cleopatra, v. 2.

          Thou art by no means valiant;
For thou dost fear the soft and tender fork
Of a poor *worm.*   *Measure for Measure*, iii. 1.

          Whose self-same mettle
Engenders the black toad and adder blue,
The gilded newt and eyeless venom'd *worm.*
                                        Timon of Athens, iv. 3.

Lest, being suffer'd in that harmful slumber,
The mortal *worm* might make the sleep eternal.
                                        Henry 6, P. 2, iii. 2.

WORSHIP. *Eminence; dignity; reputation;
credit; authority.*

His cup-bearer, whom I from meaner form
Have bench'd, and rear'd to *worship.*
                                        Winter's Tale, i. 2.

My train are men of choice and rarest parts,
That all particulars of duty know,
And in the most exact regard support
The *worships* of their name.   *King Lear*, i. 4.

Turn from me then that noble countenance,
Wherein the *worship* of the whole world lies.
                                        Antony and Cleopatra, iv. 14.

To WORSHIP. *To honour; to dignify.*

Or else our grave shall have a tongueless mouth,
Not *worshipp'd* with a waxen epitaph. *Henry* 5, i. 2.

WORST. *Lowest; meanest; poorest.*

          Hence, be gone!
If thou hadst not been born the *worst* of men,
Thou hadst been a knave and flatterer.
                                        Timon of Athens, iv. 3.

Now, if you have a station in the file,
And not i' the *worst* rank of manhood, say't;
And I will put that business in your bosoms,
Whose execution takes your enemy off.
                                        Macbeth, iii. 1.

WORTH. *Wealth; means; fortune; birth;
rank; full weight; pennyworth.*

They are but beggars that can count their *worth.*
                                        Romeo and Juliet, ii. 6.

He that helps him take all my outward *worth.*
                                        King Lear, iv. 4.

Ay, my good lord, I know the gentleman
To be of *worth,* and worthy estimation.
                                        Two Gentlemen of Verona, ii. 4.

But, were my *worth,* as is my conscience, firm,
You should find better dealing. *Twelfth-Night*, iii. 3.

                      And as sorry
Your choice is not so rich in *worth* as beauty,
That you might well enjoy her. *Winter's Tale*, v. 1.

          He hath been us'd
Ever to conquer, and to have his *worth*
Of contradiction.   *Coriolanus*, iii. 3.

WORTH. *Suitable for; fit for; worthy of.*

          For I can sing,
And speak to him in many sorts of music,
That will allow me very *worth* his service.
                                        Twelfth-Night, i. 2.

          You have obedience scanted,
And well are *worth* the want that you have wanted.
                                        King Lear, i. 1.

WORTHILY. *Justly; not without cause.*

The king is present: if't be known to him
That I gainsay my deed, how may he wound,
And *worthily,* my falsehood!   *Henry* 8, ii. 4.

WORTHY. *Just; well-merited; sufficient;
noble; valuable; wise; prudent.*

          Your master, Pindarus,
Hath given me some *worthy* cause to wish
Things done, undone.   *Julius Cæsar*, iv. 2.

He has much *worthy* blame laid upon him for shaking off so good a wife and so sweet a lady.
All's well that ends well, iv. 3.

In the mean time,
Let me be thought too busy in my fears,—
As *worthy* cause I have to fear I am,—
And hold her free, I do beseech your honour.
Othello, iii. 3.

I'm sorry for't; not seeming
So *worthy* as thy birth. *Cymbeline,* iv. 2.

The ruin speaks that sometime
It was a *worthy* building. *Ibid.* iv. 2.

They call him Doricles; and boasts himself
To have a *worthy* feeding. *Winter's Tale,* iv. 3.

That he should die is *worthy* policy;
But yet we want a colour for his death.
Henry 6, P. 2, iii. 1.

To WORTHY. *To render worthy; to aggrandize; to exalt.*

Being down, insulted, rail'd,
And put upon him such a deal of man,
That *worthied* him, got praises of the king
For him attempting who was self-subdu'd.
King Lear, ii. 2.

To WOT. *To know.*

But in gross brain little *wots*
What watch the king keeps to maintain the peace.
Henry 5, iv. 1.

And then you may come and see the picture,
she says, that you *wot* of.
Merry Wives of Windsor, ii. 2.

WOULD. *Would have; requires; wishes for; desires.*

Sorrow *would* solace, and mine age *would* ease.
Henry 6, P. 2, ii. 3.

WRACK. *Destruction; ruin.*

Ring the alarum-bell!—Blow, wind! come, *wrack!*
At least we'll die with harness on our back.
Macbeth, v. 5.

WRANGLER. *Opponent; adversary; competitor.*

Tell him he hath made a match with such a *wrangler*
That all the courts of France will be disturb'd
With chases. *Henry* 5, i. 2.

WRATH. *Angry; wrathful.*

For Oberon is passing fell and *wrath.*
Midsummer-Night's Dream, ii. 1.

WREAK. *Revenge.*

Then, if thou hast
A heart of *wreak* in thee . . . . .
. . . . . . speed thee straight,
And make my misery serve thy turn.
Coriolanus, iv. 5.

To WREAK. *To avenge; to revenge.*

O, how my heart abhors
To hear him nam'd,—and cannot come to him,
To *wreak* the love I bore my cousin Tybalt
Upon his body that hath slaughter'd him!
Romeo and Juliet, iii. 5.

WREAKFUL. *Indignant; angry.*

Call the creatures,
Whose naked natures live in all the spite
Of *wreakful* heaven; bid them flatter thee.
Timon of Athens, iv. 3.

WRECK. *Destruction; ruin.*

Or that with both
He labour'd in his country's *wreck*, I know not.
Macbeth, i. 3.

To WRENCH. *To wrest; to screw.*

For thy revenge
Wrench up thy power to the highest.
Coriolanus, i. 8.

WREST. *An instrument for tuning harps.*

But this Antenor,
I know, is such a *wrest* in their affairs,
That their negotiations all must slack,
Wanting his manage. *Troilus and Cressida,* iii. 3.

WRESTED. *Usurped; acquired by violence.*

And vast confusion waits,
As doth a raven on a sick-fallen beast,
The imminent decay of *wrested* pomp.
King John, iv. 3.

WRETCH. *A word of tenderness and endearment.*

Excellent *wretch!* Perdition catch my soul,
But I do love thee! *Othello,* iii. 3.

WRETCHED. *Hateful; despicable.*

The *wretched*, bloody, and usurping boar.
Richard 3, v. 2.

To **WRING.** *To writhe ; to be convulsed.*

'Tis all men's office to speak patience
To those that *wring* under the load of sorrow.
Much Ado about Nothing, v. 1.

He *wrings* at some distress. *Cymbeline*, iii. 6.

WRIT. *Writing ; composition.*

For the law of *writ* and the liberty, these are
the only men. *Hamlet*, ii. 2.

To **WRITE.** *To possess ; to be entitled to ; to call one's self ; to adopt ; to make use of.*

I'd give bay curtal and his furniture,
My mouth no more were broken than these boys',
And *writ* as little beard.
All's well that ends well, ii. 3.

I must tell thee, sirrah, I *write* man ; to which
title age cannot bring thee. *Ibid.* ii. 3.

About it ; and *write* happy when thou hast done.
King Lear, v. 3.

However they have *writ* the style of gods,
And made a push at chance and sufferance.
Much Ado about Nothing, v. 1.

WRITHLED. *Wrinkled.*

It cannot be this weak and *writhled* shrimp
Should strike such terror to his enemies.
Henry 6, P. 1, ii. 3.

WRONG. *A wronger ; shame ; dishonour ; harm ; detriment.*

He should have found his uncle Gaunt a father,
To rouse his *wrongs*, and chase them to the bay.
Richard 2, ii. 3.

A word, good sir ;
I fear, you've done yourself some *wrong* : a word.
Tempest, i. 2.

It shall advantage more than do us *wrong*.
Julius Cæsar, iii. 1.

To **WRONG.** *To disgrace ; to bring shame upon ; to deceive.*

You *wrong'd* yourself to write in such a case.
Julius Cæsar, iv. 3.

By my fidelity, this is not well, Master Ford ;
this *wrongs* you. *Merry Wives of Windsor*, iv. 2.

Good sister, wrong me not, nor *wrong* yourself,
To make a bondmaid and a slave of me.
Taming of the Shrew, ii. 1.

That you may well perceive I have not *wrong'd* you,
One of the greatest in the Christian world
Shall be my surety. *All's well that ends well*, iv. 4.

WROTH. *Misfortune ; sorrow ; misery ; ruth.*

Sweet, adieu. I'll keep my oath,
Patiently to bear my *wroth*.
Merchant of Venice, ii. 8.

WROUGHT. *Moved ; agitated ; transported ; stirred.*

If I had thought the sight of my poor image
Would thus have *wrought* you . . . . .
I'd not have show'd it. *Winter's Tale*, v. 3.

Give me your favour :—my dull brain was *wrought*
With things forgotten. *Macbeth*, i. 3.

To **WRY.** *To step aside ; to swerve ; to err.*

You married ones,
If each of you should take this course, how many
Must murder wives much better than themselves
For *wrying* but a little ! *Cymbeline*, v. 1.

Y.

YARE. *Ready ; nimble ; dexterous ; handy ; swift ; light.*

Cheerly, cheerly, my hearts ! *yare, yare !*
Tempest, i. 1.

I do desire to learn, sir : and I hope, if you have
occasion to use me for your own turn, you shall find
me *yare*. *Measure for Measure*, iv. 2.

Yare, yare, good Iras ; quick.—Methinks I hear
Antony call. *Antony and Cleopatra*, v. 2.

Their ships are *yare* ; yours heavy.
Ibid. iii. 7.

Dismount thy tuck, be *yare* in thy preparation.
Twelfth-Night, iii. 4.

·And to proclaim it civilly, were like

A halter'd neck which does the hangman thank
For being *yare* about him.
Antony and Cleopatra, iii. 13.

YARELY. *Dexterously; skilfully.*

Fall to 't *yarely*, or we run ourselves a-ground.
Tempest, i. 1.
The silken tackle
Swell with the touches of those flower-soft hands,
That *yarely* frame the office.
Antony and Cleopatra, ii. 2.

To YAW. *To roll, as a ship does in a swell.*

Though, I know, to divide him inventorially
would dizzy the arithmetic of memory, and it but
yaw neither, in respect of his quick sail.
Hamlet, v. 2.

To YEARN. *To grieve; to vex.*

It *yearns* me not if men my garments wear.
Henry 5, iv. 3.
O, how it *yearn'd* my heart, when I beheld,
In London streets, that coronation-day,
When Bolingbroke rode on roan Barbary!
Richard 2, v. 5.

YELLOWNESS. *Jealousy.*

I will possess him with *yellowness*, for this revolt
of mine is dangerous.
Merry Wives of Windsor, i. 3.

YEOMAN. *A bailiff's follower; a kind of under-bailiff.*

Where's your *yeoman*? Is't a lusty *yeoman*?
will 'a stand to't? *Henry 4*, P. 2, ii. 1.

To YERK. *To fling out; to jerk; to strike.*

Nine or ten times
I had thought t'have *yerked* him here under the ribs.
Othello, i. 2.
And their wounded steeds
Yerk out their armèd heels at their dead masters,
Killing them twice. *Henry 5*, iv. 7.

YEST. *Foam.*

Now the ship boring the moon with her main-
mast, and anon swallowed with *yest* and froth, as
you'd thrust a cork into a hogshead.
Winter's Tale, iii. 3.

YESTY. *Frothy; foamy.*

A kind of *yesty* collection, which carries them
through and through the most fanned and winnowed
opinions. *Hamlet*, v. 2.
Though the *yesty* waves
Confound and swallow navigation up.
Macbeth, iv. 1.

To YIELD. *To render; to give; to produce.*

We'll visit Caliban my slave, who never
Yields us kind answer. *Tempest*, i. 2.
The reasons of our state I cannot *yield*.
All's well that ends well, iii. 1.

YOKE-FELLOW. *Companion.*

And thou, his *yoke-fellow* of equity,
Bench by his side. *King Lear*, iii. 6.
Yoke-fellows in arms, let us to France.
Henry 5, ii. 3.

YOND. *Yonder.*

The fringèd curtains of thine eye advance,
And say what thou see'st *yond*. *Tempest*, i. 2.

YOUNG. *New; fresh; recent.*

Marry, this is yet but *young*, and may be left
To some ears unrecounted. *Henry 8*, iii. 2.

YOUNGEST. *Latter; latest.*

Thus Eleanor's pride dies in her *youngest* days.
Henry 6, P. 2, ii. 3.

YOUNKER. *A youngster; a greenhorn; a novice.*

What, will you make a *younker* of me?
Henry 4, P. 1, iii. 3.
How like a *younker* or a prodigal
The scarfèd bark puts from her native bay!
Merchant of Venice, ii. 5.
Trimm'd like a *younker* prancing to his love.
Henry 6, P. 3, ii. 1.

YOURS. *You; yourself.*

This is a poor epitome of *yours*,
Which by th' interpretation of full time
May show like all yourself. *Coriolanus*, v. 3.

Z.

ZANY. *A buffoon; an antic; a mimic.*

Some carry-tale, some please-man, some slight zany.
Love's Labour's lost, v. 2.

I protest, I take these wise men, that crow so at these set kind of fools, no better than the fools' zanies. *Twelfth-Night*, i. 5.

ZENITH. *Meridian; extreme point of greatness or power.*

And by my prescience

I find my zenith doth depend upon
A most auspicious star. *Tempest*, i. 2.

ZODIAC. *A year.*

So long, that nineteen zodiacs have gone round,
And none of them been worn.
Measure for Measure, i. 2.

THE END.

LONDON:
ROBSON AND SON, GREAT NORTHERN PRINTING WORKS,
PANCRAS ROAD, N.W.

www.ingramcontent.com/pod-product-compliance
Lightning Source LLC
Chambersburg PA
CBHW030904270326
41929CB00008B/575